Modern Management

THEORY AND PRACTICE FOR IRISH STUDENTS

Second edition

Modern Management

THEORY AND PRACTICE FOR IRISH STUDENTS

Second edition

Siobhan Tiernan, Michael Morley, Edel Foley

Gill & Macmillan

Gill & Macmillan Ltd
Hume Avenue
Park West
Dublin 12
with associated companies throughout the world
www.gillmacmillan.ie

Contents

Preface

Managers in Ireland today face a rapidly changing global business world. Changes over the last decade in Irish business mirror developments internationally. Rapid technological developments particularly in information technology and the resultant e-business, new organisational forms and new approaches to management reflect the strategic imperative of the first decade of the twenty-first century and challenge our traditional assumptions in relation to organisation and management. In a sense, managers can no longer look to past practice in order to chart a course for the future.

Any summative account of management in Ireland of this nature cannot claim to be all-inclusive. Managerial backgrounds and styles, organisational practices and business environments vary widely. This book is intended as an introductory text for Irish students. A mixture of theory and practice has been employed in the completion of the manuscript, and theoretical principles are supported by Irish case examples, case studies at the end of each chapter and Irish data where available.

The fourteen chapters trace the history of management thought, examine the development of Irish industrial policy and business development, the current business environment, and the key managerial roles (planning, decision making, organising, motivating, leading and controlling), and discuss contemporaneous issues relating to entrepreneurship and the management of change. Readability of the text is enhanced by the inclusion of a summary of key propositions at the end of each chapter and student revision is facilitated by the provision of end-of-chapter discussion questions. There is also a glossary of key managerial terms; these are highlighted throughout the text in SMALL CAPITALS. Each chapter contains an Irish case study relevant to the material covered in the chapter, and website addresses are given for the companies around which the case is written so that students can keep up to date with current developments.

There are a number of people who have provided valuable assistance in the preparation of this book and we take this opportunity to place on record our thanks to them.

Professor Noel Whelan, Dean of the College of Business, Professor Donal Dineen, Head of the Department of Economics, Jim Dalton, Head of the Department of Management and Marketing, Joe Wallace, Head of the Department of Personnel and Employment Relations, Professor Tom Kennedy, Head of the Department of Accounting and Finance, Professor Paddy Gunnigle, Helena Lenihan, Una Brady, Camilla Noonan, Terence Sheridan, Eugene Power, Noreen Heraty, Tom Garavan, Patrick Flood, Brega Hynes, Jim Donoughue, Roy Hayhurst, Sarah Moore, Tom Turner, Josephine Igoe, Dave Maguire and all those in the College of Business at the University of Limerick who constantly provide support for our endeavours. Anto Kerins, Sinead

Dunne and Herbie Lawton at the Dublin Institute of Technology. Margaret Whelan, Project Development Centre, DIT. Paul Beatty, Co-Operation Ireland. Dun and Bradstreet, Excellence Ireland.

The wonderful staff of the Library at the University of Limerick and the Dublin Institute of Technology whose patience and understanding always managed to locate that vital document or annual report.

The staff at Forfas, Industrial Development Authority, Ireland, and Enterprise Ireland, especially the following: Helena Acheson (Forfas); Peter D. Coyle, Michael Leahy and Darragh Kelly, all of Enterprise Ireland.

Jim Kelly for his immense knowledge of companies operating in the Dublin area.

The staff at the following institutions were always courteous and helpful when dealing with our enquires: The Government Publications Office; The Central Statistics Office; The Department of Enterprise and Employment; The Labour Relations Commission; Shannon Development Company.

Siobhan Tiernan
Michael Morley
Edel Foley

Limerick & Dublin
May 2001

Dedication

To Kevin, Luke and Meadbh (ST)
To Noreen, Oisín and Alannah (MM)
To Mary (EF)

Chapter 1 Management: Concepts and Evolution

1.1 Introduction

This chapter provides an introduction to the topic of MANAGEMENT and its evolution. First, a definition of management is provided and its nature and importance in modern society explained. The main functions of all managers are outlined along with the various skills they typically use. The different roles played by managers at the top, middle and bottom of the organisation are explained, and the characteristics of effective managers are then considered. The historical evolution of management is also considered, starting with the traditional classical approaches to management right through to current approaches.

Drucker (1988), one of the most influential management theorists, stated that over the last 150 years management has revolutionised the social and economic fabric of the developed regions of the world. Management has also made the structure of modern industry possible. Prior to the advent of management, society could only support small groups of workers. Management has permitted the use of large numbers of knowledgeable and skilled employees to achieve organisational goals. As a result effective management has become one of the most important resources of the developed world and one which most of the developing regions eagerly seek.

Finding an adequate definition of management is not always easy due to the fact that it has often been used in a variety of different ways. The word can refer to:

▶ the process that managers go through to achieve organisational goals

▶ a body of knowledge which provides information about how to manage

▶ individuals who guide and control organisational activities

▶ a career involving the task of guiding and controlling organisations.

For the purposes of this book, management is viewed as *the process in which managers engage to achieve organisational goals*. In this respect numerous definitions of management exist within the literature, but most definitions have three characteristics in common:

▶ Management is viewed as a process or series of continuing and related activities.

▶ Management is viewed as involving the achievement of organisational goals.

▶ Management reaches such organisational goals by working with and through people.

One of the best definitions of management available at present defines management as:

the process of achieving desired results through an efficient utilisation of human and material resources. (Bedeian 1993:4).

Managers can then be viewed as individuals within organisations whose principal aim is to achieve organisational goals by holding positions of AUTHORITY and making decisions about the allocation of resources.

All managers operate within an organisation of some sort. An organisation can be viewed as a system which is designed and operated to achieve specific organisational objectives. Organisations are consciously and formally established to achieve goals that their members would be unable to achieve by working on their own. Management is universal in that it occurs in all types of organisation whether public or private, large or small, profit- or non-profit-making. While the techniques and emphasis may vary depending on the organisation, the general principles of management can be used in all organisations.

As all organisations exist for a purpose, managers have the responsibility of combining and using organisational resources to ensure that the organisation achieves its purpose. If these activities are designed effectively, the production of each individual worker represents a contribution to the achievement of organisational goals. Management tries to encourage individual activity that will lead to the achievement of organisational objectives, and tries to discourage individual activity that hinders organisational goal attainment.

1.2 The functions of management

In order to achieve organisational goals all managers perform several major functions or activities. The key management functions are planning, organising, staffing and personnel, leading, and controlling.

1.2.1 Planning

Planning is the process of establishing goals and objectives and selecting a future course of action in order to achieve them. Plans are developed throughout the organisation including business units, work groups and individuals. Such plans can have a long-term orientation of between five and fifteen years, a medium-term orientation of one to five years, or may have a short-term orientation of less than one year. Managers have responsibility for gathering and evaluating the information on which the plans are based, setting the goals that need to be achieved and deciding how such goals should be achieved through the implementation of plans.

1.2.2 Organising

Once the plans have been established it is necessary to allocate adequate resources to ensure that the plans can be achieved. Organising therefore constitutes the next logical step in the management process. It involves dividing tasks into sub-tasks and allocating resources to achieve such tasks and finally co-ordinating employees. In addition organising involves establishing managerial authority.

1.2.3 Staffing

The staffing and personnel function ensures that effective employees are selected, trained, developed and, finally, rewarded for the accomplishment of organisational goals.

1.2.4 Leading

The fourth main function of management is leading, which involves inducing individuals or groups to assist willingly and harmoniously in the attainment of organisational goals. Leading usually means that the manager has to direct, motivate and communicate with employees. The leading function is almost entirely concerned with managing people within the organisation.

1.2.5 Controlling

The final function of management is controlling, which is the process of monitoring progress made by the organisation, business unit or individual and, where necessary, taking action to ensure goals match targets. The other management functions focus on developing plans, organising the resources needed to put the plans into practice and directing and motivating employees towards their realisation. However, good plans, solid organisation and effective leaders are no guarantee of success unless the various activities are measured, evaluated and corrected. Successful organisations pay close attention to the control function to make sure that they are on target for the achievement of goals.

The five management functions are carried out by all managers and are interrelated. They make up a set of interdependent activities that shape the MANAGEMENT PROCESS, as shown in Figure 1.1.

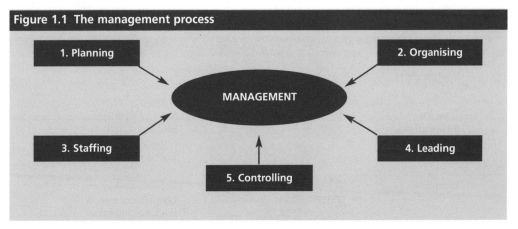

Figure 1.1 The management process

Although the various functions take place concurrently throughout most organisations, they follow a logical sequence. Planning establishes the direction of the organisation. Organising divides organisational activities among work groups, and co-ordinates results. Staffing allocates the required people to achieve tasks. Leading motivates employees to achieve organisational goals. Finally, control measures and evaluates organisational performance.

1.3 Management levels and skills

Managers are located at different levels in the organisations. Typically managers at different levels perform a range of different activities. Three distinct but sometimes overlapping levels of management can be identified in most organisations, as shown in Figure 1.2.

Figure 1.2 Levels of management

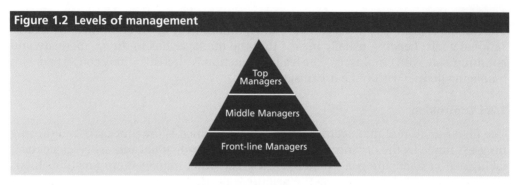

TOP MANAGERS, sometimes referred to as strategic managers, are the top executives of an organisation. Top managers include the chief executive officer, president, chairman, chief operating officer, directors and members of the board. These managers are responsible for the overall mission and direction of the organisation. Top managers shape organisational goals, provide resources, monitor progress and make strategic decisions. In this sense they act as the interface between the organisation and its external environment. They represent the organisation at outside meetings and develop customer and supplier relationships.

Mintzberg (1973) identified 10 different but interrelated roles that top managers typically undertake in the course of their activities, as shown in Figure 1.3.

Figure 1.3 Roles performed by top managers

Interpersonal	Figurehead
	Leader
	Liaison
Informational	Monitor
	Disseminator
	Spokesperson
Decisional	Entrepreneur
	Disturbance handler
	Resource allocator
	Negotiator

Top managers have an important interpersonal role which usually comes from their formal authority. They are figureheads serving as organisational representatives in the social, economic and legal arenas; they are leaders in the sense that they have to influence the activities of employees; and they have a liaison function, interacting with peers and other colleagues in other organisations.

Another major role performed by top managers is an informational one. Top managers are monitors in that they collect information that enables them to deal with both internal and external developments; they disseminate information to those inside the organisation; and they act as a spokesperson for the organisation, dealing with external bodies.

The role of top managers is also a decisional one. As entrepreneurs, top managers initiate changes to improve organisational performance. As disturbance handlers they deal with unforeseen events. As resource allocators, they decide where an organisation should allocate its resources. As negotiators, top managers bargain with influential groups such as trade unions.

MIDDLE MANAGERS are also called tactical managers and are responsible for translating the general plans and objectives developed by top managers into specific objectives and activities with which to achieve the organisational objectives. In this way, middle managers occupy positions above front-line managers and below top managers. Middle managers include plant managers, business unit managers, operations managers and superintendents and senior supervisors. Middle managers integrate the activities of different work groups to ensure co-ordination. As the link between top managers and front-line mangers, they communicate and transfer information between all levels. In recent years middle managers have become more involved in strategy formulation; however, top managers still have primary responsibility for strategic planning and decision making.

During the 1980s, many middle managers lost their jobs as organisations downsized and delayered. The main casualties in these delayering programmes were superintendents and senior supervisors. Such moves were caused by the need for organisations to reduce costs and to become more competitive. Developments in information technology have meant that middle managers are no longer required to serve as information and communications channels between top managers and front-line managers and many organisations have not replaced the middle managers they eliminated previously; it is unlikely that they will do so in the future.

FRONT-LINE MANAGERS, sometimes referred to as operational managers or supervisors, form the largest group of managers in most organisations. They are responsible for directly supervising and managing operating employees and resources. They make sure that the plans developed by top managers are fulfilled by the employees who actually produce the organisation's goods and services. They are a critically important managerial group as they are the link between management and non-management personnel. How they interpret information and pass it on to employees has an important impact on employees' reactions.

While the number of middle managers has been reduced, the role of front-line managers has also changed. Many of the responsibilities of the traditional middle manager have been passed on down to the front-line manager who has become increasingly responsible for shop-floor operations and has been given more authority and responsibility. Some observers have predicted that no job is going to change more during this decade than that of the front-line manager.

While management functions are the cornerstone of the manager's job, certain skills are needed to ensure that managers are effective in the execution of their functions. Skills are the abilities that managers develop as a result of knowledge, information, practice and aptitude. Management skills can be divided into three categories:

▶ technical

▶ interpersonal

▶ conceptual.

A technical skill is the ability to perform a specialised task involving a particular method or process. Most employees develop a set of technical skills as they start their careers. For example, business graduates have technical skills in relation to accounting, finance, marketing and HUMAN RESOURCE MANAGEMENT (HRM). The daily activities of most managers involve the use of some technical skills. However, as managers rise within the organisation they spend less time using technical skills. For example, an engineer, when recruited, relies heavily on technical skills, but as s/he is promoted and manages other employees, other skills become more important.

In order to work well with other people a manager needs good INTERPERSONAL SKILLS which are sometimes called human skills. Most top managers spend about half of their time dealing with other people (Mintzberg 1975). If managers are to deal with employees effectively they must develop their abilities to motivate and communicate effectively with those around them. Interpersonal skills are required by all managers as they all have to deal with other people.

CONCEPTUAL SKILLS involve the ability to see the organisation as a whole, recognising complex and dynamic issues, examining factors that influence these problems and resolving such situations. As managers are promoted up the organisation they depend more and more on conceptual skills. In fact most managers are promoted on the basis of their ability to make sound decisions and their vision and ability to chart the organisation's future. While conceptual skills are used by most managers, top managers require them most of all, particularly when making strategic decisions.

Figure 1.4 shows the variations in skills necessary at different management levels. As the diagram shows, for front-line managers the most important skills are technical and interpersonal. For middle managers, interpersonal skills are the most important with medium amounts of technical and conceptual input. For top managers the most important skills are conceptual and interpersonal, with little need for technical input.

Figure 1.4 Management skills at different levels

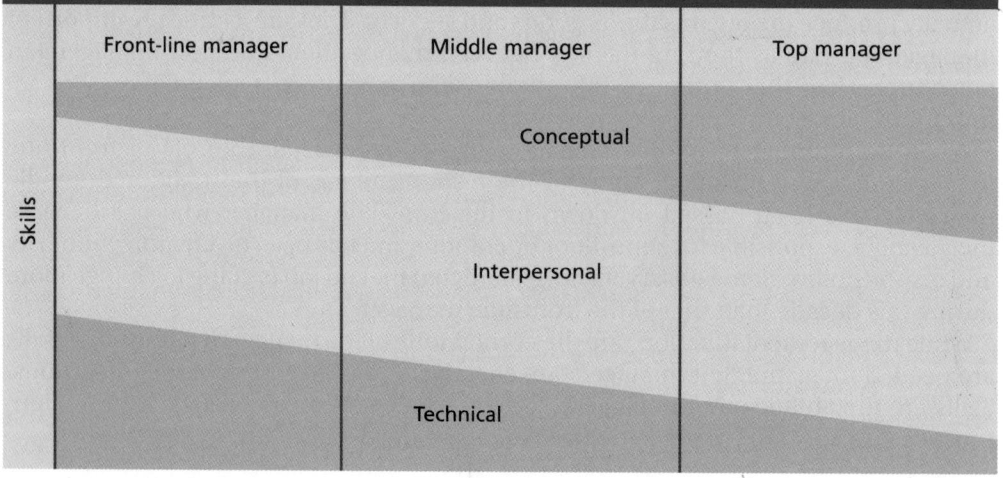

Front-line manager	Middle manager	Top manager

Skills

Conceptual

Interpersonal

Technical

1.4 Effective managers

In addition to the execution of the five management functions with the use of three types of skills, EFFECTIVE MANAGERS have a number of important characteristics. Bateman and Zeithhaml, (1993) argue that effective managers are active leaders who create both the opportunity and the INCENTIVE to achieve high performance, as shown in Figure 1.5.

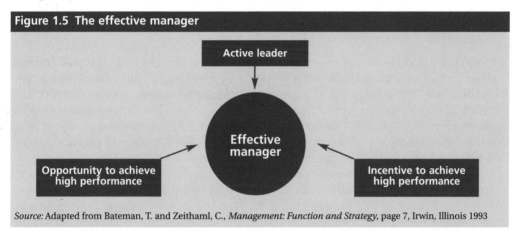

Figure 1.5 The effective manager

Source: Adapted from Bateman, T. and Zeithaml, C., *Management: Function and Strategy*, page 7, Irwin, Illinois 1993

To be effective a manager should be an active leader. As we have seen, leading is one of the key functions of management. The main difference between managers and leaders is that managers do things right whereas leaders do the right things (Bennis and Nanus 1985). In this way leaders have a vision which they successfully communicate to employees. Active leaders concentrate on achieving the task at hand in an active rather than passive manner. They participate in the activities of the organisation at work-group and BUSINESS UNIT level. In this way they are highly visible to employees and demonstrate their thorough knowledge of the business. Examples of managers who are active leaders include Michael Smurfit of the Smurfit Group and Fergal Quinn of Superquinn.

In order to provide the opportunity for high performance, both managers and employees must understand their jobs and what they do, as opposed to what they *should* do. They must also have a sense of the future for their particular task. Involving employees in the design and execution stages is one method of providing the opportunity to achieve high performance. The Japanese have used this philosophy very effectively, especially in relation to QUALITY CIRCLES. Japanese managers work closely with employees to plan and implement changes for the benefit of everyone. Managers can also provide the opportunity to achieve high performance by making sure that all employees have the necessary resources. Effective managers are constantly searching for ways to help employees do their jobs well and to focus their activities and efforts on production matters.

In order to provide incentives for employees to achieve high performance, the manager needs to identify the factors that motivate employees and build those factors into the work environment. Incentives can include rewards such as money and promotion, a challenging job or relationships with co-workers. Having identified the factors that motivate employees, the manager needs to link these factors to clear objectives. In other words, effective managers identify the important objectives they need to achieve and they focus everyone's efforts towards the achievement of those objectives.

Before becoming too focused on the managers role in a modern business organisation it is important first to consider historical approaches to the study of management. It is only by studying previous methods that we can learn from and build on their limitations to reach an integrated view of the concept of management.

1.5 Early management thought

Attempts to understand and develop a THEORY of management can be traced back to the earliest efforts of man to achieve goals by working in groups. However, the Industrial Revolution heightened awareness and interest in management theory and practice as managers sought to achieve internal EFFICIENCY. The opportunities created at the turn of the twentieth century by the Industrial Revolution led to a period of considerable debate on the most effective management theory and practice, which resulted in what we now call CLASSICAL MANAGEMENT.

A thorough knowledge and understanding of the classical approaches to management is necessary due to the fact that they laid the foundations for many of the modern theories on management. In fact the most modern approaches to management have integrated and expanded the key concepts developed within the classical approaches. The following sections will examine the earliest contributions to management thought, the classical approaches to management and, finally, the modern approaches available to managers today.

For thousands of years man has been faced with the same issues and problems that continue to confront managers today. The earliest thoughts and ideas in relation to management can be traced back to the written records of the Sumerians (5000 BC) who documented the formation of their government, their tax-gathering systems and their conduct of commerce. The clearest example of such management thought lies with the ancient Egyptians (4000–2000 BC) who used managerial skills to build vast pyramids, giving rise to the first real nation state. The construction of the Great Pyramids involved over 100,000 workers of various trades and, using levers and rollers, took nearly 30 years to complete. In achieving such a vast undertaking, managers had to plan in advance the type and size of stone required, organise available staff and resources, provide leadership and finally control the process to ensure that the end result matched the original plans. The Egyptians developed managerial skills to organise human labour and found that the best way to delegate the multitude of tasks required to complete the undertaking was through a hierarchy.

Greek civilisation (*circa* 500–300 BC) also contributed to early management thought with the development of separate courts, an administration system and an army, highlighting the need for different management functions. Early Greek philosophers such as Socrates differentiated between management and other technical functions, providing the first written example of the concept that management was a separate and specialist skill.

The Roman Empire (*circa* 300 BC–AD 300) provides further evidence of the development of management thought. Due to the fact that the Roman Empire extended over such a vast area the Romans were faced with the problem of the management and control of their conquests. In order to effectively manage the empire, DELEGATION of power and the SCALAR PRINCIPLE of authority were used, coupled with a system of communication between the outposts and the central command. This ensured that the Roman Empire could maintain control over regions due to its tight organisation. One of the most enduring examples of early management thought and certainly the most prevalent in Ireland can be found in the Catholic Church, which combined managerial skills with a spiritual message to successfully convey its objectives. Managerial techniques employed by the Catholic Church included a strict hierarchy of authority and the SPECIALISATION of members along a functional basis. The hierarchical structure still employed by the Catholic Church includes five main levels; Parish Priest, Bishop, Arch Bishop, Cardinal and Pope. The concept of centralisation of authority in Rome remains the same today as when it was first introduced in 2 AD. The Catholic Church became a model for the management of other religious organisations and also for the army, who further developed the concepts of LEADERSHIP, UNITY OF COMMAND, LINE AUTHORITY and STAFF AUTHORITY.

In the 1300s, Venetian merchants made their contribution to management thought by establishing the legal foundations of the enterprise. Financial records were formalised into double-entry book-keeping, first described by Pacioli in 1494. Machiavelli, who published *The Prince* in 1532, further developed management thought in relation to the political organisation. He suggested that the prince or leader should build a cohesive organisation, binding his allies with rewards and making sure they knew what was expected of them. Machiavelli's ideas on leadership and consent of the masses for effective rule still have relevance in today's environment.

Collectively, the contributors to the development of early management thought have produced many ideas and concepts that have relevance for modern theory and practice. However, early managers tended to operate on a trial and error basis. Communication and transport problems prevented the widespread growth of business ventures which meant that advances in management techniques and skills could not significantly improve performance. The advent of the Industrial Revolution changed the situation and led to the development of management as a formal discipline.

1.6 The Industrial Revolution

The Industrial Revolution marked a major watershed in the development of management thought. Up until the 1700s large organisations were mainly military, political or religious, rather than industrial. Instead of by large industrial organisations, most skilled work was performed by craft workers who, working alone using fairly simple tools, produced clearly identifiable goods such as watches or clothing. These goods were then sold directly to individual customers within the locality of the craft worker.

The Industrial Revolution significantly changed this pattern of industrial activity. The invention of machines such as Watt's steam engine (1765), Arkwright's water frame (1769) and Cartwright's power loom (1785) effectively transferred skills from the craft worker to the machine. These new machines required only an unskilled worker to insert raw materials and extract the finished goods. Eventually fully automated machines were developed which no longer required worker input. Such developments also made possible the establishment of large-scale factories which stood in marked contrast to the local nature of craft work.

As a result of these advances the productive capability of humans and indeed animals was greatly increased. PRODUCTIVITY began to increase steadily and industry started to feel the benefits of ECONOMIES OF SCALE, whereby the average unit cost of producing an item decreases as the volume of production increases. Consequently prices fell and consumption rose. Developments in transportation and communications further opened up new markets and promoted economic growth. Industry and commerce boomed and entrepreneurs formed the new social class—the bourgeoisie. The growth of industry gave people the opportunity to leave the land and move into the cities to avail themselves of industrial work. The social implications of the Industrial Revolution were enormous as people had to leave their homes to work long hours for poor pay and conditions.

Prior to the Industrial Revolution, in Ireland, agriculture was the main form of occupation with some of the larger towns having small water-powered factories producing beer, whiskey and flour. Only about one in 10 people lived in towns, most of whom were craft workers. The impact of the Industrial Revolution in Ireland was less evident than in the UK or the USA in terms of industrialisation. In fact Irish industry suffered from competition by the UK, particularly in the woollen and cotton industries, which virtually collapsed in the mid 1800s. However, in the linen industry, production moved from the home to large-scale factories. Nonetheless, Ireland remained an agricultural economy and only experienced the shift to industrial employment in the 1950s (for further discussion, see Chapter 2).

As industry and commerce expanded to capitalise on new markets and production processes, organisations became increasingly large and complex. Such size and complexity meant that new management techniques would have to be developed to cope with the problems and opportunities presented by industrialisation. As early as 1776, Adam Smith advocated in *The Wealth of Nations* that the key to profitability lay in the specialisation of labour, whereby workers should be assigned a specific task to complete, ensuring a sharp division of labour.

The Industrial Revolution created huge opportunities for MASS PRODUCTION and, coupled with the increasing size and complexity of organisations, resulted in an upsurge of systematic thought on the key managerial problems presented by industrialisation, namely production, efficiency and cost savings. An era of renewed interest and debate on management ensued which led to the emergence of management as a formal discipline distinct from other technical areas.

The evolution of management thought since the Industrial Revolution can be divided into classical and modern approaches. Figure 1.6 provides a historical picture of the evolution of management thought. Many of the approaches were developed simultaneously and have therefore affected one another, but some of the approaches were developed as a direct response to some of the weaknesses of earlier approaches. The remainder of the chapter will concentrate on the contribution of both the classical and the modern approaches to the study of management.

1.7 The classical approaches

The classical approach to the study of management was born at the end of the nineteenth century as a response to the managerial challenges posed by over a century of intense industrialisation. The major approaches associated with this era are scientific management, bureaucracy, administrative management and human relations, and they were generally developed from the personal experiences of key contributors. In order to avoid confusion about dates which apply to each approach, it is important to distinguish between:

❶ the date a particular work was written

❷ the date it was translated into English

❸ the date the work became popular in management thought.

For many of the approaches each of these categories will have a different date.

Figure 1.6 The evolution of management thought

1700s	Industrial Revolution
Classical approaches	
1898	Scientific management
1916	Administrative management
1920s	Bureaucracy
1927	Human relations
Modern approaches	
1950s	Systems theory
1960s	Contingency theory
1970s	Total quality management
1980s	Organisational culture

The year associated with each school of thought is the year that the approach began. The beginning of the next school of thought does not however denote the end of the previous one.

1.7.1 Scientific management

SCIENTIFIC MANAGEMENT is concerned with the development of one best way of performing a task through the application of SCIENTIFIC METHODS. The birth of scientific management is attributed to Frederick Taylor (1856–1917), whose ideas were developed in two books, *Shop Management* (1903), and *Principles of Scientific Management* (1911); both of these books were combined and published in 1947 under the title *Scientific Management*. Taylor trained in the USA as an engineer and having finished his apprenticeship joined the Midvale Steel Company where he rose to the rank of chief engineer. His first-hand experience at Midvale led him to conclude that both productivity and pay were poor, operations were inefficient and wasteful, and relations between workers and management were antagonistic—a picture which he believed reflected the wider state of industry at the time.

According to Taylor the principle objective of management should be to secure the maximum prosperity for the employer coupled with the maximum prosperity of each employee (Taylor 1947). This prosperity meant not only monetary profit, but also the development of each employee to perform to the highest level that s/he was able. In order to achieve this, Taylor advocated that scientific methods should be used to analyse the one best way, scientifically, to do tasks.

In 1898 Taylor was employed as a consultant by the Bethlehem Steel Works Company, where he applied his principles of scientific management most visibly. Production within the company focused on two processes, the first of which was the handling of pig-iron blocks on to railroad cars and, second, shovelling fuel (sand, limestone, coal and iron ore) into blast furnaces. Pig-iron handling was a very physical job and the management at Bethlehem found that they could do nothing to induce workers to work faster. By studying pig-iron handlers over a period of time Taylor concluded that with better, less tiring, work methods and frequent breaks, daily output per worker could be quadrupled. In order to do this a piece-rate pay system was developed whereby workers would be paid extra when they produced above a standard level of output. The results were staggering; not only did output per worker increase from 12.5 to 47.5 tons, but wages per day increased from $1.15 to $1.85.

Taylor then proceeded to tackle the problem of shovelling, which was completed by work groups of 50–60 under a single foreman. Time and motion studies were used by Taylor to establish the one best way of shovelling, including the type of shovel to be used, which Taylor believed depended on the raw material used. As a result of his findings a tool-room was established and each morning workers were given written instructions stating what tools were needed for the day. A piece-rate system was also introduced. Once again the results were outstanding. Tons shovelled per day increased from 16 to 59 and wages increased from $1.15 to $1.88.

Taylor's experience at Bethlehem led him to develop four main principles of management which became the cornerstones of scientific management.

▶ **The development of a true science of work**. Taylor believed that both management and workers were essentially unaware of what a fair day's work was and this consequently gave employers room for complaint about employee inadequacies. Taylor therefore argued that rules of thumb should be replaced by a scientific approach to work, whereby each task could be broken down into basic movements which could be timed to determine one best way of doing the task. In this way a worker would know what constituted a fair day's work, for which he would receive a fair day's pay. The level of pay would be higher than the average worker would get in unscientific factories, but if workers failed to perform they would lose income.

▶ **The scientific selection and development of workers**. Taylor was aware of the importance of hiring and training the appropriate worker for the job with regard to physical and mental aptitudes. Once properly matched to the job the worker could then be developed to the highest capacity by a piece-rate system of pay. Taylor believed that as workers were motivated by money, both workers and managers would benefit by increased productivity.

▶ **The co-operation of workers and management in studying the science of work**. Taylor believed that management and workers should co-operate to ensure that the job, plans and principles all matched. To achieve this end he advocated standardised tools, instruction cards to assist workers and breaks to reduce tiredness.

▶ **The division of work between management and the workforce**. Taylor believed that workers and those in management should do the tasks for which they were best equipped: managers would therefore direct and allocate work, and workers would complete the tasks.

The principles of scientific management were widely accepted and one of the most famous applications of the approach was Henry Ford's Model T factory. Other proponents of scientific management included Henry Gantt and Frank and Lillian Gilbreth. Gantt (1861–1919) was a contemporary and acquaintance of Taylor who modified some of his ideas. Gantt proposed that every worker should be entitled to a set wage rate, with a bonus if output was exceeded. This would allow supervisors to spend more time coaching the less able worker—in other words, this is the application of the principle of MANAGEMENT BY EXCEPTION. Such an approach left room for more initiative and discretion.

Frank Gilbreth (1868–1924) and his wife Lillian (1878–1972) were also contemporaries of Taylor. They were primarily concerned with the elimination of waste and, like Taylor, discovering the one best way of doing a job. They believed that in finding the one best way an individual's personal potential could best be achieved. Frank Gilbreth, who owned a construction company in Boston, began to analyse each task he did , constantly trying to eliminate unnecessary work movements. He identified 17 hand motions which he called *therbligs* (a slightly altered backward spelling of the family name). Frank believed that by isolating the therbligs in a task one could eliminate or shorten them. In applying this system to bricklaying he reduced the motions or therbligs from 18 to 4.5.

After her husband's death, Lillian continued his pioneering work. As an industrial psychologist, she emphasised the need for understanding workers' personalities and needs and pioneered the development of human resource management. Her interests lay in the human factor and the scientific selection, training and development of workers. The Gilbreths proved to be a formidable team in terms of their contribution to management thought, the handling of materials, monotony, and modern human resource management.

Scientific management and its advocates had a phenomenal effect on managerial practices at the turn of the century. Taylor's *Principles of Scientific Management* was first published in 1911 and within a few years had been translated into eight different languages. Scientific management spread as far as the Soviet Union, where the principles were incorporated into the various five-year development plans. Scientific management dramatically improved productivity and efficiency in manufacturing organisations and introduced scientific analysis into the world of work. The piece-rate pay system gained wide acceptance due to the link between effort and reward. Scientific management instilled a sense of co-operation between workers and management and finally the concept of a management specialist gained widespread acceptance.

However, scientific management was not without its critics. In emphasising the link between worker effort and monetary reward, Taylor assumed that man/woman was motivated solely by money. Worker motivation is however far more complex, and involves job-related social and psychological factors which Taylor ignored. In advocating one best way of completing tasks, work activities frequently became routine and machine-like which led to boredom and apathy among the workforce.

Trade unions strongly opposed scientific management techniques. They viewed the piece-rate system as a return to 'sweat shop' exploitation of labour by management. Scientific management techniques frequently resulted in lay-offs and, as a result, unions feared that its application would lead to widespread job losses. Scientific management also ignored the role of senior management within the organisation. While dealing with the issues of internal efficiency it failed to deal with the relationship between the organisation and the environment, such as competitors and regulators, especially at the senior level of the organisation.

Despite these criticisms the legacy of scientific management is pervasive. It formally established management as a specialist area, introduced scientific analysis to the workplace and provided a framework for solving the managerial problems of efficiency and productivity. While Taylor was accused of causing unemployment, his real aim was to cause a mental revolution so that both sides would take their eyes off the division of the surplus as the all-important matter, and, together, turn their attention towards increasing the size of the surplus (Taylor 1947).

1.7.2 Administrative management

Administrative management was based on the personal experiences of its key advocates. It focused on senior managers and the policy issues faced by them. In doing so, administrative management offered UNIVERSAL PRINCIPLES OF MANAGEMENT. The most important contributor to administrative management was Henri Fayol (1841–1925), commonly known as the father of modern management. Unlike previous management theorists who were American, Fayol was French, and worked independently during the same period that scientific management was gaining momentum. Fayol worked as a mining engineer and came to realise that managing an ENTERPRISE required a host of skills apart from technical ones. In 1916 he produced *Administration Industrielle et Générale*, later published in English during the 1930s as *General and Industrial Management*, which established him as the pioneer of European management in the early 1900s.

Unlike Taylor who concentrated on work group management, the focus of Fayol's work was the senior executive of the organisation, which reflected his managerial experiences. Concentrating on the problems faced by the senior executive in managing an organisation Fayol concluded that all business activities could be divided into six essential areas:

▶ technical (production and manufacturing)

▶ commercial (buying, selling and exchange)

▶ financial (funding and using capital)

▶ security (guarding property)

▶ accounting (costing and stock-taking)

▶ managerial (planning, organising, controlling, commanding and co-ordinating).

The inclusion of management as a separate business activity with five main functions gained Fayol widespread recognition. Fayol believed that the six groups of activities were interdependent and all needed to be running effectively for the organisation to prosper. Figure 1.7 outlines the manager's main activities according to Fayol. It is interesting to note the similarity between Fayols five main managerial activities and the modern five functions of management (planning, organising, staffing, leading and controlling) discussed in Section 1.2.

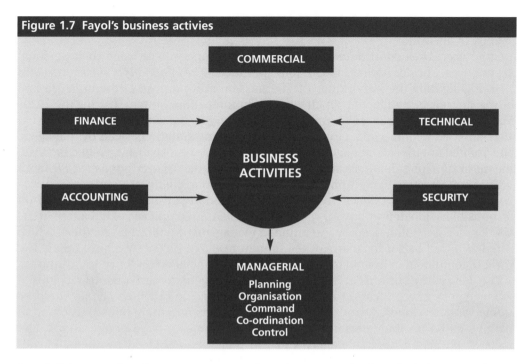

Figure 1.7 Fayol's business activies

COMMERCIAL

FINANCE → BUSINESS ACTIVITIES ← TECHNICAL

ACCOUNTING → ← SECURITY

MANAGERIAL

Planning
Organisation
Command
Co-ordination
Control

In addition to the five management functions, Fayol identified fourteen basic principles of management which he had found to be most useful during his career. Figure 1.8 presents Fayol's management principles.

Figure 1.8 Fayol's fourteen management principles

1. **Division of labour:** Divide work into specialised tasks and assign responsibility to individuals.
2. **Authority:** Equal delegation of responsibility and authority.
3. **Discipline:** Establish clear expectations and penalties.
4. **Unity of command:** Each employee should report to one supervisor.
5. **Unity of direction:** Employee efforts should be guided to achieve organisational goals.
6. **Subordination of individual interest to general:** Group interests should not precede the general interests of the group.
7. **Remuneration:** Equitable rewards for work.
8. **Scalar chain:** Lines of authority and communications from the highest to the lowest level.
9. **Order:** Order tasks and materials to support organisational direction.
10. **Equity:** Treat employees fairly.
11. **Stability of tenure:** Minimise turnover to ensure loyalty of personnel.
12. **Initiative:** Employees should have freedom and discretion.
13. **Esprit de corps:** Unity of interest between management and workers.
14. **Centralisation:** Decide the importance of superior and subordinate roles.

Fayol emphasised that such principles of management should be applied in a flexible manner. Fayol's principles remain important not only because of the influence of

Fayol on succeeding generations of managers, but also because of the continuing validity of his work.

Other executives contributed to administrative management using their personal experiences. Chester Barnard (1886–1961) produced *The Functions of the Executive* in 1938 highlighting the importance of: the mission and purpose of the organisation; hiring specialists; and having an effective communications system. During the 1920s Mary Parker Follet (1868–1935) produced *The Dynamic Administration* (published in 1941 after her death) which emphasised the changing situations faced by managers. She pointed out that all managers want flexibility, and she also distinguished between the motivation of individuals and groups. In 1947 Lyndall Urwick published *Elements of Administration* which emphasised the social responsibility of managers towards employees. Urwick produced 10 principles for good organisation which focused on responsibility, job definition and spans of control. As an employee of Rowntree in the UK, Urwick was influenced by the humane management policy he saw there, which acted as a trail blazer for many of the human resource policies we have today. The earliest companies in Ireland to adopt these policies included Cadbury and Guinness.

The key contributions of administrative management are that it recognised management as a profession much like law or medicine in which people could be trained and developed. Advocates of administrative management offered recommendations based on their personal experience of managing large organisations, and focused on senior-level managers and the policy issues faced by them. Finally, administrative management offered universal principles of management, in other words principles that were believed to work in all situations.

The main criticism levelled at the approach is that universal principles do not take account of variations in the environment, technology or personnel, which may require alternative management action. Administrative management is remembered for its enormous influence on successive generations of managers and because of the continued relevance and validity of its principles, particularly those of Fayol.

1.7.3 Bureaucracy

Max Weber (1864–1920) was a German sociologist who wrote most of his work at the turn of the century, though this was only translated into English during the 1920s. While Taylor's and Fayol's attention focused on the problems of effectively managing an organisation, Weber concentrated on how to structure organisations for success. Weber outlined key elements of an ideal form of structure which he believed would promote efficiency and called it BUREAUCRACY. It is important to note that while the term 'bureaucracy' may have negative connotations in today's society, at the beginning of the twentieth century, bureaucracy was viewed as the ultimate structure to provide efficiency and stability.

The ideal bureaucracy which Weber advocated had six main elements:

▶ **Division of labour**. Tasks were divided and delegated to specialists so that responsibility and authority were clearly defined.

▶ **Hierarchy**. Positions were organised in a hierarchy of authority from the top of the organisation to the bottom, with authority centralised at the top of the organisation.

▶ **Selection**. Employees were recruited on the basis of technical qualifications rather than favouritism.

- ▶ **Career orientation**. Managers were viewed as professionals pursuing careers rather than having ownership in the organisation.
- ▶ **Formalisation**. The organisation was subject to formal rules and procedures in relation to performance.
- ▶ **Impersonality**. Rules and procedures were applied uniformly to all employees.

Weber's ideal bureaucracy gained widespread acceptance as soon as his work was translated in the 1920s and 1930s. The structure became extensively used in large-scale organisations world-wide due to the fact that it allowed such organisations to perform the many routine activities necessary for survival. Bureaucracy was particularly popular for public organisations and civil service-type organisations. Many of the early Irish semi-state bodies and the civil service were structured along bureaucratic lines, including Aer Lingus and Iarnrod Éireann (formerly part of CIE).

The bureaucratic structure had a number of important advantages for large organisations. The division of labour increased efficiency and expertise due to the continued repetition of the task. Hierarchy allowed a CHAIN OF COMMAND to develop in line with Fayol's scalar chain idea. Formal selection meant that employees were hired on merit and expertise and no other criteria would be used. Career orientation ensured that career professionals would give the organisation a degree of continuity in operations. Rules and procedures controlled employee performance, increasing efficiency. The impersonality of the organisation ensured that rules were applied across the board without personality or other influence getting in the way.

While bureaucracy might be an extremely rational and efficient form of organisation, it has a number of disadvantages. The extensive rules and procedures can sometimes become ends in themselves. In other words obeying rules at all costs becomes important irrespective of whether such action helps to achieve organisational goals. Bureaucracy promotes stability but over time things can become very rigid. Rules and procedures are blindly applied to all situations even though they may not be the most appropriate. Consequently the organisation comes to believe that what has worked well in the past will continue to do so in the future, despite changed conditions.

Delegation of authority in the bureaucratic organisation can lead to a situation where the goals of the work groups become more important than organisational goals, adversely affecting the organisation in the long run. The strict division of labour can lead to routine and boring jobs where workers feel apathetic and demotivated. The extensive rules can lead to the establishment among workers of a minimum acceptable standard as laid down by the rules, above which workers will not go. So, instead of acting as a controlling device, the rules actually reduce performance.

The fact that elements of Weber's bureaucratic structure can be found in so many organisations today is testimony to the importance of his work. Bureaucracy is both rational and efficient. However, organisations need to understand bureaucracy in order to avoid being controlled by it. Like that of Taylor and Fayol, Weber's work had enormous influence on management thought and is still relevant in today's business environment particularly for organisations operating in a stable environment such as McDonald's.

1.7.4 Human relations

The human relations (or behavioural) approach to management emerged in the 1920s and 1930s. In contrast to previous approaches, the human relations movement concentrated on the human side of management and sought to understand how psychological and social factors interacted with the work environment in influencing performance. The approach built on the ideas and concepts developed by the foregoing approaches, most notably Gantt and the Gilbreths' scientific management.

The human relations approach emerged from a research study that began as a scientific management application to determine the impact of working conditions on performance and ended up discovering the effect of the human factor on productivity. Elton Mayo (1880–1949) and Fritz Roethlisberger, both Harvard researchers were employed in 1927 by the Western Electric Company to study the effect of physical working conditions on worker productivity and efficiency. Commonly known as the Hawthorne Studies, and chronicled by Roethlisberger and Dickson (1939) in *Management and the Worker*, they marked one the most important watersheds in the evolution of management thought.

Western Electric (now AT&T Technologies) manufactured equipment for the telephone industry. Between 1924 and 1932 a series of studies were carried out within the company. The Hawthorne Studies can be divided into three main phases, with each phase adding to the knowledge acquired in the previous one:

❶ The Illumination Experiments 1924–27

❷ The Relay Assembly Room Experiments 1927–32

❸ The Bank Wiring Observation Room Experiments 1931–32.

The Illumination Experiments 1924–27

Prior to the arrival of Mayo and his research team, an investigation had been made by the US National Research Council which marked the first stage of the Hawthorne Studies. Between 1924 and 1927 the Illumination Experiments were conducted in several departments employing female coil-winders, relay assemblers and small-parts inspectors. The investigation was designed to determine how the level of lighting affected worker output and the researchers expected that better lighting would increase output. Two groups were isolated and the conditions in one were held constant, while the level of light was systematically changed in the second group. The results, however, showed that output increased in both groups. When Mayo and his research team were employed in 1927 they concluded that there was no simple cause-and-effect relationship between illumination and productivity and that the increase in output was caused by the fact that the workers were aware of being observed. This phenomenon was called the Hawthorne Effect whereby workers were influenced more by psychological and social factors (observation) than by physical and logical factors (illumination).

The Relay Assembly Test Room Experiments 1927–32

The Relay Assembly Test Room (RATR) Experiments were designed to study the effects of rest breaks, work-day length, refreshments and incentive payments on productivity. Six skilled women involved in the assembly of phone relays were selected and placed in a test room without their normal supervisor. An observer was placed in the test room to record observations and to create a friendly and relaxed atmosphere. The various changes were introduced with the women's knowledge and consent. The result was that output increased. The next stage was to return the women to their original conditions (a 48-hour, 6-day week, no refreshments, no incentives and no pauses) by withdrawing the concessions, and once again output increased.

In trying to explain such results Mayo concluded that unintentionally the research team had changed the human relations of the work group under observation. They found that the test room was significantly different to regular departments in four main ways.

First, the supervisory style in the test room, with the absence of a formal supervisor, was more open and friendly and workers enjoyed being the centre of attention. Second, the test room was less controlled than regular work groups and the women actually participated in decisions affecting the job and could set their own work pace. Third, group formation resulted in a cohesive group which was loyal and co-operative. Finally, the attitudes of the women were different as they no longer felt part of a large department subject to managerial control but felt involved. This consequently affected their job satisfaction.

Mayo was rather puzzled and surprised by the results of his observations and decided to interview the factory workers about their conditions. From this he found that many of the management's problems were related to human factors. In other words, people were underproductive because of things they felt were wrong, rather than because of ignorance about the company's objectives. This contradicted Taylorism, which claimed that once a worker was convinced of the one best way, s/he would adopt it.

The Bank Wiring Observation Room Experiments 1931–32   *Hawthorne Studies.*

The Bank Wiring Observation Room (BWOR) Experiments involved fourteen men who were kept in their natural work setting (i.e. non-experimental) with an observer but with no changes in their working conditions. The aim of the study was to analyse the behaviour of the work group and how it functioned. Observation and interviewing showed that the group had well-established norms or rules of behaviour. The results showed that the men restricted their output; the group had standards for output and these were not exceeded by any worker. They had their own idea of what constituted a fair day's work and employees who exceeded the agreed daily output were called 'rate busters' and those producing below it were called 'rate chisellers'. These norms were enforced by the group through sarcasm and 'binging' whereby a group member hit another on the arm to show displeasure. Group members were united in their opposition to management and were indifferent to the financial incentives offered for higher output. All of these observations led Mayo to conclude that informal work-group relations had enormous influence on motivation and performance. When Mayo reviewed the overall findings, he concluded that an 'informal' organisation existed among the workers, in addition to the 'formal' organisation recognised by management.

The important contribution made by the Hawthorne Studies was that social needs took precedence over economic needs and that the informal work group could exert control over employee behaviour and performance. Consequently Mayo argued that managers should focus on motivation, communications and employee welfare to gain the co-operation of the group and promote job satisfaction and norms consistent with the goals of the organisation. However, in recent years doubt has been cast on the authenticity of a 'Hawthorne Effect' with researchers (see, for example, Jones 1990, 1992; Rice 1982; Yunker 1993; Carey 1967) arguing that we have naively taken on board the assumption, when in reality the evidence does not support its existence. The case at the end of this chapter debates this point more fully. Whatever our feelings on this debate there can be no doubt that the Hawthorne Studies played a monumental role in the development of managerial thought by voicing concerns about the role human beings play in the organisation.

Another key contributor to the human relations approach to management was Abraham Maslow. Maslow (1943) was concerned with the issue of worker motivation and sought to explain how workers could be motivated to achieve higher performance. Maslow's studies led him to propose a theory of human motivation which is still referred to in current discussions of management. Maslow believed that people try to satisfy a hierarchy of needs, as shown in Figure 1.9.

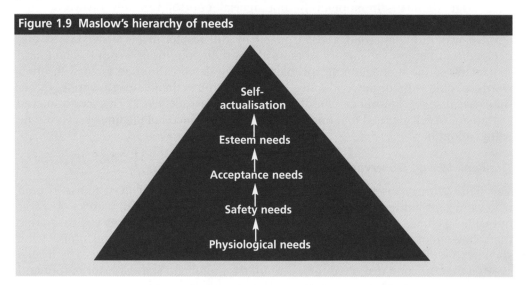

Figure 1.9 Maslow's hierarchy of needs

The various needs which he identified start with physiological needs which include food and shelter. Safety needs refer to the need to feel secure and physically protected; acceptance needs are concerned with the need to relate to and be accepted by other people; esteem needs include the need for self-respect and for the esteem of others; and self-actualisation refers to the needs for self achievement and fulfilment. The first three have been termed 'deficiency needs' because they need to be satisfied for basic comfort, while the top two are growth needs, as they focus on growth and development.

Maslow argued that people try to satisfy their needs systematically, starting from the bottom and working up so that once a given level of needs has been satisfied it no longer acts as a motivator and people move onto the satisfaction of higher order needs. Therefore people try to satisfy food and shelter needs before considering love and esteem. It is possible to apply these basic needs to the organisational setting which offers more insight into how people can be motivated. Figure 1.10 provides an example of Maslow's hierarchy of needs as applied to the organisation and shows what basic needs the worker has and what has to be satisfied before moving on to the next level.

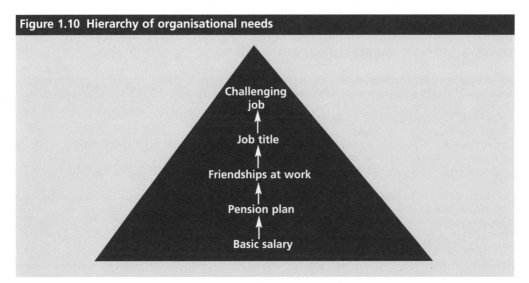

Figure 1.10 Hierarchy of organisational needs

It has been concluded that in many instances managers help workers to satisfy the first three needs but neglect the last two. Consequently many employees remain undermotivated. Maslow's research gave important managerial insights into how people seek self-actualisation in their work. Many regard work as a way of satisfying physiological and safety needs, and seek self-fulfilment in their hobbies or interests.

Other researchers belonging to the human relations school of thought include Herzberg and McGregor, both of whom will be discussed in detail in Chapter 9 on Motivation. The primary contribution of the human relations movement was that it emphasised the importance of the human factor in the work environment. It highlighted the role played by social and psychological processes and the satisfaction of needs in determining performance. Like the previous approaches it also drew criticism. The Hawthorne Studies it was claimed were unscientific in that many of the conclusions reached did not necessarily follow the evidence. The human relations approach in general has been criticised for its apparent neglect of the more rational side of workers and the important characteristics of the formal organisation. Despite such criticisms the human relations movement has had a phenomenal impact on management thought, encouraging managers and researchers to consider psychological and social factors that might influence performance.

1.7.5 The classical approaches: a summary

The various classical approaches to the study of management laid the foundations for the management of organisations that still exist today. Figure 1.11 provides a summary of the main contributions and limitations of the various approaches.

The approaches sought to provide managers with skills and techniques to confront the important issues of the time, namely, productivity and efficiency. Primarily based on the personal experience of key contributors, they focused on the basic managerial functions, co-ordination of work and supervision. Apart from the human relations school and elements of administrative management, they concentrated on the formal aspects of the organisation. With the benefit of hindsight, some of the approaches take a simplistic view of the needs and interests of workers and fail to address the important issue of the role of the external environment in determining success. The more modern approaches to the study of management attempt to further these basic concepts and overcome key criticisms.

Figure 1.11 The classical approaches: a summary	
School of thought:	Scientific management: 1898–present day
Proponents:	Taylor, Gantt and the Gilbreths
Contribution:	Application of scientific principles to the study of work through work studies and incentives
Limitations:	Simplistic view of motivation and ignored the role of the external environment
School of thought:	Administrative management: 1916–present day
Proponents:	Fayol, Follet, Barnard and Urwick
Contribution:	Universal principles of management for senior executives
Limitations:	Ignored environmental differences
School of thought:	Bureaucracy: 1920s–present day
Proponents:	Weber
Contributions:	Bureaucratic structure emphasising efficiency and stability
Limitations:	Ignored the human element and the role of the external environment
School of thought:	Human relations: 1927–present day
Proponents:	Mayo, Roethlisberger and Maslow
Contributions:	Importance of social and psychological factors in influencing work performance
Limitations:	Ignored the role of the formal work group and worker rationality

1.8 Modern approaches

Since the 1950s, modern approaches to the study of management have sought to build on and integrate many of the elements of the classical approaches and, in so doing, provide a framework for managing the modern organisation. As industries have matured and evolved and competition has steadily increased, researchers and practitioners have become more concerned about how to manage for competitive success. As a result there has been an ever-increasing amount of literature on management, to such an extent that Koontz referred to the 'management theory jungle' (1980:175). Rather than an exhaustive list of all of the contributions, the next section concentrates on systems theory, contingency theory, total quality management, and organisational culture, which are four critically important approaches, representing the most dominant and influential of modern management theories.

1.8.1 Systems theory

The systems approach to the study of management originated in the work of Barnard (1938) and came to the fore of management literature in the 1950s. Many of the classical approaches had ignored the role of the external environment and tended to concentrate on particular aspects of the organisation rather then viewing it as a whole. In the 1950s, management theorists began to consider the organisation as a whole system and developed systems theory as a means of interpreting organisations.

A SYSTEM is a set of interdependent parts or elements which function as a whole in achieving certain goals or objectives. Systems theory argues that organisations should be seen as systems that transform inputs from the external environment into outputs to the external environment. Figure 1.12 outlines the basic model of systems theory.

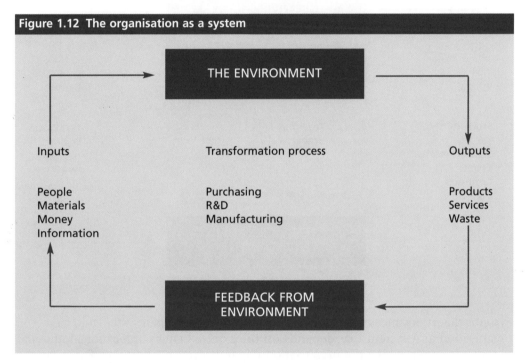

Figure 1.12 The organisation as a system

THE ENVIRONMENT

Inputs — Transformation process — Outputs

People / Materials / Money / Information

Purchasing / R&D / Manufacturing

Products / Services / Waste

FEEDBACK FROM ENVIRONMENT

The inputs an organisation uses are commonly termed 'factors of production' and include materials, money, information and people. The organisation transforms such inputs into outputs in the form of goods or services which are then exchanged in the external environment. Such outputs to the environment provide feedback for the organisation, enabling it to begin the whole process again. Figure 1.13 provides an example of the application of systems theory to an Irish University or third-level institution and shows how an organisation can be viewed as a system using various inputs and producing outputs to the external environment through its transformation process.

The cycle of inputs, transformation and outputs must be maintained if the organisation is to stay in existence. So the organisation has to be able to produce outputs that will result in energy or feedback from the environment to enable it to begin the process again. An organisation will be profitable when the value created, or what customers are willing to pay, is greater than the cost of inputs and transformation.

One of the key elements of systems theory was that organisations should be viewed as OPEN SYSTEMS rather than CLOSED SYSTEMS. Many of the classical approaches treated organisations as closed systems which meant that the organisation did not depend on interactions with the external environment for survival and in this sense acted as a closed entity. The classical approaches, in concentrating on closed systems and internal efficiency, ignored the fact that an organisation depends on the environment for inputs and on a market for outputs.

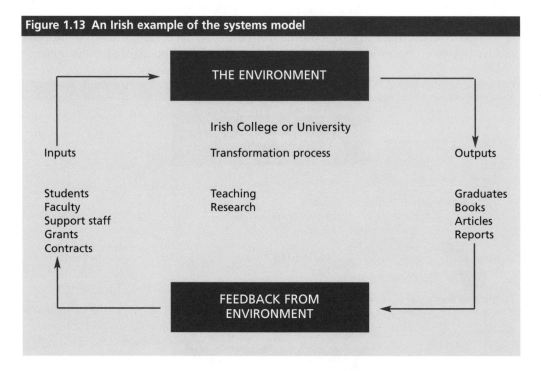

Figure 1.13 An Irish example of the systems model

THE ENVIRONMENT

Irish College or University

Inputs	Transformation process	Outputs
Students	Teaching	Graduates
Faculty	Research	Books
Support staff		Articles
Grants		Reports
Contracts		

FEEDBACK FROM ENVIRONMENT

Systems theory advances the idea of the organisation as an open system and views the organisation as a system that depends on the external environment for inputs *and* outputs. In other words, the organisation depends on other systems. For example, universities or third-level institutions all depend on inputs in the form of students and faculty. In addition, they are dependent on the environment to sell or market their outputs in the form of graduates and research. So if the organisation is to survive it must not only be aware of, but also respond to, systems that supply it and in turn those which it supplies.

In viewing organisations as closed systems many of the classical approaches were solely concerned with internal efficiency. By taking an open systems view another important dimension for managers becomes apparent—EFFECTIVENESS. Effectiveness is the extent to which the organisation's outputs match the needs and wants of the external environment. The effectiveness of, for example, the university or third-level institution mentioned above can be determined by the extent to which the external environment needs and wants students and research. If the environment does not need or want the outputs then the organisation cannot be effective no matter how efficient it is.

As all systems tend to have SUB-SYSTEMS, the organisation can be viewed as a series of sub-systems that comprise of a whole system—the organisation. Each sub-system itself can be viewed as a system having its own sub-systems.

The organisation can also be viewed as a sub-system of a wider system. For example, the world economy can be viewed as a system with each of the national economies as sub-systems. In turn the Irish national economy is made up of various sub-systems including industries. In the case of Glanbia, for instance, this organisation is a sub-system of the wider food industry. The realisation that the organisation is both a system and a sub-system encourages it to think in whole terms. As a result, it should be easier for the organisation to see the effect any single action it takes will have on its ability to achieve wider organisational goals.

Systems theory also highlights the point that if the performance of the organisation is the product of interactions of its various parts it is possible for the action of two or more parts to achieve more than either is capable of individually. This concept is referred to as SYNERGY and means that the creation of a whole is often greater than the sum of its parts. Therefore the performance of an organisation as a whole depends more on how well its parts relate than on how well each operates. The implication for management is that organisations need to be managed in terms of their interactions, not on the basis of their independent actions.

The most important contribution made by systems theory is its recognition of the relationship between an organisation and its environment, especially in terms of achieving organisational effectiveness. Viewing an organisation as an open system emphasises the importance of the external environment both for inputs and for markets for outputs. As a system the organisation also has various sub-systems which must interact well with each other, sometimes achieving a synergy where the whole is greater than the sum of the parts. One limitation of this approach, however, is that it does not provide details on the functions and duties of managers working in open systems. Nonetheless, systems theory marked a step away from a sole focus on internal operations to one which incorporated the external environment.

1.8.2 Contingency theory

The second modern approach to the study of management attempts to integrate the concepts of earlier approaches, especially systems theory. CONTINGENCY THEORY advocates that managerial practice depends on the situation facing an organisation. Advocates of contingency theory, and therefore CONTINGENCY MANAGEMENT, argue that it is impossible to specify a single way of managing that works best in all situations because circumstances facing organisations are varied and continually changing. Consequently, contingency theory rejects the idea of universal principles of management which can be applied in every case.

Contingency theory accepts that every organisation is distinct, operating in a unique environment with different employees and organisational objectives. Such differences mean that managers have to consider the circumstances of each situation before taking any action. The different circumstances or situations facing organisations are called CONTINGENCIES. Managerial response depends on identifying key contingencies in an organisational setting. The main contingencies are:

▶ the rate of change and complexity of the external environment
▶ the types of technology, tasks and resources used by the organisation
▶ the internal strengths and weaknesses of the organisation
▶ the values, skills and attitudes of the workforce.

These various contingencies affect the type of managerial action required by the organisation and its degree of success. For example, a universal strategy of low-cost products will only be effective if the market is cost-conscious. If the market emphasises QUALITY then such a strategy will not be effective for the organisation. In this example the success of the strategy is contingent upon the demands of the external environment. It should be noted, however, that low costs do not necessarily lead to poor quality but high quality is usually associated with higher costs.

Only when a manager understands the contingencies facing the organisation, is it possible to identify which situations demand particular managerial action. Depending on the situation at hand or the contingency, the organisation can categorise the situation and use an appropriate form of structure, managerial process or competitive strategy. Much of the research conducted within the contingency framework concentrated on how different environments and technologies affect the structure and processes of the organisation.

Lawrence and Lorsch (1969), both from the Harvard Business School, argued that the structure of an organisation is contingent upon the environment within which it operates. Their approach to structure is based on research undertaken in 10 organisations in three different industrial sectors—plastics (six organisations), food (two) and containers (two).

In order to deal effectively with the external environment, organisations develop segmented units to deal with specific aspects of the environment. For example, organisational functions are typically divided into production, sales, research and development (R & D) and finance, each of which has to cope with different sub-sections of the environment. Lawrence and Lorsch used the term DIFFERENTIATION to describe this SEGMENTATION or breaking down of functions. They defined differentiation as 'the differences in cognitive and emotional orientation of managers in various functional areas' (1969:11).

However, organisations also need to be co-ordinated to achieve effective transaction with the environment. Such CO-ORDINATION and collaboration is achieved through integration, which Lawrence and Lorsch define as 'the quality of the state of collaboration existing among departments that are needed to achieve unity of effort demanded by the environment' (1969:11). Integration can be achieved through mechanisms such as direct managerial contact, hierarchy, formal and informal communication and through more sophisticated devices such as permanent integrating teams and integrative departments.

During the course of their research Lawrence and Lorsch found that the greater the level of uncertainty in the environment the greater the diversity or differentiation among organisational sub-units. For example, organisations in the plastics industry, faced by a high degree of uncertainty, significantly differentiated between sales, R & D, finance and production. In contrast organisations in the container industry which faced a more certain environment employed less differentiation.

Greater differentiation, however, creates the potential for conflict between sub-units as the specialist groups develop their own ways of dealing with uncertainty in the environment. Highly differentiated organisations consequently require appropriate methods of integration and conflict resolution. Lawrence and Lorsch found that the greater the degree of differentiation the greater the need for integration. For example, high-performing organisations within the plastic sector which had the highest level of differentiation used a variety of integrative mechanisms including direct managerial contact, hierarchy, communications, permanent cross-functional teams and integrative departments. In contrast the container industry's lower levels of differentiation required less integration in the form of direct managerial contact, hierarchy and communications.

Lawrence and Lorsch concluded that effective organisational functioning depended on an appropriate three-way relationship between uncertainty and diversity within the environment, the degree of differentiation and the state of integration achieved. In this way the structure of a successful organisation was contingent upon its environment, as shown in Figure 1.14.

Figure 1.14 The Lawrence and Lorsch framework

Contingency: Environmental stability/certainty

Environmental uncertainty and instability ———▶ High differentiation and integration

Environmental certainty and stability ———▶ Less differentiation and integration

---

In relation to technology, Burns and Stalker (1961) argued that the structure of the organisation was contingent upon the rate of technological change, as shown in Figure 1.15. Based on research in the UK they found that if the rate of technological change was slow the most effective structure is mechanistic, but if the rate of change is rapid then a more flexible—organic—type of structure is required, which allows flexibility as demanded by the pace of change.

Figure 1.15 The Burns and Stalker framework

Contingency: Rate of technological change

Slow rate of change ——————————————————▶ Mechanistic structure

Fast rate of change ——————————————————▶ Organic structure

A mechanistic form of structure in mainly hierarchical in nature with communications and interaction occurring vertically. In this form of structure knowledge is concentrated at the top and continued membership of the organisation is based on obedience and loyalty. Therefore the mechanistic form of structure is similar to a bureaucracy. In contrast, the organic structure is like a network with interactions and communications occurring both horizontally and vertically. Knowledge is based whereever it is most suitable for the organisation and membership requires commitment to the organisation.

Lawrence and Lorsch, Burns and Stalker and another influential theorist on the relationship between structure and technology—Woodward, will be discussed in more detail in Chapter 6 on organising.

An example of an Irish company which took a contingency approach to its structure can be found in Team Aer Lingus. Up until 1990, Team was the Maintenance and Engineering (M & E) Department of the national airline involved in aircraft maintenance of the Aer Lingus fleet and outside contracts. The external environment facing M & E remained relatively stable during the 1960s and 1970s which suited the department's bureaucratic structure. However, once the environment became more dynamic and competitive in the mid-1980s it was forced to change its structure in order to take advantage of market opportunities within the environment. As a result Team was formed as a separate company with its own internal business unit structure. Layers of hierarchy were eliminated and job design was widened in an attempt to provide more flexibility to meet the demands of the competitive environment.

The main contribution of contingency theory is that it recognised the limitations of universal principles of management and identified contingencies under which different actions are required. These ideas gained widespread acceptance, especially in relation to the role of technology and the external environment. The main problem associated with the approach is that it may not be applicable to all managerial issues and it is almost impossible to identify all contingencies facing organisations. Despite these problems, contingency theory is still popular today, because it emphasises the need for managers to be flexible and to adapt to changing conditions. In recognising that the world is too complex for one best way of managing to exist, contingency theory has provided much food for thought in contemporary management.

1.8.3 Total quality management

Improving the quality of products and services is not a new idea but since the 1950s there has been an upsurge of interest in the role quality improvement can play in organisational success. Traditionally, quality was seen as the responsibility of the quality control department, whose role was to identify and weed out mistakes after they had occurred. However, seeking to control mistakes after they had been made meant that many quality defects were already embedded in the product and were essentially hidden and difficult to locate. Organisations, therefore, did the best they could to uncover mistakes but were resigned to the fact that certain mistakes would remain undetected. Total quality management (TQM) emphasised preventing mistakes rather than finding or correcting them. In order to achieve this, responsibility for quality shifted from those in quality control to all members of the organisation. This led many organisations to fundamentally alter their operations.

The fathers of the Quality Revolution were both American, W. Deming and J. Juran, though it was the Japanese who in the 1950s embraced their ideals. Much of Japan's postwar manufacturing success has been attributed to both Deming and Juran. Deming believed that by improving quality costs would decrease due to less reworking, fewer mistakes, fewer delays and better all round use of time. This would, he believed, result in greater productivity and enable the organisation to capture a larger share of the market with a lower price and higher quality as illustrated in Figure 1.16. Therefore the more quality became embedded in the organisation the less it would cost over time.

Deming produced a list of fourteen points which he believed were essential ingredients for achieving quality within an organisation. He emphasised that organisations should cease to rely on inspection to ensure quality—quality should be built into every stage of the production process with statistical controls to prevent, rather than detect, defects. Deming also believed that the cause of inefficiency and poor quality lay with the systems used and not the people using them. Therefore, it was management's responsibility to correct the systems to achieve high quality. He further stressed the importance of reducing deviations from standards and distinguished between special causes of variation (correctable) and common causes of variation (random).

Figure 1.16 Deming's model of quality improvement

Improve quality
↓
Decrease costs due to:
↓
1. Less rework
2. Fewer mistakes
3. Fewer delays
4. Better all-round use of time
↓
Greater productivity
↓
Larger market share
Lower price and higher quality

Juran also taught quality to the Japanese and argued that 80 per cent of quality defects were correctable and therefore controllable by management. Consequently he believed it was management's responsibility to correct this problem. Quality, he believed, revolved around three areas:

▶ quality planning to identify the processes which would be capable of meeting standards.

▶ quality control to highlight when corrective action was required

▶ quality improvement to identify ways of doing things better.

The successful application of these concepts in Japan by the 1970s was evidenced by their increasing power in the US steel, auto and electronics markets. As a result, organisations world-wide attempted to enjoy the same success as the Japanese and took total quality initiatives on board with the aim of helping organisations cope with increased competition.

Total quality management has come to refer to an organisation's philosophy and its efforts to achieve a total quality product/service through the involvement of the entire organisation from top to bottom, with customer satisfaction as the driving force. The TQM approach involves a number of steps, shown in Figure 1.17.

Figure 1.17 The TQM approach

1. Finding out what the customer wants
↓
2. Designing a product/service that meets/exceeds customer requirements
↓
3. Designing a production process so that tasks are done correctly first time
↓
4. Keeping track of performance results
↓
5. Extending this approach to suppliers and distributors

Source: Stevenson, W. *Production/Operations Management,* p. 104. Irwin, Illinois 1989.

The first step involves finding out about customer requirements. This can be achieved through the use of surveys and focus-group interviews. Following on from this a product/service is designed to meet customer requirements focusing on easy use and easy production. The production process must then be designed to determine where mistakes are likely to occur, and to prevent them. Performance results are gathered and monitored to make sure that continuous improvement takes place. Finally, organisations that have developed TQM attempt to extend the principles to those who supply their raw materials and those who distribute the final good/service.

An important feature of the TQM approach is that the entire organisation is involved in the search for quality improvement and nothing is regarded as untouchable. Members of a TQM organisation view themselves as internal customers; different sections within an organisation will be viewed as customers of other sections. For example, the materials department supplies the production department with raw materials, so the production department becomes a customer of the materials department. By focusing on what is needed in order to satisfy internal customers it is quite frequently possible to improve the system, thereby increasing external customer satisfaction.

Within a TQM system each employee is responsible for the quality of his/her work and is expected to produce goods/services that meet specifications, and to find mistakes that occur. The emphasis is on producing goods and services correctly the first time, rather than identifying faults that have already been made. In this way, each employee becomes a quality inspector for his/her own work. When the work is then passed on to the next internal customer in the process the employee is certifying that the good/service meets the agreed quality standards.

Dean and Bowen (1994) have usefully viewed TQM in terms of its principles, practices and techniques as shown in Table 1.1.

Table 1.1 The principles, practices and techniques of total quality management

Principles	Practices	Techniques
1. Customer focus	Direct customer contact and information gathering	Customer survey and focus group
2. Continuous improvement	Process analysis, reengineering, problem solving	Flow charts, statistical process control
3. Teamwork	Team formation, training and establishment of arrangements	Team-building mechanisms

Source: Adapted from Dean and Bowen (1994:4).

The TQM philosophy rests on three principles, customer focus, continuous improvement and teamwork. Each principle is implemented through a set of practices which are in turn supported by a variety of techniques. The principle of customer focus is implemented through promoting direct contact with customers, collecting information about customer expectations and distributing this information throughout the organisation. Techniques used to achieve this include customer surveys. This practice is extended to include internal customers.

Continuous improvement requires a commitment to search for improvements to both technical and administrative processes within the organisation (Dean and Bowen 1994). Practices include process analysis and reengineering which can be achieved through the use of flowcharts and statistical process control. Teamwork is the final principle and is based on the idea that organisations as systems must all strive to achieve a common goal rather than pursue sub-goals. Teamwork practices include identifying the needs of all teams and finding arrangements of mutual benefit to all involved. This is often achieved by introducing cross-functional teams. These principles are mutually reinforcing and are devised to ultimately meet customers needs.

Total quality, as originally advocated by Deming and Juran, has become a vital ingredient for corporate success. It has become one of the most important tools in achieving competitive advantage and is seen as an important way for an organisation to differentiate itself from competitors. However, as Reger *et al.* (1994) point out, a successful move to a TQM philosophy requires radical organisational change and this is something that organisations find difficult to achieve in the short term. On the whole TQM has created a revolution in the way quality can be managed and improved and has become a cornerstone in modern management thought.

1.8.4 Organisational culture

The final approach which will be examined in this chapter is organisational culture and its affect on management. An organisation's culture is concerned with the shared values, beliefs and assumptions held by members of the organisation and commonly communicated through symbolic means. Schein (1985:14) provides a useful definition of organisational culture:

Organisational culture is the pattern of basic assumptions that a given group has invented, discovered or developed in learning to cope with its problems of external adaptation and internal integration.

The culture of an organisation develops over time from a unique blend of three interdependent elements, as shown in Figure 1.18. First, an organisation's culture is developed by the prevailing national culture within which the organisation operates. Second, the nature of the industry acts as a determinant of an organisation's culture. Specific industries contain certain cultural characteristics which become manifest in an organisation's culture. Gordon (1991) argues that organisational culture is shaped by the competitive environment and the degree to which the organisation is in a monopoly situation or faced by many competitors. Similarly, customer requirements in the form of reliability versus novelty shape an organisation's culture. Finally, society holds certain expectations about particular industries which influences the values adopted. Both the role of national culture and industry characteristics reflect the view that the organisation is shaped by its environment in line with the open systems theory of Katz and Kahn (1966). The final element shaping an organisation's culture is the role of the founders of the organisation. Founder members shape organisational culture by their own cultural values which they use to develop assumptions and theories in establishing the organisation. Organisational culture is therefore developed from three interdependent sources all of which influence the beliefs, values and assumptions of the organisation.

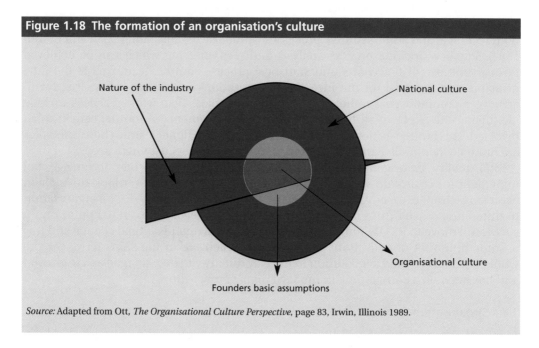

Figure 1.18 The formation of an organisation's culture

Nature of the industry

National culture

Organisational culture

Founders basic assumptions

Source: Adapted from Ott, *The Organisational Culture Perspective,* page 83, Irwin, Illinois 1989.

Organisational culture was catapulted to the forefront of management literature with the publication of four books in the early 1980s—*The Art of Japanese Management* (Pascale and Athos 1981), *In Search of Excellence* (Peters and Waterman 1982), *Theory Z* (Ouchi 1981) and *Corporate Cultures* (Deal and Kennedy 1982). These and subsequent authors have tried to explain why some organisations are more successful than others and have pinpointed aspects of culture which they argue contribute to organisational performance. The organisational culture perspective, therefore, believes that many of the behaviours within an organisation are predetermined by the patterns of basic assumptions in the organisation—its culture. Effective management therefore should focus on the culture of an organisation rather than on the structures and systems of the organisation.

Ouchi (1981) analysed the organisational cultures of three groups of organisations which he characterised as typical American organisations, typical Japanese organisations and Type Z American organisations. Through his analysis Ouchi developed seven cultural factors on which these three types of organisation could be compared. Ouchi believed that the cultures of the typical Japanese organisation and the Type Z American organisation were very different to the typical American organisation. Ouchi argued that the differences in culture explained the success of Japanese and Type Z organisations at the expense of typical American organisations. The seven points of cultural comparison developed by Ouchi are shown in Figure 1.19.

Figure 1.19 The Ouchi framework

Cultural value	Japanese Co.	Type Z	Typical US Co
Commitment to employees	Lifetime employment	Long-term employment	Short-term employment
Evaluation	Slow and qualitative	Slow and qualitative	Fast and quantitative
Careers	Very broad	Moderately broad	Narrow
Control	Implicit and informal	Implicit and informal	Explicit and formal
Decision-making	Group concensus	Group concensus	Individual
Responsibility	Group	Group	Individual
Concern for people	Holistic	Holistic	Narrow

Source: Ouchi, W, *Theory Z: How American Business can meet the Japanese Challenge,* Addison-Wesely Massachussetts 1981

Peters and Waterman (1982) focused more specifically than Ouchi on the relationship between organisational culture and performance. Peters and Waterman chose a sample of highly successful organisations and tried to describe the management practices that led these organisations to be so successful. They identified eight cultural values that led to successful management practices which they called excellent values. Figure 1.20 lists the eight excellent cultural characteristics.

Figure 1.20 The Peters and Waterman framework

Characteristics of the excellent organisation

1. **Bias for action**: Managers are expected to make decisions even if all the facts are not available
2. **Stay close to the customer**: Customers should be valued over everything else
3. **Encourage autonomy and entrepreneurship**: The organisation is broken into small, more manageable parts and these are encouraged to be independent, creative and risk-taking
4. **Encourage productivity through people**: People are the organisation's most important asset and the organisation must let them flourish
5. **Hands-on management**: Managers stay in touch with business activities by wandering around the organisation and not managing from behind closed doors
6. **Stick to the knitting**: Reluctance to engage in business activitiesoutside of the organisation's core expertise
7. **Simple form, lean staff**: Few administrative and hierarchical layers and small corporate staff
8. **Simultaneously loosely and tightly organised**: Tightly organised in that all organisational members understand and believe in the organisation's values. At the same time, loosely organised in that the organisation has fewer administrative overheads, fewer staff members and fewer rules and procedures

The organisational culture perspective therefore argued that successful management resulted from the development of key cultural values rather than any innovations in structure and systems. The key contribution made by the approach was that it recognised the important role that organisational culture plays within an organisation.

The limitations of the approach are associated with it being an unscientific approach, that organisational cultures are not easily identifiable and that many of the excellent organisations identified in the research (especially by Peters and Waterman) have subsequently performed badly. The approach also largely ignores the role of structures and systems within the organisation and their role in achieving organisational success.

1.8.5 The modern approaches: a summary

Systems theory, contingency theory, total quality management and organisational culture have dominated the field of management thought since the 1950s and are still influential, both in theory and practice. The key contributions and limitations of the various approaches are outlined in Figure 1.21.

Figure 1.21 Modern approaches: a summary	
School of thought:	Systems theory: 1950s–present day
Proponents:	Barnard and Katz and Khan
Contribution:	Organisation seen as open system interacting with the environment; organisation is both a system and a sub system; synergies exist and multiple ways to achieve the same outcome
Limitations:	No specific guidelines on the functions and duties of managers
School of thought:	Contingency theory: 1960s–present day
Proponents:	Burns and Stalker and Lawrence and Lorsch
Contribution:	Appropriate managerial action depends on situational contingencies; no one best way of managing
Limitations:	Not possible to identify all contingencies; may not applyto all managerial issues
School of thought:	Total Quality Management: 1970s–present day
Proponents:	Deming and Juran
Contribution:	Quality is an important means of achieving competitive advantage; emphasises total quality management throughout the organisation and on doing things right first time
Limitations:	Ignores other issues such as structure and strategy
School of thought:	Organisational Culture: 1980s–present day
Proponents:	Peters and Waterman, Ouchi, Deal and Kennedy and Pascale and Athos
Contribution:	Highlighted the importance of organisational culture in an organisation's success
Limitations:	Largely unscientific approach, culture difficult to identify and some research within the school has been discredited

Systems theory recognised the organisation as an open system depending on the external environment for survival, and emphasised that efficiency alone was not sufficient for survival. In order to be successful organisations have to be effective in ensuring a match between what they produce and what the external environment wants and needs.

Contingency theory argues that best management practice depends on or is contingent upon the situation at hand. The technology employed by the organisation and the environment within which it operates often influence the managerial action required for success.

Total quality management emphasises the importance of improving quality to achieve competitive advantage. It was argued that TQM could significantly reduce costs, focus on customer satisfaction and lead to huge quality gains, all of which benefit the organisation. In terms of management the focus is on building total quality into every aspect of the organisation and at every level so that quality becomes everyone's responsibility, not just the responsibility of those concerned solely with quality control.

Organisational culture emphasises the role that an organisation's culture can play in shaping organisational success. It is argued that managers should shift their focus from structures and systems and concentrate their efforts on developing and sustaining cultural values that contribute to organisational success.

These approaches arc still popular today in the field of management thought and represent four of the most critical issues facing managers as they try to achieve competitive advantage in the increasingly competitive external environment. Systems theory highlights the importance of the environment for organisational survival. Contingency theory emphasises that best management practice depends on the situation and that must be evaluated by the manager. TQM focuses on the role quality can play in reducing costs and improving quality. Finally, organisational culture emphasises the importance of the organisation's basic values and assumptions and the important role they play in organisational success. All of these factors need to be adequately addressed by managers in today's environment if the organisation is to be successful. These points will be further developed throughout the book.

1.9 Summary of key propositions

▶ Management has been largely responsible for the development of the pattern of industry as we know it today. Management has facilitated the co-ordination of people with different skills and knowledge to achieve organisational goals.

▶ Management is the process of achieving desired results through an efficient utilisation of human and material resources. Managers are individuals within organisations who are responsible for the process of management.

▶ Management typically has five main functions which logically follow on from one another: planning involves establishing what needs to be done; organising establishes how tasks should be completed; staffing and personnel ensures the availability of human resources to achieve such tasks; leading involves directing and motivating employees towards the attainment of organisational goals; and control involves measuring actual performance against desired performance and taking corrective action.

▶ The earliest contributions to management thought can be traced back to the Sumerians, the ancient Egyptians and the Romans. One of the most enduring examples of early management practice is the Catholic Church.

▶ The Industrial Revolution marked a watershed in the development of management thought. As industries expanded to take advantage of new markets and techno-logical innovations, organisations became larger and more complex. This led to the development of new management techniques to cope with the issues presented by industrialisation, namely, production, efficiency and cost savings.

▶ In response to the managerial challenges posed by industrialisation, what has been termed the 'classical' approach to management emerged at the turn of the century. The major schools of thought associated with the classical approach are scientific management, administrative management, bureaucracy and human relations.

▶ Scientific management emphasised the development of one best way of performing a task through the application of scientific methods. The birth of scientific management is attributed to Taylor and his pioneering work in the Bethlehem Steel Works.

▶ Administrative management was based on the personal experiences of its key proponents and focused on senior managers and the policy issues they faced. The father of administrative management is Henri Fayol, who identified management as a separate business activity with five functions. Fayol also developed fourteen principles of management.

▶ Max Weber concentrated on how organisations should be structured to ensure efficiency. He developed what he perceived to be the ideal form of structure and called it bureaucracy. The bureaucratic structure emphasised detailed rules and procedures, hierarchy and impersonal relationships between organisational members.

▶ The human relations movement concentrated on the human side of management and tried to understand how social and psychological factors influence performance. Mayo and his associates conducted the Hawthorne Studies which proved that social needs took precedence over economic needs and that the informal work group exerts control over employee performance.

▶ The modern approaches to management have developed from the 1950s and include systems theory, contingency theory, total quality management and organisational culture. Systems theory argues that organisations should be viewed as systems that transform inputs into outputs to the environment. Consequently, the organisation constantly interacts with its environment. Key advocates of this approach include Barnard and Katz and Kahn.

▶ Contingency theory argues that there is no one best way of managing due to the different situations or contingencies facing organisations. The most common contingencies are the external environment, technology, internal strengths and weaknesses of the organisation and the values and skills of the workforce. Burns and Stalker and Lawrence and Lorsch examined the contingencies affecting structure.

▶ Total quality management was pioneered by Juran and Deming working in Japan. They argued that quality was the key to organisational success. The TQM approach they developed emphasised prevention rather than the correction of mistakes. In order to achieve this, responsibility for quality shifted from the quality control department to all members of the organisation.

▶ The organisational culture approach emphasises the importance of culture in influencing behaviour within the organisation. Advocates of this approach, such as Peters and Waterman and Ouchi, argue that effective management should focus on culture rather than structures and systems.

▶ All of the issues raised by the various approaches need to be considered by managers when striving to compete in the present business environment.

Discussion questions

❶ What is scientific management? Why was it so popular?

❷ What effect did the Industrial Revolution have on management?

❸ Compare and contrast scientific and administrative management.

❹ What were the Hawthorne Studies? Why were they so important to the development of management thought?

❺ What are the main elements of bureaucracy? What are its advantages and disadvantages?

❻ How did systems theory try to overcome the limitations of earlier approaches?

❼ Explain why contingency theory has become so popular.

❽ What is total quality management? What does it try to achieve?

❾ How do the modern approaches to management differ from the classical approaches?

❿ Taylor and Fayol have both been accused of seeking a one best way of managing organisations. To what extent is this statement true?

⓫ Why is an organisation's culture important for managers to consider?

Concluding case: The Hawthorne Effect—fact or myth?

The enduring legacy of the famous Hawthorne Studies, conducted in Western Electric in the 1920s and 1930s, is the Hawthorne Effect, which is generally accepted to describe the fact that the behaviour of subjects during an experiment changes due to the fact that they are aware of observation. No other set of experiments in the field of social science has had such a remarkable and pervasive influence as the Hawthorne Studies and yet, despite their widespread acceptance, little research has been conducted into the quality and validity of the original experiments.

The experiments

The Illumination Experiments predate the actual Hawthorne Studies and sought to establish the relationship between levels of lighting and performance. Mayo and Roethlisberger concluded, when they first arrived at the plant, that these initial studies 'failed to answer the specific question of the relation between illumination and efficiency'; nonetheless, 'they provided great stimulus for more research in the field of human relations' (Roethlisberger and Dickson 1939).

The best known of the Hawthorne Studies were the Relay Assembly Test Room (RATR) Experiments which took place over a period of six years (270 weeks) although the first two years and two months (114 weeks) are considered to be the most important as they influenced subsequent studies carried out. The first 13 experimental periods in the RATR can be divided into:

❶ An introductory phase (periods 1–3)

❷ A rest-pause phase (periods 4–7)

❸ A shorter work-day and week phase (periods 8–13).

The female subjects involved in the study were not chosen randomly but one of the operators was asked to choose four other assemblers and she picked a friend and three others that she knew. A layout operator was chosen by management to service the five assemblers. The women were placed in a test room separated from their department and supervisor. Here their output of relays was recorded while changes to their working conditions were made; these included less variation in the task, shorter hours, the introduction of rest pauses, more friendly supervision and an incentive payment system. These changes were introduced cumulatively and no control group was established for comparative purposes.

At the end of the two-year period output had increased by 30 per cent, but not all the periods under examination had yielded the same result. In periods 2, 6, 10 and 12, hourly group production actually declined. However, by this time the researchers were confident of the fact that the physical conditions had little to do with the results, which they believed were caused by a change in mental attitude by the six participants as a result of less supervision, the formation of a cohesive group, etc. The standard report of the study, however, recognises that any of a number changes could hypothetically cause this change in mental attitude chief among them:

- ▶ changes in character and physical context of work task
- ▶ reduction in fatigue and monotony due to introduction of rest pauses and reduced hours of work
- ▶ change in payment system
- ▶ changes in supervision and group relations.

The second stage of the RATR involved the introduction of a new incentive scheme only. Five girls who, under normal factory conditions, were employed on the same sort of task as the girls in stage 1 were given a preferred incentive scheme which had been used throughout stage 1 whereby the earnings of each participant was related to the average of each participant and not the average of an entire department. Output increased by 12.6 per cent but the experiment caused so much upset among the remainder of the workforce that it had to be discontinued after nine weeks. When the participants returned to their normal payment scheme their output dropped by 16 per cent. These results would perhaps lead us to conclude that the incentive scheme had an effect on performance. However, the researchers involved concluded that it was due to inter-group rivalry resulting from the establishment of this second group. The increased output from stage 2 showed that in nine weeks as much was produced as under stage 1 in nine months. This point was never discussed.

The Bank Wiring Observation Room (BWOR) was the final experiment in the Hawthorne Studies and involved 14 men being placed in a special room for observation. Men were chosen for this study because it was felt they might act differently to women. The participants were told to work normally and were assured that nothing done in front of the observers would be used against them. The observers discovered that two informal groups existed in the room. One group consisted of those who assembled connector equipment and the other consisted of those involved with selector equipment. Product figures assumed a straight-line function when plotted over consecutive work days. Essentially the wiremen felt as they had in the main department that two completed pieces of equipment per day should be their standard output. The men admitted that they were capable of producing more than this. However, with the effects of the depression approaching they were afraid of working themselves out of a job.

Problems with the study

❶ In relation to the Illumination Experiments, according to later accounts, the women in each of these experiments worked progressively faster regardless of increases or decreases in lighting. But the only account of these experiments published at any time was a brief summary in an engineering journal. No detailed or documented report ever came out and the original research data disappeared.

❷ In relation to the BWOR experiements, the men were being observed yet there is no documented evidence of an increase in output which we would expect to find where there is a Hawthorne Effect in operation.

❸ An oft-unmentioned factor associated with the RATR experiments is the fact that two out of the five participants had to be replaced mid-experiment for talking too much and for slow output. This point seriously contaminates any subsequent findings of increased output by the group.

❹ Claims of continuing gains in productivity do not stand up under careful examination. The group's hourly output actually fell during periods when rest breaks were withdrawn and work-day length increased, although it cannot be denied that overall productivity increased by 30 per cent.

❺ In the RATR experiment in stages 1 to 3, there was no attempt to establish sample groups representative of any larger population than the groups themselves. Therefore generalisation is not possible. There was no attempt to employ control data from the output records of the women who were not put under special experimental conditions. Even if both of these points had been met the experiments would still have been of only minor scientific value since a group of five subjects is too small to yield scientific and statistically reliable results.

❻ The idea that being aware of observation and special attention affects people's behaviour has not been supported in subsequent tests (see Adair 1984). In addition baseline data was gathered by the researchers for both the RATR and BWOR before the experiments began. Inspection of the production data shows that baseline data for the relay assemblers in period 1 did not differ from data in period 2 after the women were chosen and placed in a separate room. Similarly the production data for the BWOR participants during an 18-week baseline period did not differ from their production data once they were chosen. This evidence alone seems to discredit the 'special attention' explanation of the Hawthorne Effect.

❼ There are numerous other possible explanations that could have accounted for the results which have not been given adequate consideration. Researchers never considered the possibility that output rose over a five-year period because the women became more skilled and therefore faster at their work. As their level of output was not measured on their return to their old department, it is impossible to test this theory. Another possibility is that output increased throughout the Hawthorne Studies due to the onset of the depression in the 1930s as people worked harder because they needed more money.

The Hawthorne Effect still generates much controversy and debate among researchers in the field of social science. However, from a historical viewpoint the importance of the reliability and validity of the original experiments comes only a poor second when compared to the interest stimulated by such experiments in the role of the human factor within organisations. It is the impact of these series of experiments rather than their academic justification that secure a place for the Hawthorne Studies in the history of management.

Case adapted from Rice (1982); Jones (1990); Jones (1992); Carey (1967); Yunker (1993).

Case questions

❶ What are the most fundamental problems associated the existence of a Hawthorne Effect?

❷ What improvements could possibly be made to the original studies to rectify some of the problems?

❸ Are any of the alternative explanations plausible in your opinion?

Bibliography

Adair, J. (1984) 'The Hawthorne Effect: A Reconsideration of the Methodological Artefact', *Journal of Applied Psychology*, 69, 334–45.

Barnard, C. (1938) *The Functions of the Executive*. Cambridge, Mass: Harvard University Press.

Baughman, J.(ed.) (1969) *The History of American Management Thought*. New Jersey: Prentice Hall.

Burns, T. and Stalker, G. (1961) *The Management of Innovation*. London: Tavistock.

Carey, A. (1967) 'The Hawthorne Studies: A Radical Criticism', *American Sociological Review*, 32, 403–16.

Deal, T. & Kennedy, A. (1982) *Corporate Culture: The Rites and Rituals of Corporate Life.*, Mass: Wesely.

Dean, J. and Bowen, D. (1994) 'Management Theory and Total Quality: Improving Research and Practice Through Theory Development', *Academy of Management Review*, 19 (3), 392–427.

Deming, W. (1982) *Quality Productivity and Competitive Position*. Cambridge, Mass: MIT.

Drucker, P. (1980) *Managing in Turbulent Times*. London: Heinemann.

Drucker, P. (1949) *The Frontiers of Management*. London: Heinemann.

Fayol, H. (1949) *General and Industrial Management*, translation of *Administration Industrielle et Générale* (1916). London: Pitman.

Gordon, G. (1991) 'Industry Determinants of Organisational Culture', *Academy of Management Review*, 16 (2), 339–58.

Handy, C. (1993) *Understanding Organisations*. London: Penguin.

Jones, S. (1990) 'Worker Interdependence and Output: The Hawthorne Studies Re-evaluated', *American Sociological Review*, 55, April, 176–90.

Jones, S. (1992) 'Was There a Hawthorne Effect?', *American Journal of Sociology*, 98 (3), 451–68.

Juran, J. (1986) 'The Quality Trilogy', *Quality Progress*, 19 (8), 19–24.

Katz, D. and Kahn, R. (1978) *The Social Psychology of Organisations*. New York: John Wiley.

Koontz, H. (1980) 'The Management Theory Jungle Revisited', *Academy of Management Review*, April, 175–87.

Lawrence, P. and Lorsch, J. (1969) *Organisations and Environment: Managing Differentiation and Integration*. Illinois: Irwin.

Machiavelli, N. (1985) *The Prince*. London: Penguin. Originally published 1532.

Maslow, A. (1954) *Motivation and Personality*. New York: Harper Row.

Maslow, A. (1943) 'A Theory of Human Motivation', *Psychological Review*, 50 (2), 370–96.

Mayo, E.(1949) *The Human Problems of an Industrial Civilisation*. New York: Macmillan.

Metcalf, H. and Urwick, L. (eds) (1941) *Dynamic Administration: The Collected Papers of Mary Parker Follet*. New York: Harper & Brothers.

Ott, M. (1989) *The Organisational Culture Perspective.*, Illinois: Irwin.

Ouchi, W. (1981) *Theory Z: How American Business Can Meet the Japanese Challenge*. Mass: Wesely.

Parsons, H. (1978) 'What Caused the Hawthorne Effect?' *Administration and Society*, 10, 259–83.

Parsons, H. (1974) 'What Happened at Hawthorne?', *Science*, 183, 922–32.

Parsons, H. (1992) 'Hawthorne: An Early OBM Experiment', *Journal of Organisational Behaviour Management*, 12 (1), 27-43.

Pascale, R. and Athos, A. (1981) *The Art of Japanese Management: Applications for American Executives*. New York: Harper Row.

Peters, T. and Waterman, R. (1982) *In Search of Excellence*. New York: Harper Row.

Pugh, D. and Hickson, D. (1989) *Writers on Organisations*. London: Penguin.

Reger, R., Gustafson, L., Demarie, S., and Mullane, J. (1994) 'Reframing the Organisation: Why Implementing Total Quality is Easier Said Than Done', *Academy of Management Review*, 19, (3), 565–85.

Rice, B. (1982) 'The Hawthorne Defect: Persistence of a Flawed Theory', *Psychology Today*, February, 70–74.

Roethlisberger, F. and Dickson, W. (1939) *Management and the Worker*. Cambridge, Mass: Harvard University Press.

Schein, E. (1985) *Organisational Culture and Leadership*. California: Jossey Bass.

Schein, E. (1985) 'The Role of the Founder in Creating Organisational Culture', *Organisational Dynamics*, Summer, 14.

Smith, A. (1937) *An Inquiry Into the Nature and Causes of the Wealth of Nations*. New York: Modern Library. Originally published 1776.

Stevenson, W. (1993) *Production/Operations Management.*, Illinois: Irwin.

Sunday Business Post. Selected articles, April to July 1993.

Taylor, F. (1947) *Scientific Management*. New York: Harper Row.

Urwick, L. (1973). *The Elements of Administration*. London: Pitman.

Weber, M. (1947) *The Theory of Social and Economic Organisation*, translation, Henderson and Talcott. New York: Free Press.

Weihrich, H. and Koontz, H. (1993) *Management: A Global Perspective*. New York: McGraw Hill.

Yunker, G. (1993) 'An Explanation of Positive and Negative Hawthorne Effects: Evidence from the Relay Assembly Test Room and Bank Wiring Observation Room Studies'. Paper presented to the Academy of Management Annual Meeting, Atlanta, Georgia.

Chapter 2   The Development of the Irish Business Sector

2.1 Introduction

This chapter charts the development of the Irish business sector from its earliest industrial activity right up to current events. Historical approaches to industrial development, from early protectionism to free trade and foreign direct investment are considered. The role played by membership of the EC in 1973 is also highlighted. Economic recession and subsequent recovery during the 1990s is explained. The chapter concludes by discussing the key sectors in Irish business and their future prospects.

2.2 The early years

Ireland was largely unaffected by the Industrial Revolution, which swept through the UK and the USA, changing the pattern of industrial development. Despite this fact, according to the 1821 Census of Population, more than one-third of Irish counties (six of which were outside Ulster) had a significant number of people involved in manufacture, trade or handicraft. The census also indicated that 700,000 people were employed in the Irish textile industries, most notably cotton and linen (O'Malley 1980). During this period the country's per capita income rose steadily, averaging at 40 per cent of the UK level in the 1840s, increasing to 60 per cent in 1913. In fact, Irish incomes were higher than those in Finland, Italy and Portugal (Fitzpatrick 2000). Population levels, however, continued to decline in the post-famine era falling from 6.6 million in 1851 to just over 4 million in the early 1900s.

The first census of production in Ireland (32 counties) was undertaken in 1907 and found that industrial activity came a poor second to agriculture in terms of employment and output. However, notwithstanding this fact, Irish industry employed about a 20 per cent of the entire workforce and 50 per cent of industrial output was exported. The country had also earned world-wide recognition in key industrial sectors such as linen, shipbuilding, distilling and brewing, with names like Guinness, and Harland and Wolfe, well-established in their industrial sectors. In addition, Ireland's volume of trade per capita was higher than the British figure. It is important to note, however, that the bulk of industrial activity was centred around the six north-eastern counties.

Acknowledgement

I would like to thank Mr. Peter D. Coyle, Executive Director, Enterprise Ireland for his comments on earlier drafts of this chapter. The opinions expressed and any errors contained within remain the author's.

An important challenge confronted by Irish businesses in the early years of the nineteenth century was the emergence of an organised labour movement. Most European businesses were also faced by similar challenges. The development of a strong labour movement particularly in Dublin and Cork posed difficulties for Irish industry. The growing tensions between management and unions culminated in the now famous Dublin Lockout of 1913. Dublin employers led by William Martin Murphy came into conflict with the Transport Union led by Jim Larkin. When workers refused to sign statements undertaking not to acquire or retain union membership, workers went on strike and were subsequently locked out by their employers. At its height, 20,000 workers from 300 different companies were involved. After six months the workers drifted back to work but the experience radicalised many workers (Fitzpatrick 2000).

2.3 The Irish Free State 1922

With the emergence of the Irish Free State in 1922, Ireland was not only politically but also in theory economically independent. The extent of such economic independence has to be qualified by the fact that the Irish economy remained closely dependent on the UK. The currency tie between the two countries remained and the UK market was the largest Irish export market. In addition much industry in Ireland at the time took the form of UK subsidiary companies.

The most pressing task for the new government was that of building a nation. The country inherited a fully developed banking system, a reasonable communications system, schools, hospitals and valuable external assets (Fitzpatrick 2000). It also inherited the devastation ravaged on the country by both the War of Independence and later the Civil War. The population had also fallen significantly to 3.1 million in 1922.

In terms of industry the most devastating blow to Ireland was the loss of the industrialised north-east, especially the thriving region of Belfast. By the 1920s the industrial labour force amounted to just over 100,000 workers or about 7 per cent of the total labour force (O'Malley 1980). The lack of entrepreneurial tradition within Ireland further undermined the prospects for the fledgling economy. The reasons for the lack of entrepreneurship centre around the ex-colonial status of the economy which by definition meant that the native population was given limited access to business opportunities and managerial positions. In addition, the recent turbulent environment meant that in many cases the 'brightest and best' opted for the relatively safe employment of the civil service, rather than establishing business or seeking employment in the private sector.

The government adopted a conservative approach to both economic and industrial development and received the backing of the banks, large farmers and the Anglo-Irish community, which provided a useful base from which to construct the new state. The government managed to avoid the mistakes made by other countries such as Poland and Germany who printed their own money and consequently suffered severe inflation.

In terms of economic development the government very firmly prioritised the agricultural sector, which at the time employed 50 per cent of the workforce, and was the country's largest exporter. Key members of the government believed that what was good for agriculture would automatically be good for industry. In this sense agriculture was viewed as a vehicle for economic and industrial growth. STATE INTERVENTION in industry was, therefore, kept to a minimum.

Despite its conservative stance on the economy and the development of the industrial sector, the government was responsible for the establishment of an electricity supply service. The decision to construct a hydro-electric plant at Ard na Crusha was taken in 1924 and was largely the brain child of Dr T. McLaughlin, an Irish engineer who had been approached by the government in 1923 to survey Ireland's electricity capacity. The government established the ESB in 1927 to supervise the distribution of electricity nationally. The Shannon Scheme, when it became operational in 1929 was an immediate success. The scheme was so significant that is changed the face of rural Ireland with the introduction of electricity. In the decades that followed, industry also benefited from this ambitious development which added significantly to the Irish industrial infrastructure. The Agricultural Credit Corporation was also established in 1927 to finance the development and expansion of farming and agri business.

The early years of the state, while prioritising agriculture, nonetheless made important inroads into providing a base from which industry could, many years later, develop. However, in this period the development of a vibrant export-driven industrial economy was still a distant hope.

2.4 Self-sufficiency and protectionism: 1932–58

In 1932 Fianna Fail came to power and began to pursue an entirely different approach to industrial policy, one that was economically, but also politically, motivated. This marked the first occasion on which a native Irish government had a coherent economic philosophy. PROTECTIONISM and self-sufficiency was particularly espoused by Arthur Griffith, and based in theory on Frederick List's infant industry argument which advocated a protectionist policy. Like many other countries in Europe at the time, De Valera's government possessed a strong ideological belief in self-sufficiency. For Ireland self-sufficiency was viewed as a means of ensuring economic growth but was also a measure of political independence achieved by the state. Self-sufficiency effectively meant that domestic industries were protected from competition by placing high TARIFFS on imported goods, thereby rendering them more costly than domestic produce. Such tariffs rose to as much as 45 per cent in the following years and only countries like Spain and Germany had higher barriers. A number of new industries, such as car assembly, successfully grew up behind tariff barriers during this period. The Control of Manufacturers Act (1932) required that more than 50 per cent of the equity in new companies should be Irish owned.

Exhibit 2.1 Difficulties with tariffs

Imposing tariffs wasn't the simple thing that many thought. The 1934 budget for instance, was forced to address the problem that brush handles were escaping duties by masquerading as duty-free handles for chimney scrapers. However, the most persistent problem was with the importation of rosary beads. Despite a 33.3% duty, imports continued to be stubbornly strong. A minimum duty of 2d per rosary was imposed to stop the deluge. Soon, however, cunning types began to import beads with a full 15 decades on each (presumably to encompass Glorious, Sorrowful and Joyful Mysteries in one compendium). The government countered this threat to the national endeavour by slapping a 3.4d tax on every decade of imported foreign rosaries. That put a stop to the gallop of the bead importers.

Source: Fitzpatrick (2000).

The 1930s were characterised by severe depression in the aftermath of the Wall Street Crash in 1929 and the government found the IR£3 million annual payment to the UK in land annuities a serious drain on public finances. In 1932 the government withheld payment and the UK responded by imposing duties on the importation of Irish livestock, meat and diary products. The Irish government in turn imposed additional tariffs on UK goods and as a result the Economic War ensued between the two countries until agreement was reached in 1937. The Irish economy fared badly during the Economic War with cattle exports to the UK falling from 750,000 in 1930 to 500,000 in 1934. Total agricultural exports fell from €454 million in 1929 to €17.6 million in 1935. As a result the cattle industry was severely hit, farm incomes dropped and unemployment and emigration both increased.

However, the Economic War also affected industry. One of the most negative consequences saw Ireland's largest brewer, Guinness, establish manufacturing operations outside of Ireland for the first time. The reasons behind the move by Guinness were clear. American Prohibition had increased the company's reliance on the UK market. However, with the introduction of tariffs, the UK market came under significant threat. Rather than put trade with the UK at risk, Guinness decided to establish its first brewery outside Ireland. Eventually, Guinness was no longer viewed as an Irish company (Fitzpatrick 2000).

Throughout the period of protectionism, pragmatic decisions to develop the economic infrastructure were undertaken by the government. Many semi-state bodies were established to provide essential services that the market might fail to do (Aer Lingus 1936, CIE 1944 and Irish Shipping 1951), and to exploit natural resources (Bord na Mona 1946 and Comhlucht Siucra Éireann 1933). In 1933 the Industrial Credit Corporation (ICC) was established to provide capital for the development of industry. The ICC essentially acted as an underwriter to issues of new companies.

Despite high rates of emigration and the effects of the Economic War, the 1930s brought both growth in industrial employment and output. The extent of growth is, however, a debatable issue. According to official figures gross industrial output rose from €63.4 million in 1931 to €114.2 million in 1938. Industrial employment rose from 162,000 to 217,000 over the same period. However, it has been suggested that these figures merely reflect improved enumeration procedures and that the real increase is considerably less. Lee (1989) concludes that while growth in recorded employment in the industrial sector overstates the real increase, a substantial improvement occurred between 1931 and 1938. In the absence of the new protectionist policy there is little doubt that Irish industry would have suffered enormously from intensified UK competition in key markets. In this sense the government's achievements during this period were impressive, despite the self-inflicted wounds of the Economic War.

With the onset of the World War Two self-sufficiency was no longer a choice but became an economic necessity. The period 1939-45 in Ireland was termed the Emergency and was a particularly difficult time for the economy. One of the main problems was importing raw materials and supplies, the sources of which were limited to the UK and the USA, as the Germans occupied most of Europe. The war caused extreme hardship for some industries that depended on imported raw materials, for example, car assembly (Ford), soap making (Creans) and candle manufacturing (Rathbornes).

The war further heightened economic divisions between the North and South of the country. While the North had been particularly badly affected by the Great Depression of the 1930s, the situation changed completely with the start of the war, which meant rearmament and huge ship-building projects. The economy of the North benefited from such orders, however the South failed to experience the same economic boom. In the South incomes only grew by 14 per cent between 1939 and 1947, while in the North they grew by 84 per cent over the same period (Fitzpatrick 2000).

The immediate post-war years continued to provide problems for the government, who had envisaged a fast economic recovery. However, Ireland continued to experience rising unemployment, high emigration (125,000 people emigrated between 1945 and 1948), increasing prices, and rationing. The late 1940s were characterised by bad harvests and public-sector strikes. The winter of 1946/47 was particularly harsh and a fuel crisis during the early part of 1947 crippled industry and transport. A national teachers' strike in 1948 further intensified problems.

In 1949 the government established the Industrial Development Authority (IDA) which had a dual function, namely:

▶ to advise the Minister for Industry and Commerce on industrial development
▶ to promote greater investment in Irish industry.

The passing of the Underdeveloped Areas Act 1952 introduced financial grants for industries to set up in undeveloped areas, mostly in the western and midland regions. In the same year the government decided to separate the grant-giving function of the IDA from the promotion of new industry. As a result, two organisations were established: the IDA now promoting new investment; and An Foras Tionscal awarding grants and incentives. In 1956, Export Profits Tax Relief was introduced in the Finance Act. This gave 50 per cent tax remission on export sales, increased to 100 per cent two years later.

There were some success stories from the protectionist self-sufficiency years in Ireland's development, the most famous of which is Jefferson Smurfit. In the 1930s Jefferson Smurfit set up a box-making business in Dublin. During the war years, as Smurfit's supplies all but disappeared, he pioneered the development of a machine to use waste paper, and through this was able to keep his business growing. The company continued to expand through ACQUISITIONS, both domestically and internationally, and by 1964 the company was quoted on the Irish Stock Exchange (Fitzpatrick 2000). The experience of the Smurfit Group, however, is at odds with the more familiar spectre associated with Irish industry in the 1950s.

Economic difficulties continued throughout the 1950s; this period has often been referred to as the Great Slump. Emigration continued at an alarming rate with 400,000 people leaving the country between 1951 and 1961. Almost 90 per cent of exports were to the UK, which marked an extreme overreliance on one market. Living standards failed to increase and the move to international FREE TRADE by other countries during the early 1950s passed Ireland by.

The situation in Ireland during the 1950s was unique in comparison to other European countries, all of whom were rebuilding and experiencing growth. The late 1950s were a period of great prosperity in the UK, prompted in part by the need for post-war recovery and facilitated by a strong manufacturing base. In contrast, Ireland in the 1950s was characterised by a deep conservatism generated by the influence of the Catholic Church and close linkages between political and church leaders. The political scene was still dominated by the War of Independence/Civil War generation, unlike the familiar left–right divide which was experienced in many other countries at the time.

Domestic companies were small and uncompetitive, sheltering behind high tariff walls where there was no incentive to become efficient and effective. The industrial base simply was not large enough to employ surplus labour and to reduce unemployment through job creation. By 1950 manufactured goods only accounted for 6 per cent of exports with food and food products making up 73 per cent. A sizeable proportion of the labour force, 44 per cent, was employed in agriculture compared to only 15 per cent in industry (Lee 1989). Ireland was faced with growing BALANCE OF PAYMENTS crises fuelled in part by devaluation of Sterling and both the Korean War and Suez Crisis.

2.5 The move to free trade and foreign direct investment (1958)

By the late 1950s Ireland was facing economic crisis which began to threaten the economic viability of the country as a separate entity. Given the huge volume emigrating to seek work and success elsewhere, people began to question whether the country could survive independently on a long-term basis. Since the foundation of the state 1 million people had emigrated. In the mid-1950s the government set up the Capital Investment Advisory Committee to examine ways of improving the economy. T. K. Whitaker, the new Secretary of the Department of Finance was appointed Chairman. In 1958 Whitaker produced a report called *Economic Development* which advocated a reversal of the protectionist policy that had been pursued since 1932. The thrust of industrial policy should, according to the report, concentrate on free trade and reflect a move by the government towards productive rather than social investment. The document also recommended that a policy of FOREIGN DIRECT INVESTMENT (FDI) should be pursued. This meant that the country should encourage foreign companies to invest in Ireland. Whitaker's *Economic Development* was implemented by the government through a series of economic programmes, starting with the First Programme for Economic Expansion plan running from 1959 to 1964. The main elements of the First Programme were:

► increased state expenditure on productive investment areas
► an export drive in both agriculture and industry
► the encouragement of FDI in Ireland
► the adaptation of Irish industry to modern markets and methods of production.

The implementation of the First Programme was therefore a huge change in industrial policy, one that would open up Ireland's small closed economy and develop important links with other countries, thereby promoting industrial and economic growth. It was followed by a second programme designed to cover 1964 to 1970, but this was shelved in 1967.

According to Kennedy (1998) this new outward-looking policy was composed of three main strategies which the government pursued during the 1960s.

► Protectionism was gradually replaced by free trade and greater market access, which culminated in the Anglo-Irish Free Trade Area Agreement (AIFTAA) in 1965 and EEC membership in 1973.

▶ The IDA was given the task of actively generating FDI in Ireland to aid job creation and further develop the export orientation espoused in Whitaker's report.

▶ Financial grants and incentives were given to encourage the development of an export-focused manufacturing industry.

Each of these strategies was vigorously pursued by different means throughout the 1960s. In relation to the first strategy of promoting free trade, Ireland joined the World Bank and the International Monetary Fund (IMF). The transition to free trade was eased by two developments—the AIFTAA in 1965 and Ireland's 1961 application and subsequent membership of the European Economic Community (EEC) in 1973. The French vetoed Britain's entry in 1961 and it was considered too risky for Ireland to enter without its largest trading partner. The AIFTAA was signed in December 1965 and resulted in a phased reduction of tariffs between Ireland and Britain. It consisted of the following terms:

▶ Irish industrial goods were guaranteed tariff-free access to British markets.

▶ Irish store cattle were given a guaranteed market and butter import quotes to Britain were increased.

▶ Ireland reduced tariff barriers on British imports annually by 10 per cent, reaching free trade after a period of ten years in 1975.

The time frame associated with the agreement was sufficiently long as to allow Irish industry time to adapt to changed circumstances. The AIFTAA can be viewed as a stepping-stone to membership of the General Agreement on Tariffs and Trade (GATT) which Ireland secured in 1967, along with eventual EEC membership in 1973.

The second strategy of increasing FDI was handled by the IDA and was viewed as critical to the IDA's efforts to promote Ireland as a foreign-investment location. The IDA attempted to provide a one-stop shop for potential investors, providing packages to initially attract them, and then once located in Ireland, maintaining the investment through communication with the foreign parent and the Irish facility. In 1958 the Control of Manufacturers Act 1932, which had placed restrictions on foreign ownership of industry in Ireland, was eased.

Traditionally the main source of foreign investment in Ireland had come from UK firms hoping to avoid high tariffs in the Irish market. Throughout the 1960s the UK remained the single largest source of foreign investment and resultant job creation, until the USA overtook it in the 1970s. In the late 1950s and the early 1960s West German companies were particularly interested in Ireland. Marshall Aid had helped West German companies to recover from the ravages of World War Two and they were ready to consider new locations. These West German companies were the first foreign-owned businesses to build new factories where the output was produced solely for export purposes. Examples of such companies include Krups (Limerick), Faber Castell (Cork) and Liebherr (Kilkenny).

In the 1960s the pattern of FDI began to change as a result of the IDA's promotional efforts in the USA. General Electric established two electronic industries, EI in Shannon (1963) and Ecco in Dundalk (1966) (White 2000). Another US giant, the Pfizer Corporation, set up a chemical plant in Ringaskiddy, Cork, in 1969. The promotional campaigns undertaken by the IDA produced results. During the 1960s

450 foreign companies established facilities in Ireland and employed 34,000 people by 1972 (IDA Annual Reports).

Despite IDA success in promoting FDI through its home base and network of six foreign offices, there was a feeling that the twin agencies (IDA and An Foras Tionscal) were suffering from the civil service employment structure they operated within. It was argued that such a structure prevented the agencies from developing. A report published in 1967 reflected these fears and recommended that IDA staff should no longer be regarded as civil servants. The report was accepted by the Minster for Industry and Commerce and implemented through the Industrial Development Act 1969, which gave the IDA a mandate to act under the minster as a body having responsibility for industrial development. The IDA now had sole responsibility for the allocation of grants and incentives and provision of factories and industrial estates, and could for the first time take an equity stake in selected companies. Coupled with this role, the IDA now held responsibility for the promotion in Ireland of INDIGENOUS COMPANIES, especially small start-ups. The change in the IDA from civil service to state-sponsored body marked a major transition in the IDA's development. Almost all civil servants previously employed in the IDA returned to the Department of Industry and Commerce when the new agency was established.

In pursuing the third and final strategy of developing an export-focused manufac-turing industry the government set up the Committee on Industrial Organisation (CIO) in 1961 in order to generate adjustment measures for Irish industry. The CIO carried out detailed analyses of the levels of efficiency across many different industrial sectors and recommended various aids and incentives for Irish companies (Fitzgerald 1968). Irish companies were left in no doubt that they had to adapt to the concept of export-led growth or face decline and extinction. Some Irish companies responded to the challenge laid down by the changes. Companies such as Youghal Carpets and Waterford Glass saw a significant growth in earnings, boosted by generous tax relief from the government (Fitzpatrick 2000). Others, however, were less successful, and the sugar confectionery business provides a good example of the failure of Irish companies to develop with free trade. Throughout the 1940s and 1950s Lemon's had become a highly successful sweet manufacturer, with the company's image successfully displayed through a very effective advertising campaign. The campaign consisted of a series of line drawings accompanied by the slogan, 'This is Saturday—time for your Lemon's pure sweets'. Lemon's competed against foreign companies such as Cadbury and Rowntree-Mackintosh, and also engaged in competition with other domestic companies such as Urneys of Tallaght and Milroys (manufacturer of the famous toffee bars).

These domestic sweet manufacturers produced confectionery for the Irish public behind tariff walls. However, they had no ECONOMIES OF SCALE when compared to their UK rivals. Instead they produced a large variety of products for a small-scale unexpanding market. When the tariffs ended after the change in industrial policy so too did the small Irish independents. Lemon's was eventually bought out by a UK manufacturer and subsequently closed in 1983. Urneys was taken over by a US company in 1963 and latterly by Unilever. However, this company was also closed eventually when, in common with Lemon's, it failed to develop a strong export business (Fitzpatrick 2000).

Throughout the 1960s further developments ensued which greatly enhanced current and potential competitive infrastructure. The Irish banking industry went through a period of amalgamation to produce two major banking groups the Allied Irish Bank and the Bank of Ireland. The banks were willing to lend money to industry and the growing range of financial services offered by the banks provided the corporate customers with a complete range of business financial services (Fitzpatrick 2000).

Ireland became more aware of the importance of management training and the existence of deficiencies in Irish management. The types of management skills required to operate in a free trade export-led industry are obviously very different to those required to operate in a small, sheltered, domestic sector. Recognition of this resulted in the establishment of the Irish Management Institute (IMI) to provide management training for organisations in Ireland.

Developments in the educational sector during the 1960s, however, were to have an enormous impact in later years. By the 1960s Ireland lagged behind most of Europe in relation to the development of the educational system. Apart from the Vocational Education Act 1930, the system remained largely unchanged since the foundation of the state. Educational opportunities at second and third level were limited to those who could afford to pay the fees, rather than the most intellectually gifted. However, in the early 1960s an report by the Organisaton for Economic Co-operation and Development (OECD) entitled *Investment in Education* was produced which was highly critical of the existing educational system. It highlighted the lack of opportunity available to poorer students to enter secondary and third-level education. It also argued that the system did not foster talent due to the low intellectual, yet high cost, requirements for education. An immediate response to the report was the decision to establish comprehensive schools in areas where adequate secondary schooling was unavailable. However, the most significant change to education occurred from 1965 to 1967 by Donagh O'Malley, Minister for Education. In 1966 O'Malley announced the free secondary-school education scheme for all children. The scheme also provided free transport for all children living over five kilometres from the nearest school. These developments marked a decisive step forward for Irish education. As a direct result of the scheme the numbers electing to avail themselves of secondary education increased from 104,000 in 1966 to 144,000 in 1969 (Lee 1989). In addition the government provided support for capital expenditure in schools.

The third-level sector also witnessed change. The government established the Higher Education Authority (HEA) in 1969 to help guide expenditure in third-level education. Polytechnic-style initiatives were promoted to cater for aspects of education neglected by the universities at the time. As a result, a number of Regional Technical Colleges were established and in 1972 the National Institute for Higher Education was established in Limerick followed by another in Dublin in 1976. The full impact of these developments in education was to be felt in subsequent decades when they significantly affected promotional policies of the IDA. This point will be elaborated on later in the chapter.

As the pace of growth accelerated and national self-confidence increased, the issue of regionalism was much debated. In relation to the direction of Irish regional policy, two contrasting approaches emerged. One such approach involved a growth-pole strategy which envisaged the concentration of resources for development in a small number of large centres. This view was most notably espoused in the famous Buchanan Report (1968). The contrasting approach favoured a general dispersal of economic development. The debate culminated in the development of the IDA's

Regional Industrial Plan (1973) which effectively rejected the growth-pole strategy in favour of attempting to get jobs into a variety of towns rather than just around poles of development.

As part of the regional development drive, the first industrial estates were established by the IDA in the early 1970s in Galway and Waterford. It is interesting to note that Dublin was not specifically promoted as a location for FDI until the late 1970s, when the clothing industry which had thrived in inner Dublin collapsed due to stiff competition and recession. It was only in 1976 that the IDA began actively to promote Dublin by developing industrial estates on the periphery of the city such as Coolock, Santry and Clondalkin.

The 1960s can be viewed as a decade of prosperity and economic boom for the country. The economy grew at a rate of 4 per cent between 1959 and 1964, compared to the figure of 1 per cent for the preceding years. Between 1958 and 1970 the economy grew by 61 per cent. During the 1960s Ireland began to discover industry and business and gradually the country became less agricultural and more industrial. Industry rather than agriculture came to be viewed as the vehicle for economic growth. Table 2.1 shows the annual average growth rate of each of the key sectors from 1959 to 1969.

Table 2.1. Growth rates and contribution to GNP by sector 1958–69			
	Annual growth rate (%)	Contribution to GNP (%)	
		1958	1969
Agriculture	1.8	24.4	18.9
Industry	6.8	27.2	35.7
Distribution, transport and communication	4.8	15.5	16.6
Public administration and defence	2.0	5.4	4.3
Other domestic	2.8	21.3	18.3

Source: Ireland, National Income and Expenditure 1969 (1970).

The marked increase in the relative importance of industry in the Irish economy is clear, amounting to 35.7 per cent of GROSS NATIONAL PRODUCT (GNP) in 1969. The expanding export market, particularly in manufacturing, accounts for much of the growth during this period. Exports increased from €187 million in 1960 to €222.2 million in 1961 as shown in Table 2.2.

Table 2.2 Total value of Irish exports 1954–61 (€ million)	
1954	142.2
1956	132.05
1957	161.2
1960	187.9
1961	222.2

Source: Adapted from Lee (1989:356–7).

There were also important changes in the value and composition of exports. Manufacturing exports in 1959 amounted to €44.4 million and by 1960 had reached €55.8 million, surging ahead of the previous record of €33 million. The value of manufacturing exports had trebled between 1953 and 1960 and according to Lee (1989) this was no mere recovery but a shift in trajectory. The changing role of manufacturing exports is shown in Table 2.3 which documents the degree to which manufacturing exports contribute to overall exports.

Table 2.3 Manufacturing exports 1958–69

Manufactured exports % of total		Contribution of manufactured exports to growth in total exports (%)
1958	1969	1958–69
49.7	70	82

Source: Cooper and Whelan (1973:10).

The table shows that the relative importance of manufacturing exports increased from 49.7 per cent in 1958 to 70 per cent in 1969. There was also a change in the pattern of manufacturing exports, with growth occurring in the newer, modern industry sectors, such as chemicals and machinery, marking a shift in the balance of power within manufacturing. Such new, modern industries, however, do not use large quantities of raw materials, and have a high import content; that is, these industries import a large proportion of their raw materials.

Also during the 1960s the population of the country increased, reaching 2.98 million in 1971. Emigration continued to fall as shown in Table 2.4.

Table 2.4 Irish emigration 1956–71

1956–61	43,000 per annum
1962–66	16,000 per annum
1966–71	11,000 per annum

Source: Lee (1989:359).

Employment was the only area not recording a significant improvement, mainly due to the continuing reduction in the numbers employed in agriculture, as shown in Table 2.5.

Table 2.5 Total number at work by sector 1961–71

	1961	1966	1971
Agriculture	379,000	334,000	273,000
Industry	257,000	293,000	323,000
Services	415,000	438,000	459,000

Source: Lee (1989:360).

There can be no doubt that in terms of economic performance and industrial development the 1960s were heady years. However, there is less consensus among commentators in relation to the causal relationship between the new policies introduced after 1958, and the phenomenal growth rate. Some have argued that even in the absence of free trade and FDI, the Irish economy would still have grown. It seems unlikely, however, that such a scale of economic growth could have been achieved without the changes in industrial policy. Kennedy and Dowling (1975) argue that other factors contributed to the favourable outcome of economic growth. They point out that the First Programme was extremely conservative and that the good fortune of improved terms of trade in 1958–59, combined with good weather in 1959–60 affected agricultural output, thereby enabling the economy to advance rapidly. Lee (1989) concludes that, while difficult to quantify, policy played a preponderant role in turning recovery into growth, concluding that the policy makers were lucky in that the new policy coincided with favourable international circumstances.

The industrial policy pursued by the IDA during this period was not without its critics. The Cooper and Whelan Report published in 1973 (co-authored by Noel Whelan who was later to become Secretary to the Department of An Taoiseach in 1979), expressed concern about the long-term impact of the heavy reliance on foreign investment. The report concluded that:

▶ Dependence on foreign enterprise should be more selective and there should be a more complete cost–benefit comparison of the advantages of foreign as opposed to Irish enterprise.

▶ Foreign enterprise should be conceived of as providing a complementary source of technology rather than substituting for the development of Irish skills.

▶ Support for Irish enterprise should shift from the present policy of attempting marginal improvements within the existing structure of inefficient, protected, small firms to the creation of a new structure of production.

While some of the suggestions were taken on board by the IDA, the issue of the lack of Irish enterprise development was to re-emerge in the early 1980s. The next most immediate challenge to face Ireland was ascension to the European Economic Community.

2.6 Membership of the European Economic Community 1973

In January 1973, Ireland along with the UK and Denmark joined the EEC. In 1951 the European Coal and Steel Community (ECSC) had been established by the main European countries to foster co-operation. This was followed in 1957 by the formation, under the Treaty of Rome, of the European Economic Community (EEC) and the European Atomic Energy Community (EAEC or EURATOM). As the three communities were managed by common institutions they were collectively referred to in the singular as the European Community (EC). The term European Community came to replace the term European Economic Community, and as a result the former is used from here on in the text.

Membership of such a large economic community opened up enormous opportunities for indigenous Irish companies to develop Continental markets, thereby reducing reliance on UK markets. In addition, membership of the EC became a highly significant selling point for the IDA when promoting Ireland as an investment location, particularly in the USA. Ireland could now be sold as a European base for foreign MULTINATIONAL CORPORATIONS (MNCs) to enter into the European market. For farmers the COMMON AGRICULTURAL POLICY heralded the end of their reliance on the UK market.

Membership of the EC had significant benefits in relation to state aid programmes; however, the EC COMMISSION was required to control state aid by member states in order to avoid competitive advantage based on national interest. EC state aid policy is laid down in Article 87.1 of the Treaty of Rome. This article provides that state aid is, in principle, incompatible with the common market. Under Article 88, the EC Commission is given the task to control state Aid. This Article requires Member States to inform the Commission in advance of any plan to grant State aid.

The Treaty does not try to control all types of measures that could affect companies. Community state aid rules apply only to measures that satisfy all of the criteria listed in Article 87.1:

► There must be a transfer of state resources. This includes aid that may be granted by private bodies appointed by the state. Financial transfers include not just grants or interest subsidies but also loan guarantees, capital allowances, tax rebates, etc.

► The aid should constitute an economic advantage that the recipient would not have received in the normal course of business.

► The aid must be selective, and thus affect the balance between certain firms and their competitors.

► The aid must have the potential to effect competition between member states.

Throughout Europe, different countries have developed a myriad of state aid schemes. This created a significant problem for the EC Commission in trying to control all the different types of aid. The Commission, in order to try and limit the level and type of support, and its own workload, has over the years produced a range of guidelines for aid for investment/job creation, aid for research and development aid for training, etc. These guidelines provide guidance for the Member States when they are developing a scheme.

Ireland received monetary transfers under both the European Social Fund and the Regional Development Fund throughout the 1970s and, by 1980, had been funded the equivalent of 5 per cent of national income. Such programmes were designed to assist countries, particularly those in peripheral locations. In later years, Ireland continued to receive funds through the Structural and Cohesion Funds which greatly assisted the development of Irish infrastructure. Specific R & D funding for industry is provided on an ongoing basis through the EU's four-year R & D Framework Programmes. The thrust of the programmes is to give European industry an advantage over its US competitors. These funds are technically in conflict with the terms of the GATT agreement; however, Europe would argue that US companies are subverted by US military spending.

Since 1973 Irish reliance on UK markets declined substantially and by 1981 almost a third of exports were destined for other EC countries. The reduction in the share of Irish exports to the UK paved the way for Ireland's membership of the EUROPEAN MONETARY SYSTEM (EMS) whereby the direct link with Sterling was eliminated. The structure of the Irish economy has undergone a significant change in this regard, especially when compared to the post-1922 era of UK dependence.

During the 1970s additional foreign investment was attracted to Ireland particularly from the USA. By 1979 Ireland received 2.5 per cent of US manufacturing investment in the EC, while Irish GNP only amounted to 0.7 per cent of the EC total (Haughton 1987). In 1978 the government abolished Export Profit Tax Relief and introduced a 10 per cent rate of corporation tax for all manufacturing from 1981–2000. The IDA strategy at this time involved a DIRECT MARKETING approach targeting companies in the electronics, pharmaceutical and chemicals area. Companies investing in Ireland in the early 1970s included Snia Vicossa, Asahi, Courtaulds, Gilette-Braun, Syntex, Merck Sharpe and Dohme and Warner Lambert.

However, the first oil crisis of 1973 severely hampered investment in Ireland, as companies become more risk-averse and the numbers locating in Ireland dropped from 80 in 1973 to 45 in 1975. But the late 1970s saw the arrival of Mostek, Wang Laboratories, Verbatim and Apple Computers. In 1979 the IDA approved 105 new projects, 40 of which were American (IDA Annual Report 1979). Bausch and Lomb in Waterford, IMED in Letterkenny, Kostal in Limerick and Fujitsu in Tallaght soon followed in early 1980. This, however, was the last wave of investment before deepening recession changed industry fortunes.

While the 1970s marked a period of significant foreign investment, indigenous industry failed to make significant advances. Of the net increase in industrial jobs of 27,000 during the period 1973–1980, just 5,000 of them were in the indigenous sector which failed to increase its share of output or significantly reduce its reliance on the UK market.

The industrial legacy of the 1930s was characterised by small domestic-market-focused companies without the capital, experience or skills to expand and develop international markets. The transformation of farmers CO-OPERATIVES into major food companies was only at an early stage of development and actually involved significant job losses and increased capitalisation in the food industry. Irish-owned industry across many sectors contracted, with job losses occurring in the traditional manufacturing sector. The employment increases secured by the modern manufacturing sector, (most of which were foreign) did little to keep pace with the overall losses. IDA policies were focused on grants for the acquisition of new capital equipment, as obsolete equipment was perceived to be the major weaknesses associated with indigenous companies. However, the response by the IDA to the domestic industry situation was, with the benefit of hindsight, unimaginative and concentrated too heavily on the capital equipment needs of the industry.

During the 1970s Irish economic growth was dampened by the two oil crises, and the rate of growth of GDP for 1973–81 was 0.5 per cent below that for the preceding 12 years. However, in the late 1970s the Irish economy grew faster than the EC average for two main reasons. First, the positive inflow of US FDI; and second, the increase in spending through external borrowing by the public sector from 1977 onwards. This development created an expansionary stimulus for the domestic economy which led to increased output but a deterioration in the trade deficit. In 1979, debt rose from €377.1 million to €1,382 million. The deficit in the balance of payments increased from 2.4 per cent of GNP in 1978 to 10.1 per cent in 1979 (Lee 1989).

2.7 Recession and retrenchment 1980–86

The situation continued to deteriorate until 1981 when the debt/GNP ratio stood at 94 per cent and the balance of payments deficit was 12.5 per cent. The increased balance of payments deficits, and contrasts with average EC rates, are shown in Table 2.6.

Table 2.6 Balance of payments deficits 1978–1981 (% GDP)

	Ireland	EC
1978	2.4	–
1979	10.1	0.5
1980	8.3	1.5
1981	12.5	1.5

Source: Lee (1989:489).

Wages and inflation also continued to grow during this period as shown in Table 2.7.

Table 2.7. Wages and inflation 1978–80 (%)

	Wages	Inflation
1978	14.6	7.6
1979	16.6	13.2
1980	20.5	18.2
1981	18.4	20.4

Source: Lee (1989:489).

This represented a growing crisis, which demanded immediate action. The Fine Gael–Labour coalition (1982–87) pursed a strategy of increasing taxation to reduce government borrowing and the level of debt. Unemployment increased from 7.3 per cent in 1980 to 17.7 per cent in 1985 (Eurostat). Emigration resumed and economic growth did not materialise. Despite the fact that Ireland had received a positive inflow of funds from the EC, the employment numbers had only increased by 4 per cent since 1973. Between 1980 and 1986 employment fell by 76,000.

The FDI effort was hampered by the deepening recession in the USA which resulted in a sharp drop in US inward investment. Another possible explanation for the timing of the slow-down was that the pace of US FDI in the 1970s was a one-off adjustment to Ireland's EC membership and that this had levelled off by 1980. In addition, other countries provided favourable packages designed to induce companies to establish operations with them. The IDA increasingly found that the business of attracting foreign companies was becoming cut-throat.

In January 1981 the government extended the 10 per cent tax on profits for foreign companies until 2010. This was soon followed by the launch of IDA's Strategic Plan (1982–92). The focus of the IDA's new strategy concentrated on attracting companies with high output, using the best available technology while spending significant amounts on Irish materials and services. In this way, it was envisaged that these companies would not only generate jobs in their own areas, but would also feed demand for related services and raw materials which would lead to increased employment. This was a reversal of the former IDA policy of attracting the most labour intensive industries. The industrial sectors targeted for promotion included biotechnology, healthcare, software and electronics.

Promotional strategies also changed in the 1980s. The focus of promotion moved from financial grants and incentives towards the importance of human capital. The existence of a young educated workforce became a huge selling point for the IDA. The change of focus launched a new advertising campaign entitled 'We are the young Europeans.'

Despite the recession some companies decided to locate in Ireland during this period, including Fruit of the Loom (1985) and Yamanouchi (1985). However, there were losses within the foreign sector. In 1983, Telectron (owned by AT&T) and Black and Decker both announced they were to close, with the loss of 1,000 jobs.

Focusing on the service sector a new International Services Programme was launched which was designed to attract service companies. It was recognised that such companies would require a different set of financial incentives. As a result, the Industrial Development Act No. 2 was passed in 1981 which gave the IDA the power to give employment grants unrelated to investment in capital goods. The programme saw many companies setting up premises in Ireland including IBM Software Centre (1983), Lotus Software (1984) and Microsoft Software (1985). This highly significant development helped to further the concept of Ireland as a world-class centre for software.

This period was also marked by a growing concern that indigenous Irish companies had failed to develop. It had originally been hoped that Irish industry would develop alongside a thriving foreign sector, supplying them with raw materials and related services. However, by the early 1980s it became clear that this would not be the case. In response, a report to evaluate industrial policy was commissioned by the government. The Telesis Report (1982) criticised industrial policy for allowing a situation to arise where there was an overreliance on the foreign sector, rather than a more even balance between foreign and indigenous. The report made a number of recommendations:

▶ a shift towards indigenous companies
▶ recognition of the constraints inherent in indigenous industry and generating resources to deal with this
▶ the concentration of a small number of indigenous companies to build strong indigenous companies
▶ a reduction in the grants for foreign companies
▶ a greater role in industrial policy for the Department of Industry and Commerce
▶ the focus on capital grants should be reduced.

The report was never implemented in full and it was not until the early 1990s that the challenge posed by Telesis was taken up. However, debate continued in relation to the failure of an Irish ENTERPRISE sector to develop. Lee (1989) offers a means of explaining why enterprise had not sufficiently developed. He argues that societies can be shaped or founded on two different principles—the performer versus the possessor. Where the possessor principle is dominant, Lee argues, a person is judged in life by what they possess, whereas the performance principle means that a person is judged on their performance. Lee (1989) further argues that due to our mainly agrarian society until the 1950s, Ireland had a predominance of the possessor principle well into the second half of the twentieth century. Consequently, Lee states, this provides little real incentive to achieve or to become an entrepreneur.

During the 1980s there were some significant developments in relation to indigenous industry. New programmes such as the Company Development Programme, National Linkage Programme and the Management Development Programme were introduced. The motivation for such a move was to encourage companies to think strategically about their business direction rather than merely seeking capital grants for expansion. This point is reiterated in the Telesis Report.

The employment breakdown by sector in 1986 is shown in Table 2.8. Job gains of 16,388 are offset by losses of 19,068, which led to a reduction by 1.3 per cent.

Table 2.8 Employment 1986 by sector

	Employment	% change	Number of companies
Modern sectors			
Metals and chemicals	62,504	-0.44	2,119
Chemicals	13,162	-1.23	271
Natural resource sectors			
Food	40,668	-2.5	984
Timber and furniture	10,161	-6.93	1,022
Drink and tobacco	9,077	-1.58	107
Traditional sectors			
Clothing, footwear and leather	16,863	+0.15	534
Paper and printing	13,979	-0.77	418
Non-metallic minerals	13,598	-4.93	518
Textiles	10,902	-1.05	303
Miscellaneous industries	10,430	+1.69	634
Grant-aided service industries	6,886	+6.57	305
TOTAL	**208,232**	**-1.3**	**7,223**

Source: IDA Annual Report (1986:8).

Manufacturing output for 1986 by sector is shown in Table 2.9. Growth in the manufacturing industry was slow at 2.8 per cent. However, there was strong growth in the modern sectors at 4.6 per cent. The losses were mainly from the traditional sector. Overall the period from 1980 to 1986 was a very difficult one for industry, with high INTEREST and exchange rates and little growth in domestic demand.

Table 2.9 Manufacturing output 1985–86 by sector

	% change 1985–86
Modern sectors	
Chemicals	-0.7
Metals and engineering	+7.4
Office and data processing	+23
Total	**+4.6**

Table 2.9 Manufacturing output by sector 1986–86 *contd.*

	% change 1985–86
Natural resource sectors	
Food	+4.7
Drink and tobacco	-1.3
Timber and wooden furniture	+6.9
Total	**+3.4**
Traditional sectors	
Non-metallic minerals	-11.1
Textiles	-0.2
Clothing, footwear and leather	-1.0
Paper and printing	-1.0
Miscellaneous industries	+4.9
Total	**-2.5**
Total all manufacturing	**+2.8**

Source: IDA Annual Report (1986:8).

2.8 Recovery and social partnership 1987–90

In 1987 a political consensus on fiscal policy started to emerge, largely as a result of the publication by the NESC (National Economic and Social Council) of *Strategy and Development 1986–1990*. This document argued that the national debt had to be reduced through public spending cuts as a matter of priority. The NESC document was widely welcomed by trade unions, farmers' organisations, employers and the opposition. The main opposition party, led by Alan Dukes, agreed to support the minority government as it pushed through measures that were in the country's best interests. Such a bold and daring strategy reflected the growing concerns of all involved.

The development of the social partnership model in 1987 laid the foundations for recovery. The programme was the first of four highly successful centralised agreements. It was the first time that an agreement on wages was tied to agreement on a range of economic and social policy issues underpinned by political consensus. Under the Programme for National Recovery (PNR) (1987) the government agreed to reduce income tax (to increase the real take-home pay of workers) in return for moderate pay increases (to increase competitiveness and employment in Irish industry). Such income tax concessions totalled €285.6 million over the course of the PNR and were designed to bring two-thirds of earners onto the standard rate of taxation. The most important feature of the agreement was the fact that it was the product of a social partnership whereby all parties—government, unions, employers and farmers—were all given a role in aspects of economic policy, which denoted a greater sense of realism by all involved.

Between 1987 and 1990 employment continued to grow as shown in Table 2.10.

Table 2.10 Total employment 1987–90

1987	1,080,000
1988	1,091,000
1989	1,090,000
1990	1,120,000

Source: IDA Annual Report (1990:7).

Emigration continued and, coupled with increased employment, led to a reduction in unemployment, from 225,000 in 1987 to 174,500 in 1990. Table 2.11 provides a summary of employment figures in 1990 by sector.

Table 2.11 Employment in industry 1990 by sector

	Employment	Number of firms
Food	29,949	912
Metals and engineering	27,151	1,770
Paper and printing	11,924	401
Clothing, footwear and leather	9,327	494
Timber and furniture	8,678	834
Non Metallic Minerals	8,531	414
Miscellaneous industries	7,773	708
Non-manufacturing grant-aided	6,004	478
Chemicals	4,084	206
Textile industry	3,297	256
Drink and tobacco	2,623	86
Total	**119,341**	**6,559**

Source: IDA Annual Report (1990).

The overall figures show a reduction of 2.6 per cent mainly due to losses in clothing, footwear, leather, drink and tobacco. Table 2.12 provides a summary of manufacturing output, which was up by 4.7 per cent on the previous year.

Table 2.12 Manufacturing output 1990 by sector

	Volume growth (%)
Modern sectors	
Chemicals	+2.9
Pharmaceuticals	+2.0
Metals and engineering	+6.6
Office and data processing	+5.8
Electrical engineering	+9.5
Instrument engineering	+10.2
Natural resource sectors	
Food	+3.7
Drink and tobacco	+0.3
Timber and wooden furniture	+5.8

Table 2.12 Manufacturing output 1990 by sector *contd.*

	Volume growth (%)
Traditional sectors	
Non-metallic mineral products	+4.9
Textiles	+7.2
Clothing, footwear and leather	+1.0
Paper and printing	+1.5
Miscellaneous industries	+7.1
Total	**+4.7**

Source: IDA Annual Report (1990:4).

By 1990, as the PNR came to a close, the budget deficit had fallen to 0.7 per cent of GNP, down from 8.3 per cent in 1986. This period also witnessed changes to the tax incentives for business. It was concluded by the government that the tax incentives were too generous and the high relief's available encouraged investment in fixed assets rather than job creation. The 1988 budget introduced a broader tax base with fewer reliefs. This marked the first step on the road to the reform of corporation tax.

Throughout the late 1980s the IDA capitalised on the pace of recovery in its FDI promotion. Motorola, Teradata, Intel, Stratus, EDS and Sandoz all established facilities in Ireland during this period. The Intel investment was seen as particularly significant, reinforcing the important role Ireland had come to play in the world-wide electronics sector. At the end of 1991 indigenous industry employed 120,000 while foreign accounted for 94,000 (IDA Annual Report 1992).

2.9 A time for change 1990–93

In 1990 economic growth stood at 7.8 per cent yet by 1991 the figure had dipped to 2.2 per cent. The primary reasons for such a decline were the Gulf War and subsequent recession in both the USA and UK economies. In addition, German reunification added a considerable cost burden to the newly reunited country. All of these factors led to increased INTEREST RATES, while at the same time unemployment levels began to creep upwards.

In 1991 the Maastricht Treaty was signed by EC member states, which committed them to the establishment of a common currency—European Monetary Union (EMU)—by the end of 1999 at the latest. In order to qualify for membership in the first round countries had to meet stringent convergence criteria, which included:

▶ no devaluation of currency for at least 2 years prior to entry
▶ low inflation
▶ strict budget deficit/GDP and debt/GDP ratios.

As a result there was a change in focus by the government away from sole preoccupation with public finances to making sure that the economy could meet the convergence criteria. The social partnership model developed with the PNR was continued with the second centralised agreement in 1991 called the Programme for

Economic and Social Progress (PESP). The PESP, which covered the years 1991 to 1993, broadly followed the same concepts developed under the PNR. Wage moderation was guaranteed in return for tax concessions to boost competitiveness and growth. Fiscal targets in the PESP were designed to ensure qualification for EMU membership.

In 1992 the UK left the EUROPEAN EXCHANGE RATE MECHANISM (ERM) and this posed serious difficulties for Ireland. The resultant sharp reduction in UK interest rates led to a weaker Sterling currency. This in effect meant that the Irish punt was overvalued in relation to Sterling. This led to a loss of competitiveness for Irish industry as companies exporting to the UK market now found that their produce was more expensive. In addition, domestic operators found that UK imports were now cheaper and the sale of their goods increased at the expense of Irish goods. Consequently the punt was devalued by 10 per cent in 1993. In 1993 the European Community (EC) changed title to become the European Union (EU), reflecting moves towards greater integration in Europe.

In 1991 Des O'Malley, the Minster for Industry and Commerce commissioned a further review of industrial policy. This was the first occasion since Telesis in 1982 that radical reform of policy was given due consideration. Many of the issues and challenges that Telesis raised, particularly for Irish indigenous industry, were echoed in the report which followed. The Industrial Policy Review Group (chaired by Jim Culliton) firmly believed that growth in output is the key to employment growth. Growth in output can only be achieved by increased efficiency and competitiveness. This underlying premise guided the findings and recommendations, which were subsequently produced.

The Culliton Report, as it came to be known, was published in 1992 and argued that in relation to the formulation and evaluation of industrial policy a much broader approach was required (1992:9):

It must go beyond traditional departmental DEMARCATION LINES to take account of all the major relevant factors including notably the level and structure of taxation, the cost and quality of infrastructure, the relevance and effectiveness of education and training.

The report highlights a number of important findings and recommendations, the most significant of which are summarised below:

❶ **Tax reform**. The report found that there was an urgent need for tax reform. The current system encourages unproductive tax avoidance activities and holds back industrial progress. The Personal income tax system also stifles enterprise. *The report recommends that a programme of reform be undertaken to broaden the tax base and to extend the standard rate band.*

❷ **Infrastructure**. Some deficiencies are being tackled with the aid of EUROPEAN UNION (EU) STRUCTURAL FUNDS but continued improvements in access and efficiency of transport is crucial. Organisational changes are needed to promote low-cost transport and communications links. Energy prices are kept unduly high by uncompetitive arrangement. *The report recommends a variety of measures to improve energy services, ports, communications, transport—road and air—and environmental issues.*

❸ **Education**. The current system has gaps in the area of technology and vocational education. Management training is underused and consequently skill deficiencies exist. The role of FAS requires clarification and institutional reform. *The need for productive enterprise should be a primary issue at all educational levels. A higher priority must be attached to the acquisition of usable skills. An institutional reorganisation of FAS should take place.*

❹ **Technology**. Ireland's low ranking in R & D spending should be helped by available Structural Funds. However, there is a danger that this spending will be too remote from industrial application. *The Department of Industry and Commerce and the implementing agencies should ensure that the EU funds are applied as effectively as possible. Industrialists with relevant experience should be actively involved. Greater emphasis should be placed on the acquisition of product quality and competitiveness in industry.*

❺ **Industry and enterprise**. The widespread use of grants for indigenous companies is counterproductive. It encourages a hand-out mentality instead of fostering market-led production oriented enterprise. Gaps exist in available finance especially in the area of venture capital. It is desirable to develop clusters of related industries. Grant aid for mobile international industry should be reduced. *The grant aid budget for internationally mobile industry should be reduced. Shift decisively from grants for home-managed industry to the use of equity to meet financial gaps. Focus the reduced grant-aid budget on fostering industrial clusters.*

❻ **Institutional**. The present structure for industrial policy and implementation is inadequate. The department is unduly focused on operational matters. The supports for indigenous industry are scattered across a variety of agencies. *The department should have a greater role in industrial policy. The IDA should be restructured with a new agency dealing with indigenous industry.*

The report also recommended the establishment of a task force reporting to the Taoiseach on how the report should be implemented. The Moriarty Task Force Report subsequently reported to the government on how Culliton could be implemented. Throughout the decade the recommendations of the Culliton report were gradually implemented. In 1993 and again in 1998 the state agencies involved in industrial development were restructured as illustrated in Figure 2.1.

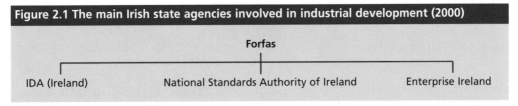

Figure 2.1 The main Irish state agencies involved in industrial development (2000)

Forfas

IDA (Ireland)   National Standards Authority of Ireland   Enterprise Ireland

Forfas is responsible for overall policy advice and co-ordination. Forfas employs its own staff and that of both Enterprise Ireland and IDA Ireland. As a result, staff are frequently transferred between the three bodies. In 1993 Forbairt received responsibility for the promotion and development of Irish industry. Forbairt was the outcome of a merger between the domestic industry development side of the old IDA and Eolas which was the government's long-standing body for the promotion of SCIENCE and the provision of various technical industrial services. IDA (Ireland) was given responsibility for the promotion and development of foreign investment with the title Industrial

Development Authority changing to Industrial Development Agency. When in 1998 the structure was again revised Forbairt, the Irish Trade Board and the in-house training function of FAS were merged to form Enterprise Ireland which concentrates on fostering indigenous enterprise. The structural revision of 1998 also saw the development of the National Standards Authority of Ireland. Shannon Development has responsibility on an agency basis for Enterprise Ireland activities in the Mid-West Region and North Kerry and South Offaly. It also undertakes similar activities for IDA (Ireland) in that area as well as having wider responsibilities for tourism development. Údarás na Gaeltachta has specific responsibility for the Gaeltacht regions.

2.10 The emergence of the Celtic tiger

Government taxation policy changed significantly with the new coalition government with Labour and Fianna Fail. The emphasis was now firmly placed on broadening the tax bands and allowances to help lower income earners. The Programme for Competitiveness and Work (PCW) was agreed in 1994 and, like its two predecessors, involved a trade-off between pay moderation and tax concessions designed to increase after tax income and employment levels. In addition, to encourage employers to recruit more lower-paid staff, employers' payroll costs were reduced with a 9 per cent employer PRSI levy on income introduced on incomes below €11,428.

In December 1994 the standard rate of corporation tax was cut to 12.5 per cent. The economy grew by 9 per cent in 1995 and 6 per cent in 1996. In 1995, 11,254 new jobs were created by IDA-supported companies, a record level, as shown in Table 2.13.

Table 2.13 New jobs by sector in 1991–95 (IDA-supported companies)

Sector	1991	1992	1993	1994	1995
Metals and engineering	3,363	3,506	4,098	5,420	7,243
Chemical/pharmaceuticals	841	944	1,177	1,032	789
Textiles, clothing, footwear	433	558	488	580	326
Miscellaneous	383	323	522	693	518
Grant-aided services	1,383	1,433	1,720	2,079	2,648
Total new jobs	6,403	6,764	8,005	9,804	11,524
Total job losses	5,729	5,756	5,586	4,699	/

Source: IDA Annual Report (1995:7).

Total employment was up by 7.9 per cent between 1994–95 as shown in Table 2.14

The destination of manufacturing exports changed markedly between 1970 and 1995 with a decline in the reliance on the EU, as shown in Figure 2.2.

The components of manufacturing exports also changed significantly during this period as shown in Figure 2.3. The increasing importance of the pharmaceutical and electronics sector is evident.

Table 2.14 Total employment by sector 1991–95

Sector	1991	1992	1993	1994	1995	% change
Metals and engineering	38,724	39,041	40,264	42,997	47,894	+11.4
Chemicals/pharmaceuticals	11,294	12,038	12,745	13,355	13,930	+4.3
Textiles, clothing and foowear	9,821	9,393	8,768	8,752	8,326	-4.9
Miscellaneous	7,433	7,297	7,296	7,656	7,677	+0.3
Grant-aided services	7,101	7,612	8,727	10,145	11,653	+14.9
Total	**74,373**	**75,381**	**77,800**	**82,905**	**89,480**	**+7.9**

Source: IDA Annual Report (1995:8).

Figure 2.2 Destination of Manufactured Exports

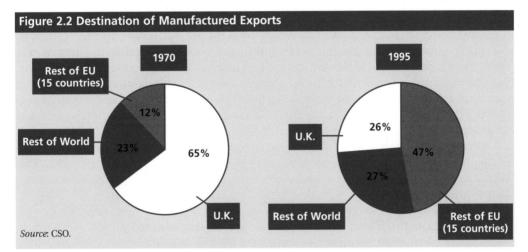

Source: CSO.

The emphasis on broadening tax bands and allowances continued as the standard rate was cut to 26 per cent in the 1997 budget. Other developments included employers' PRSI which was cut to 9 per cent on the first €15,237 of income for each employee. For employees, the first €63.40 of weekly income was free from PRSI contributions.

Figure 2.3 Components of Manufactured Exports

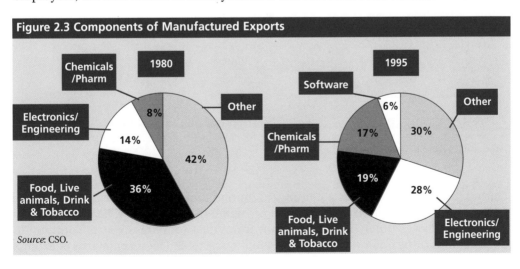

Source: CSO.

During this period the government was in a position to finance the tax cuts without resorting to borrowing or inflation. They also benefited significantly from Structural Funds received from the EU. The scale of recovery in the early 1990s was due partly to the influx of funds received under two rounds of Structural Funds amounting to €9.52 billion 1989–2000. In particular, the Delors 1 round (1989-1993) helped to finance much of the infrastructural development. Other significant developments on the European front during this period included the launch of the EU common currency, the euro. In January 2002 the euro replaces the individual currencies of those EU member states who have signed up for membership of the single currency.

Partnership 2000, covering the years 1997–99, followed the same guidelines as the first three programmes, including additional measures at the enterprise level to reduce unemployment. In the 1997, after the change of government there was a move back to reducing tax rates. The 1999 budget made a new departure with the introduction of a tax credit system which brought greater equity to the system by providing a standard rating to personal allowances. This ensured that any increases in allowances amounted to the same value to all taxpayers irrespective of their income. For an economy experiencing rapid growth coupled with labour shortages, and therefore running the risk of wage inflation, the move to a tax credit system was appropriate (MacSharry and White 2000). Easing the tax burden helped to increase the supply of labour, as people were better off working, than receiving benefits.

Another measure that increased confidence in the business community was the decision to reduce capital gains tax (CGT) from 40 to 20 per cent in 1998. This stimulated a more productive use of assets and at the same time increased revenues for the government.

In 12 years the Irish economy has undergone a remarkable recovery. The budget surplus amounted to €2.53 billion in 1998 compared to a deficit of €1.77 billion in 1986. Rapid economic growth has ensued with five years of stunning economic performance between 1994 and 1999. No other OECD member country has been able to match the level of growth in Ireland, as shown in Table 2.15.

Table 2.15 Real GDP growth in the EU (1999)	
	Real GDP growth (%)
Ireland	9
UK	8.6
France	1.7
Germany	2.4
Netherlands	3.0
Spain	3.7
Portugal	3.1

Source: OECD Economic Outlook, December 1999.

During this period there was a net inward immigration of 38,000 between 1996 and 1998. In addition, inflation has remained no higher than 5 per cent. Real GDP growth has averaged over 9 per cent per annum from 1994 to 1999. Exports continue to outstrip imports by €56.8 million to €39.4 million in 1998. The components of exports are shown in Table 2.16.

Table 2.16 Components of exports: January–August 1999	
Chemicals	32.4%
Computer equipment	22.2%
Machine and various equipment	16.3%
Food and live animals	9.4%
Miscellaneous manufacturing	13.7%
Other	6%

Source: Central Statistics Office, December 1999.

The trends in permanent full-time employment from 1990 to 1999 for both Irish and foreign-owned companies are shown in Table 2.17.

Table 2.17 Trends in permanent full-time employment: overall Irish and foreign-owned components—IDA Ireland, Enterprise Ireland, Shannon Development and Údarás na Gaeltachta										
	1990	1991	1992	1993	1994	1995	1996	9917	1998	1999
Overall total	214,938	214,956	215,143	217,224	224,173	234,816	247,273	263,124	277,609	290,600
Irish-owned	119,203	117,872	117,507	117,082	118,859	122,382	127,166	133,009	138,376	142,654
Foreign-owned	95,735	97,084	97,636	100,142	105,314	112,434	120,107	130,115	139,233	147,946

Source: Forfas Employment Survey 1999.

Overall permanent full-time employment (i.e. for manufacturing, internationally traded and financial services and other activities supported by the agencies) increased by 75,662 (35.2 per cent) over the 10-year period 1990–99. In 1999, overall total permanent full-time employment amounted to 290,600, and increase of 12,991 (4.7 per cent) over 1998. Foreign-owned companies accounted for 8,713 (67.1 per cent) of the net employment increase in 1999, with Irish-owned companies contributing 4,278 (32.9 per cent).

Over the past 10 years, permanent full-time employment in foreign-owned companies grew by 52,211 (54.5 per cent) with employment in Irish-owned companies increasing by 23,451 (19.7 per cent). Permanent full-time employment in foreign-owned companies now accounts for 50.9 per cent of total employment in manufacturing, internationally traded and financial services and other activities supported by the agencies compared with 50.2 per cent in 1998 and 44.5 per cent in 1990. Table 2.18 illustrates the employment trends in by sector.

Over the 10-year period 1990–99, permanent full-time manufacturing employment rose from 201,412 in 1990 to 237,749 in 1999, an increase of 36,337 jobs (18.0 per cent). In 1999, an increase of 3,480 jobs (1.5 per cent) was recorded. Permanent full-time employment in internationally traded and financial services companies displayed consistent year-on-year growth from 10,788 in 1990 to 49,206 in 1999, a rise of 356 per cent. This accounted for 38,418 (51.4 per cent) of the rise in total employment in manufacturing and internationally traded and financial services companies of 74,755 over the 10 years. The increase in internationally traded and financial services employment was 9,518 (24.0 per cent) in 1999, and accounted for 73.3 per cent of the rise in total employment of 12,991 in 1999. Such trends in employment are in line with overall industry patterns away from manufacturing to a post-manufacturing knowledge-based industry. These developments however raise issues for labour supply and reskilling into the future.

Table 2.18 Trends in permanent full-time employment 1990–99: manufacturing/internationally traded and financial services/other activities—IDA Ireland, Enterprise Ireland, Shannon Development and Údarás na Gaeltachta

	1990	1991	1992	1993	1994	1995	1996	9917	1998	1999
Manufacturing	201,412	200,189	199,681	200,249	204,811	212,598	219,724	228,950	234,269	237,749
Internationally traded/financial services	10,788	12,044	12,606	14,184	16,455	19,038	24,078	30,560	39,688	49,206
Mining/quarrying and other activities	2,738	2,723	2,856	2,791	2,907	3,180	3,471	3,614	3,652	3,645
Overall total	214,938	214,956	215,143	217,224	224,173	234,816	247,273	263,124	277,609	290,600

Source: Forfas Employment Survey (1999).

Total employment by overseas companies, supported by IDA Ireland is shown in Table 2.19. It is important to note that these figures relate only to IDA Ireland assisted companies and therefore, exclude companies handled by Shannon Development and Údarás na Gaeltachta.

Table 2.19 Overall employment in overseas companies 1989–98 (IDA-Ireland-supported companies)

	1989	1990	1991	1992	1993	1994	1995	1996	9917	1998
New jobs	7,744	7,641	6,608	7,040	8,225	9,890	11,689	13,273	14,836	15,996
Number of companies	750	812	844	856	877	912	965	1,047	1,111	1,140
Full-time employment	70,620	73,833	74,723	78,889	78,571	83,524	90,037	97,279	107,171	115,981
Net change %	+7.7	+4.6	+1.2	+1.6	+3.5	+6.3	+7.8	+8.0	+10.2	+8.2
Job losses as % total jobs	3.8	6	7.7	7.7	7.1	5.8	5.8	6.2	4.6	6.2

Source: IDA Ireland Annual Report (1999).

Sales and exports from overseas industry (both manufacturing and internationally traded services) grew by over 16 per cent with sales of €35.5 billion and exports of €33.01 billion. In the manufacturing sector sales grew by 10 per cent. The origins of IDA supported overseas investment is shown in Table 2.20. The predominance of American companies is evident.

Table 2.20 Origins of IDA-supported-companies 1999

Country of origin	Number of companies	Employment
USA	497	78,521
UK	198	12,956
Germany	172	11,070
Rest of Europe	291	13,642
Asia/Pacific	57	4,949
Rest of world	64	3,526
Total	1,279	124,664

Source: IDA Ireland (1999).

2.11 The Irish business sector 2000

The Top 10 companies by turnover in Ireland in 1999 are shown in Table 2.21. The Top 10 ranking includes six indigenous Irish companies (CRH, Jefferson Smurfit, Glanbia, Kerry Group, Fyffes and Dunnes) and four overseas branches of global MNCs (Dell, Intel, Microsoft and Oracle).

Table 2.21 The Top 10 companies in Ireland by turnover (1999)

	Turnover (€ billion)	Employees
1. Dell	5.76	3,800
2. CRH	5.21	22,708
3. Intel	5.08	4,300
4. Microsoft	3.72	1,500
5. Jefferson Smurfit	3.67	6,000
6. Glanbia	2.92	12,000
7. Kerry Group	2.20	12,500
8. Oracle Europe	1.90	720
9. Fyffes	1.86	3,170
10. Dunnes	1.84	18,000

Source: Adapted from Business and Finance Top 1000 Companies, February (2000).

The growth experienced by Dell, Intel, Oracle and Microsoft reflects that fact that the high-technology sector still has enormous potential. All of the leading companies have an international presence in many markets, adopting a PORTFOLIO approach so that if one geographical sector performs poorly, other sectors can compensate. Dell secured the number one spot with an increase in turnover of €761.8 million. The Kerry Group's good performance was mainly due to strong domestic and international sales. Dunnes managed to generate €1.841 billion in turnover despite extreme competition from Musgrave's (SuperValu and Centra) and Tesco Ireland. Oracle, a leading software company saw European sales increase by 69 per cent over the period 1998–99. Both Glanbia and Fyffes recorded a slight reduction in turnover in 1999, although both still justify their position in the Top 10. Table 2.22 shows the Top 10 Irish companies in 1999.

Table 2.22 The Top 10 Irish organisations (1999)

	Turnover (€ billion)	Employees
1. CRH	5.21	22,708
2. Jefferson Smurfit	3.67	6,000
3. Glanbia	2.92	12,000
4. Kerry Group	2.20	12,500
5. Fyffes	1.86	3,179
6. Dunnes	1.84	18,000
7. Eircom	1.82	11,560
8. Irish Diary Board	1.81	3,117
9. ESB	1.60	7,800
10. Musgrave's	1.49	2,600

Source: Adapted from Business and Finance Top 1000 Companies, February (2000).

A consistently high performer is CRH recording a 28 per cent increase in turnover, earning itself the number one spot. CRH is a huge company and is twice the size of Jefferson Smurfit. The strength of this international concrete, cement and aggregates group is illustrated by its appetite for new acquisitions and the gap opening up with the rest of the league in turnover. In recent years CRH had advanced from making a series of small to medium-sized acquisitions to larger deals which have produced such a successful recipe. The secret to their success lies in the ability to make earning enhancing acquisitions most notably in Poland and Eastern Europe (Business and Finance 2000).

The Top 10 high-technology companies in Ireland are listed in Table 2.23, and contain the major international players in the world.

Table 2.23 The Top 10 technology companies in Ireland (1999)

	Turnover (€ billion)	Employees
1. Dell	5.76	3,800
2. Intel	5.08	4,300
3. Microsoft	3.72	1,500
4. Oracle Europe	1.90	720
5. 3Com	1.40	1,800
6. EMC BV	1.31	935
7. Apple Computer	0.69	600
8. Gateway 2000	0.69	2,000
9. Motorola BV	0.51	1,700
10. Nortel Networks	0.44	1000

Source: Adapted from Business and Finance Top 1000 Companies, February 2000.

While these remain the key operators in the world-wide business there are also many smaller companies which occupy a sub-stratum of the information technology sector. These companies are mainly Irish and are creating leading-edge technologies. Companies such as Iona Technologies, Baltimore Technologies, Trintech and WBT are all examples of smaller indigenous operations successfully involved in the high-technology sector.

The companies just examined are the big players in Irish business today. However, to solely examine them at the expense of many smaller and medium-sized companies would be to disguise the true picture of Irish business. The business sector is made up a myriad of both, Irish and overseas, small to medium-sized enterprises (SMEs). The Task Force on Small Businesses (1993) found that there were 160,000 non-farm organisations in Ireland. While this amounts to a significant number of organisations, most of them are extremely small, with 98 per cent of companies employing less than 50 employees. Less than 1 per cent of companies employ more than 500 people. As a result there are thousands of small and medium-sized companies operating in Ireland, whose growth in recent years can be attributed to favourable economic conditions. However, the main difference between the large-scale companies examined earlier and the SMEs, lies in the ability of the former to grow through acquisition, while the latter face more organic growth.

2.12 Key business sectors in 2000

There are a number of key sectors in Irish business, which will be discussed in greater detail. The sectors chosen do not represent all sectors within the business community, but have been chosen on the basis of their contribution to economic growth.

2.12.1 The pharmaceutical sector

Ireland has become a key location for both pharmaceutical and chemicals. Over 120 overseas companies employ over 17,000 people and export $18 billion annually. This figure represents over 25 per cent of total exports from Ireland making the country one of the world's largest exporters of pharmaceuticals and fine chemicals in the world (IDA Ireland 2000).

The pharmaceutical industry was one of the first successes of the sectoral approach adopted by the IDA back in the 1960s. Early successes included Leo Laboratories (Danish), the Pfizer Corporation (USA) and Squibb Linson (USA). Promotional activity was facilitated by the small number of companies involved which meant that they were easy to initially identify, and subsequently to target. Companies involved in this sector require a large capital investment and as a result are more likely to make a long-term commitment to a country, once initially established. Throughout the 1970s and 1980s companies like Syntex, Merck Sharpe and Dohme, SmithKline and Allergan established facilities in Ireland.

The pharmaceutical sector is highly sophisticated, with advanced manufacturing technology, state of the art equipment and strict quality control. The total investment by overseas pharmaceutical companies is estimated to be in the region of $7 billion. The sector is quite diversified with some investment in fine chemical plants producing bulk active materials, and newer investment in finished product pharmaceutical operations. There are currently 47 finished pharmaceutical plants in Ireland. The main companies involved in sector are listed in Table 2.24.

Table 2.24 The main companies involved in the pharmaceuticals sector

	Turnover (€ million)	Employees
Janssen Pharmaceuticals	1,047.5	600
Swords Laboratories	876.1	358
United Drug	600.6	800
Schering Plough	380.9	680
SmithKline Beecham	380.9	288
Pfizer	253.9	320
Allergan Pharmaceuticals	241.3	900
Organon Ireland	184.1	450
Warner Lambert	184.1	300

Source: Adapted from Business and Finance Top 1000 companies, February 2000.

2.12.2 The healthcare sector

Companies involved in this sector develop and manufacture high-technology medical products ranging from catheters and orthopaedic implants to disposable contact lenses. The industry is viewed as a highly desirable one to develop, with its ultra-clean facilities and laboratory-style image. There are currently 80 companies including 10 of the worlds top 15 medical device companies located in Ireland, employing over 16,000 workers. These companies export over $2.5 billion annually. The first wave of these companies came in the 1970s and included Baxter Travenol, Abbott Laboratory, Hollister and Becton Dickinson. Bausch and Lomb and Sherwood Medical followed these in the 1980s and the industry quickly built up a solid reputation for providing stable jobs. The successful pattern has been continued into the 1990s with the location of Boston Scientific to Galway and Cork.

Table 2.25 The main companies involved in the healthcare sector

	Turnover (€ million)	Employees
Baxter Healthcare	228.6	800
Howmedica	199.3	300
Medtronic	146.0	900
Boston Scientific	139.7	400
Oral B Labs	127	450
Becton Dickinson	114.2	510
Bausch & Lomb	107.9	1,000
Mallinkrodt	101.6	300
Millipore	88.9	300
Guidant Corp	50.8	380

Source Adapted from Business and Finance Top 1000 Companies, February 2000.

The sub-sectors of the industry in Ireland include interventional products, medical equipment, dental, vision and healing products, orthopaedics, disposable support products and services. The main companies involved in the healthcare sector are listed in Table 2.25

2.12.3 The electronics sector

The development of a vibrant electronics sector has been at the heart of Ireland's economic development. This sector currently represents the largest single overseas investment sector in Ireland. Over 300 electronics companies develop, market and manufacture a range of products in Ireland. The industry is made up of the following sub-sectors: components, computers, contract manufacturing, semi-conductors, telecommunications and data communications services.

During 1997 high-technology companies exported €10.1 billion from Ireland which marked rise of 22 per cent over the previous year and represented 36 per cent of the total exports. In addition these companies spend in the region of €2.79 billion in the Irish economy each year in wages, raw materials and services (IDA Ireland 2000). The overseas electronics sector accounts for 14 per cent of the total number of overseas companies in Ireland. US companies form the largest part of the electronics sector accounting for 61 per cent of companies. A strong high-quality support structure and infrastructure has also developed which meets the needs of electronics companies in Ireland.

The development of modern digitally based telecommunications system and the establishment of a National Microelectronics Centre for research at UCC were to prove crucial in developing the sector in later years. Companies such as Apple, Verbatim, Amdahl and a little later Sun Micro Systems, Motorola and Intel all established facilities in Ireland. When computers and telecommunications converged to produce the Internet boom, the IDA moved to attract new leaders such as 3Com and Cabletron. Some of the main companies currently involved in the sector are listed in Table 2.26.

Table 2.26 The main companies involved in the electronics sector		
	Turnover (€ million)	Employees
Dell	5,763.3	3,800
Intel Irl	5,079	4,300
Motorola	507.9	1,700
Compaq	393.6	520
Analog Devices	304.7	1,500
Siemens	253.8	600
Sun Microsystems	50.79	200

Source: Adapted from Business and Finance Top 1000 Companies, February 2000.

2.12.4 The software sector

Ireland is the second largest exporter of software in the world after the USA. The top 10 independent software companies have a presence in Ireland and over 40 per cent of all PC package software sold across Europe is produced in Ireland. The software sector in Ireland is made up of 550 companies (120 overseas) employing 15,000 people. These companies to carry out a broad range of activities including core software development, product customisation, software testing and fulfilment.

The software that is being developed in Ireland has a huge number of applications including mobile communications, electronics, engineering, banking, DATABASE management, insurance solutions and Internet security (IDA Ireland 2000). An increasing number of companies involved in this sector are also providing technical support to customers though the establishment of call centres in Ireland which provide toll free advice. A number of software companies in Ireland, some of which originated as small start-ups are leading their market with innovative middleware and Internet solutions. The main companies involved in the sector in Ireland are listed in Table 2. 27.

Table 2.27 The main companies involved in the software sector		
	Turnover (€ million)	Employees
Microsoft	3,714	1,500
Lotus Development	412.7	550
Informix Software	254	150
Visio International	76.2	120
ADC	127	229
Iona Technologies	84.2	300
Sun Microsystems	50.8	200
Oracle	1,904.6	720
Baltimore Technologies	31	450

Source: Adapted from Business and Finance Top 1000 Companies, March 2000.

2.12.5 The teleservices sector

Ireland has recently established a strong presence in the call centre market with over 60 companies opting for Ireland as a base for their new European call centres. These global operators employ 6,000 people in Ireland and carry out many of their key business functions here, ranging from handling customer queries, taking orders and providing technical support on a pan European level. These multilingual centres provide services to clients across Europe, 24 hours a day, 365 days of the year. One-third of teleworkers operating in Europe are located in Ireland (O'Dea 1999).

The challenge for the IDA in promoting newer service opportunities like call centres lay in convincing companies that they would save costs and provide a better service to customers from Ireland than anywhere else. Ireland's new digital-based telecommunications which gradually became available in the 1980s allowed the IDA to combine three elements into their promotional package:

► Eircom's technical advantage
► Eircom's low call charges for volume users
► the availability of staff with European languages.

It was designed to attract the marketing, customer and technical support services of the computer and electronic companies in Ireland. Ireland's status as a call centre provider was further enhanced by the decision by IBM to invest €253.9 million in a European call centre in Dublin. By 1996 there were 26 teleservice projects including American Airlines, Hertz, ITT Sheraton Hotels and Citibank.

2.12.6 The financial services sector

By far the most significant development in relation to this sector has been the International Financial Services Centre (IFSC), which was established in 1987 in Dublin. Since its inception the centre has played a pivotal role in the development of the economy. It currently employs 4,000 people and indirectly effects demand for a host of other related business services.

The IFSC is now the preferred location for a number of financial service activities including, banking and asset financing, corporate treasury, insurance, securitisation and mutual funds. Table 2.28 provides a list of some of the main international players in the IFSC.

Table 2.28 The main international companies in the IFSC		
	Assets (€ billion)	Employees
DE Pfa Bank Europe	20.04	60
Banque Nationale de Paris	13.60	100
Rabobank	8.88	45
Merrill Lynch Capital Markets	6.19	150
Commerzbank Europe (Irl)	4.10	25
Scotia bank of Ireland	3.40	35
Hypo Vereinsbank Ireland	3.31	–
SCZ Bank Ireland	3.16	18
Bank Gesellschaft	2.63	25
Haleba Dublin Landesbank	2.07	30

Source: Business and Finance Top 1000 Companies, March 2000.

2.12.7 The engineering sector

There are 170 foreign-owned engineering companies in Ireland employing 15,000 people. Many of these companies export most of their output, which accounts for about 8 per cent of Irish exports. The main activities carried out include automotive components, materials handling, mechanical engineering, electrical equipment, building products, aerospace and engineering services.

Automotive components and aerospace technology are two of the most important and rapidly growing sectors in Ireland. Ireland exports $1 billion-worth of auto-components alone. The engineering industry is a vibrant sector of the economy with many world-class manufacturing operations based in Ireland. The industry is supported by a strong indigenous sub-supply base and close links are fostered between industry and third-level institutions, particularly in the area of advanced manufacturing technology. Some of the main companies involved in the sector are listed in Table 2.29.

Table 2.29 The main companies involved in the engineering sector

	Turnover (€ million)	Employees
Barlo Group	223.3	1,400
Kostal	171.4	1,200
Xilinx Ireland	168.9	200
Willamette	92.2	200
Wellman International	90.2	430
Allied Signal Ireland	82.5	600
Carey Bros	22.9	350
Liebherr	44.4	400
ABS Pumps	39.9	327
Donnelly Mirrors	41.4	475

Source: Adapted from Business and Finance Top 1000 Companies, February 2000.

2.12.8 The consumer products sector

This sector mainly comprises 100 companies producing consumer goods. Products range form domestic appliances to clothing and leisure goods. Two sports specialists, Penn Racquet Sports and Tretorn, supply more than half of all first-class tennis balls sold in Europe. Other recognised leaders with their main facilities in Ireland include Hasbro (games), Giro (cycle helmets), Wilson (sport socks) and Atari (electronic games. Some of the main companies operating in this sector are listed in Table 2.30.

Table 2.30 The main companies involved in the consumer products sector

	Turnover (€ million)	Employees
Glen Dimplex	825.3	6,000
Unilever	289.5	550
Hasbro	52.1	480
Yves Rocher Irl	34.9	250
Goblin Ireland	28.6	170
Penn Raquet	22.9	153

Source: Adapted from Business and Finance Top 1000 Companies, February 2000.

2.12.9 The food and drinks sector

The food and drinks sector has consistently remained one of the most important industrial sectors. Unlike many of the other sectors examined, the food and drinks sector is largely dominated by Irish companies and in part reflects the role played by Irish agriculture. The main companies involved in the sector are listed in Table 2.31.

Table 2.31 The main companies involved in the food and drinks sector

	Turnover (€ million)	Employees
Glanbia	2,922	12,000
Kerry Group	2,200	12,500
Fyffes	1,864	3,179
Irish Diary Board	1,808	3,117
Guinness Ireland	1,152	2,300
Irish Distillers	965	2,010
Irish Food Processors	889	2,950
Greencore	864	1,675
IAWS Group	850	950
Golden Vale	736	2,010

Source: Adapted from Business and Finance Top 1000 Companies, February 2000.

Glanbia is the largest company in the food and drink sector although the Kerry Group is a close rival. Glanbia is currently a major player on both the domestic and international market.

2.13 Future prospects

The success of the Irish economy in the 1990s was phenomenal. Ambitious targets for employment and growth were not only achieved but surpassed in many sectors. Some will say that Ireland may become a victim of its own success and that strategies designed to consolidate rather than continue unrestrained growth would be more prudent.

Irish economic growth has been driven by two main factors. First, the growth experienced by Ireland's trading partners (USA, UK and more recently Germany) which has had an obvious impact on Irish growth. Second, the major internal engine for Irish economic growth has been FDI. One of the most immediate challenges facing the Irish economy is to reduce the effect that a world-wide recession and slow-down would have on the country, largely due to dependence on FDI. There is little doubt that a world-wide recession would have an enormous impact on employment levels in the major players in Ireland such as Intel and Dell.

One of the main priorities for IDA Ireland is to minimise this possibility by attempting to attract new FDI which is higher up the value chain than, for example, call centres, which are susceptible both to changes in Irish costs and technological developments. Consequently, the focus of IDA Ireland for the year 2000 was to switch from quantity to quality in its job creation programme. It reduced its target for new jobs in 2000 to 12,000 which is down roughly 30 per cent on the 1999 figure of 18,079. Reflecting the declining unemployment in the state, this was the first time the Agency reduced its job creation targets. IDA Ireland is now remodelling itself as an economic development agency with particular interest in regional aid and E-BUSINESS. Its focus is no longer on the quantity of jobs it helps create but on the quality of these positions and their location. Its performance is being measured in terms of income and wealth. In 1999 some 9,392 IDA Ireland jobs were lost mainly in the 'low end' sectors.

The closure of the Fruit of the Loom plant in Co. Donegal is typical of the decline in the textile sector. The shift in the IDA strategy is indicative of the urgent need for consensus on the need to balance economic growth and development against the need for infrastructural development in roads, communications, electrical power generation and distribution and the provision of mobile telephony and waste management services. Labour shortages in key areas and the resultant increase in labour costs will make the FDI process more demanding and challenging.

In addition, all industrial development, both indigenous and FDI effort faces further challenges due to the fact that the overall EU industrial incentives package has changed. Less support is now available and it has become narrower in extent, with the emphasis placed on capability rather than capacity development. Ireland is now required to submit all proposed state aid schemes to the Competition Directorate for approval prior to implementation. This introduces another level of administration that can slow down the implementation of an initiative.

A further complicating factor for Ireland is the division of the country into two regions—the Border, Midlands and West (BMW) region which has Objective One Status which gives the state the right to grant the maximum levels of aid for the period 2000/06. The remainder of the country has Objective One in Transition Status and that puts lower limits on the levels of state aid allowable. In developing new schemes for the future, greater inventiveness will be required in utilising the maximum scope of the EU guidelines.

IDA Ireland wants to develop Ireland as a world and European hub for e-business. The success of this strategy will be heavily dependent on among other things, the provision of low-cost, high-bandwidth communications for Internet access. In mid-1999 a series of related government measures were announced designed to get Ireland into a leading position in the E-COMMERCE business. These included a deal with the Global Crossing Company of America to provide dramatically improved telecommunication connections between the USA, Ireland and 24 European cities. The trans-Atlantic cable would surface in the first National Digital Park dedicated to e-commerce companies. Citywest Business Campus and IDA Ireland are developing this. The national e-commerce and Internet infrastructure now being put in place should enable the IDA Ireland to succeed in its ambition to make Ireland a leading European centre for the extensive range of new age industries needing these facilities.

Although the final phase of deregulation in the communications sector was brought forward by a year to December 1998, the unbundling of the local loop (i.e. allowing competitors to use the part of the network known as the 'final mile', or the cable connecting the subscriber to the local exchange) is still a difficult challenge for the fledging privatised Eircom to accept. Already, some European countries notably Spain, have experience of the impact of various high-speed cable services such as ADSL (asymmetric digital subscriber line) services. Early indications are that the forecast growth levels in BUSINESS TO BUSINESS (B2B) and BUSINESS TO CUSTOMER (B2C) content over these networks are indeed well justified. In the European competitive environment the recent success of the Irish economy will be watched closely by its neighbours. There is therefore a very high level of urgency if Ireland is to succeed in its ambitions in this area.

On the indigenous side, the challenge faced by Enterprise Ireland in its role as the body charged with the responsibility for the development of Irish Enterprise is to work with Irish-owned or controlled enterprises in the manufacturing, natural resources and internationally traded services sectors to:

► create profitable new businesses
► build share of international markets
► harness new technologies
► improve R & D capability
► build people skills and capabilities.

The core of the Enterprise Ireland vision for the next 10 years is that locally controlled business, trading internationally will have doubled their sales form €25.39 billion to €50.78 billion in this period. In order to achieve this they have set their priority on assisting growth-oriented companies in the process of business development, internationalisation and innovation. The approach is to focus on solutions and services rather than programmes and processes. Each client firm will have a dedicated client advisor, who will act as the primary point of contact and give the client access to the full range of Enterprise Ireland solutions. The client will be helped to source expertise both from within Enterprise Ireland and externally and it is foreseen that these services will be delivered as part of a structured development process agreed with the client. There is no doubt that this will lead to the creation of a family of professional consultants in the financial, legal, marketing and business domains. The primary assumption is that the entrepreneurs will be extracted from industry and the educational institutions by an aggressive targeting campaign. The advisors will create the appropriate, legal financial and corporate structures around them and the opportunity to grow will ensue.

In the area of financial assistance there is a clear shift of policy towards supporting capability development at the expense of expanding capacity. Enterprise Ireland's finance policy is based on:

► rationalisation of the range of financial support instruments to six main business development areas
► differentiation between the requirements of firms in the regions
► creating the conditions where the private sector becomes the primary source of equity for expanding companies.

Enterprise Ireland has identified a number of critically important issues which have a large impact on the future development of indigenous industry, with specific relevance to the internationally traded services area. Some of the issues reviewed below are also relevant to the overseas sector; however, the discussion will focus on indigenous industry.

The importance of R & D. This has remained a key issue for indigenous industrial development for many years. Expenditure on R & D has grown from 0.5 per cent of sales in 1988 to 1.1 per cent in 1997; however, this is low in the context of the competitive need for product and process innovation. Gross domestic expenditure on R & D (GERD) is well below OECD averages and in 1997 was just under $1.1 billion of which $237 million was state-funded.

Telecommunications and infrastructure costs. Internet and broadband applications offer significant opportunities for indigenous software and service companies who require fast high-capacity telelcommunications facilities. It is vital that these facilities are available at a competitive price. In this regard, the introduction of flat-rate charges for different levels of high-speed Internet access is important.

Tightening labour market. Labour market and skills gaps are arising due to the near full-employment conditions and a low (*circa* 4.7 per cent) rate of unemployment. Labour market shortages typically increase the cost of labour which in the medium to long run could seriously undermine Ireland's competitive position.

Education system. The education system needs to keep pace with business models and concepts, as well as technological developments, and embrace new disciplines.

Infrastructure. A fundamental requirement for continued economic and regional development is access to an adequate infrastructure—roads, rail, airports and serviced accommodations. The lack of adequate transport facilities (mainly roads) inhibits further development. Very significant investment is required to bring the transport infrastructure to EU standards.

Regulations governing e-business. Fears about security and fraud have to be addressed. The e-business regulatory regime needs to deal with issues relating to security.

Access to finance. The availability of seed and VENTURE CAPITAL is critically important for the development of high-tech companies. The key issues include the level of support needed at each stage of development, a balance between grants and repayable funds, and matching the form and the amount of funds to the specific developmental needs of the company.

The attention of the state agencies involved in the development of indigenous industry has focused on strategies designed to achieve many of the critical success factors discussed above.

Globalisation has intensified competition and increasingly competitiveness is achieved through knowledge-based technological innovation. The business world is moving into a post-manufacturing era where high-knowledge-content industries are driving competition. New technologies and the people who develop, apply and manage them—referred to as intellectual capital is fast becoming the most important factor of production. The availability, cost and quality of intellectual capital is becoming critically important. In order to develop high-technology companies which embody a high knowledge content Irish industry requires the following:

▶ investment in R & D, especially basic (or generic) research which is high risk
▶ investment in people—leading edge researchers
▶ investment in enabling processes for effective technology transfer to facilitate profitable commercialisation of Intellectual property rights.

The importance of building such scientific and technological capability for the future is a fundamental part of the Technology Foresight Ireland document, which was published by Forfas and the Irish Council for Science Technology and Innovation in 1999. Indeed the document (1999:5) states that:

Knowledge is one of the main drivers of prosperity and well-being. Ireland needs to evolve rapidly to a knowledge society. Enterprises that are focused on their customers, employ educated workers, encourage innovation throughout their business and know more and learn faster than their global competitors are the most likely to succeed and grow. Societies that maximise opportunities for individuals and enterprises to develop knowledge-age skills and access knowledge-age services are the most likely to be cohesive and successful.

Technology Foresight is a process for gathering together scientists, engineers, industrialists and government officials and other interested parties to identify areas of strategic research and the emerging technologies likely to create the greatest economic and social gains. The initiative therefore attempts to link investment in research, science and technology with the drive to develop Ireland as a knowledge society. The report concludes that the Irish economy needs to reposition itself—from predominantly production-oriented plants to research, knowledge-based and innovation-driven firms. To achieve this goal a vision of the type of economy and enterprises the country wishes to develop and the supporting policies and investment are required to make it happen.

The government's response to the recommendations saw the establishment of a €711.05 million Technology Foresight Fund to contribute to the development of world-class research capability in *informatics* (the combination of information and communications technologies) and biotechnology. Both informatics and biotechnology are viewed as key foundation-enabling technologies which fuel the growth of many other related sectors. The key challenge for agencies like Enterprise Ireland is to create initiatives that maximise the commercial effects of these drives through successful spin-off and commercialisation of research outputs.

Outside of informatics and biotechnology R & D expenditure in indigenous industry while improving still remains low. The R & D intensity (R & D spend to gross output) of indigenous manufacturing was 1.1 per cent in 1997 up from 0.5 per cent in 1991. There are also signs of a slowing down in the growth rate of business sector R & D activity. The growth rate in R & D expenditure in real terms between 1995 and 1997 was 15 per cent per annum which is lower than that for the period 1991–95 which stood at 20 per cent (Forfas Annual Report 1999). Overall, in terms of expenditure on R & D there remains room for improvement.

Enterprise Ireland is also trying to influence and effect change so that the business environment enables enterprise to thrive. In order to develop and expand companies require access to adequate sources of finance on reasonable terms. The shortage of seed and venture capital and long-term credit finance for emerging companies is a critical issue for enterprise development in Ireland. Part of the reason for the shortage of seed and early-stage capital is the limited ability of investment and support bodies generally in Ireland to assess the commercial viability of emergent high-tech companies. The major asset held by such companies is intellectual property rather than fixed assets that LENDING AGENCIES have relied on in the past for security (Forfas Annual Report 1999).

Steps have been taken to rectify the venture capital shortage. The EU Seed and Venture Capital Measure under the Operational Programme for Industrial Development 1994–99 was set up to establish Venture Capital Funds to provide early-stage, SME-growth-oriented enterprises with equity capital. The programme provided €41.9 million for investment through venture capital intermediaries, matched by €41.9 million from the private sector. Enterprise Ireland implemented the policy of forming partnerships with private-sector institutions and venture capitalists to set up the Venture Capital Funds. There are currently 15 such funds in operation in Ireland including Trinity Venture Fund, ICC Software Fund Limited and ACT Enterprise Limited Partnership. In 1999 investments of €25.52 million were made in 51 companies in return for an equity stake. Of that €25.52 million 82 per cent went to start up and early stage companies. It would appear that Irish companies are developing a wider acceptance of venture capital. Alternative sources of finance for the development stage of companies is likely to be achieved by accessing public funding through the process of flotation on alternative investment markets. Examples of these markets include the London-based Alternative Investment Market (AIM) and the Dublin based Developing Companies Market (DCM). This trend is likely to continue in the future.

In 1999 Enterprise Ireland commissioned a major study of the Internationally Traded Services (ITS) sector in Ireland which resulted in the ITS 2007 strategy document. It involved an examination of global opportunities, an identification of areas with greatest potential for Ireland, and the development of recommendations for policies and interventions which would enable Irish companies to realise potential. The ITS sector is viewed as having greater potential than any other indigenous sector for creating wealth, growth in value-added, exports and high-quality employment. The strategy document presents a range of initiatives to be undertaken by Enterprise Ireland aimed at developing high value-added, knowledge-intensive industries and helping them achieve fast growth. The strategy has two objectives:

▶ the development of ITS businesses in the regions
▶ the development of sectors that present the best opportunities.

ITS 2007 concentrates on four sectors—informatics, e-business, healthsciences and digital media (film, TV, radio production and post-production, animation, special effects, music, advertising and multimedia), as they offer the greatest growth opportunities. In terms of regional development the strategy proposes to establish a number of technology hubs to address difficulties associated with early and rapid growth. Such technology hubs to be known as *webworks* are designed to provide office facilities and management structure for technology-based companies. A key element of the concept is that the webworks environment should be conducive to networking and promote mutual learning. It is envisaged that each webwork will concentrate on a broad technology area, housing companies in one of the target sectors. The networks will support new businesses across a wide range of sectors, exploiting the new business models facilitated by Internet and global e-business growth.

Central to the webworks concept is the idea that campus companies incubating in local universities and institutes of technology can be accommodated along with local companies and non-campus-based initiatives. The webworks could evolve in response to clusters of established companies, building on strengths. A certain critical mass of companies is necessary to create the cluster effect which will be located in main regional urban centres—Limerick, Cork, Galway, Waterford and smaller webworks in locations such as Letterkenny, Sligo, Castlebar and Athlone. An experienced manager will head each and be co-ordinated through a national *webworks networking team*.

The strategy document also makes sector specific recommendations, the most fundamental of which centre around informatics. This sector includes software, communications and hardware and includes design, development, support and service activities. It is characterised by knowledge intensity and export orientation and currently accounts for about 85 per cent of ITS sales from Ireland. Continued development of this sector is therefore important for the entire service sector particularly digital media and e-business which rely on the developments in informatics. The strategy for the informatics sectors focuses on moving companies up the value chain by improving productivity and competitiveness and concentrating on higher-value activities, so that Irish companies don't have to engage in PRICE COMPETITION with lower cost economies.

The National Software Directorate is to be expanded to encompass non-software informatics companies as well and will be known as the National Informatics Directorate. This directorate will work closely with webworks and webworks network teams. It is envisaged that the Informatics Programme will cater for informatics, e-business and digital media in seeking to focus the national research agenda on areas that are capable of commercialisation by Irish companies through the following mechanisms:

▶ influencing the operation and prioritisation of the state and EU R & D schemes for industry

▶ providing input to the basic research agenda in informatics funded under Technology Foresight

▶ directing an applied research programme geared to the needs of the informatics sector

▶ directing the collaborative and strategic research grant schemes.

The ITS 2007 strategy documents concluded by prioritising a number of specific recommendations:

▶ webworks—support in the form of clusters of flexible highly wired office accommodation and management supply for clusters of high-technology companies

▶ E-Business Learning Centre—to help both new and existing businesses to adopt new business models, centrally and in the Border, Midlands and West

▶ technology exploitation initiatives—to ensure that the results of investment in research are exploited as far as possible within Ireland

▶ Digital Media District in Dublin—to help establish Ireland as a leader in the emerging digital media industry

▶ international market initiatives—to help Irish companies develop global markets.

Through these initiatives, and others detailed in the report, it is envisaged that Irish ITS could increase sales by €2.03 billion, exports by €2.28 billion and employ an additional 8,500 by 2007.

The future prospects for industrial development in Ireland are on balance very good. The current IDA Ireland approach to FDI, focusing on quality of jobs rather than quantity, should result in a pattern of investment higher in the value chain than at present. The threat of recession, labour shortages and infrastructure constraints continue to pose the greatest problems for continued development of FDI in Ireland.

On the indigenous front, the need to create an industrial development environment which positively promotes the development of home-grown intellectual property poses a challenge for all involved. The foundation for sustainable growth in the modern global economy requires a marriage between finance, innovation and entrepreneurial creativity. Support and reward for the innovator will prove to be the critical success factor in the years to come.

2.14 Summary of key propositions

- ▶ With the establishment of the Free State in 1922 a conservative approach was taken to the development of industry, with little state involvement. The development of agriculture was prioritised during the period.

- ▶ From 1932 to 1958 a policy of self-sufficiency and protectionism was pursued which was motivated by both economic and political factors. Protectionism meant that Irish companies were protected from external competition by the imposition of high tariffs on imported goods. Such tariffs ensured that foreign imports were more expensive than Irish goods.

- ▶ In 1958 Whitaker produced a document called *Economic Development* which altered the course of industrial development. The document advocated a move to free trade and a policy of foreign direct investment, and was later translated into the First Programme for Economic Expansion.

- ▶ In 1969 the IDA was restructured under the Industrial Development Act. As a result of the changes the IDA assumed sole responsibility for the development of industry, both indigenous and foreign.

- ▶ In 1973 Ireland joined the EEC. Membership of the EEC became a highly significant selling point for the IDA, when promoting Ireland as an investment location, particularly in the USA. Ireland could now be sold as a European base for foreign MNCs who could serve the European market. In addition it also opened a market of 250 million people, for Irish indigenous companies.

- ▶ The recession of the early 1980s forced the IDA to rethink their strategy. The main thrust of the new approach adopted was to concentrate on attracting companies with high output using the best technology while spending significant amounts on Irish materials and related services. The IDA introduced a new International Services Programme and changed the promotional efforts away from offering financial grants to the importance of human capital in Ireland.

- ▶ The Telesis Report published in 1982 heavily criticised industrial policy for an over reliance on the foreign sector at the expense of Irish indigenous companies. The report argued that there should be more of a balance between the two sectors.

- ▶ The period 1987 onwards is characterised by economic and industrial recovery through social partnership and fiscal rectitude. Under the PNR (1987) wage moderation was agreed in return for significant cuts in taxation. The PNR was followed by the PESP (1991), the PCW (1994) and Partnership 2000 (1997). All of these centralised deals marked a greater degree of involvement and realism among the social partners.

▶ Economic policies of the early 1990s were heavily influenced by events in Europe. The Maastricht Treaty (1991) signalled an intent to establish a common currency by 1999. In order to gain membership strict criteria had to be met.

▶ In 1992 the Culliton Report was published which argued that a much broader approach should be taken to industrial policy. It offered a number of recommendations concerning taxation, infrastructure, education, technology, industry, enterprise and institutional arrangements.

▶ As a result of the Culliton Report the IDA was restructured in 1993 and again in 1998. It now consists of IDA (Ireland) to promote overseas investment, Enterprise Ireland to promote indigenous industry, Shannon Development, Údarás na Gaeltachta and Forfas for policy advice and co-ordination.

▶ Between 1987 and 2000 the economy underwent something of a miraculous recovery. Budget deficits were converted into surpluses, emigration became immigration, employment increased and inflation was kept at a manageable level.

▶ The key business sectors in Ireland are pharmaceuticals and chemicals, healthcare, electronics, software, teleservices, financial services, engineering, consumer products and food and drink.

Discussion questions

❶ Explain the pattern of early industrial development in Ireland prior to 1958.

❷ Explain the significance of Whitaker's *Economic Development* document for the subsequent move to free trade and direct foreign investment.

❸ How did membership of the EEC in 1973 affect industrial policy performance?

❹ Why were the changes that were introduced to the educational system in the late 1960s and early 1970s so important in later years?

❺ What were the main strategies pursued by the IDA during the period 1980–86? Critically evaluate their success.

❻ Why was the move to a social partnership model so important for economic and industrial recovery?

❼ Why was the Culliton Report (1992) viewed as a watershed in the development of industrial policy?

❽ How did EU membership affect economic and industrial policy during the 1980s and 1990s?

❾ Account for Ireland's economic recovery from 1994 onwards.

❿ Discuss the fortunes of the various business sectors in the 1990s.

⓫ Six out of the top 10 companies in Ireland are indigenous companies. Account for their success.

⓬ What future direction should Irish industrial policy take?

Concluding case: The International Financial Services Centre (IFSC)

In 1987 the government established the International Financial Services Sector in the Customs House Docks area of Dublin. The IFSC is currently a $640 million development consisting of 1,200,000 square feet of high-quality office space. The IFSC is an integral and crucial part of the Irish economy. It employs close to 4000 people directly and indirectly effecting demand for a host of other related services including legal, accounting, security and catering. There are almost 400 international financial services companies located in the Centre with 350 companies conducting business under the IFSC programme.

Prior to 1987 the idea of establishing a world-class international financial services centre in Dublin seemed an impossible dream. In terms of financial markets and mere presence in the financial services sector, Dublin was completely overshadowed by its neighbour, London. As London was the third largest financial centre in the world, the thought of building up a presence in the market must have appeared daunting. However, in the late 1980s four factors emerged which presented Ireland with the opportunity to become a player in the industry.

▶ Financial markets became global and increasingly interdependent. Invested funds could be traded around the world easily, multinational corporations were trading on stock exchanges around the world and international financial instruments developed. In addition, operations were now conducted round the clock.

▶ Technological advances had led to the emergence of the electronic market place for financial services, which offered enormous opportunities for companies.

▶ The global deregulation of financial services meant that companies could now offer products outside of their traditional markets, thereby increasing the range of financial services available on an international basis.

▶ There was also a rapid growth in the financial services sector world-wide at the end of the 1980s.

The original concept of developing a specialised centre for internal financial services can be traced back to Dermot Desmond (NCB Stockbrokers) who argued that the international financial services sector presented a great opportunity for Ireland. A feasibility study of the concept was undertaken in 1986 and concluded that the project had enormous potential. Chief among the critical success factors possessed by Ireland was lower operating costs when compared to London, a plentiful supply of educated young people, a modern digital-based telecommunications network, the English language and presence in the same time zone as London. All of these factors conspired to produce an opportunity ripe for the taking.

The development of the IFSC is largely the result of a unique combination of factors. One of the key proponents of the concept was the then Taoiseach Charles Haughey who pioneered much of the early development. In May 1987 a 27-acre site at the Customs House Dock was selected for the IFSC. An International Financial Services Committee was set up to oversee the development of the centre. This committee was unique in that its composition reflected both public and private sector characters. Heads of key government departments, the Revenue Commissioners, Central Bank and leaders from the private sector all worked together to achieve a common goal— the establishment of a world-class financial centre.

A licensing mechanism was quickly established which was designed to ensure that only the most desirable projects were chosen, ones in which jobs and economic activity would result. Unlike previous developments no cash grants were given for investment in the IFSC. A 10 per cent corporation tax rate was given to all licensed companies establishing facilities and this was included in the Finance Act (1987). Irish companies were encouraged to set up in the centre provided that they generated business and jobs. The Central Bank agreed to supervise activities within the centre and strived for integrity.

Strong political momentum was given to the project by the enduring commitment of Charles Haughey. He brought to the project a degree of allure and charisma. The IDA, in collaboration with the private sector, undertook initial promotion of the concept, which was a new departure. Showpiece seminars were conducted world-wide during 1988–89 including in Frankfurt, Tokyo, London and New York. These seminars were produced jointly by the IDA and the Financial Services Industry Association.

By the end of 1987 the IDA had granted approval for 18 projects to set up facilities in the IFSC. Despite such early success the government decided to change the promotional approach by establishing a Government Representative Group to market the IFSC to the highest levels internationally. The government group consisted of three high-profile men, O'Cofaigh, (former Governor of the Central Bank), Pairceir (former Chairman of the Revenue Commissioners) and Hogan (former second Secretary at the Department of Finance) and became known as the 'wise men'. This group was to be highly successful in its promotion of the IFSC particularly given their financial backgrounds. They were responsible for attracting the Dutch Rabobank and ABN-AMRO, and the German Dresdner Bank to locate in the IFSC. By April 1989 60 projects had been approved and the group retired.

Despite the budgetary cutbacks associated with this period the government found alternative ways of promoting the concept which did not involve large sums of money. In parallel with the approach employed by the wise men, journalists from the international financial media were invited to Dublin and the IFSC became a growing news story. By the end of 1989 95 projects had been approved including Chase Manhattan (USA), Commerzbank (Germany), Banque Bruxelles and Lambert (Belgium), Mitsubshisi Trust and Sumitomo Bank (Japan). At the end of 1990 150 projects had been approved.

The IFSC is currently a highly desirable and growing location for a range of international financial services, which includes international banking and asset financing, corporate treasury, insurance, securitisation and mutual funds. The IFSC owes its success to many factors not least of which was the proactive approach to its development, which was adopted by the various parties involved.

Case adapted from White (2000); IDA (Ireland) website: www.idairleand.com.

Case questions

❶ Account for the success of the IFSC.

❷ How does the strategy for developing the IFSC fit into the overall industrial development policy in Ireland?

❸ What does the future hold for the IFSC?

Keep up to date

You can keep up to date on the main developments in the Irish business sector by consulting the following websites:

www.Enterprise-Ireland.com
www.idaireland.com.

Bibliography

A Time for Change: Industrial Policy for the 1990s (1992). Report of the Industrial Policy Review Group. Stationary Office, Dublin. Also termed the Culliton Report.

Annual Competitiveness Report (1999). The National Competitive Council. Forfas, Dublin.

Buchanan, C. and partners (1968) *Regional Studies in Ireland.* United Nations Consultants.

Business and Finance (2000), 'Ireland's Top 1000 Companies', February.

Cooper, C. and Whelan, N. (1973) *Science, Technology and Industry in Ireland.* Report to the National Science Council. Stationary Office, Dublin.

Duffy, D., Kearney, I. and Smyth, D. (1999) *Medium Term Review 1999–2005.* The Economic and Social Research Institute, Dublin.

Economic and Social Development 1976-1980. Stationary Office, Dublin.

Employment through Enterprise: The Response of the Government to the Moriarty Task Force on the Implementation of the Culliton Report (1993). Stationary Office, Dublin.

Enterprise Ireland Annual Report and Accounts (1999). Enterprise Ireland, Dublin.

Enterprise Ireland: Strategy 1999–2001. Enterprise Ireland, Dublin.

Enterprise Ireland: Working with Irish Industry to grow profitable sales, exports and employment (2000). Enterprise Ireland, Dublin.

Fitzgerald, G. (1968) *Planning in Ireland.* Dublin: Institute of Public Administration.

Fitzpatrick, M. (2000) 'A Century of Irish Business', *Sunday Independent*, January 2, 18L–19L.

Forbairt Annual Report 1997.

Forfas Annual Report and Accounts (1999). Forfas, Dublin.

Haughton, J. (1987) 'The Historical Background', in J. O'Hagan (ed.) *The Economy of Ireland.* Dublin, MIMI.

IDA Annual Reports 1970–95.

IDA Ireland Annual Reports 1997–99.

Ireland: National Development Plan 1989–93. Stationary Office, Dublin.

Ireland: National Income and Expenditure 1969 (1970). Central Statistics Office, Dublin.

ITS 2007: Opportunities for Irelands High-Technology Internationally Traded Services Sector to 2007. Enterprise Ireland 2000, Dublin.

Kennedy, K. (1998) *From Famine to Feast: Economic and Social Change in Ireland 1847–1997.* Institute of Public Administration, Dublin.

Kennedy, K. and Dowling, B. (1975) *Economic Growth in Ireland: The experience since 1947.* Dublin: Gill & Macmillan.

Lee, J. (1989) *Ireland 1912–1985: Politics and Society.* UK: Cambridge University Press.

MacSharry, R. and White, P. (2000) *The Making of the Celtic Tiger: The Inside Story of Ireland's Boom Economy.* Dublin, Mercier Press.

Moran, A. (2000) 'Economic Pills and Potions'. *Ireland 2000*, Dublin.

Mulrennan, F. (2000) 'Irish Financial Services: Industry Structure'. *Ireland 2000*, Dublin.

O'Dea, C. (1999) 'Republic is home to one-third of Europe's army of Teleworkers', *Irish Times*, 8 October 2000.

O'Malley, E. (1980) *Industrial Policy and Development: A Survey of the Literature from the Early 1960s.* National Economic and Social Council, Dublin.

Regional Development and Industrial Location in Ireland (1973) An Foras Forbatha, Dublin.

Ryan, W. (1966) 'Industrial Development in National Economic Expansion'. Proceedings of the Seminar on Industrial Development and the Development Plan. An Foras Forbatha, Dublin.

Seed and Venture Capital Measure of the Operational Programme 1994–1999. Enterprise Ireland, Dublin.

Submission on Industrial Policy: A Report by the Central Bank to the Policy Review Group. Stationary Office, Dublin.

Technology Foresight Ireland: An ICSTI Overview (1999). Forfas, Dublin.

White, P. (2000) 'The Evolution of the IDA', in MacSharry, R. and White, P. *The Making of the Celtic Tiger.* Dublin, Mercier Press.

Chapter 3
The Business Environment
....

3.1 Introduction

This chapter analyses the business ENVIRONMENT within which all organisations operate. It is possible to consider the external environment from two significant points of view—the macro environment and the task environment. In the current business environment the most important area is that of competitors or rivals. Competitive analysis can be undertaken to determine the degree of competition in the market place and to assess whether the environment is favourable or unfavourable. Based on this analysis, the organisation can then make attempts to manage its external environment.

3.2 The business environment

Organisations, regardless of their size, whether they are public or private enterprises, domestic or international, all operate within the context of an external environment. The external business environment includes all factors that affect the organisation yet which lie outside the organisation's boundary, that is, all factors that are external to the organisation. In order to fully understand the challenge faced by managers it is important to come to terms with the relationship between an organisation and its external environment.

Systems theory, which was introduced and discussed in Chapter 1, highlighted the importance of the external environment in viewing an organisation as an open system. All organisations must have inputs (people, money, information and materials) from their external environment and in turn exchange the finished goods and services they produce to provide energy for continued existence. Managerial performance is often dependent on knowing how the organisation influences, and is influenced by, its external environment. No organisation can be viewed as having enough power and influence to enable it to ignore environmental pressures.

Factors contained in the external environment are essentially uncontrollable from an organisation's point of view. For example, there is very little an organisation can do to prevent the onset of a recession. However, this does not mean that an organisation can ignore such factors. For example, many Irish organisations were severely affected by past interest rate and currency crises. To survive in the current business environment the organisation needs to be able to manage its environment by being constantly aware of developments, and, where possible, anticipating future developments, to ensure a speedy and accurate response to the situation at hand.

The external business environment consists of two main elements. First, the organisation operates within a macro environment, which is the most general part of the environment, containing, for example, the political and economic contexts and other fundamental factors that generally affect all organisations. Second, the organisation also operates within a more specific task environment, which includes competitors, suppliers, customers, trade unions and regulators all of whom interact with the organisation. Figure 3.1 illustrates the external environment facing organisations.

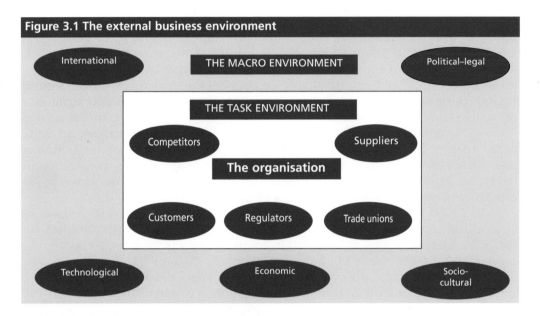

Figure 3.1 The external business environment

International

THE MACRO ENVIRONMENT

Political–legal

THE TASK ENVIRONMENT

Competitors

Suppliers

The organisation

Customers

Regulators

Trade unions

Technological

Economic

Socio-cultural

3.3 The macro environment

The macro environment within which an organisation operates contains general factors that affect all organisations and includes the international, political–legal, economic, technology and socio-cultural contexts. The macro environment is quite similar for most organisations, given the general nature of the various factors. For example, developments in the international context affect most organisations. How organisations perceive and react to these factors, however, accounts for the variations in organisational performance in relation to the external environment. Each of the elements of the macro environment will be discussed below.

3.3.1 The international context

The international context is concerned with events of an international nature, that is, those which transcend national boundaries. Developments in the international environment have important ramifications for organisations operating in international markets. However, domestic organisations should also be aware of developments on the international front, in order to facilitate future decisions on international expansion and to keep abreast of developments that may lead to new entrants in the domestic market.

Events on an international scale typically occur in three main regions of the world, which warrant closer examination—Europe, the Americas and the Asia/Pacific region.

In 1992 the member states of the EUROPEAN UNION (EU) integrated economically to form the biggest market in the world. Economic integration has meant that trade barriers between the member states have been eliminated and that capital and labour can flow freely between the states with no restrictions. The EU is emerging as a key global player operating from a market of 375 million people, compared to 220 million in the USA and 120 million in Japan. Therefore in terms of sheer size the EU is a force to be reckoned with.

As a result, the EU has emerged as one of the largest markets in the world covering 15 different countries. The trend towards enlargement of the EU is expected to continue, with the entrance of some Commonwealth of Independent States (CIS) republics and some eastern European countries. If the current trends towards enlargement continues then membership of the EU could consist of 25 countries across Europe. In 1999 the euro was accepted by 11 of the 15 member states including Ireland. The remaining four countries either failed to meet the qualification criteria or decided to take an opt-out clause.

The EU is also becoming far more competitive on a global basis, pursuing an active policy to enhance its competitiveness in a number of key industries including information technology, defence, and aerospace. An example is the success of Airbus Industries, involved in the manufacture of civil aircraft, which has captured a 30 per cent share of the world-wide market since its formation in the early 1970s.

While the EU is becoming a more potent force in the global market in terms of its competitiveness, its development also presents threats and opportunities for individual member states like Ireland. In terms of opportunities for a country like Ireland, the establishment of the Single European Market has opened up vast European markets for Irish organisations. Non-EU countries have come to view Ireland as an important base from which to aggressively pursue the EU market. For example, many US organisations, especially in the aerospace and electronics industries, have set up operations in Ireland as a strategic base to capture EU market share, as seen in Chapter 2.

Events in the remainder of Europe also affect the business community. The CIS has replaced the Soviet Union. Germany has been reunified and many of the former communist nations such as Romania and Poland have denounced communism and moved towards capitalism with the PRIVATISATION of many state industries. These developments offer both threats and opportunities for countries like Ireland. On the one hand, they are providing huge previously untapped markets for goods and services. Organisations world-wide are investigating new business and investment opportunities. Many Irish organisations have also sought to expand in order to capture market share in these markets. An example of an Irish company expanding into eastern European markets is Beeline Healthcare, established in 1989 to produce vitamins and supplements. The company has recently developed markets in both the Czech and Slovak Republics, Hungary and Poland (Finn 1994). Sales of Guinness have also grown significantly in eastern Europe, and the region has become an important target export market. So the opening up of the eastern Europe market has brought many opportunities for Irish organisations.

However, along with such opportunities there are threats. The former communist countries are potential competitors for Irish companies in many markets, with their huge sources of labour and raw materials. Therefore, developments in the EU and the rest of Europe have afforded Ireland numerous opportunities, but at the same time

Irish markets have been increasingly opened up to EU competitors who represent an important threat to established Irish markets.

The next international area to consider is the Americas. Canada, the USA and Mexico have signed an agreement, which links them in an economic alliance. The agreement is termed the North American Free Trade Agreement (NAFTA) and allows the free movement of money, trade and investment within the region in much the same way as in the EU. Despite difficulties which emerged during the course of negotiations between the various countries, the agreement marks the first stage in the establishment of an American economic community.

Many countries in central and Southern America are also planning for future expansion. Countries such as a Bolivia, Brazil, Paraguay and Argentina have signed an economic agreement called MERLOSOR, while the Caribbean countries have formed CARICOM. The possibility therefore exists for the formation of a large economically integrated unit to rival the EU. This would offer both opportunities and threats for companies throughout the remainder of the world.

Financial difficulties have dominated the attention paid to the Asia/Pacific region in recent years. However, the region's historically strong growth should not be ignored. During the 1970s and 1980s the Japanese threatened US dominance in many US markets, particularly the auto business. A decade later the 'four dragons' of South Korea, Taiwan, Singapore and Hong Kong emerged as strong challengers on the international front. Currently Thailand, Malaysia, Indonesia and the Philippines are continuing to display long-term potential for growth and expansion. In line with development in Europe and the Americas, the Asia/Pacific region has joined together to form the Asia Pacific Economic Cooperation (APEC), which is a regional economic alliance. China remains the largest world market at 1.2 billion; however, it has a poor human rights record and businesses have encountered difficulties with commercial activities.

While these three areas provide the focus for world-wide economic activities at present, the African continent offers the potential for long-term growth. While currently suffering from poor growth, unrest and poverty, it has long-term potential for economic growth. Many areas are rich in natural resources and could emulate post-apartheid South Africa which has experienced economic recovery and attracted significant overseas investment.

All of these developments present similar challenges—increased global competition, increased opportunities to develop new markets and the increased threat of new entrants into traditional markets. In meeting the opportunities afforded by these developments an organisation can choose from a number of different international business strategies:

▶ **Importing and exporting** is usually the most basic type of international business in which an organisation becomes involved. Exporting involves a producing a product/service in a domestic market and then selling to another country, while importing is buying a product/service from another country. As a first step to international business this strategy offers small cash outlay and low risk.

▶ **Franchising** is another strategy often pursued and involves getting another organisation in an overseas country to produce their product/service under a special arrangement. This effectively allows another organisation to use the original organisation's brand name, trademark and technology. The franchisee pays a fee for this arrangement.

▶ **Strategic alliances or joint ventures** have become increasingly popular for international business. A strategic alliance is an agreement between two or more organisations to co-operate to achieve specific goals in order to prosper (Ohmae 1989). No equity is involved in this type of arrangement. Strategic alliances are very common in the airline industry, the two largest being Oneworld (Aer Lingus belongs to this alliance) and Star Alliance. Joint ventures, on the other hand, involve joint ownership of a project where both partners share the costs and rewards. This type of shared ownership limits overall control held by any one party.

▶ The final strategy is that of **foreign direct investment** (FDI) and occurs when an overseas company decides to invest in another country by establishing a subsidiary. This tactic is usually used to avail of cheaper labour and raw materials. The IDA pursued a policy of attracting FDI as outlined in Chapter 2.

3.3.2 The political–legal context

The political–legal context is shaped by the activities of governments at both national and international levels. Governments of different countries can have an enormous impact on the business environment in terms of economic policies, international trade policies and tax laws. The economic environment is also shaped by the activities of various governments and will be discussed in the next section. On a national level, a government can affect business through its policies in relation to industrial/services development and in particular by the tax incentives, capital grants and expansion schemes available. On an international level, the political environment influences business through policies in relation to international trade and deregulation/liberalisation.

One of the main ways that individual governments seek to influence international trade is through their input into the General Agreement on Trade and Tariffs (GATT) and its successor the World Trade Organisation (WTO). Both past and present bodies recognise the right of governments to levy duties to offset export subsidies or dumping (selling goods and services at less than a fair value.) The last round of GATT negotiations took place in 1994. Individual governments and international agencies such as the United Nations (UN) can also impose trade embargoes or sanctions on trade with particular countries. Examples of countries which have had sanctions placed on trade include Iraq, South Africa and Libya.

The political environment has also affected the business environment with moves towards deregulation in certain markets. Deregulation attempts to remove restrictions on trade within particular industries. Recent developments in the EU have seen moves towards the deregulation of financial markets, public utilities and the airline industry, with the aim of removing protective restrictions on operations in order to allow greater competition. In Ireland the airline and public utility industry sector have all been deregulated in recent years allowing new entrants to compete in the marketplace. Moves towards deregulation have opened up market opportunities for other companies. PostNet, which is an American franchise with outlets in 15 countries, has recently been established in Ireland by a former An Post manager. PostNet offers a range of post-related service to small businesses and individual customers. It also provides customers with a mailbox service and takes delivery of goods from any carrier. Due to the fact that PostNet is a franchise it can avail itself of discounts offered to the parent company by suppliers and these can then be passed down through the buyer chain to the customer (O'Halloran 2000(b)).

Due to the fact that Ireland is an export-dominated economy, the Irish government, at both national and international levels, tries to promote trade to ensure that Ireland can increase its exports to other markets. Ireland currently has a BALANCE OF TRADE surplus, which means that, as a country, more goods are exported than imported. The government tries to promote exports by ensuring a stable exchange rate, which affects the cost of our exports abroad, and also tries to keep inflation down to stimulate demand and to keep exports competitive.

The developments in the political environment, including moves towards deregulation and liberalisation, all result in the opening up of new markets and increased competition in existing markets.

3.3.3 The economic context

The economic environment is shaped by the general state of individual economies, by the economic policies pursued by their respective governments (as seen in Chapter 2), and finally by the position of the various economies in relation to others, particularly trading partners. In effect the economic environment consists of complex interconnections between the economies of different countries.

Governments pursue different economic policies which affect key areas like inflation (changes in prices levels from one year to the next), interest rates (the cost of borrowing money) and wage rates (levels of pay). Variations in these key areas have important effects on the business environment. Interest rates determine the extent of an organisation's loans and investments. In general, high interest rates deter organisations from heavy investment. Inflation and wage rates can be considered together. Increased inflation is usually followed by demands for increased wages on the part of the workforce, the reason being that as inflation increases the purchasing power of the consumer declines. In other words, wages buy fewer products and services.

Wage levels affect an organisation's cost structure in that high wages mean high costs and they also determine the amount of disposable income, that is, the amount customers can spend on goods and services which affects demand for the organisation's PRODUCT. Finally exchange rates have a huge impact on organisations which export large amounts of their produce and/or import large quantities of raw materials. When the value of the home country's currency rises in relation to the country to which they export, an organisation's goods and services become more expensive, thereby reducing its competitiveness. Therefore, variations in these areas greatly affects the business environment within which organisations operate.

The current Irish economic environment has improved since the early 1980s and economic growth is stronger than in other EU member states. Inflation is low and stable (although there are signs that it is once again rising), government borrowing has been brought under control and the balance of payments is in surplus. Irish economic policy has centred on keeping finances under control, a firm exchange rate and low inflation to ensure growth. Wage increases under the Programme for National Recovery (PNR) in 1987 and the subsequent Programme for Economic and Social Progress (PESP) in 1991, the Programme for Competitiveness and Work (PCW) in 1994 and Partnership 2000 (1997), involved modest wage increases which were designed to ensure that Irish products were competitive. This means that Irish organisations should be operating in an environment which allows them to compete favourably on the international market with competitive wage rates and a stable exchange rate.

One of the most important developments in relation to the economic environment has been the emergence of global interdependencies between different economies. This development is particularly important given that Ireland is a SMALL OPEN ECONOMY. No longer do national economies operate in isolation; today they share an interdependence with other national economies. In other words, events in one economy impact on other economies.

For example, a recession in the UK is not solely confined to the UK in terms of its impact, but affects the economies of other countries, particularly Ireland which has close trading links with the UK. Within the EU the currency crisis of 1993 highlighted how interdependent the various national economies had become. In the case of Ireland, a devaluation of the punt was necessary to restore competitiveness in the Irish export market. Similarly, German interest rates have a huge impact on interest rates within Ireland through the exchange rate mechanism of the EU. Therefore developments in one economy have enormous implications for others, which means that organisations have to keep up to date on growth and recession both domestically and internationally. Organisations which operate on an international basis must be aware of the economic conditions in both their parent and host nations. The main result of growing interdependencies between economies is that the complexity of conducting business increases.

3.3.4 The technological context

The technological environment is concerned with technological developments and the pace of such developments. It is a critically important part of the macro environment due to the fact that no organisation is immune to the effects of technological developments. Technology generally affects organisations in three ways. First, technological innovation, such as the development of the Walkman by Sony, leads to the creation of new industries, markets and COMPETITIVE NICHES. Therefore, the advent of new technology can create a whole new industry such as the personal computer (PC), compact disk (CD) and the digital versatile disk (DVD) have done. Technological innovation is currently occurring at a far greater pace than in previous decades, and this has an enormous impact on markets and whole industries. The lead-times associated with such innovation are also decreasing. Lead-time refers to the amount of time between the inception of the idea and its final production. One of the key results of the increase in the pace of technological change is that organisations can no longer rely on a technological innovation to provide them with long-term success. Due to the increased pace of change, competitor organisations can quickly imitate the innovation, thereby eliminating any advantage the innovating organisation had. Therefore, organisations have to stay at the leading edge of technological change in order to enjoy any form of long-term success.

Second, technology affects the production techniques used by organisations as they produce products and services. Technological innovations in the use of computers have resulted in computers being increasingly used for product design and manufacturing. A technique called computer-aided design (CAD) uses computer graphics for product design. Computer-aided manufacturing (CAM) uses computers to assist in the manufacture of goods and services. Both CAD and CAM techniques are widely used in the automotive and electronics industries. Guinness has recently replaced its older brewing equipment and has installed state-of-the-art technology. Such new technology, particularly information technology and computers, has resulted in the complete automation of the brewing production process.

Third, technology affects how an organisation is managed and how communications take place in the organisation. The more sophisticated the technology, the easier it is to communicate and thereby manage large organisations. Systems such as financial information systems (FIS) and management information systems (MIS) mean that information can be acquired at the push of a button rather than sifting through mounds of paper to identify the correct information to be used. Such systems also permit calculations to be computed on the data, something which previously took a long time to achieve.

As a result of all of these changes, the technological environment is becoming increasingly complex and organisations need to keep up to date with developments, and as the pace of technological change increases, they need to be aware of the leading role technology is playing. In the current business environment organisations must incorporate technology into strategies to ensure survival. This is especially important for organisations involved in the technological industries but it also has implications for all organisations in terms of production techniques and communications. Examples of Irish-based subsidiaries of US firms that are technological leaders in their industries include Intel, which is involved in the manufacture of microchips, and Motorola, which is involved in the manufacture of mobile phones.

The emergence of e-business

One of the most significant changes in recent years has been the advent of electronic (e-)business. E-business can be defined (Kalakota and Andrews 1997:1) as the:

interchange of goods, services or property of any kind through an electronic medium.

Its effects have been so profound that it warrants its own section for discussion. The means of transaction for this type of business is electronic rather than the face-to-face style of older types of business transactions. To engage in e-business a company has to set up a website which provides others with information about available products or services. Visitors to the website should also be able to serve themselves with a range of data concerning the company, finally purchasing products or services on line.

The first stage of the Internet revolution occurred in 1994 with the extension of the Internet to the World Wide Web. As a result BUSINESS-TO-CONSUMER (B2C) Internet business flourished. We are currently in the second stage of the revolution which is concerned with BUSINESS-TO-BUSINESS (B2B) transactions. The e-business sector is growing at a phenomenal rate world-wide. In the USA B2C e-business sales were up 1.2 per cent to $5.26 billion in the first quarter of 2000. In relation to the retail sector B2C revenues in the US increased by 120 per cent to $33.1 billion in 1999. The online retail market in Europe is predicted to expand significantly as shown in Table 3.1.

It is predicted that by 2005 the number of Internet users in western Europe will have increased from 20 million to 85 million. However, the real growth area lies with B2B. An analysis of the global B2C market is said to be worth between $175–300 billion by 2003. In contrast the B2B market is expected to grow from $1.8 trillion to $3.2 trillion in the same period. As can be seen from the predictions, B2B market is likely to be ten times the size of the B2C market.

Table 3.1. Predictions for growth in online retail in Europe	
	Predicted value (€ billion)
2000	8
2001	14.7
2005	64

Source: Irish Times (2000).

In Ireland the B2C e-business market is valued at €48.2 million (McCall 2000). It is predicted to grow to €934.5 million by 2002. Following the international pattern, B2B is by far the bigger market with a value of €120.6 million currently, predicted to grow to €3.352 billion in 2002.

Growing internationalisation of Irish companies has forced them to enter the e-business market. However, Ireland is still in the early stages of development, certainly in comparison to the USA. A study undertaken by Amarach, cited in the *Irish Times* (2000) in relation to the use of e-business found the following results:

► 9 per cent of companies surveyed had an active e-business sales channel

► 14 per cent had a procurement channel

► 26 per cent had an e-business presence

► 73 per cent felt they were e-business capable.

Despite the fact that Ireland is still only in the relatively early stages of development numerous companies have become well established in the e-business market, particularly in the B2C area. RyanAir (www.RyanAir.com) has pioneered the use of the Internet for booking airline seats. As a result the traditional travel agent who played an intermediary role has been eliminated from the value chain (Kennedy 2000(a)). Both AIB and the Bank of Ireland have introduced e-banking services. Church and General subsidiary First Call Direct offer motor insurance on line. Exhibit 3.1 provides some other examples of how former high street stores have responded to the Internet challenge.

Exhibit 3.1 From high street to Internet

Books. In the USA sales of antique books over the Internet has increased rapidly. In Ireland a similar trend is occurring with Hodges Figgis, Waterstone's and Kenny's all becoming involved in Internet retailing. Internet use opens up the potential customer base from local to global with obvious benefits.

Flowers. Shiela's Flowers closed down their premises on Lower Baggot Street, Dublin, to concentrate on Internet trade. The company has found that Irish business has increased 50 per cent and that processing orders is much easier.

Food. Luxury food is well suited to Internet sale and in the UK supermarkets have introduced Internet trade for weekly shopping.

Wine. Sale of wine over the Internet has become popular with companies like Mitchell's, Oddbin's and O'Brien's Fine Wines all developing e-sales.

Estate agents. Sherry Fitzgerald and Gunne have both recently started promoting the use of the web for property sales.

Source: Adapted from Oram (2000).

There has also been activity by Irish companies in the B2B market. E-procurement is one of the fastest-growing areas in e-business, and many Irish companies now offer e-procurement. Buying on line saves companies time and money and as a result their operations are more efficient. When purchasing materials through traditional means at least three quotes would have to be required initially, then a decision made on the source, followed by a placement for an order. All of this takes days or in some cases even weeks. Online purchasing means this process is cut down to minutes. There are some fears that this trend could lead to price fixing and an abuse of dominant positions by big suppliers (Kennedy 2000(b)).

Build-Online was the first B2B portal site in Ireland offering supplies to the construction industry. 1,000 companies now purchase supplies through this medium, representing 50 per cent of the construction market. Fyffes offer a B2B portal—worldoffruit.com—for purchasers of fresh produce. Esat Net and ICL launched a B2B portal providing online credit-checking facilities, auctions and web-based training (Kennedy 2000(b)).

Many of the points outlined above will be further developed in Chapter 14 which examines factors forcing organisations to change.

3.3.5 The socio-cultural context

The socio-cultural context is concerned with the demographics, attitudes and behaviour of the members of society. Demographics are concerned with identifying the characteristics of the people making up the social units of society. Demographic groups include work groups, organisations, countries, markets and societies, and can be measured in terms of age, gender, family size, education and occupation. These are the measures which are normally used in a population census.

Demographics impact on the business environment in two important ways—through the workforce employed by organisations and the consumers who purchase final goods and services. Organisations must be aware of the workforce demographics when formulating plans for the recruitment, selection, training and motivation of staff. The shortage of skilled labour in key industrial sectors means that the labour market is currently a seller's market. As a result, organisations need to focus very clearly on manpower requirements and how to satisfy demand.

Consumer demands are largely a function of the demographics of a society. Large numbers of lone-parent and dual-income families with children have led to the establishment of crèche facilities, and disposable items such as nappies and ready-made baby foods are commonplace. Demographics also effects demand for services such as radio stations like 98 FM and FM 104, which specifically cater for the musical tastes of the large proportion of the population who grew up in the 1960s and 1970s. Therefore, demographics affect human resource policies and the nature of the products and services available.

Developments in the wider social environment that affect people's attitudes and behaviour are also critically important for organisations to understand. As with demographics, developments in the social environment have implications for organisations in two main areas—the attitudes and behaviour of the workforce and of consumers. In relation to the workforce, the major social change has been the emergence over the last decade of large numbers of mothers working outside of the home. This has meant that organisations have had to introduce supportive policies regarding maternal and paternal leave, flexible working hours and childcare. In 1994, for example, paternal leave became compulsory in Sweden for working fathers. In Ireland parental leave has recently been introduced whereby additional unpaid leave is available for new parents.

Social changes in relation to consumer demand have been equally important. Among the main developments has been the emergence of a more environmentally aware consumer. Such developments have seen the development of whole new industries such as vegetarian and organic food markets. An Irish example can be seen in the expansion of the Dublin Trading Co-Operative which has a sizeable market in organic food produce (O'Raghallaigh 1994). Other organisations have also been forced to become more environmentally aware by using recyclable materials, particularly for packaging.

Increasing crime and violence in society is also driving change with the emergence of whole new industries and the development of existing ones. For example, in the USA increasing crime has led to the emergence of a new industry producing non-lethal devices to fight crime. Honeywell, ADT Security and AT&T are all concentrating on the burglar alarm market where sales increased from $4 billion in 1986 to $6 billion in 1993 (Serwer 1994).

Taken collectively, the five components of the macro environment are giving rise to an increasingly competitive, complex and changing business environment. In order to survive, organisations operating in both domestic and international markets need to be aware of such developments and adopt strategies which reflect these developments.

3.4 The task environment

The task environment consists of factors which are directly relevant to the organisation. In contrast to the macro environment which is a broad environment, the task environment is the more immediate environment in which the organisation operates. All organisations operating in a similar industry will have the same task environment facing them. It is important to remember that while we can clearly distinguish between macro and task environments, the boundaries between them should not be viewed as static. Changes in the macro environment inevitably force change in the task environment. For example, the Gulf War in 1992, a feature of the macro environment, had a huge affect on the task environment of many organisations, particularly the tourist business which suffered greatly as demand plummeted.

As with the macro environment, the task environment has several key elements which warrant discussion.

3.4.1 Competitors

The first component of the task environment, and probably the most important one given the increased competitiveness of the macro environment, consists of competitors. Unless operating in a monopoly situation, organisations will face competition. When organisations compete for the same customers and the same market they must react to and anticipate their competitors' actions in order to remain competitive.

In attempting to compete with other organisations a company tries to develop what is called a *competitive advantage*. In other words, it must develop some form of advantage over its rivals. Porter (1985:3) explains the concept of competitive advantage as follows:

Competitive advantage grows fundamentally out of the value a firm is able to create for its buyers that exceeds the firm's cost of creating it. Value is what buyers are willing to pay, and superior value stems from offering lower prices than competitors for equivalent benefits or providing unique benefits that more than offset a higher price.

Therefore, to achieve competitive advantage, an organisation must either provide equal product value but operate more efficiently than rivals which will enable it to charge a lower cost—this is called COST LEADERSHIP—or operate in a unique manner that creates greater product value which in turn commands a premium price—DIFFERENTIATION. Organisations that are unable to develop competitive advantage through either cost leadership or differentiation will find that the law of the marketplace dictates that they will either have to change their product line or risk going out of business.

In order to compete effectively in a product market and develop a sustainable competitive advantage, an organisation clearly has to analyse its competitive environment, as it plays such an important role in a company's task environment. Competitive analysis is examined in detail in Sections 3.5 and 3.6.

3.4.2 Suppliers

In line with systems theory, organisations obtain inputs from the external environment and convert these into products and services to be sold. Suppliers provide the sources of raw materials, for example, schools and universities (people), banks and other LENDING AGENCIES (capital) and producers, wholesalers and distributors (inputs required for the manufacturing process). Therefore, organisations are extremely dependent on the suppliers of raw materials, who form an integral part of the task environment. Choosing suppliers is a critically important decision for any organisation. Favourable supplier relations can lead to improved quality, better shipping arrangements, improved manufacturing time, early warning of price changes and information about developments in the marketplace.

As discussed earlier, e-business has changed relationships within the supply chain as companies can now purchase on line thereby saving time and money. The advent of e-business also facilitates disintermediation whereby intermediaries in the value chain are eliminated. This has serious consequences for suppliers in the middle of the value chain who face the prospect of losing business. Individual sectors are also experiencing change. In the retail sector world-wide there is a trend towards increasing the control of retailers over the supply chain through centralised distribution. It has been estimated that up to 50 per cent of food distribution in Ireland may be centralised over the next three to four years (Wall 2000). Suppliers face the challenge of forming links with other suppliers from different sectors to provide a value-added package to retailers and to consider the potential for international cross group sales. For example, sales to Tesco UK could be helped by back-loading on delivery containers returning from Ireland (Wall 2000).

3.4.3 Customers

Customers are the people who buy the product or service produced by the organisation and consequently are a critically important element of the task environment. Final customers are those who purchase a final product such as a car or a meal. Intermediate customers buy wholesale products and then sell to a final customer. An example of this is a clothes wholesaler who buys from the manufacturer and then sells to specific clothes outlets. However, the trend towards disintermediation mentioned above, particularly in the clothing sector, will eliminate the layers of potential customers. For example, the Belfast located company Hugo Thomas, which provides an Italian tailoring service, deals directly with the Italian manufacturers whereas previously the company would have had to deal with three or four more layers. Each additional layer would have added signifi-cantly to the price rather than the value of the product. The Internet, which enhances price transparency, is further contributing to this development.

In competitive markets, organisations realise that giving the customer a top-quality service is critically important if the organisation is to get repeat trade. Providing a quality customer service includes the speed of filling and delivering of the order, willingness to meet emergency requests, products delivered in good condition, willingness to rectify faults quickly and the availability of a repair and/or spare parts service. In order to develop customer loyalty the organisation needs to be fully aware of who the customers are and what products and services they need.

Many organisations are turning to customer groups themselves to find answers. A key example of an Irish organisation with a strong customer focus is Superquinn. In striving to improve the quality of the product and service, customer groups are frequently interviewed and asked for their suggestions.

3.4.4 Regulators

Regulators are generally government organisations whose function is to regulate and control aspects of certain industries. Due to the fact that regulatory bodies deal specifically with certain issues, they form part of the immediate task environment rather than the political environment.

Regulatory bodies exist at both national and international levels. An example of an international regulatory body is the International Civil Aviation Organisation (ICAO), which is the intergovernmental body, concerned with technical and safety issues for the airline industry. On a national level, Irish regulatory bodies include, for example, the Employment Equality Agency whose function is to ensure equal employment opportunities, the Environmental Protection Agency whose function is to ensure environmental awareness and the Office of the Director of Telecommunications Regulations (ODTR) whose function is to police the telecommunications airwaves.

3.4.5 Trade unions

As many employees world-wide are trade union members, unions form an important part of an organisation's task environment. The role of trade unions is to recruit members, collect dues and represent and protect employees. Unions aim to ensure that employees are treated fairly in their jobs.

Traditionally, manufacturing has been the most unionised industrial sector. However, clerical workers, teachers, nurses and professionals are also catered for by trade unions. Many organisations find that their employees are represented by many different trade unions, according to the different classifications of workers.

Historically, relations between organisations and trade unions have been adversarial. Poor industrial relations create costs for the organisation, especially when strikes and go-slows occur. More recently trade unions and organisations have tried to work together to ensure that the organisation survives. This trend is particularly noticeable in the USA where companies such as General Motors and Ford have allowed more union involvement in decision making.

In Ireland, 44 per cent of the workforce is unionised and consequently unions represent a key element in the task environment of many organisations, particularly semi-state bodies. These organisations including Aer Lingus, Iarnrod Éireann, Bus Éireann and Dublin Bus have to deal with numerous trade unions and tend to have a poor record of industrial relations. Other newer organisations like Shannon Aerospace have just one union representing their workforce—SIPTU, in an attempt to have more manageable and better industrial relations. Trade unions will be discussed further in Chapter 7.

3.5 Competitive analysis

The most widely used technique for analysing the competitive environment has been developed by Michael Porter in his famous books *Competitive Strategy: Techniques for Analysing Industries and Competitors* (1980) and *Competitive Advantage: Creating and Sustaining Superior Performance* (1985). Porter is a professor at the Harvard Business School and has had a phenomenal impact on management thinking and practice in the past decade. Porter believes that the most important thing for an organisation to consider when formulating strategy is how to deal with the competition. Porter argues that five forces shape the degree of market competition operating within an organisation's task environment:

❶ the degree of rivalry among existing competitors

❷ the threat of substitute products and services

❸ the threat of new entrants into the market

❹ the bargaining power of suppliers

❺ the bargaining power of buyers/customers.

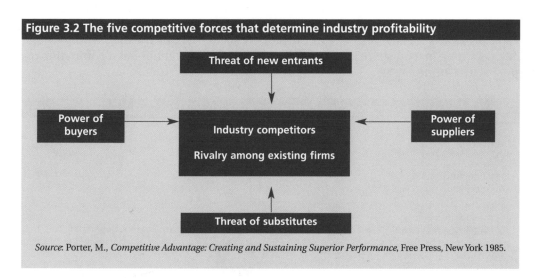

Figure 3.2 The five competitive forces that determine industry profitability

Threat of new entrants

Power of buyers → Industry competitors ← Power of suppliers

Rivalry among existing firms

Threat of substitutes

Source: Porter, M., *Competitive Advantage: Creating and Sustaining Superior Performance*, Free Press, New York 1985.

The combined power of these five forces determines the profit potential of an industry by shaping the price an organisation can charge and the costs and investment required to compete. Figure 3.2 illustrates Porter's five forces model for competitive analysis.

3.5.1 Rivalry among existing firms

Organisations in direct competition with each other use tactics such as price competition, advertising campaigns, new product launches and increased customer service or warranties to gain an advantage over rivals. Rivalry occurs because at least one competitor comes under pressure or feels that there is an opportunity to gain market share. Competition and rivalry are most intense when there are many direct competitors (domestic or international) and when the industry is a slow-growth industry. New high-growth industries offer organisations the opportunity to make good profits.

An example of a high-growth industry sector in Ireland was the cinema in the 1990s. Ireland has the highest level of cinema attendance in western Europe. In 1990 7.5 million cinema seats were sold compared to 12.4 million in 1999. This represents a growth rate of 65 per cent. The high growth rate has attracted additional competitors and screen facilities increased from 171 in 1990 to 296 in 1999 (O'Halloran 2000(a)). The increase in screen facilities also contributed to high growth. The main players in the industry are UCI (a joint venture between Universal and Paramount) with 7 per cent of the country's screens and Virgin and Ster Century with 3 per cent of screens. In terms of profitability, in 1997 gross box office revenues were €45.07 million and jumped to €63.4 million in 1998.

However, as an industry matures the excess profits attract new entrants, thereby making the industry more competitive. As the industry then reaches maturity the intense competition causes an industry shakeout, whereby weaker companies are eliminated and the stronger ones survive.

In industries characterised by a high degree of rivalry, market actions by one competitor provoke countermoves by others. In Ireland, an example of a highly competitive industry is the supermarket sector with Dunnes Stores, and Tesco Ireland engaged in intense rivalry. Price wars have been a constant feature of this industry sector with each competitor attempting to match price reductions by their rivals. Table 3.2 shows the market share of the grocery sector held by the main competitors. Tesco's strong market share is primarily due to the fact that it has been competing on price with Dunnes.

Table 3.2 Market share in the Irish supermarket industry 2000	
	Market share (%)
Dunnes	23.3
Tesco Ireland	23.3
Musgrave's Group*	18.9
Superquinn	8.6

*Musgrave's Group is made up of Centra, SuperValu and Roches Stores Grocery Departments

Source: Business and Finance, 6 April 2000, 48.

Other highly competitive industry sectors include mobile phones (Esat, Eircom and Meteor), newspapers and magazines and cars. However, rivalry and its associated intense competition, should not necessarily be viewed as a bad thing. Good competition can actually improve an organisation's performance due to the fact that competition can serve to stimulate and motivate an organisation. For example, if faced with a healthy competitor, an organisation has a strong impetus to reduce costs, improve the quality of goods and services and keep pace with technological developments.

3.5.2 The threat of substitutes

Organisations compete not only with other organisations providing similar products and services but also with those which produce SUBSTITUTE PRODUCTS and services. For example, shipping companies like Irish Ferries and Sealink compete directly with each other and also with organisations involved in substitute forms of transport such as airlines.

The availability of substitutes can severely limit the industry's potential, unless organisations become involved in aggressive marketing campaigns and continue to improve product quality. For example, the manufacturers of butter like Glanbia, Kerrygold and Mitchelstown have to compete directly with substitute products like alternative dairy spreads and Flora. The market share for dairy spreads has increased significantly since their introduction at the expense of butter. In order to compete more effectively the butter manufacturers have run successful advertising campaigns to promote the sale of butter.

3.5.3 The threat of new entrants

New entrants enter an industry segment and compete directly with existing organi- sations. If many factors prevent new companies from entering the industry the threat to established organisations is less serious. However, if there are few barriers to entry, the threat of new entrants can become serious.

The government can limit or prevent new entrants from entering a particular industry. This is most notable in the airline industry. However, deregulation is making this less of a problem. Capital requirements for certain industries can be so high that organisations will be unable to raise sufficient capital to finance set up costs. Airlines typically experience high start-up costs although recent trends towards leasing and franchising are making this less of a problem. Another barrier to entry is brand identi- fication which means that new organisations would have to spend considerable amounts of money on advertising to develop customer loyalty. For example, the brand name Tayto is synonymous with potato crisps, so much so that frequently customers ask for Tayto's when referring to crisps. New entrants like Sam Spudz have had to spend a lot of money on advertising to develop market share. Goldenvale have successfully established Cheesestrings as a speciality branded product designed to encourage children to eat cheese. Bailey's Irish Cream, however, remains one of the world's strongest brand names.

Cost advantages also act as a barrier to entry in that existing organisations may have favourable locations or existing assets which give them a cost advantage over newer rivals. Finally, distribution channels act as a barrier to entry for new entrants in getting their products and services to customers. For example, existing supermarket products are allocated a certain shelf-space and position and if a new entrant is to make headway it will have to undertake promotions, price cuts and intensive selling to displace existing products.

If an organisation can overcome the barriers to entry and break into a market, the result is normally an increase in the supply of the product, with the new entrant using considerable resources to gain market share. As a result market prices usually fall and this has a negative impact on the profitability of all organisations, serving to further increase competition.

3.5.4 The bargaining power of suppliers

Suppliers are critically important to the organisation because of the resources they supply. Suppliers can exert power on an organisation by threatening to raise prices or to reduce product quality. In relation to price increases, if the organisation is unable to recover the increased costs through price increases on its own products, then its long-term profitability will suffer, making it all the more difficult to compete.

An organisation is at an extreme disadvantage if it is overly dependent on one supplier. In contrast, the supplier is in a powerful situation if the organisation has few sources of supply or if the supplier has many other customers. It is also very powerful if it has built up switching costs—these are fixed costs that organisations face if they change supplier. For example, if a company is used to purchasing and operating a particular brand of computer, changing to another type may involve switching costs if the existing software packages also have to be changed.

However, organisations can be in a strong situation if they are the dominant customer for a supplier. In situations like this the organisation can demand credit arrangements and that the supplier goes through inspection and education processes to ensure acceptable quality of supplies. Some suppliers may find themselves in a weak position if there are many suppliers in the market all seeking market share. In the brewing industry, for example, the 'big four' dominate the market—Guinness (Carlsberg, Budweiser, Harp and Guinness), Murphy's (Heineken and Murphy's), Beamish Crawford (Beamish Stout) and Showerings (Bulmers). Smaller suppliers in this industry find it difficult to compete against the big four for pump space in Irish pubs, which typically offer 20 or more different draught beers and ciders. Kilkenny and Caffreys, for example, have relatively weak positions as suppliers and consequently have little bargaining power.

The emergence of e-business has given some companies the opportunity to seriously weaken the bargaining power of their suppliers. By moving their purchasing operations online, some of the larger car companies in the US are reported to have saved thousands of dollars on the cost of each car they produce (Johns 2000). E-business also allows companies to compare prices on alternative suppliers and streamline stock control processes.

3.5.5 The bargaining power of buyers

Buyers or customers are extremely important for an organisation's success because without a market organisations go out of business. Customers can put pressure on organisations by demanding lower prices, higher quality or additional services. Customers can also play off competitors against one another. For example, when purchasing durable goods of a high cost or even negotiating a mortgage, a buyer can collect different offers and negotiate for the best possible deal.

Organisations have problems if they depend on a few strong customers. Customers are powerful if they make large purchases of the product either in monetary or volume terms, or if they can easily find alternatives. When the customer is powerful s/he can exert pressure on an organisation and is more likely to be able to negotiate a better deal than a minor customer. When there are many customers who purchase small amounts of the product, the organisation has strong bargaining power. In the mobile phone industry, for example, customers exert little power over the price and in this sense have little bargaining power over companies like Eircom, Esat or Meteor.

Analysing the five environmental factors described above enables an organisation to identify its competitive strengths and weaknesses in relation to the external environment and to understand the nature of the competitive environment in which it is located. A competitive analysis helps to guide strategic decisions such as whether to acquire a company in another industry or whether to divest a particular business interest. It also facilitates an evaluation of the potential for different business ventures by assessing their competitive environment.

Based on this analysis, it is possible to identify favourable and unfavourable competitive business environments that may confront organisations. Figure 3.3 outlines the characteristic features of both types of environment. It should be noted that frequently an organisation's competitive environment will contain elements of both favourable and unfavourable environments and consequently the organisation will have to make sound decisions on future directions. However, the classification serves as a useful guideline.

Figure 3.3 Favourable and unfavourable competitive environments

Factor	Favourable	Unfavourable
1. Competitors	Few; high growth industry	Many; low growth industry
2. Threat of new entrants	Low threat, many barriers	High threat, few barriers
3. Substitutes	Few	Many
4. Power of suppliers	Many, low bargaining power	Few, high bargaining power
5. Power of customers	Many, low bargaining power	Few, high bargaining power

Source: Porter, M., *Competitive Advantage: Creating and Sustaining Superior Performance*, Free Press, New York 1985.

Porter concludes, that when formulating strategies based on competitive analysis, organisations should consider moving into industries with limited competition and many customers and suppliers. Organisations should similarly avoid industries in more difficult or unfavourable competitive environments.

3.6 Competitive analysis: The Irish retail pharmacy industry

It is possible to apply Porter's five forces model to analyse the nature of the competitive environment in any industry. To illustrate its application an Irish industry sector has been chosen—retail pharmacy. According to Hoban (1999) there are three different classifications of pharmacies operating in Ireland. Class C pharmacies, of which there are only 250, have a turnover in excess of €888,816. Class B pharmacies have a turnover of between €400,000–700,000, and there currently 500 of those in operation in Ireland. Class A pharmacies are the smallest with a turnover of less than €400,000.

3.6.1 The rivalry of existing competitors

Traditionally there has been little dangerous competitive rivalry between pharmacies in Ireland. This was mainly due to the actions of The Irish Pharmaceutical Union and the Pharmaceutical Society who collectively advocated a professional approach to the conduct of business rather than the cut-throat competition found in other industries (Hoban 1999). There has been little evidence of head-to-head battles in relation to price or service between Irish pharmacies. However, there may be evidence to suggest that this might change in the future with the entrance into the market of UK multiples such as Boots, who, in addition to pharmaceutical services, provide a large retail outlet. The introduction of the larger multiples into the market will inevitably affect smaller pharmacies in the long run. Overall, unlike almost any other industry structure there remains little aggressive competitive rivalry within the pharmacy sector in Ireland.

3.6.2 The threat of new entrants

In assessing the potential threat posed by new entrants, the barriers to entry need to be considered. In the retail pharmacy industry a number of important barriers to entry exist. Regulatory barriers limit the number of new entrants who can operate within a specific area based on geographical location and urban/rural classifications. To set up a pharmacy a LICENSE must be granted, without which the pharmacy cannot operate. Due to regulations governing entrance to the industry the potential threat of new entrants is significantly reduced.

Economies of scale within the retail pharmacy industry also represent a barrier to entry. Pharmacies that are well established within their industry, in terms of size and market share, will experience cost savings when compared to smaller start-ups. Economies of scale in the retail pharmacy industry exist within the marketing and advertising, human resources and purchasing functions. Larger pharmacies experience lower unit costs in those key areas. For example, running a nation-wide advertising campaign will cost the same irrespective of whether it involves a chain of pharmacies or one small pharmacy. Cost savings also relate to areas such as setting up a website, which again is more cost-effective for larger or chains of pharmacies. In general, the larger the competitor the smaller the cost base, and therefore, the greater the risk of rival competitive advantage.

The development of a highly differentiated branded product or service can also reduce the threat of new entrants. New entrants would have to invest heavily in advertising to reduce customer loyalty to the branded product. Boots, for example, has a very well-known range of own branded goods particularly in relation to cosmetics, baby products and over-the-counter medicines. The final barrier to entry with direct relevance to the retail pharmacy industry is the amount of capital required to set up. The capital cost of buying/leasing premises and equipment is not as high as for some other industry sectors; however, the cost of acquiring an established pharmacy is increasing, and this places further pressures on potential purchasers.

3.6.3 The power of suppliers

There are four main sources of supply for the pharmacy industry—proprietary drug manufacturers (sole manufacturers of patented products such as Zantac by Glaxo Smithkline), generic manufacturers (manufacturers of products like paracetamol), wholesalers (domestic) and suppliers of the outer shop area (toiletries and sundries). In relation to the first group their supplier power is somewhat reduced in that they engage in negotiations with the Department of Health to agree on prices. Prices are, therefore, agreed before the margins at retail and wholesale level are introduced.

The generic companies feel that the pharmacy exerts power over them due to their influence on brand selection. Therefore these suppliers have little bargaining power. Domestic wholesalers are few in number but their service is not greatly differentiated. They tend have low bargaining power as the pharmacy can change from one supplier to the next without incurring high switching costs. Suppliers to the outer shops have tended to be the most problematic for the pharmacies, being viewed as an unnecessary layer between major supplier and the pharmacy. They have little control over the pharmacy and in this sense their bargaining power is low. Overall, across the four different categories, suppliers have very little bargaining power.

3.6.4 Buyer power

The key question at this point is: Who is the buyer of the product/service provided by the pharmacy? There are in fact two main groups of buyers. One is obviously the individual patient/customer, who exerts very little power in terms of price or service. In addition, this kind of customer is great in number, buying small quantities of the goods. The second is the government through the Department of Health which is a large purchaser of the product. However, the situation is unusual in that the Department of Health also plays a role in price negotiations with the drugs manufacturers. Consequently, the Department of Health has considerable influence and power. In relation to overall buyer power the picture is mixed.

3.6.5 The threat of substitutes

There is no real prospect of any other means of providing this service. The mail order alternative has worked well in the USA but is unlikely to have the same impact in Europe due to language difficulties and the lack of economies of scale. The Internet and e-commerce, however, remain a possibility for the future.

In conclusion, the competitive position facing those involved in the retail pharmacy industry is favourable. A summary of the main findings is shown in Table 3.3. In four out of five of the main criteria the industry has a favourable position. Only in relation to the bargaining power of buyers is the situation slightly different, due to the unique role played by the Department of Health. Overall, the competitive position within this industry sector is highly favourable. The fact that the Department of Health has a role to play in establishing prices, however, may mean that excess profits are unlikely in this industry.

Table 3.3. Competitive environment for the Irish retail pharmacy industry

Rivalry among competitors	Low but increasing
Threat of new entrants	Low
Bargaining power of suppliers	Low
Bargaining power of buyers	Medium
Threat of substitutes	Low

3.7 Managing the external environment

Having analysed the macro and task environments within which it operates, the organisation can then move on to consider ways of managing the external environment. ENVIRONMENTAL MANAGEMENT refers to strategies aimed at changing the environmental context within which the organisation operates. Zeithhaml and Zeithhaml (1984) suggest that there are three methods that organisations can employ when managing their external environment.

3.7.1 Strategic manoeuvring

This involves the organisation attempting to alter the boundaries of its task environment. Typical ways of doing this involve diversification into different types of business (for example, different geographic regions, different products or using different technologies), mergers or acquisitions, selling one or more businesses or finally entering markets with limited competition and high growth. Aggressive competitors constantly seek to change the boundaries of the task environment, thereby placing other competitors under pressure to respond.

3.7.2 Independent strategies

In contrast to strategic manoeuvring which involves changing the boundary of the external environment, organisations can also seek to change the existing environment within which they operate. An independent strategy means that the organisation acts on its own to alter the environment. Examples of such approaches include public relations exercises to reinforce a favourable image of the company in the public mind, political action to create a more favourable business climate or to reduce competition or, finally, taking legal action against a competitor.

3.7.3 Co-operative strategies

While the previous two approaches involve organisations working alone, co-operative strategies involve two or more organisations working together to change their environment. The rationale for joint strategies is that joint action will reduce the costs and risks, and co-operation should increase power. Examples of this type of approach include the emergence of JOINT VENTURE arrangements in almost all sectors of industry or, alternatively, the formation of industry associations.

In choosing which of strategy to pursue, organisations should attempt to change appropriate elements of the environment, choose appropriate strategies that focus on important elements of the environment and implement strategies which are most beneficial at the lowest cost. The bottom line for all organisations, however, as they attempt to manage their environment, is the need to achieve competitive advantage. As the nature of the external business environment is constantly changing, this task becomes all the more daunting for organisations which have to constantly update their strategic decisions. The importance of the changing nature of the business environment and the need to achieve competitive advantage is a recurring theme throughout this book.

3.8 Summary of key propositions

▶ All organisations operate within an external business environment which is a critically important area to consider. The external environment has two main components—a macro environment and a task environment.

▶ The macro environment is made up of factors that affect all organisations and in this sense is very broad. Factors included in the macro environment are the international, political–legal, economic, technological and socio-cultural environments. All of these factors are forcing change for organisations by increasing competitiveness and complexity.

▶ The task environment is the immediate environment facing the organisation. Organisations operating within the same industry will have a similar task environment. Factors included in the task environment are competitors, suppliers, customers, regulators and trade unions.

▶ As the current business environment has become increasingly competitive, organisations need to undertake a competitive analysis of their industry to work out how they can achieve a competitive advantage.

▶ When analysing the competitive environment, five factors have to be considered: the degree of rivalry among existing competitors, the threat of new entrants and substitute products and services, and the bargaining power of suppliers and customers.

▶ Favourable competitive environments are high-growth industries which have few competitors, high barriers to entry, few substitute products and services and suppliers and customers with little power over the organisation.

▶ Unfavourable competitive environments are low-growth industries which have many competitors, few barriers to entry, many substitute products and services, and customers and suppliers with strong power over the organisation.

▶ Having analysed the external environment, from both macro and task points of view, and considered the nature of the competitive environment, organisations can examine ways of managing the external environment.

▶ Strategic manoeuvring means that the organisation tries to alter the boundaries of its task environment by either diversifying or merging.

▶ Independent strategies mean that the organisation tries to change the existing environment within which it operates. This can be done through public relations exercises or political action.

▶ Co-operative strategies mean that the organisation works with another organisation to change its environment. This can be done by entering into a joint venture with another organisation to reduce costs and spread risks.

Discussion questions

❶ What do you understand by the term 'business environment' and why is it important for organisations to consider it?

❷ Explain the difference between the macro and the task environments.

❸ Of the three main changes in the international environment, which one do you consider to be the most important for Irish organisations?

❹ Select a company that you are familiar with and describe the macro environment within which it operates.

❺ Select a company that you are familiar with and describe the task environment within which it operates.

❻ Why are competitors so important for organisations to consider?

❼ Apply Porter's five forces model of competitive analysis to any Irish organisation/industry.

❽ Consider the soft drinks market in Ireland. Evaluate whether the current competitive environment is favourable or unfavourable.

❾ How would you characterise the rivalry between your nearest competing supermarkets. What action has been taken recently by one competitor that has provoked countermoves by others?

❿ You are considering setting up your own pizza restaurant in your home town. Undertake a competitive analysis of the industry in the locality and examine whether you would establish a business there or not, based on your analysis.

⓫ Overall, how would you describe the external business environment affecting Irish organisations operating domestically or internationally?

⓬ How can organisations try to manage their external environments?

Concluding case: The Irish airline industry—the Dublin–London route

The world-wide airline industry has grown rapidly in the last 25 years, with an average growth rate of 5.5 per cent per annum. The Irish airline industry has also enjoyed strong growth over the same period. The Dublin–London route is now the busiest international route in Europe. In 1991 1.7 million passengers travelled on the route but by 1998 that number had increased to 4 million.

The Ireland–UK market is one of the most competitive markets in Europe and is one of the most keenly contested. The Dublin–London route is served by five direct competitors—Aer Lingus, RyanAir, British Midland International (BMI), Cityflyer Express (a British Airways franchisee) and Cityjet (a Virgin franchisee). All of these airlines are fiercely competitive in the battle to achieve market share on the key Dublin–London route. The airports served by each of the main competitive rivals are shown below.

	Heathrow	Gatwick	Luton	City	Stansted
Aer Lingus	*	*		*	
Cityflyer Express	*	*			
RyanAir		*	*		*
BMI	*				
Cityjet				*	

It should be noted that Cityjet operates a codeshare arrangement with Jersey European on their Dublin–London City route. This means that while they market and sell the airline seats they do not actually service the flight.

The intense competition and rivalry is mainly caused by the fact that airlines have high fixed costs in terms of wages, fuel and insurance and this puts pressure on airlines to fill to capacity on their flights. The main competitive strategies used by the airlines are PRICE COMPETITION and product DIFFERENTIATION. All of the five airlines engage in price competition offering many different types of fares on the Dublin–London route. RyanAir pursues a 'no frills' type of service and not surprisingly offers the lowest fares for both business and non-business passengers. The use of a cost leadership strategy by RyanAir is evident in its fare structure as shown below:

RyanAir fares on key routes from Dublin, summer 2000

	Fare (€)
Bristol	11.42
Cardiff	11.42
Liverpool	11.42
Manchester	11.42
Leeds	24.12
Luton	36.8
Stansted	36.8
Gatwick	36.8
Brussels	36.8
Paris	74.9

While RyanAir tends to be the cost leader all of the other airlines are engaged in price competition with their rivals. While RyanAir concentrates on the leisure passenger, the other main rivals, most notably Aer Lingus and BMI, target the business traveller. Examples of some of the business fares offered by Aer Lingus are shown below:

Business fares (€) offered by Aer Lingus, summer 2000

From Dublin to	Heathrow	Gatwick	City
Off-peak economy	140.9	142.2	267.9
Budget*	374.5	–	151
Premier budget*	378.3	373.3	373.3
Premier excursion*	372	372	372
Premier	220.9	220.9	220.9
Premier Europe	260.2	260.2	260.2

*denotes return fare

The airlines also compete with each other in terms of product/service differentiation. Aer Lingus, British Midland International and Cityflyer Express mainly undertake competition based on product differentiation. RyanAir operates a cost leadership strategy and does not engage in product differentiation to any great extent. The remaining four airlines compete in terms of the frequency of flights, airports served and in flight entertainment. For example, Aer Lingus has tried to differentiate its product by having regular hourly flights from Dublin to Heathrow and by providing good in-flight meals. Aer Lingus also has a frequent flyer programme, Travel Award Bonus (TAB), designed to build up customer loyalty. Aer Lingus is now a member of the Oneworld Alliance which extends the frequent flyer miles to include those flown with other airline members of the alliance. This is particularly attractive to frequent business travellers. With airlines engaging in both price competition and product/service differentiation strategies, competition between rivals is intense in this market.

The airlines are also engaged in competition with other modes of transport including the services offered by road, rail and sea. On the Dublin–London travel route the airlines compete with Irish Ferries and Stena Sealink. The substitutability of the airline product depends very much on price. When RyanAir and Aer Lingus were engaged in strong price competition in 1986, the demand for sea travel declined significantly. The product offered by the substitute companies has one drawback and that is the length of time taken by the trip. Air travel is much quicker than sea travel—it takes three hours just to cross the Irish Sea, one and a half with the Sea Cat. Either way, travelling by air could have the customer at his/her final destination rather than in either Fishguard or Holyhead. This is inappropriate for business travellers and is the least preferred option for leisure travellers. As long as the additional cost of flying can be offset against the timesaving, then the power of alternative forms of travel is limited. The only advantage that sea travel has is the ability to bring a car. However, car rental companies offer good deals on car rentals, which diminishes the advantage.

Increased liberalisation of the Ireland–UK market means that the route is open to the threat of new entrants. However, the barriers to entry into the airline industry are still very high by industry standards. There are a number of significant entry barriers, which would deter new entrants from entering the market. First, the capital requirements of entry are extremely high and include the costs of acquiring aircraft, maintenance provisions, training of crew and landing slots at airports. RyanAir have estimated that their start-up costs were in the region of €25.39 million. Economies of scale represent another barrier to entry. Economies of scale refer to the advantages attached to large-scale organisations. Examples in the aviation industry include bulk discounts in purchasing fuel, maintenance and catering supplies. If organisations already within the industry exhibit economies of scale it will act as a deterrent to potential new entrants, because it will force them to come in at a larger scale or to accept cost disadvantages.

The final barrier to entry is brand identity. Organisations, which have established brand names or high levels of customer loyalty, present a huge barrier to a new entrant. In effect it means that the new entrant will have to invest heavily in advertising and promotion to develop the market. So, while deregulation is encouraging new entrants on to the market, the barriers to entry are still extremely high.

Airlines operating the Dublin–London route have five main sources of supply—aircraft leasing companies, fuel suppliers, catering companies, airport management companies and travel agents. Purchasing an aircraft and its related equipment is one means of acquiring an aircraft, the alternative is leasing. Many airlines now lease aircraft rather than purchase them outright. There are many specialist companies as well as individual airlines involved in leasing. Overall, there are a large number of suppliers with little power.

The power of suppliers of aviation fuel can be high in times of oil shortages. However, under normal conditions there is an abundant supply of distributors who do not wield significant power. Catering companies are plentiful, offering a wide choice for the airlines. In addition the switching costs are low.

Airport management companies can possess significant power in determining which airline flies into which airport. For example, slots at Heathrow are in great demand, thereby increasing the power of airport management companies. The final source of supply for an airline is the travel agent who traditionally has been the intermediary between the airline and the passenger. However, one of the most dramatic changes to this established relationship has occurred as a result of online ticket sales. This approach is being pioneered by low-cost airlines such as RyanAir and Virgin Express (operating on the Shannon–London routes). Passengers can now book their flight directly with the airline thereby eliminating the travel agent's role. This should result in more control by the airline of their reservation systems.

The buyers of the airline product tend to make small purchases and are large in number. As a result they do not engage in any form of bargaining on price or quality. The airlines servicing the Dublin–London route do not cater for the charter market to not deal with much group travel and therefore would not offer discounts of any nature. Executive travellers, however, have a higher degree of buyer power if they have corporate accounts with airlines. Corporate accounts can play off the different airlines against one another in the hope of lowering the price or getting a better deal.

Case adapted from Jones (1999); Wall (2000b; 2000c).

Case questions

❶ Prepare a competitive analysis of the Dublin–London airline industry.

❷ Based on the above analysis advise both Aer Lingus and RyanAir on their competitive positions within the industry.

Keep up to date

www.AerLingus.ie
www.BritishAirways.com
www.BritishMidlandco.uk
www.RyanAir.com
Cityjet have no website address but you can contact www.klmuk.co.uk.

Bibliography

Barrett, S. (1993) 'International Competitiveness and the Semi State Sector'. Paper presented to the Economics Workshop, Kenmare.

Business and Finance (2000) 'ePS: Reducing Costs', Special Supplement, 6 April.

Business and Finance (1994) 'Cityjet joins the Fray', 6 January.

Doganis, R. (1993) *Flying Off Course: The Economics of International Airlines.* London: Routledge.

Finn, G. (1994) 'Beeline: The New BuzzWord', *Checkout*, 20, March, 8–9.

Hepojoki, N. (2000) 'E Business: Making Business Simpler', *Business and Finance*, 1 June, 36.

Hoban, F. (1999) 'Economics of Pharmacy: An Analysis of Industry Structure', *IPU Review*, January.

Irish Times (2000) Special Supplement on E-Business, 28 June.

Johns, C. (2000) 'Ireland: The Next New Hampshire', *Business and Finance*, 1 June.

Jones, L. (1999) 'Taking to the Air', *Ireland 2000*, Dublin.

Kalakota, R. and Andrews, W. (1997) *Electronic Commerce: A Managers Guide.* Reading, MA: Addison-Wesley.

Kennedy, J. (2000a) 'Fare is Fare on the Internet', *Business and Finance*, 2 March.

—(2000b) 'E Procurement: Lubricating Trade or Squeezing Suppliers', *Business and Finance*, 23 March, 6.

McCall, B. (2000) 'The Future is E', Special Supplement on E-Business, *Irish Times*, 28 June.

Mooney, A. (2000) 'The Italian Job', *Business and Finance*, 8 June, 23.

O'Halloran, B. (2000a) 'No End to this Affair', *Business and Finance*, 2 March, 12.

— (2000b) 'Post Haste', *Business and Finance*, 6 April, 21.

Ohmae, K. (1989) 'The Global Logic of Strategic Alliances', *Harvard Business Review*, 67 (2), 143–154.

O'Raghaillaigh, L. (1994) 'Food for Thought', *Checkout*, 20, March, 20–21.

Oram, H. (2000) 'E-Tailors display their Wares', Special Supplement on E-Business, *Irish Times*, 28 June, 3.

Peters, T. (1993) 'Prometheus Barely Unbound', *Academy of Management Executive*, 4 (4), 70–84.

Porter, M. (1980) *Competitive Strategy: Techniques for Analysing Industries and Competitors.* New York: Free Press.

—(1985) *Competitive Advantage: Creating and Sustaining Superior Performance.* New York: Free Press.

Quinn, F. (1990) *Crowning the Customer: How to become Customer Driven.* Dublin: O'Brien Press.

Serwer, A. (1994) 'Crime Stoppers make a Killing', *Fortune*, 4 April, 67–70.

Wall, V. (2000a) 'Price Benefits for Consumers as Retail Sector Continues to Grow', *Business and Finance*, 6 January, 4.

—(2000b) 'Sky's the Limit', *Business and Finance*, 30 March, 11–13.

—(2000c) 'Why you should buy Aer Lingus Shares', *Business and Finance*, 15 June, 20–23.

Zeithaml, C. and Zeithaml, V. (1984) 'Environmental Management: Revisiting the Marketing Perspective', *Journal of Marketing*, 48 (2), 46–53.

Chapter 4
Planning

....

This chapter focuses on the first managerial function—planning. It considers the importance of planning for an organisation, the types of planning that can be undertaken and the various approaches that can be used to facilitate planning. Drawing all of these factors together, the planning process is presented and outlines the numerous stages that an organisation goes through in order to plan successfully. Corporate and business-level planning and strategies are then discussed in more detail focusing on key strategies and management techniques.

4.2 The nature and importance of planning

Planning is perhaps the most basic of all management functions. It can be defined as (Jones 1974:3):

the systematic development of action programmes aimed at reaching agreed business objectives by the process of analysing, evaluating and selecting among the opportunities which are foreseen.

Planning is therefore the process of establishing aims and objectives and choosing a course of action to ensure that they are achieved. This process serves to bridge the gap between where an organisation currently is and where it would like to be. Consider the examples of planning outlined in Exhibit 4.1.

Exhibit 4.1 Planning in some organisations in Ireland

Deutsche Bank plans to expand: the IFSC's largest fund administration operation Deutsche Bank plans to set up a second funds operation outside Dublin creating at least 200 jobs.

Princes plans digital television next month: Princes Holdings will launch its 60-channel digital television service next month and will be offering phone services to the Dublin market by the end of the year.

Dunnes may drop G25.3 million plan: speculation is increasing that the retailer has abandoned its €25.3 million plan for a new corporate headquarters and shopping complex in the centre of Dublin.

Source: Sunday Tribune (2000).

In the case of Deutsche Bank the plan centres on expansion of facilities, whereas the case of Princes is concerned with launching a new television service. Plans are not necessarily always followed through to implementation, as is the case with the Dunnes Stores example. However, the important point is that a company is engaged in forward planning, which can on occasions highlight key areas an organisation is less interested in.

Planning is undertaken by all managers, irrespective of their position in the hierarchy; it is one of the most important managerial functions. Planning generally precedes all other management functions. In other words, before an organisation can organise, staff, lead and control, it has to identify its objectives and how to achieve them. Only by planning can the organisation decide what form of organisational structure, what people, what form of leadership and what means of control will be most effective.

Planning seeks to reduce the amount of uncertainty faced by the organisation. While no organisation can predict future events with certainty, without planning, the organisation is leaving things to chance, or as Michiels (1986:259) states 'an enterprise without a plan is like a ship sailing in dense fog without any navigational means—the only thing it can possibly be sure about is whether it is afloat or not.' Organisations therefore need plans to guide future action.

Planning sets up the skeleton around which the organisation's activities can be built. It sets the scene for the type of business that will be conducted and the STRATEGY which will be pursued. If, for example, it is foreseen that demand for the organisation's present product range will remain buoyant, this will have a positive effect on the forecast of net income, profit and cash flow. It might also enable the organisation to pursue a strategy of DIVERSIFICATION into product lines complimentary to its existing PORTFOLIO.

It is important for managers to remember that planning should at all times be perceived as a means and not an end in itself. Organisations have on occasion become so involved in specific details of planning that they have failed to respond to critically important events in the business environment. This happens because the organisation becomes bureaucratic in nature, focusing on filling out forms and having all plans in a perfect condition. This is often referred to as 'paralysis by analysis' and essentially means that the organisation analyses too deeply and fails to take action.

4.3 Types of planning

There are three main types of planning undertaken by an organisation:

▶ **Strategic planning** involves issues of strategic direction and normally takes place at the top level of the organisation. Strategic planning therefore has a long-term orientation (greater than five years) and focuses on the organisation's basic mission, establishing organisational objectives, conducting internal analysis, assessing the external environment and developing strategic business plans. It serves to guide issues such as MERGERS, acquisitions, investment and divestiture and areas for future expansion.

▶ **Tactical planning** is concerned with the current operations of the various component parts of the organisation and has a medium-term orientation (one to five years). This type of planning normally takes place at middle-management levels. It involves interpreting the strategic plans by formulating tactical plans to achieve strategic objectives, outlining functional roles and responsibilities and developing tactical responses to medium-term business problems facing the organisation, such as a decline in market share for a particular product.

▶ **Operational planning** is concerned with short-term planning of day-to-day functions and serves to guide immediate action undertaken by the organisation. Consequently, it is undertaken by front-line supervisors who are in a position to make plans about short-term operations. Operational planning involves establishing short-term business unit or departmental targets, budgets and specific programmes of action geared towards the achievement of tactical plans.

An example of all three types of planning and the resultant plans for a small supermarket chain is shown in Figure 4.1.

Figure 4.1 Strategic, tactical and operational plans for a small chain of supermarkets

Mission
Our mission is to establish this chain of supermarkets as the best in the region, providing high quality service at a reasonable price, with due care for the natural environment

Strategic plans
- to increase market share
- to reduce costs and improve productivity of staff
- to provide an adequate return on investment—15%

Tactical plans
- to increase the number of retail outlets from 5 to 9 over a period of 4 years
- to introduce a scanning system in all outlets within two years
- to increase outlet sales 10% by the end of the year
- to embark on a long-term advertising and promotional campaign

Operational plans
- to investigate over the next three months other outlets where scanning facilities are already established
- to retrain staff in the area of customer service over six months
- to hire a new training manager with immediate effect to deal with the move to scanning techniques
- to price advertising on local radio as soon as possible.

Most organisations use all three types of planning to guide their future actions. However, for these programmes to be successful, each level of planning must be strongly related. In other words operational plans must be related to and reflect tactical plans. Similarly, tactical plans must reflect overall strategic plans. All managers are involved in planning. However, as we have seen, the type of planning undertaken depends on the manager's position in the hierarchy.

The amount of time spent on planning also varies depending on the manager's position. Top management has the overall responsibility for seeing that the planning function is carried out. They generally have time to devote to planning, usually have the best understanding of the organisational situation as a whole, and are therefore best equipped to make long-term strategic plans. Middle managers spend less of their time planning than top managers as they focus more on operational issues of the various business units. Middle managers have the best knowledge of the operations of the various areas and are therefore in a better position to make medium-term plans. Finally, lower-level front-line supervisors spend less time again in planning than either top or middle managers because they have to focus on day-to-day operations. Such a focus means that they are best able to determine what can be achieved in the short-term to achieve organisational objectives. Figure 4.2 shows the increase in time spent by managers on planning as one moves from front-line supervisors to top managers.

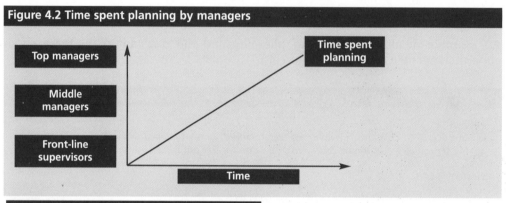

Figure 4.2 Time spent planning by managers

4.4 Contingency planning

In addition to strategic, tactical and operational planning, organisations also undertake contingency planning. It involves the generation of alternative courses of action should unexpected events occur in the business environment (Froot *et al.* 1994). Organisations usually develop different sets of plans depending on the economic forecasts. In this sense their plans for a recession scenario would be very different to that of a boom scenario. Contingency planning depends on the ability of the organisation to correctly identify and predict alternative scenarios (Foster 1993). If these are incorrectly generated then the contingency plans will have little practical use for the organisation.

In the current business environment organisations typically have a number of different contingency plans which can be put into operation depending on the situation, thus ensuring that the organisation is prepared for all eventualities. Plans, therefore should have in-built flexibility, so that they can take account of unforeseen events, such as changes in the price of raw materials.

An example of an Irish organisation which accurately foresaw changes in its product market and made appropriate contingency plans is Dawn Farm Foods situated in Naas, Co. Kildare. The company is involved in the manufacture of ingredient meats and toppings for branded ready meals, most notably Green Isle and Heinz. Recently the company began to realise that the principal manufacturers they supplied were increasingly outsourcing ingredients and reducing their involvement in final assembly and product marketing. In response to these trends Dawn began to develop contingency plans, developing its research and development, introducing international quality standards (see Chapter 11), WORLD-CLASS MANUFACTURING and long-term relationships with clients. These plans paid off when Dawn Farm Foods won a contract with Pizza Hut to supply meat topping to its 800 outlets in Europe, the Middle East and Africa, beating six major European competitors. Planning for such market changes was therefore critical to Dawn's success.

4.5 Types of plans

A plan is a statement of action to be undertaken by the organisation aimed at helping it achieve its objectives. Planning results in the formation of statements of recommended courses of action, namely, plans. According to Kast and Rosenweig (1985) plans have a number of important dimensions: repetitiveness, time, scope and level:

▶ The **repetitiveness** dimension concerns the extent to which a plan is used over and over again. Some plans apply to certain situations only and tend to have a short time frame and so are essentially non-repetitive. However, some plans apply to many situations and have a longer time frame. Such plans are repetitive by their very nature. This distinction is also referred to as single-use versus standard plans. Single-use plans are generally tailored to a specific situation and are usually strategic in nature. Standard plans are more routine in nature and tend to be operational plans.

Figure 4.3 The hierarchy of plans

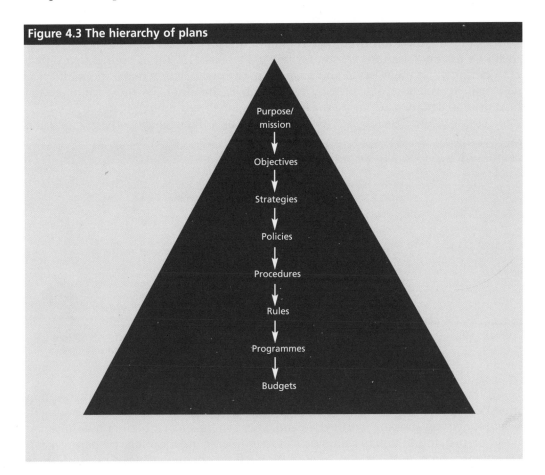

▶ The **time** dimension refers to the length of time associated with the plan. Some plans are short term and associated with operational planning, while others have a longer time frame and are associated with strategic planning.

▶ **Scope** refers to the elements of the organisation that are affected by the plan. Some plans have a broad nature and serve to guide the organisation as a whole. Others focus on particular functions or departments and therefore have a narrower scope.

▶ The **level** dimension refers to the level of the organisation towards which the plan is directed. Plans differ in the extent to which they focus on the top, middle or lower levels of the organisation. However, most plans, irrespective of the level they are aimed at will have an affect on all levels due to the interdependence of plans.

Organisations typically use a wide variety of plans to assist their planning process. Weihrich and Koontz (1993) argue that planning can be a difficult process when managers fail to recognise that there are a number of different types of plans, all of which have a future orientation. They state that there are eight different types of plans which form a hierarchy as shown in Figure 4.3. Each of the different types of plans is discussed below.

4.5.1 Purpose or mission

David (1989) defines a mission as an enduring statement of purpose that distinguishes one organisation from other similar enterprises. The mission or purpose is therefore the organisation's reason for being. Drucker (1973) has argued that only a clear definition of the mission and purpose of the organisation makes possible clear and realistic business objectives. The mission is therefore the most fundamental organisational plan of all, laying the foundation for all subsequent plans.

The mission or purpose involves looking at the scope of the business the organisation

Figure 4.4 Examples of Irish organisations' mission statements	
Aer Rianta:	Aer Rianta wants to establish itself as the best organisation in the world in the field of managing airports and related commercial activities.
Ballygowan:	To substantially grow the Irish bottled water market and to grow Ballygowan's share of that market.
Irish Permanent:	To provide better retail financial services and to become and remain more profitable than the associated banks.
ESB:	We in the ESB will provide our customers with quality energy services at a competitive price with due care for the natural environment. We will also promote national economic progress by engaging in profitable ancillary activities.
Golden Vale:	Golden Vale will be a major force in the European dairy food market and acknowledged by all customers as innovative and responsive, a socially and environmentally responsible leader, trustworthy and fun to do business with.

is involved in and the organisation's future direction. Consequently an organisation must decide what directions for growth are desirable, what market niches are sought, what pioneering aims are worthwhile and what synergism's with other missions can be developed. In addition to a mission statement, some organisations prepare a vision statement which outlines the organisations fundamental values and ambitions

(Quigley 1994). Figure 4.4 provides examples of the mission statements of a number of Irish organisations, which outlines their basic mission as an organisational entity.

4.5.2 Objectives/goals

Objectives and goals are terms often used interchangeably to describe what must be undertaken by the organisation to achieve its basic mission or purpose. Objectives provide specific aims that the organisation is to achieve within the broader framework of its goals and usually involve a specific time frame. Objectives, therefore, outline more precisely how the organisation seeks to achieve its mission. According to Thompson and Strickland (1990), they breathe life into the mission by training the energies of each part of the organisation on what needs to be achieved.

Objectives can be general, applied to the whole organisation (corporate objectives) or specific, focusing on one functional area. An example of a corporate objective would be 'to achieve a return on investment of 15 per cent at the end of the financial year'. An example of an objective specific to a production area would be 'to increase production by 50 per cent by 1 June 1996 without additional costs at the current level of quality'. According to Drucker (1954) there are a number of areas in which objectives and performance need to be set, including: market standing; physical and financial resources; innovation; productivity; profitability; manager performance and development; worker performance and attitude; and public responsibility.

It is possible for objectives/goals to be in direct conflict with each other. For example, the organisation might have set a goal to reduce costs and at the same time improve product/service quality. The basic conflict in this example is that improving product quality can lead to increased costs and, similarly, reducing costs can have a negative effect on quality. In this case the organisation has to either strike a balance between the two or drop one entirely (Vancourver *et al.* 1994).

4.5.3 Strategies

The fundamental plans that an organisation devises in order to achieve goals and objectives are termed 'strategies' (Shivastava 1994). Strategy is the programme of activities formulated in response to objectives. In other words it answers the question: how are we going to get where we want to go? Many dictionaries quote the meaning of strategy in relation to military operations and this metaphor is accurate for business. Strategy preparation means that the organisation must examine its own strengths and weaknesses and analyse the external environment to find out how both can be harnessed to achieve objectives.

The main purpose of strategy is to build on the objectives and to communicate through a system of major objectives and policies where the organisation wants to go. Strategies by their very nature do not attempt to outline exactly how the organisation is to specifically accomplish its objectives. This role is achieved by numerous other major and minor supporting plans. Strategies therefore serve as important guides for planning.

4.5.4 Policies

Policies are general guidelines for decision making throughout the organisation. They provide a direction for managers when using their judgement in achieving objectives. Policies help to establish consistency in decision making. However, they are only broad guidelines and managers can exercise discretion in their interpretation. For example, a policy might state that preference should be given to Irish raw materials suppliers when ordering stock. A policy written in such terms allows a degree of managerial discretion to determine the extent and degree of preference.

Policies can be couched in two forms, namely, express and implied. An express policy is a written or verbal statement which guides managers in their decision making. For example, the personnel manual may state that the organisation is an equal opportunities employer. Implied policy is inferred from looking at the organisation's behaviour and actions, and, in this example, an analysis of the workforce may reveal that all employees are white middle-class males and that there are no female managers, which means that the expressed policy is not being adhered to but has been replaced by an implied policy of hiring and promoting white middle-class males. Sometimes expressed and implied policies may conflict or contradict each other, with the organisation pursuing an expressed policy openly yet privately applying an implied policy, as in the above example.

4.5.5 Procedures

Procedures are plans that outline methods for handling certain situations. In this sense they serve to guide thinking rather than action and detail the precise manner in which activities are to be carried out. Policies and procedures are quite similar in that they both seek to influence certain decisions. However, procedures frequently involve a series of related steps which have to be undertaken, and differ from policies that address single issues. For example, an organisation may have a stated policy in relation to grievance and discipline. Backing up this policy the organisation will have set procedures for dealing with issues of grievance and discipline which normally follow a step-by-step approach. Other examples of procedures include purchasing equipment, hiring staff and the authorisation of travel expenses. Procedures therefore leave little room for discretion and ensure that all similar situations are handled in the same manner producing consistency.

Procedures exist at all levels of the organisation but are more prevalent at the lower levels, mainly due to the need for tighter control. Weihrich and Koontz (1993) argue that procedures become more numerous at lower levels due to the economic advantages of spelling out actions in detail for employees; because managers at lower levels need less leeway; and because routine jobs can be completed most effectively when management details the best way to carry them out.

Well-established procedures are commonly termed 'standard operating procedures'. These are procedures that the organisation uses in a routine manner. However, it should be remembered that procedures should be updated and reviewed to ensure that they are always appropriate for the organisation. Mistakes frequently occur when procedures become obsolete and no longer contribute to the achievement of organisational objectives.

4.5.6 Rules

Rules are statements that either prohibit or prescribe certain actions by clearly specifying what employees can and cannot do. Rules apply to situations regardless of the particular individuals involved, such as a 'no smoking' rule. Rules differ from both policies and procedures in a number of important areas. Unlike procedures discussed above, rules do not contain a specific time sequence. In fact, procedures can be viewed as a series of rules. And unlike policies, rules allow no discretion in their interpretation. So, while personal judgement can be used when applying policies, no such judgement is permitted with rules. The only element of discretion associated with rules concerns whether the rule applies to certain situations. Organisations experience problems when they fail to clearly distinguish between rules, procedures and policies, which leads to confusion on the part of employees.

4.5.7 Programmes

Programmes are plans designed to accomplish specific goals, usually within a fixed period of time. They can be broad in nature, such as an energy conservation programme undertaken by an organisation. Similarly, programmes can be narrow in nature focusing on particular areas within the organisation, such as a management development programme for executives.

The introduction of a programme within an organisation may lead to the development of numerous supporting programmes. Using the example of an energy conservation programme, supporting programmes may include searching for alternative sources of energy, better building insulation, better and more economical use of existing energy supplies and designing more efficient equipment. One of the key prerequisites for the successful implementation of programmes is that all of the various supporting programmes are well co-ordinated and contribute to the original programme's aims.

4.5.8 Budgets

A budget is a numerical expression of a plan which deals with the future allocation and utilisation of resources over a given period of time. Budgets are normally expressed in financial terms, person hours, productivity or any other measurable unit. The budget can be seen as a tool for translating future plans into numerical terms. Examples of budgets include revenue and expense budgets, and time, space, material and product budgets.

A budget also serves as an important control mechanism (see Section 10.7). However, for it to act as a standard of control it must reflect plans. One of the major advantages of a budget is that it forces people to plan in a precise way. Since budgets are normally developed for an entire organisation, budgeting is an important device for consolidating organisation-wide plans.

The different types of plans very clearly form a hierarchy. Placed at the top of the hierarchy is the organisation's mission or purpose, which states in the broadest sense where the organisation is going. As one moves further down the hierarchy the plans become more specific and focused until we reach budgets which are probably the most precise and specific form of planning in which the organisation engages.

4.6 Management by objectives

Management by objectives (MBO) is a particular approach to setting objectives and ensuring their achievement. The technique can be used in conjunction with the planning process outlined above. It was developed by a group of management consultants, Urwick, Orr and Partners and was strongly advocated by theorists such as Drucker (1954) and Humble (1972). It came to prominence in the 1960s when it was put into practice by a number of major organisations. However, the turbulent business environment of the last two decades has resulted in the usefulness of the approach being called into question, but the principles of the approach remain valid.

Instead of imposing goals or objectives on employees, MBO proposes that each subordinate be free to set goals within the framework provided by his/her superior (Carroll and Tosi 1973). The process originates at the top of the organisation with managers taking the decision to pursue the MBO approach. The reasons behind the decision must be communicated to the staff involved. The MBO process must also be consistent with the overall organisational goals, otherwise inconsistencies are likely to occur. The process involves the following steps:

❶ The superior or manager sets performance standards which must be met by the subordinate.

❷ The subordinate proposes his/her own goals depending on how s/he feels s/he can reach or exceed standards.

❸ Goals are then quantified and assigned a specific time frame and finally agreed between the superior and subordinate.

❹ At agreed intervals the superior reviews performance with the subordinate. The manager's role should be like that of a counsellor, helping the employee to achieve goals. The degree of goal attainment should be discussed and the causes of success or failure should be analysed.

The MBO process was widely adopted by organisations. The process assumes that individual managers are capable of assessing the goals and objectives which they can realistically expect subordinates to reach. Much depends on how MBO is communicated to those whose co-operation is required. If it is used as a 'big stick' then MOTIVATION will suffer. The objective is to improve corporate performance, and this is achieved by every individual having a part in the objective-setting process. According to Odiorne et al. (1980), to be worthwhile an MBO programme needs complete support throughout the organisation. It also needs effort to monitor its implementation. The following advantages associated with MBO have been identified:

▶ The employee gains a clearer understanding of the goals s/he is expected to work towards.

▶ Planning should improve as there is greater commitment to goals.

▶ Control should be easier as performance standards now exist.

▶ Motivation should improve as subordinates feel they have input in the objective setting process.

▶ Employee appraisal is simplified by reference to each individual's objectives.

However, MBO also has disadvantages associated with it (Kondrasuk 1981):

▶ If MBO is not sold properly throughout the organisation employees may feel they are being coerced.

▶ The focus on objectives can lead the business to strive towards incompatible goals.

For example, a finance manager may have agreed to cut operating costs, while the marketing manager's objective is to promote the product more strongly.

▶ There may be a focus on easily measurable objectives and these are not always the best ones. For example, a businessperson might want to improve the quality of his/her customer service. This is a difficult thing to measure and s/he may end up aiming for a reduction in the number of complaints, which is not necessarily the same thing.

▶ Agreement on objectives can cause inflexibility when the environment changes. When time has been invested in hammering out objectives it is difficult to abandon them even when circumstances change.

▶ When goals are imposed rather than negotiated with employees, resentment and lack of commitment by employees can result.

4.7 The planning process

Planning is the process of examining all aspects of the organisation in an effort to formulate strategy, incorporating strategic, tactical and operational planning, aimed at preparing the organisation for the future. It is possible to identify certain steps that organisations typically go through in their efforts to plan—we call this the planning process and it is illustrated in Figure 4.5.

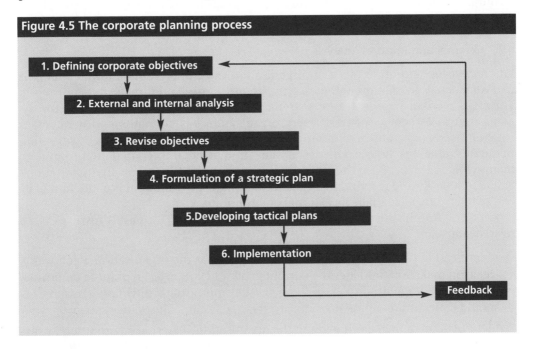

Figure 4.5 The corporate planning process

1. Defining corporate objectives
2. External and internal analysis
3. Revise objectives
4. Formulation of a strategic plan
5. Developing tactical plans
6. Implementation
Feedback

4.7.1 Defining corporate objectives

The first step in the corporate planning process is establishing corporate objectives. The previous section on objectives can be amplified in the light of corporate objective setting. Most organisations have just a few objectives, in general terms, which they hope to achieve over a long period of time. It is necessary that these objectives are clarified and documented so that they can be understood by those who are trying to further the planning process.

Economists have suggested two common types of objectives found in organisations: profit maximisers and profit satisficers. The profit-maximising organisation's aim is to make the highest possible profit, and this aim is connected to all other objectives. The profit-satisficing organisation, on the other hand, only seeks sufficient profits to allow it to fulfil other aims, for example, to invest in new production, to enjoy a high public profile, or to allow the owner to have a good lifestyle. Many smaller businesses turn away from the chance to optimise profits in order to keep the business personal or to allow the management more free time.

Two management theories worth noting in this context are shareholder theory and stakeholder theory. *Shareholder theory* holds that all organisational objectives should be geared to maximising the return to shareholders. In a public enterprise the shareholders are a wide and diverse group including customers, employees, the government and all other interest groups whose needs have to be considered. *Stakeholder theory* holds that objectives have to be related to all those who have a stake in the organisation, which includes customers, suppliers, employees, the government and the public in general. The interests of all these groups have to be considered when setting organisational objectives. So, for example, a pharmaceutical company may be concerned with selling its products for a certain profit, providing employees with a favourable working environment, sourcing materials from local suppliers, complying with local and voluntary codes of practice and making contributions to local activities.

4.7.2 External and internal analysis

When devising corporate plans an organisation must analyse its internal strengths and weaknesses in relation to the external opportunities and threats that confront it. The assessment of an organisation's strengths, weaknesses, opportunities and threats is referred to as a SWOT ANALYSIS. Every organisation has strengths and weaknesses which it needs to be aware of in order to capitalise on them. Unless an organisation frequently analyses its weaknesses it may find itself unprepared to respond to unanticipated threats from the environment. As noted in Chapter 3 an organisation's ability to identify and respond to opportunities in the environment is a function of its ability to effectively manage its external environment.

According to Johnson and Scholes (1993) a typical SWOT analysis involves three related steps:

❶ Identification of the current strategy/strategies that the organisation is following. Decision makers should identify current goals and strategies in order to determine whether the organisation is moving in the appropriate direction. This review should concentrate on the mission, strategic goals and corporate strategy.

❷ Identification of the key changes in the organisation's external environment, using the techniques described in Chapter 3. The organisation should thoroughly analyse both its macro and task environment, focusing on the relative importance of each of the components for the organisation and the extent to which they are changing. This process is sometimes referred to as a PEST analysis. PEST is an acronym for political–legal, economic, socio-cultural and technological analysis of environmental influences. In this sense it corresponds to an analysis of the primary features of the macro environment. Due to the increasingly competitive nature of the external environment, a competitive analysis of the industry within which the organisation operates has become critically important. Chapter 3 provides details of how an organisation should undertake such a task.

❸ A resource profile of the organisation should be undertaken to identify the key capabilities (strengths) and key limitations (weaknesses). In order to exploit opportunities in the external environment it is necessary to know what competencies and weaknesses exist inside the organisation. This analysis can be undertaken by considering resources under the following headings:

- ▶ **Human resources**. Human resources in this case refer to the structure and quality of the workforce. A human resource analysis might consider the age structure of employees, levels of skill, experience, staff turnover, promotion and replacement. A young highly skilled workforce is an enormous asset, but this group also demands a lot from the organisation in high salaries, promotion and good working conditions, for example. The analysis should focus on future manpower requirements, so that areas of scarcity and surplus can be identified.

- ▶ **Financial resources**. A financial audit of resources includes the financial structure and current borrowing capacity of the organisation. Balance sheets, RATIO ANALYSIS, forecasted cash flow and WORKING CAPITAL have to be examined.

- ▶ **Organisational resources**. Examining organisational resources involves considering the strengths and weaknesses of each business unit and department. A critical examination of each area will reveal certain strengths and shortcomings. For example, a print firm might have a highly trained production staff, but this may be a drawback for the organisation in terms of its cost and the difficulty of introducing new technology.

- ▶ **Technological resources**. Every organisation has to decide whether to be leader or a follower in the area of technological capability. This will have implications for the level of production costs, which have to be traded against the capital cost of acquiring new technology. Most Irish organisations are not renowned for being on the leading edge of technology, and rely on craft skills to allow them to sell high-quality goods. This is in marked contrast to less developed countries like Korea, which exploited its late industrialisation as an opportunity to acquire the latest technology. When coupled with low wages, this gave it a unique advantage which has been exploited in its motor and electronics industries.

One of the main aims of an internal organisational analysis of strengths and weaknesses is that it enables the organisation to see where it can develop a competitive advantage. In the current business environment an organisation must be able to carve out a special and distinct advantage which will endure over time.

A SWOT analysis can be performed by any organisation and the example of ESAT Digifone is provided at this point. Sales of mobile phones world-wide have increased steadily over the last five years mainly due to advances in information technology. The use of mobile phones for both personal and business use has provided a real alternative to the use of faxes, e-mails, video conferencing, pagers and portable PCs with modems and faxes, allowing the individual a greater degree of flexibility.

The mobile phone industry in Ireland has grown at a phenomenal rate over the last few years. In 1999 there was a 20 per cent growth in the market which compares to an average EU growth rate of 12 per cent. At the end of 1999 43.4 per cent of the population had a mobile phone.

Eircell began operations in 1985 with an analogue service (088 numbers) and in 1993 added a GSM digital service (087 numbers) which can be used abroad. During this period Eircell enjoyed a monopoly on the supply of mobile phones in Ireland. This situation changed as the government granted a second mobile phone license to ESAT Digifone who started providing an alternative service to Eircell in March 1997. Eircell and ESAT have since been joined in the market by Meteor who were granted the third mobile phone license in 2000. A SWOT analysis of ESAT Digifone is shown in Figure 4.6.

Figure 4.6 SWOT analysis of ESAT Digifone

Strengths:
- competitive price structure
- customer service provided by the company
- dropped call compensation and per second billing
- highly qualified staff
- range of services offered to the market
- lean organisational structure with few hierarchical levels.

Weaknesses:
- initial billing problems
- customers experienced coverage problems
- high start-up costs on entering the market; estimated that ESAT spent up to €114.2 million.

Opportunities:
- continue the strong growth experienced by the organisation over the last two years
- increase the range of services and options available to the customers; for example, Wireless Access Protocol (WAP) services
- ESAT's new majority owner British Telecom has allowed the company a seamless roaming arrangement for ESAT customers between the UK and Ireland; in addition, the BT connection opens up numerous opportunities for ESAT to further develop services.

Threats:
- emergence of true competition in the market with the entrance of Meteor; the new market entrant poses a threat for both of the incumbents
- current growth rates will not last as mobile phone saturation is reached
- fears exist in relation to the health of residents living close to masts erected by the mobile phone companies.

4.7.3 Revising objectives

In the light of the foregoing external and internal analyses, the unique competitive advantage an organisation can develop should be clear. If no distinct advantage emerges, then strategy formulation should centre on developing some competitive edge. Such advantages could include a unique product, market leadership, and quality of manufacturing reputation or service back-up. Developing some form of leading edge often means a complete revision of the objectives previously defined.

4.7.4 Formulating strategies

At this stage, the building blocks are in place, to be cemented together in the form of a strategic plan. Strategic plans, discussed earlier, are usually developed along two lines: first, deciding the direction of the organisation's activities (expansion, contraction, diversification or merger); second, finding the resources to facilitate these activities (human and financial). The starting point for a strategic plan is the formulation of a strategy statement. This proposes how objectives are to be fulfilled and sets the guidelines for the development of tactical plans. Organisations typically formulate strategies on two levels—corporate and business level. Corporate level strategies are those strategies relating to the conduct of business across several industries and are broad in nature. Business level strategies relate to the conduct of business in one particular industry sector. These will be examined in more depth at the end of this chapter.

4.7.5 Formulating tactical plans

Tactical plans are formulated for every function or business unit within the organisation and normally have a medium-term orientation of perhaps one year, but this may vary from organisation to organisation. Tactical plans interpret the strategic plan to produce more medium-term plans to achieve strategic objectives. In this sense they are more precise formulations of plans. An example of a tactical plan for a specific functional area, in this case, production, might include the following:

▶ to improve productivity in the production area
▶ to improve communications in the production area.

Tactical plans should be flexible enough to be altered as contingencies warrant.

4.7.6 Formulating action/operational plans

When tactical plans are finally agreed it is then necessary to formulate specific action plans to implement planning decisions. The link between tactical planning and implementation is the various operational or action plans that deal with the day-to-day functioning of the organisation. Action or operational plans to achieve the tactical plans outlined in the previous section could include the following:

▶ to increase productivity by 10 per cent by 1 June 2002
▶ to issue a three-page monthly newsletter by 30 June 2002.

Effective implementation means providing the necessary resources, motivating staff and holding regular (usually monthly) meetings to review how targets are being met. These meetings provide the basis for feedback to all levels of the organisation on how effective the planning process has been.

The planning process, just outlined, is a complex and highly important process for any organisation. The process is a demanding one requiring that the organisation consciously determines courses of action and bases decisions on purpose, knowledge and considered estimates.

Having completed the planning process, the organisation has clearly identified objectives, strategies and various types of plans to achieve those goals. The organisation is then in a position to make decisions about other managerial functions, such as organising and controlling, which will contribute to organisational efficiency.

4.8 Business-level planning and strategies

Business level strategies refer to the operation of a single business. A single business or STRATEGIC BUSINESS UNIT (SBU) produces a particular line of goods/services which are marketed to a clearly identifiable customer group. A number of different approaches have been taken to the classification of the various strategies available to single business organisations.

4.8.1 The Miles and Snow typology

Raymond Miles and Charles Snow (1978) identified four different categories of business level strategies:

❶ A company pursuing a **prospector** strategy is typically involved in a high growth innovative industry and continually looks for new opportunities and market sectors. This type of organisation embraces change and rewards risk taking.

❷ Companies pursuing a **defender** strategy maintain growth levels by protecting their current markets and keeping customers well served. Organisations using this style tend to be less aggressive and less entrepreneurial in style.

❸ A combination of both prospector and defender strategies can be found with the **analyser** strategy. In this case the organisation keeps its current market and customers with a moderate degree of change and innovation. Organisations opt for this strategy as they do not want to miss out on certain opportunities should they arise within the business environment.

❹ The final strategy is a **reactor** strategy whereby the organisation has no clear approach, merely reacting to the changes introduced by competitors rather than anticipating potential changes. Such organisations often fail to notice changes in the business environment until it is too late.

The Miles and Snow typology can be applied to the retail clothing sector in Ireland and is shown in Figure 4.7.

Figure 4.7 The Miles and Snow typology: the Irish retail clothing sector

Strategy	Organisation
Defender	Roches Stores
Prospector	NEXT
Analyser	Dunnes Stores
Reactor	Marks and Spencer

4.8.2 Porter's generic strategies

Michael Porter provides the second approach to the classification of business level strategies. In line with his model of competitive analysis, he argues that organisations can follow one of three generic strategies: differentiation, cost leadership and focus.

▶ Organisations pursuing a DIFFERENTIATION strategy try to make their products and services unique and distinctive by enhancing product quality. Customers as a result are willing to pay more because they perceive that the product/service is more valuable. An example of an organisation pursuing such a strategy is Superquinn in the supermarket business.

▶ Organisations can also pursue COST LEADERSHIP whereby the organisation offers the lowest-cost product/service by reducing manufacturing and other costs. By keeping costs low the organisation can offer its product/service at the lowest price. Both Tesco and Dunnes Stores pursue this strategy.

▶ A FOCUS strategy enables the organisation to concentrate on a specific regional market, product line or group of customers. The strategy could have a differentiation focus whereby it concentrates on providing high-quality goods and services at a premium price, or a cost leadership focus whereby it concentrates on providing the lowest-cost product within a specific sector. Some of the local and regional supermarkets adopt this approach by only catering for particular regional markets.

4.8.3 The product life cycle approach

This approach argues that products go through a specific life cycle consisting of four stages. The strategies pursued by the organisation will differ depending on what stage of the life cycle the product is placed (Anderson and Zeithaml 1984). The four stages are illustrated in Figure 4.8.

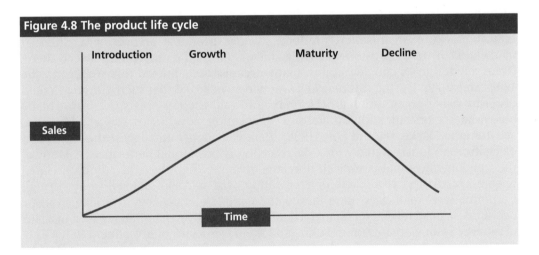

Figure 4.8 The product life cycle

At the introduction phase, demand for the new product is high, even possibly outstripping organisational capacity. Normally at this stage the organisation concentrates on hiring employees and managing stock and cash levels. As the product enters the growth stage, sales continue to increase but other organisations start to enter the market. At this stage, the organisation may start to consider differentiation strategies to make its product unique from competitors. After a period of growth the product enters the maturity phase where demand for the product stabilises. Both product differentiation and maintaining low cost are important at this stage. The final stage in the product life cycle is decline. Total sales and demand for the product fall off considerably. Saturation of demand may occur at this stage where consumers are only buying replacement products. Organisations at this stage should keep costs low and continue to differentiate their product.

4.9 Corporate-level planning strategies

Organisations can also develop strategies at the corporate level that may extend across many industry sectors. At the corporate level the key strategic issue for an organisation concerns the nature and degree of DIVERSIFICATION. Diversification is the number of different business activities conducted by an organisation and the extent to which those activities are related or not (Lubatkin and Chatterje 1994).

It is possible to identify two main types of CORPORATE-LEVEL STRATEGIES which can be pursued by an organisation.

4.9.1 Related diversification

The organisation in this case produces a variety of similar products and services which are linked in some way. Organisations pursuing related diversification normally compete in the same market, have the same distributors, technology, brand name and reputation. Proctor and Gamble pursue a related diversification strategy. Its main advantages are that it spreads the organisations risk evenly, provides economies of scale and lower overhead costs and finally facilitates the development of synergy.

4.9.2 Unrelated diversification

In this case the organisation produces diverse products across many different markets. Many of the business activities have no logical connection between them. Often referred to as conglomerates, many organisations pursed this strategy in the 1960s and 1970s. During this period it was widely believed that such a strategy could result in stable organisational performance in that the risk was spread over many industrial sectors. In addition, resource allocation advantages existed. However, according to Hoskisson and Hitt (1994) there is evidence to suggest that unrelated diversification is associated with a decrease in organisational performance. Many of the conglomerates that embraced unrelated diversification have hived off unrelated business activities. Unrelated diversification was hard to manage and control. Corporate-level managers often lacked the complete knowledge to make strategic decisions, instead relying on financial data. Unrelated diversification resulted in a lack of synergy among organisational units and there was a lack of investment in R & D.

4.9.3 Managing diversification strategies

Organisations can manage their diversification strategies by using portfolio management techniques, the most famous of which is the Boston Consulting Group (BCG) matrix. This matrix is a framework for making conclusions about the performance of key businesses performed by the diversified organisation. In evaluating business performance the BCG matrix considers the rate of growth within the market and the market share held by the organisation. The matrix concludes that rapidly growing sectors where the organisation already possesses a strong market share performs best. The least attractive option is where the growth rate is slow and the organisation has a small share of the market. The matrix classification is illustrated in Figure 4.9.

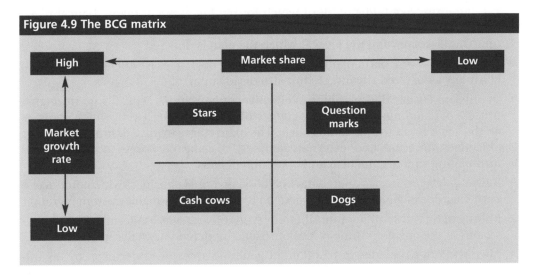

Figure 4.9 The BCG matrix

Stars are businesses that have the largest share of the market in a rapidly growing market. Cash cows are businesses with a large market share which is not likely to increase in the near future. These businesses usually generate profits which can be invested in stars. Question marks are businesses that have a small share of a growing market. The future outlook in these sectors is often unpredictable. Dogs are sectors where the business has a small share of a low-growth market. The matrix advises organisations to sell dogs and invest the money in other sectors.

The BCG matrix has been used by many diversified organisations as a means of effectively managing their portfolio of business investments. However, despite its appealing nature the BCG matrix has one main disadvantage: its analysis is limited to two criteria—that of market growth and market share held by the organisation. It is widely recognised that other factors influence organisational performance, and these are not included in the matrix. Despite its faults, however, the BCG matrix has greatly enhanced the power of organisations to control their diversified investments.

4.10 Summary of key propositions

▶ Planning has been defined as a process of establishing aims and objectives and choosing a course of action to ensure that these objectives are achieved. Planning is a critically important function for all organisations providing the framework for all subsequent management functions.

▶ Planning takes place at various levels of the organisation involving all managers to a greater or lesser degree. Strategic planning takes place at the top of the organisation, tactical at middle levels and operational at lower levels.

▶ In addition to the three main types of planning, organisations also engage in contingency planning. This involves the generation of alternative courses of action should unexpected events occur in the business environment.

▶ When planning, organisations can use a variety of different plans to guide future action, ranging from the most basic, the mission statement, to more precise and specific forms like budgets, all of which form a hierarchy of plans. Typical plans used by an organisation differ across four criteria: the degree of repetitiveness; the time frame; scope; and the level at which the plan is directed.

▶ An example of one particular process for setting objectives is MBO. This approach has many associated advantages but also disadvantages.

▶ In order to ensure that planning is effective, organisations typically go through a process of planning, involving a sequence of stages, the success of which depends on the accuracy of the preceding stage. The main stages involve defining corporate objectives, internal and external analyses, revising corporate objectives and formulating strategic, tactical and operational plans.

▶ Business-level strategies refer to the operation of a single business which produces a particular line of goods/services marketed to a clearly identifiable customer group.

▶ Miles and Snow identified four different types of strategies undertaken by organisations at the business strategy level: prospector; defender; analyser; reactor.

▶ Michael Porter provides three different generic strategies undertaken by organisations: differentiation; cost leadership; and focus.

▶ The final approach to business-level strategies is the product life cycle which argues that the strategies pursed are dependent upon the products stage in its life cycle.

▶ Organisations can also develop strategies at the corporate level and these may extend across many industry sectors. At the corporate level the key strategic issue for an organisation is the extent of diversification.

▶ Organisations typically pursue one of two kinds of diversification strategy. Related diversification means that the organisation produces a variety of products/services which are connected. In contrast unrelated diversification involves the production of diverse products/services across different markets with no logical connection.

▶ Organisations have sought to manage their diversification strategies by using portfolio management technique, the most famous of which is the BCG matrix.

Discussion questions

❶ Explain why planning is one of the most important managerial functions.

❷ Distinguish between strategic, tactical and operational planning.

❸ Identify any four types of plans and explain their importance to the planning process.

❹ Explain why the planning process is necessary.

❺ Conduct a SWOT analysis for an organisation with which you are familiar.

❻ What are the main advantages and disadvantages associated with the MBO approach?

❼ Find some recent examples of plans announced by organisations in Ireland and evaluate their nature and characteristics.

❽ Explain why organisations engage in contingency planning.

❾ Explain the Miles and Snow typology for business-level strategies and apply it to a market sector with which you are familiar.

⑩ Explain the main differences between Porter's generic strategies and the product life cycle approaches to strategy.

⑪ What are corporate-level strategies and why are they important for planning?

⑫ Find examples of organisations in Ireland pursuing related and unrelated diversification strategies and evaluate their success.

Concluding case: The Irish newspaper industry

The Irish newspaper market has grown significantly in the late 1990s. In 1994 330,000 newspapers were sold daily in Ireland, but by 1999 that figure had risen to 341,000 representing a 3.5 per cent growth rate. The Independent News and Media Group (INM) led by Tony O'Reilly produces a number of newspapers in the Irish market and occupies a strong position. The INM Group is a global company with subsidiaries operating around the world. The key titles produced by the INM Group include its flagship, *Irish Independent*, and the *Sunday Independent, Star, Evening Herald, Sunday World*, and a 29.9 per cent stake in the *Sunday Tribune*. Other significant players in the daily broadsheet market include the *Irish Times* and the *Irish Examiner*. In addition, there is a significant tabloid market which is dominated by British newspapers such as the *Irish Sun* and the *Irish Mirror*. A Sunday newspaper market also exists including both broadsheet and tabloid. The breakdown of market share and circulation for both tabloid and broadsheet is shown in the table below:

Circulation of newspapers in Ireland (2000)		
	Circulation	Market share (%)
Daily broadsheet market		
Irish Independent	165,000	48.5
Irish Times	114,000	33.5
Irish *Examiner*	62,000	18
Daily tabloid market		
Irish Sun	107,000	39
Star	92,000	34
Irish Mirror	72,000	27
Sunday broadsheet market		
Sunday Independent	318,000	51
Sunday Tribune	85,000	13
Sunday Times	85,000	13
Ireland on Sunday	70,000	11
Sunday Business Post	49,000	9
UK titles	16,000	3
Sunday tabloid market		
Sunday World	310,000	53
News of the World	158,000	27
Sunday People	65,000	11
Sunday Mirror	48,000	9

As can be seen from the table, INM, through their main titles, have a strong share of all sectors of the market. The overall newspaper industry as a whole has undergone a period of growth. The healthy state of the economy has resulted in increased advertising and promotions, all of which translate into increased revenues for the newspapers. In terms of profitability the main newspaper groups are in a sound financial position. The *Independent* had pre-tax profits of €142.7 million in 1999, the *Irish Times* €17.9 million and the *Examiner* parent Thomas Crosbie Holdings (TCH), €5.2 million. However, in common with many other high-growth industry sectors, there is intense competition among the main rivals.

The newly rebranded and relaunched *Irish Examiner* (formerly the *Cork Examiner*) is attempting to increase its share of the daily morning market. The company has spent €1.27 million on the relaunch with the specific aim of broadening their customer base beyond the Munster area. INM have retaliated by targeting former *Cork Examiner* readers. Traditionally the Cork area had lower levels of *Irish Independent* (18 per cent) readership than the national average (20 per cent+). Similarly the *Irish Examiner* has a low percentage of its circulation in Dublin (2 per cent) and Leinster (1 per cent). The market share split between the *Independent* and the *Times* is shown in the table below:

Market share by region (%)		
	Irish Independent	*Irish Times*
Dublin	30	55
Leinster	22	23
Connaught-Ulster	22	9
Munster	18	10

For the *Irish Independent* a key potential growth area is Munster, while the *Examiner* is concentrating on other areas outside of its traditional heartland. The newspapers are therefore, likely to compete head to head, which will place a drain on finances. In this regard the *Independent* is in a stronger position as it has more global financial reserves to fight a market share battle.

The *Irish Times*, which has traditionally been perceived as a Dublin newspaper, has tried to develop a broader appeal in recent years. Additional regional corespondents have been appointed, and the editorial focus places a greater emphasis on regional affairs than it previously did. The *Irish Times* also has a strong readership in Northern Ireland and is poised to capitalise on this by increasing its market share.

A significant selling point for the *Irish Times* is its excellent foreign affairs coverage. The newspaper has plans to further develop its coverage particularly in eastern Europe. The *Irish Times* has also secured a strong lead over rivals in the electronic publishing market with its Ireland.Com Internet site. The *Irish Times* has started publishing a Saturday magazine to compete directly with that of the *Irish Independent*. The *Irish Independent*'s Saturday magazine has been very successful, attracting increased readership and advertising revenue.

The tabloid sector of the market has also experienced growth in recent years, largely related to the economic recovery. Between 1994–99 sales grew from 188,000 to 271,000, which was a 40 per cent growth rate. This was due to the fact that the wage levels and job prospects of the traditional tabloid readership improved and, as a result, more of their disposable income was spent on newspapers.

The three main Irish newspaper groups are all establishing new printing facilities. Both the *Independent* and the *Times* are locating their print facilities in Citywest at a cost of €59.6 million and €57.1 million respectively, while the *Examiner* is looking to invest €25.3 million in a facility in the Munster region. It is likely, however, that this development will lead to an overcapacity which will have to be filled by some means. One approach involves subcontract work, and given the fact the INM and TCH both have subsidiaries that print UK newspapers for distribution in Ireland, this could provide a solution. In fact, the INM Group is such a global operation that economies of scale also arise from its operations which creates a competitive advantage for the group.

One of the main threats to INM's dominance of the market is its level of cross-media ownership. The INM Group controls a large portion of the market through its titles. For example, in relation to the market for Sunday newspapers the Group controls 60 per cent of the broadsheet market through the *Sunday Independent* and the *Sunday Tribune*, and a further 50 per cent of the tabloid market with the *Sunday World*. The issue of cross-media ownership came to the fore in the 1990s when the group tried to acquire a 29.9 per cent stake in the doomed Irish Press Group. Given that the group wish to expand and purchase titles in Northern Ireland, this issue is one that is likely to occur again.

The recent boom in newspaper circulation and readership is related to Ireland's economic recovery and the emergence of the 'Celtic Tiger'. The improved economic fortunes not only increase sales but also increase the revenue generated from advertising and promotional features. However, a key question for the future remains: Can Ireland's small economy and small population sustain its highly competitive newspaper sector?

Case adapted from O'Halloran (2000).

Case questions

❶ Prepare a SWOT analysis for the INM in Ireland including broadsheet, tabloid and Sunday market sectors.

❷ What future strategies should the organisation adopt to capitalise on opportunities while reducing potential threats in Ireland?

Keep up to date

www.Independent.ie

Bibliography

Anderson, C and Zeithaml, C (1984) 'Stage of the Product Life Cycle, Business Strategy and Business Performance', *Academy of Management Journal*, 27 (1), 5–24.
Carroll, S. and Tosi, H. (1973) *Management by Objectives*. New York: MacMillan.

Connecting With the Future: ESB Strategies for the 1990s. Dublin, March 1990.

David, F. (1989) 'How Companies Define their Missions', *Long-Range Planning*, 22 (1), 90–97.

Drucker, P. (1973) *Management Tasks, Responsibilities and Practices.* New York: Harper Row.

Drucker, P. (1954) *The Practice of Management.* New York: Harper Row.

Foster, J. (1993) 'Scenario Planning for Small Businesses', *Long Range Planning*, 26 (1), 123–29.

Froot, K., Scharfstein, D. and Stein, J. (1994) 'A Framework for Risk Management', *Harvard Business Review*, 63 (6), 91–102.

Hoskisson, R. and Hitt, M. (1994) *Downscoping: How to Tame The Diversified Firm.* New York: Oxford University Press.

Humble, J. (1972) *Management by Objectives.* USA: Teakfield.

Johnson, G. and Scholes, K. (1993) *Exploring Corporate Strategy.* London: Prentice Hall.

Jones, H. (1974) *Preparing Company Plans: A Workbook for Effective Corporate Planning.* New York: Wiley.

Kast, F and Rosenweig, J. (1985) *Organisation and Management: A Systems Approach.* New York: McGraw Hill.

Kondrasuk, J. (1981) 'Studies in Management by Objectives Effectiveness', *Academy of management Review*, July, 419–30.

Lubatkin, M. and Chatterje, S. (1994) 'Extending Modern Portfolio Theory into the Domain of Corporate Diversification. Does it Apply?', *Academy of Management Journal*, 37, 109–36.

Michiels, R. (1986) 'Planning, an Effective Management Tool or a Corporate Pastime', *Journal of Marketing Management*, 1 (3), 259–264.

Miles, R. and Snow, C. (1978) *Organisational Strategy, Structure and Process*, New York: McGraw Hill.

Moorehead, G and Griffin, R. (1989) *Organisational Behaviour.* Boston: Houghton Mifflin.

Odiorne, G., Weihrich, H. and Mendelson, J. (eds) *Executive Skills: A Management by Objectives Approach.* Iowa: Brown and Co.

O'Halloran, B. (2000) 'Newspaper Tigers', *Business and Finance*, 1 June, 12–15.

Porter, M. (1980) *Competitive Strategy: Techniques for Analysing Industries and Competitors.* New York: Free Press.

Quigley, J. (1994) 'Vision: How Leaders Develop It, Share It and Sustain It', *Business Horizons*, September–October, 37–41.

Shivastava, P. (1994) *Strategic Management: Concepts and Cases.* Cincinatti: South Western.

Sisk, H. (1973) *Management and Organisation.* Cincinnati: South Western.

Sunday Tribune (2000) Business Section, 16 July, 1–3.

Thompson, A and Strickland, A. (1990) *Strategic Management: Concepts and Cases.* Illinois: Irwin.

Vancourver, J., Millsap,R. and Peters,P. (1994) 'Multi-level Analysis of Organisational Goal Congruence', *Journal of Applied Psychology*, 79 (5), 666–79.

Weihrich, H. and Koontz, H. (1993) *Management: A Global Perspective.* New York: McGraw-Hill.

Chapter 5

Decision Making

5.1 Introduction

Decision making can be viewed as an integral part of planning in that key decisions have to taken throughout the planning process. This chapter focuses on many of the issues which arise when making organisational decisions. The nature and importance of decision making is explained, along with the different types of decisions made by organisations. The discussion then moves on to consider different decision-making conditions. There are four main approaches to understanding how organisational decisions are made: the rational model; the bounded rationality model; the political model; and the escalation of commitment model. The chapter concludes by examining group and individual decision making.

5.2 The nature and importance of decision making

Weihrich and Koontz define decision making as 'the selection of a course of action from among alternatives' (1993:199). In this sense decision making is at the heart of planning: for plans to be formulated and implemented, decisions on certain courses of action have to be taken. Some commentators (see Priem 1994) have even argued that decision making can be viewed as the most fundamental managerial activity of all. Decision making in this chapter is discussed primarily within the context of planning. However, despite the linkage with planning, decision making is a fundamental element of the entire management process.

Organisations make literally hundreds of decisions each day as they fulfil their operational requirements. Some of these decisions are small and minor and can be completed quickly, for example, the size and colour of envelopes required by the organisation. Others are more complicated and far-reaching and require more detailed analysis, such as whether to expand into foreign markets. Decision making, which takes place at all levels of the organisation, is therefore a central part of the manager's role.

5.3 Types of decision

Making decisions in an organisational context requires good judgement and diagnostic skills, and most managers advance within the organisation as a result of their ability to make good decisions. According to Huber (1980), there are two main types of decision made by managers: PROGRAMMED DECISIONS and NON-PROGRAMMED DECISIONS.

Programmed decisions tend to be well structured, routine and repetitive, occurring on a regular basis. Programmed decisions usually take place at lower levels in the organisation, have short-term consequences and are based on readily available information. Due to the fact that the organisation is frequently presented with the decision, a decision rule can be developed that tells the organisation or decision maker which alternative to choose once the information is available. The decision rule ensures that a definite method for obtaining a solution can be found and that the decision does not have to be treated as something new each time it occurs. Frequently simple formulae can be applied to the situation. Examples of programmed decisions include the ordering of raw materials or office supplies and the calculation of holiday pay, sick pay or redundancy payments, which frequently take place in Irish organisations.

Non-programmed decisions, in contrast, are new and unstructured and consequently prevent the application of a previously established decision rule. In other words, the organisation has no established procedures or records for dealing with the decision, which can therefore appear to be highly complex. Non-programmed decisions tend to occur at higher levels in the organisation, have long-term consequences and require a degree of judgement and creativity (Agor 1986).

Examples of non-programmed decisions include the decision to try an unproven technology or to expand into a previously unknown market. Allegro, the Irish distribution company took a major non-programmed decision in deciding to launch the American snack 'Pringles' on to the Irish market. This product is very different from traditional snack foods in that it is marketed in its distinctive tube packaging which ensures that the product is unbroken and has a long shelf life of 18 months. The decision however paid off with Pringles capturing 15 per cent of the market, a figure far in excess of the targeted 5 per cent. Figure 5.1 outlines the main characteristics of each type of decision.

Figure 5.1 Characteristics of programmes and non-programmed decisions

Programmed	Non-programmed
Well-structured	Poorly structured
Routine	New
Information available	Little information
Taken at lower levels	Taken at higher levels
Short time frame	Long time frame
Decision rules and set procedures used	Judgement and creativity used

While these two types of decisions are clearly distinguishable, they represent a continuum from programmed to non-programmed rather than being exclusive categories. Many decisions will have elements of both types of decisions.

5.4 Decision-making conditions

In general there are three different types of conditions under which managers take decisions (Huber 1980; Bass 1983; March 1994; Harrison 1994). The first condition is certainty, which means that the available alternatives and their costs or benefits are certain. In other words managers know with certainty that particular alternatives will lead to definite outcomes and there is no element of doubt. Given the current turbulent business environment it is not surprising that very few decisions can be made with certainty. Only the most minor of decisions can be taken under a condition of complete certainty.

The second decision-making condition is that of risk. Under the risk condition all of the available choices and their potential costs and benefits are known, but the outcomes are sometimes in doubt. So, while the alternatives are known, the outcomes are unknown. An example of a risk condition is the throw of a dice—the alternatives (one to six) are known but the outcome is not known in that there is a one-in-six chance of each number coming up. The probability of certain events can be calculated by the organisation using statistical techniques. OBJECTIVE PROBABILITY is the likelihood of an event occurring based on hard quantitative data, normally statistical. In contrast, SUBJECTIVE PROBABILITY is the likelihood of an event occurring based on personal judgement. In today's business environment, risk taking has become critically important for organisations.

The final condition is that of uncertainty when the available alternatives, the likelihood of their occurrence and the outcomes are all unknown. Decisions made under uncertainty are consequently the most difficult to take due to the lack of concrete knowledge. Such decisions tend to be ambiguous, intangible and highly unusual (Boynton 1993). In the current business environment more and more decisions are taken under uncertainty. Managers when making decisions under uncertain conditions require intuition and judgement.

The decision-making conditions represent a continuum from certainty to uncertainty as shown in Figure 5.2.

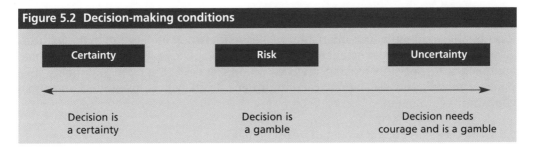

Figure 5.2 Decision-making conditions

| Certainty | Risk | Uncertainty |

Decision is a certainty

Decision is a gamble

Decision needs courage and is a gamble

While decisions taken under conditions of certainty tend to be the easiest to make and the most successful, decision failures can occur in relation to any type of decision. Given the additional problems associated with risk and uncertainty conditions it is not surprising that there are decision failures. Whyte (1991) argues that any decision can suffer from adverse conditions and bad luck, but attributes much decision failure to decision-making procedures which are under the manager's control.

Decisions can be framed either in terms of gains or losses, by a reference point against which the various options can be evaluated. A manager normally applies a decision frame to a decision. A decision frame refers to the perception held by the manager in terms of gains or losses associated with the outcome of a decision (Tversky and Kahneman 1981). Consequently, the same outcome could be viewed as a gain or a loss depending on the perception and reference point used. For example, if an employee received an €1,000 bonus while everyone else receives an €2,000 bonus, should this be viewed as a gain or as a loss? The answer depends on the individual and whether the reference point is with the employee's original salary (gain) or on comparisons with others (loss).

In the mid-1980s Coca-Cola was the biggest-selling soft drink world-wide yet the company decided to change the formula and introduce a 'new' Coca-Cola on to the market. The result was disastrous, as consumers disliked the new formula, preferring the old one. As a result the company had to reintroduce the old formula after three months using the brand name Coca-Cola Classic. What events led to the company taking such a poor decision? The decision was the product of a negative decision frame. Coca-Cola's share of the market had been steadily declining and the company's options were to make no changes and continue to decline, or to take the risky option to change the formula. In essence, the choice was between certain loss or risk, and the company chose the latter. As it turned out, though, the decision the company made resulted in more short-term losses than anticipated.

The nature of decision framing is important because managers usually tend to avoid risky options, though, when faced with a choice between losses, managers will tend to opt for a risky alternative. Choosing between losses is a choice between risky alternatives, that is, certain loss or possibly even greater loss. Whyte (1991) argues that decision framing may be responsible for many decision failures in that risky decisions which normally go wrong are the product of a choice between losses. The result is a strong preference for risk rather than perceived certain loss. This motivates managers to take risks in order to avoid losses. Although such behaviour might sometimes avoid loss, the typical result is actually to increase it.

5.5 Approaches to decision making

It is possible to identify four main approaches to the study of decision making; these vary depending to a great extent on the theorist's perspective. The four most popular approaches to decision making are: the rational model, bounded rationality, the political model, and escalation to commitment. Each will be examined and their contribution evaluated.

5.5.1 The classical rational model of decision making

Rationality in relation to decision making refers to a process that is perfectly logical and objective, whereby managers gather information objectively, evaluate available evidence, consider all alternatives and eventually make choices which will lead to the best outcomes for the organisation. The rational approach to decision making has its foundations in traditional economic theory which argues that managers attempt to maximise benefits and have the capacity to make complex decisions quickly. Such a rational approach to decision making assumes that four conditions are fulfilled:

❶ There is prefect knowledge of all the available alternatives.

❷ There is perfect knowledge of all of the consequences of the available alternatives.

❸ Managers have the capacity to objectively evaluate the consequences of the available alternatives.

❹ Managers have a well structured and definite set of procedures to allow them to make optimum decisions.

Although managers rarely have total control over all of the factors that determine how successful decisions will be, they can ensure a degree of control over the process that they use for making decisions. In attempting to make rational decisions managers typically go through six steps in the decision-making process as outlined in Figure 5.3. Throughout the various steps in the decision-making process the Aer Lingus decision to lease brand new Airbus 330 aircraft for its transatlantic route, will be used as an example.

Figure 5.3 The decision-making process

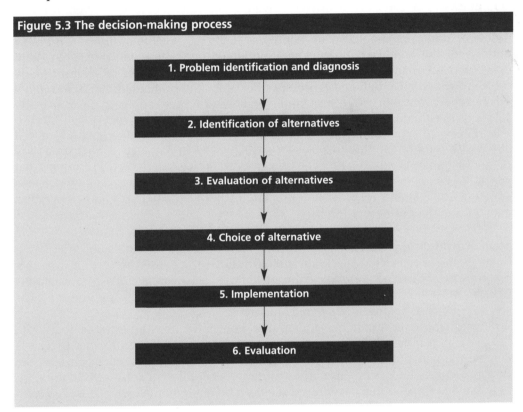

Step 1: **Problem identification and diagnosis**. The first stage of the decision-making process is recognising that a problem exists and that action has to be taken. A problem is a discrepancy between the current state of affairs and the desired state of affairs. Unless the problem is identified in precise terms solutions are very difficult to find. In seeking to identify a problem, managers can use various sources of data including comparing organisational performance against historical performance, the current performance of other organisations or departments or future expected performance.

Problem identification must be followed by a willingness to do something to rectify the situation. Before taking action the problem needs to be diagnosed. Diagnosis involves assessing the true cause of the problem by carefully selecting all relevant material about a problem and discarding information which is not relevant to the problem at hand.

For Aer Lingus the problem identification and diagnosis stage was quite simple and routine. The problem arose from the fact that the existing Boeing 747s used on the transatlantic route were starting to age. Aer Lingus had a total of three 747s in operation, all of which had been purchased in the late 1960s and early 1970s. As the average life of a jet aircraft is between 20 and 25 years these aircraft would have to be retired form service in the early 1990s. The problem did not arise suddenly, but was something which Aer Lingus was aware of from an early stage. However, as the retirement date loomed, action was needed and a quick problem identification and diagnosis was therefore required in order to place orders for new aircraft.

Step 2: Identification of alternatives. Having identified and diagnosed the problem the next step for an organisation is to identify a range of alternatives to solve the problem. Managers should try to identify as many as possible in order to broaden options for the organisation. In generating alternatives the organisation may look towards ready-made solutions which have been tried before, or custom-made solutions which have to be designed specifically for the problem at hand. In today's business environment more and more organisations are applying custom-made solutions to enhance competitive advantage.

In seeking to solve the ageing aircraft problem, Aer Lingus identified a range of alternative solutions to their problem. The first concerned the issue of whether new or an old aircraft should be considered as replacements. Second, Aer Lingus considered whether the aircraft should be purchased outright or leased. Finally the company considered a range of aircraft types, including the Boeing range of 747, 757, and 767 and the Airbus 330 and 340.

Step 3: Evaluating alternatives. Having identified the available alternatives a manager needs to evaluate each alternative in order to choose the best one; consideration should therefore be given to the advantages, disadvantages, costs and benefits of each. Most alternatives will have positive and negative aspects and the manager will have to try to balance anticipated outcomes.

Depending on the situation, evaluation of alternatives may be intuitive (based on gut feeling) or based on SCIENTIFIC ANALYSIS. Most organisations try to use a combination of both. When evaluating alternatives managers may consider the potential consequences of alternatives under several different scenarios. In doing so they can develop contingency plans, which can be implemented with possible future scenarios in mind.

In evaluating the alternatives available to Aer Lingus in relation to whether the replacement aircraft should be purchased or leased, or old or new, the costs and benefits of each of the scenarios was examined. In evaluating which aircraft type to choose, Aer Lingus considered numerous factors including:

- ▶ the size of the market
- ▶ the length of the routes to be served
- ▶ the frequency of service
- ▶ aircraft size in terms of seats and the split between classes (economy and business)
- ▶ the design and physical performance of the aircraft
- ▶ maintenance requirements
- ▶ availability of spare parts
- ▶ the amount of training required for cabin crew, pilots and maintenance engineers.

Step 4: Choice of alternative. Having evaluated the various alternatives the next step is to choose the most suitable one. If for some reason none of the options considered are suitable then the manager should revert back to Step 2 of the process and begin again. Where there are suitable alternatives and Steps 2 and 3 have been conducted skilfully, selecting alternatives should be relatively easy. In practice, however, alternatives may not differ significantly in terms of their outcomes, and therefore decisions will be a matter of judgement. In coming to a decision the manager will be confronted by many conflicting requirements which will have to be taken into account. For example, quality versus acceptability of the decision, and political and resource constraints.

Based on an evaluation of alternatives, Aer Lingus finally opted to lease brand new aircraft as opposed to purchasing old or new aircraft or leasing older ones. The particular aircraft type chosen was the Airbus 330 costing €88.8 million.

Step 5: Implementation. Once the decision has been made it needs to be implemented. This stage of the process is critical to the success of the decision and is the key to effective decision making. The best alternative is worth nothing if it is not implemented properly. In order to successfully implement a decision, managers must ensure that those who are implementing it fully understand why the choice was made and why it is being implemented and are fully committed to its success.

Decisions often fail at the implementation stage because managers do not ensure that people understand the rationale behind the decision and are fully committed to it. For this reason many organisations are attempting to push decision making further down the organisation to ensure that employees feel some sense of ownership in decisions that are made.

In the case of Aer Lingus the implementation of the decision involved the lease of the aircraft from a leasing company which in turn involved lengthy negotiations, the training of staff, ensuring the availability of spare parts and finally putting the aircraft into service.

Step 6: Evaluation. Having implemented the decision it then needs to be evaluated to provide feedback. The process of evaluation should take place at all managerial levels. This step allows managers to see what the results of the decision have been and to identify any adjustments which need to be made. In almost all cases some form of adjustment will be made to ensure favourable results.

Evaluation and feedback are not one-off activities, however; they form part of an ongoing process. As conditions change, decisions taken should be re-evaluated to ensure that they are still the most appropriate for the organisation. This also helps managers learn to make sound decisions taking past experience into account. In the case of Aer Lingus, an evaluation of the decision now occurs at regular intervals with assessment of the ongoing costs and benefits of the choice taken into consideration. In this process, Aer Lingus managers are able to use their experience of previous aircraft selection processes.

The model presented in Figure 5.3 seeks to provide a useful framework for managers taking decisions. It must be recognised, however, that the process is seldom as neat and sequential as outlined above (Czander 1993; Payne *et al*. 1993). The process is subject to various biases and pressures. Managers frequently allow their SUBJECTIVE biases to interfere with objective decision making. Pressures of time also affect the process and managers may be involved in the various steps simultaneously to ensure that a quick decision is made. Following each of the steps in the rational model is no guarantee of success. Indeed many of the most successful decisions have been taken without the aid of the rational model, particularly those of an innovative nature (Imparato *et al.* 1995).

5.5.2 Bounded rationality

As we saw in the previous section, decisions are made under varying conditions ranging from certainty and risk to uncertainty. In the current environment managers seldom make decisions under conditions of certainty which would be needed to apply a completely rational model. For many managers today the rational approach represents an ideal approach but one that is simply not attainable under current conditions of risk and uncertainty.

Given the fact that managers cannot always make decisions under certainty conditions, in a rational manner, they have to apply a less than perfect form of rationality. Simon (1976) called this bounded rationality, arguing that decisions taken by managers are bounded by limited mental capacity and emotions and by environmental factors over which they have no control. Due to these limitations managers rarely maximise or take ideal decisions with the best possible outcomes (Martin, Kleindorfer and Brashers 1987).

Intuition and judgement are therefore used by the manager to solve problems and make decisions. Taking a rational approach to problem solving and decision making involves clear identification of goals, objectives, alternatives, potential consequences and their outcomes. Each of these is in turn evaluated in terms of contribution to the overall aim. Decision making based on judgement is very different as Simon (1987:57) explains:

In judgmental decision making, the response to the need for a decision is usually rapid, too rapid to allow for an orderly sequential analysis of the situation, and the decision maker can not usually give a veridical account of either the process by which the decision was reached or the grounds for judging it correct.

For example, a manager might have to make a decision about where to establish a subsidiary office of the organisation. When making the decision the manager could be influenced by personal opinions, emotions and personal bias in favour of one location over another. This might be particularly noticeable if the manager is subsequently going to work in the office as the choice might be heavily influenced by his/her desire to live in one location. In this way, total rationality is not applied as the manager may choose a location which he/she favours and this will not not necessarily be the most rational choice.

Another integral part of the bounded rationality approach is the notion that managers seek to SATISFICE, that is, settle for an alternative which is satisfactory, rather than continuing to search for the optimal solution. Satisficing occurs because the manager may tire of the decision-making process and seek to quickly resolve the problem with the first minimally acceptable solution rather than search further for a better one.

Managers may also be unable to handle large amounts of complex information. Bounded rationality also recognises that managers may not have full and complete information and may experience problems processing information. Problems with INFORMATION PROCESSING clearly affects a manager's ability to make optimal decisions (Saunders and Jones 1990). Decisions made under bounded rationality may not always be the best; however, on occasion good decisions have been made on the basis of judgement and gut feeling.

Therefore the rational approach associated with traditional economic theory proposes that managers seek to maximise benefits and in this sense outlines how managers should behave. Bounded rationality, however, concentrates on how managers actually behave in practice when making decisions, and argues that limitations placed on managers mean they will seek to satisfice rather than maximise.

5.5.3 The political model

While the previous approaches have concentrated on the role played by rationality in the decision-making process, the political model concentrates on the impact of organisational politics on decision making. Power and politics play an important role in the decision-making process. Power is the ability to influence others. Within the context of an organisation power can be viewed as the ability to exert influence over individuals, work groups or departments. There are five main types of power found within the organisational setting:

▶ **Legitimate power** originates from the manager's position within the organisation's hierarchy. The power is inherent in the hierarchical position the manager occupies.

▶ **Reward power** originates from the manager's ability to withhold rewards from others.

▶ **Expert power** derives from the expert knowledge and information that an individual/manager has amassed.

▶ **Referent power** originates from the charisma or identification that a manager has developed.

▶ **Coercive power** is associated with emotional of physical threats to ensure compliance.

Within the decision-making process those who possess power are clearly an important dynamic. Political decision processes are used in situations where uncertainty, disagreement and lack of information are common. Within organisations it is common to find different COALITIONS, all of which possess varying degrees of power depending on the situation at hand. Coalitions can be formed by particular work groups, teams, managers, functional specialists, external stakeholders and trade unions. Each particular group brings with it certain ideas and values, coupled with power in relation to the decision under discussion. It is common for each coalition to defend their own territory and to ensure that any decisions made do not negatively impact on their members (both formal and informal). The presence of coalitions therefore adds an important ingredient to the decision-making process.

Different coalitions are likely to possess different and conflicting objectives. Depending on the relative power of each coalition, negotiation and compromise will feature strongly. In some cases the compromise and outcome will be a win–lose situation which means that one coalitions gain is another's loss. In other cases a win–win situation can be generated.

The political model recognises that, apart from actually making the decision, many other factors are at work, including negotiation, compromise and power struggles. Political forces within the decision-making process can be beneficial if a wider range of issues is considered and greater input and commitment is achieved. On the other hand, power struggles may lead to a lack of focus on key issues and produce narrowly defined decisions largely following the self-interests of particular groups within the organisation.

5.5.4 Escalation of commitment

While not explaining much about how decisions are made, this approach concentrates on why people continue to pursue a failing course of action, that is, why commitment to a poor decision often escalates after the initial decision has been made.

This approach is particularly concerned with decision makers who, even in the face of failure, continue to invest resources in a failing decision. For example, an organisation may decide to enter a particular market by introducing a certain product. After a little while it may become obvious that the product is not suited to that market. The organisation however, continues to increase spending on advertising and marketing rather than exiting from the market.

Such escalation of commitment to a failing decision is often attributed to self-justification and a feeling of personal responsibility for the decision. Staw (1976:39) concluded that 'when individuals are personally responsible for negative consequences they may decide to increase investment of resources to a previously chosen course of action'. Subsequent researchers (Brockner 1992; Staw and Ross 1987; Bobocel and Meyer 1994; Bowen 1987) have explained the effect on the grounds of self-justification or COGNITIVE DISSONANCE.

Organisations therefore, have to strike a balance between persevering with a decision and recognising when a decision is failing and should be abandoned. Not all organisations fall into the escalation of commitment trap. In the example of Coca-Cola above, the organisation realised that the decision to change the formula was incorrect and subsequently altered their course of action.

5.6 Group decision making

Task forces, teams and boards are all examples of where decision making occurs in a group setting. The basic idea behind group decision making is the notion that two heads are better than one. Much research (Shaw 1981; Hill 1982; Sussman and Deep 1984) has been conducted on the subject of whether groups make better decisions than individuals acting alone. Generally the diversity of groups facilitates better-quality decisions. However, Hill (1982) found that groups could be inferior to the best individual. In some cases groups will provide the best-quality decisions and in others the individual will do better (Locke, Schweiger and Latham 1986). In coming to a conclusion about the efficiency of groups it is necessary to consider the advantages and disadvantages of group decision making.

5.6.1 Advantages of group decision making

▶ Group decision making allows a greater number of perspectives and approaches to be considered, thereby increasing the number of alternatives that can be drawn up.

▶ Groups generally facilitate a larger pool of information to be processed. Individuals from different areas can bring varied information to the decision-making setting.

▶ By increasing the number of people involved in the process it is more likely that a greater number of people will understand why the decision was made and this facilitates implementation.

▶ Group decision making allows people to become involved and produces a sense of ownership of the final decision which means that people will be more committed to the decision.

▶ Using a group to arrive at a decision means that less co-ordination and communication is required when implementing the decision (Iaquinto and Fredrickson 1997).

5.6.2 Disadvantages of group decision making

▶ Group decisions take longer to arrive at and this can be problematic when speed of action is key.

▶ Groups can be indecisive and opt for satisficing rather then maximising. Indecision can arise from lack of agreement among members. Satisficing occurs when individuals grow tired of the process and want it brought to a conclusion, leading to satisficing rather than maximisation.

▶ Individuals who have either a strong personality or position can dominate groups. The result is that a particular individual can exert more influence than others. The main problem with such a situation is that the dominating person's view of the decision need not necessarily be right; and if his/her view is the right one, convening a group for discussion is a waste of time.

▶ Groups inevitably have to compromise to reach a decision and this can lead to mediocre decisions. Mediocrity results when an individual's thinking is brought into line with the average quality of a group's thinking. This is called the LEVELLING EFFECT.

▶ Groups can lead to GROUP THINK. Irving (1982) defines group think as 'a mode of thinking that people engage in when they are deeply involved in a cohesive group, when members' strivings for unanimity override their motivation to realistically appraise alternative courses of action'. Group think happens in situations where the need to achieve consensus among group members becomes so powerful that it takes over realistic evaluations of available alternatives. Criticism is suppressed and conflicting views are not aired for fear of breaking up a positive team spirit. Such groups become over confident and too willing to take risks.

5.6.3 Individual versus group decision making

Having considered the advantages and disadvantages of group decision making it is clear that group decision making is well suited to certain circumstances. Sussman and Deep (1984:120) contrast individual with group decision making by outlining ten factors which favour each method, and their lists can be useful in determining the most appropriate problem-solving method to use in a given set of circumstances.

Factors favouring individual decision making include:

❶ Short time frame.

❷ Decision is relatively unimportant to the group.

❸ Manager has all the data needed to make the decision.

❹ One or two members of the group are likely to dominate.

❺ Conflict is likely.

❻ People attend too many meetings.

❼ The data is confidential.

❽ Group members are not sufficiently qualified.

❾ The manager is dominant.

❿ The decision does not directly affect the group.

Factors favouring group decision making include:

❶ Creativity is required.

❷ Data is held by the group.

❸ Acceptance of the solution by group members is important.

❹ Understanding of the solution is important.

❺ The problem is complex and needs a broad range of knowledge.

❻ The manager wants to build commitment.

❼ More risk taking is involved.

❽ Better understanding of group members is needed.

❾ The group is responsible for the decision.

❿ The manager wants feedback on ideas.

5.7 Improving group decision making

In order to avoid the disadvantages associated with group decision making and to build on the advantages, three main ways of improving group decision making have been developed (Moorehead and Griffin 1989).

▶ **Brainstorming** became popular in the 1950s and was developed by Alexander Osborn to facilitate the development of creative solutions and alternatives. Brainstorming is solely concerned with idea generation rather than evaluation, choice or implementation. The term effectively means using the brain creatively to storm a problem. It is based on the belief that when people interact in a more relaxed and less restrained setting they will generate more creative ideas. The acceptance of new ideas is also more likely when the decision is made by the group involved with its implementation (Summers and White 1976).

In brainstorming the group members are normally given a summary of the problem prior to the meeting. At the meeting members come up with various ideas which are recorded in full view of all other members. None of the alternatives are evaluated or criticised at this stage. As members produce new ideas and alternatives this serves to stimulate other members in the hope that a truly good solution can be identified. The concept of Bailey's Irish Cream was developed from a brainstorming session.

▶ **The Delphi technique** was developed by Dalkey and Helmar in the early 1960s as a means of avoiding the undesirable effects, while retaining the positive aspects, of group interaction. The technique got its name from Delphi which was the seat of the Greek god Apollo who was renowned for his wise decisions.

The Delphi technique consists of a panel of experts formed to examine a problem. Rather than physically meeting, the various members are kept apart so that social or psychological pressures associated with group behaviour cannot influence them. In order to find out their views they are asked to complete a questionnaire. A co-ordinator then summarises the findings and members are asked to fill out another questionnaire to reevaluate earlier points. The technique presumes that, as repeated questionnaires are conducted, the range of responses will narrow to produce a consensus. The Delphi technique is particularly useful where experts are physically dispersed, anonymity is required and where members have difficulty communicating with each other. On the negative side, however, it reduces direct interaction among group members.

▶ **Nominal grouping** was developed by Delbecq and Van de Ven (1971) and, in contrast to brainstorming, does not allow a free association of ideas, tries to restrict verbal interaction and can be used at many other stages of the decision-making process apart from just idea generation. With nominal grouping members are given a problem and are asked to think of ideas individually with no discussion. They then present these ideas on a flip chart. A period of discussion follows which builds on the ideas presented. After the discussion, members privately rank the ideas. Generation of ideas and discussion proceeds in this manner until a solution is found.

The main advantage of this approach is that it overcomes differences between members in terms of power and prestige and it can also be used at a variety of stages in the overall decision-making process. Its main disadvantages are that its structure may limit creativity and it is costly and time-consuming.

5.8 Summary of key propositions

▶ Decision making is the selection of a course of action from a range of alternatives. It plays an integral part in planning but is also a fundamental part of the entire management process.

▶ Organisations make hundreds of decisions each day which can be classified as programmed and non-programmed. Programmed decisions are well structured, routine, repetitive, occurring on a regular basis. Non-programmed decisions are new, unstructured and have no established procedures for making them.

▶ Decisions are taken under different conditions ranging from complete certainty to risk and uncertainty.

▶ Certainty means that the available alternatives and their costs or benefits are certain: managers know with certainty that particular alternatives will lead to definite outcomes and there is no element of doubt.

▶ Under the risk condition all of the available alternatives and their potential costs and benefits are known, but the outcomes are sometimes in doubt. Therefore while the alternatives are known the outcomes are unknown.

▶ Uncertainty is when the available alternatives, the likelihood of their occurrence and the outcomes are all unknown. Decisions made under uncertain conditions are consequently the most difficult to take due to the lack of concrete knowledge. In the current business environment more and more decisions are being made under conditions of uncertainty.

▶ The four most popular approaches to decision making are: the rational model, bounded rationality, escalation of commitment and the political model.

▶ Rationality in relation to decision making refers to a process that is perfectly logical and objective, whereby managers gather information objectively, evaluate available evidence, consider all alternatives and ultimately make choices which will lead to the best outcomes for the organisation.

▶ The rational model of decision making contains six key steps: problem identification and diagnosis; identification of alternatives; evaluating alternatives; choice of alternative; implementation; and evaluation.

▶ Decisions can be taken by either groups or individuals depending on the nature of the decision.

▶ Group decision-making has a number of advantages: a greater number of perspectives, a larger pool of information, greater commitment and ownership; less co-ordination required for implementation.

▶ Group decision making also produces a number of disadvantages: length of time to reach a decision; satisficing; dominant individuals; compromise and the levelling effect; group think.

▶ The quality of group decisions can be enhanced by three main techniques including brainstorming, the Delphi technique and nominal grouping.

Discussion questions

❶ Explain the nature and importance of decision making.

❷ Explain using your own examples the differences between programmed and non-programmed decisions.

❸ Explain the different decision-making conditions under which decisions are taken.

❹ What do you understand by the rational model of decision making?

❺ Explain the term 'bounded rationality'.

❻ What role do political forces play in organisational decision making?

❼ Apply the rational model of decision making to your decision about how to spend next year's summer holiday. Evaluate its effectiveness.

❽ Outline the advantages of group decision making.

❾ Outline the disadvantages of group decision making.

❿ Explain the terms 'group think' and the 'levelling effect'.

⓫ Evaluate group versus individual decision making.

⓬ How can group decision making be improved?

Concluding case: Glanbia—key decisions

Glanbia was formed from the merger of Avonmore Foods and Waterford Foods in 1997. It is an Irish company involved in food processing with a strong market presence in Ireland, the UK, Europe and the USA. In 1999 Glanbia had a turnover of €2,922 million and profits of €53.3 million. It ranks among the world's leading dairy businesses, in addition to strong regional meat markets. Glanbia is one of the world's top five cheese producers and is the largest producer of functional pizza cheese in Europe. Glanbia is the largest dairy processor in Ireland and the UK with number one positions in milk, cheese, fresh dairy products, fresh soups and sauces. In addition, Glanbia is the second largest pig meat producer in the UK and Ireland. Glanbia's mission statement reads as follows:

Glanbia will be a world-class company with leading positions in food ingredients and consumer markets. We deliver value for all our stakeholders through excellence in customer service, innovation, uncompromising quality and operational efficiency.

Glanbia is structured into four main divisions:

▶ **Agribusiness**. This division is involved in animal feed manufacture, pig production and Glanbia agribusiness which is the primary link between the company and its farmer supply base.

▶ **Meat**. Glanbia's meat division concentrates on processing pig meat and lamb and supplying consumer ready products to the market.

▶ **Consumer foods**. Glanbia's consumer foods division produces branded and own-label consumer dairy products in Ireland, the UK and other EU markets. The main products include yoghurts, fromage frais and soups.

▶ **Food ingredients**. This division produces dairy-based ingredients to the world-wide food and nutritional industries. The main markets served include Europe, USA, Canada, Latin America and Africa.

Following the 1997 merger Glanbia decided to create a single brand identity in 1999. The brand name Glanbia now replaces the previous use of both Avonmore and Waterford. This decision was designed to reduce consumer confusion, especially in the UK market, and also to reduce internal divisions between the former Avonmore and Waterford staff.

Glanbia's current strategy is to secure and enhance its strong market leadership in key sectors by continuous development in innovation, market knowledge, operations and technological quality standards. In pursuit of this strategy, and in response to events in the competitive marketplace, Glanbia has taken a number of important decisions in recent times. Some of these decisions are expansionary in nature, others are responses to strong market competition and unfavourable environmental conditions.

Glanbia's overall strategy is to concentrate efforts in a number of key sectors, the two most significant of which are cheese and nutritional products. The cheese sector involves the USA, pizza cheese production for the EU market and the Irish and UK retail cheese market. The US cheese business is based in Idaho and is expected to thrive due to its low cost location and the scale advantages accruing to Glanbia. This market is driven by a strong demand for food services. Glanbia cemented the commitment to the US market when it invested $35 million to increase capacity to 120,000 tonnes.

However, in the UK Glanbia retail cheese operations have been badly affected by the UK's strong currency. Prices in both the mature and mild cheese markets have been considerably reduced which affects Glanbia's margins. Further difficulties have been created for Glanbia by the price wars between the main supermarkets, which once again reduces margins. The cheese business is critical for Glanbia, particularly in terms of profit; however, the nutritional products market may provide more long-term potential.

Nutrition is a high-growth area and Glanbia have become involved in supplying ingredients such as lactose, casein, milk proteins, formulated products and cream base. The world-wide market is valued at $15 billion and Glanbia is placed number two in the world after Nestlé. Glanbia is exploring opportunities for alliances and joint ventures for further expansion and development of this market.

The competitive position of some of Glanbia's other divisions, however, has been deteriorating and this has presented the company with some tough decisions. Many of the problems have centred on the UK market where the strength of Sterling, price wars among supermarkets and strong competition among suppliers have all negatively affected Glanbia. In 1999, the liquid milk business in the UK provided Glanbia with many problems as the company found one of its traditional markets under severe price pressure. Glanbia lost an important account with ASDA-Walmart and continued to face strong competition from other suppliers. In addition, the supermarkets began a process of rationalising the number of suppliers they traded with. Under such competitive pressure Glanbia decided to sell the liquid milk business in the UK to Express Dairies.

The global meat market has also been faced with oversupply and falling demand. From 1998 onwards demand from Russia and Asia declined. This was coupled with increased international competition. The extent of oversupply in the international pig meat market in the EU and the USA led Glanbia to dispose of its beef operations to Dawn Meats. Glanbia also plans to sell the sheep meats division.

In Ireland in the consumer products division competition has intensified. International players such as Danone have provided stiff competition to Yoplait and Avonmore products. Glanbia has managed to maintain market share but the future could be more problematic. The liquid milk division in Ireland lost money in 1999 and four plants were closed. The food ingredients sector in Ireland still suffers from high costs.

While the future for some divisions looks promising the situation facing others is very uncertain. Some key strategic decisions have already been made but Glanbia have to take further decisions to ensure that the company maintains competitive strength.

Case adapted from the Glanbia website and Micheau (2000).

Case questions

❶ Identify the key decisions that have been made by Glanbia.

❷ What type of decisions were they?

❸ Under what conditions were they made?

❹ How successful have the decisions been?

❺ What decisions will Glanbia have to make in the future?

Keep up to date

www.Glanbia.com.

Bibliography

Agor, W. (1986) 'How Top Executives Use Their Intuition to Make Important Decisions', *Business Horizons*, 29 (2), 49–53.

Bass, B. (1983) *Organisational Decision Making*. Illinois: Irwin.

Bobocel, D. and Meyer, J. (1994) 'Escalating Commitment to a Failing Course of Action: Separating the Roles of Choice and Justification', *Journal of Applied Psychology*, 79 (3), 360–63.

Bowen, M. (1987) 'The Escalation Phenomenon Reconsidered: Decision Dilemmas or Decision Errors?', *Academy of Management Review*, 12, 52–66.

Boynton, A. (1993) 'Management Search Activity: the Impact of Perceived Role Uncertainty and Threat', *Journal of Management*, 19 (4), 725–48.

Brockner, J. (1992) 'The Escalation of Commitment to a Failing Course of Action: Toward Theoretical Progress', *Academy of Management Review*, 17, 39–61.

Czander, W. (1993) *The Psychodynamics of Work and Organisations*. New York: Guilford.

Dalkey, N. and Helmar, O. (1963) 'An Experimental Application of the Delphi Methods to the Use of Experts', *Managerial Science*, 9, 458–67.

Delbecq, A. and Van de Ven, A. (1971) 'A Group Process Model for Problem Identification and Programme Planning', *Journal of Applied Behavioural Science*, 7, 466–92.

Harrison, F. (1994) *The Managerial Decision Making Process*. Boston: Houghton Mifflin.

Hill, G. (1982) 'Group Versus Individual Performance: Are n + 1 Heads Better than One', *Psychological Bulletin*, 91, 517–39.

Huber, G. (1980) *Managerial Decision Making*. Illinois: Scott Foresman.

Iaquinto, A. and Fredrickson, J. (1997) 'Top Management Team Agreement about the Strategic Decision Process: A Test of some of its Determinants and Consequences', *Strategic Management Journal*, 18, 63–75.

Imparato, N. and Harari, O. (1995) Jumping the Curve: Innovation and Strategic Choice in an Age of Transition. San Francisco: Jossey Bass.

Irving, J. (1982) *Group Think*. Boston: Houghton Mifflin.

Locke, E., Schweiger, D. and Latham, G. (1986) 'Participation in Decision Making: Should it be used?', Organisation Dynamics, 14 (3), 65–79.

March, J. (1994) *A Primer on Decision Making: How Decisions Happen*. New York: Free Press.

Martin, J. Kleindorfer, G. and Brashers, W. (1987) 'The Theory of Bounded Rationality and the Problem of Legitmation', *Journal for the Theory of Social Behaviour*, 17, 63–82.

Micheau, E. (2000) 'Glanbia—O'Sullivan's Poisoned Chalice', *Business and Finance*, 9 March, 20–23.

Moorehead, G. and Griffin, R. (1989) *Organisational Behavious*. Boston: Houghton Mifflin.

Osborn, A. (1963) *Applied Imagination: Principles and Procedures for Creative Problem Solving*. New York: Scribner.

Payne, J., Bettman, J. and Johnson, E. (1993) *The Adaptive Decision Maker*, New York: Cambridge University Press.

Priem, R. (1994) 'Executive Judgement, Organisational Congruence and Firm Performance', *Organisational Science*, August, 421–32.

Saunders, C. and Jones, J. (1990) 'Temporal Sequences in Information Acquisition for Decision-Making: A Focus on Source and Medium', *Academy of Management Review*, 15, 29–46.

Schoemaker, P. and Russo, J. (1993) 'A Pyramid of Decision Approaches', *California Management Review*, 36 (1), 9–31.

Schwenk, C. (1984) 'Cognitive Simplification Process in Strategic Decision Making', *Strategic Management Journal*, 5 (2), 111–28.

Shaw, M. (1981) *Group Dynamics: The Psychology of Small Group Behaviour*. New York: McGraw-Hill.

Simon, H. (1976) *Administrative Behaviour: A Study of Decision Making Processes in Administrative Organisations*. New York: Free Press.

Simon, H. (1987) 'Making Management Decisions: The Role of Intuition and Emotion', *Academy of Management Executive*, February, 57–64.

Staw, B. (1976) 'Knee Deep in the Big Muddy: A Study of Escalating Commitment to a Chosen Course of Action', *Organisational Behaviour and Human Performance*, 16, 27–44.

Staw, B. and Ross, J. (1987) 'Behaviour in Escalation Situations: Antecedents, Prototypes and Solutions', in Cummings, L. and Staw, B. (eds) *Research in Organisational Behaviour*, 9, 39–78).

Summers, I. and White, D. (1976) 'Creativity Techniques: Towards Improvement of the Decision Process', *Academy of Management Review*, 1 (3), 99–107.

Sussman, L. and Deep, S. (1984) *COMEX: The Communication Experience in Human Relations*. Cincinnati: South Western.

Tversky, A. and Kahneman, D. (1981) 'The Framing of Decisions and the Psychology of Choice', *Science*, 59, 453–8.

Voyer, J. (1994) 'Coercive Organisational Politics and Organisational Outcomes: An Interpretative Study', *Organisation Science*, 5 (1), 72–85.

Weihrich, H. and Koontz, H. (1993) *Management*. New York: McGraw-Hill.

Whyte. G. (1991) 'Decision Failures: Why They Occur and How to Prevent Them', *Academy of Management Executive*, 5 (3), 23–31.

Chapter 6

Organisational Structure
and Design

This chapter examines the second function of management—organising. Organising is the process of dividing the tasks to be achieved and then co-ordinating them. The framework used for organising is called organisational structure. Organisational structure has a number of components which are examined. Organisational design is concerned with how the various components of structure are drawn together to produce particular structural forms. Following this, historical approaches to structure and design are considered along with some more recent additions. Recent developments in structure and design have been triggered by changes in the business environment. As a result, three new types of structure have been developed and used by organisations, depending on their requirements. The three new forms are the network organisation, the cluster organisation and the high-performance organisation.

6.2 The nature and importance of organising

The second function of management is organising. Organising is the process of dividing the tasks between groups, individuals and departments and CO-ORDINATING their activities to achieve organisational goals. The process usually starts with a reflection on the plans and objectives devised at the planning stage followed by the establishment of the major tasks that need to undertaken to achieve such goals. These tasks are then subdivided into sub-tasks and resources are allocated to them. Finally, the outcomes of the process are evaluated and corrections made. The function of organising creates relationships between organisational areas that outline when, where and how resources are to be used.

As a result of the organising process the organisation's activities are broken down and departmentalised. Connections and means of co-ordination are then established. The pattern of how activities are divided and later co-ordinated is called organisational structure. Organisational structure can be defined as the system of task, reporting and authority relationships within which the work of the organisation is completed (Moorehead and Griffin 1989). The purpose of any form of structure is to co-ordinate the activities of employees in order to achieve organisational goals.

In recent years, organisational structure and design has undergone a revolution. As a result of the changes in the business environment organisations have come to realise that in order to survive their structures must be flexible and adaptive, to enable the organisation to respond to and anticipate change (Nadler and Tushman 1997). Therefore, having an effective form of organisational structure has become an important source of competitive advantage. Organisations that do not adapt their structures to meet changing needs will face extinction. Those that change their structural design to reflect changed circumstances will achieve the flexibility and creativity necessary for survival. Before examining the various approaches to organisational design, including recent developments, it is necessary to understand the components of an organisation's structure.

6.3 Components of organisational structure

The main components of an organisation's structure can be divided into two main areas:

- ▶ structural configuration
- ▶ structural operation.

Structural configuration refers to the size and shape of the structure and concentrates on the size of the hierarchy, spans of control, division of labour and means of co-ordination. The structural configuration of an organisation can be clearly seen from its ORGANISATIONAL CHART. In contrast, structural operation concentrates on the processes and operation of organisational structure, including decision making, formalisation, responsibility and authority. Taken together, structural configuration and operation provide a full picture of the various component parts of an organisation's structure. Each element is shown in Figure 6.1 and will be examined in turn.

Figure 6.1 Components of organisational structure

Structural configuration	Structural operation
Division of labour	Formalisation
Spans of control	Decision making
Hierarchical levels	Responsibility
Departmentalisation	Authority

6.3.1 Structural configuration

The *division of labour* within an organisation is the extent to which the work of the organisation is broken down into different tasks, to be completed by different people. It is also referred to as JOB SPECIALISATION meaning that one person is specialised in doing one particular task. A clear example of division of labour can be found in McDonald's where staff are either assigned to cleaning up the lobby areas, making fries, making burgers or serving the public. In this case the division of labour is quite narrow in that each person completes one particular task. A wider division of labour in this example could mean that each person looked after customers throughout their visit, from serving them, to preparing food, and cleaning up after them.

It was hoped that narrow divisions of labour and job specialisation would lead to efficient use of labour, increased standardisation and the development of employee expertise through repetition of the task. However, very narrow job specialisation can lead to reduced job satisfaction and motivation, as people have to complete the same routine task over and over again (Sherman and Smith 1984). It can also lead to absenteeism, high turnover and poor-quality output.

Spans of control are the number of employees directly reporting to a supervisor. A narrow span of control means that the supervisor is in charge of a small number of employees, whereas a wide span of control means that the supervisor is in charge of a large number. Figure 6.2 shows an example of both wide and narrow spans of control. Supervisor A has only three employees directly reporting to him/her which is a very narrow span. In contrast, supervisor B has nine employees reporting to him/her which is a much wider span.

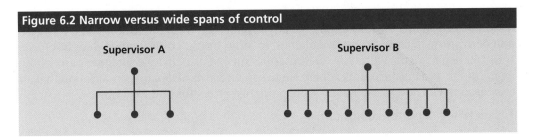

Figure 6.2 Narrow versus wide spans of control

With wider spans of control employees tend to have more freedom and discretion. In contrast, narrow spans of control usually lead to a high levels of supervision, as managers can keep their eyes on the activities of all employees under their control. Effective spans of control are those where employees can be given a degree of freedom, while at the same time having some form of guidance from a supervisor should assistance be required. Many theorists have tried to identify what the optimal span of control should be (see Urwick 1956; Haimann and Scott 1970; Koontz and O'Donnell 1964; Van Fleet and Bedeian 1977). Mintzberg (1979) concludes that the size of the span depends on a number of factors, not least the degree of specialisation, the similarity of tasks, the type of information available, the need for autonomy, direct access to supervisors and the abilities and experience of both supervisors and employees. Consequently there can be no universal prescriptions in relation to the optimal span of control that hold true across all situations.

The number of levels and the extent of *hierarchy* outlines the reporting relationships within the organisation from the top to the bottom. Organisations which have relatively few levels in their hierarchy are called flat structures while those with many levels are called tall structures. A relationship exists between the number of levels in the hierarchy and the spans of control, as shown in Figure 6.3.

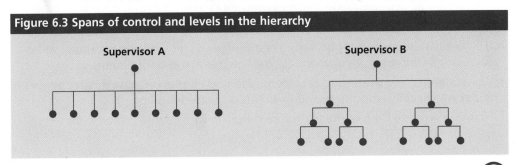

Figure 6.3 Spans of control and levels in the hierarchy

On the left-hand side of the figure it can be seen that with wide spans of control less levels in the management structure are required. In this case the span of control is 19 and only one hierarchical level is required. However, if the spans are very narrow as shown on the right-hand side of the figure, then more supervisors and managers are needed, which increases the number of levels in the hierarchy. In this case, the span of control is two and there are three hierarchical levels in the structure. Therefore, as the span increases the hierarchy decreases and conversely as the span decreases the hierarchy increases.

The final element of structural configuration is concerned with co-ordinating the various activities of the organisation. This has been traditionally known as *departmental-isation* as departments were normally set up to co-ordinate activities. In recent years business units or even separate divisions of companies have tended to replace traditional departments as the primary co-ordinating mechanism. However, the term 'departmen-talisation' can still be usefully applied to any means used by organisations, be it business unit or division, to co-ordinate its activities. In other words, co-ordination does not focus solely on departments within the organisation but can also include separate parts of the organisation and business units. There are five main forms of departmentalisation that an organisation can adopt, each possessing particular strengths and weaknesses:

▶ functional departmentalisation
▶ product departmentalisation
▶ geographical departmentalisation
▶ matrix departmentalisation
▶ mixed departmentalisation.

Probably the most popular form of departmentalisation until recent years is FUNCTIONAL DEPARTMENTALISATION which organises the separate units of the organisation according to the functions they perform. Functional departmentalisation is usually structured around the traditional organisational functions of manufacturing, marketing, finance, engineering and personnel. Figure 6.4 provides an example of a functional approach to departmentalisation used by SDS, a subsidiary of An Post, providing courier services and the distribution of special parcels. As can be seen from the chart SDS is structured around the main functions involved in its activities, which are finance, sales and marketing and operations.

The main advantages associated with functional departmentalisation include:

▶ The functions of each individual are emphasised allowing people to concentrate their efforts.
▶ Resources are used efficiently by grouping the various functions and gaining economies of scale and reductions in overheads.
▶ A clear and simple communication and decision-making system is possible.
▶ The measurement of output and performance of the various functional areas is facilitated. Consequently performance standards are easier to maintain.
▶ The training given to specialists is simplified and employees have greater opportu-nities for specialised training and in-depth skill development.
▶ Status is given to each of the main functional areas.
▶ Control by the top of the organisation is facilitated.

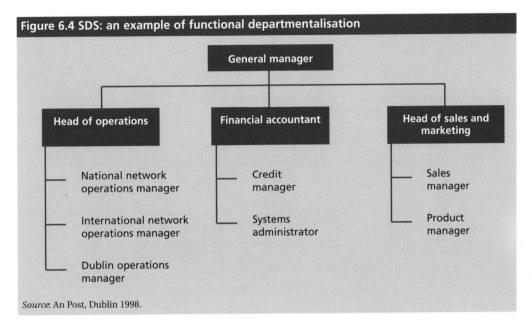

Figure 6.4 SDS: an example of functional departmentalisation

General manager

Head of operations

- National network operations manager
- International network operations manager
- Dublin operations manager

Financial accountant

- Credit manager
- Systems administrator

Head of sales and marketing

- Sales manager
- Product manager

Source: An Post, Dublin 1998.

However, there is a number of disadvantages associated with this form of departmentalisation:

▶ If departments are large then it becomes difficult to co-ordinate the various departments.

▶ Employees tend to focus on departmental goals rather than wider organisational goals due to their limited outlook.

▶ It can be quite costly to co-ordinate the activities of the various functions.

▶ Such a structure makes it difficult to develop managers with experience in a wide variety of areas.

▶ Competition and rivalry between departments can develop.

▶ Such a structure can lower customer satisfaction when compared to alternative means of departmentalisation.

The second form of departmentalisation is PRODUCT DEPARTMENTALISATION. Instead of structuring the organisation around functional areas, it is structured on the basis of the products produced. Business units in many organisations are structured in this manner. Product departmentalisation is frequently introduced by large organisations who have found that it was too difficult to co-ordinate functional departments. An example of product departmentalisation used by Glanbia is shown in Figure 6 5.

The main products of the organisation such as consumer foods, food ingredients, meat and agribusiness become the focus of the structure. Each product line contains the various functional activities that it requires, such as personnel and marketing. This form of departmentalisation is also commonly used by organisations operating in the service sector, including CIE, who structure their activities into the main services that they provide. Figure 6.6 illustrates the service style of departmentalisation used by CIE which focuses on key service areas namely Iarnrod Éireann, Bus Éireann, Bus Atha Cliath and Ancillary Business Services.

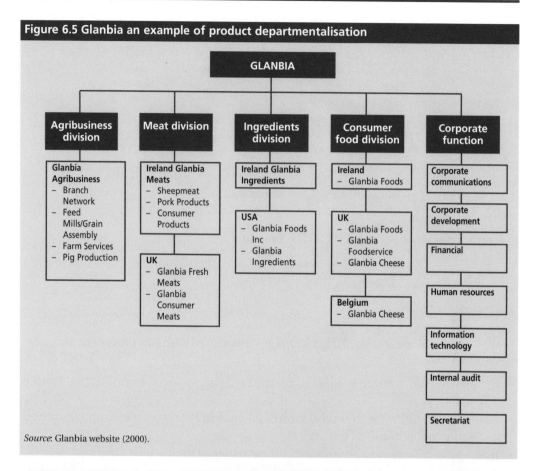

Figure 6.5 Glanbia an example of product departmentalisation

Source: Glanbia website (2000).

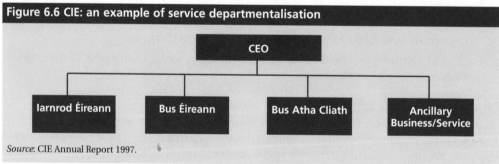

Figure 6.6 CIE: an example of service departmentalisation

Source: CIE Annual Report 1997.

This form of structure has a number of advantages:

▶ Product areas or business units can be evaluated as profit centres.

▶ Additions to the product line can be easily facilitated which allows for growth. In the same way a product can be discontinued and resources reallocated to another product.

▶ It allows co-ordination and communication between functions working on a product to occur quickly.

- ▶ The structure focuses on the needs of the clients.
- ▶ The structure develops managers with a wide experience of various functions.
- ▶ Employees develop full time commitment to a particular product line.

It also has a number of disadvantages:

- ▶ Co-ordination among specialised product areas can be problematic.
- ▶ There is a duplication of functional services for each product.
- ▶ Less communication and interaction occurs between functional specialists.
- ▶ The emphasis tends to be on product objectives rather than wider organisational objectives.

The next form of departmentalisation is called GEOGRAPHICAL DEPARTMENTALISATION. In this case the organisation is structured around activities in the various geographical locations. An example of geographical departmentalisation used by the Smurfit Group is shown in Figure 6.7.

This form of structure is particularly suitable for organisations selling in many different countries where there are significant difference in markets and customer needs. The main advantages of this form of structure are as follows;

- ▶ It encourages logistic efficiency.
- ▶ It allows divisions to adapt to local markets.
- ▶ Legal, cultural and political differences can be minimised.
- ▶ It provides a good training ground for managers.

This form of structure also has a number of disadvantages:

- ▶ It needs a large number of general managers.
- ▶ Top management loses a degree of control over operations.
- ▶ A duplication of support services is inevitable.
- ▶ Employees may focus on regional objectives at the expense of wider organisational goals.

Another form of departmentalisation is called a MATRIX STRUCTURE (or MATRIX DEPART-MENTALISATION). In effect the matrix structure is a combination of functional and product departmentalisation. It was first implemented by TRW Inc. in the USA who found that traditional functional departmentalisation was inadequate for managing complex technological developments. With a matrix structure employees are both members of a functional group and also a product group. So in effect they have two supervisors, one from their core functional area and one from the particular project area. However, when employees are involved in specific projects the project manager is the reporting supervisor. The most remarkable feature about the matrix structure is that functional and product lines of authority are overlaid to form a grid. This form of structure is usually found in organisations with diverse activities, or used for project management. Private industry has found this structure attractive, particularly for projects with a high capital investment and R & D requirement.

Figure 6.7 The Smurfit Group: an example of geographical departmentalisation

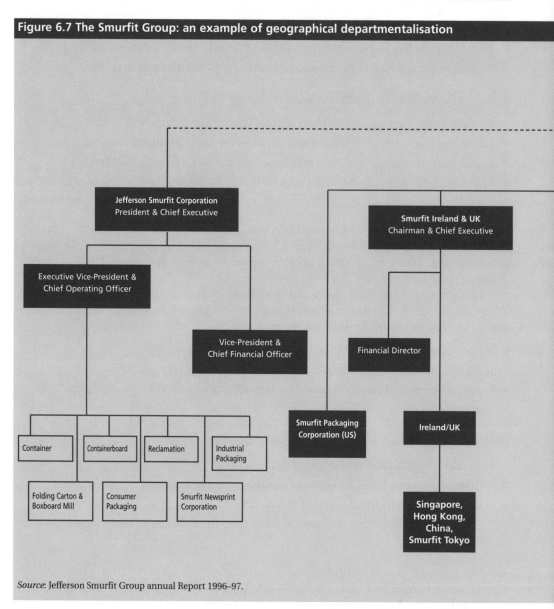

Source: Jefferson Smurfit Group annual Report 1996–97.

An example of a matrix structure is shown in Figure 6.8. As can be seen from the diagram employees belong to both a functional group, either engineering, sales or finance, and at the same time are also members of a particular project group.

Figure 6.8 An example of a matrix structure

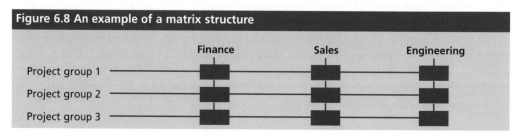

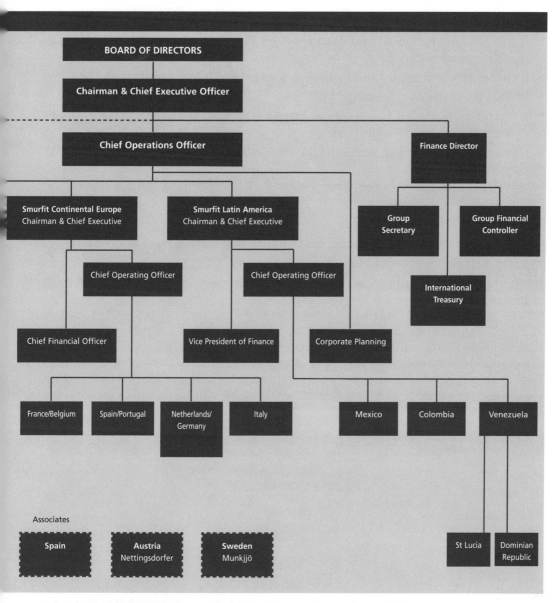

This form of structure has a number of important advantages:

▶ The interdisciplinary nature of the project teams contributes to a high rate of new-product innovation.

▶ It establishes the project manager as a focal point for all matters involving a particular project.

▶ It maximises the use of a limited pool of specialists.

▶ It makes specialised functional assistance available to all projects.

▶ It provides a good training ground for potential managers of diversified organisations.

According to Davis and Lawrence (1977) there are also a number of disadvantages:

▶ It leads to interpersonal and command conflict with the existence of a dual reporting relationship.
▶ It creates power struggles among project managers and functional area heads.
▶ It slows down decision making.
▶ It can promote narrow viewpoints associated with specific projects at the expense of wider organisational objectives.
▶ It can be difficult to trace accountability and authority.

Grinnel and Apple (1975) have argued that the matrix structure is only appropriate in certain circumstances:

▶ when the organisation produces short-run complex products
▶ when complicated product design needs innovation and timely completion
▶ when many kinds of sophisticated skills are needed
▶ when a rapidly changing marketplace requires changes even in the period between design and delivery.

The final form of departmentalisation is MIXED DEPARTMENTALISATION. Many large organisations use a mixture of the various approaches to gain the advantages associated with the different means of departmentalisation. For example, a bank might have a geographical structure in several countries with a functional structure in each bank. An example of mixed departmentalisation can by found in the ESB, as illustrated in Figure 6.9.

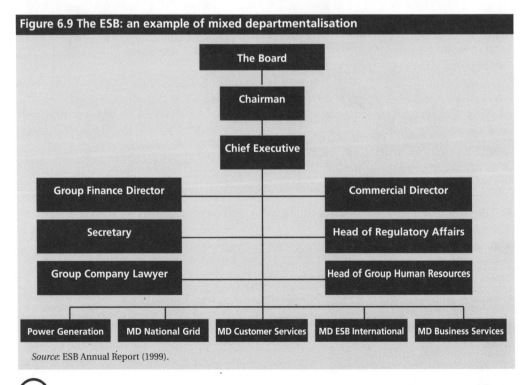

Figure 6.9 The ESB: an example of mixed departmentalisation

Source: ESB Annual Report (1999).

The organisational chart clearly shows that the structure is a mixture of functional and product/service departmentalisation. The main functions performed include finance, commercial, regulatory affairs and HRM, while the main product/service business units are Power Generation, National Grid, ESB International and Customer and Business Services.

6.3.2 Structural operation

Formalisation refers to the degree to which rules and procedures shape the jobs and tasks completed by employees. Organisations are said to be highly formalised if their work activities are governed by many rules and procedures. On the other hand, if the activities are governed by few rules and procedures then the structure is said to have low formalisation. According to Mintzberg (1979), the main purpose of formalisation is to predict and control how employees behave on the job.

High formalisation is designed to ensure standardisation of work and also to ensure a high quality product or service. Organisations involved in the manufacture or maintenance of transport vehicles typically display high levels of formalisation due to the requirements of stringent safety and engineering standards. On the negative side, high formalisation leads to a lack of AUTONOMY, freedom and initiative as people come to blindly follow rules without considering whether or not they benefit the organisation.

Decision making can either be centralised or decentralised. Centralisation refers to a decision-making policy where authority resides at the top of the organisation. Decentralisation, on the other hand, means that decisions are taken at all levels of the organisation. Centralisation ensures a greater uniformity of decisions as they are all taken by the same group. Those at the top of the organisations have the best knowledge and understanding of the issues facing the organisation and are, therefore, in a better position to take decisions. On the other hand, decentralisation ensures that lower-level problems can be solved and decisions taken on the spot. It also gives lower-level employees the opportunity to develop decision-making skills. It can also increase motivation, and spreads the work more evenly throughout the organisation.

Responsibility can be viewed as an obligation to do something under the expectation that some act or output will be achieved. In an organisational setting managers and supervisors are responsible for achieving certain organisational goals and also for the conduct of their subordinates. Passing on responsibility is usually referred to as DELEGATING. Most organisations delegate responsibility for certain tasks to those lower down in the organisation. Top managers cannot cope with responsibility for all tasks and consequently delegate.

AUTHORITY is power that has been legitimised within a certain social context (Pfeffer 1981), or in other words, the right to performance on command. In the case of organisational authority, the social context is the organisation and the authority is associated with the hierarchical position. This is referred to as position power or LEGITIMATE POWER. Specialists within the organisations may also possess power which arises from their expert knowledge. This is referred to as EXPERT POWER. Authority and responsibility are related in that for responsibility to be truly delegated the authority associated with such responsibility should also be passed on. However, frequently managers or supervisors pass on the responsibility for a certain task but not the authority to see it through. The end result is confusion and inefficiency.

Organisational structures, therefore, have clearly identifiable components. Structural configuration can be seen from an organisational chart and includes the division of labour, spans of control, hierarchy and departmentalisation. Structural operation focuses on the actual operation of the structure and includes formalisation, decision making, responsibility and authority.

6.4 Universal approaches to organisational design

- he in with people

Having discussed the main components of organisational structure it is possible to move on to consider the various approaches that have been taken in relation to organisational design. Structural components are the building blocks which are used to configure organisational design forms in much the same way as building materials are used to produce a house. The manner in which the components are drawn together produces different types of organisational design, in a similar fashion to building materials producing different house designs. Organisational design therefore, refers to the structural components and relationships which are used to achieve organisational goals.

Universal approaches to organisational structure argued that there was always one best way of structuring an organisation's activities. In this sense, they offered prescriptions which were designed to work in all situations. These approaches concentrate almost entirely on the formal organisation and its associated structure, and ignore the role of the informal organisation (for a discussion on the importance of the informal organisation see Krackhardt and Hanson 1993). Factors such as the organisation's external environment, size and technology were, therefore, largely ignored by advocates of the universal approach. The three most popular and influential universal approaches are the classic principles advocated by Fayol, Weber and Likert.

As we saw in Chapter 1, Fayol is considered the father of modern management. He was the first person to identify what roughly corresponds to the modern five functions of management—planning, organising, commanding, co-ordinating and controlling. Fayol also identified 14 principles of management which he considered vitally important for managers. Fayol's classical principles were widely applied in many organisations and therefore it is not surprising that they have had an impact on organisational structure.

Fayol's principles have served as a basis for the development of principles of organising. The application of Fayol's unity of command meant that employees should only receive instructions from one person, while the unity of direction meant that tasks with the same objective should have the same supervisor. Fayol also advocated division of labour and a clear system of responsibility. Taken together these principles have laid the foundation for both structural configuration and structural operation.

Over time these principles have been criticised for ignoring the human element in organisations, such as motivation, job satisfaction and the informal organisation. The application of these principles leads to a rather rigid mechanical form of structure, whereby people are slotted into areas irrespective of their abilities or motivation. Fayol also neglected to outline how his principles should be put into operation to ensure success. Finally, Fayol's principles were based not on scientific analysis but on his own personal experiences which have led many people to question their general applicability.

The second universal approach and probably the most well known and enduring is that of bureaucracy. Weber used the term 'bureaucracy' at the turn of the century to describe what he perceived as the preferred form of structure for business and government. Weber's bureaucratic organisation was designed to minimise the personal influence of individual employees in decision making, thereby co-ordinating the large number of decisions to be taken by the organisation. It was also designed to facilitate the allocation of scarce resources in an increasingly complex society. The bureaucratic structure advocated by Weber had six main characteristics which were discussed in Chapter 1 and are summarised here:

▶ division of labour
▶ managerial hierarchy
▶ formal selection
▶ career orientation
▶ formal rules and procedures
▶ impersonality.

Organisational structures based on Weber's principles of bureaucracy quickly developed. Such structures emphasised a narrow division of labour, narrow spans of control, many levels of hierarchy, limited responsibility and authority, centralised decision making and high formalisation. The bureaucratic structure was particularly popular in large organisations as it allowed such organisations to perform the various routine activities needed for effective operation. This structure became the dominant form of structure used by the majority of organisations, as it appeared to offer an efficient form of structure and was technically superior to any other form.

The bureaucratic structure has a number of important advantages:

▶ The strict division of labour advocated by Weber increased efficiency and expertise due to repetition of the task.
▶ The hierarchy of authority allowed a clear chain of command to develop which permitted the orderly flow of information and communication.
▶ Formal selection meant that employees were hired on merit and expertise which eliminated the nepotism associated with managerial practices in the early days of the Industrial Revolution.
▶ Career orientation ensured that career professionals would give the organisation a degree of continuity.
▶ Rules and procedures controlled employee performance and, therefore, increased productivity and efficiency.
▶ The impersonality of the organisation ensured that rules were applied across the board, eliminating personal biases and ensuring efficiency.

Over time bureaucracies have produced a number of unintended negative outcomes, particularly associated with individual behaviour. The main disadvantages are as follows:

▶ The behaviour of employees becomes segmented and insular, with employees only focusing on their own task with little awareness of what is going on in other areas. As a result, effective co-ordination becomes very difficult.

▶ The extensive rules and procedures used by the organisation can sometimes become ends in themselves. Consequently, obeying rules at all costs becomes important irrespective of whether such action is to the organisation's advantage or not.

▶ Bureaucracy also promotes rigidity and leads to a situation where the organisation is unable to react quickly or change when necessary. Bureaucratic organisations come to believe that what has worked well in the past will continue to do so.

▶ Delegation of authority and the insular nature of bureaucracy can lead to a situation where employees identify more with the objectives of work groups, at the expense of the objectives of the wider organisations. This is referred to as GOAL DISPLACEMENT.

▶ The extensive hierarchy makes communications particularly difficult. Middle managers frequently become overloaded with information, and bottlenecks are created.

▶ Innovation rarely occurs in a bureaucratic structure, due to the fact that new ideas take so long to filter up the hierarchy. Each level in the hierarchy acts as a further barrier.

▶ The strict division of labour can lead to routine and boring jobs where workers feel apathetic and demotivated.

▶ The extensive rules and procedures provide minimum standards above which employees normally will not go. So, instead of acting as a controlling device the rules actually reduce performance.

Despite its inherent disadvantages, the bureaucratic form of organisational structure has been very successful for large organisations operating in stable and simple external environments. Its rationality and efficiency are entirely suitable for this type of environment which may explain why so many organisations have used a bureaucratic structure.

The final universal approach to structure was advocated and developed by Likert (1967) with his concept of the 'human organisation'. As Likert had strongly criticised both Fayol and Weber for ignoring human factors, he emphasised the importance of employee participation, supportive relationships and overlapping work groups. Supportive relationships mean that employees should experience self-worth and importance at work. Overlapping work groups are work groups linked together by managers. Such managers also belong to management groups, which facilitate co-ordination throughout the organisation. Likert believed that the most successful structure was one composed of highly cohesive groups, aligned with organisational goals by effective co-ordination and communication. To highlight his arguments Likert developed four systems of organising as follows:

❶ exploitative authoritarian

❷ benevolent authoritarian

❸ consultative authoritarian

❹ participative group.

System 1, exploitative authoritarian, corresponds to the classical bureaucratic structure. Managers in this system are autocratic with little trust in subordinates.

Decision making is centralised and communication takes place from the top downwards. System 2 managers tend to have patronising confidence and trust in employees, motivating through rewards and fear of punishment. Within this system there is limited delegation of decision making and some upward communication. In System 3, managers have substantial trust in employees and try to use employee opinions. Motivation is achieved through rewards and occasional punishment. Decision making is somewhat decentralised and both upward and downward communication takes place. System 4 was the most preferred structure advocated by Likert and consisted of eight key characteristics:

▶ Managers and leaders have trust in subordinates and their ideas.
▶ The organisation recognises and channels employee motivations towards organisational goals.
▶ Communication is both vertical and horizontal and occurs frequently.
▶ Much interaction and influence occurs between work groups.
▶ Decisions are made throughout the organisation in a decentralised manner.
▶ Goals are set by work groups.
▶ All levels are involved in the control process.
▶ Top management set high-performance goals for the organisation.

System 4 heavily contradicts both the unity of command and the hierarchical chain of command. Likert believed that work groups should overlap horizontally and vertically and he favoured a 'linking pin' concept of overlapping groups for co-ordination, rather than the hierarchical chain of command, as shown in Figure 6.10.

Figure 6.10 Likert's overlapping work groups: the linking pin organisation

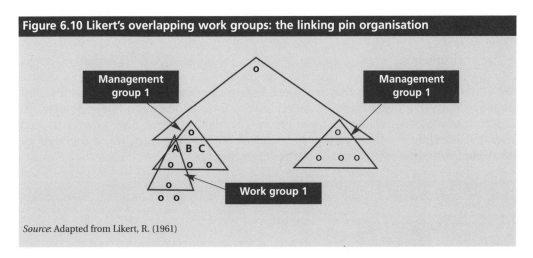

Source: Adapted from Likert, R. (1961)

Managers serve as linking pins between the various workgroups. Each manager (except those at the top of the organisation) is a member of two groups—a work group which s/he manages and a management group composed of the manager's peers and colleagues. For example, manager A is both a member of work group A and management group 1. Co-ordination and communication are facilitated by managers who perform the linking function by sharing problems and information. Likert, therefore, firmly believed that people worked best in highly cohesive work groups linked together by managers.

While Likert focuses on human aspects, his approach as been criticised for focusing exclusively on individuals and groups and not dealing with structural factors (Katz and Kahn 1978). The cause-and-effect relationship between System 4 and positive outcomes has also been questioned. Miner (1982) has argued that the positive elements such as high productivity and positive attitudes could have already been present in the organisation and facilitated the introduction of the System 4 structure rather than being outcomes of the approach.

Taken as a whole, the universal approaches to structure, while laying the foundations for further development and analysis, were heavily flawed. Both Fayol and Weber concentrated too heavily on formal aspects of the organisation which led to a rigid mechanistic type of structure. At the other extreme, Likert focused too heavily on individuals and groups to the detriment of concrete structural principles. All three approaches, in advocating universal principles, ignored the role of the organisations size, technology and external environment.

6.5 Contingency approaches to organisational design

Contingency approaches to organisational design became popular in the 1950s and 1960s and were developed to overcome many of the inadequacies associated with the universal approaches. Essentially contingency approaches argue that there is no one best way of structuring an organisation. The most appropriate structure depends on a number of contingencies or circumstances, the four most popular being:

▶ size

▶ organisational life cycle

▶ technology

▶ the environment.

CONTINGENCY THEORY argues that the most appropriate structure for an organisation depends on its size, organisational life cycle, technology and environment (referred to as STRUCTURAL IMPERATIVES), as shown in Figure 6.11. Each of these imperatives has been widely researched by different theorists and no single theorist or researcher can be attributed with the formulation of contingency theory.

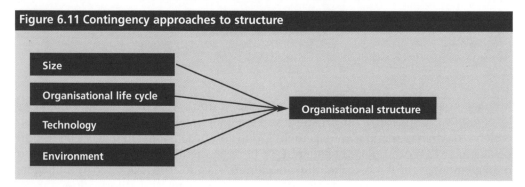

Figure 6.11 Contingency approaches to structure

6.5.1 Size

The size imperative argues that the most appropriate structure for an organisation is determined by its size. Kimberly (1976) has argued that when considering the issue of size, the measurement of size is important and can include employees, profit, turnover and sales. Larger organisations are generally more complex and bureaucratic (Blau and Schoenherr 1971). According to Robey (1991), when compared to smaller organisations, larger organisations have a number of important differences (see Figure 6.12):

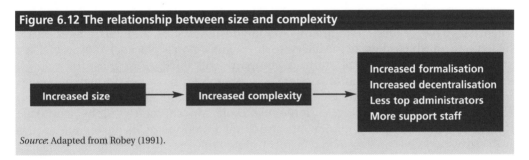

Figure 6.12 The relationship between size and complexity

Increased size → Increased complexity →
- Increased formalisation
- Increased decentralisation
- Less top administrators
- More support staff

Source: Adapted from Robey (1991).

▶ Large organisations are more complex. More specialisation of labour exists and groups of specialists develop, which makes the organisation more difficult to co-ordinate and control. As a result, more hierarchical levels are created to ensure that spans do not become too large.

▶ Large organisations have more formalisation. To handle increased complexity organisations typically become more bureaucratic and create more rules and procedures to ensure efficiency.

▶ Larger organisations tend to be more decentralised. Due to its size, decisions get pushed down to lower levels where appropriate information is readily available.

▶ Larger organisations have more top administrators arising from increased formalisation and more support staff due to the increased need for co-ordination and communication.

Increased size, therefore, leads to more complexity which in turn leads to more bureaucratic structures to facilitate control (Robey 1991). Size is an important contingency that determines the most appropriate type of structure. As the organisation increases in size, the original structure is simply unable to handle the complexity. Similarly, a small organisation does not need so many bureaucratic structures and controls to operate effectively. While the role of size in relation to an organisation's structure is widely accepted, Hall *et al.* (1967) have argued that a more accurate picture is painted from an examination of both size and technology. So, while size on its own is important, other issues also need consideration.

6.5.2 Organisational life cycle

All organisations go through a clearly identifiable cycle which has been termed the 'organisational life cycle'. The life cycle refers to the various stages through which organisations progress as they evolve and develop over time. Many models of the organisational life cycle have been developed (see Greiner 1972; Katz and Kahn 1978; Quinn and Cameron 1983; Bluedorn 1993), most of which point to the existence of four key stages in the life of an organisation:

❶ **Birth and creation**—the organisation is initially established.

❷ **Youth and growth**—the youthful organisation expands its operations and resources.

❸ **Mid-life**—the organisation becomes more stable.

❹ **Maturity**—the organisation has reached stability and may enter into decline.

Theorists have argued that organisational design issues and challenges differ depending on which stage of the life cycle the organisation is placed. For example, key structural issues for a small start-up company will differ from those of a large, established, mature organisation. Generally, as organisations evolve through the stages in the life cycle they become larger and more bureaucratic. According to Baker and Cullen (1993) the early stages of the life cycle are characterised by work-role delineation, policy implementation and structural development. As the organisation is in its early stages it is not hampered by institutional roles or the momentum associated with older organisations and as a result structures are changeable. In the second and third stages of the life cycle organisations grow and begin to experience problems with co-ordination and control. To increase efficiency, roles become more specialised and jobs more differentiated and both formal and informal rules increase (Quinn and Cameron 1983). In the fourth stage organisations face more complex internal and external environments. Institutionalised rules, regulations and formal structures are further developed. Organisations in the final stage of the life cycle may enter into decline and reduce significantly in size. Such organisations typically occupy narrow, long-standing niches and have well-established relationships with customers.

Clearly an organisation's position in the life cycle will have an impact on the types of structural issues which confront it. The size imperative, discussed earlier, is also related to the organisational life cycle in that it is common for organisations to increase their size as they go through stages 1 to 3 of the life cycle and then to reduce in size as they reach maturity and decline. Therefore, the already established relationship between size and structure is further developed and made more significant by the role of the organisational life cycle.

6.5.3 Technology

The most influential work within the technology imperative was completed by Woodward (1958 and 1965). Woodward sought to examine whether spans of control and hierarchical levels have universal application. She studied the performance and structure of 100 UK manufacturing organisations and concluded that different technologies create different kinds of demands on organisations, which are met by different types of structure. In other words, the most appropriate structure was dependent upon the technology used.

Woodward identified three different types of technology:

▶ UNIT PRODUCTION occurs where one or a small number of finished goods are produced according to a customer specification; for example, tailor-made clothes or specially printed cards or invitations.

▶ MASS PRODUCTION occurs where large batches of standardised goods are produced on an assembly line by assembling parts in a particular way; for example, car manufacturers.

▶ CONTINUOUS PROCESS PRODUCTION occurs where raw materials are transformed into finished goods using a production system whereby the composition of the raw material changes; for example, the manufacture of pharmaceuticals.

Based on this classification Woodward found each technology was associated with a particular form of structure as shown in Figure 6.13. For example, organisations using unit production technology had flatter structures, fewer managers and smaller spans, than organisations using a continuous process technology.

Figure 6.13 Woodward's relationship between technology and structure

Unit production	Flat structures
	Few managerial employees
	Few policies
	Medium-sized spans of control
Mass production	Wide spans of control
	Distinctions between line and staff units
	High formalisation
Continuous process production	Tall structures
	Narrow spans of control
	High number of managers

Woodward concluded that successful organisations displayed an appropriate fit between the technology used and the structure. Burns and Stalker (1961) also investigated the relationship between technology and structure. They examined 20 manufacturing organisations in the UK, and came to the conclusion that the rate of technological change determined the most suitable structure for an organisation. If the rate of technological change is slow, then the most suitable form of structure is a mechanistic one. On the other hand, if the rate of technological change is fast then an organic structure is more appropriate. The characteristics of both mechanistic and organic structure are shown in Figure 6.14.

Figure 6.14 Characteristics of mechanistic and organic structures

Mechanistic
Hierarchical structure
Vertical information systems
Employees instructed on work directions by supervisors
Knowledge and information resides at the top

Organic
Network Structure
Lateral communications
Work directions issued through advice and communications
Information and knowledge dispersed throughout the organisation

The Aston Studies conducted by Hickson, Pugh and Pheysey (1969) found an association between size, technology and organisational structure. They found that technology affected the structure of smaller organisations more. In large organisations they found that structure depended more on size than on technology. It would, therefore, appear that size and technology are both important elements in determining an organisation's structure and should be considered together.

In addition to the actual technologies it is also possible to examine the degree and type of technological interdependence within an organisation. Technological interdependence refers to the degree of co-ordination necessary between departments and work groups to successful transfer inputs into outputs (Keller 1994). Different technologies have different types of internal interdependence. Three types of technological interdependence exist as organisations go through their transformation processes:

▶ **Pooled interdependence** involves a minimal amount of information and resource sharing within or between departments as illustrated in Figure 6.15. Each department or work unit operates in an independent manner towards the achievement of a specific output. An example of pooled interdependence can be found in banking organisations.

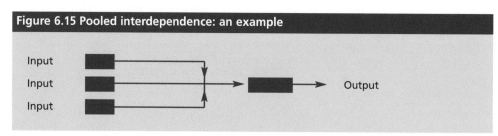

Figure 6.15 Pooled interdependence: an example

Organisations using pooled interdependence achieve co-ordination by the establishment of standards and rules for each department or work area.

▶ **Sequential interdependence** exists when there is a flow of information and resources between departments and work groups. The output of one area is the input of another and as a result some areas depend on others for output before they can begin their work operations. Sequential interdependence is found in car manufacturing and is shown in diagrammatic form in Figure 6.16.

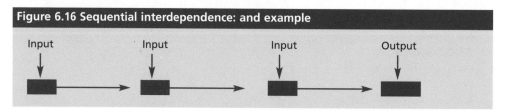

Figure 6.16 Sequential interdependence: and example

To ensure co-ordination organisation using sequential interdependence must have rules in place to schedule when parts arrive and leave each work area.

▶ **Reciprocal interdependence** occurs when information and resources are passed back and forth between work groups and departments until the work is completed.

Each area depends on others and is in turn depended upon for work flow. An example is shown in Figure 6.17. Hospitals use this form of interdependence. Co-ordination is achieved by mutual adjustment achieved through regular work group meetings.

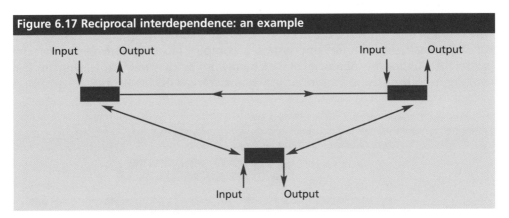

Figure 6.17 Reciprocal interdependence: an example

Each type of technology presents organisations with different structural challenges and leads to differences in organisational design. Organisations involved in the service sector have different technologies compared to the typical manufacturing-type technologies discussed above. As they produce a service rather than a product they are faced with a different set of structural challenges. It is possible to distinguish between routine and non-routine service technologies (Hellriegal and Slowm 1996).

Routine service technologies are used by service organisations operating in stable environments with customers who are sure of their needs. Examples of organisations operating routine service technologies include retail and fast food outlets. In these cases the tasks are standardised and relatively simple, with close customer contact for short periods of time.

In contrast, non-routine service technologies are used by service organisations operating in a complex environment with customers who are not always aware of their needs. Tasks are not standardised and in many cases each client may demand something slightly different. Examples include advertising agencies. Organisations using non-routine service technologies tend to have organic structures with decentralised decision making coupled with informal rules and procedures. Routine service technologies are more mechanistic in nature with low specialisation and centralised decision making.

As we have seen, both the type of technology and the degree of technological interdependence has an impact on the types of structure that organisations use.

6.5.4 The environment

All organisations operate within an external environment. It is, therefore, an important area to consider when designing an organisation's structure. The environmental imperative argues that organisations face different types of environments which determine the most appropriate type of structure. Duncan (1972) has identified two factors along which environments differ—the rate of environmental change and ENVIRONMENTAL COMPLEXITY.

The rate of environmental change facing an organisation can either be fast or slow. In a DYNAMIC ENVIRONMENT, things change rapidly and it is difficult for managers to forecast the future and plan effectively. Static environments, on the other hand, are characterised by less rapid change. In the current business environment, very few organisations operate within a static environment.

Environments also differ depending on the degree of complexity. In a simple environment only a few factors need to be considered before making a decision, all of which are easily identifiable. In contrast, a complex environment means that many factors have to be considered, all of which may not be easy to identify. Duncan (1972) combined both of these factors into a single framework measuring ENVIRONMENTAL UNCERTAINTY as shown in Figure 6.18

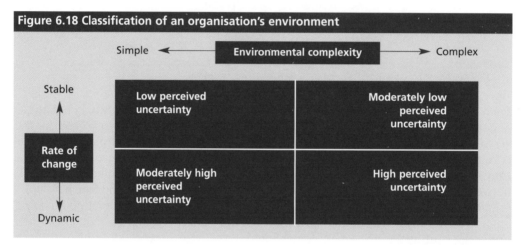

Figure 6.18 Classification of an organisation's environment

This framework, in using environmental complexity and the rate of change, allows an organisation to assess the degree of environmental uncertainty that it is facing. Environmental uncertainty exists when managers have very little information about events in the environment and their potential impact on the organisation, and corresponds to the uncertainty condition associated with decision making. As is seen in Figure 6.18, organisations whose environment is characterised by little change and is simple in nature, face a low perceived environmental uncertainty, whereas those facing a lot of environmental change and a complex environment face high perceived uncertainty in their external environment. Examples of industries facing high uncertainty include the airline, computer and telecommunications industries.

It has been established that organisational environments have different character-istics. Therefore, it is important that an organisation clearly identifies what type of external environment it operates within. Having done that, it can consider the structure most appropriate for that set of environmental conditions. The environment imperative, therefore, argues that the most suitable structure depends on the nature of the external environment. Lawrence and Lorsch (1969), both Harvard professors, made an important contribution to the study of the relationship between the external environment and organisational structure.

Lawrence and Lorsch examined the relationship between the external environment and two elements of an organisation's internal structure—differentiation and integration. Differentiation arises from job specialisation and the division of labour and is the extent to which an organisation's activities are structured into separate areas which are different from each other. Differentiation is high when there are many different departments, sub-units and specialists who all complete different tasks. Lawrence and Lorsch found that organisations with a complex uncertain environment (plastics industry) developed a high degree of differentiation in their structures. Organisations operating within a stable environment (container industry) used much lower levels of differentiation. Organisations operating in an environment mid-way between the other two had intermediate levels of differentiation.

Lawrence and Lorsch found the structural difference that distinguished successful from less successful organisations. They referred to this as integration and found that in complex environments demanding high differentiation, high integration was also found in successful organisations. Integration is the degree to which differentiated units work together and co-ordinate their divided efforts. While all organisations need integration to achieve organisational goals, it becomes more difficult if a high level of differentiation is also needed in line with environmental demands. Lawrence and Lorsch found that organisations in complex environments were more likely to fail if they appropriately differentiated but neglected to integrate.

These researchers concluded that the nature of the external environment influenced the most appropriate form of structure. In stable and static environments organisations needed less specialisation and division of labour, and consequently integration to achieve organisational goals is easier. On the other hand, those involved in complex and uncertain environments needed more differentiation, and consequently overall integration is more difficult.

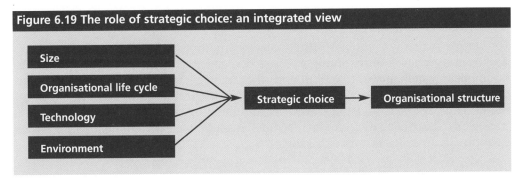

Figure 6.19 The role of strategic choice: an integrated view

Size

Organisational life cycle

Technology

Environment

Strategic choice → Organisational structure

In addition to the four main structural imperatives another dimension needs to be examined—that of STRATEGY and the role of strategic choice. Theorists like Chandler (1962) have highlighted the link between the strategy employed by the organisation and its structure. Chandler argued that structure followed strategy, observing that growth strategies were normally accompanied by decentralisation through a division-alised structure. Managers and decision makers also affect the structure of the organisation in that they assess the environment, technology and size factors, before deciding on a particular strategy, and in this sense form an intermediary stage between the imperatives and structure. Figure 6.19 shows how strategic choice follows on from an assessment of the structural imperatives and leads to a decision about which form of structure to adopt. Bobbitt and Ford (1980) have argued that managerial choice in relation to structure is determined by the organisation's purposes and goals, the imperatives and the manager's personality, value system and experience. Strategic choice theorists conclude that for organisations to be successful there must be a fit between the structure, imperatives and the strategy.

Contingency theory has been criticised on a number of grounds. It has been argued that it is impossible to identify all of the contingencies facing an organisation. In addition, it is unrealistic to expect managers to observe a change in one of the contingencies and to make a rational structural change. Schoonoven (1981) has also criticised contingency theory for containing vague language that blurs the nature of the interactions being studied and makes it more difficult for researchers to test the theories. In defence of contingency theory Donaldson (1987) has argued that it is logical and reasonable to expect that organisations will respond to poor performance caused by a change in one or more contingencies. Despite its criticisms, contingency theory has remained popular.

6.6 The Mintzberg framework

Building on contingency theory, Mintzberg (1979, 1981) identified a range of structures and situations in which they are most commonly found. Mintzberg argued that a vitally important consideration in structuring an organisation was to achieve a match or fit between the various parts. There must be a fit between the structure, the structural imperatives (size, technology, environment and organisational life cycle), the organisations strategy and the various components of structure (co-ordination, division of labour, formalisation and decision making). If these elements do not fit together, then the structure will be ineffective (Mintzberg 1981). Mintzberg identified five types of structure.

6.6.1 Simple structure

The simple structure is found in small relatively new organisations that operate in a simple and dynamic environment. Direct supervision is the main co-ordinating mechanism, which means that a supervisor or manager co-ordinates the activities of employees. The structure is quite organic with little specialisation and little formalisation. The CEO holds most of the power and decision-making authority. Due to its simple yet dynamic environment, it must react quickly to changing events. An example is a small local shop or a garage.

6.6.2 Machine bureaucracy

A machine bureaucracy corresponds to a typical bureaucracy and can be found in large mature organisations operating in a stable and simple environment. Standardisation of work processes is the main co-ordinating mechanism, which means that the methods employees use to transform inputs into outputs are standardised. There is strong division of labour, high formalisation and centralised decision making. Due to its stable and simple environment the machine bureaucracy does not have to change or adapt quickly. An example of a machine bureaucracy is the civil service or any large mass production organisation.

6.6.3 Professional bureaucracy

Professional bureaucracies are usually professional organisations located in complex and stable environments. The primary co-ordinating mechanism is the standardisation of employee skills which means that the skills or inputs into the various processes are standardised. The division of labour is based on professional expertise and little formalisation exists. Decision making is decentralised and occurs where the expertise is based. An example of a professional bureaucracy is a hospital or university.

6.6.4 Divisionalised structure

The divisionalised structure is found in old and large organisations operating in simple and stable environments with many distinct markets. It could in fact, be a machine bureaucracy divided into the different markets that it serves. Decision making is split between headquarters (HQ) and the divisions, and standardisation of outputs is the main co-ordinating mechanism used. Due to the fact that control is required by HQ a machine bureaucracy tends to develop in each of the divisions. The most famous example of a divisionalised structure can be found in General Motors, who pioneered the design in the 1920s.

6.6.5 Adhocracy

An adhocracy is found in young organisations operating in complex and dynamic environments, normally in a technical area. Co-ordination is achieved by mutual adjustment, which means that employees use informal communication to co-ordinate with each other. Decision making is spread throughout the organisation, and there is little formalisation. Specialists are placed in project teams to achieve the work of the organisation. This form of structure is designed to encourage innovation which is very difficult to do with the other structures. Examples of organisations that use adhocracies in certain areas of their organisation are Johnson and Johnson, Proctor and Gamble and Iona Technologies.

Mintzberg's framework provides guidelines for the choice of an appropriate structure depending on the age of the organisation, its external environment and the nature of its employees.

6.7 Recent trends in organisation design

Trends.

There have been two major evolutions in organisational structure to date. The first occurred in the early 1900s and involved a recognition of the independent roles and function of management and ownership. The second evolution took place some 20 years later and introduced the command and control organisation, more commonly called a bureaucracy, with which we are so familiar today. Now organisations are coming to terms with the third evolutionary period. The shift this time is from bureaucratic, hierarchical forms to more flexible and adaptable forms. Clegg (1992) has referred to this as a move from modernist to post-modernist forms.

Bureaucracy has been the dominant form of organisation structure used by organisations. The main reason for its dominance is that it is a rational and efficient form of structure when the environment is simple and stable. However, when the external environment becomes complex and dynamic, the rigidity of the bureaucratic structure hampers its ability to be flexible and adaptive. Recent trends in organisational structure have centred on the need to achieve competitive advantage in an increasingly complex, dynamic and competitive environment.

The extent of the changes in the business environment have meant that bureaucratic and hierarchical structures are no longer effective. Such forms of structure thrive on stability and certainty, a state which characterised previous environments but not the environment within which most organisations now operate. The bureaucratic model, with its extended hierarchy, narrowly segmented job design, rule-bound procedures and lack of individual autonomy and responsibility, is no longer appropriate for effective organisation. The structures and systems associated with such organisational forms do not adapt readily to change and are not flexible enough to anticipate change.

Many of the developments have built on the idea advocated by contingency theory and further developed by Mintzberg—that the nature of the business environment shapes the most appropriate form of structure. Drucker (1992) has argued that, due to the nature of the current business environment, organisations are now undertaking fundamental changes to their structures. To achieve competitive advantage organisations must be flexible and adaptive, to respond to and anticipate change in the business environment. Many organisations have looked to organisational structure as a means of providing such flexibility and adaptability. As a result of the nature of the business environment and the ineffectiveness of traditional bureaucratic structure, organisations have experimented with four main structural trends, as shown in Figure 6.20 (Tiernan 1993).

Figure 6.20 Recent trends in organisational structure

1. Changes in job design
2. Flatter hierarchies
3. Team mechanisms
4. Increased responsibility and decision making authority

The first trend has been towards flatter, less hierarchical, structures. Reducing the layers in the hierarchy is designed to reduce costs, free up information flows, speed up communications and allow more innovative ideas to flourish. Organisations, therefore, are reducing hierarchy to more manageable levels. However, hierarchy has not been eliminated totally as this would be both impractical and in contravention of all time-tested laws of management and leadership. An example of an organisation that has reduced levels in the hierarchy is Team Aer Lingus. Team was the former Maintenance and Engineering (M & E) Department of Aer Lingus and operated with nineteen hierarchical levels in the late 1980s. After its establishment as a separate subsidiary the number of levels was reduced to seven, most of which occurred at the middle-management level.

Organisations have also widened the traditional division of labour. Previously individuals were boxed into segmented and isolated work tasks with little knowledge or training in other areas. Due to the need to be more flexible, many organisations have now widened job categories and trained employees to be multiskilled. An example of increased job scope can be seen at Dublin Bus with its introduction of driver-only buses. Previously both a driver and a conductor were used to operate the service. Currently the driver completes both tasks, thereby having a wider job design.

Changing attitudes among the workforce has led to the creation of new structures which allow individuals more responsibility and authority over their work and a larger role in decision making. In order to meet these demands organisations have pushed responsibility downwards. For example, workers have been allowed to inspect work where previously they were only allowed to manufacture products. Amdahl Ireland have introduced more participative decision-making structures to ensure that employees are more involved and that their skills are fully used.

The final trend has been to move away from segmented and isolated work to team-based operations. Organisations are experimenting with task forces for short-term problem-solving exercises and with cross-functional and cross-hierarchical teams to achieve longer-term objectives. Organisations are also introducing team mechanisms for completing tasks. Such team mechanisms have been called SELF-MANAGED TEAMS or autonomous work groups and they complete the work of the organisation with the guidance of a supervisor. For example, Bausch and Lomb who manufacture sunglasses and contact lenses have begun to introduce self-managed teams to complete tasks in a teams rather than in isolation. As organisations have experimented with these four structural trends, new types of organisational structures have emerged.

6.8 New forms of organisational design

No new means of managing an organisation arrives fully fledged and ready to be implemented, but generally evolves as a result of the actions taken by innovative organisations. In this respect three different types of structure demand our attention:

6.8.1 The network organisation

According to Baker (1992) a network organisation is a market mechanism that allocates people and resources to problems and projects in a decentralised manner. The network organisation seeks to manage complex relationships between people and departments within the organisation and sometimes groups such as suppliers and customers external to the organisation. Such relationships are established through lateral communication, decision making and goal setting. Rather than allocating responsibility and authority in line with the traditional hierarchy, the network organisation mutually shares authority, responsibility and control among people and units that facilitates the co-operation necessary to achieve organisational goals (Powell 1990; Chisholm 1998). A key element of the network organisation is its ability to redesign itself-to accommodate new tasks and problems and changing environmental circumstances. The network organisation is thus designed to be flexible enough to change as tasks and goals change (McCann 1991). Organisations which have experimented with such forms of internal networks include General Motors Saturn Corporation and Ericsson of Sweden.

The use of networks to establish relationships with external groups has also become popular. Such networks frequently include suppliers, customers, trade unions and even competitors. In some cases these networks can be used to establish alliances with traditional competitors. An example of an external network is shown in Figure 6.21.

A dynamic network is arranged so that its major component parts can be assembled or reassembled to meet changing requirements. The traditional business functions such as manufacturing, marketing and distribution are no longer carried out by a single organisation but by independent organisations within the network. Each part of the network is therefore able to pursue its distinctive competence. Due to the fact that each business function is not necessarily part of the same organisation, a broker is used to assemble and co-ordinate the various contributions. The various networks are held together by contracts, which are market mechanisms, rather than a hierarchy. The use of information technology, whereby networks can hook themselves together in a continually updated information system further facilitates such developments.

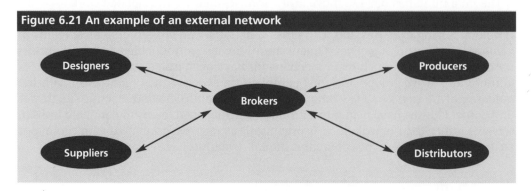

Figure 6.21 An example of an external network

The illustration of an external network can be applied to the case of the manufacture of sports clothing. A sports kit could be designed in Italy for the North American market, specifically meeting its local demand, manufactured in Singapore, then sold and distributed by a transnational network. Each of the main functions, from design to manufacture, sales and distribution is conducted by a different organisation. More and more organisations are adopting this type of structure and it is a well-known fact that brand leaders such as Nike are not involved in the actual manufacture of their products.

There are some potential problems associated with the recent move towards network structures. While developments in information technology have facilitated the development of complex business contacts and relationships, these can become difficult to co-ordinate and control, posing difficulties for those involved with this form of structural design. In addition, there is little hands-on control as the network operations are geographically dispersed. Continuity can also be a problem for the network organisation as it constantly redefines itself-using different network partners.

6.8.2 The cluster organisation

The cluster organisation is a radical and innovative form of organisational structure in which groups of employees are arranged like grapes growing on a vine. A cluster is a group of employees from different disciplines who work together and are undifferentiated by rank or job title. No direct reporting relationships exist within the clusters and support areas only have a residual hierarchy.

The cluster is accountable for its business results and has a customer focus. It develops its own expertise, shares information broadly and pushes decisions towards the point of action. The central element of the cluster organisation is the business unit which is a profit centre. The cluster organisation contains other forms of clusters including project teams, alliance teams, change teams and STAFF UNITS. In the cluster organisation staff units run their own businesses selling to internal and external customers where possible.

Quinn Mills (1991) documents the case of British Petroleum Engineering (BPE) which he presents as a good example of a cluster organisation. BPE consists of 1000 professional engineers and support staff who provide technical support, engineering, procurement and contractual services to BP, its partners and outside organisations. Figure 6.22 illustrates the cluster structure found at BPE.

Figure 6.22 BPE: an example of a cluster organisation

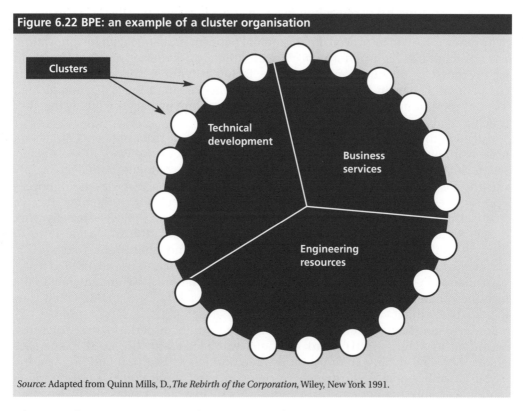

Source: Adapted from Quinn Mills, D., *The Rebirth of the Corporation*, Wiley, New York 1991.

Clusters of engineers, ranging from 30 to 60 members, form the core of the organisation. These clusters are supported by three functional areas—Business Services, Engineering Resources and Technology Development. Each cluster has one senior consultant whose responsibilities include co-ordinating and integrating between functional areas and cluster members. No direct reporting relationships exist within the cluster. Engineers, therefore, are expected to be self-managing on the basis of their skills and experience. Each of the three functional areas assigns individuals to service the clusters. Engineering Resources contain resource managers who review assignments and career progress. Business Services provide people to handle contracts and to solicit business on behalf of clients and Technology Development assigns people to handle technical issues.

The cluster organisation has become popular in professional organisations, but it is unlikely that the cluster organisation would suit all organisations. High-volume, low-variance activities are poorly suited to clusters since the work cannot be made more challenging and interesting. In such a situation there is little scope for increasing responsibility and discretion. It is also difficult to see how traditional assembly-line organisations could adopt such a structure as it would involve eliminating all hierarchy and job titles. The cluster organisation, therefore, may be the most appropriate structure for professional organisations rather than for mass-production organisations.

6.8.3 The high-performance organisation

The high-performance organisation has a distinctive structure which is designed to provide employees with skills, incentives, information and decision-making responsibility that will lead to improved organisational performance and facilitate innovation. The trend towards high-performance organisational structures is most noticeable in high-technology organisations and those facing stiff international and domestic competition. The main aim of the high-performance organisation is to generate high levels of commitment and involvement of employees and managers working together to achieve organisational goals (Lawler 1991).

Instead of the traditional structure of tasks, this form of structure concentrates on team work by introducing self-managed teams to achieve the work of the organisation. Such teams make decisions about the tasks to be completed and deal directly with the customer. In this way the structure ensures that even lower-levels employees have a direct relationship with customers or suppliers and, therefore, receive feedback and are held accountable for a product or service. Employees usually work in self-managing teams. The organisational structure is flatter but some form of hierarchy still exists. The structure is decentralised and built around customers, products or services. Task forces, study groups and other techniques are used to foster participation in decisions that affect the entire organisation. Also fundamental to the high-performance organisation is continuous feedback to participants about how they are performing.

Bord na Mona has in recent years experimented with high-performance structures. According to Magee (1991), Bord na Mona was faced with the need to increase productivity and quality, improve motivation and job satisfaction and improve the overall organisational performance. In order to meet these targets Bord na Mona introduced autonomous enterprise units (AEU). Instead of working in isolation employees became group members. Between four and six employees were selected as AEU leaders. Production and equipment was then assigned to the AEU along with the responsibility and authority to complete tasks. The AEUs are responsible for managing the seasonal workforce and are free to decide hours worked, allocation of work and the methods of work. Members of the AEUs are remunerated on a payment-by-results basis. In addition to the introduction of teams, Bord na Mona also reduced the levels in the hierarchy. The AEUs are then overlaid on the delayered hierarchy as shown in Figure 6.23.

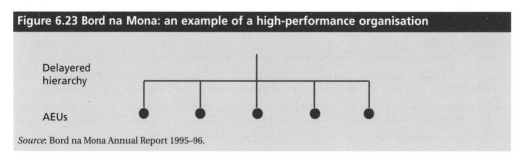

Figure 6.23 Bord na Mona: an example of a high-performance organisation

Delayered hierarchy

AEUs

Source: Bord na Mona Annual Report 1995–96.

6.9 Summary of key propositions

▶ Organising is the process of dividing the organisational tasks between groups, individuals and departments and co-ordinating their activities to achieve organisational goals. The pattern of how activities are divided and later co-ordinated is called organisational structure. Organisational structure is the system of task, reporting and authority relationships within which the work of the organisation is done.

▶ Organisational structure can be broken down into structural configuration and structural operation. Structural configuration is the size and shape of the structure. It includes the division of labour, spans of control, hierarchy and departmentalisation. Structural operation is the process of the structure and includes formalisation, decision making, responsibility and authority.

▶ Five main types of departmentalisation exist: functional; product; geographical; matrix; and mixed. The most suitable form of departmentalisation depends on the nature of the organisational activities.

▶ Traditional approaches to organisational design were universal in that they offered principles which were designed to work in all situations. The most popular universal approaches were Fayol's classical principles of management, Weber's bureaucracy and Likert's human organisation. All three theorists argued that their particular form of structure worked well for all organisations.

▶ In contrast to the universal approaches to design, contingency theory argues that there is no one best way to structure an organisation. The design depends on a number of contingencies: size; life cycle; technology; and the environment. Strategy and strategic choice has also recently been included in the theory. Despite its critics, contingency theory has remained popular.

▶ Mintzberg identifies a range of structures: a simple structure; a machine bureaucracy; a professional bureaucracy; a divisionalised structure; and an adhocracy. Mintzberg concludes that there must be a fit between the structure, the structural imperatives, the organisation's strategy and components of the structure.

▶ Bureaucracy has been the dominant form of structure since it became popular in the 1930s and 1940s. However, it is primarily suited to stable and simple environments. The external environment is currently complex and unstable and as a result bureaucracies have become less effective.

▶ Four main trends in organisational design have developed in response to the realisation that bureaucracy can no longer cope with a changing business environment. Hierarchical levels have been reduced, the division of labour has been widened, teams have been introduced and responsibility and decision-making authority has been pushed down the organisation.

▶ Three different forms of organisational design have been introduced depending on the degree of experimentation with the four trends. Network organisational structures have been created which are designed to manage complex relationships. Networks can be formed between work groups and departments; these are called internal networks. Networks can also be formed with outside organisations such as suppliers and customers, and these are called external networks. Networks are flexible and can be redesigned as circumstances change.

▶ Cluster organisations have also developed. Such organisational designs are arranged in clusters consisting of employees undifferentiated by job title or rank. No direct reporting relationships exist within the clusters who carry out the work of the organisation. Clusters deal directly with customers.

▶ Organisations have experimented with high-performance designs which are designed to provide employees with skills and responsibilities which will lead to improved performance. High-performance designs typically reduce hierarchy, introduce team-based work and increase responsibility and decision-making authority.

Discussion questions

❶ Explain the terms 'organising' and 'organisational structure'.

❷ Explain the terms 'division of labour', 'span of control' and 'hierarchy'.

❸ Explain the elements of structural configuration.

❹ Discuss the different types of departmentalisation an organisation can use. Which one do you think is most appropriate for a large organisation competing in many different and widespread markets?

❺ Critically evaluate the universal approaches to the study of organisational design.

❻ Examine the contingency approach to design. Which imperative do you think is most important in determining an organisation's structure?

❼ What role do strategy and strategic choice play in determining an organisation's design?

❽ Discuss Mintzberg's contention that effective structure arises from a fit between the structural imperatives, strategy and the components of the structure.

❾ Outline the most recent trends in organisational design. Find an example of a company that has introduced any of these changes.

❿ Why have bureaucracies become less efficient in the current business environment?

⓫ What is the difference between a network and a cluster organisation?

⓬ What are the key characteristics of the high-performance organisation? What is it designed to achieve?

Concluding case: Bureaucracy and the business environment at Team Aer Lingus (Team FLS)

The Maintenance and Engineering (M & E) Department of Aer Lingus,(now called Team FLS since it was purchased by FLS Aerospace) was established in 1936 to provide technical support for the newly formed national airline, Aer Lingus. It was involved in the maintenance and overhaul of the Aer Lingus fleet. Mirroring growth in the airline itself M & E grew in size and strength throughout the 1950s and 1960s, employing roughly 1000 maintenance craft workers. During the late 1960s M & E expanded into third-party maintenance and began to overhaul aircraft belonging to other airlines, especially those in the African region. By 1975 over 40 airlines were using the expertise of M & E, which now comprised 1500 employees.

The environment of the 1970s was quite stable and static for M & E with plenty of opportunities for them to break into the African market. M & E produced excellent technical quality for its customers and was reasonably fast at overhauling the aircraft. However, M & E was quite expensive but due to the fact that demand was strong customers were willing to accept this. Despite Aer Lingus making huge losses during this period, M & E made a steady profit and significantly contributed to the Aer Lingus group as a whole.

During this time M & E, like many other companies involved in maintenance, had a typically bureaucratic structure. The division of labour in M & E was very narrow with employees completing very narrow and specialised tasks. Eleven different trades or craft worker classifications existed in M & E, ranging from painters and carpenters to sheet-metal workers, electricians and mechanics. Each of these trades pursued narrowly defined tasks and never encroached on another trades working area. Spans of control were also very limited and stood at 3.5:1. This meant that for every 3.5 employees 1 person directly supervised their tasks. M & E was also very hierarchically based with 10 different rungs on the internal hierarchy ranging from the General Manager at the top to the tradesmen at the bottom. The Department was co-ordinated along functional lines.

Decision making was highly centralised with all but the most minor of decisions being taken at the top of the organisation. M & E was also highly formalised with many rules and procedures in operation. Both responsibility and authority were centralised at the top of the organisation. Employees were given virtually no authority and responsibility and were simply required to complete their work with no concern about anything else.

This bureaucratic structure worked very well for M & E during the 1960s and 1970s as can be seen from the fact that the Department continued to expand and make a profit. However, in the mid-1980s the business environment began to change rapidly. The introduction of new technology aircraft presented M & E with a challenge. The emergence of new high-technology aircraft (for example, the Boeing 737-300) resulted in a reduced demand for maintenance from all such aircraft types. These aircraft by their nature are more advanced and their designs have been refined over time and therefore they require less maintenance than older aircraft. Aer Lingus had already purchased two Boeing 737-300s and had put in place a fleet-replacement programme, whereby more new technology aircraft would be purchased.

The net result was that the Aer Lingus demand for maintenance was projected to decline substantially from demanding 320,000 man hours of maintenance in 1987 to an expected figure of 200,000 in the early 1990s. M & E was therefore faced with the realisation that Aer Lingus would need less maintenance in future and that such a trend would be reflected in the world-wide maintenance business, making it more difficult to attract and retain customers.

The nature of demand for maintenance also started to change, and the competitive position of M & E concerning its approach to the provision of products and services began to deteriorate. The aircraft types where M & E had particular strength were projected to decline significantly over the coming years. M & E was, therefore, under pressure to change the range of products and services catered for, to meet the changing nature of the demand. In addition, M & E were faced with the loss of their traditional business. M & E had, during the 1970s, relied heavily on a few African customers (who had accumulated bills of €38.9 million by 1986). However, such reliance became a problem in the mid-1980s when several existing African customers ceased trading with M & E. Many of them developed their own on-site maintenance facilities, such as Zambia and Nigeria Airways. Such indigenisation of skills (that is, native countries learning to overhaul their own aircraft), not only eroded traditional markets, but increased competition in the maintenance market.

World-wide maintenance capacity also started to increase. Like Aer Lingus, many major European airlines were modernising their fleet resulting in less demand for maintenance, and thereby, creating an increase in capacity in the marketplace, further increasing competition for M & E. In anticipation of the increased competition within the industry, many of M & Es competitors became more sophisticated and streamlined their approaches to maintenance. Alliances were becoming a major force in the market, diverting trade away from M & E. Significant alliances in Europe included KSSU (KLM, SAS, Swissair and UTA) and AFRAA (Association of African Airlines).

The demands of the customers were also changing. While quality considerations had always been important for customers, they now turned their attention to the areas of costs and TURNAROUND times. Increasingly customers demanded not only quality but quality at a low cost and at a fast pace. This created problems for M & E, due to the fact that the annual cost of maintaining the Aer Lingus fleet was too high. To be more competitive and meet changing requirements M & E needed to cut €19 million off net maintenance costs. They also needed to improve turnaround times.

Faced with these unprecedented changes in the industry environment Aer Lingus was faced with the growing realisation that their M & E section was uncompetitive in its current configuration. M & E made little attempt to differentiate itself from competitors, incorporated little or no cost strategy and was unfocused in that it attempted to overhaul as many types of aircraft as it could. M & E was therefore faced with a stark choice: it either had to change to meet new industry requirements, or remain as it was and face the consequences.

Case questions

❶ Why do you think that the bureaucratic structure worked well for M & E?

❷ Why, in the mid-1980s did the structure become less effective?

❸ Suggest new alternative forms of organisational design that could possibly be introduced into the organisation.

Keep up to date

Visit the FLS website at www.FLSAerospce.com.

Bibliography

Baker, W. (1992) 'The Network Organisation: Theory and Practice', in Nohria and Eccles (eds) *Networks and Organisations: Structure, Form and Action*. MA: HBS Press.

Baker, D. and Cullen, J. (1993) 'Administrative Reorganisation and Configurational Context: The Contingent Effects of Age, Size and Change in Size', *Academy of Management Journal*, 36, 1251–77.

Blau, P. and Schoenherr, R. (1971) *The Structure of Organisations*. New York: Basic Books.

Bluedorn, A. (1993) 'Pilgrims Progress: Trends and Convergence in Research on Organisational Size and Environments', *Journal of Management*, Summer, 163–91.

Bobbitt, H. and Ford, J. (1980) 'Decision Maker Choice as a Determinant of Organisational Structure', *Academy of Management Review*, 5 (1), 13-23.

Burns, T. and Stalker, G. (1961) *The Management of Innovation*. London: Tavistock.

Chandler, A. (1962) *Strategm and Structure: Chapters in the History of American Industrial Enterprise*. Mass: Mit Press.

Chisholm, R. (1998) *Developing Network Organisations: Learning from Practice and theory*. Reading, MA: Addison Wesely.

Clegg, R. (1992) 'Modernist and Post Modernist Organisations', in G. Salaman (ed.) *Human Resource Strategies*. London: Sage.

Davis, S. and Lawrence, P. (1977) *Matrix*. Reading, Mass.

Donaldson, L. (1987) 'Strategy and Structural Adjustment to Regain Fit and Performance: In Defence of Contingency Theory', *Journal of Management Studies*, 8, 1–24.

Drucker, P. (1992) 'The Coming of the New Organisation', *Harvard Business Review*, 66, 33–5.

Duncan, R. (1972) 'Characteristics of Organisations Environments and Perceived Uncertainty', *Administrative Science Quarterly*, 17, 313–27.

Fayol, H. (1949) *General and Industrial Management*, translation of *Administration Industrielle et Generale* (1916), London: Pitman.

Greiner,L. (1972) 'Evolution and Revolution as Organisations Grow', *Harvard Business Review* 50, 37–46.

Grinnel, S. and Apple, H. (1975) 'When Two Bosses are Better than One', *Machine Design*, 9 January.

Haimann, T. and Scott, W. (1970) *Management in the Modern Organisation*. Boston: Houghton Mifflin.

Hall, R., Haas, E., and Johnson N. (1967) 'Organisational Size, Complexity and Formalisation', *American Sociological Review*, 903–12.

Hellriegel, D. and Slowm, J. (1996) *Management*, Ohio: South Western College Publishing.

Hickson, D., Pugh, D., and Pheysey, D. (1969) 'Operations Technology and Organisational Structure: An Empirical Reappraisal', *Administrative Science Quarterly*, 14, 378–94.

Katz, D. and Kahn, R. (1978) *The Social Psychology of Organisations*. New York: Wiley.

Keller, R. (1994) 'Technology Information Processing Fit and the Performance of R & D Project Groups: A Test of Contingency Theory', *Academy of Management Journal*, 37, 167–79.

Kimberly, R. (1976) 'Organisational Size and the Structuralism Perspective : A Review, Critique and Proposal', *Administrative Science Quarterly*, 21 (2), 571–97.

Koontz, H. and O'Donnell, C. (1964) *Principles of Management*. New York: McGraw-Hill.

Krackhardt, D. and Hanson, J. (1993) 'Informal Networks: The Company behind the Chart', *Harvard Business Review*, July–August, 104–11.

Lawler, E. (1991) 'Executive Behaviour in High Involvement Organisations', in Kilmann, R. (ed.) *Making Organisations Competitive*. CA: Jossey Bass.

Lawrence, R. and Lorsch, J. (1969) *Organisation and Environment: Managing Differentiation and Integration*. Illinois: Irwin.

Likert, R. (1967) *The Human Organisation: Its Management and Values*. New York: McGraw-Hill.

Magee, C. (1991) 'A Typical Work Forms and Organisational Flexibility'. Paper presented to the IPA Personnel Conference, 6 March.

McCann, J. (1991) 'Design Principles for an Innovating Company', *Academy of Management Executive*, 5 (2), 76–93.

Miles, C. and Snow, C. (1986) 'Network Organisations: New Concepts and New Forms', *California Management Review*, 28 (3), 62–73.

Miner, J. (1982) *Theories of Organisational Structure and Process*. Illinois: Dryden.

Mintzberg, H. (1979) *The Structuring of Organisations: A Synthesis of Research*. News Jersey: Prentice Hall.

Mintzberg, H. (1981) 'Organisational Design: Fashion or Fit', *Harvard Business Review*, 59, 103–16.

Moorehead, G. and Griffin, R. (1989) *Organisational Behaviour*. Mass: Houghton Mifflin.

Nadler, D. and Tushman, M. (1997) *Competing by Design: The Power of Organisational Architecture*. New York: Oxford University Press.

Pfeffer, J. (1981) *Power in Organisations*. Mass: Pittman.

Powell, W. (1990) 'Neither Market nor Hierarchy: Network Forms of Organisation', in Staw, B. and Cummings, L. (eds) *Research in Organisational Behaviour*. CA: JAI Press.

Quinn Mills, D. (1991) *The Rebirth of the Corporation*. New York: Wiley.

Quinn, R. and Cameron, K. (1983) 'Organisational Life Cycles and Shifting Criteria of effectiveness: Some Preliminary evidence', *Management Science*, 29, 33–51.

Robey, D. (1991) *Designing Organisations*. Illinois: Irwin.

Schoonoven, C. (1981) 'Problems with Contingency Theory: Testing Assumptions Hidden within the Language of Contingency Theory', *Administrative Science Quarterly*, 26, 349–77.

Sherman, J. and Smith, H. (1984) 'The Influence of Organisational Structure on Intrinsic and Extrinsic Motivation', *Academy of Management Review*, 27 (4), 877–85.

Tiernan, S. (1993) 'Innovations in Organisational Structure', *IBAR*, 14 (2), 57–69.

Urwick, L. (1956) 'The Span of Control: Some Facts about the Fables', *Advanced Management*, 21, 39–49.

Van Fleet, D. and Bedeian, A. (1977) 'A History of the Span of Management', *Academy of Management Review*, July, 356–72.

Weber, M. (1947) *The Theory of Social and Economic Organisation*. Henderson and Talcott translation. Free Press, New York.

Woodward, J. (1958) *Management and Technology: Problems of Progress in Industry*. London: HM Stationary Office.

Woodward, J. (1965) *Industrial Organisations: Theory and Practice*. London: Oxford University Press.

Chapter 7
Managing Human Resources

....

Managing human resources is one of the key elements in the co-ordination and management of an organisation. An organisation's workforce represents one of its most valuable resources. However, human resources are also potentially the most difficult to manage, principally because of individual differences. Nevertheless, it is said that the extent to which the workforce is managed effectively may be a critical factor in improving and sustaining organisational effectiveness and efficiency and, according to Mabey and Salaman (1995:1), 'may offer ways out of the perennial characteristic dysfunctions of organisations, dysfunctions and limitations which are all too apparent to us as employees, consumers, citizens, shareholders, human beings'. In this vein, the management of the human resource may be one of those pivotal factors that distinguishes the high-performance organisation from the average performer (Morley and Garavan 1993; Hanna 1988, Buchanan and McCalman 1989). Indeed, Flood *et al.* (1996) in their treatise on managing without traditional methods argue that human resources represent the single most important untapped source of potential organisational competitive advantage. Without labour, capital is inert, and without capital, labour is inert. Poole and Jenkins (1996:1) note that:

There are many ways in which companies can gain competitive edge or a lasting and sustained advantage over their competitors, among them being the development of comprehensive human resource management policies. Indeed, the adoption of sophisticated human resource management policies and practices is seen as one of the major keys to competitive advantage in the modern world. This is not least because such practices can be formidable weapons in highly competitive environments because of the inability of competitors to formulate an effective response in the short term.

Similarly, Grundy (1998) argues that while a human resources strategy in itself might not be effective, the integration of corporate strategy and human resource matters into an 'organisation and people strategy' might prove more effective. In all commercial organisations human resources, effectively managed, add some value to the production process.

It is to this critical issue of 'people management' that we now turn. Variously referred to as PERSONNEL MANAGEMENT or HUMAN RESOURCE MANAGEMENT (HRM), this dichotomy presents a difficulty inherent in any discussion in this area. It is a particularly complex issue, given that neither of the two are viewed as completely homogeneous concepts (Clifford *et al.* 1997:1). In order to avoid getting into major ideological debates, or stereotypical characterisations of differences between human resource versus personnel management which are beyond the scope of this text, here we follow Monks (1996) who, in a reflective piece on the role carried out by those who are responsible for managing the 'people' function within organisations, argues that whether the incumbents are called personnel or HR managers is not necessarily important; what is much more important is to give recognition and expression to the complexity of the task that faces those who have to take responsibility for 'people matters'. Thus, we can suggest that the expressions 'human resource management' or 'personnel management' may be interpreted in specific or general terms. In its specific or narrow interpretation, the expression refers to the professional specialist function performed by human resource or personnel managers who are responsible for devising and executing the organisation's policies and strategies relating to the attraction, selection, rewarding, employment and welfare of people (Gunnigle *et al.* 1997; Tyson and York 1992). More generally, the literature on the subject also clearly indicates that the management of the human resource may relate to any and all of those who have responsibility for people matters in their various organisational roles—a responsibility that most managers, across all functions have to fulfil (Torrington and Hall 1987). Again, accepting, of course, that the management of the human resource may be a function of all who have a responsibility for others, for the purpose of this chapter, it is necessary to take a narrow interpretation and to concentrate on the specialist function and its activities. In Section 7.2 we provide a short historical overview of the development of the specialist HR function in Ireland. In Section 7.3 we discuss each of the main activities of the human resource function, incorporating Irish research data where available. In this section HUMAN RESOURCE PLANNING, RECRUITMENT, SELECTION, pay and benefits, PERFORMANCE APPRAISAL, training and development are all examined as core HR activity areas. Finally, Section 7.4 examines employee relations (traditionally the most significant area of personnel activity in Ireland: see, for example, Shivanath 1987) as a separate people management activity focusing on the different actors and institutions that exist in the EMPLOYEE RELATIONS domain.

7.2 The historical development of the HR function

In order to properly understand the current nature of HR activity and the specialist function, it is necessary to provide a thumbnail sketch of its historical development. This overview will highlight the major transitions that personnel management has gone through and give some indications of how HRM has developed as a specialist management function. Monks (1996) notes that it is difficult to pinpoint exactly when personnel management first appeared in Ireland, but she refers to Barrington (1980) who, in his account of the development of the Irish administrative system, indicates that a personnel function had been established in the civil service after World War One. Monks suggests that its official recognition in the private sector is probably best dated to the setting up of the Irish branch of the Institute of Labour Management in Dublin in 1937. This body was the forerunner to the current Chartered Institute of Personnel and Development (CIPD). For the purpose of the short historical account presented here, we distinguish between the following key phases: the early 1900s; the mid-1900s; the centralised pay-bargaining period during the 1970s; and the human resource management (HRM) debate from the 1980s onwards.

7.2.1 The early 1900s

Prior to the 1930s, two key traditions can be identified. They represent the first prominent influences on managerial practice relating to human resources and, as such, lay the foundation for the development of personnel management as we now understand it (Gunnigle *et al.* 1997; Foley and Gunnigle 1993).

Welfarists. The origins of personnel management lay in the Protestant work ethic and a concern, among a few enlightened employers, for the alleviation of the abhorrent working conditions witnessed after the Industrial Revolution. In Britain, the first recorded appointment of a welfare worker in 1896 was formal recognition of the need for specialist individuals to deal with people management issues. The early years of the twentieth century brought with them the appointment of a number of welfare workers among Irish employers. Prominent Irish examples include Jacobs and Maguire & Paterson in Dublin. However, the depression that followed World War One, coupled with large-scale unemployment, led to the abandonment of much of this work.

Taylorists. As welfarism was increasingly becoming a victim of the depression, Taylorism and its associated notions of labour efficiency became an increasingly popular alternative. The quest for efficiency and profitability among employers led to the standardisation of work systems and to a more systematic approach to a wide range of managerial activities.

7.2.2 The mid-1900s

If some developments in Taylorism caused personnel practitioners to develop a more calculative approach to managing employees, this was partially redressed by a growth in the behavioural sciences (Gunnigle and Flood 1990). This period was marked by a trend towards increasing organisational size and complexity and the application of personnel management practice to increasingly wide areas of management. The emerging behavioural sciences established a body of knowledge to underpin many aspects of personnel work, such as selection, training, motivation, INDUSTRIAL RELATIONS and payment systems. The increasing complexity during this period led to the emergence of two different traditions:

► bureaucrats
► consensus negotiators.

Bureaucrats. As organisations became increasingly complex, the range of personnel activities widened, which, in turn, led to the need to formalise procedures. Under this tradition, personnel embodied activities in the areas of employment, wages, joint consultation, health and safety, welfare and education/training. Personnel functions largely became custodians of the procedures which regulated the operation of these activities within the organisation.

Consensus negotiators. Following the lifting of the Emergency Powers Order in 1946, trade union density in Ireland accelerated sharply, as money and real wages began to rise for the first time since 1939 (Roche and Larragy 1986). Foley and Gunnigle (1993) argue that this 'new unionism' was to have a large impact on both the organisational environment and on the functioning of specialist personnel departments for a number of reasons. First, trade unions enjoyed a period of legitimacy in the eyes of employers and among government, highlighted best, perhaps, by the establishment of the Labour Court in 1946. Second, with increasing union density came an enhanced ability to engage in industrial action in the pursuit of collective objectives. An indicator of this is the very large number of days lost in the period 1947–51 (1.742 million). The emphasis on collective bargaining required, on the part of personnel managers, a wide range of specialist skills. This ever expanding specialist skills base served not only to justify and enhance the role of the personnel specialist, but also that of the personnel function as a whole.

7.2.3 The 1970s: centralised pay bargaining

The return to centralised pay bargaining in 1970 did not result in a decline in the importance of the personnel specialist as union negotiators switched their focus to other negotiable issues at the level of the workplace, such as employment conditions and productivity. It resulted in the necessity for the personnel specialist to become a legal expert. The 1970s brought with them an unprecedented wave of legislation which sought to protect employees and provide for redress in cases where rights had been infringed. In turn, this required that personnel functions have a high level of expertise in all aspects of employment law. This development, in particular, added a strong impetus to the drive for greater professionalism in the field of personnel management. Clearly, interest in greater professionalism in personnel management cannot be absolutely confined to this period, although it was during this period that it received a much stronger impetus. The Donovan Commission on industrial relations (1968) highlighted the need for greater expertise in the operation of the employer/employee relationship and in 1970, the Institute of Personnel Management (IPM—now CIPD) developed an exam-only scheme as a route to membership in an attempt to regularise and improve standards within the personnel management profession.

7.2.4 The 1980s: the transformation of personnel management?

The 1980s was clearly a decade of change. It was a period of reappraisal for personnel management. A depressed economic climate since the beginning of the decade, together with increased competitive pressures, led to a slump in business activity. These developments helped to change both the focus of personnel management and the nature of personnel activities. Internationalisation, Japanisation, excellence theories, new technology and economic pressures combined to set new priorities, forcing the personnel function to act under tighter cost controls, dismantle historical rigidities, build flexibility and accommodate a greater range of work, with little by way of extra resources (Morley *et al.* 1995; Storey 1995; Berridge 1992; Lawler 1988; Keating 1987; Tyson 1987; Foley and Gunnigle 1993). The personnel function increasingly turned to more innovative practices, the most important being human resource management (HRM) which Guest (1989) argues is slowly, but inevitably, replacing personnel management. Human resource management essentially refers to the development of a strategic corporate approach to workforce management. It has its roots in US industry which has been receptive to the application of organisational psychology and behavioural science principles in an attempt to improve organisational performance. The central contention is that organisations incorporate human resource considerations into strategic decision making, establish a corporate human resource philosophy and develop personnel strategies and policies to improve human resource utilisation (Grundy 1998; Poole and Jenkins 1996; Lundy and Cowling 1996; Mabey and Salaman 1995; Guest 1987; Beer *et al.* 1985; Fombrun *et al.* 1984). To many the implications of this ongoing development for personnel management are unclear. Some contributors argue that human resource management as a development merely involves a retitling exercise (Keenoy 1990; Horwitz 1990), while others feel it could involve a complete reorientation of the personnel function, depending on how strategic it actually is (Foley *et al.* 1996; Storey 1992). At least, according to Beardwell and Holden (1994), there is some conflict among academic commentators as to the substance and nature of the shift in the way employees are managed. Whatever the truth of the matter, the potential for optimising competitive advantages from human resources has emerged as one of the most significant debates in this new order and can be broadly seen to be related to three key features of a firm's human resources:

▶ A firm's workforce must add value to the product or service provided.

▶ Levels of individual performance must matter.

▶ A firm's human capital investment cannot be easily imitated.

7.3 Activity areas in human resource management

Thus far in this chapter, we have provided a brief historical overview of the development of personnel management and the specialist human resource function in Ireland. This discussion is intended to serve as a general background for the remainder of this chapter which focuses on specific activities of human resource management and the context for managing the employment relationship.

The variety of human resource management activities that may be undertaken by an organisation is extensive and, as a result, the role of the specialist HR function clearly may vary between organisations. As Gunnigle and Flood (1990:14) suggest:

Many are basic activities common to all types of organisation, such as recruitment. Others may be appropriate in certain organisational contexts (for example, collective bargaining in unionised firms), while still others are optional in character and their use related to managerial perspectives on personnel management (such as an emphasis on personal career development).

Thus, this section of the chapter will cover human resource planning, recruitment, selection, pay and benefits, performance appraisal and training and development as the major activity areas within managing the human resource.

7.3.1 Human resource planning

Before launching into more mainstream HRM activities, such as recruitment or training, an organisation must decide on a human resource strategy that fits with its present and future needs. The importance of planning the material resources of an organisation has never been called into question. However, planning for people as a resource—the human resource—has never been accorded the same status. Because people are, arguably, the single most important resource available to an organisation, it is important that sufficient numbers of the appropriate calibre of people are available to the organisation in pursuit of its objectives. In other words, it is crucial to plan for people, much like any other resource. Bowey (1974) defines human resource planning as:

an effort to anticipate future business and environmental demands upon an organisation and to provide the personnel to fulfil that business and satisfy those demands.

The major objectives of HR planning are:

▶ to ensure that the organisation finds and retains the quantity and quality of human resources that it requires

▶ to ensure that the organisation makes the best possible use of its human resources

▶ to ensure that the organisation can manage the human resource implications of employee surpluses or deficits.

Thus, HR planning by definition is not simply about numbers of people but also, as Cole (1986) points out, about the quality of personnel and how they are deployed throughout the organisation in an attempt to ensure optimum organisational effectiveness and efficiency. It is a process which affects every aspect of human resource management (recruitment, selection, performance appraisal, training and development, industrial relations etc.), and one which must be aligned with the corporate objectives/mission and strategic plans of the organisation.

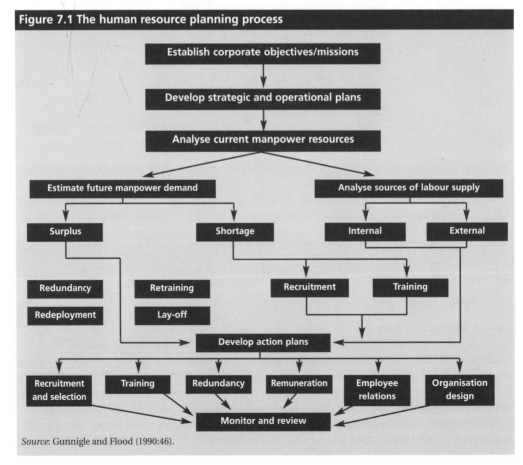

Figure 7.1 The human resource planning process

Source: Gunnigle and Flood (1990:46).

Tyson and York (1992) suggest that sound HR planning needs to be based on the following six principles and actions which are necessary prerequisites for any organisation:

❶ The plan has to be fully integrated with the other areas of the organisation's strategy and planning.

❷ Senior management must give a lead in stressing its importance throughout the organisation.

❸ In larger organisations a central HR planning unit responsible to senior management needs to be established, the objective of which is to co-ordinate and reconcile the demands for human resources from different departments

❹ The time span to be covered by the plan needs to be defined.

❺ The scope and details of the plan have to be determined.

❻ The plan must be based on the most comprehensive and accurate information that is available.

The major stages in the process are:

Stage 1: demand analysis

Stage 2: supply analysis

Stage 3: estimating deficits/surpluses

Stage 4: developing action plans

Stage 1: Demand Analysis. This stage of the process is concerned with estimating the quantity and quality of human resources required to meet the objectives of the organisation. It is based upon a thorough understanding of the organisations strategy and its implications for the workforce, planned technological changes, a detailed inventory of employee characteristics (age, sex, marital status, tenure, skill level, qualifications, promotion potential and performance levels) and the attrition rate among current resources. The most common techniques employed when conducting a demand analysis are managerial estimates/judgements, statistical methods/techniques and work study methods/techniques (Gunnigle *et al.* 1997; Heraty *et al.* 1997; Cole 1986).

Managerial estimates are the most straightforward method and are often the most commonly used. Typically, individual managers, based upon their knowledge of the situation, draw up estimates of human resource requirements. Managerial estimates are often collected at different levels in the organisational hierarchy, with managers at lower levels in the organisation submitting estimates that are passed up through the hierarchy for discussion and consideration. Clearly, since these estimates rely entirely upon personal judgements, their major weakness is one of subjectivity.

Statistical techniques are now more commonly used for making estimates. However, techniques such as regression analysis or econometric models are often only employed by larger organisations that have particular difficulties with manpower planning.

Work study is the systematic analysis of work in terms of people, skills, materials and machines and, in particular, the man hours needed per output unit to achieve maximum productivity (Tyson and York 1992). Work study is a particularly useful form of analysis for tasks that lend themselves to measurement and, consequently, work study methods are often employed for estimating the demand for 'direct' employees.

Stage 2: Supply Analysis. Supply analysis is concerned with estimating the quantity and quality of manpower that is likely to be available to the organisation. In this instance there are two major sources to be examined, namely, the internal labour market (existing employees) and the external labour market (the potential supply of manpower that is available outside the organisation). Table 7.1 summarises the issues on which a typical supply analysis might focus.

Table 7.1 Supply analysis: the areas to be considered		
Existing staff	**Potential staff**	**Leavers**
Numbers	Location	Retirements
Categories	Categories	Wastage rates
Skills	Skills	Redundancies
Performance	Trainability	Dismissals
Flexibility	Attitudes	
Promotability	Competition	

Source: Cole (1986:46).

With respect to supply analysis, one of the most common factors which complicates the task of human resource planning is labour wastage. Both planned and unplanned losses must be accounted for. Planned losses might be those that relate to retirements for example. Unplanned losses are more difficult to deal with. The most typical source of unplanned loss is through voluntary wastage, that is, when employees leave of their own accord. Useful indices for calculating wastage are provided in the Table 7.2.

Table 7.2 Indices used in HR planning		
Labour turnover index	=	$\dfrac{\text{Number of Employees leaving in period}}{\text{Average number employed in period}} \times 100$
Labour stability index (extent to which experienced employees are being retained)	=	$\dfrac{\text{Number of employees with more than one year's service}}{\text{Number employed one year ago}} \times 100$

Finally, with respect to the supply analysis, there are external factors that need to be taken into account. Factors such as the nature of the competition for labour, population trends, education/training opportunities, Government policies etc. will all have an impact on the external labour market.

Stage 3: Estimating Deficits/Surpluses. As a result of conducting both a demand and supply analysis, it is now possible to compare the results in order to determine whether the supply of labour available matches the demand for labour. Equally, it is possible that the supply of labour exceeds or falls short of the estimates required. Depending on the result achieved at this stage of the process, an action plan will be prepared.

Stage 4: Preparing an action plan. This last stage is based on the information that the preceding stages have yielded. The purpose of this action plan is to ensure that the day-to-day human resource needs of the organisation are satisfied. Plans emanating from the process will cover what the organisation must do, and how it will manage recruitment, selection, training and development, promotions and so on.

7.3.2 Recruitment

Information arising from the process of human resource planning will be used to make decisions about the planned level of recruitment. Recruitment is concerned with attracting a group of potential candidates to apply for the vacancy that the organisation has available. Effective recruitment procedures are a prerequisite to the development of an effective workforce. Clearly, in recent years, there has been an ever increasing emphasis on the recruitment of employees that are committed to the goals of the organisation. Influential contributors, such as Plumbley (1985), suggest that the profitability and even the survival of an enterprise will usually depend upon the calibre of the workforce, while Pettigrew, Hendry and Sparrow (1988) indicate that human resources represent a critical means of achieving competitive advantage. Heraty *et al.* (1997) note that a deal of the recent literature has emphasised the necessity for the recruitment and selection of employees who are committed to the goals of the organisation. The terms 'recruitment' and 'selection' refer to comple- mentary, but distinct processes in employment. Thus, as Anderson and Shackleton (1986) indicate, the quality of the new recruits depends upon an organisation's recruitment practices, while the relative effectiveness of the selection phase is inherently dependent upon the calibre of the candidates attracted.

The key choice in relation to recruitment is whether to recruit internally or externally. There are advantages and disadvantages associated with both and the choice largely depends on the position being filled. Smith, Gregg and Andrews (1989) suggest that the benefits of recruiting internally from current employees are that it is good HR practice, there is a reduction of induction time and the costs and uncertainties of recruiting from outside are reduced. However, there are also drawbacks as it limits the potential range of candidates from the wider labour market, and may lead to employee frustration, should employees feel that they have been overlooked for promotion. Gunnigle *et al.* (1997) suggest that the apparent desire among some Irish organisations to focus on the internal labour market may be linked to 'soft' HRM practices, such as career planning, counselling and employee development, in place there.

Two key stages can be identified in the recruitment process: first, what can be called the 'background' stage, and second, the actual recruitment stage.

Background stage. This involves the conducting of what is termed a 'job analysis'. Job analysis may simply be defined as 'specifying the job and defining what the job demands in terms of employee behaviour'. Typically, two important products are derived from the process of job analysis:

- the job description
- the person specification.

The JOB DESCRIPTION is a statement of the main tasks and responsibilities of the job. It is clearly an important aspect of the background stage of recruitment, because the ideal individual is derived from the contents of the job description. If an inaccurate job description is prepared, then the individual characteristics subsequently specified may also be inaccurate or inappropriate. Therefore, in order to achieve the best possible 'job–person fit', an accurate job description is essential. Organisations may take different approaches to the preparation of the job description. Some organisations ask current employees to keep diaries of their daily job activities and draw up a job description accordingly, while in other instances the task of compiling the details of the job description may be reserved for managers and supervisors.

The PERSON SPECIFICATION details the skills, qualifications, knowledge and experience the individual should possess in order to best match the job. The person specification may often distinguish between those characteristics considered essential and those considered desirable.

Among the things that it might take account of are:

❶ attainments, education/qualifications/experience

❷ general intelligence

❸ special aptitudes

❹ interests

❺ motivation

❻ adjustment.

In this way the person specification can be useful for focusing our thoughts on the desired characteristics of potential employees that may need to be specified in the background phase. It may also be helpful in the preparation for, and conducting of, interviews in the subsequent selection phase.

Recruitment stage. Equipped with a job description and a person specification, as a result of conducting a job analysis, the task now becomes one of attracting a pool of potential candidates. In considering possible sources of labour, it is in some ways easy to assume that these are inevitably external. However, as mentioned earlier, they may be either internal or external. Internal sources may come about through transfers, promotions or, indeed, demotions. Potential external sources include schools, regional technical colleges, universities and other educational establishments, FAS, employment agencies, unsolicited applications previously received, advertising (local/national media, professional/technical journals) and management consultants/executive search agencies. Each of these sources should be evaluated, particularly with respect to their suitability to yield the right candidate, and the costs involved. Table 7.3 highlights the major costs associated with different sources of recruitment.

In the Irish context, the data from both the 1992 and 1995 rounds of the Cranet E Survey in Ireland (see Note, page 232), suggests that a broad spectrum of recruitment methods are being utilised by organisations and what is currently happening in Irish recruitment is, for the most part, relatively unsurprising, though the tightening of the labour market in recent years has meant that recruitment has become a far more competitive game (Heraty and Morley 1998(b)). Table 7.4, drawing upon data from the Cranet E Survey, highlights the recruitment methods used to fill vacancies for different managerial grades.

Table 7.3 Costs associated with different sources of recruitment

	Direct costs
Internal sources	
Transfer	
Promotion	
Demotion	None
External sources	
Existing workforce: recommendations from friends, relatives etc.	Minimal
Casual applications: unrequested CVs	Minimal
Advertising: local, national media, professional/technical journals etc.	Expensive (depending on media used)
Schools and colleges: contacts, careers officers, 'milk round'	Low (except for travel costs)
FAS	None (can receive financial benefits for employing some categories of workers)
Employment agencies	Expensive (10–25% of starting salary)
Management consultants/executive search agencies	Very expensive (25%+ of starting salary)

Source: Gunnigle and Flood (1990:73).

Table 7.4 Usual method of filling vacancies (N = 261)

	Senior management	Middle management	Junior management
Internally	57%	75%	77%
Recruitment consultant	52%	38%	22%
National newspaper	47%	49%	37%
Professional magazine	12%	13%	5%
International newspaper	12%	7%	2%
Word-of-mouth	7%	10%	14%

Source: Heraty and Morley (1998).

The data suggest a combination of recruitment methods are being used by responding organisations to fill managerial positions. Utilising the internal labour market for recruitment purposes appears to be the most common recruitment method at all managerial levels. However, some variation is evident between the different managerial levels where, for example, middle and junior managerial vacancies are more likely to be filled internally than senior management positions. In terms of where the actual HR manager is recruited from, in our survey, 36 per cent of respondents indicated that their most senior HR manager is a non-personnel specialist who has been recruited from within the organisation, while 34 per cent recruited their HR manager from outside the organisation.

Regardless of the method of recruitment used to source applicants, the organisation requires details on the skills, abilities, aptitudes etc. of the candidates. Typically, the choice here is between asking the applicants to submit their own curriculum vitae (CV) or to have all applicants complete a standard application form. From the point of view of getting standardised information and assessing candidates against the same parameters, application forms are preferred. An individual CV gives scope for creativity but may also include some irrelevant information, whilst excluding some essential facts. A compromise situation lies between both of these alternatives: design an application form specific to the job, but allow some blank space for supporting information.

7.3.3 Selection

The selection process effectively begins when application forms are received. Selection tools available to organisations range from the more traditional methods of interviews and references, through to the more sophisticated techniques such as biographical data, aptitude tests and psychological tests. The degree to which a selection technique is perceived as effective is determined by its reliability and validity. *Reliability* is generally synonymous with consistency, while *validity* refers to what is being measured, and the extent to which those measures are correct (Muchinski 1986).

The interview is widely held to be the most commonly used selection technique. For example, McMahon (1988), researching in Ireland, found that over 90 per cent of job categories were filled with the assistance of an interview. Often described as a 'conversation with a purpose' (or as McMahon (2000) suggests, a contrived, interrogative conversation involving a meeting, usually between strangers, which rarely lasts for more than an hour), the interview can take a number of different forms. The three most common types are one-to-one interviews, panel interviews and group interviews/assessment. In a one-to-one situation, there will be one interviewer and one interviewee/candidate. This type of interview tends to be less formal than a panel interview and facilitates the development of rapport between interviewer and interviewee. It also makes a lower demand on management time. Perhaps its greatest weakness is the potential for subjectivity and bias. In a panel interview, there will normally be a number of interviewers (often up to seven people) and one interviewee. The key advantage of such an interview is that it is more objective than the one-to-one and reduces the opportunity for bias. However, it may prove difficult to co-ordinate from the organisation's perspective and it clearly increases the demand on management time and resources. Finally, a group interview/assessment, which is not an interview in the strict sense of the word, attempts to assess a group of candidates together. A relatively informal process, in some respects, it attempts to observe and assess the individuals' behaviour in a group situation. It is often used as a preliminary selection tool.

Regardless of the type of interview being conducted, the interviewer(s) should have three constant objectives:

▶ to obtain enough information about the candidate to determine how s/he will fit the job

▶ to ensure that the applicant has enough information about the vacancy and the organisation

▶ to leave the applicant with the genuine impression that s/he has been treated fairly.

It is important for interviewers to adequately prepare for an interview and to have a set plan when interviewing. The interview has a poor track record in predicting job performance. Most managers have little training in interviewing, and yet they rely on the process to find the most suitable person for the job. McMahon (2000) notes that the effectiveness of the interview process is influenced by a host of factors, including the number of interviewers, their professionalism, and the time of day or the day of the week the interview is held! Table 7.5 highlights the interviewing errors that most frequently occur.

Table 7.5 Common interviewing errors

Inadequate preparation:
- little job analysis
- inadequate interview preparation
- poor planning and administration.

Absence of interview structure

Premature judgement:
- arriving at early decisions on candidate suitability and using interview to justify such decisions.

Interviewer dominance:
- interviewer talking too much
- interviewer not listening, observing or analysing.

No rapport:
- atmosphere too intimidating
- interviewer being overly critical and judgemental.

Halo/horns effect:
- allowing favourable/unfavourable characteristics or reports to influence final decision.

Interviewer bias:
- allowing prejudices or subjective opinions to influence selection decisions.

Structural rigidity:
- adhering slavishly to a pre-planned structure
- not adapting to the needs of individual candidates.

Source: Gunnigle and Flood (1990:89).

The whole objective of the exercise is to establish a rapport with the interviewee, and to obtain all the information relevant to the post. The interviewer must be wary of allowing his/her own biases and interests to influence the decision. Clearly, since interviews are likely to retain an important role in employee selection, management should make every effort to gain the best possible results from their use.

A number of selection tests are available to assist in making selection decisions. Owing to the subjective nature of the interview, such tests are sometimes used to give a more objective rating. The most common types of tests are:

▶ **Intelligence tests**. These measure one's mental capacity and potential. They are particularly useful for giving an insight into a person's ability to learn. However, they are not a good indicator of subsequent job performance.

▶ **Aptitude tests**. These are generally used in an attempt to predict areas of special aptitude and to examine a candidate's suitability for particular types of work. However, as with intelligence tests, they cannot, in absolute terms, predict subsequent job performance.

▶ **Proficiency tests**. Otherwise known as ability tests of achievement, they can be a good measure of specific knowledge or skills.

▶ **Personality tests**. These tests strive to ensure that the successful candidate has the most appropriate type of personality for the job being filled. While these tests do give a measure of an individual's suitability for certain jobs, their reliability and validity is rather low.

Reference checking typically forms a part of most selection processes. Indeed, McMahon (1988) found that after interviewing, reference checking is the next most popular selection technique. It helps to validate information already obtained and allows a picture of the individual's previous performance to be formed. References may be sought in different ways:

▶ writing a standard business letter, detailing the position and asking the referee to give his/her opinion of the candidates suitability

▶ forwarding a standard form, asking the referee to give details of the candidate's past experience and character

▶ requesting information over the telephone about the candidate's past performance etc.

Regardless of the method used, the object is the same: to seek independent corroboration of the facts as presented by the applicant. Typically, the reference is used as a 'rubber stamp' in approving the final decision (McMahon 1988).

Table 7.6. Selection methods most commonly used in Ireland					
	Every appointment (%)	Most appointments (%)	Some appointments (%)	Few appointments (%)	Not used (%)	N =
Interview panel	41	28	18	6	7	235
One-to-one interview	37	14	23	14	12	217
Application form	59	20	12	3	6	241
Aptitude test	6	13	37	15	29	201
Psychometric test	4	9	27	11	49	199
Assessment centres	2	2	9	8	79	181
Graphology	0.6	0.6	4	1	94	169
References	70	22	5	1	2	230

Source: Heraty and Morley (1998).

The data generated by the Cranet E Survey in 1992 indicated that relatively little use was being made of what were considered the more 'sophisticated' selection techniques by Irish organisations. The picture that emerges from the 1995 data presented in Table 7.6 confirms that finding and indeed the earlier work by McMahon

(1988), and highlights that the application form, the interview and reference checks remain the most commonly used selection methods in Ireland. Yet the research in the extant literature indicates that these remain selection tools with low validity and reliability (Heraty and Morley 1998; Makin and Robertson 1986, Attwood 1989). Biodata, assessment centres and testing are increasingly being viewed as consistently valid predictors and, while their usage remains rather low in Ireland, the feeling is that they may become more widespread in the future. Group selection methods and graphology remain the least utilised techniques in Ireland. Graphology has been criticised on the grounds of low reliability and validity and there is some difficulty associated with assessing the performance of an individual in a group context during the selection stage (Arnold *et al.* 1991, Smith and Robertson 1986).

7.3.4 Pay and benefits

An organisation's REWARD SYSTEM is a powerful indicator of its philosophy and approach to workforce management. The design and implementation of an effective reward system has proven a difficult task for many organisations. Beer (1985) *et al.* suggest that many employee grievances and criticisms of reward systems may actually mask more fundamental problems. Dissatisfaction with aspects of the employment relationship, such as the supervisory style or opportunities for personal development, may manifest themselves in dissatisfaction with aspects of the reward system. Consequently, organisations experiencing problems with their reward system should examine decisions taken on other personnel issues such as selection or work design, rather than making piecemeal changes to their compensation system (Gunnigle *et al.* 1997).

Employee rewards are usually classified under two broad headings:

▶ intrinsic rewards

▶ extrinsic rewards.

Intrinsic rewards spring from the job itself and include such things as autonomy, responsibility and challenge. Extrinsic rewards are more tangible in nature and include pay, job security and working conditions. The relative importance of intrinsic over extrinsic rewards, and vice versa, is a much debated issue, rooted in the various theories of motivation (for a fuller discussion of theories of motivation, see Chapter 9).

An organisation's reward system may attempt to incorporate the motivational principles underlying the various motivation theories in an attempt to improve or reinforce performance. Actual reward satisfaction will be one of the key determinants of performance improvements. Lawler (1977) concluded that the following five key factors influence satisfaction with a reward:

❶ Satisfaction with a reward depends on the amount received versus the amount the individual feels he should receive.

❷ Comparisons with what happens to others influences people's feelings of satisfaction.

❸ Employees' satisfaction with both the intrinsic and extrinsic rewards received from their jobs affects overall job satisfaction; individuals who are dissatisfied with the reward system are likely to express dissatisfaction with their jobs overall.

❹ People differ widely in the rewards they desire and in what value they attach to those rewards; effective reward systems should meet workers' needs.

❺ Many extrinsic rewards satisfy workers only because they lead to other rewards; for example, increased pay may only satisfy because of what it can buy.

Turning specifically to payment systems, the choice of a payment system is an important consideration for organisations. The money that a person receives for carrying out work can be a major source of motivation and therefore it is imperative that an organisation maintains an appropriate and equitable payment system. The particular package offered will be determined by a variety of factors, not least among them the organisation's ability to pay, labour market conditions, comparable rates/levels elsewhere and possibly the bargaining strength of the TRADE UNION (Morley *et al.* 1999; Morley and Gunnigle 1997). There are numerous options in the type of payment system an organisation might adopt. The more common types of payment systems utilised in Irish organisations are:

▶ **Flat rate only**. Flat rate schemes are by far the most popular, and involve a fixed hourly, weekly or monthly rate. Such schemes are simple, easy to administer, easily understood and provide stability of earnings for the employee. Flat rate schemes are typically used in jobs where specific performance criteria are difficult to establish.

▶ **Flat rate + individual, group or company-wide payment by results**. Schemes of this kind are becoming more popular. It is estimated that over one-third of manufacturing establishments in Ireland operate some type of wage incentive scheme for direct manual employees. While schemes of this kind often act as a good motivator due to the immediacy of the reward, they are often difficult to establish and administer and indeed may be a source of conflict due to felt inequities.

▶ **Merit rating**. Under merit rating schemes employees receive bonus payments based on a systematic assessment of their performance. Thus performance is evaluated against specified objectives and, on this basis, merit payments are made. While such systems are positive because they reward good performance and do not solely involve the basis of production factors, it is clearly difficult to find an accurate measure of overall performance.

▶ **Profit/gainsharing**. Under schemes of this kind, employees receive a bonus related to improved company performance. That bonus/reward may take the form of money or company shares. While schemes of this nature create greater employee awareness of the organisation's overall performance and may go some way towards increasing their employees' commitment to the organisation, take-up in Ireland has been low.

▶ **Piecework**. In this instance, employees are only paid for the work that they have completed. Payment is based solely on performance in this respect. As a payment system it may be a major source of conflict as it does not guarantee any minimum income.

Mooney (1980), in a study of wage payment systems in Ireland, found that the flat rate system was by far the most popular, particularly for indirect employees.

Table 7.7 Payment systems in Ireland

Payment system	Utilisation (%)	Direct manual employees	Indirect employees
Flat rate only	70.5	53.4	66.3
Flat rate + individual PBR	15.3	27.4	6.2
Flat rate + group PBR	8.6	12	15.8
Flat rate + company PBR	2.6	3.9	6
Piecework	3	3.3	0.2

Source: Mooney (1980).

More recent research evidence suggests that incentive schemes seem to be experiencing increased popularity in many Irish organisations.

Table 7.8 Use of incentive schemes in Ireland (1992 and 1995)

1992 N=269; 1995 N=244	Managerial %		Professional/ technical %		Clerical %		Manual %	
	1992	1995	1992	1995	1992	1995	1992	1995
Share options	20.4	23	11.9	13.8	8.2	11.5	7.8	9.6
Profit sharing	15.2	19.2	11.5	13.4	10	12.6	8.9	10.0
Group bonus schemes	13	20.1	11.5	15.7	9.7	16.1	12.6	15.3
Merit/performance-related pay	46.1	50.3	39	44.8	28.6	36.8	13.4	15.3

Source: Cranet E Surveys (Ireland), University of Limerick (1992, 1995).

The growth of incentive schemes in Ireland has been inexorably linked to the trend towards relating pay more closely to performance. However, the take-up of incentive schemes is correlated with the organisational ownership. Thus, in the Irish context, US-owned organisations on the whole appear far more likely to utilise incentives than their counterparts, particularly Irish indigenous organisations who demonstrate a low take-up across the range of incentives (Gunnigle, Foley and Morley 1993).

Table 7.9 Employee benefits (statutory and voluntary)

Maternity leave	Child care facilities	Career breaks
Paternity leave	Parental leave	
Holidays (above the statutory minimum)	Additional holiday pay	Sick pay
Health insurance	Company cars	
Sports/recreation facilities	Pension schemes	

When planning pay systems, an approach that takes account of all the benefits and their interrelations is to be preferred (Tyson and York 1992). Pay should not therefore be examined without giving at least some consideration to the other benefits that may apply. The nature of voluntary fringe benefits provided to employees varies between organisations. In general, it is estimated that fringe benefits (both statutory and voluntary) constitute an additional 25–30 per cent on top of basic weekly pay for manual grades. For clerical, administrative and managerial grades, a figure of 15–30 per cent should be added (Gunnigle, Foley and Morley 1993). Table 7.9 lists a range of benefits, some of which are common in Irish organisations.

7.3.5 Performance appraisal

Assessing the work of employees is a key function in human resource management, and indeed a central aspect of all managerial work. The objective is to achieve and sustain high performance standards in an attempt to ensure organisational survival and success. Designed to complement the continuous evaluation and reward of people at work, performance appraisal has been defined as:

a procedure and process which assists in the collection, checking, sharing and use of information collected from and about people at work for the evaluation of their performance and potential for such purposes as staff development and the improvement of that work performance. (McMahon and Gunnigle 1994:1)

It can therefore be seen as a periodic assessment of the performance of the individual dedicated to reviewing the past performance of the individual, as well as examining the individual's future potential. Such a review and examination allows decisions to be made with respect to the training and development needs of an individual and also the reward where salary increments, bonuses, etc., are awarded on the basis of individual performance.

Tyson and York (1992) identify six major objectives of the performance appraisal process:

▶ to determine how far people are meeting the requirements of their jobs and whether any changes or action are required for the future.
▶ to determine developmental needs in terms of work experience and training.
▶ to identify people who have potential to take on wider responsibilities.
▶ to provide a basis for assessing and allocating pay increments and similar rewards.
▶ to improve communication between managers and their staff.
▶ to develop motivation and commitment by providing regular and scheduled opportunities for feedback on performance and discussion of work, problems, suggestions for improvement, prospects, etc.

In their study of performance appraisal in Ireland, McMahon and Gunnigle (1994) identified a number of central objectives of performance appraisal in Irish organisations.

The results reveal that in the Irish context, there are on average more than eight objectives for each appraisal system, which, as the authors point out, is somewhat ambitious, given that some of the objectives may not be compatible; for example, appraiser playing judge and counsellor together. Morley and Gunnigle (1997), once again drawing upon the Cranet E data from 1995, suggest that, in a majority of cases, performance appraisal is used to identify individual training needs. The identification of promotion potential and career development are also important outcomes of the appraisal process.

Table 7.10 Objectives of performance appraisal in the Republic of Ireland

Objectives	%
Improve future performance	98
Provide feedback on performance	96
Agree key objectives	95
Identify training needs	95
Strengthen appraisee commitment and motivation	89
Improve communication	84
Assess promotion/potential	82
Career counselling	77
Assist personnel decisions	70
Aid salary review	64
Secure feedback on supervisory/managerial effectiveness	63

Source: MaMahon and Gunnigle (1994).

Accompanying the large number of objectives which performance appraisal may attempt to fulfil is an equally large number of appraisal methods. The method(s) selected will be a major determinant in the success or otherwise of the process. Selection of a particular method should be based upon a stringent assessment of the strengths and weaknesses of the methods and the relevance of the methods to the organisation's circumstances. Table 7.11 summarises the characteristics of the more common appraisal methods and highlights some of the strengths and weaknesses associated with each.

With regard to the methods of appraisal used in Irish organisations, research by MacMahon and Gunnigle (1994) suggests that the performance/objective or results-oriented appraisal method is the most widely used. Rating on the basis of traits that the appraisee possesses and the free-form descriptive essay also feature prominently (see Table 7.12).

Finally, research suggests that many organisations opt to combine the key features of different appraisal schemes into one, particularly using self-appraisal as a component of most other appraisal techniques.

7.3.6 Training and development

Helping employees to become effective in their jobs is one of the fundamentally important tasks in human resource management that any work organisation has to undertake (Tyson and York 1992). The initiative for providing this help lies in training and development. Recent years have witnessed considerable efforts to improve the national system of training and development and, in line with developments in many other economies, much of this renewed effort has been instigated by heightened international competition, technological advancements leading to the emergence of skills gaps in certain areas and renewed efforts to provide increased incentives for organisational-level training (Heraty *et al.* 2000; Heraty and Morley 1998).

Garavan, Costine and Heraty (1995) in their text on training and development in Ireland draw a clear distinction between these two concepts. They define training as a planned, systematic effort to modify or develop knowledge, skills and attitudes through learning experiences in order to achieve effective performance in an activity

Table 7.11 Appraisal techniques

Method	Characteristics	Strengths	Weaknesses
Ranking	Appraiser ranks workers from best to worst based on specific characteristics or overall job performance	Simple, facilitates comparisons	Little basis for decisions, degrees of difference not specified, subjective
Paired comparison	Two workers compared at a time and decisions made on which is superior resulting in a final ranking order for full group	Ease of decison-making, simple	Difficult with large numbers plus weaknesses attributed to ranking
Critical incident	Appraiser/supervisor observes incidents of good/bad performance. These are used as a basis for judging and assessing/discussing performance	Job related; more objective	Needs good observation skills; time-consuming
Free-form/ narrative	General free-written evaluation by appraiser	Flexible	Subjective; difficulty of comparison
Self-assessment	Appraisees evaluate themselves using a particular format/structure	Participative; facilitates discussion; promotes self-analysis	Danger of lenient tendency; potential source of conflict between appraiser and appraisee.
Assessment centre	Appraisees undergo a series of assessments (interviews, tests etc.) undertaken by trained assessors	Range of dimensions examined; objective	Expensive; not necessarily job specific
Performance/ objectives-oriented systems	Appraiser evaluates degree to which specific job targets/standards have been achieved	Job-related; objective; partici-pative	Needs measurable targets; danger of collusion
Rating	Appraiser specifies on a scale to what degree relevant characteristics (normally related to job-related behaviour or personality) are possessed by appraisee	Ease of comparison, range in complexity from very simple to very involved using descriptions of behaviour/ performance	Subjective; personality/behavioural traits difficult to measure

Source: Gunnigle and Flood (1990).

Table 7.12 Performance appraisal schemes used in Ireland

	%
Results-oriented	62 (45)
Trait rating scales	51 (37)
Descriptive essay	44 (32)
Critical incident	22 (16)
Ranking	10 (7)
Other (e.g., peer and group appraisal, assessment centre)	21 (15)

Source: MaMahon and Gunnigle (1994).

or range of activities. They view development as a broader concept referring to the general enhancement and growth of an individual's skills and abilities through conscious and unconscious learning, with a view to enabling them to take up a future role in the organisation. In some quarters training and development was often seen as an optional extra—something to be indulged in when times are good but one of the first areas to suffer when cutbacks are required. However, it is generally becoming more recognised that there is a strong correlation between organisational success and investment in training and development. In recent times, the academic literature has witnessed a resurgent interest in the whole area of training and development, with much of the literature, according to Heraty (1992) focusing on the strategic development of human resources as a means of increasing the effectiveness of organisations. Much of this interest has perhaps occurred through the popularisation of Porter's (1980) notion of competitive advantage, and the emergence of the 'excellence' literature (Peters and Waterman 1982). This notion of excellence has been expanded into an analysis of the management of human resources generally and more specifically into the development of human resources in an attempt to achieve competitive advantage (Heraty, Morley and Turner 1993). In the Irish context, the Advisory Committee on Management Training (1988) documented case histories of Allied Irish Bank, Howmedica Inc., Blarney Woollen Mills, the Department of Social Welfare, the Electricity Supply Board and Guinness to demonstrate and highlight the relationship between investment in training and development and improved performance.

A number of factors external to the organisation are also partly responsible for the increased interest in training and development. These include the pervasive spread of new technologies (Walton 1985), increasing global competition resulting in the need for greater flexibility (Barrow and Loughlin 1992), and the emergence of skills gaps in certain industries (Collins and Sinclaire 1991).

At national level, responsibility for training in Ireland currently lies with FAS which has as its primary objectives the co-ordination, promotion and the provision of training activities in Ireland. Table 7.13 provides a historical overview of training in Ireland.

Clearly, training and development is an issue that has to be faced by every organisation. At this juncture it is necessary to distinguish between what we mean by *training* and *development*. For the purposes of this discussion, training is taken to be that activity which is concerned with the development of the knowledge, skills and attitudes that are required by the individual in order for him/her to execute his/her job in an effective and efficient manner. Development, on the other hand, is seen as a broader concept relating to the individual and his/her future career in the organisation, as well as the organisation's own future. It is not concerned with immediate performance; rather, future potential. In practice, process distinctions are rarely made between training and development except when it comes to choosing the particular interventions themselves.

Table 7.13 Historical overview of training in Ireland		
1098	Norman Invasion	Introduction of the Guild System of operation
1879	Industrial Revolution	Evolution of factory system of production
1896	Agricultural and Technical Instruction (Irl) Act	First form of regulated apprenticeship in Ireland
1930	Vocational Education Act	Established VECs to provide a nation-wide system of continuing education
1931	Apprenticeship Act	Set up Apprenticeship Committees to regulate apprenticeship training
1959 ordinate	Apprenticeship Act	Established An Cheard Chomhairle to co- and regulate the apprenticeship system
1967	Industrial Training Act	Set up AnCO to assume full responsibility for all industrial and commercial training, including apprenticeships. Also to promote training at all levels in industry
1987	Labour Services Act	Established FAS—the amalgamation of AnCO, NMS and the YEA. Function to provide, co-ordinate and promote training activities in Ireland.

Source: Heraty (1992)

With respect to the actual process of training and development, it should be thought of as a logical sequence of events, beginning with the establishment of a policy, followed by the identification of training needs, subsequently planning and conducting the training and finally evaluating the process.

Formulating a training policy. The objective here is that those responsible for training and development in the organisation, in conjunction with other managers, agree a definite policy with specific objectives achievable within a given time frame. The policy should clearly establish what the organisation is prepared to do with respect to the training and development of its employees. The policy should ensure that employees can find solutions to their training and development needs and that training and development is put into action through the creation of a facilitative atmosphere backed up with the necessary resources.

Identifying training needs. Accurate identification of training needs is vital for the development of effective, relevant, timely training and development interventions. It should aim to identify what is currently happening and what should actually be happening. It is, in some ways, a rather subjective area as training needs for a particular job are open to different interpretations. The most common method used to identify training needs is a survey. Typically, the survey centres around identifying:

▶ Who needs to be trained—numbers and types of employees?
▶ What standards of performance is the training expected to achieve?
▶ What are the present training arrangements?
▶ What are the suggestions for improvements?

Planning and conducting the training. This refers to the actual planning of the training which is to take place and deciding on the most appropriate methods. There is a whole range of training methods from which a suitable selection can be made, for example:

▶ on-the-job
▶ coaching
▶ counselling
▶ mentoring
▶ secondment
▶ project work
▶ formal lectures
▶ group discussions
▶ case study
▶ computer-assisted training.

When choosing a particular intervention, the guiding principle should be the facilitation of high learning transfer; in other words, seeking activities or interventions which focus as closely as possible on the job to be performed.

Evaluating training and development activities. Evaluation of training and development activities ensures that control is maintained over the total process and allows a considered assessment of the outcomes, methods and overall impact of any particular training and development programme (Gunnigle and Flood 1990). Training evaluation can take place at a relatively informal level, for example, simply asking participants how they felt about the programme and judging their reactions; or at a more formal level, using questionnaires or tests to assess what the participant has actually learned, for example.

The choice of training delivery method available to organisations is considerable. Therefore organisations, when deciding on the most appropriate method to use, should take account of the principles of learning, the particular needs of those to be trained and the logistics of training that affect every organisation. All training delivery methods have their own particular strengths and can be modified to suit organisational requirements. The most important criterion in determining the choice of training delivery method is the extent to which it meets the particular objectives that have been established through the training needs analysis. In her study of training and development practices in Ireland, Heraty (1992) found that on-the-job training was the most frequently used training strategy. Internal and external formal training and development programmes and part-time professional training were also regularly used by respondent organisations. However, more longer-term developmental methods, such as secondment and special projects, were used in a much smaller number of cases.

Table 7.14 Training and development methods used in Irish organisations	
Methods	% (N = 58)
On-the-job training and development	91
External formal T & D programmes	83
In-house formal T & D programmes	78
Part-time professional training programmes	74
Open/distance learning	45
Special projects/task force participation	36
Secondment	19

Source: Heraty (1992).

More recent data (Cranet E, Ireland 1995) indicate that organisations are reluctant to rely solely on one training delivery strategy and appear to strike a balance between formal and informal delivery mechanisms in an effort to maximise efficiency returns. However, on-the-job training retains its popularity. The data also suggest that there has been an increase in the use of computer-based packages as a training delivery mechanism, while mentoring and coaching emerged as the least likely to be used, arguably due to the large commitment of time, and resources required for such interventions. Significantly however, it is precisely these interventions that have been lauded for their critical contribution to strategic employee development (see, for example, Wexley and Latham 1991).

7.4 The employee relations context

So far in this chapter we have argued that recent years have brought with them a concerted effort by many organisation to establish a competitive edge through improvements in quality, service and performance. We have noted that one key source of competitive improvement has been an increased emphasis on the more optimal utilisation of human resources, something which can be potentially leveraged through a focus on a core set of HRM activities, namely, human resource planning, recruitment, selection, pay and benefits, performance appraisal and training and development. One other critical factor influencing success or failure in the leveraging of organisational advantage in this area is the nature of the relationship between the parties to the labour process. It is to this relationship, encompassing the spectrum of employee, employer and state interactions, that we now turn. The way in which this relationship is set up and managed defines the climate of employee relations in the organisation, and serves as a strong enabler for all HR activity.

At the outset it is important to clarify what is meant by industrial employee relations as the term itself is a source of some confusion. There are, as Salman (1987) observed, almost as many definitions of the concept as there are writers on employee relations matters. The majority of classical definitions of industrial/employee relations emphasise the rules, or job regulations mechanisms that govern the employment relationship in the workplace. For example, Dunlop (1958:5) defines industrial relations as 'the study of employment rules and their variation over time'. This early perspective set a broad and integrated agenda for the discipline of industrial relations. Accordingly, the parties to the labour process, namely, management, trade unions and government agencies, established a network of rules for the workplace and the work community. The central task of industrial relations is therefore to explain why these particular rules are actually established and how they are administered. The rules are divided into procedural rules and substantive rules. Procedural rules refer to methods for formally handling specific issues that might arise, such as trade union recognition, disciplinary issues or dispute resolution. Substantive matters refer to detailed outcomes of negotiations, such as percentage pay increases, extra holidays, etc.

The traditional management focus has been on the pluralist concept of industrial relations, encompassing the premise that a basic conflict of interest exists between management and labour and that this conflict can be optimally handled through collective bargaining between employers and trade unions over divisive issues, particularly pay and working conditions. Collective bargaining refers to the process through which agreement on negotiable issues is reached between organised employees and management representatives. The pluralist approach therefore recognises that a coalition of various interests exists, and management's role is to achieve a balance between these differing interests. Because of the existence of this coalition of interests, conflict is likely to arise and management's role is to plan for the handling of this conflict and reconcile the conflicting interests.

During the 1980s it became evident that although this definition aptly described management–worker relations in many organisations, it did not encapsulate organisations where the focus was more unitarist in perspective. Unitarism as a philosophy of industrial relations is based on the existence of a mutuality of interests between the parties to the labour process. The organisation's goals are the fundamental ones and it is management's prerogative to manage. Consequently, this latter approach places the emphasis on dealings with individual employees using various mechanisms such as elaborate communications, career development, quality circles and merit pay.

In this chapter, employee relations are seen in generic terms as incorporating all employer, employee and state interactions on employment matters. The focus is therefore on the nature of the relationship between the parties to the labour process and the term includes both pluralist and unitarist models and encapsulates both state and organisational-level arrangements. Having established the meaning of employee relations it is now pertinent to turn to the actors involved in the process, namely, trade unions, management associations and state institutions and their role in employee relations in Ireland

7.4.1 Trade unions

Essentially a trade union can be viewed as a body that aims to unite workers with common interests. It seeks to define those interests, express them and collectively advance them (Gunnigle, Garavan and Fitzgerald 1992). Its basic strength lies in its ability to organise and unite. While employees join trade unions for a host of reasons, among the most common are a desire to influence pay claims, to have protection against arbitrary management actions and because they fundamentally believe in the function and the role of trade unions in society. By joining unions, employees provide themselves with the collective means and the strength to redress the imbalance in bargaining power which normally exists between the individual employee and the employer. Table 7.15 highlights the major objectives of trade unions in Ireland.

Table 7.15 Trade union objectives in Ireland

- Achieving satisfactory levels of pay and conditions of employment and providing members with a range of services.
- Replacing individual bargaining with collective bargaining thereby redressing the balance of bargaining power in favour of employees and reducing management prerogative in employment related matters.
- Facilitating the development of a political system where workers have a greater degree of influence on political decisions resulting in an economic and social framework which reflects employee needs rather than those of employers/management.

Source: Gunnigle, Garavan and Fitzgerald (1992).

Irish trade unions are normally organised on an occupational basis and may be loosely grouped into three broad categories:

▶ craft unions
▶ general unions
▶ white-collar unions.

Craft unions cater for workers who possess a particular skill in a trade where entry is restricted through apprenticeship or otherwise. Craft unions have traditionally been protective of their trade by ensuring that only people holding union cards carry out certain types of skilled work. This has often led to criticisms of restrictive and inefficient work practices and sometimes to demarcation disputes. Increased mechanisation and consequent de-skilling have had a detrimental impact on the membership and power of craft unions as reflected in the reduction of their share of union members. Examples of craft unions in Ireland are the Electrical Trade Union (ETU), and the National Union of Sheet Metal Workers of Ireland (NUSMWI).

General unions cater for workers, regardless of skill or industry. However, they have traditionally catered for semi-skilled and unskilled workers. They are typically the largest unions and account for approximately half of all trade union members. They are common in all types of organisations and in all industrial sectors. The best known is the Services, Industrial, Professional and Technical Union (SIPTU) which is by far the largest union in Ireland.

White-collar unions normally cater for professional, supervisory, clerical and managerial grades. Unions of this type experienced significant growth in membership in the latter years as reflected in their increased share of membership from 24 per cent in 1940 to over 35 per cent in the late 1980s. The Manufacturing, Service and Finance Union (MSF) and the Association of Secondary School Teachers of Ireland (ASTI) are examples of white-collar unions.

There are essentially three different levels within the trade union structure in Ireland (see Figure 7.2).

▶ workplace level
▶ branch level
▶ national level.

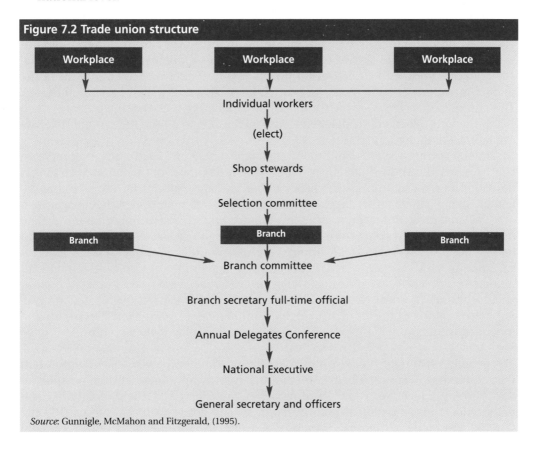

Figure 7.2 Trade union structure

Source: Gunnigle, McMahon and Fitzgerald, (1995).

At the workplace level, shop stewards are the main trade union representatives. The steward is charged with the responsibility of acting on the membership's behalf on industrial relations matters at the organisational level. Fellow trade union members at annual elections elect the steward. The steward must perform his job like all other employees as well as acting as steward. In this respect stewards are given reasonable time off from work for union business. The major functions of the shop steward are:

▶ to recruit new members into the union
▶ to collect union subscriptions from members
▶ to negotiate with management on behalf of the members
▶ to liaise with the unions central office
▶ to represent workers in grievance and disciplinary situations.

The section committee is a group of trade union members elected by fellow trade union members who work in a specific section of the organisation. The section committee's main activity is to help shop stewards to perform their tasks effectively. On a committee of this kind all of the stewards are from the same trade union. If they are members of different trade unions, the committee is known as a joint shop stewards committee. Such a committee can regulate conflict between unions and support individual stewards. They also constitute a more powerful body for negotiating with management.

A trade union branch is typically made up of employees from different organisations located in the same geographical area. The branch manages the internal affairs of the union and strives for improvements in the terms and conditions of the branch members. The affairs of the branch are managed by the branch committee. This committee is elected at the Annual General Meeting (AGM) of the branch, which is also the forum for electing delegates from the branch to attend the Annual Delegate Conference of the union.

A branch secretary serves both the branch committee and the branch members. In larger unions, this individual may be a permanent employee of the union. If so s/he is described as a full-time branch official, whose role is to administer the affairs of the branch and negotiate terms and conditions for all branch members with management.

At national level, the election of union officers takes place at the Annual Delegate Conference. Motions concerning the union and its policies are discussed and voted upon. These motions are usually branch resolutions and a motion that is approved at the Annual Delegate Conference becomes a resolution of the conference and ultimately union policy. The Annual Delegate Conference consists of branch delegates and the unions' National Executive. The National Executive is responsible for carrying out the decisions of the Annual Delegate Conference. In particular, it appoints the unions full-time branch officials and appoints staff employed by the union.

The general officers of the union are usually full-time employees of the union and they do not have another job. In some unions they are appointed to their position by the National Executive, while in others they are elected at the Annual Delegate Conference or by a ballot of union members. The general officers are usually the General President, a General Secretary, a General Vice-President and a General Treasurer.

The IRISH CONGRESS OF TRADE UNIONS (ICTU) is the central co-ordinating body for the Irish trade union movement, with over 90 per cent of trade unionists in membership of unions affiliated to Congress. Individual unions maintain a large degree of autonomy and the ICTU relies on the co-operation of affiliated unions in promoting its overall goals. The annual conference of the ICTU consists of delegates from affiliated unions. The ICTU plays a critical role at national level, representing union views to government. Along with the other social partners (government, employer representatives, farmer federations), it is involved in national negotiations on pay and other aspects of social and economic policy.

7.4.2 Employer organisations

The major driving force for the development of employer organisations was the perceived need on the employers' side to organise collectively in order to counterbalance and deal effectively with emerging trade unions. Employer organisations in Ireland are of two types: employer associations and trade associations. Employer associations were established to aid in the conduct of employee relations, whereas trade associations were established with trade and commercial reasons in mind.

Employer associations have the following broad objectives:

- to effectively represent employers' views to government and to other appropriate bodies so as to preserve and develop a political, economic, social and cultural climate in which business objectives can be achieved
- to create an environment/climate that supports free enterprise and enshrines managerial prerogative in decision making
- to ensure the existence of a legislative and procedural environment that supports and co-ordinates employers' views on employee relations matters and to provide assistance to affiliated employers.

The largest employer association in Ireland is the Irish Business and Employers' Confederation (IBEC), which was formed in 1993 through an amalgamation of two previously separate institutions, namely, the Federation of Irish Employers (FIE) and the Confederation of Irish Industry (CII). IBEC represents the alliance of a large number of companies and organisations which recognised the need for a single cohesive force capable of providing effective leadership and representation in the current turbulent business environment. IBEC is dedicated to promoting a favourable climate for economic growth, investment and employee/industrial relations. IBEC has offices in Dublin, Cork, Limerick, Waterford, Galway, Donegal Town and Brussels. Among its services are:

- representation in relations with government, trade unions and EU institutions on commercial, economic and industrial and employee relations issues
- membership of an appropriate sector organisation with direct links to the corresponding European association
- conferences, seminars, specialist publications, statistics, business-sector profiles and customised research
- a range of additional consultancy services on, for example, human resource management, health, safety and environment, training and development issues.

At the national level, IBEC has a strong regional membership structure through which the views of members are co-ordinated on national issues and representation can be made on matters of regional interest. At European level, through its Brussels office, IBEC seeks to influence EU economic and social policy, represent Irish interests in the Union of Industry and Employer Confederations in Europe (UNICE), and produce a range of specialist publications, including *EU Business Opportunities* and *EU Monthly Report*. The Confederation also represents members' interests in many international organisations, such as the International Labour Office and the International Organisation of Employers.

7.4.3 State institutions

Traditionally, the role of the state in employee relations in Ireland has been restricted to the establishment of legislative ground rules and the provision of mediation and arbitration services, leaving employers and employees relatively free to develop work rules and procedures to suit particular organisational contexts. In recent years, the role of the state in employee relations has increased, particularly through a process of reforming the system of employee relations and also through being a party to national agreements such as the Programme for National Recovery (PNR), the Programme for Economic and Social Progress (PESP), the Programme for Competitiveness and Work (PCW), Partnership 2000, and the Programme for Prosperity and Fairness (PPF).

The state provides a number of specific institutions—the LABOUR RELATIONS COMMISSION, the LABOUR COURT, RIGHTS COMMISSIONERS, EQUALITY OFFICERS and the EMPLOYMENT APPEALS TRIBUNAL (EAT)—all charged with various responsibilities for employee relations matters.

The Labour Relations Commission. Formally established by the then Minister for Labour in January 1991, the Labour Relations Commission's statutory authority and functions derive from Section 24 and Section 25 of the Industrial Relations Act 1990. It is a tripartite body with employer, trade union and independent representation and has been charged with the general responsibility of promoting good industrial relations practice. The Commission provides a comprehensive range of services designed to prevent the occurrence of disputes and, where they do occur, some mechanisms for resolution. The key services provided by the Labour Relations Commission are:

- ▶ a conciliation service
- ▶ an industrial relations advisory service
- ▶ the preparation of codes of practice relevant to industrial relations after consultation with unions and employers organisations
- ▶ providing guidance on codes of practice
- ▶ the appointment of equality officers and the provision of an equality service
- ▶ the selection and nomination of persons for appointment as rights commissioners
- ▶ the commissioning of research into matters relevant to industrial relations
- ▶ the review and monitoring of developments in the area of industrial relations
- ▶ assisting joint labour committees and joint industrial councils in the exercise of their functions.

The conciliation service was formally provided by the Labour Court. The service can be seen as a proactive measure to resolve disputes before they require full Labour Court investigation. The role of the advisory service is broader than that of the conciliation service and is designed to help in the identification of general problems which may be giving rise to employee relations difficulties. The advisory service brings with it a new dimension to the services available to Irish employers and trade unions. It has as its central brief the task of preventing industrial disputes by encouraging good industrial relations policies, practices and procedures in organisations facing management–labour difficulties. The service becomes involved in assignments either on the basis of union/management agreement or on the initiative of the Labour Relations Commission with the agreement of the parties concerned. In 1992 the advisory service undertook eight projects of which two involved private sector companies and six involved private-sector employments.

The Labour Court. Established in 1946 by the Industrial Relations Act, it is a central institution in the Irish system of employee relations. The role of the Court has changed significantly as a result of the 1990 Industrial Relations Act. Its central role is investigating and making recommendations on cases referred to it by parties in dispute. If the conciliation service provided by the Labour Relations Commission fails to resolve a dispute, both parties can ask the Labour Court to hear their case. The Industrial Relations Act 1990 provides that the Labour Court may normally investigate a dispute only in the following situations:

❶ If it receives a report from the Labour Relations Commission that no further efforts on its part will help resolve the dispute.

❷ If it is notified by the Chairperson of the Commission that the Commission has waived its function of conciliation in the dispute.

❸ If it is hearing an appeal in relation to a recommendation of a Rights Commissioner or an Equality Officer.

❹ If it decides after consultation with the Commission that the exceptional circumstances of the case warrant a Labour Court investigation.

❺ If it is referred to under Section 20 of the Industrial Relations Act 1969.

❻ If it is requested by the Minister for Enterprise and Employment to do so.

A Labour Court hearing normally consists of an independent chairperson and an employer and a trade union representative. Hearings typically involve both written and oral submissions and some element of cross examination. When the Court has fully investigated the case it will issue a recommendation which is not legally binding.

Rights Commissioners and Equality Officers. Rights Commissioners are appointed by the Minister for Labour under the auspices of the Industrial Relations Act 1969. They deal with disputes concerning individual employees. Originally established under the operation of the Labour Court, the Rights Commissioner Service now operates as part of the Labour Relations Commission. Commissioners remain completely independent in the performance of their functions. Rights Commissioners investigate disputes under the Industrial Relations Act 1969, the Unfair Dismissals Act 1977, the Maternity Protection Act 1981 and the Payment of Wages Act 1991. A Rights Commissioner will only deal with a dispute if it involves:

▶ a dispute that is not connected with the pay and conditions of a collective group of workers

▶ a dispute that has not been or is not already being investigated by the Labour Court

▶ a party to the dispute who does not object in writing.

Generally, a Rights Commissioner will investigate disputes concerning individual employees only. Recent legislation in the form of the Industrial Relations Act 1990 provides that an objection to an investigation by a Rights Commissioner must be notified in writing to the Commissioner within three weeks. An appeal against a recommendation from a rights Commissioner must be notified in writing to the Labour Court within six weeks from the date of the recommendation.

Historically, Equality Officers dealt with issues relating to discrimination under legislation such as the Anti-Discrimination (Pay) Act 1974 and the Employment Equality Act 1977. Such Officers operated under the auspices of the Labour Relations Commission, but were independent in the performance of their duties. More recent legislation in the form of the Employment Equality Act 1998 repeals the Anti-Discrimination (PAY) Act 1974 and the earlier Employment Equality Act 1977. Under the 1998 Act, discrimination occurs where a person is treated less favourably than another person. It is forbidden on the grounds of gender, marital status, family status, sexual orientation, religious belief, age, disability, race and membership of the travelling community. The recently established Equality Authority facilitates the enforcement of the Act. It is charged with the responsibility of promoting equality under the Act. Equality Officers now operate within the Office of the Director of Equality Investigations. This Office is now the first place where individuals seeking redress under the Act will go.

Employment Appeals Tribunal. The current Employment Appeals Tribunal (EAT) was initially established as the Redundancy Appeals Tribunal under the terms of the Redundancy Payments Act 1969, and was later renamed the Employment Appeals Tribunal under the Unfair Dismissals Act 1977. The EAT consists of a chairperson, who must be a practising barrister or solicitor, seven vice-chairpersons and a panel of ordinary members drawn equally from employer associations and the ICTU. The EAT operates in divisions consisting of a chairperson or vice-chairperson and two other members, one from the employers' side and one from the trade union side. The EAT adjudicates upon a number of Acts including the Redundancy Payments Acts 1967–89, the Terms of Employment Act 1994 (replacing the Minimum Notice and Terms of Employment Act 1973), the Unfair Dismissals (Amendment) Act 1993 and the Unfair Dismissals Act 1977, and the Maternity (Protection of Employees) Act 1981.

Overall, state institutions play a major role in employee relations in Ireland. Operating within the framework of the Industrial Relations Act 1990 and earlier legislation, state institutions are largely concerned with conciliation and arbitration.

7.5 Summary of key propositions

▶ This chapter introduced the historical development of human resource management in Ireland, discussed each of the major activity areas in HRM, namely, HR planning, recruitment, selection, performance appraisal, pay and benefits and training and development. It also outlined the context for the conduct of employee relations in Ireland, examining the role of trade unions, employers' organisations and the machinery of the state involved in employee relations. Historically, HR management has gone through a number of major transitions, the most prominent being the Welfarist and Taylorist phases in the early 1900s, the move towards bureaucracy and negotiators in the mid-1900s, the increased legislation in the 1970s, and the increasingly strategic role of more recent years, culminating in the emergence of HRM.

▶ Human resource planning is concerned with the quantity and quality of manpower available to an organisation and how this manpower is deployed throughout the organisation in an attempt to ensure organisational effectiveness and efficiency. The major stages in the manpower planning process are demand analysis, supply analysis, estimating deficits/surpluses and developing action plans.

▶ Recruitment is concerned with attracting a group of potential candidates to apply for the position that the organisation has available. Two key stages can be identified in the recruitment process. First, the background stage which is concerned with the conducting of a job analysis. Second, there is the actual recruitment stage which is concerned with attracting a pool of potential candidates from either the internal or the external labour market.

▶ Selection is concerned with choosing the most suitable candidate from the pool that has been attracted during the recruitment phase. The most common methods of selection include the interview, the reference and the aptitude test.

▶ The choice of payment system is an important consideration for organisations as the money a person receives for carrying out work can be a source of motivation. The most common types of payment systems used in Irish organisations include flat rate only, flat rate + bonus, merit rating, profit sharing and piecework.

▶ Performance appraisal is the process of reviewing an individual's performance and progress in a job and assessing his/her potential for future promotion. The results-oriented appraisal method is the most commonly used in Irish organisations. Rating and free form are also frequently used.

▶ Training and development is aimed at helping employees to become more effective on the job and developing their potential. Good training practice should begin with the development of a policy, followed by the identification of needs, then planning and conducting the training and finally evaluating the process. On-the-job training is the most commonly used training method in Ireland.

▶ Pluralism in employee relations refers to the existence of a conflict of interest between management and labour which can best be handled through collective bargaining. Unitarism refers to the existence of a mutuality of interests between the parties to the labour process.

▶ A trade union can be defined as a continuous association of wage earners with the objective of improving or maintaining conditions of employment. There are three major types of trade unions in Ireland, namely, craft unions, general unions and white-collar unions. Employer organisations in Ireland are of two types: employer associations and trade associations.

▶ The major state institutions involved in employee relations in Ireland are the Labour Relations Commission, the Labour Court, Rights Commissioners, Equality Officers and the Employment Appeals Tribunal.

Discussion questions

❶ What are the main phases in the history of human resource management in Ireland?

❷ Define human resource planning and give reasons why it should be linked to an organisation's overall strategic plan.

❸ Identify and describe the main phases in producing a manpower plan.

❹ What should be included in a job description and person specification?

❺ What are the major sources of recruitment available to an organisation?

❻ Describe the different types of selection interview that you are familiar with and highlight the advantages and disadvantages associated with each.

❼ What factors will influence an employee's satisfaction with the rewards s/he receives?

❽ Describe the different types of payment system that an organisation could adopt. What factors will influence the choice of payment system?

❾ Define performance appraisal and identify some of the major objectives of the performance appraisal process.

❿ Describe the methods of performance appraisal that you are familiar with including their advantages and disadvantages.

⓫ Distinguish between training and development and identify the factors that are responsible for the increased interest in training and development in recent years.

⓬ Describe each of the main stages involved in systematic training and development.

⓭ Outline the main aims of trade unions and discuss the key strategies that are employed to achieve these aims.

⓮ Consider the Irish Business and Employers' Confederation, focusing on its role and the advantages and disadvantages of membership from an organisation's perspective.

⓯ Discuss the role of both the Labour Court and the Labour Relations Commission in Irish employee relations.

Concluding case: Change at Leeway and the implications for human resource management and development

Leeway, a unionised organisation with headquarters in the USA, is a leading manufacturer of computer systems and associated equipment. The company operates in highly competitive circumstances, and its external environment is both complex and dynamic. The company and its management appreciate that organisational change and adaptation is necessary in order to remain competitive and continue as a market leader.

In the past, Leeway has come to recognise the need to become a more employee-centred organisation. While it started out as what might be termed 'organic' in nature, a number of negative features have manifested themselves in the course of time: several layers of supervision; large growth in the number of technical specialists and support staff; a growth in the number of procedures and rules, leading to a deal of inflexibility; weakened general decision making with relatively little input from employees; a fall off in the level of innovation; poor communication and duplication of certain activities.

Overall the organisation was out of tune in terms of what was being demanded of it by its external environment. The negative features combined to form what the company had labelled the traditional organisation, one not conducive to high levels of performance and effectiveness.

Following a series of meetings at various levels throughout the organisation, a number of features of the new organisation scenario were identified, and can be summarised as follows: greater optimisation of technical and human resources; implementation of a philosophy whereby human assets are to be viewed as resources to be developed rather than as expendable spare parts (agents, not objects); the achievement of optimum task groupings and multiple, broad flexible skills; the promotion of ownership and responsibility lower down the organisation and the utilisation of internal controls and self-regulating sub-systems and groups; the achievement of a flatter organisation structure and a more participative management style; the encouragement of a degree of innovation and intrapreneurship; a more proactive stance in relation to the external environment.

Case questions

❶ Reflect on the characteristics of the new organisation scenario and what it represents relative to the tradition within Leeway.

❷ Discuss the implications of the implementation of each aspect of the new scenario on each of the functional aspects of HRM.

Bibliography

Advisory Committee on Management Training (1988) *Managers for Ireland: The Case of the Development of Irish Managers*. Government Publications Office.

Anderson, N. and Shackleton, V. (1986) 'Recruitment and Selection: A Review of Developments in the 1980s', *Personnel Review*, 15 (4).

Arnold, J., Robertson, I. and Cooper, C. (1991) *Work Psychology: Understanding Human Behaviour in the Workplace*. London: Pitman.

Attwood, M. (1989) *Personnel Management*. Basingstoke: Macmillan.

Barrington, T. (1980) *The Irish Administrative System*. Dublin: Institute of Public Administration.

Barrow, M. and Loughlin, H. (1992) 'Towards a Learning Organisation: 1. The Rationale', *Industrial and Commercial Training*, 24 (1).

Beardwell, I. and Holden, L. (1994) *Human Resource Management: A Contemporary Perspective*. London: Pitman.

Beer, M. *et al.* (1985) *Human Resource Management: A General Manager's Perspective*. The Free Press/Macmillan.

Berridge, J. (1992) 'Human Resource Management in Britain', *Employee Relations*, 14 (5).

Bowey, A. (1974) *Manpower Planning*. Oxford: Heinemann.

Buchanan, D. and McCalman, J. (1989) *High Performance Work Systems: The Digital Experience*. London: Routledge.

Clifford, N., Turner, T., Gunnigle, P. and Morley, M. (1997) 'Human Resource Management in Ireland: An Overview', in Gunnigle, P., Morley, M., Clifford, N. and Turner, T. (1997) *Human Resource Management in Irish Organisations: Practice in Perspective*, Dublin: Oak Tree Press.

Cole, G. (1986) *Personnel Management: Theory and Practice*. London: DP Publications.

Collins, D. and Sinclaire, J. (1991) 'The Skills Time Bomb: 1', *Leadership and Organisation Development Journal*, 12 (1).

Cranet E Surveys (Ireland) (1992, 1995), University of Limerick.

Flood, P., Gannon, M. and Paauwe, J. (1996) *Managing Without Traditional Methods*. Wokingham: Addison Wesley.

Foley, K. and Gunnigle, P. (1993) 'The Personnel/Human Resource Function and Workplace Employee Relations', in Gunnigle, P., Flood, P., Morley, M. and Turner, T. *Continuity and Change in Irish Employee Relations*. Dublin: Oak Tree Press.

Foley, K., Gunnigle, P. and Morley, M. (1996) 'Personnel Management in Ireland: A New Epoch?', *The International Journal of Employment Studies*, 4 (2).

Fombrun, C., Tichy, N. and Devanna, M. (1984) *Strategic Human Resource Management*. New York: John Wiley & Sons.

Garavan, T., Constine, P. and Heraty, N. (1995) *Training and Development in Ireland: Context, Policy and Practice*. Dublin: Oak Tree Press.

Grundy, T. (1998) 'How are Corporate Strategy and Human Resources Strategy Linked?', *Journal of General Management*, 23 (3), 49–58.

Guest, D. (1987) 'Human Resource Management and Industrial Relations', *Journal of Management Studies*, May.

Guest, D. (1989) 'Personnel and HRM: Can You Tell the Difference?', *Personnel Management*, January.

Gunnigle, P. (1992) 'Human Resource Management in Ireland', *Employee Relations*, 14 (5).

Gunnigle, P. and Flood, P. (1990) *Personnel Management in Ireland: Practices, Trends and Developments*. Dublin: Gill & Macmillan.

Gunnigle, P., Foley, K. and Morley, M. (1993) 'A Review of Organisational Reward Practices in Ireland', in Gunnigle, P., Flood, P., Morley, M. and Turner, T. *Continuity and Change in Irish Employee Relations*. Dublin: Oak Tree Press.

Gunnigle, P., Garavan, T. and Fitzgerald, G. (1992) *Employee Relations and Employment Law in Ireland*, University of Limerick.

Gunnigle, P., Heraty, N. and Morley, M. (1997) *Personnel & Human Resource Management in Ireland: Theory & Practice*. Dublin: Gill & Macmillan.

Gunnigle, P., Morley, M., Clifford, N. and Turner, T. (1997) *Human Resource Management in Irish Organisations: Practice in Perspective*. Dublin: Oak Tree Press.

Hanna, D. (1988) *Designing Organisations for High Performance*. New York: Addison Wesley.

Heraty, N. (1992) 'Training and Development: A Study of Practices in Irish Based Companies'. University of Limerick: Unpublished MBS Thesis.

Heraty, N. and Morley, M. (1998a) 'In Search of Good Fit: Policy and Practice in Recruitment and Selection in Ireland', *Journal of Management Development*, 17 (9).

Heraty, N. and Morley, M. (1998b) 'Training and Development in the Irish Context: Responding to the Competitiveness Agenda', *Journal of European Industrial Training*, 22 (4), 190–204.

Heraty, N., Gunnigle, P. and Clifford, N. (1997) 'Recruitment and Selection in Ireland', in Gunnigle, P., Morley, M., Clifford, N. and Turner, T. *Human Resource Management in Irish Organisations: Practice in Perspective*. Dublin: Oak Tree Press.

Heraty, N., Morley, M. and McCarthy, A. (2000) 'Vocational Education and Training in the Republic of Ireland: Institutional Reform and Policy Developments Since the 1960s', *Journal of Vocational Education and Training*, 52 (2), 177–98.

Heraty, N., Morley, M. and Turner, T. (1993) 'Trends and Developments in the Organisation of the Employment Relationship', in Gunnigle, P., Flood, P., Morley, M. and Turner, T.

Continuity and Change in Irish Employee Relations. Dublin: Oak Tree Press.

Horwitz, F. (1990) 'HRM: An Ideological Perspective', *Personnel Review*, 19 (2).

Keating, M. (1987) 'Personnel Management in Ireland', in *Industrial Relations in Ireland*. Department of Industrial Relations. Dublin: University College.

Keenoy, T. (1990) 'Human Resource Management: A Case of the Wolf in Sheep's Clothing?', *Personnel Review*, 19 (2).

Lawler, E. (1977) 'Reward Systems', in Hackman, J. and Suttle, J. (eds.) *Improving Life at Work: Behavioural Science Approaches to Organisational Change*. New York: Goodyear.

Lawler, E. (1988) 'Human Resource Management: Meeting the New Challenge', *Personnel*, January.

Lundy, O. and Cowling, A. (1996) *Strategic Human Resource Management*. London: Routledge.

Mabey, C. and Salaman, G. (1995) *Strategic Human Resource Management*. Oxford: Blackwell.

Makin, P. and Robertson, I. (1986) 'Selecting the Best Selection Technique', *Personnel Management*, November.

McMahon, G. and Gunnigle, P. (1994) *Performance Appraisal: How to Get it Right*. Productive Personnel Limited in association with IPM (Ireland).

McMahon, G. (1988) 'Personnel Selection in Ireland: Scientific Prediction or Crystal Ball Gazing?', *IPM News*, 3 (3), October.

McMahon, G. (2000) 'Choosing the Right Kind of Interview for the Job', *Irish Times*, 9 October.

Monks, K. (1996) 'Ploughing the Furrow and Reaping the Harvest: Roles and Relationships in HRM'. The 1996 Examiner/University College Cork Lecture in Human Resource Management, University College Cork, September.

Mooney, P. (1980) 'An Inquiry into Wage Payment Systems in Ireland', ESRI/European Foundation for the Improvement of Living and Working Conditions.

Morley, M. and Garavan, T. (1993) 'The New Organisation: It's Implications for Training and Development'. Paper presented to the Irish Institute of Training and Development 24th National Conference, The Emerging Organisation, Galway, April.

Morley, M. and Gunnigle, P. (1997) 'Compensation and Benefits', in Gunnigle, P., Morley, M., Clifford, N. and Turner, T. *Human Resource Management in Irish Organisations: Practice in Perspective*. Dublin: Oak Tree Press.

Morley, M., Gunnigle, P. and Heraty, N. (1995) 'Developments in Flexible Working Practices in the Republic of Ireland: Research Evidence Considered', *The International Journal of Manpower*, 16 (8).

Morley, M., Gunnigle, P. and Heraty, N. (1999) 'Constructing the Reward Package,' *International Journal of Employment Studies*, 7 (2).

Muchinski, P. (1986) 'Personnel Selection Methods', in Cooper, C. and Robertson, I. (eds), *International Review of Industrial and Organisational Psychology*. New York: John Wiley.

Munro-Fraser, J. (1954) *A Handbook of Employment Interviewing*. New York: MacDonald & Evans.

Peters, T. and Waterman, R. (1982) *In Search of Excellence*. New York: Harper Row.

Pettigrew, P., Hendry, C. and Sparrow, P. (1988) 'Linking Strategic Change, Competitive Performance and Human Resource Management'. Results of a UK-based Empirical Study, University of Warwick.

Plumbley, P. (1985) *Recruitment and Selection*. London: Institute of Personnel Management.

Poole, M. and Jenkins, G. (1996) 'Competitiveness and Human Resource Management Policies', *Journal of General Management*, 22 (2), 1–14.

Porter, M. (1979) 'How Competitive Forces Shape Strategy', *Harvard Business Review*, March/April.

Purcell, J. (1982) 'Macho Managers and the New Industrial Relations', *Employee Relations*, 4 (1).

Roche, W. and Larragy, J. (1986) 'The Trend of Unionisation in the Irish Republic', in *Industrial Relations in Ireland: Contemporary Issues and Developments*. University College Dublin.

Rodger, A. (1952) *The Seven Point Plan*. UK: National Institute of Psychology.

Shivanath, G. (1987) 'Personnel Practitioners 1986: Their Role and Status in Irish Industry', University of LImerick: Unpublished MBS Thesis.

Smith, M. and Robertson, I. (1986) *The Theory and Practice of Systematic Staff Selection*. Basingstoke: Macmillan.

Smith, M., Gregg, M. and Andrews, D. (1989) *Selection and Assessment: A New Appraisal*. London: Pitman.

Storey, J. (1992) *Developments in the Management of Human Resources*. Oxford: Blackwell Publishers.

Storey, J. (1995) 'Human Resource Management: Still Marching On, or Marching Out', in Storey, J. (ed.) *Human Resource Management: A Critical Text*. London: Routledge.

Torrington, D. and Hall, L. (1987) *Personnel Management: A New Approach*. Prentice Hall International.

Torrington, D. (1986) 'Will Consultants take over the Personnel Function?', *Personnel Management*, September.

Tyson, S. and York, A. (1992) *Personnel Management*. Oxford: Butterworth-Heinemann.

Tyson, S. (1987) 'The Management of the Personnel Function', *Journal of Management Studies*, September.

Walton, R. (1985) *From Control to Commitment in the Workplace*, Harvard Business Review, March/April.

Wexley, K. and Latham, G. (1991) *Developing and Training Human Resources in Organisations*. New York: Harper-Collins.

Note

What was originally called the Price Waterhouse Cranfield Project, now known as the Cranet E Project on International Strategic Human Resource Management, was established in 1989 and is designed to analyse the nature of human resource management practices at enterprise level in Europe. It is designed around a tri-annual survey in some 22 participating countries. The project is co-ordinated by Professor Chris Brewster and a dedicated team of researchers at Cranfield University School of Management in the UK. The Republic of Ireland participated in the survey for the first time in 1992 and in subsequent rounds of the survey. The Irish component of the study is located at the Department of Personnel and Employment Relations in the College of Business at the University of Limerick and is co-ordinated by Professor Patrick Gunnigle, Dr Michael Morley and Thomas Turner. For more details on the European-wide findings, see Brewster, C., Mayerhofer, W. and Morley, M. (2000) *New Challenges for European Human Resource Management*, London: Macmillan; and Brewster, C. and Hegewisch, A. (1994) *Policy and Practice in European Human*

Resource Management: The Price Waterhouse Cranfield Project, London: Routledge. For more detailed accounts of the findings from Ireland, see Gunnigle, P., Morley, M., Clifford, N. and Turner, T. (1997), *Human Resource Management in Irish Organisations: Practice in Perspective*, Dublin: Oak Tree Press; and Gunnigle, P., Flood, P. Morley, M. and Turner, T. (1994), *Continuity and Change in Irish Employee Relations*, Dublin: Oak Tree Press.

Chapter 8
Leadership

8.1 Introduction

Leadership, according to Cunningham (1992), is a concept worthy of global concern, especially in the context of the ever increasing internationalisation of business. But what are the characteristics of a good leader? Well, that's a good question! There is little doubt that leadership is a skill that is respected and admired, but it appears rather elusive to many people. It is also widely talked about and, at the same time, is somehow puzzling. Nicholls (1990) suggests that leadership is a seductive word that has a multitude of meanings, while, Leavy (1995:40) notes that 'few areas in management and in the wider purview of society and social organisation are more engaging and intriguing than leadership'. One potential reason for the appearance of confusion in the literature might lie in Flanagan and Thompson's (1993:9) observation that 'leadership research and teaching are fast moving fields'. They note that:

While big ideas—traits, behaviours, cognition—do not come along very frequently, intense energy goes into the 'normal science' of applying these ideas to diverse situations and changing circumstances. The results can often portray a very fragmented picture or, worse, a series of pictures whose relationship is by no means clear.

There are many studies and a considerable body of knowledge on leadership, the impetus for this, some would say, arising from an underlying dissatisfaction with many theories. The diversity of the body of knowledge on leadership is reflected in the breadth of the literature. Among the diverse issues investigated are the qualities of the exceptional leader; the relationship between personality dimensions and successful leadership; the extent of the charisma possessed by the leader and its usefulness in effecting change in organisations; confidence, in particular, overconfidence among leaders; leadership perception; the effect of leadership on group behaviour and performance; trust between leaders and followers; decision making among leaders; vision creation and leadership; the role of leadership in individuals withdrawing from organisational life; the motivational consequences of different leadership approaches; the degree of emotional intelligence possessed by the leader, in particular, its relationship with transformational abilities; the relationship between demonstrated leadership and organisational performance; the language patterns of leaders which are said to have the potential to provide unique insights into their thoughts and actions; to the actual physical fitness of the leader, something which Neck *et al.* (2000) have recently suggested might hold the key to effective executive leadership.

The sheer diversity of the field has led Hitt (1993:5) to suggest that trying to 'piece together' a comprehensive theory of leadership from the numerous threads running through the extensive literature is 'like trying to find one's way out of a jungle without a map'. But with or without a map, making the journey and exploring the nature of leadership is important because, as Sarros and Woodman (1993) point out, while the determinants of leadership success are far from clear, numerous studies have indicated that leadership can make a difference to organisational performance.

In making the exploratory journey the reader will discover that the broad sweep of the literature on the subject concerns itself with the characteristics of so-called effective leaders and the things that set them apart, the power sources of the leader, and the nature of the influence that they possess and how they wield it. In this way, House and Aditya (1997) suggest that many of the varied contributions to the extant literature have been cumulative, each building upon the other, and a good deal is now known about the leadership phenomenon. This chapter examines the nature of leadership and its significance in organisational life. We introduce the distinctions between management and leadership framed in the literature, outline the multiple roles that a leader might adopt in the organisation, and review the different schools of thought on leadership. Early trait theory, followed by behavioural, contingency and more recent charismatic models are presented. As you will see, trait theory has its origins in the elaborate search for characteristics, dispositions and tendencies which set leaders apart from others. An assumption underpinning the thought of many of the researchers working in this trait tradition is that leaders are born, not made. The behavioural school takes as its starting point not the identification of traits, but the actual behaviours exhibited by the leader. Several major contributions in this tradition point to two major dichotomous leadership behaviours, namely, task- and people-oriented. The contingency school concerned itself with the differing demands made on leaders, depending on the context in which they are operating. And charismatic models of leadership broadly focus on how leaders enact the achievement of highly significant accomplishments in organisations. However, before we present these different schools in greater detail, the definitional and role aspects of leadership, which abound in the literature, will be explored.

8.2 Leadership defined

House and Aditya (1997:409) note that though the leadership phenomenon has a long pedigree, the 'systematic social scientific study of leadership did not begin until the early 1930s'. Since that time, 'the burning cry in all organisations', according to Perrow (1973), 'has been for good leadership'. However, he also notes that we have learned that, beyond a threshold level of adequacy, it is extremely difficult to know what good leadership is. While leadership means different things to different people, it is generally regarded as a critical factor in the success of any kind of social activity (Statt 1994) and more directly in business performance (Schultz 2000; Edgeman and Dahlgaard 1998).

The ability to provide effective leadership is one of the most important skills that a manager can posses. Thus there is little doubt that leadership is a skill that is respected and admired, but it appears rather elusive to many people. Mullins (1991) argues that leadership may be interpreted in simple terms such as 'getting others to follow', or interpreted more specifically, for example, as 'the use of authority in decision making'. It may, he suggests, be exercised as an attribute of position, or because of personal knowledge or wisdom. Pettinger (1994:31) maintains that:

Leadership is that part of the management sphere concerned with getting results through people, and all that entails and implies—the organisation of the staff into productive teams, groups, departments; the creation of human structures; their motivation and direction; the resolution of conflicts at the workplace; creating vision and direction for the whole undertaking; and providing resources in support of this.

Thus, getting results through people is a demanding and complex engagement. In this way, Selznick (1957) noted that leadership goes beyond simple efficiency or arguments about efficiency and more fundamentally establishes the basic mission of the enterprise and creates and nurtures a functioning social unit capable of fulfilling that core mission. This can be seen to provide the backdrop to Hitt's (1993) conception of the leadership phenomenon. He notes that leadership can be best thought of in terms of 'influence', the art or process of influencing people so that they will strive willingly towards the achievement of group goals. A slightly narrower interpretation is advanced by Tannenbaum *et al.* (1961) when they suggest that leadership is an interpersonal influence that is exercised in a situation and directed specifically through the communication process towards the attainment of a specified goal. More recently, Edgeman and Dahlgaard (1998) present the concept of systematic leadership as a combination of core values and core competences which allow the right course of action in a given situation to be chosen. Systematic leadership of this nature, they suggest, is related to business excellence. Dess and Picken (2000) in their treaties on leadership in the twenty-first century observe that the foundation of wealth creation is changing from capital intensive manufacturing industry to information intensive businesses and that a change of this nature and magnitude requires a new and distinct form of leadership dedicated to simultaneously fostering innovation and respon-siveness. These attributes of innovation and responsiveness are, they suggest, best attained by leadership behaviours dedicated to institutionalising employee empowerment, knowledge sharing and enabling creativity. Trevelyan (1998) suggests that leadership should be a balance between a directive style which shows the way, and a softer, devolved style which seeks to maximise the potential of individuals. The most effective leadership, she suggests, promotes motivation, creativity and performance, while also sustaining support, managerial control and expert input. In this way the leader is viewed both as enabler and constrainer.

8.3 Distinguishing leadership and management

Leadership is an essential and integral part of good management. Contrary to popular belief, leadership is not an optional extra. Managers who do not lead are failing to fulfil their function as managers. When lacking its leadership dimensions, management is reduced to mere administration. Generally, organisations that are managed without leadership perform poorly—they are bureaucratic, unresponsive and inefficient. (Nicholls 1993:1)

In drawing attention to the distinction between leadership and management, Nicholls (1993:7) refers to the 'paradox of managerial leadership', while Bennis (1989) argues that in order to survive in the twenty-first century, 'we are going to need a new generation of leaders—leaders, not managers. The distinction is an important one. Leaders conquer the context—the volatile, turbulent, ambiguous surroundings that sometimes seem to conspire against us and will surely suffocate us if we let them—

while managers surrender to it.' 'Managers', according to Bennis and Nanus (1985), 'do things right', while, 'leaders do the right things'. Similarly, Yukl (1994) notes that while one individual might perform both managerial and leadership functions, the two activity domains involve separate and relatively distinct processes. Thus, managers, Yukl suggests, are oriented towards stability, while leaders are innovation oriented. Furthermore, while managers typically get individuals to do things with ever increasing efficiency, the goal of the effective leader is to get individuals to agree about what things should actually be done.

Vaughan (1989:34) notes that while managers typically want to portray themselves as skilled professionals as well as inspirational leaders, these roles are 'basically incompatible'. He goes on to suggest that:

Attempts to combine both can cause confusions and misunderstandings about management responsibilities and motives, and can result in serious errors of judgement. It is occasionally difficult to decide whether some advertisements for management positions, such as the one ... that was addressed to 'aggressive motivated accountants', are dangerous or merely absurd in the way they combine personal and professional requirements. It [this paper] does not agree that the substitution of professionalism with personal leadership and persuasion offers the best means of ensuring good relations.

Exhibit 8.1 Workplace conversations on the nature of leadership

- Two machinists are chatting over coffee in the canteen during a break from work:

  1st voice: It's a funny thing but Bob seems much better as section head than I thought he would be.

  2nd voice: How do you mean?

  1st voice: Well, I had my doubts when they promoted him last year, but he has turned out really well. He seems to adjust to suit everyone. If you know how to do something, he lets you get on with it—providing you show willing, of course.

  2nd voice: He certainly doesn't let you get away with things! If something is wrong, he gets in there to sort out why.

  1st voice: Too true! But at the same time he is very flexible. Some things I'm good at so he never watches me closely or interferes. But he is helping me a lot with the new milling machine. I'm really getting the hang of it.

  2nd voice: Yes, its funny how the job seems to have brought out his leadership talents—I wouldn't have thought it possible.

- Two executives of the same medium-sized company are talking at the water-cooler on the seventh floor of their smart headquarters:

  1st voice: I hear Harry Coleman's finally decided to retire next year. The place won't be the same without him.

  2nd voice: You're right! I can't think of many others who could have pulled us through the things we've just faced in the last couple of years.

  1st voice: It's amazing how he sorted out the mess old Fred lad left us in. He seemed to have an instinct for what had to go and what to hang on to.

  2nd voice: Mind you, he trod on a few toes in the process. He'd never have got all those new projects going if he hadn't. But, by George! The medicine worked!

  1st voice: That's the whole point. He didn't mind whose nose he put out of joint. If he felt it was right he would go for it. After he'd cleared out the dead wood at head office, the others soon got the message.

  2nd voice: Too right! We'd have gone right under without his leadership. He really turned us around.

Exhibit 8.1 Workplace conversations on the nature of leadership *contd.*

- The company's manufacturing director is talking to the personnel director before a board meeting:

  Manufacturing Director: Susan's done a magnificent job with the management services division since she took over last year.

  Personnel Director: They've really found their feet. It seems to me they have a much clearer idea of their role.

  Manufacturing Director: Yes, she's shifted the emphasis to helping the operating divisions perform better and make better decisions—not imposing systems on them like they used to.

  Personnel Director: Not only that, everyone seems to be pulling together. She's managed to overcome the traditional rivalry between design and operations. They actually talk to each other now!

  Manufacturing Director: That's it. There's a real enthusiasm that was never there before. I bumped into Joe Thompson, their chief systems analyst, the other day. He tell me that everyone now feel that they are really able to give their best. Sometimes they get so stuck into things that he actually has to throw them out at night!

  Personnel Director: Sue really knows how to get people turned on. We could do with a bit more leadership like hers around here.

  Commentary: In these examples, Bob, Harry and Sue are performing at widely different levels in their organisations, and the speakers have focused on markedly different aspects of their behaviour as managers. Hearing them one after the other like this, our impression is of three very different activities, yet each is referred to as leadership. No wonder Humpty Dumpty finds it a confusing word!

Source: Extract from Nicholls (1990).

While both leadership and management can be conceived of as being essentially about influence and the use of power, there is a strong argument to be made that leadership is a broader concept than management per se. Critically, it is not axiomatic that every leader is a manager, though conversely Mintzberg (1973) argues that leadership behaviour can be an integral part of a manager's job; in his research he identifies 10 main roles grouped into three areas (see Table 8.1).

Table 8.1 Managerial Roles identified by Mintzberg

Interpersonal	Figurehead
	Leader
	Liaison
Informational	Monitor
	Disseminator
	Spokesman
Decisional	Entrepreneur
	Disturbance handler
	Resource allocator
	Negotiator

Source: Mintzberg (1973).

Obviously, according to Statt (1994), chief executives will spend much more of their time on the interpersonal roles than would more junior managers. However, this does not mean that they will be any more effective as leaders. He argues that the job titles and the job descriptions, and the amount of time the job demands for activity defined as leadership simply tells us what is done. It does not tell us how it is done—and that is where leadership ability and effectiveness comes in (1994:337):

But in any organisation we tend to look automatically at the apex for evidence of leadership. Indeed the greatest fallacy of leadership is that it always comes from the top down. It most certainly does not.

Many believe management and leadership to be more delineated as organisational and/or societal roles (Mullins 1991:421):

Management is more usually viewed as getting things done through other people in order to achieve stated organisational objectives. The manager may react to specific situations and be more concerned with solving short-term problems. Management is regarded as relating to people working within a structured organisation and with prescribed roles. To people outside of the organisation the manager might not be seen in a leadership role. The emphasis of leadership is on interpersonal behaviour in a broader context. It is often associated with the willing and enthusiastic behaviour of followers. Leadership does not necessarily take place within the hierarchical structure of the organisation. Many people operate as leaders without their role ever being clearly established or defined. A leader often has sufficient influence to bring about long-term changes in people's attitudes. Leadership can be seen primarily as an inspirational process.

Table 8.2 Distinguishing between a manager and a leader

Manager	Leader
Motivates people and administers resources to achieve stated organisational goals	Motivates people to develop new objectives
Short-range view	Long-range perspective
A copy	An original
Maintains	Develops
Focuses on system and structure	Focuses on people
Implements	Shapes
Relies on control	Inspires trust
Eye on the bottom line	Eye on the horizon
Narrows down horizons	Opens up horizons
Rational	Emotional
Classic good soldier	Own person
Accepts the status quo	Challenges the status quo
Does things right	Does the right thing

Source: Adapted from Bennis (1989); Statt (1994:340).

Zaleznik of the Harvard Business School (1977) argues forcefully that there is a difference between leadership and management and highlights a number of differences associated with their motivation, personal history and how they actually think:

▶ Managers tend to adopt impersonal or passive attitudes towards goals. Leaders adopt a more personal and active attitude towards goals.

▶ In order to get people to accept solutions, the manager needs to continually co-ordinate and balance in order to compromise conflicting values. The leader creates excitement in work and develops choices that give substance to images that excite people.

▶ In their relationships with other people, managers maintain a low level of emotional involvement. Leaders have empathy with other people and give attention to what events and actions mean.

▶ Managers see themselves more as conservators and regulators of the existing order of affairs with which they identify, and from which they gain rewards. Leaders work in, but do not belong to, the organisation. Their sense of identity does not depend upon membership or work roles and they search out opportunities for change.

While many of the differences cited are not scientifically derived, arguably an individual can be a leader without being a manager and a manager without being a leader. Indeed, Flanagan and Thompson (1993) suggest that there may have been an overemphasis on the creative, transformational component—vision, charisma, meaning, empowering—and what is needed is a balance of 'leadership' and 'management'. In this way Sarros and Woodman (1993) suggest that what is probably clear is that successful organisational leadership relies on a sympathetic combination of traits, skills, attitudes, environmental and intra-environmental conditions and when one or more of these components is missing, leadership goes awry.

8.4 Multiple leadership roles

As far back as 1962, Krech *et al.* identified fourteen leadership functions that demonstrate the complexity of leadership:

❶ The leader as executive—top co-ordinator of the group activities and overseer of the execution of policies.

❷ The leader as planner—deciding the ways and means by which the group achieves its ends through both short-term and long-term planning.

❸ The leader as policy maker—establishing group goals and policies.

❹ The leader as expert—a source of readily available information and skills.

❺ The leader as external group representative—the official spokesperson for the group, the representative of the group and the clearing house for outgoing and incoming information.

❻ The leader as controller of internal relations—determining specific aspects of the groups structure.

❼ The leader as purveyor of rewards and punishment—having control over group members by the power to provide rewards and apply punishments.

❽ The leader as arbitrator and mediator—controlling interpersonal conflict within the group.

❾ The leader as exemplar—a model of behaviour for members of the group, setting an example of what is expected.

❿ The leader as symbol of the group—enhancing the group unit by providing some kind of cognitive focus and establishing the group as a distinct entity.

⓫ The leader as substitute for individual responsibility—relieving the individual member of the group from the necessity of, and responsibility for, personal decision.

⓬ The leader as ideologist—serving as the source of beliefs, values and standards of behaviour for individual members of the group.

⓭ The leader as father figure—serving as focus for the positive emotional feelings of individual members and the object for identification and transference.

⓮ The leader as scapegoat—serving as a target for aggression and hostility of the group, accepting blame in the case of failure.

More recently Dawson (1996:218) assembles what she describes as a 'long and incomplete list' of leadership functions. From a review of the extant literature she argues that the list can be classified into five key areas:

▶ task functions
▶ cultural functions
▶ symbolic functions
▶ political functions
▶ relational functions.

Task functions are largely concerned with task completion, while cultural functions are associated with creating and sustaining a performance culture and climate in the organisation. Symbolic functions are seen to be important arguably because leaders are important for what they stand for as much as for what they actually do. Political functions are associated with the leaders role in relation to outsiders, while relational functions deal with the nature of the relationship between the leader and the followers.

The notion of what constitutes effectiveness in leadership trait, behaviour or action is also highly variable in the literature. Table 8.3, adapted from Hitt (1993) highlights contrasting views of effectiveness advanced by prominent contributors to the leadership literature.

In a recent contribution on the qualities of an exceptional leader, Schultz (2000) draws upon the work of Deming, Shewart and Tribus, all of whom are viewed as masters in their field, to examine those qualities needed by the exceptional leader and identifies three basic ways in which leaders contribute to excellent organisational performance, namely, leadership, direction and action. Schultz suggests that these fundamentals are necessary before the appropriate concepts and techniques can be identified that will support the strategies which can deliver the required performance. Conversely, Dulewicz (2000) points to the importance of emotional intelligence on the part of the effective leader. He suggests that there is little doubting its important for working as part of the top management team in an organisation and is likely to be a key factor in determining successful corporate leadership in the new millennium. Finally, Brown (1994:10) argues that a good deal of leadership effectiveness lies in organisational change know-how. He concludes that the derivation of competitive advantage calls for a sophisticated understanding of organisational change processes, something which is the job of the leader: 'the transformational leader, who, through the judicious use of dramatic rites, can encourage the relearning necessary for radical change'.

Table 8.3 Notions of effective leadership	
Plato:	Effective leaders are philosopher kings
Machiavelli:	Effective leaders are power-wielders, individuals who employ manipulation, exploitation and deviousness to achieve their own ends
Weber:	Effective leaders have charisma—that special spiritual power or personal quality that gives an individual influence over large numbers of people
Taylor:	Effective leaders view management as a science
DePree:	Effective leaders view management as an art
Drucker:	Effective leaders are able to carry out the functions of management—planning, organising, directing and measuring
Appley:	Effective leaders have mastered the art of getting things done through others
McGregor:	Effective leaders understand the human side of enterprise
Likert:	Effective leaders are able to establish effective management systems
Blake and Mouton:	Effective leaders choose a leadership style that reflects a concern for both production and people
Iacocca:	Effective leaders focus on the three 'p's, people, product and profit, in that order
Bradford and Cohen:	Effective leaders develop people
Block:	Effective leaders empower others
Kanter:	Effective leaders are change masters
Bennis and Nanus:	Effective leaders have vision and are able to translate the vision into action
Burns:	Effective leaders are able to lift followers into their better selves
Deming:	Effective leaders help others do quality work

Source: Hitt (1993).

8.5 Different leadership schools of thought

Here we introduce and discuss four major schools of thought on leadership, namely:

▶ the trait approach
▶ the behavioural approach
▶ the contingency approach
▶ the charismatic approach.

8.5.1 Trait theories of leadership

It is almost a truism to suggest that good leadership is essential for business performance. But what makes a good leader? Among the earliest theories of leadership were those which focused on traits (Gibb 1947; Stogdill 1948). The earliest TRAIT THEORIES, which can be traced back to the ancient Greeks, concluded that leaders are born, not made. Up to around 1950 most studies sought to identify leadership traits, principally because prominent leaders seemed to posses certain 'exceptional characteristics'. Also known as the 'great man' theory, the assumption was that it is possible to identify a unifying set of characteristics that make all great leaders great and so psychologists set about looking for the personality characteristics or traits that distinguished leaders from other people. If the concept of traits were to be proved valid, there would have to be specific characteristics in existence that all leaders possess. The trait theories argued that leadership is innate, the product of our parents, given at birth. The chosen individuals are born with traits (particularly personality traits, though physical traits possibly had a role to play) which caused them to be self-selected as leaders. The findings emanating from this early work tend to disagree on what sets of traits distinguish leaders from followers. Among the characteristics identified are:

▶ intelligence
▶ initiative
▶ dependability
▶ lateral thinking ability
▶ self-assuredness
▶ maturity
▶ visionary ability
▶ social well-being
▶ need for achievement
▶ need for power
▶ goal-directedness.

The vast amount of research effort expended by psychologists on this topic, up to the middle of the twentieth century, was reviewed in what Statt (1994:326) refers to as 'a very important article' written by Stogdill (1948). Stogdill found that such people did tend to be higher in certain characteristics than other people—for example, intelligence, level of activity and social participation—but that this relationship was inconsistent and, even where it was found, it was a lot less influential than had generally been assumed. He therefore concluded that, while any useful theory of leadership had to say something about personal characteristics, by themselves they explained very little about leadership behaviour in organisations (Statt 1994:326):

Leadership was much more a matter of context and situation, Stogdill suggested. People who exhibited behaviour in one situation might not do so in another ... the reason for this was that whatever leadership may be it is always a relationship between people.

Overall, the research effort dedicated to the search for universal traits possessed by leaders resulted in little truly convincing evidence. Robbins (1991) goes so far as to say it resulted in 'dead ends'. Certainly much of the research work has identified lists of traits which tend to be overlapping or contradictory with few significant correlations between factors. As Luthans (1992) points out only intelligence seemed to hold up with any degree of consistency and when these findings were combined with those of studies on physical traits, the overall conclusion was that leaders were more likely to be bigger and brighter than those being led, but not too much so! Despite this, Stogdill, argued that it was not entirely appropriate to abandon the study of traits, and that the best way forward was to introduce an interactional element into the equation whereby traits and their significance/universality would be considered in the context of the situational difficulties or demands facing the leader.

However, this view that leaders are born and not made is much less widely held today. There has been an incremental shift away from this thinking for a number of reasons. First, the enormous range of traits potentially affecting leadership ability is problematic and there is a difficulty associated with measuring their existence. This appears a critical weakness according to House and Aditya (1997) largely because there was little empirically substantiated personality theory to guide the search for leadership traits. The lists of traits tend to be exceptionally long and there is not always agreement on how their content should be prioritised. This resulted in an inability to produce many replicative investigations. Second, if we were to rely on birth alone to produce leaders, then potentially we would not have enough leaders to go around. Third, there is a growing body of evidence on the influence of nurturing and life experiences in this area. Fourth, our leadership needs are diverse and vary enormously and are commonly dispersed throughout society, with the result that if the specific situational demands of the leader are taken into account, the replication problem once again raises its head. Overall, many psychologists remain unconvinced that there is any link between any specific characteristics and any form of leadership. Finally, from a methodological perspective, there will very likely be some subjective judgement in determining who is regarded as an effective, 'good' leader (see Yetton 1984).

8.5.2 Behavioural theories of leadership

As convincing evidence failed to accumulate through trait-based research, increasingly researchers began to seek out behaviours that specific leaders exhibited. The central hypothesis in this school of thought was that critical specific behaviours differentiate leaders from non-leaders. Extensive research studies on behavioural classifications of leadership were conducted at Ohio State University (Stogdill and Coons 1957) and the University of Michigan (Likert 1961).

Ohio State University leadership studies. These studies, which began in the 1940s, sought to identify and classify independent dimensions of leader behaviour. Questionnaires were designed containing a list of items detailing specific aspects of leadership behaviour. From a list of more than one thousand dimensions, they eventually consistently identified two categories that accounted for most of the leadership behaviour. These two dimensions were labelled *initiating structure* style and *considerate* style. Initiating structure style reflects the extent to which the leader defines and structures his/her role and the roles of the followers in achieving established organisational goals. The considerate style reflects the extent to which the leader focuses on establishing trust, mutual respect and rapport between him/herself and the followers and among the group of followers.

Both styles were found to be uncorrelated, thus potentially giving rise to four possible types of leadership behaviour (see also Figure 8.1):

▶ low on initiating structure style/low on considerate style
▶ high on initiating structure style/low on considerate style
▶ high on initiating structure style/high on considerate style
▶ low on initiating structure style/high on considerate style.

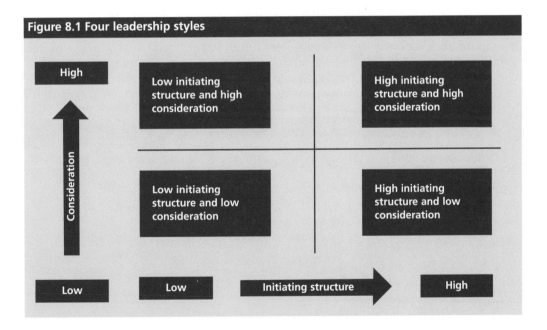

Figure 8.1 Four leadership styles

Though criticised on methodological grounds, particularly for their reliance on questionnaires, the research demonstrated that leaders high in initiating structure style and high in considerate style were generally more likely to achieve superior performance among their followers. Followers were also more likely to describe higher feelings of satisfaction when compared with their counterparts operating under the leadership of those who were low on either style, or both.

University of Michigan studies. Similar to the work done at Ohio, the Michigan studies, under the direction of Rensis Likert, sought to examine the nature of the relationship between the behavioural characteristics of leaders and performance effectiveness. The research resulted in a two-way classification of leadership, namely, *employee-oriented* and *production-oriented* styles, with employee-oriented leaders emphasising interpersonal relations in the workplace, while production-oriented leaders concentrate on the technical aspects of the work. The results of the studies demonstrated that employee-oriented leaders consistently achieve higher productivity and higher job satisfaction among their work groups. Conversely, production-oriented leaders are more likely to be associated with lower group productivity and lower job satisfaction. However, it also emerged that the employee-oriented and production-oriented approaches need to be balanced. Those employee-oriented leaders taking part in the studies who achieved superior results consistently recognised that production was one of the main responsibilities of their work!

The managerial grid. The managerial grid advanced by Blake and Mouton (1962) has been particularly influential as a two-dimensional model of leadership and is generally viewed as an extension and advancement of the earlier work of the team at Ohio State University. Thus, the grid which has two axes (concern for people and concern for production) which can be taken to represent the initiating structure style and the considerate style of the Ohio research or indeed the employee-oriented and production-oriented dimensions of the Michigan work. Blake and Mouton's writings begin from the assumption that a manager's job is to foster attitudes about behaviour which promote performance, creativity and intrapreneurship and innovation within the enterprise. Such managerial competence can be taught and learned. Their managerial grid provides a framework for understanding and applying effective leadership (see Figure 8.2).

Figure 8.2 The Blake and Mouton grid

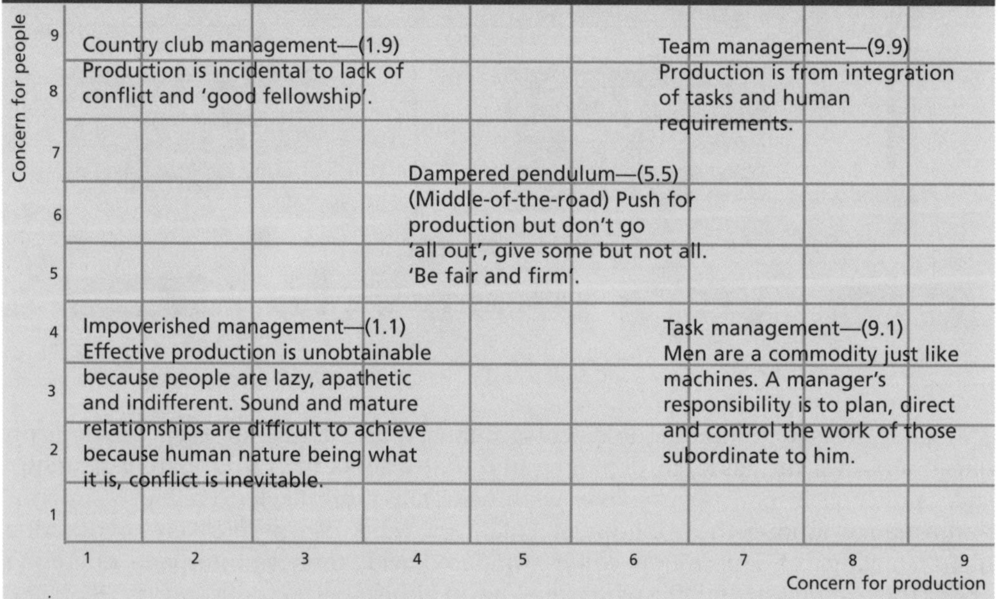

Source: Blake and Mouton (1962).

The grid results from combining two fundamental ingredients of managerial behaviour, namely, a concern for production and a concern for people. Any manager's approach to their job will show more or less of each of these two fundamental constituents. They may show a high degree of concern for one or the other of these, or there is the possibility that the might lie in the middle with an equal concern for both. Different positions on the grid represent different typical patterns of behaviour. The grid indicates that all degrees of concern for production and concern for people are possible. Only five key styles are isolated for illustration.

9,1: Management focuses almost exclusively on production issues. This type is one who expects schedules to be met and has a desire for the smooth running of production operations in a methodical way. Interruptions in this schedule are viewed as someone's mistakes. Disagreement is viewed as being dysfunctional and is seen as insubordination.

1,9: This management style—'country club style'—almost exclusively emphasises people concerns. People are encouraged and supported in their endeavours as long as they are doing their best. Conflict and disagreement is to be avoided and even constructive criticism is not seen as helpful as it interrupts the harmonious relationship.

1,1: This style, known as impoverished management, signals little concern for either production or people. These managers avoid responsibility and task commitment. Leaders of this kind avoid contact and where possible display little commitment to problem solving.

5,5: These managers display the 'middle of the road' style; they push enough to get acceptable levels of production, but in the techniques and skills that they use they also demonstrate a concern for people. They show a firm but fair attitude and have confidence in their subordinates.

9,9: This manager demonstrates a high concern for production and a high concern for people issues. This is a team manager whose goal is one of integration. S/he aims for the highest possible standard and insists on the best possible result for everyone. There is usually maximum involvement and participation and the achievement of difficult goals is viewed as a fulfilling challenge. It is accepted that conflict will occur. When it happens it is handled in an open and frank manner and is not treated as a personal attack. This style, Blake and Mouton argue, is always the best style to adopt since it builds on long-term development and trust. In order to be truly effective, this style of leadership requires an appropriate cultural fit. The value set of the whole organisation must seek to support this style of leadership.

8.5.3 Contingency leadership theory

Contingency theories are based on the premise that the predicting of leadership success and effectiveness is more complex than the simple isolation of traits or behaviours. Situational variables, or the context in which leadership is occurring, are also viewed as having strong explanatory power. Both Fiedler's investigations, in particular his concepts of the *least preferred co-worker* (LPC) and House's *path–goal theory* can be seen to be in the tradition of CONTINGENCY THEORY.

Fiedler's theory. In the 1970s Fred Fiedler conducted a series of studies dedicated to the leadership of work groups. Beginning with the assumption that anyone appointed to a responsible leadership position of this kind will posses the requisite technical expertise, his research question was: What is it about leadership behaviour that leads to effective group working?—'effective' meaning how well the group performs the primary task for which it exists. Fiedler's research identifies two main leadership styles, namely, *relationship-motivated leaders* and *task-motivated leaders*. The former obtain satisfaction from having good relationships with others. They usually encourage participation and involvement and are always concerned about what the other team members think of them. Conversely task-motivated leaders are strongly focused on the task. Their emphasis is on proceduralisation and task completion.

Fiedler subsequently developed an instrument to classify these two styles. The instrument asks leaders to review all people with whom they have ever worked and think of the one with whom they could work least well. They are then asked to rate this LPC along a number of dimensions. Fiedler found that relationship-motivated leaders will score relationship issues high in spite of their problems with the LPC. Conversely task-motivated leaders rate the LPC low on all dimensions. Fiedler emphasises that both these leadership styles can be useful and effective in appropriate situations. He argues that it is necessary to have a contingency perspective on leadership because effective leadership will be contingent on the nature of the tasks to be completed and the context in which this is to be done.

Exhibit 8.2 Least-preferred co-worker

Think of the person with whom you work least well. S/he may be someone you work with presently, or may be someone you knew in the past. S/he does not have to be the person you like least well, but should be the person with whom you now have or have had the most difficulty in getting a job done. Describe this person as s/he appears to you by placing an 'x' at the point you believe best describes that person. Do this for each pair of adjectives.

Pleasant	8 7 6 5 4 3 2 1	Unpleasant
Friendly	8 7 6 5 4 3 2 1	Unfriendly
Rejecting	8 7 6 5 4 3 2 1	Accepting
Helpful	8 7 6 5 4 3 2 1	Frustrating
Unenthusiastic	8 7 6 5 4 3 2 1	Enthusiastic
Tense	8 7 6 5 4 3 2 1	Relaxed
Distant	8 7 6 5 4 3 2 1	Close
Cold	8 7 6 5 4 3 2 1	Warm
Co-operative	8 7 6 5 4 3 2 1	Uncooperative

Exhibit 8.2 Least-preferred co-worker *contd.*

Supportive	8 7 6 5 4 3 2 1	Hostile
Boring	8 7 6 5 4 3 2 1	Interesting
Quarrelsome	8 7 6 5 4 3 2 1	Harmonious
Self-assured	8 7 6 5 4 3 2 1	Hesitant
Efficient	8 7 6 5 4 3 2 1	Inefficient
Gloomy	8 7 6 5 4 3 2 1	Cheerful
Open	8 7 6 5 4 3 2 1	Guarded

Scoring. Your score on the LPC scale is a measure of your leadership style and indicates your primary motivation in a work setting. To determine your score, add up the points (1 through 8) for each of the 16 items. If your score is 64 or above, you are a high LPC person or relationship-oriented. If your score is 57 or below, you are a low LPC person or task-oriented. If your score falls between 58 and 63, you will need to determine for yourself in which category you belong.

Source: Fiedler and Chemers (1974).

House's path–goal theory. Advanced by Robert House (1971) as a contingency theory of leadership, path-goal theory extracts critical elements from EXPECTANCY THEORY of work motivation and the Ohio State University research on behavioural aspects of leadership. Specifically it was intended as a contribution that would reconcile the conflicting findings concerning task-oriented and person-oriented leadership. House (1971) argues that leaders are effective if they can help subordinates to identify a goal and then enable them to achieve it. The terminology 'path–goal' is used as a result of the belief that effective leadership is about clarifying the path to help others get from where they are to the achievement of their work goals and to smooth the journey along the path by reducing and/or eliminating blocks and pitfalls. House identifies four leadership styles—directive, supportive, participative and achievement-oriented—and two classes of situational variables that influence the leadership behaviour–outcome relationship—the personal characteristics of the subordinates and the environment of the subordinates. These situational variables are seen to influence the perceptions and motivations of subordinates, and consequently the leader is advised to adopt the style which in the given circumstances is most likely to result in the identification and achievement of appropriate goals. Robbins (1991:370) outlines a number of useful hypotheses that have emerged from path–goal theory research:

▶ Directive leadership leads to greater satisfaction when tasks are ambiguous or stressful than when they are highly structured and well laid out.

▶ Supportive leadership results in high employee performance and satisfaction when subordinates are performing structured tasks.

- ▶ Directive leadership is likely to be perceived as redundant among subordinates with high perceived ability or with considerable experience.
- ▶ The more clear and bureaucratic the formal authority relationships, the more leaders should exhibit supportive behaviour and de-emphasise directive behaviour.
- ▶ Directive leadership will lead to higher employee satisfaction when there is substantive conflict within a group.
- ▶ Subordinates with an internal locus of control (those who believe they control their own destiny) will be more satisfied with a participative style.
- ▶ Subordinates with an external locus of control will be more satisfied with a directive style.
- ▶ Achievement-oriented leadership will increase subordinates' expectancies that effort will lead to high performance when tasks are ambiguously structured.

Overall, in evaluating the significance of contingency theory and research in that tradition, House and Aditya (1997:429) note that:

While some of the major predictions of contingency and path–goal theory were supported by meta-analyses, ... the theories did not fare well overall, and the interest of leadership scholars in these theories waned.

In particular they suggest that they were criticised for the conceptual base from which they were drawing and because of the degree of inconsistency that characterised the empirical findings that were produced. However, as both House and Aditya also highlight, research in this domain did eventually lead to other work which proved more influential in the field. Significantly, later work by Fiedler and Garcia (1987) proved significant and House's path–goal theory eventually led to significant developments in the charismatic research tradition.

8.5.4 Charismatic leadership theories

Much like some of the early work associated with trait theory and behavioural theory, studies on charismatic leadership have been directed at identifying behaviours that differentiate charismatic leaders from their non-charismatic counterparts. House (1977) suggests that charismatic leaders are exceptionally self-confident, strongly motivated to attain and assert influence, and have strong conviction in the moral correctness of their beliefs. In the tradition of trait theory, these personality traits are believed to be antecedents to charismatic leadership. Conger and Kanungo (1988) define it in the context of followers making attributions of heroic or extraordinary leadership abilities when they observe certain behaviours. Popper and Zakkai (1994:6) note that the growth and development of charismatic leadership in organisations is related to the presence of circumstances which deviate from organisational routine circumstances connected with crisis situations or major changes. Particularly significant here are transformational leadership and SUPERLEADERSHIP (see below).

Transactional and transformational leadership. From the 1970s research attention was paid to the hypothesis that more successful organisations (using objective performance indicators) have better top-management leadership than less successful organisations. Dedicated to identifying 'charismatic' characteristics of leaders, it was viewed as important in the context of organisations attempting to transform traditional systems, methodologies and approaches in an attempt to meet the emerging strategic imperative. Bryman (1993) refers to the work in this area as the 'new leadership theories'. Research work emanating from both the USA and the UK lent support to the hypothesis (see Peters and Austin 1985 and Goldsmith and Clutterbuck 1984). The single factor that made the crucial difference was what Burns (1978) coined as 'transformational leadership'. This, according to Dulewicz (2000:8) remains 'the model currently attracting widespread support'. Burns identified two types of political leadership, *transactional* and *transformational* (see Table 8.4).

Table 8.4 Approaches of transactional versus transformational leaders	
Transactional leader	
Contingent reward	Contracts exchange of rewards for effort, promises rewards for good performance, recognises accomplishments.
Management by exception (active)	Watches and searches for deviations from rules and standards, takes corrective action.
Management by exception (passive)	Intervenes only if standards are not met.
Laissez-faire	Abdicates responsibilities, avoids making decisions.
Transformational leader	
Charisma	Provides vision and sense of mission, instils pride, gains respect and trust.
Inspiration	Communicates high expectations, uses symbols to focus efforts, expresses important purposes in simple ways.
Intellectual stimulation	Promotes intelligence, rationality and careful problem-solving.
Individual consideration	Gives personal attention, treats each employee individually, coaches, advises.

Source: Bass (1990).

The more traditional transactional leadership involves an exchange relationship between leaders and followers which 'becomes possible when there is no outstanding sense of impending threat or anxiety' (Popper and Zakkai 1994:6), but transformational leadership is more about leaders adjusting the values, beliefs and needs of their followers. Bass suggests that transactional leadership is largely a prescription for mediocrity, while transformational leadership consistently leads to exceptional performance in organisations that really need it. The core functions of the transformational leader are:

▶ to be a charismatic role model
▶ to be an inspirational motivator
▶ to provide intellectual stimulation
▶ to show concern and consideration for followers' needs, particularly those relating to achievement and growth (see Bass 1985 and 1990).

He argues that the development and utilisation of transformational leadership through a sustained focus on the human resource policy areas of recruitment, selection, promotion, training and development will yield dividends in the health, well-being, and effective performance of the modern organisation. Brown (1994:1) suggests that transformational leaders are a very important asset when tackling technical change in organisations. He notes that 'major change requires transformational leaders and one of their principle tools are social rites—elaborate, dramatic, planned sets of activities that promote change in individuals'. He continues (2):

The transformational leader operates by moulding the psychology and behaviour of his or her colleagues and subordinates. At the psychological or cognitive level the transformational leader is especially concerned to shape the values, beliefs and assumptions that employees have about their tasks, their colleagues and their organisation. At the behavioural level the transformational leader strives to create social situations which dramatically and powerfully communicate significant messages to others. It is the means by which this social and psychological leadership can most effectively be accomplished in the cause of technological change management.

Transformational leadership theory has been criticised on a number of accounts. Statt (1994:339) describes it as the 'Loch Ness monster' of leadership theory. He accepts that while a number of perfectly sober observers claim to have seen it, he has never witnessed it. Furthermore, he suggests that upon close observation, transformational leadership represents a reversion back to the much-maligned notion of 'great man' theory. Robbins (1991:354) agrees that it does represent a return to traits, but from a different perspective. 'Researchers are now attempting to identify the set of traits that people implicitly refer to when they characterise someone as a leader. This line of thinking proposes that leadership is as much style—projecting the appearance of being a leader—as it is substance.' A more serious criticism questions the methodological foundations of the theory. Most of the research to date has relied on Bass's original questionnaire, which has been criticised, or on qualitative research that largely describes leaders through interviews. In relation to the latter, Luthans (1992) cites Tichy and Devanna's (1986) research which, through a series of interviews with top managers in major companies revealed that transformational leaders share the following characteristics:

- ▶ They identify themselves as change agents.
- ▶ They believe in people.
- ▶ They are courageous.
- ▶ They are visionaries.
- ▶ They have an ability to tolerate ambiguity, complexity and uncertainty. ·
- ▶ They are value-driven.

Table 8.5 gives an indication of the conditions taken to be conducive to transactional and transformational leadership.

Table 8.5 Conditions conducive to transactional and transformational leadership	
Leadership pattern	**Conditions conducive to the predominance of the pattern**
Transactional	Routine situations where the basic level of anxiety is not high, there is no acute sense of impending crisis or major changes.
Transformational	Situations where the basic level of anxiety is not high and attention is given to the developmental needs of the led. In general, this leadership pattern depends more on the leader's view of him/herself as transformational and less on the organisational context than does transactional leadership.

Source: Popper and Zakkai (1994).

SuperLeadership: leading for self-leadership. More recently it has been argued that leadership style may be better interpreted as being arranged along a continuum, with leadership approaches ranging from a completely 'strong man' approach, dedicated to the issuing of strict instructions and tight supervision, to one that is based on the principle of SuperLeadership, the objective of which is to lead others to lead themselves.

Figure 8.3 presents a perspective on different approaches to leadership.

The authors argue that viewpoints on what constitutes successful leadership in organisations have changed over time. The 'STRONG MAN' THEORY of leadership is the earliest dominant form. Based on the principle of autocracy, the emphasis is on the strength of the leader. The expertise for knowing what should be done rests entirely with the leader and his/her power stems entirely from his/her position in the organisation. The second view of leadership is based on that of the transactor. The emphasis here is on the rational exchange process (exchange of rewards for work performed) in order to get employees to do their work. The focus, according to the authors, is on goals and rewards and the leader's power stems from his/her ability to provide followers with rewards. The third type of leader identified is that of the visionary hero. The emphasis here is on the ability of the leader to create highly motivating and absorbing visions. The focus in the relationship is on the leader's vision and the leader's power is based on the followers' desire to relate to the vision. The final view of the leader is that of the SuperLeader. Rather than using the title to create a larger than life type of figure, the authors argue that ironically the emphasis in this relationship is largely on the followers. The objective of the leader is to help the followers become self-leaders. Power is more evenly shared between the leader and the followers, the objective being to ensure that all followers experience commitment and ownership of their work.

8.6 Recent Irish evidence

The Global Leadership and Organizational Behavior Effectiveness Program (GLOBE) directed by Bob House at the Wharton School of Management, University of Pennsylvania, is focused on trying to establish how societal cultural variables influence organisational values, organisational practices, culturally endorsed norms, implicit theories relevant to leadership and the exercise of leadership in each of the

Figure 8.3 Four types of leader

	Strong Man	Transactor	Visionary Hero	SuperLeader
Focus	Commands	Rewards	Visions	Self-leadership
Type	Position/ of power	Rewards authority	Relational/	Shared inspirational
Source of leader's wisdom and direction	Leader	Leader	Leader	Mostly followers (self-leaders) and then leaders
Followers' response	Fear based compliance	Calculative compliance	Emotional commitment based on leader's vision	Commitment based on ownership
Typical leader behaviours	Direction command	Interactive goal setting	Communication of leader's vision	Becoming an effective self-leader
	Assigned goals	Contingent personal reward	Emphasis on leader's values	Modelling self-leadership
	Intimidation	Contingent material reward	Exhortation	Creating positive thought patterns
	Reprimand	Contingent reprimand	Inspirational persuasion	Developing self-leadership through reward and constructive reprimand
				Promoting self-leading teams
				Facilitating a self-leadership culture

Source: Manz and Sims (1989).

cultures studied. As part of this global study of leadership, which will redress the US cultural bias of much of the extant literature, a group of researchers from the School of Business at Trinity College Dublin (see Keating *et al.* 1996), employing a pluralist methodology, report new important data on several Irish leadership behaviours.

Using questionnaire data from a sample of 156 middle managers from the food-processing and financial services industries, the authors rank the leadership behaviours in the Irish context (see Table 8.6).

The scale scores reflect the validity of the leadership behaviour and the higher the score the more favourable the behaviour is perceived.

Table 8.6 Irish leadership attributes

Leadership attributes	Mean (7-point scale)
Self-centred	1.99
Face-saving	2.48
Autocratic	2.48
Bureaucratic	3.50
Status-conscious	3.62
Individualist	3.95
Humanely oriented	5.01
Possessing equanimity	5.11
Charismatic	5.11
Diplomatic	5.44
Collective	5.46
Procedural	5.60
Decisive	6.14
Having integrity	6.19
Inspirational	6.29
Visionary	6.33
Performance orientated	6.38

Source: Keating, Martin and Donnelly-Cox (1996).

In a qualitative phase of this study, participants were asked to define management and leadership, to identify the behavioural characteristics of an average manager, an above-average manager and an outstanding leader (Keating *et al.* 1996: 6):

The leadership behaviours given prominence by the groups included vision, charisma, competence, inspiration, persistence and risk-taking. There was great dissent in the groups as to whether successful business persons on both the Irish and international stage were in fact outstanding leaders. None of the participants identified an excellent Irish business leader. Reference to outstanding leaders tended in general to refer to figures outside the Irish context. The participants suggested the inability to give credit to successful business people reflected the Irish culture. Contrasting with their lack of confidence in Irish leadership figures, there was a general belief amongst them that Irish managers are extremely adaptable and perform well abroad.

8.7 Summary of key propositions

▶ Leadership may be interpreted in simple terms, such as 'getting others to follow', or more specifically, for example, as 'the use of authority in decision making'. It may be exercised as an attribute of position, or because of personal knowledge or wisdom.

▶ Leadership behaviour can be an integral part of a manager's job.

▶ Leadership activities can be classified into five key areas: task functions; cultural functions; symbolic functions; political functions; and relational functions.

▶ Leadership trait theory argues that leaders are born and not made. Also known as the 'great man' theory, the assumption was that it is possible to identify a unifying set of characteristics that make all great leaders great.

▶ Behavioural theories argue that specific behaviours differentiate leaders from non leaders. Critical studies include the Ohio and Michigan studies and the managerial grid.

▶ Contingency theories are based on the premise that the predicting of leadership success and effectiveness is more complex than the simple isolation of traits or behaviours. Situational variables, or the context in which leadership is occurring are also viewed as having strong explanatory power.

▶ Charismatic leadership has been directed at identifying behaviours that differentiate charismatic leaders from their non-charismatic counterparts. Transformational leadership has been influential here.

Discussion questions

❶ Distinguish between leadership and management.
❷ Outline and describe 10 key roles that a leader should perform in an organisation.
❸ In what way would you say effective leadership can impact on an organisation?
❹ Name two business leaders you consider to be particularly effective. Compare and contrast their leadership styles, setting down those particular traits and behaviours which you deem to be important to their leadership abilities.
❺ Leaders are born, not made. Discuss.
❻ What are the main problems with trait theory of leadership?
❼ What is the managerial grid?
❽ What do you understand by contingency theory of leadership?
❾ How might an organisation go about adopting the principle of SuperLeadership?
❿ From your reading of the chapter, outline three areas for future research in the leadership area that you think could prove fruitful to further building knowledge in this area.

Concluding case: The rise and fall of Leadmore Ice Cream

Back in the 1940s, operating from his farm at Leadmore, Kilrush, George Glynn was looking towards the future. He was selling his farm's produce from a downtown outlet. Innovative by nature, he believed that anything he did, he should do properly. The farm had two acres of land under glass for vegetable production and a separate unit for mushrooms and tomatoes. The glasshouse was heated by an engine he had constructed himself.

George also supplied milk to the townspeople. Even at a time of little emphasis on quality control, he carried out a regular bacteria count. Leadmore Farm provided West Clare with its first taste of homogenised bottled milk. During a glass shortage, he provided a service whereby the customer could take milk from the churn with their own containers as he ventured door-to-door. George saw how this could potentially lead to health problems so he imported cartons from Sweden, becoming one of the first distributors of pasteurised milk cartons in the country.

By 1946, the company, now called Leadmore Dairies, faced a surplus of milk, but George viewed this as an opportunity to realise a life-long ambition to commercially produce ice cream. He had already done much research on the idea but now, with the possibility of realising the ambition, he began to tour ice cream plants in Ireland and the UK. Once he was fully satisfied that he had the know-how, he began production of ice cream at the farm, and brought it to his downtown shop. He laid emphasis on experimentation and quality control. On numerous occasions throughout the 1950s, 60s and 70s, Leadmore Dairies won awards for excellence in competitions held by the Ice Cream Alliance. By the 1960s Leadmore Ice Cream was distributed throughout the Clare–Limerick region. George had a marketing-oriented approach towards his business and developed the market for his ice cream in this area. A logo of two Eskimos was developed and much point-of-sale material was distributed including posters, stickers, badges and flags. Within company resources, a significant marketing effort was carried out until the 1980s.

In 1969 demand for Leadmore had far outgrown supply so George oversaw the construction of a new modern plant with sufficient production and storage capacity to facilitate nation-wide distribution. George had this operational by 1971. Furthermore, during the 1970s, George sought to acquire several depots throughout the Republic and Northern Ireland.

The 1980s began on a high note. With Peter Glynn in full control of his father's company, a new brand image and some significant interests within the UK, the company was gaining much penetration within stores. In-store refrigeration was constantly updated, with state-of-the-art freezers coming from Gramp Corporation of Denmark. A succession of two poor seasons, due to bad weather conditions, lay at the heart of the decision to rely more on agents to decrease distribution costs. During the busier seasons, however, the smaller the distribution network they had to control themselves, the less costly it was for the firm. Agents seemed to be performing to a capacity which production could barely meet. The factory was manufacturing for the peak months over six days a week, 24 hours a day, to meet demand. In 1989, a heatwave in early August was a godsend for the company.

After this successful season, Peter Glynn oversaw a major investment into refrigeration in order to maintain the quality of the ice cream. The decision was taken to reconstruct the enormous cold storage facility in order to maximise wind-chill factors and minimise temperatures. New freezer compressors were purchased and new deliver trucks invested in.

Disaster struck with a run of five bad seasons, due again primarily to poor weather. In response, some emergency management decisions were made, such as changing the company name, this time from Leadmore Ice to Leadmore Farm, and more investment in quality, in particular the introduction of foil wrapping, creamier recipes and changing the one-pint brick wrap to the same colour as a competitor's product.

In 1993, due to the increasingly poor health of his mother, Peter took the decision to step back from the day-to-day running of the company and he engaged marketing consultants to do an overall review of the company's strategy. The study was carried out by James Hoblyn and Peter O'Hara of Grant Thornton Consulting Limited. James Hoblyn proposed himself as the person who could implement a turnaround strategy. In October 1993, he took up the position of managing director of the company.

In addition to appointing this new MD, fresh equity of approximately £75,000 was put into the company by family members. The board faced 1994 with confidence in the new management and the potential for an upturn in company fortunes.

Mid-way through the summer of 1994 it became apparent that targets were not being reached and that a serious cash-flow problem had developed. The company was left with two key options: either secure outside investment or sell the company in its entirety. Creditors were demanding payment. Little progress was made and on 9 December 1994, protective notice was served to employees. The company was liquidated in 1995.

Case adapted from Garavan, T. and Garavan, M. (1997) 'Leadmore Ice Cream', in Garavan *et al.* (eds.) *Entrepreneurship and Business Start-Ups in Ireland: Vol 2: Cases.* Dublin: Oak Tree Press.

Case questions

Compare and contrast the leadership styles of George and Peter.

Bibliography

Bantel, K. and Jackson, S. (1989) 'Top Management and Innovations in Banking: Does the Composition of the Top Team Make a Difference?', *Strategic Management Journal*, 10, 107–24.

Bass, B. (1990) 'From Transactional to Transformational Leadership: Learning to Share the Vision', *Organizational Dynamics*, Winter 1990, 22.

Bass, R. (1985) *Leadership and Performance Beyond Expectation.* New York: Free Press.

Bennis, W. and Nanus, B. (1985) *Leaders: The Strategies for Taking Charge.* New York: Harper Row.

Bennis, W. (1989) 'Managing the Dream: Leadership in the 21st Century', *Journal of Organisational Change Management*, 2 (1), 7.

Blake, R. and Mouton, J. (1962) 'The Managerial Grid', *Advanced Management Office Executive*, 1 (9).

Brown, A. (1994) 'Transformational Leadership in Tackling Technical Change', *Journal of General Management*, 19 (4), 1–10.

Bryman, A. (1993) 'Charismatic Leadership in Business Organisations: Some Neglected Issues', *Leadership Quarterly*, 4, 289–304.

Burns, J. (1978), *Leadership.* New York: Harper Row.

Conger, J. and Kanungo, R. (1988), *Charismatic Leadership.* San Fransisco: Jossey Bass.

Cunningham, I. (1992) 'The Impact of Leaders: Who They Are and What They Do', *Leadership and Organization Development Journal*, 13 (2), 7–10.

Dawson, S. (1996) *Analysing Organisations.* London: Macmillan.

Dess, G. and Picken, J. (2000) 'Changing Roles: Leadership in the 21st Century', *Organisational Dynamics*, 28 (3), 18–35.

Dulewicz, V. (2000) 'Emotional Intelligence: The Key to Future Successful Corporate Leadership', *Journal of General Management*, 25 (3), 1–14.

Edgeman, R. and Dahlgaard, J. (1998) 'A Paradigm for Leadership Excellence', *Total Quality Management*, 9 (4/5), 75–80.

Fiedler, F. (1967) *A Theory of Leadership Effectiveness.* New York: McGraw-Hill.

Fiedler, F. and Chemers, M. (1974) *Leadership and Effective Management.* New York, Scott, Foresman and Co.

Fiedler, F. and Garcia, J. (1987) *New Approaches to Effective Leadership: Cognitive Resources and Organizational Performance.* New York: John Wiley and Sons.

Finkelstein, S. and Hambrick, D. (1996) *Strategic Leadership: Top Executives and their Effects on Organisations*. St Paul: West Publishing Company.

Flanagan, H. and Thompson, D. (1993) 'Leadership: The Swing of the Pendulum', *Leadership and Organizational Development Journal*, 14 (1), 9–15.

Flood, P. and Smith, K. (1994) 'Top Management Team Cohesiveness: Impact on Company Performance'. Paper presented to College of Business Conference, Building and Effective and Cohesive Top Management Team, University of Limerick, May.

Flood, P., C. Min Fong, K. Smith, P. O'Regan, S. Moore and Morley, M. (1997) 'Top Management Teams and Pioneering: A Resource-based View', *International Journal of Human Resource Management*, 8 (3).

Garavan, T. and Garavan, M. (1997) 'Leadmore Ice Cream', in Garavan *et al.* (eds.) *Entrepreneurship and Business Start-Ups in Ireland: Vol. 2: Cases*. Dublin: Oak Tree Press.

Gibb, C. (1947) 'The Principles and Traits of Leadership', *Journal of Abnormal and Social Psychology*, 42, 267–84.

Goldsmith, W. and Clutterbuck, D. (1984) *The Winning Streak*. London: Weidenfeld and Nicolson.

Hambrick, D. (1994), 'Top Management Groups: A Conceptual Integration and Reconsideration of the "Team" Label', *Research in Organizational Behaviour*, 16, 171–213.

Hambrick, D. and Mason, P. (1984) 'Upper Echelons: The Organization as a Reflection of its Top Managers', *Academy of Management Review*, 9, 193–206.

Hitt, W. (1993) 'The Model Leader: A Fully Functioning Person', *Leadership and Organisation Development Journal*, 11 (7), 4–11.

House, R. and Aditya, R. (1997) 'The Social Scientific Study of Leadership: Quo Vadis?', *Journal of Management*, 23 (3), 409–73.

House, R. (1971) 'A Path–Goal Theory of Leader Effectiveness', *Administrative Science Quarterly*, 16, September, 321–38.

House, R. (1977) 'A 1976 Theory of Charismatic Leadership', in Hunt, J. and Larson, L. (eds) *Leadership: The Cutting Edge*, Carbondale Il: Southern Illinois University Press.

Keating, M., Martin, G. and Donnelly-Cox, G. (1996) 'The GLOBE Project: A Case for Interdisciplinary and Intercultural Research', in *Proceedings of the 1st Irish Academy of Management Conference*, Management Research in Ireland: The way Forward, University College Cork, 12–13 September.

Krech, D., Crutchfield, R. and Ballachey, E. (1962) *Individual in Society*. New York: McGraw-Hill.

Likert, R. (1961) *New patterns of Management*. New York: McGraw-Hill.

Luthans, F. (1992) *Organizational Behaviour*. New York: McGraw-Hill.

Manz, C. and Sims, H. (1989) *SuperLeadership: Leading Others to Lead Themselves*. New York: Prentice Hall.

Manz, C. and Sims, H. (1991) 'SuperLeadership: Beyond the Myth of Heroic Leadership', *Organisational Dynamics*, Summer, 56–78.

Mintzberg, H. (1973) *The Nature of Managerial Work*. New York: Harper Row.

Morley, M., S. Moore and P. O'Regan (1996) 'The Impact of the Top Management Team on the Sales Growth Performance of International Divisions of US Multinational Enterprises Operating in the Republic of Ireland', *Journal of Irish Business and Administrative Research*, 17 (1).

Mullins, L. (1991) *Management and Organisational Behaviour*. London: Pitman.

Neck, C., Mitchell, T., Manz, C., Cooper, K. and Thompson. E. (2000) 'Fit to Lead: Is Fitness the Key to Effective Executive Leadership?', *Journal of Managerial Psychology*, 15 (8), 833–40.

Nicholls, J. (1990) Rescuing Leadership from Humpty Dumpty, *Journal of General Management*, 16 (2), 76–19.

Nicholls, J. (1993) The Paradox of Managerial Leadership, *Journal of General Management*, 18 (4), 1–14.

Perrow, C. (1973) *Organizational Dynamics*, Summer, 2–15.

Peters, T. and Austin, N. (1985) *A Passion for Excellence: The Leadership Difference*. New York: Random House.

Pettinger, R. (1994) *Introduction to Management*. London: Macmillan.

Popper, M. and Zakkai, E. (1994) 'Transactional, Charismatic and Transformational Leadership: Conditions Conducive to their Predominance', *Leadership and Organisational Development Journal*, 15 (6), 3–7.

Robbins, S. (1991) *Organizational Behavior: Concepts, Controversies, and Applications*. Englewood Cliffs, NJ: Prentice Hall.

Sarros, J. and Woodman, D. (1993) 'Leadership in Australia and Its Organisational Outcomes', *Leadership and Organisation Development Journal*, 14 (4), 3–9.

Schultz, L. (2000) 'Qualities of an Exceptional Leader', *Human Systems Management*, 19 (2), 93–102.

Selznick, P. (1957) *Leadership in Administration*. New York: Harper Row.

Statt, D. (1994) *Psychology and the World of Work*. London: Macmillan.

Stogdill, R. and Coons, A. (1957) *Leader Behaviour: Its Description and Measurement*. Columbus OH: Ohio State University Press of Bureau for Business Research.

Stogdill, R. (1948) 'Personal Factors Associated with Leadership: A survey of the Literature', *Journal of Psychology*, 25, 35–71.

Tannenbaum, R., Weschler, I. And Masserik, F. (1961) *Leadership and Organization*. New York: McGraw-Hill.

Tichy, N. and Devanna, M. (1986) 'The Transformational Leader', *Training and Development Journal*, July, 30–32.

Trevelyan, R. (1998) 'The Boundary of Leadership: Getting it Right and Having it All', *Business Strategy Review*, 9 (1), 37–44.

Vaughan, E. (1989) 'The Leadership Obsession: An Addendum to Mangham's "In Search of Competence"', *Journal of General Management*, 14, (3), 26–34.

Yetton, P. (1984) 'Leadership and Supervision', in Gruneberg, M. and Wall, T. (eds.) *Social Psychology and Organizational Behaviour*. Chichester: Wiley.

Yukl, G. (1994) *Leadership in Organizations*. Englewood Cliffs, NJ: Prentice Hall.

Zaleznik, A. (1977) 'Managers and Leaders: Are they Different?', *Harvard Business Review*, May–June, 67–78.

Chapter 9

Motivating Job Performance

9.1 Introduction

Motivation is typically viewed as a set of processes that activate, direct and sustain human behaviour dedicated to goal accomplishment and, according to Osteracker (1999(a)), can be considered to have three dimensions: physical, social and mental. It is an important concept and has much relevance to the practising manager. How to be better at motivating people continues to be an important theme in published literature (see, for example, Allan 1999; Hiam 1999; Ritchie and Martin, 2000). However, as Nelson (1999) suggests, although the term 'motivation' is widely used, many managers do not understand how to motivate their employees. Nelson's research highlights several incongruities and inconsistencies between what is commonly practised and what actually works. This trail of dichotomous evidence leads him to emphasise the importance of recognition, suggesting that recognition for a job well done is the top motivator of employee performance. Nelson further suggests that managers should strive to ensure that employees feel appreciated because attempting to regenerate flagging morale is a much more demanding task than doing relatively straightforward things regularly to maintain it at an acceptable level. In exploring the area of motivation, this chapter highlights definitional aspects of motivation and outlines the key theoretical perspectives that have been adopted in relation to this concept. The long pedigree of the concept in the management cannon is established through the examination of both content and process theories of motivation. Hierarchy of needs theory, EXISTENCE–RELATEDNESS–GROWTH (ERG) theory, achievement motivation theory, TWO-FACTOR THEORY, EXPECTANCY THEORY, equity theory and goal theory are all treated. These can be considered classic seminal contributions on motivation and they remain highly significant in the extant literature. Thus while Osteracker (1999) believes that the motivational theories that do exist, which were originally applied to a relatively static environment, need to be adjusted to take account of the DYNAMIC ENVIRONMENT of organisations today. As Ambrose and Kulik (1999) conclude in their review of empirical work on motivation published during the 1990s, while some new motivational theories have been introduced, the traditional ones appear firmly entrenched and continue to receive considerable empirical support. The importance of pay and the structuring and design of work to motivation in the workplace are also considered as motivation theory locates its analysis of employee performance on how work and its rewards satisfy individual employee needs.

9.2 The ongoing centrality of motivation in organisational life

Motivation at work has been the object of sustained attention since the emergence of the industrial society. Steers and Porter (1987) advance a number of factors that account for the prominence of motivation as a focal point of interest. First, they suggest that managers and organisational researchers cannot avoid a concern for the behavioural requirements of the organisation. The necessity of attracting the right calibre of employee and engaging them in such a way as to ensure high performance remains a central concern of the productive process. Second, they argue that the pervasive nature of the concept itself has resulted in it remaining a central area of inquiry. As a complex phenomenon it impacts upon a multitude of factors and any worthwhile understanding of organisations requires a deal of attention to be focused on this array of factors and how they interact with one another to create certain outcomes. Third, the competitive trends of the business environment coupled with increased business regulation has forced organisations to seek out any mechanisms which might improve organisational effectiveness and efficiency. The ability to direct employees efforts towards these twin goals of effectiveness and efficiency are seen as crucial. A fourth reason for the sustained interest in motivation concerns the issue of technological advancement. An organisation must continually ensure that its workforce is capable of and willing to use advanced manufacturing technologies to achieve organisational goals. A final reason, according to Steers and Porter, centres around the issue of planning horizons. Taking a longer-term perspective of the human resource in an attempt to build up a reservoir of well-skilled, enthusiastic employees brings the concept of motivation right into the fore.

9.3 Motivation defined

Marcum (2000) argues that motivational theory, rooted in psychological thought, mirrors the growth in a more humanistic approach to workplace behaviour, replacing the 'carrot and stick' with a focus on rewards and participation. The word 'motivation' was originally derived from the Latin word *movere* meaning to move. Modern interpretation of motivation is somewhat more all-encompassing, expressing various understandings of how we view people and organisations. Thus, while Vroom (1964) conceptualises motivation as a process governing choices made by persons or lower organisms among alternative forms of voluntary activity, DuBrin (1978) suggests that motivation centres on the expenditure of effort toward achieving an objective the organisation wants accomplished. Arnold *et al.* (1995), using a mechanical analogy, suggest that the motive force gets a machine started and keeps it going; they argue that motivation concerns the factors that push or pull us to behave in certain ways. Bennet (1991) suggests that an employee's motivation to work consists of all the drives, forces and influences—conscious or unconscious—that cause the employee to want to achieve certain aims, while, similarly, Forrest (2000) considers that motivation can be simply defined as 'consistently putting effort, energy and commitment into desired results'. Most of the early work on motivation was centred around getting more out of the employee, although many of the theorists were also concerned with finding an answer to the problem that was consistent with the essential dignity and independence of the individual. Motivation theory bases its analysis of employee performance on how work and its rewards satisfy individual employee needs. Numerous theories have been developed over the years to aid management in identifying employee motives and needs, the most influential of which will be discussed here.

The study of motivation at work has been based on analysing employee behaviour at work and thus motivation theory is essentially concerned with explaining why people behave as they do, or why people choose different forms of behaviour in order to achieve different ends. However, there is no simple answer to the crucial question: How do you motivate people? Nevertheless, achieving and maintaining high levels of motivation remains vital, especially in competitive industry, primarily because, according to Pettinger (1994:49):

There is a correlation between organisations that go to a lot of trouble to motivate their staff, and profitable business performance ... The ability to gain the commitment and motivation of staff in organisations has been recognised as important in certain sectors of the business sphere. It is now more universally accepted as a critical business and organisational activity, and one that has highly profitable returns and implications for the extent of the returns on investment that is made in the human resource.

Among the long list of things considered to be important motivational drivers are the human needs for interesting and stimulating work, achievement, self-development, variety, creativity, power and influence, social relations and social contact, appropriate rewards, traction, structure and rules and long-term relationships (see Ritchie and Martin, 2000). Conversely, Bent *et al.* (1999) identify the major causes of demotivation as repetitive work, low pay, long hours, poor communication, poor training and being offered little or no responsibility.

Overall, therefore, motivation theory has a role to play in assisting managers in formulating strategies and approaches for achieving high levels of performance. There is an onus on managers to begin to understand what motivates. Indeed Fox *et al.* (1999) have identified that employee disenchantment continues to exist as one of the major conditions that prevent organisations from realising the highest possible benefits from performance improvement initiatives. If employees' core motives can be identified and satisfied then the first major step has been taken towards achieving effectiveness and efficiency and realising the potential benefits of workplace initiatives. With this in mind, the following theories help to throw some important light on motivational structures, processes and outcomes.

9.4 Content theories of motivation

Content theories of motivation focus on the question: What initiates or stimulates behaviour? Content theorists implicitly assume that needs are the most important determinant of individual levels of motivation.

9.4.1 Maslow's hierarchy of needs

Most managers will be familiar with the hierarchical classification of human needs first proposed by Maslow (1943) which, according to Forrest (2000), continues today to offer a basis for understanding individuals' goals or needs. Maslow, who was a clinical psychologist, suggested that human motivation was dependent on the desire to satisfy various levels of needs. Maslow's hierarchy of needs is perhaps the most publicised theory of motivation. Based on the existence of a series of needs that range from basis instinctive needs for sustenance and security to higher-order needs, such as self-esteem and the need for self-actualisation, it seeks to explain different types and levels of motivation that are important to individuals at particular times in their lives.

In all, Maslow suggests that there are five levels of needs ranked in the order shown in Figure 9.1 as this is the order in which the individual will seek to satisfy them.

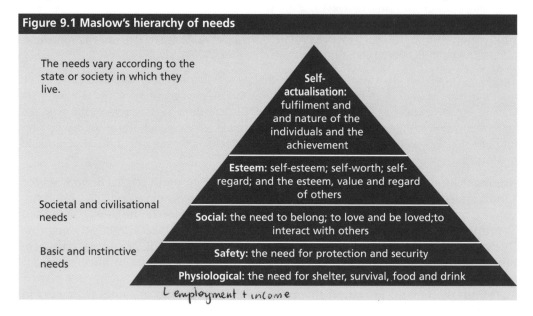

Figure 9.1 Maslow's hierarchy of needs

The needs vary according to the state or society in which they live.

Self-actualisation: fulfilment and and nature of the individuals and the achievement

Esteem: self-esteem; self-worth; self-regard; and the esteem, value and regard of others

Societal and civilisational needs

Social: the need to belong; to love and be loved;to interact with others

Basic and instinctive needs

Safety: the need for protection and security

Physiological: the need for shelter, survival, food and drink

└ employment + income

Physiological needs include such things as food, shelter, clothing and heat. These basic needs must be satisfied for the person to survive. In modern society it is employment and the income it generates that allows an individual to satisfy these needs.

Safety needs refer to things such as security at home, tenure at work and protection against reduced living standards. Only when physiological needs have been satisfied will the individual concentrate on safety needs.

Social or love needs refer to people's desire for affection and the need to feel wanted. Our need for association, acceptance by others and friendship, companionship and love would be included here.

Esteem needs cover the desire for self-esteem and self-confidence and also the need for recognition, authority and influence over others.

Self-actualisation refers to the need for self-fulfilment, self-realisation, personal development and fulfilment of the creative faculties.

Hierarchy of needs theory states that a need that is unsatisfied activates seeking/searching behaviour. Thus, the individual who is hungry will search for food; s/he who is unloved will seek to be loved. Once this seeking behaviour is fulfilled or satisfied, it no longer acts as a primary motivator. Needs that are satisfied no longer motivate. This clearly illustrates the rationale for arranging these needs in a hierarchy. The sequential ascending order implies that it is the next unachieved level which acts as the prime motivator. However, need propensity means that higher-order needs cannot become an active motivating force until the preceding lower-order need is satisfied. However, individuals will seek growth when it is feasible to do so and have an innate desire to ascend the hierarchy. Such higher-order needs will act as a motivator when lower-order needs have been satisfied. Self-actualisation is the climax of personal growth. Maslow (1943) describes it as the desire for self-fulfilment, the desire to become increasingly what one is, to become everything that one is capable of becoming.

Maslow's hierarchy of needs theory recognises that needs motivate people in different ways and assumes that if someone experiences deficiency needs, they will not be motivated to grow or to develop until those needs have been satisfied. Furthermore, it identifies important categories of individual needs and encourages us to consider the variety of needs which at different times stimulate or initiate behaviour. However, Maslow's theory has been the subject of much commentary and criticism over the years and it is generally agreed that the theory has a number of deficiencies. First, Maslow's work was based on general studies of human behaviour and motivation and as such was not directly associated with matters central to the workplace. Arising from this the theory is extremely difficult to apply because of the illusive nature of the needs identified, particularly in the context of the workplace. Researchers have also found little support for the concept of exclusive pre-potency. There is plenty of evidence to suggest that needs are not organised in the hierarchical structure suggested in Maslow's framework. On a regular basis, people sacrifice lower-order needs in order to satisfy those at a higher level on the hierarchy. For example, people who have risked their lives to save other people (ignoring their own needs for safety in favour of say attachment or esteem needs); people who have gone on hunger strike (depriving themselves of their basic survival needs in order to satisfy a higher-order need); or even someone who has stayed up all night to study for an exam (bypassing the need for sleep in order to fulfil their individual potential) all provide clear evidence that the need order is not as straightforward or as linear as the hierarchy suggests. A more realistic scenario is that individuals have several active needs at the same time which implies that lower-order needs are not always satisfied before one concentrates on higher-order needs. An implicit assumption of Maslow's hierarchy is that need deprivation is what motivates people's behaviour. The theory is based on a 'fulfilment progression' dynamic that indicates that when a need has been sufficiently satisfied, it no longer acts as a motivator. There is a connotation inherent in this assertion that suggests that in any attempts to motivate people, needs should be deprived in order to sustain motivated behaviour. Both intuitively and empirically, this implication points to a flaw in the theory. Need deprivation may motivate for a certain length of time, after which its effects may yield quite the opposite reaction. If people are continually denied an opportunity to satisfy needs that they are experiencing, this eventually leads to demotivated, apathetic and disheartened behaviour. Finally, it has also been suggested that the theory attempts to demonstrate an imputed rationality in human actions which may not necessarily exist. The conceptualisation of our needs in such a logical sequential fashion, while useful as a frame of reference to which we can all compare ourselves, has not resulted in convincing evidence among the research community.

The strongest implication emerging from the hierarchy is that unless people's basic deficiency needs are satisfied, they will not be motivated to pursue goals that relate to higher-order needs. Therefore, activities that demand the organisationally popular dimensions of teamwork, 'empowerment', creativity, innovation, or knowledge enhancement will not be relevant or important to people who don't earn enough money to survive, or who are not sufficiently protected from danger in their workplace. According to Maslow's theory people in low-paid work or who face hazardous or dangerous environments in the workplace will be less interested in developing social networks, achieving high status in their jobs or realising their potential in other ways.

9.4.2 Existence–relatedness–growth theory

Existence–relatedness–growth (ERG) theory developed by Alderfer (1969) reduces Maslow's hierarchy of needs into a three-fold taxonomy (see Figure 9.2).

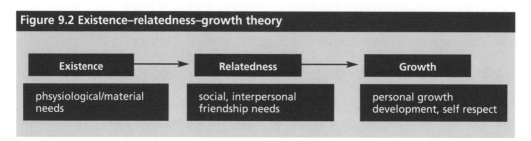

Figure 9.2 Existence–relatedness–growth theory

Building upon Maslow's work, ERG theory avoids some of the issues that have caused criticism of Maslow's work. Here there is no emphasis on a hierarchical structuring of needs. Instead, needs are arranged along a continuum, giving them all equal status in terms of their ability to serve as a goad to action at a particular point in time. Alderfer suggests that motivated behaviour can be activated either via 'need fulfilment progression' or by another dynamic referred to as 'need frustration regression'. Fulfilment progression refers to a situation where once a need is satisfied in someone, s/he ceases to be motivated by that need category and moves on to another, higher-order, category of need, while frustration regression refers to the situation where, if a need is consistently frustrated, an individual 'regresses' to being motivated by lower-order needs that are already being fulfilled to a sufficient degree. Therefore, another important difference is the proposition that an already satisfied need may be reactivated as a motivator when a higher-order need cannot be satisfied. Furthermore, more than one needs category may be important and influential at any one time and thus the notion of pre-potency is rejected here.

9.4.3 McClelland's achievement theory

McClelland (1960) concentrated on developing and identifying motivational differences between individuals as a means of establishing which patterns of motivation lead to effective performance and success as work. The needs identified by McClelland can be useful in helping managers to recognise the diversity of behaviours that people display at work. According to this theory, needs that people experience can be directly related to people's work preferences. McClelland's theory of achievement motivation argues that the main factor in willingness to perform is the intensity of an individual's actual need for achievement. He proposes that the organisation offers an opportunity to satisfy three sets of needs:

▶ the need for achievement (nAch) which is a desire for challenging tasks and a good deal of responsibility

▶ the need for affiliation (nAff) which refers to the need for developed social and personal relations

▶ the need for power (nPow) which refers to the need for dominance.

These are need categories that are learned through life experiences, and a person will tend to be driven more or less by any one of the three needs identified. McClelland's research has shown that people who are mainly driven by a need for achievement will have distinctly different work preferences than those driven by a need for power or by a need for affiliation. Individuals with a high need for achievement tend to view organisational membership as a means of solving problems and providing a platform from which they can excel. Individuals with a high nAch tend to take personal responsibility for providing solutions to problems and desire feedback on their performance. Persons who have a high nAff desire to participate in tasks that allow them to frequently interact with others. Those who demonstrate a high nPow view the organisation as a means of providing them with status through the position they occupy. McClelland suggests that these needs are acquired throughout one's life and thus may be triggered and developed through the appropriate environmental conditions.

The motivation of those with a high need achievement is then a product of the task responsibilities, how attainable the task goals are and the nature and regularity of the feedback that they receive. Hitt *et al.* (1989) maintain that people are often motivated by tasks that give them a feeling of competence. This, they find, is especially true of people who have a high nAch. Such individuals tend to work at tasks that lead to difficult but achievable goals. Achieving difficult goals causes them to feel competent, while goals that are too easy to achieve or that are unattainable do not. Finally McClelland maintains that individuals can actually learn to increase their nAch. This may be achieved through exposing them to human resource development programmes that place an emphasis on achievement and that are didactic with respect to the methods that can be put in place for achieving.

9.4.4 Two-factor theory

Herzberg's (1962) research involved questioning people about those factors that led to either extreme satisfaction or extreme dissatisfaction with their jobs, the environment, the workplace. His original study was based on intensive interviews with a sample of 200 engineers and accountants. The factors that resulted in satisfaction, Herzberg labelled MOTIVATORS, while those that resulted in dissatisfaction he labelled HYGIENE FACTORS (see figure 9.3).

Like McGregor (see below), Herzberg was concerned with the impact of the job and the environment on an individual's motivation. His objective was to identify the factors at work that led to the greatest levels of satisfaction and dissatisfaction in an attempt to design work that provided job satisfaction and promoted high levels of performance. The motivators he identified were:

▶ achievement

▶ recognition

▶ the work itself

► responsibility
► advancement
► growth.

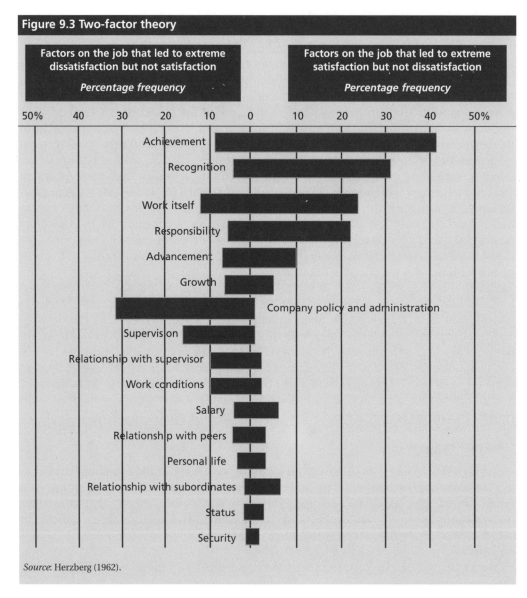

Figure 9.3 Two-factor theory

Source: Herzberg (1962).

The implication is that management can stimulate employee motivation by structuring work to incorporate these dimensions. The hygiene factors he identified were:

► company policy
► supervision

- ▶ salary
- ▶ peer and subordinate relationships
- ▶ status
- ▶ security.

These, according to Herzberg, are factors that, where good, will not of themselves make people feel satisfied. Thus, if they are good, dissatisfaction is removed but satisfaction does not accrue. However, if these aspects of work are poor, then extreme dissatisfaction is experienced. Herzberg's findings indicate that satisfaction and dissatisfaction are not at opposite ends of the same spectrum. Rather, they are on two separate spectra. The opposite of satisfaction is not *dis*satisfaction but *no* satisfaction; similarly the opposite of dissatisfaction is *no* dissatisfaction. Thus, pleasant or good working conditions do not actually produce motivation—as hygiene factors, they simply prevent dissatisfaction.

The major criticisms levelled at Herzberg's work centre around the extent to which his original study was methodologically sound; for example, the extent to which accountants and engineers are actually like all other workers.

9.5 Process theories of motivation

The work of the process theorists proposes that people are more complex, more pragmatic and more contemplative than the need theorists suggest, or at least imply, and that motivation at work is subject to more than an individual's needs. In researching what motivates people at work, process theories seek to establish not only what people want from their work situations, but how they believe they can actually achieve it and what influences the process.

9.5.1 Theory X, theory Y

Figure 9.4 Theory X, theory Y	
THEORY X	**THEORY Y**
Employees are inherently lazy, dislike work and will do as little as possible.	Employees like work and want to undertake challenging tasks.
Consequently, workers need to be corrected, controlled and directed to exert adequate effort.	If the work itself and the organisational environment is appropriate, employees will work willingly without need for coercion or control.
Most employees dislike responsibility and prefer direction.	People are motivated by needs for respect, esteem, recognition and self-fulfilment.
Employees want only security and material rewards.	People at work want responsibility. The majority of workers are imaginative and creative and can exercise ingenuity at work.

Marcum (2000) comments that there has been a renewed interest in theory X and theory Y in recent years. Advanced by McGregor (1960) in his seminal writing, *The*

Human Side of Enterprise, it is an attempt to focus on managerial assumptions about employees and the implications of such assumptions for subsequent managerial behaviour, particularly with respect to how managers seek to motivate their subordinates. McGregor outlined two sets of assumptions concerning human nature that a manager might adopt. Labelled theory X and theory Y, autocratic managers, McGregor suggested, were likely to subscribe to the assumptions of theory X, while those that were less bureaucratic were likely to work with the assumptions of theory Y (see Figure 9.4).

This dichotomous framework is particularly useful for allowing us to classify differing managerial styles. McGregor himself maintained that in the majority of circumstances theory Y assumptions were the most accurate reflection of employee attitudes towards work because work is natural to the human species and those who perform work will normally devote their attention to the completion of a task. Consequently, to the extent that these theory Y assumptions are valid they should be reflected in organisational structures, systems and practices. Thus Bennet (1991:165) suggests that:

This implies that employee participation in decision making, the joint determination of subordinates' targets by the manager and the worker concerned, and relatively flexible organisational structures that allow for job enrichment, overlapping responsibilities and the motivation of junior staff.

9.5.2 Expectancy theory

Associated with Vroom (1964), this theory identifies important expectations that individuals bring to the workplace and focuses on the relationship between the effort put into the completion of particular activities by the individual and the expectations concerning the actual reward that will accrue as a result of expending the effort. Expectancy theory attempts to combine individual and organisational factors that impact on this causal effort–reward relationship. Broadly, this theory argues that individuals base decisions about their behaviour on the expectation that one behaviour or another is more likely to lead to needed or desired outcomes. The relationship between one's behaviour and particular desired outcomes is affected by individual factors such as personality, perception, motives, skills, abilities, etc., and by organisational factors such as culture, structure, managerial style (the context in which one is operating). Thus, expectancy theory avoids attempts to isolate a definitive set of employee motives, but seeks to explain individual differences in terms of goals, motives and behaviours. It postulates that employee motivation is dependent on how the employer perceives the relationship between effort, performance and outcomes.

Figure 9.5 Expectancy theory

Motivation = Expectancy × Instrumentality × Valence

EXPECTANCY (see Figure 9.5) is the probability assigned by the individual that work effort will be followed by a given level of achieved task performance (value = 0 to 1).

INSTRUMENTALITY is the probability assigned by the individual that a given level of achieved task performance will lead to various work outcomes (rewards) (value = 0 to 1).

VALENCE is the value attached by the individual to various work outcomes (rewards) (value = -1 to +1).

Therefore the motivational appeal of a given work path is drastically reduced whenever any one or more of the factors approaches the value of zero. The model suggests that an individual's level of effort (motivation) is not simply a function of rewards. The individual must feel that s/he has the ability to perform the task (expectancy), that this performance will impact on the reward and that this reward is actually valued. Only if all conditions are satisfied will employees be motivated to exert greater effort. It is thus critical that individuals can see a connection between effort and reward and that the reward offered by the organisation will satisfy employees' needs. However, there is no simple formula since individuals possess different preferences for outcomes and have different understandings of the relationship between effort and reward. They may well be motivated in very different ways. Among the criticisms levelled at the theory are the difficulty associated with testing the theory empirically, and the fact that it assumes a type of rationality, which may not actually exist, with respect to how the individual thinks and behaves.

Porter and Lawler have extended the original work of Vroom and advanced a revised 'expectancy framework' (see Figure 9.6). They examine the role that abilities and role perceptions play in producing various outcomes and, drawing upon earlier motivation theory, highlight the differences between intrinsic and extrinsic rewards, the former being rewards that are generated by the individuals themselves (for example, a sense of achievement, personal satisfaction, a feeling of pride in work, and so on) and the latter being rewards that are provided from external sources (pay, promotion, praise, recognition, etc).

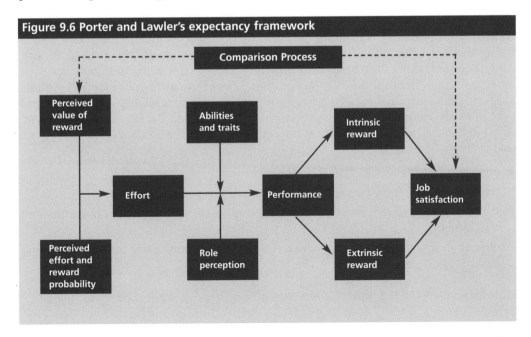

Figure 9.6 Porter and Lawler's expectancy framework

Like the original expectancy theory, Porter and Lawler also highlight that before people make a decision to exert effort, they need to value the rewards that are available and to feel that, if they do exert effort, the rewards will be available to them.

In relation to the implications of expectancy theory for management, Vroom (1964) suggests that managers must seek to understand individual employee goals and motives, ensure these are clearly and positively linked to desired performance levels which in turn are achievable from the employee's perspective. Nadler and Lawler (1979) go a little further and highlight specific areas for management action:

- ▶ Establish what the valued outcomes are.
- ▶ Specify desired and achievable performance levels.
- ▶ Ensure there is a clear link between effort, performance and desired outcomes.
- ▶ Ensure adequate variation of outcomes available.
- ▶ Ensure equity and fairness for the individual employee.

Expectancy theory does not attempt to identify a universal set of motivational factors. Rather, it highlights the importance of a range of potential motivational factors. These may be either intrinsic or extrinsic. Intrinsic outcomes are those originating from doing the job (sense of achievement, satisfaction), while extrinsic outcomes are those provided by other people, particularly management, and include pay, promotion, etc.

9.5.3 Equity theory

The concept of a fair day's work for a fair day's pay is often utilised to express how the parties to the labour process wish to perceive the employment relationship. Equity theory, sometimes referred to as justice theory, resembles expectancy theory in that it sets down the individual's cognitive process that determines whether or not s/he will engage in the effort–reward bargain within the framework of the social exchange process.

Developed by Adams (1965), the equity theory of motivation is based on the comparison between two variables: inputs and outcomes. Inputs refer to that which the individual brings to his/her employment and include things such as effort, experience and skills. Outcomes describe the range of factors the employee receives in return for his/her inputs—pay, recognition, fringe benefits, status symbols. Adams suggests that individual expectations about equity correlations between inputs and outcomes are learned during the process of socialisation in the home or at work and through comparison with the inputs and outcomes of others. Adams (1965) suggests that individual's can:

- ▶ change inputs—reduce effort if underpaid
- ▶ try to change their outcomes—ask for a pay rise or promotion
- ▶ psychologically distort their own ratios by rationalising differences in inputs and outcomes
- ▶ change the reference group to which they compare themselves in order to restore equity.

Huseman *et al.* (1987) enumerate the core propositions of equity theory as follows:

❶ Individual's evaluate their relationships with others by assessing the ratio of their outcomes from, and inputs to the relationship against the outcome–input ratio of another comparable individual.

❷ If the outcome–input ratios of the individual and the comparable other are deemed to be unequal, then inequity exists.

❸ The greater the inequity the individual perceives (in the form of either over-reward or under-reward), the more distress the individual experiences. In this respect, there are two types of perceived inequity that people can experience:

▶ negative inequity—when people feel that the unfair treatment affects them in negative ways such as less pay, or fewer positive work outcomes than other people in the same or similar work situations

▶ positive inequity—when individuals feel that the unfair treatment affects them in positive ways such as when they receive more positive work outcomes than their colleagues, including pay.

❹ The greater the distress an individual experiences, the harder s/he will work to restore equity. Among the possible equity restoration techniques the individual might use are: distorting inputs or outcomes; disregarding the comparable other and referring to a new one; or terminating the relationship.

Thus, employees will formulate a ratio between their inputs and outcomes and compare it with the perceived ratios of inputs and outcomes of other people in the same or a similar situation. If these two ratios are not equal then the individual will take actions in an attempt to restore a sense of equity.

An amount of research interest has been generated in testing the relationships advanced by Adams, particularly those relationships which focus on employee reactions to pay. Overall, the research highlights support for Adams's theory about employee reactions to wage inequities. Mowday concludes that the research support for the theory appears to be strongest for predictions about under payment inequity. Furthermore, equity theory appears to offer a useful approach to understanding a wide variety of social relationships in the workplace.

9.6 Motivation and pay

The utility of using pay to motivate and promote performance has been a subject of debate for many years, with some support for both sides of the argument. Most managers instinctively believe that money is a motivator, even though empirical evidence to support this is far from conclusive. Perhaps the key point that may be drawn from the available evidence is that pay is a complex, multifaceted issue which serves as both a tangible and intangible motivator, offering intrinsic and extrinsic rewards. Thus, the applicability of pay-related incentive schemes across a wide range of organisational contexts is difficult to generalise on and is largely dependent on organisational circumstances, employee profile and prevailing conditions.

Kohn (1993) suggests that punishment and rewards are two sides of the same coin. Rewards have a punishment effect because they, like outright punishment, are manipulative. 'Do this and you'll get that' is not very different from 'Do that and here's what will happen to you.' In the case of incentives, the reward itself may be highly desired but, by making that bonus contingent on certain behaviours, managers manipulate their subordinates, and the experience of being controlled is likely to assume a punitive quality over time. Similarly, others have argued that just because too little money can irritate and demotivate does not mean that more money will bring about increased satisfaction, much less, increased motivation. Doubtless, pay is important to employees. It provides the means to live, eat, and achieve other personal or family goals. It is a central reason why people hold down and move between jobs. However, a key question is not the importance of financial incentives as such, but whether they motivate employees to perform well in their jobs.

Once an individual has been attracted to the organisation and the job, the role of money as a motivator is debatable. Clearly money, or the lack of it, can be a source of dissatisfaction, grievance, etc. However, if an employee is reasonably happy with his/her income, does that income induce him/her to perform at high levels of performance? Many of the theoretical prescriptions suggest that money is important in satisfying essential lower-order needs, such as basic physiological and security needs. This line of argument suggests that once such lower-order needs are satisfied, it is factors intrinsic to the job that are the prime motivators, especially at the self-actualisation level. Others suggest that money is important at all levels and may be a prime motivator where it is a valued outcome and where there is an obvious or tangible link between effort, performance and the achievement of greater financial reward.

During the 1960s and 1970s many organisation behaviour theorists emphasised the importance of job enrichment and organisation development and it became popular to discount the importance of money as a motivator (Biddle and Evenden 1989). The current emphasis on performance, productivity and cost reduction has tended to focus on primary job values like employment security, benefits and, more particularly, the pay package. Most managers will agree that remuneration—especially the money element—has an important role in motivating employees. However, it is only one factor in the total motivation process. Clearly many people are not primarily motivated by money but by other factors such as promotion prospects, recognition or the job challenge itself. All employees do not have a generalised set of motives. Rather, an organisation's workforce will be made up of people with varying sets of priorities relating to different situations and work contexts resulting in differing employee motives and goals. These motives and goals will vary from one employee to another and also within the experience of individual employees over time. For example, a young single person may prioritise basic income and free time and the job itself may not hold any great interest. Later, that person, now married and with a mortgage, may be more concerned with job security and fringe benefits such as health insurance and a pension plan.

Arguably, there are four key issues that should be considered when exploring the extent to which employees are motivated by pay:

❶ It is clear that employees must value financial rewards. If people are paid at a very high level, or simply not concerned with financial rewards, higher pay would have little incentive value for employees. Other factors related to the job and work environment must have the potential to motivate employees.

❷ If money is a valued reward, employees must believe that good performance will allow them to realise that reward. This suggests that pay should be linked to performance and differences in pay should be large enough to adequately reward high levels of performance. This approach obviously rejects remuneration systems that reward good, average and poor performance equally, such as regular pay increments based on seniority.

❸ Equity is an important consideration. Employees must be fairly treated in their work situation especially in terms of the perceived equity of pay levels and comparisons with fellow employees. They will be keen that rewards (pay, incentives and benefits) adequately reflect their input (effort, skills, etc.). Should employees feel they are not being treated fairly on these criteria, performance levels may fall.

❹ Employees must believe that the performance levels necessary to achieve desired financial rewards are achievable. The required performance criteria and levels should be clearly outlined and communicated to employees. Organisations must also ensure that employees have the necessary ability, training, resources and opportunity to achieve such performance levels. Otherwise, employees will either not be able, or else will not try, to expend the necessary effort.

Thus, from the motivational perspective, effective payment systems should:

▶ Be objectively established.

▶ Clarify performance levels required and rewards available.

▶ Reward the achievement of required performance levels adequately and quickly.

▶ Ensure employees have the ability, training resources and opportunity to achieve the required performance level(s).

▶ Recognise that financial incentives are only one source of motivation and that jobs should be designed in such a way as to ensure employees can satisfy other needs through their work (for example, achievement, challenge).

▶ Take regular steps to identify employee needs and ensure these can be satisfied within the organisational environment.

Even where these factors are present, success is not guaranteed. For example, an incentive scheme based on production figures may be established to encourage employees to achieve high performance levels. However, unofficial norms established by the work group may dictate 'acceptable' performance levels and ensure this is not exceeded through various social pressures. Equally, such an approach may signal to employees that management are clearly in charge and may either lessen employee feelings of control and competence or encourage conflict over the standards set.

It should always be appreciated that while pay is an important source of employee motivation, it is not the only one.

9.7 Motivation and the design of work

Fox *et al.* (1999) suggest that the provision of meaningful work is a way of tapping into people's self-motivation and desire for achievement at work. The nature of work organisation and design will significantly influence the degree to which work is intrinsically satisfying for employees and promotes high levels of motivation. Organisations should therefore carefully consider their approach to work organisation in order to promote and maintain acceptable levels of motivation in the workplace.

Broadly conceived, the design of work refers to the way the various tasks in the organisation are structured and carried out. It reflects the interaction of management style, the technical system, human resources and the organisation's products or services. Davis (1966) defines the process of JOB DESIGN as that which is concerned with the '... specification of the contents, methods, and relationships of jobs in order to satisfy technological and organisational requirements, as well as the social and personal requirements of the job holder'. The design of individual jobs is seen to particularly impact upon employees since it influences job content, employee discretion, the degree of task fragmentation and the role of supervision. Gunnigle and Flood (1990) suggest that decisions on the organisation of work are primarily a management responsibility and the particular approach chosen will be a good indicator of corporate beliefs about how employees should be managed, jobs structured, and the role of supervision. It will also reflect the organisation's approach to many aspects of personnel management as manifested through attitudes to recruitment, employee development, motivation, rewards and management/ employee relations. The central issue therefore in Lupton's (1976) words is 'how to design for best fit'. Over the years the field of job design has been characterised by shifts from one theoretical perspective to another. The primary shifts have been from task specialisation (for example, Taylor 1911) to JOB ENLARGEMENT (for example, Walker and Guest 1952) to JOB ENRICHMENT (for example, Herzberg 1968), to socio-technical systems theory and the quality of working life (QWL) movement (for example, Cherns and Davis 1975) to high-performance work design (for example, Buchanan and McCalman 1989).

9.7.1 Task specialisation

Variously referred to as task specialisation, scientific management or Taylorism, the traditional approach to the organisation of work was dominated by a desire to maximise the productive efficiency of the organisation's technical resources. Choices on the organisation of work and the design of jobs were seen as determined by the technical system. Management's role was to ensure other organisational resources, including employees, were organised in such a way as to facilitate the optimal utilisation of the technical system. This efficiency approach is based on scientific management principles and has been a characteristic of employer approaches to job design since the beginning of the twentieth century. Jobs were broken down into simple, repetitive, measurable tasks whose skills could be easily acquired through systematic job training.

The rationale for this approach to work and job design was based on *technological determinism* where the organisation's technical resources were seen as a given constraint and the other inputs including employees had to accommodate the technical system. It also reflected managerial assumptions about people at work. Close supervision, work measurement and other types of controls indicate a belief about employees akin to McGregor's theory X discussed above. It suggests that employees need to be coerced to work productively and that this is best achieved by routine, standardised tasks.

This traditional model of job design has undoubtedly had positive benefits for many organisations. It helped improve efficiency and promoted a systematic approach to selection, training, work measurement and payment systems. However, it has also led to numerous problems, such as high levels of labour turnover and absenteeism, and most significantly in the context of our debate here, low motivation. Thus short-term efficiency benefits were often superseded by long-term reductions in organisational effectiveness. Many behavioural scientists argued that organisational effectiveness could be increased by recognising employee ability and giving them challenging, meaningful jobs within a co-operative working environment.

More recently the increased emphases on improving quality, service and overall competitiveness have led to the emergence of other schools of thought aimed at restructuring work systems to increase employee motivation and performance. Much of the focus of work of the successors to task specialisation has been on the restructuring of jobs to incorporate greater scope for intrinsic motivation. Subsequent schools questioned traditional management assumptions about why employees worked. The traditional approach saw employees as essentially instrumental in their attitudes to work. Jobs were seen as a means to an end and it was these extrinsic rewards that motivated employees. Consequently, employers created work systems that closely circumscribed jobs, supervised work and rewarded quantifiable performance.

9.7.2 Job enlargement

The job enlargement and job enrichment schools differ in their relative emphases; the former makes a job 'bigger', while the latter adds some element to the job that is dedicated to increasing the employee's psychological growth. Job enlargement grew from the arguments of humanitarians in the 1950s that production methods prevalent at the time created poor working conditions which led to high levels of job dissatisfaction. The proposed solution was job enlargement, which, when introduced, would lead to more variety and less routinised work. This assumption was drawn upon by Walker and Guest (1952) in their study of automobile assembly lines. They studied 180 workers and identified six main characteristics of MASS PRODUCTION technology:

- ▶ repetitiveness
- ▶ low skill requirement
- ▶ mechanically paced work
- ▶ little alteration of tools or methods
- ▶ low requirement for mental attention
- ▶ minute subdivision of product.

In concluding that the solution to eliminating the ills of mass production technology lay in job enlargement, their proposals have generated some debate. The disputed issues centre around meaning and methodology. Walker and Guest viewed job enlargement as 'the combination of more that two tasks into one'. However, this in no way distinguished it from 'job extension' which could possibly be nothing more that the addition of more meaningless tasks (Wall 1982). It has been argued that there is no explicit theory on which the concept of job enlargement can become a model of job restructuring. There is no motivation theory, according to Buchanan (1979), on which job enlargement stands. Aldag and Brief (1979) note that job enlargement experiments failed to use a conceptual framework of how the structuring of jobs should be actually executed. Furthermore, Buchanan (1979) argues that job enlargement studies have largely ignored external variables and people's differing attitudes towards work.

9.7.3 Job enrichment

Largely attributed to Herzberg (1966), job enrichment was developed for the advancement of the two-factor theory of work motivation discussed earlier in this chapter (see 9.4.4). The job enrichment approach suggested that employees gain most satisfaction from the work itself and it was intrinsic outcomes arising from work that motivated employees to perform well in their jobs. Herzberg (1966) establishes the concept of *vertical loading* (as a means of moving away from the addition of 'one meaningless task to the existing (meaningless) one'. Vertical loading, dedicated to the addition of more challenging dimensions to the job, remains the mainstay of job enrichment (see Figure 9.7).

Figure 9.7 Principles of vertical job loading

Principle	Motivators involved
A. Removing some controls while retaining accountability	Responsibility and personal achievement
B. Increasing the accountability of people for their own work.	Responsibility and recognition
C. Giving a person a complete natural unit of work (module, division, area, etc.)	Responsibility, achievement and recognition
D. Granting additional authority to an employee in their activity; job freedom	Responsibility, achievement and recognition
E. Making periodic reports directly available to the worker rather than to the supervisor	Internal recognition
F. Introducing new and more difficult tasks not previously handled	Growth and learning
G. Assigning people specific or specialised tasks, enabling them to become experts	Responsibility, growth and advancement

Source: Herzberg (1966).

In a similar treatise on intrinsic outcomes and job satisfaction, Hackman and Oldham (1980) enumerate three basic conditions necessary for promoting job satisfaction and employee motivation:

▶ Work should be *meaningful* for the 'doer'.
▶ 'Doers' should have *responsibility* for the results.
▶ 'Doers' should get *feedback* on the results.

This approach suggested that it was the design of the work and not the characteristics of the employee that had the greatest impact on employee motivation. Hackman and Oldham identified five 'core job characteristics' which needed to be incorporated into job design to increase meaningfulness, responsibility and feedback:

▶ skill variety—the extent to which jobs draw on a range of different skills and abilities

▶ task identity—extent to which a job requires completion of a whole, identifiable piece of work

▶ task significance—the extent to which a job substantially impacts on the work or lives of others either within or outside the organisation

▶ autonomy—freedom, independence and discretion afforded to the job holder.

▶ feedback—the degree to which the job holder receives information on their level of performance, effectiveness, etc.

Having identified the factors necessary to promote satisfaction and intrinsic motivation, the next stage is to incorporate these characteristics into jobs through various job redesign strategies. Hackman and Oldham suggest five implementation strategies to increase task variety, significance, identity, and create opportunities for greater autonomy and feedback:

▶ *Form natural work groups.* Arrange tasks together to form an identifiable, meaningful cycle of work for employees, for example, responsibility for single product rather than small components.

▶ *Combine tasks.* Group tasks together to form complete jobs.

▶ *Establish client relationships.* Establish personal contact between employees and the end user/client.

▶ *Vertically load jobs.* Many traditional approaches to job design separate planning and controlling (management functions) from executing (employee's function). Vertically loading a job means integrating the planning, controlling and executing functions and giving responsibility to employees (for example, for materials, quality, deadlines and budgetary control).

▶ *Open feedback channels.* Ensure maximum communication of job results (for example, service standards, faults, wastage, market performance, costs).

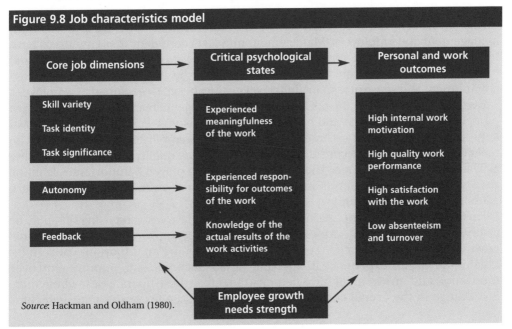

Figure 9.8 Job characteristics model

Source: Hackman and Oldham (1980).

These changes would then have positive long-term benefits for both the organisation and the individual employee. Not all employees are expected to respond favourably to such redesign initiatives. Only those with a strong desire for achievement, responsibility and autonomy will be motivated by increased intrinsic satisfaction and hence motivated to perform better. For others, such change may create a source of anxiety and lead to resentment and opposition to changes in the work system.

9.7.4 The quality of working life movement

Concern with the nature of work organisation and its potentially adverse effects on employee motivation have caused many organisations to take steps to ensure job design incorporates the intrinsic needs of employees. This has been manifested in the emergence of the quality of working life (QWL) movement aimed at eliminating many of the problems associated with traditional work systems, making work more meaningful for employees and ensuring more positive benefits for employers.

Apart from the job enrichment initiatives mentioned above, the QWL movement has also been characterised by steps to increase employee influence and involvement in work organisation and job design. Again, this challenges some traditional management assumptions about employees. It involves recognising that employees can and want to make a positive input into organisational decision making. It assumes that such involvement is valued by employees and results in increased commitment, responsibility and performance.

Increased employee influence in work system design also addresses the issue of employee supervision as an aspect of the management role. If employees are to be involved in making decisions about the organisation of work and responsible for the subsequent execution of such decisions, much of the 'control' aspect is removed from the supervisory role. It necessitates a change in attitude to workforce management. Supervisors become less concerned with monitoring and controlling employee performance and more involved in advising and facilitating employees in carrying out their jobs.

This approach requires high levels of commitment and trust both from management and employees. Management must feel confident that employees have the required competence and will use their greater levels of influence positively and to the benefit of the organisation. Employees must be happy that their increased commitment and sense of responsibility will not be abused or exploited by employers.

There are various mechanisms available to encourage increased levels of employee participation in the design and operation of work systems. Possibly the best-known approach is QUALITY CIRCLES. These are small groups of employees and managers who meet together regularly to consider means of improving quality, productivity or other aspects of work organisation. They are seen as having played a important role in the success of Japanese organisations and have been successfully applied in Western economies including Ireland.

There are numerous other participative and consultative mechanisms that may be established which can work effectively in the appropriate organisational environment. Creating such an environment has become an important concern for organisations. Past experience in applying various techniques to improve employee motivation and involvement have demonstrated that these operate best where there is a change in the overall corporate approach. The issue for senior management is how to create a corporate culture whose values, beliefs and practices establish an organisational environment within which employees are highly committed to and work towards the achievement of business goals.

9.7.5 High-performance work design

Recent commentators such as Buchanan and McCalman (1989) suggest that the heretofore limited impact of job design theories is a weakness which needs to be remedied. 'It (job design) has tended to be regarded as an isolated management technique aimed at local organisational problems and at individual jobs rather than realising that it must form part of the whole company philosophy, through all levels, if it is to be really successful.' The motive behind high-performance job restructuring is founded in the desire and the need to improve the overall competitive position of the organisation. 'The new strategic imperatives require new work organisation strategies' (Buchanan and McCalman 1989). This is clearly reflected in what is referred to as the 'high-performance' literature (Vaill 1982; Perry 1984; Lawler 1986; Buchanan and McCalman 1989), and indeed the 'excellence' literature (Peters and Waterman 1982; Moss Kanter 1983; Quinn Mills 1991). All contributors highlight the need to empower employees in an attempt to make the organisation more effective. This is achieved through a group/team-based work-structuring approach in an attempt to develop a highly skilled, flexible, co-ordinated, motivated workforce and a leaner flatter more responsive organisation. Mooney (1988) argues that this body of literature represents a basic reassessment of the value of an individual's worth to the organisation, resulting in many of the core assumptions of the traditional model of organising being jettisoned.

The high-performance concept, advocating an integrative approach to the structuring of work and the management of the human factor, has its roots in the individualistic and group approaches to job restructuring of previous decades. There is a shift in language and emphasis away from job enlargement, job enrichment and quality circles towards a more all-inclusive approach, linking individual contributions, group performance and competitive advantage, which, according to Buchanan and McCalman (1989), affords to these traditional strategies a new acceptability. Thus, they argue, the 'high performance' label reflects a strategic shift in our approach to the management of human assets, and may serve to encourage a wider understanding of the applications of traditional job restructuring techniques, variations of which have enjoyed a renaissance in recent times in light of the strategic imperative of the 1990s.

As a means of distinguishing high-performance work design from previous movements, Mooney (1988) draws upon the differences between system and value changes within organisations. As the concept implies, a system change simply encompasses changed methodology or ritual, he argues. Many of the previous job design schools were built on principle. On the other hand, value changes, according to Mooney, run deeper, involving a refocus on fundamental business tenets. Therefore, while the 'high performance' school involves system changes to accompany the new emphasis, they are driven and sustained by value changes dedicated to the creation of a revised understanding of and a new order in workplace relations.

Exhibit 9.1 How to motivate your employees

Reversing the trend.
The quest to motivate employees must be an integral part of the organisation's corporate culture. Superior companies use a variety of techniques to motivate employees and achieve their organisation goals.

Select the best. Since the source of motivation is within the individual, outstanding organisations hire only people who have the potential to be motivated in the first place. They select candidates based on more than credentials or prerequisite skills; they look for a solid system of values consistent with those of the company. All companies claim to hire superior candidates, but few actually exhibit the courage to demand — and get — the best.

Substantial time and effort must be dedicated to locating new talent. The interview process should be thorough and include assessments of personality, behaviour and management styles. Drug screening is also an imperative. Most essential of all is to identify work ethic values: discipline, desire, commitment to self-development, willingness to work hard, enthusiasm and a goal/results orientation.

The Pygmalion effect.
Outstanding managers have one thing in common: they invest psychologically in their employees. They truly believe in their people, and this confidence is irresistible. Like the teacher who puts extra effort into helping a student the teacher believes is gifted, excellent managers know their vision of an employee's performance is a self-fulfilling prophecy.

Track success. Genuine confidence and enthusiasm create energy, and specific objectives and criteria must be established to direct that energy. At the outset of employment and at regular intervals, workers should be told what is expected of them and the criteria that will be used to evaluate their performance. Excellent companies do this positively; not in a critical or demeaning fashion. Regular performance evaluations and frequent feedback can help avoid major surprises and assist each manager to focus on ways to improve and develop.

Many managers think that performance appraisals are an opportunity to punish or reprimand an employee, and the entire experience is viewed negatively by both parties. This should not be the case. At its best, the performance appraisal process can be a powerful motivating tool because it provides a structured way for a company to give workers what they really want — recognition and feedback, even in the context of constructive criticism.

Recognise contributions. A pay raise alone does not have sufficient power to motivate on a long-term basis. The best way to motivate employees is to raise their level of personal and professional self-esteem. A pay increase won't do this, but public recognition will.

A manager who adopts a policy of recognising employees' outstanding contributions at every weekly staff meeting can praise them for their accomplishments in front of their peers. Those employees will respond by

striving to achieve something important each week. It is a fact of human nature that people will spare no effort to achieve the accolades of an individual or group that they are certain truly appreciates their work.

Provide incentives and rewards. This is not to say that incentives and rewards do not play an important part in motivation. But it is essential to remember that the primary motivating factor that rewards provide is the psychological effect on the individual, not the material value of the reward.

Employees are motivated more by the boost in self-esteem that comes with public recognition than by monetary compensation. Nevertheless, when held out as a carrot, monetary incentives do motivate in the short term. However, once gained, they lose all motivating power.

Empower employees. One of the recent 'miracles' of business is the turnaround of the Ford Motor Co. How did it happen? Ford discovered and put into practice something fundamental to motivation: empowering employees.

Ford designers went directly to the people who were responsible for the company's product: its employees. They surveyed assembly-line workers, mechanics, dealers, sales representatives, satisfied customers — anyone who had 'stock' in the company (as opposed to those who owned stock but looked only at the bottom line). The combined input from all of these formerly fragmented pools of experience contributed to a winning team.

Exhibit 9.1 How to motivate your employees *contd.*

Empowering employees does not mean trading organisational structure for chaos, but just the opposite. When people feel important, they work more effectively and contentedly in any capacity, as long as they feel their contribution is meaningful.

Enhance career development. Good companies recognise that their best people — in fact, most employees — want to improve themselves. Unfortunately, employee career development is a two-edged sword. Many 'job hoppers' will stay in a company just long enough to improve their skills, then they are off to greener pastures.

This is a social reality of our times. The only way a company can combat the loss of the most productive workers in search of career development is to provide growth opportunities.

Employees cannot maintain or increase performance by staying at the same level, in the same job, preserving the status quo, indefinitely. Quality invariably suffers.

Companies must provide for career development in a variety of ways. Flexibility in scheduling can allow workers to go back to school for an advanced degree or more training. A commitment to filling positions from within the organisation provides opportunities laterally for cross-training or upwardly for promotion and advancement. Recognition and reward for workers' improvements and contributions do much to strengthen a company's reputation for caring about its employees' professional development.

Source: Dawson and Dawson (1990).

9.8 Summary of key propositions

▶ This chapter explored the concepts of motivation at work and argued that motivation as a concept continues to have a centrality in organisational life. Taking a longer-term perspective of the human resource in an attempt to build up a reservoir of well-skilled, enthusiastic employees has brought the concept of motivation to the fore.

▶ Motivation is typically viewed as a set of processes that activate, direct and sustain human behaviour dedicated to goal accomplishment. It is essentially concerned with explaining why people behave as they do, or why people choose different forms of behaviour in order to achieve different ends.

▶ The content theories of motivation focus on the needs that people experience and how these needs might drive or initiate behaviour. Maslow's hierarchy of needs, Alderfer's ERG theory, McClelland's achievement motivation theory and Herzberg's two-factor theory all attempt to explain, from a variety of perspectives, the role that needs play in motivating people's behaviour.

▶ Process theories are based on the assumption that individuals and groups think consciously about the effort that they expend at work and its relative utility in reaching valued goals. Expectancy theories and equity theories focus on how people consider or weigh up various factors which contribute to their decisions to engage in effort at work.

▶ The utility of using pay to motivate and promote performance has been a subject of debate for many years with some support for both sides of the argument. Importantly, while most managers instinctively believe that money is a motivator, empirical evidence to support this is far from conclusive.

▶ The nature of work organisation and design will significantly influence the degree to which work is intrinsically satisfying for employees and promotes high levels of motivation. Organisations should therefore carefully consider their approach to work organisation in order to promote and maintain acceptable levels of motivation in the workplace. Among the key approaches examined here were scientific management, job enlargement, job enrichment, the quality of working life movement and high-performance work design approaches, all with differing ideas on how to design work in order to keep the individual motivated in the workplace.

Discussion questions

1. What lessons does motivation theory have for practising managers?
2. Debate to what extent Maslow's hierarchy of needs has practical relevance to effective people management.
3. A manager's perceptions of the workforce will profoundly influence his attitudes in dealing with people. Discuss.
4. Compare three different need theories of motivation. In what ways are they similar and how do they differ in their approaches to motivation at work?
5. Is pay a motivator?
6. Distinguish between the different approaches to job design and highlight the aspects of each approach, if any, that were seen to be motivating.

Concluding case: Motivation case study

Kathy Murphy checks the time, logs off her computer and heads out of the office. She is late already and is supposed to be meeting her friend Paula Byrne in the nearby sandwich bar for lunch and a chat. Along the corridor she bumps into Mark O'Driscoll, the Training Manager. 'Surely it's not lunchtime already Kathy?' he queries. 'I have some memos here I want sent out before three this afternoon – I was hoping you could get them started before lunch. Also, can you drop these off to the Aine on B Shift – she's scheduling safety training for her group this afternoon.' Kathy takes the notes and assures Mark that she will attend to them as soon as she gets back and detours to Aine's desk with the safety schedules.

By the time she sits down for lunch with Paula half of her lunch break is already over and she is feeling seriously put out. 'You are cutting it fine,' says Paula. 'Don't get me started,' replies Kathy, 'you wouldn't believe the morning I've had. Honestly, some people are just too much ...' and she launches into a tirade about the running around she has had to do all day culminating in Mark's last-minute request (although she wouldn't exactly call it a request). 'I was supposed to be sitting in with Ciara for a couple of operator interviews this afternoon but I'm not going to be able to do that now as I have to type Mark's bloody memos. Oh hell, Paula, I'm so sick of it all sometimes.'

'So why don't you leave then, Kathy?' Paula retorts. 'You've been complaining for months that you are fed up with the way work is going for you and that you want to get more experience in Personnel work. Why don't you do up your CV and see what's out there?'

'I know you're right, Paula, and some days I feel that I just can't take it anymore. But I'm almost finished my Diploma course and the company is sponsoring me to do it –

I don't want to leave until I have that finished. Plus, most of the time I like working for Diamond Computing and there are lots of opportunities, if only people would give me a chance.'

'What exactly do you mean?' asks Paula. 'Well, take this afternoon, for example,' replies Kathy. 'Ciara Brennan is our Recruitment Manager and she knows I am doing the CIPD Diploma in Personnel Management [see note page 286] in the evenings at the university.

'We were talking about it last week and I was telling her that while I love the course it is often difficult to apply the theory as my job involves the administration side of the HR work and not the people side of things. Anyway, when I told her that we did a practical module on interviewing skills she asked whether I'd like to sit in with her on some interviews. I jumped at the chance but had to run it by the HR Manager first – he was fine with it, and thought it was a great idea provided I still did my regular work.'

'But I don't understand,' says Paula. 'What is the problem so?' 'Mark O'Driscoll – he's the problem,' replies Kathy. 'He's constantly calling in to me at the last minute with work that has to be done asap. Plus, he sometimes has me doing stuff that technically is not part of my job at all. Take last week. He was supposed to be designing an induction training programme for new graduates but, Paula, he hadn't a clue. He had organised a focus group with some of our graduates who have been here a while but he just didn't know what he wanted to ask them. I was involved just to take notes but I ended up feeding some ideas to him in order to get the discussion going. And then, you should have seen what he put together afterwards. It was woeful. I was putting the document together and I restructured and virtually rewrote the whole thing for him. Honestly, I know more about his job than he does.'

'I hope he was suitably grateful for you getting him out of a bind,' says Paula. 'Him? grateful? you must be joking!' retorts Kathy. 'He never mentioned it again save "thanks for typing this for me, Kathy" and "by all accounts the HR Manager really likes the final version and it's going to be introduced within the next couple of months."' 'What? He never let on that you were involved in designing it?' asks Paula disbelievingly. 'How can you bear to work for him?' 'Well, that's the thing you see,' replies Kathy. 'I don't work for Mark *per se*. Both Marjorie and myself provide general administrative assistance to the HR function, although I seem to be doing a lot more of Mark's work lately. I wouldn't mind so much except I don't really want to specialise in training. I much prefer the generalist HR side of things – you know, recruitment, rewards and the like.'

'So what are you going to do then?' asks Paula, 'wait until you finish your course, get your HR qualification and then leave?' Kathy puts on her coat and heads back to work. 'I don't know', she replies. 'What else can I do?'

Case questions

❶ How would you describe Kathy's work needs and values?

❷ At what motivation level is she working now?

❸ What would you advise Kathy to do?

❹ What practical action can the company take to improve Kathy's intrinsic motivation?

Bibliography

Adams, J. (1965) 'Inequity in Social Exchange', in Berkowitz, L. (ed) *Advances in Experimental Psychology*. New York: Academic Press.

Aldag, R. and Brief, A. (1979) *Task Design and Employee Motivation*, New York: Scott Foreman.

Alderfer, C. (1969) 'An Empirical Test of a New Theory of Human Needs', *Organizational Performance and Human Behaviour*, 4.

Allan, J. (1999)', *How to be Better at Motivating People*. London: Kogan Page.

Arnold, J., Cooper, C. and Robertson, G. (1995) *Work Psychology*. London: Pitman.

Ambrose. M. and Kilik, C. (1999) 'Old Friends, New Faces: Motivation Research in the 1990s', *Journal of Management*, 25 (3), 231–92.

Bennet, R. (1991), *Management*. London: Pitman.

Bent, R., Seaman, C. and Ingram, A. (1999) 'Staff Motivation in Small Food Manufacturing Enterprises', *British Food Journal*, 101 (9), 654–68.

Biddle, D. and Evenden, R. (1989) *Human Aspects of Management*. London: IPD.

Buchanan, D. (1979) *The Development of Job Design Theories and Techniques*. London: Saxon House.

Buchanan, D. and McCalman, J. (1989) *High Performance Work Systems: The Digital Experience*. London: Routledge.

Cherns, A. and Davis, L. (1975) *The Quality of Working Life*. London: Macmillan.

Davis, L. (1966) 'The Design of Jobs', *Industrial Relations*, 6 (1).

Dawson, K. and Dawson, Sheryl N. (1990) 'How To Motivate Your Employees', *HR Magazine*, April, 78–80.

Forrest, C. (2000) 'Motivation for the Millennium', *Training Journal*, January, 10–15.

Fox, D., Byrne, V. and Rouault, F. (1999) 'Performance Improvement: What to Keep in Mind', *Training and Development*, 52 (8), 38–41.

Gunnigle, P. and Flood. P. (1990) *Personnel Management in Ireland: Practice, Trends and Developments*. Dublin: Gill & Macmillan.

Hackman, J. and Oldham, G. (1976) 'Motivation Through the Design of Work: Test of a Theory', *Organisational Behaviour and Human Performance*, 16.

Hackman, J. and Oldham, G. (1980) *Work Redesign*. New York: Addison Wesley.

Herzberg, F. (1966) *Work and the Nature of Man*. New York: Staples

—(1968) 'One More Time: How Do You Motivate Employees?', *Harvard Business Review*, January–February.

Hiam, A. (1999) *Streetwise Motivating and Rewarding Employees: New and Better Ways*. New York: Adams Media Corporation.

Hitt, M., Middlemist, R. and Mathis, R. (1989) *Management Concepts and Effective Practice*. New York: West Publishing Co.

Huseman, R., Hatfield, J. and Miles, E. (1987) 'A New Perspective on Equity Theory: The Equity Sensitivity Construct', *Academy of Management Review*, 12.

Kohn, A. (1993) 'Why Incentive Plans Cannot Work', *Harvard Business Review*, September–October.

Lawler, E. (1986) *High Involvement Management*. San Francisco: Jossey Bass.

Lupton, T. (1976) 'Best Fit in the Design of Organisations', in Miller, E. (ed.) *Task and Organisation*. New York, John Wiley and Sons.

Marcum, J. (2000) 'Out with Motivation, In with Engagement', *National Productivity Review*, 19, 4, 57–61.

Maslow, A. (1943) 'A Theory of Human Motivation', *Psychological Review*, 50, 4.

McClelland, D. (1960) *The Achieving Society*. New York: Von Nostrand-Reinhold.

McGregor, D. (1960) *The Human Side of Enterprise*. New York: McGraw-Hill.

Mooney, P. (1988) 'From Industrial Relations to Employee Relations in Ireland', Unpublished PhD Thesis, University of Dublin, Trinity College.

Morley, M. and Heraty, N. (1995) 'The High Performance Organisation: Developing Teamwork Where it Counts', *Management Decision*, 33, 2.

Moss Kanter, R. (1983) *The Change Masters*. London: Unwin Hyman.

Nelson, B. (1999) 'The Ironies of Motivation', *Strategy and Leadership*, 27, 1, 26–33.

Osteracker, M. (1999a) 'Measuring Motivation in a Dynamic Organisation: A Contingency Approach', *Strategic Change*, 8, 2, 103–11.

Osteracker, M. (1999b) 'Measuring Motivation in a Learning Organisation', *Journal of Workplace Learning: Employee Counselling Today*, 11, 2, 73–8.

Perry, B. (1984) *Einfield: A High Performance System*. Einfield: DEC Educational Services Development and Publishing.

Peters, T. and Waterman, R. (1982) *In Search of Excellence*. New York: Harper Row.

Pettinger, R. (1994) *Introduction to Management*. London: Macmillan.

Quinn Mills, D. (1991) *Rebirth of the Corporation*. New York: Wiley

Ritchie, S. and Martin, P. (2000) *Motivation Management*, Aldershot: Gower.

Steers, R. and Porter, L. (1987) *Motivation and Work Behaviour*, New York: McGraw-Hill.

Taylor, F. (1911) *The Principles of Scientific Management*. New York: Harper.

Vaill, P. (1982) 'The Purposing of High Performance Systems', *Organizational Dynamics*, Autumn.

Vroom, V. (1964) *Work and Motivation*. New York: John Wiley and Sons.

Walker, C. and Guest, R. (1952) *The Man on the Assembly Line*. Boston: Harvard Business School Press.

Wall, T. (1982) 'Perspectives on Job Redesign', in J. Kelly and C. Clegg (eds) *Autonomy and Control at the Workplace*. London: Croom Helm.

NOTE

The Diploma course that Kathy is completing is a part-time one that is run two evenings a week for three years at the local university. The Diploma is a professional programme that provides her with membership of the Chartered Institute of Personnel and Development. The course is well respected and valued by companies and the qualification is widely recognised in the HR/personnel field.

Chapter 10

Organisational Control

10.1 Introduction

Organisational theorists have long acknowledged that processes of control are integral to the way organisations operate (Jermier 1998). Such mechanisms are central to the effective functioning of organisations and according to Baker and Jennings (1999:231) controlling is recognised as one of the major activities of managers, and generally viewed as an integral link that binds together other essential managerial functions such as planning, organising, and leading. Thus, they suggest, there is little question as to the importance of the controlling process in managerial and organisational life. While this is as true for small firms as it is for large ones (Chapman 1999; Storey 1994; Burris 1989; Lawler 1976) as well as in the not-for-profit sector (Anthony and Young 2000; Herzlinger and Nitterhouse 1999), it is being increasingly recognised that management control procedures and systems do vary between organisations, sectors and societies. Whitley (1999) notes that, in particular, four characteristics of control systems differ considerably between institutional contexts. These are:

▶ the extent to which control is exercised overwhelmingly through formal rules and procedures

▶ the degree of control exercised over how unit activities are carried out

▶ the influence and involvement of unit members in exercising control

▶ the scope of the information used by the control system in evaluating performance and deciding rewards and sanctions.

Similarly, Bhimani (1999) notes that cross-national studies of management control systems and internal accounting practices are suggestive of the existence of distinct national differences, Kald *et al.* (2000) and Nilsson (2000) identify variations in management controls depending on the actual strategy being pursued by the firm, while Modell (2000) discusses the linkage between the management controls in place and the nature of the human resource management system being followed by the organisation.

Regardless of the institutional context or variations in organisational characteristics, control ensures the achievement of organisational objectives and goals by measuring actual performance and taking corrective action where needed. In this way it can be viewed as that aspect of managerial work that ensures there is a conformance between planned and actual activities. The control process and the various types of control that can be used in organisations are examined in this chapter. Following a consideration of the characteristics of effective controls, the two main methods of control classified as financial and non-financial controls are examined. Financial controls examined include BUDGETS, BREAK-EVEN ANALYSIS and RATIO ANALYSIS. Non-financial controls looked at here include project controls, management audits and inventory, production and quality control.

10.2 The nature and importance of control

> Whenever people join forces in the name of organised action, structures of control can be found in the midst of whatever efficiency, effectiveness or coordination they achieve. This is not entirely a nefarious state of affairs. Throughout human history, configurations of control have been used to steer organised action down one path or another and, as every organisational theorist knows, organised action has been responsible for most of humanity's triumphs as well as its tragedies. (Jermier 1998:235)

The control function of modern management is the process dedicated to ensuring the efficient and effective achievement of organisational goals and objectives. Sridhar and Balachandran (1997) argue that any task assignment decision must be accompanied by an appropriately designed managerial control system as each affects the other. The control process typically involves measuring progress towards planned performance and, where necessary, applying corrective measures so that performance can be improved. Therefore, control is concerned with making sure that goals and objectives are attained. It is strongly related to planning in that for control to occur objectives and plans have to be available against which to measure performance. Similarly, planning cannot function effectively if there are no control mechanisms to correct deviations from plans. Weihrich and Koontz (1993) have likened the relationship between planning and control to that of the two blades of a pair of scissors—the scissors cannot work unless there are two blades.

Control, however, has been the most neglected and least understood function of management (Giglioni and Bedeian 1974). Kirsch (1996) notes that while much discussed, managerial control is an inadequately studied phenomenon within organisation sciences. This can be considered surprising given that it has been demonstrated that improperly implemented control mechanisms have a dysfunctional effect on organisations and only serve to obliterate both the purpose and potential of organisational advantages that should be realised under effective control processes (Baker and Jennings 1999:237). Its managerial role has frequently been equated with financial control. In this sense, control has been regarded as an activity associated with accountants and financial departments rather than as a management function. The word itself has also caused some confusion as it can mean to direct others and also the evaluation of outcomes and taking corrective action. The latter provides a more accurate description of the modern control function.

In the modern organisation, control is the function of every manager. Top-level managers are concerned about controlling sales and profits. Middle managers are concerned about controlling direct labour hours and production outputs. Front-line supervisors are concerned about controlling quality and scrap. So while the scope of control varies depending on the managerial level, all managers have responsibility for implementing plans and consequently are responsible for their control.

In recent years the control function has changed. Traditionally, the majority of organisations were involved in labour-intensive industries. However, today more and more organisations are involved in the service sector where it is more difficult to measure performance. Therefore the control function becomes more complex and at the same time more important.

Information technology has revolutionised control systems (Bruns and McFarlan 1987), but has also added complexity to the control process. Low-cost data-control systems and communications systems are now being applied to the control function, and such advancements have made possible a pan-organisational information system within which process improvements across the organisation can be made (Naveh and Halevy 2000). The result is a more flexible and speedy system. Computers allow organisations to speed up changes in strategies by revising financial plans and testing changes ahead of time by quickly running and comparing various 'what if' scenarios.

Information is now available quicker and is more accurate. As a result, information technology has revitalised the three traditional purposes that control systems serve (Bruns and McFarlan 1987):

▶ It helps managers use resources more effectively.

▶ It aligns different parts of the organisation with organisational goals.

▶ It collects data for strategic and operating decisions.

An example of the application of information technology to a control system can be found in the scanning machines in many supermarkets for purchasing goods. The most widely known example is Tesco. These electronic devices allow the organisation to:

▶ instantly identify and calculate the type, quantity and price of each individual item purchased. The control of inventory is therefore much easier as the organisation no longer has to undertake a physical stock-take as the scanners produce inventory records instantly. This system also identifies slow-moving products which may require a reduction in price to sell or perhaps should not be reordered. The system also tracks consumer tastes and patterns which facilitates reordering of stock.

▶ calculate employee productivity by assessing how many customers and items are dealt with per minute. If, for example, the checkout person is very slow this could lead to customer frustration. To prevent this, the checkout person can be sent for retraining.

▶ calculate precisely how much money or revenue is generated on an hourly, daily and weekly basis from each till, store or regional area. This makes financial control far simpler and more accurate. It is also possible to pinpoint how the organisation is deviating from budgets.

As a result of these changes, store managers have been able to lower inventory levels, boost turnover and match PRODUCT MIXES to consumers' changing tastes. These developments have all meant that the control function has assumed far greater importance.

However, while the technological revolution has increased the speed with which information can be generated, it has also introduced the necessity to control access to information, especially the protection of corporate information (Webb 2000). Barnard and Von Solms (2000) argue that such controls are variable and must be based on the specific business needs of the company concerned. In their treatise on the effective selection and evaluation of information security controls, they discuss the need for effective information security controls and how best to determine the relevant controls for an individual organisation. In their estimation, when making decisions on the information security controls necessary for an organisation, four critical areas of evaluation are worth considering:

► the functionality of the control system
► the degree of assurance of correctness
► the degree of assurance of effectiveness
► the degree of assurance of actual operation.

They conclude that the correct identification of controls and an appropriate evaluation scheme that goes beyond mere functionality are essential to an effective information security control scheme. Similarly, Matyas and Stapleton (2000) stress the need for controlling access to information generated by information and communication technologies. They introduce the notion of *biometrics* as a means of controlling access. They argue the case for biometrics as standard and they outline different phases of the process that could prove useful in controlling access to information, namely, verification, identification and enrolment.

10.3 Stages in the control process

Various frameworks for management control systems are postulated in the literature, the central objective of all being the management of organisational performance (see Otley 1999). For the purposes of this chapter, control can be considered a continuous process involving three key steps, (Daft and Macintosh 1984; Dunbar 1981; Todd 1977; Giglioni and Bedeian 1974), as shown in Figure 10.1. It is designed to ensure that employees, teams and business units meet established targets and to minimise deviations from such targets.

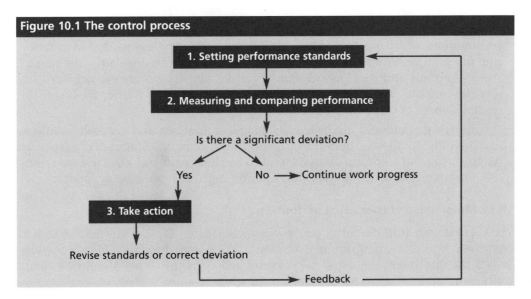

Figure 10.1 The control process

1. Setting performance standards
2. Measuring and comparing performance
Is there a significant deviation?
Yes
No ⟶ Continue work progress
3. Take action
Revise standards or correct deviation
Feedback

10.3.1 Setting performance standards

The first step in the control process is the establishment of performance standards. All organisations have goals and a standard can be viewed as the level of expected performance for a given goal (Flamholtz 1979). Standards are selected points in a planning programme which measure performance, so that managers can see how things are going without watching every step in the process (Weihrich and Koontz 1993). Therefore, standards are yardsticks for performance. Unless standards are established and enforced, performance across the various parts of the organisation is likely to vary widely. Standards of performance can be set for almost any organisational activity, as the following examples illustrate:

Market share:	Increase market share by 20 per cent.
Quality:	Product deviations should not be higher than 2.5. defects per million.
Costs:	Costs should be reduced by 15 per cent.
Innovation:	25 per cent of turnover should be generated by products less than three years old.
Employees:	Turnover should not exceed 4 per cent per month.
Customers:	All customer complaints should be answered within 24 hours.

Establishing standards of performance is a complex task, given the wide variety of standards which have to be established, but they are particularly important in the context of avoiding or rectifying poor performance (Gavin *et al.* 1995). In general, standards can be generated from three different sources—historical, comparative or engineering-based.

▶ **Historical standards** are based on the organisation's past experience. Previous production, sales, profits and costs can be used as a basis from which to establish performance standards. Standards based on historical data, however, assume that the future will be the same as the past. Given the nature of the business environment, abrupt changes render historical standards useless.

▶ **Comparative standards** are based on the experience of other organisations and competitors, which are used as benchmarks for generating standards. For instance, the financial performance of another organisation can be used to judge market value. Journals and trade associations provide information on sales, advertising expenditure and wages of competitor organisations, which further facilitates the establishment of comparative standards.

▶ **Engineering standards** are based on technical analyses and generally apply to production methods, materials, safety and QUALITY. Standards based on engineering and technical analysis tend to be numerical and objective in nature. For example, a standard of achieving 'on time' delivery rates of 95 per cent.

10.3.2 Measuring and comparing performance

The second step in the control process is to measure actual performance and to compare it against the performance standards which were developed in step one (see 10.3.1). At this stage, the 'what is' is compared with the 'what should be'. Data concerning performance can come from three main sources. First, written reports, including computer printouts, provide data which allows performance to be measured. Second, oral reports from supervisors and managers provide information about levels of performance on a day-to-day basis. Third, personal observation, which involves touring the various areas and observing activities, can provide important information about performance. However, personal observation by its very nature is subjective and does not generate sufficient quantitative data. Too much personal observation can be construed by employees as management showing a lack of trust. Despite these disadvantages, many managers still believe that personal observation provides important insights which quantitative data is simply unable to do.

Actual performance can either meet, surpass or fall below the established performance standards. If performance meets the standards then no control problem exists and the progress of work can continue. Where standards have not been reached due to exceptional circumstances such as a strike, no further action is usually taken in the control process. If performance fails to meet or exceeds expectations then further examination is required. If standards have been exceeded it is possible that standards were inappropriately set or that superior talent and effort was put in. When performance fails to meet standards this could be caused by inappropriate standards but, more worryingly, could arise from poor talent, lack of effort or failure to use resources efficiently.

In cases where actual performance falls below or exceeds standards the critical issue facing managers is how much of a deviation is acceptable before corrective action should be taken. In reality, actual performance rarely matches established performance standards and consequently deviations are the norm. Managers, however, have to know when deviations are significantly different and require corrective action. Due to the fact that managers cannot react to every deviation, performance ranges are used which state both upper and lower control limits. Managers apply the *principle of exception* by concentrating on significant deviations or exceptions from expected results. As therefore only exceptional cases need to be corrected, managers can save time and money by effectively applying the principle of exception.

10.3.3 Taking action

The final step in the control process is to take action based on the comparisons made in the previous step. At this stage of the control process, control can be clearly seen as part of the management system and can be related to the other management functions of planning organising and leading. Where a significant deviation has occurred management should take vigorous corrective action. Effective control demands that prompt action is taken to rectify the situation. An organisation can either correct the deviation or revise the standards applied. When correcting deviations, both positive and negative deviations should be examined as a basis for learning.

Corrective action can be taken by the top of the organisation, a specialist or by the operators themselves. Managers or supervisors, for example, can change procedures, introduce new technology, training, or even take disciplinary action. Further down the organisation corrective action can be taken by specialists or operators. Traditionally, specialists corrected malfunctions. However, today, operators who are multiskilled can identify and rectify their own problems as they occur. This type of control is called *operator control*. Operators are closer to the problem and therefore, can correct it closer to the source. This form of control also gives the operator more scope to use talents and skills (Wall *et al.* 1990 in refs).

An organisation can also alter or revise standards if it is felt that they are unacceptable or unrealistic. Standards which are based on historical data may no longer be appropriate due to changed environmental circumstances. Comparative standards may also prove inappropriate if based too closely on other organisations as no two organisations are identical. Finally, engineering standards also require revision to reflect changes.

Having either taken corrective action or revised standards the organisation will feed back lessons learned from the process into the first step, establishing standards, and the process continues all over again.

10.4 Types of control: feedforwarding controls, concurrent controls and feedback controls

As the control process has shown, control is necessary to identify problems, adjust plans and take action. Therefore, control is designed to regulate aspects of the organisation. Human beings are self-regulating in that when conditions change the body reacts; for example, if a person has a cold, antibodies immediately fight the germs to regulate the body's system. Self-regulating systems are referred to as *cybernetic systems* (Weiner 1949).

Unlike humans, organisations cannot regulate themselves and do not have automatic controls. As a result, their activities must be monitored to identify and adjust for deviations from established performance standards. Using the systems theory framework, an organisation's performance can be examined at three control points: before, during and after the activity has been completed. Control at each of the points corresponds to the input–transformation–output cycle associated with systems theory. Control which occurs before the activity has been completed at the input stage is called feedfoward control (Koontz and Bradspies 1980) or preliminary control (Davis 1951, Donnelly, Gibson and Ivancevich 1981). Control exerted while the activity is being completed at the transformation stage is called concurrent control. Finally, control which occurs after the activity has been completed at the output stage is called feedback control. The various types of control points are shown in Figure 10.2.

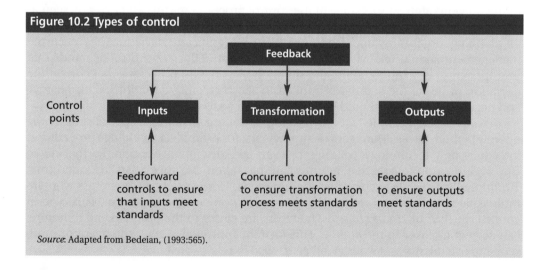

Figure 10.2 Types of control

Source: Adapted from Bedeian, (1993:565).

10.4.1 Feedforward control

Feedforward control is future-directed and aims to prevent problems before they occur. Due to the fact that managers need to react quickly to correct mistakes, control which prevents mistakes occurring is appealing for managers. Feedforward control carefully examines the various inputs to make sure that they meet the standards needed for successful transformation into outputs. Feedforward controls regulate the quantity and quality of financial, physical and human resources before they are transformed. For example, in order to prevent BAD DEBTS or loan defaults, banks ask for documentation about salary, other loans and credit history before granting loan approval. In this way they are controlling the activity of giving a loan before it is sanctioned. Similarly, in the manufacture of food products, Marks and Spencer uses extremely effective feedforward controls in relation to the quality of the supplies used. In this way Marks and Spencer make sure that all ingredients meet exacting quality standards. Feedforward control, therefore, strongly emphasises the anticipation of problems and preventative action at an early stage in the production process.

10.4.2 Concurrent control

Concurrent control occurs while inputs are being transformed into outputs. They monitor the transformation to make sure that the outputs meet standards by producing the right amount of the right products at a specified time. Concurrent controls ensure that materials and staff are available when needed, and that breakdowns are repaired speedily.

Because concurrent controls occur at the same time as the transformation process, they can cope with contingencies which were not anticipated. Concurrent controls allow adjustments to be made while the work is being done. For example, if a machine has a minor fault the manager has to decide whether to follow an alternative course or to stop and correct the situation. As a result, concurrent controls avoid waste and unacceptable outputs. Waterford Glass, Belleek China and Dublin Crystal are all examples of organisations that use particularly stringent concurrent controls to ensure the quality of the finished product.

10.4.3 Feedback control

Feedback control monitors outputs to ensure that they meet standards. This form of control takes place after the product/service has been completed. As a result, feedback control focuses on end results as opposed to inputs or transformation activities. Feedback control provides information on the return on investment, output produced, quality levels and costs, all of which are essential for planning for the future and allocating rewards for performance. Such control gives managers a basis from which to evaluate the reasonableness of organisational goals and standards, and gives insights into past performance so that important lessons can be learned.

Timing is a very important aspect of feedback control. Time-lags naturally occur when using feedback control because it takes place after the deviation has occurred. For example, when actual spending is compared with a quarterly budget there is a time-lag between spending and any corrective action that can possibly be taken. If feedback on performance is not timely and managers fail to take immediate action, serious problems can arise. An example of a feedback control can be found in the customer satisfaction surveys which Bewley's asks all customers to fill in when visiting their restaurants.

Most organisations use all three types of control to monitor their production processes. Feedfoward control helps to anticipate future problems. Concurrent control allows managers to cope with contingencies which cannot be anticipated. Feedback control ensures that the organisation does not make the same mistakes again and captures any defects.

10.5 Eight characteristics of effective control

Several criteria have been suggested as determinants of effective controls in the literature, including understandability, justifiableness, co-ordination, accuracy, timeliness, realism and acceptability (Baker and Jennings 1999). Effective controls of this nature are needed to ensure that developments conform to plans (Anthony *et al.* 1984). According to Weihrich and Koontz (1993) effective controls must be tailored to plans, positions and individuals and the requirements of organisational efficiency and effectiveness. Irrespective of the type of control being used, effective controls have a number of important characteristics in common, as shown in Figure 10.3.

Figure 10.3 Characteristics of effective controls

1. Appropriate
2. Cost effective
3. Acceptable
4. Emphasise exceptions at critical points
5. Flexible
6. Reliable and valid
7. Based on valid performance standards
8. Based on adequate information

10.5.1 Appropriateness

Controls must be suitable and appropriate for an organisation's goals and plans. In other words, controls should be tailored to the plans and various positions within the organisation. Controls should provide clear and concise information that tells managers how well plans are progressing. Effective controls should not generate information which is irrelevant in fulfilling organisational plans.

Controls should also reflect the position in which they are used. Control used by a top-level manager is very different to that used by a front-line supervisor. Different areas within an organisation require different types of control. For example, controls used within a finance department are very different to those used in marketing. Similarly, small and large organisations use different types of control. Controls should also be tailored to the individual manager, who must clearly understand them. Control should also reflect the organisational structure which shows responsibility for the execution of plans and any deviations from them.

While certain techniques for controlling finance and human resource planning have general application, none of them is completely applicable to any one situation.

Consequently, it is important to ensure that controls are tailored to the individual needs of the organisation.

10.5.2 Cost-effectiveness

The benefits achieved by control processes must offset the cost of using them. To be cost-effective, the controls used must be tailored to the job and to the size of the organisation. Larger organisations can gain economies of scale and can often afford expensive and elaborate control systems. Control techniques are economical when they show up potential or actual deviations from the minimum cost. For example, the cost of inserting electronic strips in library books which then bleep when they go through an alarm system more than offsets the cost of books lost through theft. However, employing a full-time library detective in addition to this system would probably not be cost-effective, as the cost of stolen books would not cover both forms of control.

10.5.3 Acceptability

Controls must be accepted as fair and adequate by those to whom they apply. Controls that are arbitrary or unnecessary will have little impact. Controls that are harmful to an individual's social or psychological well-being are also ineffective. For example, some organisations search their employees as they go home or come off shifts to make sure they have not stolen goods. This form of control is frequently considered unnecessary and illustrates a lack of trust in the employees. The end result is normally frustration, apathy and distrust of management and their motives. It is therefore important that controls are accepted by people as fair and necessary if they are to be effective.

10.5.4 The relative emphasis on exceptions at control points

Controls should be designed to make sure that they show up significant deviations. Controls that do so allow managers to benefit from management by exception and detect those areas that require further action. However, it is not sufficient just to identify deviations. Some small deviations in certain areas may be more important than larger deviations in other areas. For example, a 10 per cent increase in labour costs is far more worrying than a 25 per cent increase in the cost of postage stamps. As a result, exceptions must be looked for at critical points, which then facilitate corrective action.

10.5.5 Flexibility

Effective controls must be flexible enough to withstand changing circumstances or unforeseen developments. In the current business environment, the need for flexible controls has become all the more important. For example, budgets which specify how much money is to be spent on certain resources are normally based on a predicted level of sales or profits. If for some reason sales fall below the expected target the budget becomes obsolete. Unless the budget is flexible, its efficiency as a control device is questionable. Over the years it has been argued that budgets are extremely inflexible and therefore are not an effective means of control. This point will be examined in greater detail later in the chapter (see Section 10.7.1).

10.5.6 Reliability and validity

For controls to be effective they should be dependable (reliable) and must measure what they claim to measure (valid). Validity and reliability are important character-istics of effective control systems. If a control is unreliable and not valid this can cause lack of trust in the control process and lead to serious problems. For example, unreliable sales figures can lead to problems with inventory and future forecasts. Similarly, controls should be based on objective criteria rather than personal opinion. For example, a manager in charge of ordering materials who bases the order on how s/he thinks things are going is not as effective as the one who bases the order on computerised numbers of units produced and sold.

10.5.7 Controls based on valid performance standards

Effective controls are always based on accurate standards of performance. Such controls incorporate all aspects of performance. However, managers should be careful not to have too many measures as this can lead to over-control and potential resistance from employees. In order to avoid over-control, managers can make specific standards for a number of important areas and make satisfactory standards of performance for other areas. Managers can also prioritise certain targets or standards such as quality, costs and inventory. Finally, managers can establish tolerance ranges. For example, financial budgets often have optimistic, expected and minimum levels (Lawler and Rhode 1991).

10.5.8 Controls based on accurate information

Managers must effectively communicate to employees the rationale and importance of control and also provide feedback on their performance. Such feedback allows employees to take corrective action and motivates them. Operator control encourages self-control and limits the need for supervision. Therefore, information about controls should be accessible and accurate. Lawler and Rhode (1991) argue that a manager designing a control system should evaluate information systems in terms of the following questions:

❶ Does it provide people with data relevant to the decisions they need to take?

❷ Does it provide the right amount of information to decision makers throughout the organisation?

❸ Does it give sufficient information to each part of the organisation about how other related parts of the organisation are functioning?

10.6. Methods of control

Organisations use a variety of methods of control. These can be classified as either financial or non-financial. Most organisations use a variety of both types to ensure effective control of relevant areas. Figure 10.4 provides a summary of the most commonly used forms of both financial and non-financial controls, as discussed in this chapter.

Figure 10.4 The main methods of control

Financial Controls	Non Financial Controls
1. Budgetary control	1. Project controls
2. Break even analysis	2. Management audits
3. Ratio analysis	3. Inventory control
	4. Production control
	5. Quality control

10.7 Financial controls

The three main types of financial controls typically used by organisations are budgetary control, break-even analysis and ratio analysis.

10.7.1 Budgetary control

Budgetary control is one of the most widely recognised and commonly used methods of managerial control. It ties together all three types of control— feedforward, concurrent and feedback—depending on the point at which it is applied. Budgeting involves the formulation of plans for a given period in numerical terms. Budgetary control is the process of ascertaining what has been achieved and comparing this with the projections contained in the budget. Most budgets use financial data, but some contain non-financial terms such as sales volume or production output. However, a budget is predominantly a financial control device. Budgets are important because they force people to plan in a precise manner which produces a degree of order in the organisation. Budgets must reflect organisational goals and be well co-ordinated throughout the organisation if they are to serve as an effective control instrument.

According to Weihrich and Koontz (1993) there are four main types of budget:

▶ **Revenue and expense budget.** This type of budget develops projections of revenue and expenses. The most common example of a revenue and expense budget is a sales budget, illustrated in Figure 10.5. Actual revenues, expenses and sales can then be compared to the expected budgetary levels.

▶ **Time, space, material and production budget.** This form of budget develops projections for machine hours, space allocated, materials required and production output. Actual and expected levels can then be compared.

▶ **Capital expenditure budget.** This form of budget develops projections for expenditure on items such as plant and machinery. Actual expenditure can then be compared to the projected level.

▶ **Cash budget.** This form of budget develops projections about cash receipts and disbursements against which actual levels can be compared.

All budgetary control should focus on performance in what are termed KEY RESULT AREAS. These are areas which are crucial to the organisation's business, such as sales of the main product, manufacturing costs, stock levels and cash position. There are also areas where problems or failures will have repercussions elsewhere, such as supplier failures, increases in material costs and strikes or stoppages. Identifying these key result areas allows performance to be reviewed in precise terms, while allowing for some leeway elsewhere.

	January		February	
	Expected	Actual	Expected	Actual
Sales	1,500,000		2,000,000	
Expenses				
General	510,000		775,000	
Selling	292,000		323,000	
Production	377,000		425,000	
R & D	118,000		120,000	
Office	70,000		75,000	
Advertising	52,000		59,000	
Estimated gross profit	80,100		232,000	

Figure 10.5 Example of a sales budget

Note: Total expenses and gross profit = total sales expectancy

Over time, budgetary control, in certain instances, has become inflexible and cumbersome (Stewart 1990). Overbudgeting has occurred whereby managers are constrained by budgets to such an extent that they cannot use freedom and initiative in managing their areas. Frequently, abiding by budgetary forecasts becomes the overriding objective of managers at the expense of wider organisational goals. Budgets also hide inefficiencies by establishing strong precedents, especially for capital expenditure. The fact that a capital expenditure was made in the past becomes an important justification for its inclusion in future budgets, regardless of whether or not it is needed. Finally budgets can lead to inflexibility if they are formulated for long periods of time. As environmental conditions change so quickly, budgets become obsolete causing inflexibility.

New approaches to budgeting have been developed in order to overcome the inflexibility associated with traditional budgets. VARIABLE BUDGETS have been introduced by many organisations. These budgets analyse expense items to work out how individual costs will vary with the volume of output. Variable budgets distinguish between fixed and variable costs. FIXED COSTS do not vary with the volume of output and include DEPRECIATION, maintenance of plant and equipment and insurance. Costs which rise and fall depending on the volume of output are called *variable costs* and include materials and labour. Variable budgets attempt to calculate the extent to which variable costs change with given levels of output. An example of a variable budget chart is provided in Figure 10.6.

This variable budget shows the level of costs that will be incurred for different levels of output. For example, a planned production of 300 units will cost around £450. However, if actual volume increases to 600 units, costs will increase to £600, according to the budget guideline. Variable budgets therefore give the organisation a good guide as to how costs will increase with increased volume. Variable budgets work well when sales or output can be reasonably well forecast in advance. Fixed budgets can work well with good plans and sales forecasts. However, the variable budget forces the organisation to examine factors that increase as production increases.

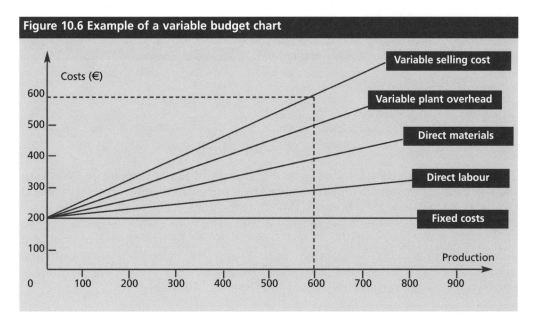

Figure 10.6 Example of a variable budget chart

Another development in budgeting is called ZERO-BASED BUDGETING and was first applied at Texas Instruments in the USA (Phyrr 1970). This approach means that managers start from zero in creating a budget each year. It is an attempt to eliminate the inefficiencies that creep in as elements are carried over from one year to the next without being questioned. Zero-based budgeting is best applied to ancillary or support areas of an organisation, such as R & D or marketing, rather than core areas like production, where certain expenses have to be carried forward every year. The main advantage of zero-based budgeting is that it forces managers to plan each year afresh.

The final development, applicable to the areas of government and public administration, is programme planning and budgeting (PPB). This sets up budgets in terms of programmes and the costs of materials and services that are required by them. This is relatively easy to do where well-established programmes exist (for example, house building, defence) but is more difficult to put into action where programmes change (for example, with a change in government or policy) or where the objectives of the programme were not well understood or well received (for example, health provision, which is usually a contentious issue).

Advances in information technology have improved the performance of budgets as control techniques. According to Bruns and McFarlan (1987) developments such as spreadsheets have speeded up the budgeting process and also improved the quality of budgets by allowing managers to view alternative scenarios and compare outcomes. In addition, managers can now continuously update budgets based on actual performance. Therefore, information technology has turned the budget into a meaningful set of instructions which can optimise an organisations performance.

Effective budgets. All budgets must be tailored to the specific task and used by all managers not just controllers, if they are to be effective. According to Weihrich and Koontz (1993) effective budgetary control is characterised by four key elements, as shown in Figure 10.7.

> **Figure 10.7 Characteristics of effective budget**
>
> 1. Top management support
> 2. Participation
> 3. Based on reliable standards
> 4. Accurate information available

To be effective budgets must first have the support of top management. When top management support the budgeting process by ensuring that budgets meet plans and require units to defend their budgets, then the organisation as a whole becomes more alert to the process. Second, all managers should participate in the process in order to ensure effective implementation. Third, budgets should be based on clear and valid standards. Finally, for budgets to work effectively managers need available information about forecasted and actual performance under budgets. Budgets displaying these characteristics will be effective control devices.

10.7.2 Break-even analysis

The second financial control technique is called break-even analysis which is another important method of managerial control. It involves the use of fixed and variable costs to analyse the point at which it becomes profitable to produce a good or service, that is, the BREAK-EVEN POINT. As noted above, fixed costs remain constant no matter how much is produced, whereas variable costs change. Fixed costs and variable costs, when added together, are referred to as TOTAL COSTS.

By analysing the level of both fixed and variable costs it is possible to identify the volume needed to break even, that is, the point at which income generated from a given volume of output breaks even with total costs. Break-even analysis has many applications in control and managerial decision making and is especially useful for decisions concerning dropping or adding product ranges and the choice of distribution channels. Figure 10.8 provides an example of break-even analysis in graphic form.

In this case, the break-even point at which revenues cover total expenses or costs is a volume of 1000 units which cost £5,000 to produce. Producing fewer than 1000 units would mean that a loss is being incurred and anything higher than 1000 units means a profit can be made.

Showing the break-even point in chart form highlights the relationship between costs and profit. The fixed costs have to be covered before anything is produced. It is assumed in Figure 10.8 that total costs increase in direct proportion to the units produced. Only when total costs are equal to the revenue earned can the organisation break even. In reality, the relationship between costs and output would probably not be linear. If an organisation upgrades a machine that produces 10,000 units to one that, for example, produces 25,000, we would expect to see a large bump in the cost curve. Similarly, the relationship between revenue and sales could be uneven because of bulk discounts or price cutting. On the whole though, break-even analysis provides a graphic illustration of how much needs to be produced before profits can be made. However, due to its simplistic approach break-even analysis is better used with other control tools rather than in isolation.

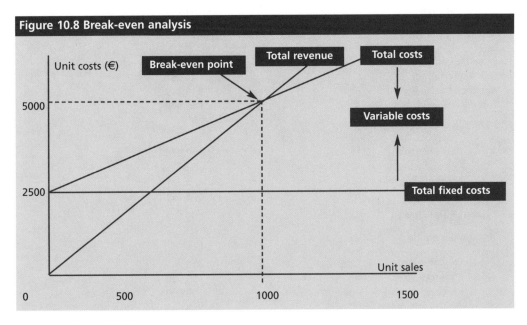

Figure 10.8 Break-even analysis

10.7.3 Ratio analysis

Several types of control have been developed for understanding and assessing an organisation's financial performance. Such guidelines for financial performance serve as control mechanisms in that they provide benchmarks for evaluation. These guidelines are commonly termed *financial ratios* and express relationships between individual or group items on an organisations balance sheet and profit and loss account. Due to the fact that they involve ratios this process has been called ratio analysis. Ratio analysis provides important mechanisms for interpreting organisational performance and allows an organisation to track its performance over time and to compare it with that of competitors. Four basic types of financial ratios exist—liquidity, activity, profitability and leverage—each of which will be discussed and calculated using the balance sheet and profit and loss statement of the fictitious Organisation ABC as shown in Figure 10.9.

Figure 10.9 ABC accounts

Balance Sheet for ABC

Assets	€
Current assets	
Cash	9,521
Accounts receivable	88,329
Inventory	401,273
Total current assets	499,123
Property and plant	161,000
Less depreciation	44,251
Net property and plant	116,749
Total assets	615,872
Liabilities and stockholder equity	
Notes payable	22,679
Accrued expenses	51,736
Accounts payable	9,321
Corporation tax payable	23,251
Total current liabilities	106,987
Stockholder equity	
Capital stock	358,885
Preferred stock	50,000
Retained earnings	100,000
Total stockholders equity	508,885
Total liabilities and stockholder equity	615,872

Liquidity ratios. An organisation's LIQUIDITY is its ability to pay for its short-term liabilities. A commonly used indicator of an organisation's liquidity is its CURRENT RATIO. The current ratio is a comparison of an organisation's CURRENT ASSETS and current liabilities. To obtain the current ratio the current assets are divided by the current liabilities. In ABC's case the figures are as follows

$$\text{Current ratio} = \frac{\text{Current assets } 499{,}123}{\text{Current liabilities } 106{,}987} = 4.6{:}1$$

A ratio of 4.6:1 means that for every €1 in current liabilities there is €4.6 in current assets to cover it. Most financial analysts believe that a ratio of 2:1 is desirable. A large current ratio as found in the case of ABC, is not necessarily a good thing as it could mean that it is not using its assets efficiently. Current ratios vary from industry to industry. Petrol and oil companies typically have a ratio of 1.6:1 whereas art galleries have 3.4:1.

Another method of assessing liquidity is the QUICK ASSET RATIO. This is preferred by some financial analysts who fear that slow-moving inventory can lead to a misleadingly high level of current assets under the current ratio method. Quick assets are those which are available to cover emergencies and therefore exclude inventory which has yet to be sold. An organisation's quick asset ratio is calculated by subtracting the value of inventory yet to be sold from the current assets and dividing that figure by the current liabilities. The larger the ratio the greater the liquidity. In the case of ABC the figures are as follows:

Quick asset ratio = Current assets 499,123
                       Less: Inventory 401,273

               = Quick assets   97,850
                  ─────────────────────────────────── = 0.91:1
                  Current liabilities 106,987

In this case for every €1 in current liabilities only €0.91 is available to cover liabilities. When the ratio is 1:1 the organisation is deemed liquid. So in this case ABC appears to be overstretched.

Activity ratios aim to show how efficiently an organisation is using its resources. There are three main activity ratios—inventory turnover ratio, asset turnover ratio and accounts receivable turnover. INVENTORY TURNOVER RATIO measures the number of times that an organisation's inventory has been sold during the year. It is, therefore, the ratio between an organisation's cost of goods sold and the current inventory. The ratio for ABC is as follows:

$$\text{Inventory turnover ratio} \quad \frac{\text{Cost of goods sold 567,215}}{\text{Current inventory 401,273}} = 1.4:1$$

ABC's inventory has therefore been sold 1.4 times during the last year. The ASSET TURNOVER RATIO assesses how well the organisation is using its assets. It is calculated as the ratio between an organisation's sales and the total assets. The figures for ABC are as follows:

$$\text{Asset turnover ratio} \quad \frac{\text{Sales 899,000}}{\text{Total assets 615,872}} = 1.45:1$$

Therefore for each €1 invested in assets, sales have generated €1.45. Capital-intensive industries tend to have small ratios. The accounts receivable turnover ratio measures an organisation's collection period on credit sales. It is calculated by dividing the sales by accounts receivable. The figures for ABC are as follows:

$$\text{Accounts receivable turnover ratio} \quad \frac{\text{Sales 899,000}}{\text{Accounts receivable 88,329}} = 10.1:1$$

If we divide the 360 (days) by 10.1 it is possible to calculate the average collection period for accounts. For ABC the figure is 35.6 days. Greater than 40 days usually indicates slow accounts receivable. However, much depends on the credit policy of the organisation.

Profitability ratios determine how profitable an organisation's performance has been and involves the use of two ratios—net profit ratio and the rate of return on assets. The net profit ratio is a good indicator of short-term profit and is the ration between net profit and sales. The net profit ratio for ABC is as follows;

$$\text{Net profit ratio} \quad \frac{\text{Net profit 41,785}}{\text{Sales 899,000}} = 0.04$$

This means that for every €1 in sales 0.04p is made in profit. In the region of 4–5 per cent is the average for successful organisations, although this obviously varies from industry to industry. The ratio of the return on assets is the ratio between an organisation's net profit and total assets and is designed to measure an organisation's efficiency in generating profit. It is calculated by dividing total assets into net profit. The figures for ABC are as follows:

$$\text{Return on assets ratio} \quad \frac{\text{Net profit 41,785}}{\text{Total assets 615,872}} = 0.06$$

This means that for every €1 invested in total assets 6p in profits is eventually made. Organisation ABC has an average ratio as the industry norm is around 0.07 or 7 per cent.

Leverage ratios attempt to identify the source of an organisation's capital. Leverage is the increased RATE OF RETURN on stockholder equity when an investment earns a return larger than the interest paid for debt financing. The most popular measure is the DEBT EQUITY RATIO which is total liabilities divided by the total equity (that is, liabilities plus stockholder equity). The ratio for ABC is as follows:

$$\text{Debt equity ratio} \quad \frac{\text{Total liabilities 106,987}}{\text{Total Equity 615,872}} = 0.17$$

This means that for every €1 in equity 17p is borrowed capital. Total liabilities should not exceed total equities.

The best Irish example of the effective use of financial controls can be found in the Jefferson Smurfit Group. The Group is involved in the packaging business where success depends on building up relationships with customers. According to Brophy (1985), strong financial control systems have always been a central part of the Smurfit approach. In the early days the organisation relied on profit and loss statements to control the business. However, as the organisation expanded, their control systems became more sophisticated. Each operating unit is now treated as a profit centre and is subjected to stringent financial controls, particularly budgets.

These systems are complemented by a corporate planning department which develops long-range and short-range plans at all levels of the organisation. It performs three central functions:

- ▶ updating and revising strategic and long-range plans at all levels
- ▶ preparation of detailed actual business plans and budgets
- ▶ review of actual results and changes to the plans where necessary.

Tight cash control has also been at the heart of the Smurfit approach. No company within the Group owns its own cash but gets its working capital from the Group Treasury and has to pay for it. This has encouraged careful and conscious working capital management. One final feature of the control system is the emphasis on cost control. Cost-reduction targets are set on a plant-by-plant basis. Smurfit has been particularly successful at reducing costs in organisations which it has taken over. All in all, the Smurfit Group is a good illustration of the effective use of financial controls.

10.8 Non-financial controls

In addition to financial control, organisations employ a range of non-financial controls. The most common forms of non-financial control are project controls including GANTT CHARTS and PERT (PROGRAMME EVALUATION REVIEW TECHNIQUE) ANALYSIS, management audits, inventory, production and quality control. Each of these key controls will be examined in this section.

10.8.1 Project controls

Project controls are designed to control the operation of certain projects undertaken by an organisation. Such controls can prevent a project going awry or can assist in extricating the organisation from a failing project (Keil and Montealegre 2000). The two most popular devices are Gantt charts and PERT analysis. Gantt charts were developed by Henry Gantt who was an advocate of scientific management (see Chapter 1). A Gantt chart is a simple bar chart that portrays the time relationship between events and their outcome. The chart therefore depicts the sequence of activities required to complete a task and allocates a time frame for each one. Figure 10.10 shows an example of a Gantt chart.

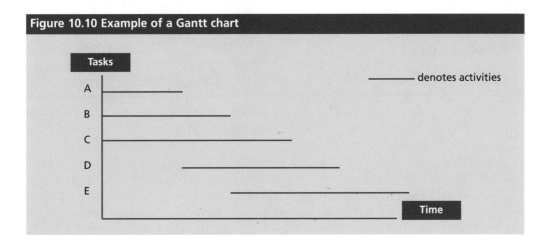

Figure 10.10 Example of a Gantt chart

All activities represented by overlapping bars can be completed at the same time. In this example, tasks A, B and C can all be completed concurrently. Activities represented by non-overlapping bars must be undertaken in the sequence illustrated. For example, task D cannot be started until task A is finished. The Gantt chart therefore represents the steps of a project over time and can be used to track whether a project is ahead, behind or on schedule. An example of a Gantt chart for the development of a particular product is illustrated in Figure 10.11.

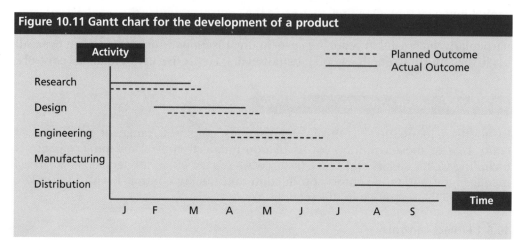

Figure 10.11 Gantt chart for the development of a product

As the chart shows, progress on the development of the new product is behind schedule at the end of the year as the product has not yet been distributed due to the fact that each stage took longer than originally planned. Gantt charts help to co-ordinate activities and the scheduling of labour. They are most useful for activities that are unrelated and are less effective when dealing with many interrelated activities.

PERT involves the development of a network which shows the most likely time needed to complete each task which is required to finish the product or project. Figure 10.12 provides an example of a PERT network.

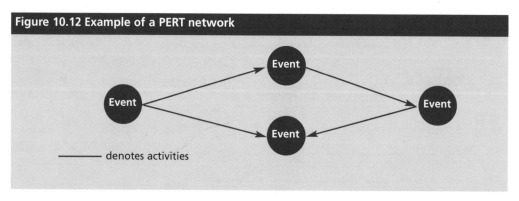

Figure 10.12 Example of a PERT network

Events are circled and represent the start and end of the various activities. An event is not completed until all activities leading to it have been finished. Activities are depicted by arrows and mark the work that has to be done. An activity cannot begin until all preceding activities to which it is connected have been completed.

In developing a PERT chart the following steps should be undertaken:

❶ Identify each event that must be completed and assign a time frame to it.

❷ Based on step 1, draw a network including the various activities which need to be done and keep in chronological order.

❸ Estimate the time needed to complete each activity usually in weeks.

❹ Estimate the total time for each activity in a sequence or path of activities. The path having the longest time is the CRITICAL PATH. The critical path is, therefore, the earliest date that a project can be finished.

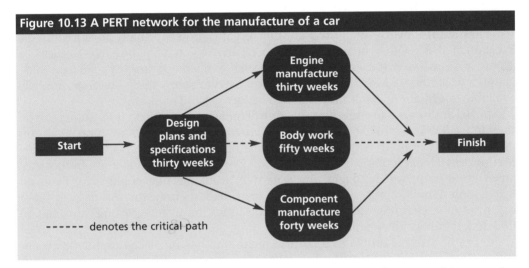

Figure 10.13 A PERT network for the manufacture of a car

- - - - - - denotes the critical path

Figure 10.13 illustrates a PERT network for the manufacture of a car. In this example, the critical path is 80 weeks. Having identified the critical path a project manager can focus on either reducing the time of the various activities or at the very least watch for any delays. PERT is widely used as an important control for undertaking projects. Figure 10.14 outlines the main advantages and disadvantages associated with its use.

Figure 10.14 Advantages and disadvantages of PERT analysis

Advantages
1. It emphasises areas where delays are most likely to occur.
2. It is a detailed means of controlling a given project.
3. It frequently stimulates alternative plans and schedules.

Disadvantages
1. Event times must be accurately calculated.
2. It can be costly.
3. It is difficult to apply stringently when outside suppliers are involved.
4. It is unsuitable for repetitive sequences of events since all events fall along a single critical path.

Whatever project control techniques are utilised by the organisation, Hutchinson (2000) notes that the objective is to help managers deliver projects that deliver business benefits on time and within budget. Consequently, what must be emphasised is the need for traceability to be built into the project so that the accuracy and speed of impact assessment is improved.

10.8.2 Management audits

According to Pomerantz (1979), management audits have developed as a means of evaluating and controlling the various elements of an organisation. Such audits can either be external or internal. With external audits, managers conduct investigations of other competitor organisations. Internal audits investigate the operations of the organisation itself. The same control techniques can be used for both.

External audits involve analysing another organisation, normally to aid strategic decision making. Other organisations can be investigated for possible MERGERS or ACQUISITIONS, to assess the strengths and weaknesses of competitors or even a possible supplier of materials. Most of the information used to assess these factors is publicly available information which simply has to be located and analysed.

External audits are a useful source of control for an organisation. Such audits can be used in feedback control (see Section 10.4.3) to discover irregularities or problems on an industry-wide basis. Similarly, audits can be used for feedfoward control (see Section 10.4.1), particularly if an organisation is planning an acquisition. In this way, an external audit will highlight any potential problems that could arise from an acquisition. Finally, audits can be used to learn lessons from the mistakes of other organisations. Learning where other organisations have gone wrong can lead to updated or enhanced concurrent controls.

The use of external audits as a control technique has increased rapidly in recent years. The nature of the current business environment, with its emphasis on cut-throat competition, has further augmented this trend. Some organisations have even gone so far as to spy on competitors (Fuld 1986). Organisations are now developing competitor intelligence, or, in other words, information about their competitors. Accountants, sales people and managers frequently collect information about opponents to aid decision making and to ensure that competitors do not get produce any nasty surprises.

Internal audits concentrate on the activities of the organisation itself. Frequently, organisations undertake reviews of their planning, organising and leading functions. Control is the essential ingredient in any internal audit. When conducting an internal audit a manager should concentrate on financial stability, production, sales, human resources and social responsibility. Problems often uncovered by an internal audit include duplication of resources, poor utilisation of resources or the uneconomical use of plant and machinery. An internal audit conducted in Aer Lingus in 1994, discovered that catering suppliers had been overpaid in the region of £12 million. As a result, the purchasing systems in Aer Lingus were reformed to ensure that the same problem would not occur again (*Sunday Tribune* 1994).

Therefore, both internal and external management audits provide vital information from which the organisation can evaluate its performance and take corrective action. In addition internal audits act as a deterrent to internal fraud.

10.8.3 Inventory control

Inventory control involves control of stock levels to ensure the organisation has stock when needed yet at the same time does not have too much money tied up in stock that is not immediately required. Up to one-third of an organisation's total costs can be tied up in storing and handling inventory. Therefore, a control system is needed to keep these costs to a minimum. A good inventory control system tries to answer three questions:

▶ How much of the required inventory items should be bought at a time?

▶ At what point should inventory items be reordered?

▶ What are the most economic order quantities of each item?

In the first instance, production experience and knowledge of the sources of supply will dictate how much inventory should be bought. Some items may be seasonal or scarce and so it may make sense to buy these in large lots. The timing of the reorder depends on two factors. First, the lead time involved, that is, the time between the placement of the order and its delivery. Second, the problem of knowing what safety stock to keep so that production will not be disrupted because of supplier transport problems. The third question is resolved by reference to the *economic order quantity* (EOQ) model. The formula for EOQ is as follows:

$$EOQ = \frac{2 \text{ x order costs x annual consumption}}{\text{annual holding costs}}$$

and is portrayed graphically in Figure 10.15.

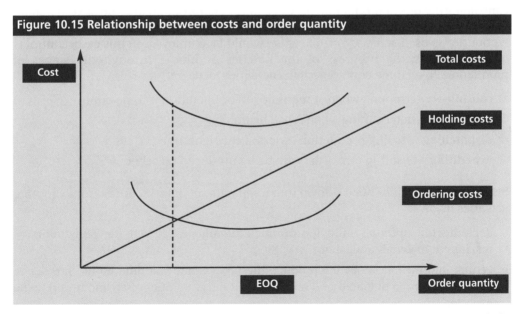

Figure 10.15 Relationship between costs and order quantity

Holding costs include storage space, handling and security. Ordering costs include administration and shipping. The most economic order quantity is where the cost of ordering the goods is not greater than the cost of holding, and the total cost curve is at its lowest point. Models like the EOQ model are removed from the real world in that they cannot take account of factors like strikes, transport problems or supplier discounts. On the other hand, they give guidelines as to how inventory costs can be reduced.

Developments in information technology have facilitated the control of inventory. New inventory tracking systems let organisations trace an order, update account balances, monitor inventory and alert suppliers of upcoming requirements. Some systems have linked their ordering function to suppliers to benefit from low inventory without shortages. An example of this can be found in the automobile industry. Automated order entry and inventory tracking can help organisations vary sales and pricing strategies between regions and customer types.

10.8.4 Production control

In the production area, planning and control systems are intertwined because the outputs of the planning system are the inputs of the control system, and vice versa. The aim of a PRODUCTION CONTROL SYSTEM is to ensure that goods are produced on time at the right cost and conform to quality standards. A good production control system should reflect the organisation's production methods and product characteristics. The type of control required in a JOB SHOP situation where there is an element of craft work will be different from that needed in an assembly line where MASS PRODUCTION takes place, but, regardless of the process employed, an effective production control process is required. The type of product will influence the control system. An organisation that makes one-off products according to buyer specifications would have a job shop where an *order control system* is used. The emphasis would be on controlling each order as it passes from design through manufacture to shipment. In assembly operations, on the other hand, the *flow control system* would be used. This involves controlling the rate of production between one assembly point and the next so that no bottlenecks or stoppages occur. In between these two systems where BATCH PRODUCTION is used, a *block control system* would be employed. In this case, control is concerned with the progress of the batches or blocks through the stages of production. In all three control systems activities focus on:

❶ **routing**—determining where a required job or operation is to be done

❷ **scheduling**—determining when it will be done

❸ **dispatching**—issuing production orders at the right time

❹ **expediting**—ensuring that orders are being produced on schedule.

Each of these activities breaks down into a separate set of tasks. For example, routing activities involve:

a. deciding the optimal route for product manufacture given the constraints of machinery, materials and labour

b. getting information about the product, the process and the time input, in order to evaluate the input of labour and materials and the amount of scrap and rework to be expected

c. preparing the forms for a production reporting system including order routing sheets, process information details and timesheets.

Advances in information technology have had an enormous impact on the production control process. One of the widest uses of information technology is in production control (Bruns and McFarlan 1987). Monitoring systems can track errors per hour, highlight down time, measure machine speeds and worker productivity. All of these advances allow managers to remedy production problems at an early stage. Previously, systems relied on a controller to spot variations. Early detection allows for early correction and improves the economics of manufacturing. According to Bruns and McFarlan (1987), one cigarette manufacturer has installed automatic control systems that pull cigarettes off the line and put them through 20 tests noting even the smallest inconsistency in quality. Before that, cigarettes were only checked after problems had occurred.

10.8.5 Quality control

Quality control and production control are intertwined in that quality control is a check on the efficiency of production. A good quality control system can offer significant cost savings due to the savings on rejected products as well as warranty and servicing costs, but, according to Davies and Kochhar (2000), its implementation and operationalisation is best guided by a number of key stages, namely:

▶ the actual identification of the need to improve operational performance
▶ the identification of best practices for the areas of performance to be improved
▶ the prioritising of practices based on the impact of specified measures of performance
▶ the assessment of predecessor practices of the practice to be implemented
▶ the implementation of the desired practices
▶ the evaluation of the improvement in operational performance.

When Japan first entered the world market its products were cheap and of inferior quality. In a drive to increase the volume and the value of its exports the Japanese decided in the early 1950s to institute a set of laws demanding that products meet certain quality standards before exportation of their products. This was backed by a campaign to make employees more aware of the need for quality. That led to the establishment of QUALITY CIRCLES, now a standard feature of the Japanese organisation. The circle or committee is staffed by shop-floor employees and supervisors, concerned with maintaining high quality and screening supplies. Another interesting facet of the Japanese system is that each employee is responsible for the quality of his/her output, reducing the need for quality control inspectors.

Quality means fitness for the intended purpose and is therefore a relative term. Quality standards are designed to be met at a reasonable cost by the producer, while at the same time presenting an acceptable face to the consumer. The relationship between quality levels and cost is shown in Figure 10.16.

As quality is improved, the cost of producing that quality goes up and the return for higher quality declines. All products have a 'most economic' quality level. So while a modern car may have lower-quality components, it is cheaper and, therefore, has a mass market. Quality control offers the benefits of reduced costs and fewer customer complaints. It also enhances the corporate image as high-quality producers are usually looked upon as leaders in the market. It must be emphasised that quality control is a continual and vigilant effort, not a sporadic effort to meet standards.

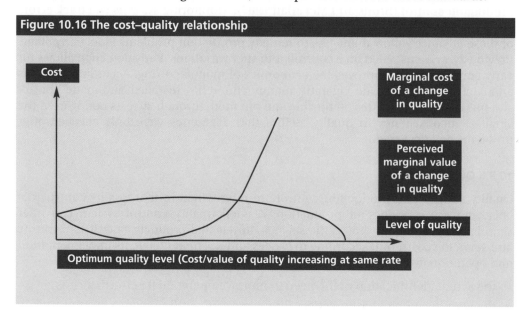

Figure 10.16 The cost–quality relationship

Cost

Marginal cost of a change in quality

Perceived marginal value of a change in quality

Level of quality

Optimum quality level (Cost/value of quality increasing at same rate

While TOTAL QUALITY MANAGEMENT (TQM) is treated in detail in Chapter 11 (see also Chapter 1), a few remarks are relevant here in order to demonstrate the significance of quality control in the broader TQM environment. The ever increasing emphasis on quality has led many organisations to adopt a TQM approach which is underpinned by six key principles, set out in Figure 10.17.

Figure 10.17 The six key principles of TQM

1. People will produce quality goods and services when the meaning of quality is expressed daily in the quality of their relations with their work, colleagues and organisation.
2. Myron Tribus said it best: 'Workers work in the system; managers should work on the system, to improve it with their help.'
3. TQM is a strategic choice made by top management and consistently translated in guidelines for the functioning of the whole organisation.
4. Each system with a certain degree of complexity has a probability of deviation, which can be understood by scientific methods.
5. Inspection of the process (or process control) is as important as inspection of the product. It can best be achieved by the workers closest to the process.
6. Envisage what you want to be as an organisation, but start working from where you actually are.

The approach must be management led, integrated into the mainstream management system, and supported by a significant communication exercise (see, for example, Van der Wiele *et al.* 2000a, 2000b; Hiyassat 2000; Gurnani 1999). A successful quality system requires the continuous commitment of the top-management team. This commitment must be translated into action and embedded in attitudes and behaviour. The approach must also apply company-wide. Quality must be the responsibility of everyone and the underlying philosophy must be one of prevention. This approach integrates detection and control into the process and directs attention towards the process rather than the outputs of the process *per se*. As Figure 10.18 demonstrates, quality control lies at the heart of this broader TQM approach and TQM represents an elaborate managerial control mechanism in the organisation (Rothschild and Ollilainen 1999).

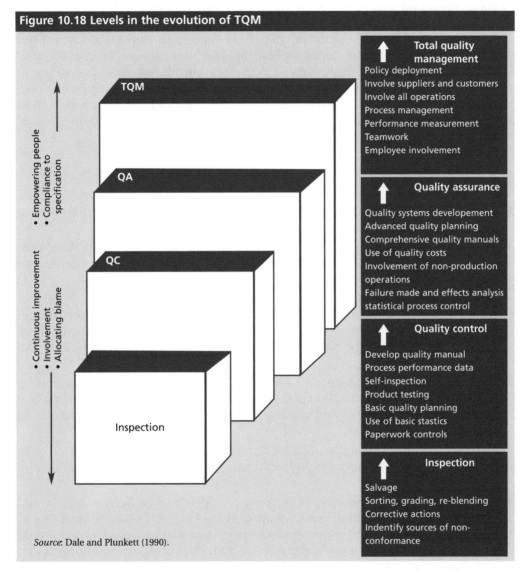

Figure 10.18 Levels in the evolution of TQM

TQM

QA

QC

Inspection

• Empowering people
• Compliance to specification

• Continuous improvement
• Involvement
• Allocating blame

Total quality management
Policy deployment
Involve suppliers and customers
Involve all operations
Process management
Performance measurement
Teamwork
Employee involvement

Quality assurance
Quality systems developement
Advanced quality planning
Comprehensive quality manuals
Use of quality costs
Involvement of non-production operations
Failure made and effects analysis
statistical process control

Quality control
Develop quality manual
Process performance data
Self-inspection
Product testing
Basic quality planning
Use of basic stastics
Paperwork controls

Inspection
Salvage
Sorting, grading, re-blending
Corrective actions
Indentify sources of non-conformance

Source: Dale and Plunkett (1990).

On the whole, with respect to non-financial controls in the form of project controls, management audits, inventory controls, production controls and quality controls, Irish companies have effectively used such controls to monitor their operations and, in particular, there are several examples of firms that have employed these approaches. Irish Distillers Group combines both production controls and quality controls to ensure that production volume matches demand and that the quality of the end product meets accepted standards. Controls on both the product flow and stock turnover are also a feature of the organisation's control system. According to Brophy (1985), these systems have endured and become a competitive strength.

Two other organisations have used quality controls to their advantage, Waterford Co-op imposed stringent quality standards in response to the EU intervention system. Due to the success of its quality control systems Waterford Co-Op became one of the first organisations to win awards from the Irish National Control Association.

Aer Lingus has also operated internal controls which satisfy both quality and safety standards. In relation to the control of safety, Aer Lingus has ensured both aircraft and staff certification and has developed sophisticated maintenance and overhaul control systems. With respect to quality, Aer Lingus has introduced control systems to monitor performance in the areas of: telephone answering times; passenger queuing; baggage handling; and reclaiming. Therefore, Irish organisations have widely used non-financial controls. The recent financial problems at Aer Lingus, however, could indicate that more stringent financial controls are required.

10.9 Summary of key propositions

▶ Control is the final management function. It is the process of ensuring the efficient and effective achievement of organisational goals and objectives.

▶ The control process involves three steps, first, establishing performance standards; second, measuring and comparing actual performance; third, taking corrective action where necessary.

▶ An organisation does not have automatic controls and therefore some form of control is needed to regulate its activities. Three types of control exist: feedfoward control; concurrent control; and feedback control. Feedfoward control monitors inputs. Concurrent control monitors the transformation process. Feedback control monitors the outputs.

▶ Effective controls have a number of important characteristics. They should be appropriate, cost-effective, acceptable, should emphasise exceptions at critical points, be flexible, reliable and valid, and based on valid performance standards and accurate information.

▶ Methods of control typically used by organisations are either financial or non-financial. Financial controls include budgetary control, break-even analysis and ratio analysis.

▶ Budgetary control is the process of ascertaining what has been achieved and comparing this with projections contained in the budget. Common examples of budgets are: revenue and expense; time; space; material and production; capital expenditure; and cash. Newer approaches to budgets include variable budgets and zero-based budgets.

▶ Break-even analysis uses both fixed and variable costs to identify the point at which it becomes profitable to produce a certain product.

▶ Ratio analysis involves the use of financial ratios to assess the financial performance of the organisation. Ratios are used to assess liquidity, profitability, activity and leverage.

▶ Non-financial controls include project controls, management audits and inventory, production and quality controls. The project controls most commonly used are Gantt charts and PERT analysis.

▶ Management audits, whether internal or external, are designed to provide information about competitor organisations to aid strategic decision making and to highlight internal problems.

▶ Inventory, production and quality control are designed to ensure that levels of inventory are appropriate, the production process is efficient and that quality standards are high. The advances made in information technology have greatly improved these controls.

Discussion questions

❶ Define control and explain its importance.

❷ Explain the three steps in the control process.

❸ Define and explain the various types of control an organisation can use.

❹ What are the characteristics of effective control?

❺ Explain the concepts of variable and zero-based budgeting.

❻ What is break-even analysis. How can it be used as a control device?

❼ Using the accounts from XYZ Company below to calculate these ratios:

Current ratio
Quick asset ratio
Asset turnover ratio
Net profit ratio
Return on assets ratio
Debt equity ratio

Balance Sheet for XYZ Company

Assets	€
Current assets:	
Cash	10,000
Accounts receivable	75,323
Inventory	327,421
Total current assets:	412,744
Property and plant	356,357
Less: Depreciation	89,462
Net property and plant	266,895
Total assets	**679,639**
Liabilities and stockholder equity	
Current liabilities:	
Notes payable	53,424

Balance Sheet for XYZ Company

Accrued expenses	87,932
Accounts payable	27,624
Corporation tax payable	56,528
Total current liabilities	255,508
Stockholder equity:	
Capital stock	224,131
Preferred stock	100,000
Retained earnings	100,000
Total stockholder equity	424,131
Total liabilities and stockholder equity	**679,639**

Profit and Loss Statement for XYZ Company

Revenues:	
Sales	1,000,000
Other income	25,000
Total	1,025,000
Costs and expenses:	
Cost of goods sold	775,000
Total expenses	200,000
Total costs and expenses	**975,000**
Profit	**50,000**

❽ Explain what Gantt charts and PERT analysis try to achieve. What is the difference between the two approaches?

❾ Critically evaluate management audits as a control technique in the current business environment.

❿ What three questions should a good inventory control system try to answer? How can it achieve this?

⓫ How have advances in information technology shaped the control function?

⓬ In the current business environment what controls should an organisation focus on?

Concluding case: Roads authority pay £2.8 million after mistake

The National Roads Authority will have to pay £2.8 million as part of a £3.15 million settlement to SIAC, a Dublin-based construction company, after a mistake made in a tender for the building of a new Limerick–Adare national primary route was spotted by Limerick County Council Staff.

The mistake in the tender put forward by the company which eventually won the £33 million contract, Pat Mulcair Contractors, was initially not noticed by county council staff, or the National Roads Authority, the secretary of the council, Mr Jim Feane, said yesterday.

Mr Feane said that during a legal dispute with SIAC over the form of the tender documents used, the error was discovered.

'The county council, in the process of preparing a defence against that particular action, was re-examining the tenders. In the exercise of re-examining the tenders, the error was detected by our staff,' he said.

The dispute over the format of documentation used, which is similar to that used by all local authorities, has not yet been resolved.

Originally eight tenders were assessed for the contract to build a 10-kilometre stretch of road which will run adjacent to the rail link between Limerick and Adare.

County council roads division staff in Mungret, Co. Limerick, in conjunction with the National Roads Authority, carried out the assessments.

'We accepted the contract subject to the approval of the National Roads Authority,' Mr Feane said.

Separately, computing errors were made by the council and new tender totals were reached for both SIAC and Pat Mulcair Contractors, with the latter winning the contract.

'SIAC would have been aware that the tender total as submitted by them would have been lower than the tender total as submitted by Pat Mulcair Contractors,' Mr Michael Tobin, Chief Executive of the National Roads Authority, said. Errors in tenders were frequent because they had to be submitted 'in ink' after being drawn up electronically, he added.

He hoped a new pilot electronic tendering process would be operational within two months.

Following a process of arbitration, with a consulting engineer as arbitrator, the settlement of £3.15 million compensation for SIAC was reached.

Mr Feane said that the Council was insured for £250,000 of the amount and would pay a further £100,000. The balance of £2.8 million will be paid by the NRA.

Case originally appeared as article by Eibhir Mulqueen, *The Irish Times*, 20 July 2000.

Case questions

❶ Drawing upon the theory of control, analyse the nature of the control breakdowns in this case.
❷ Outline what controls you would put in place to avoid such errors being made in the future.

Bibliography

Anthony, R., Dearden, J. and Bedford, N. (1984) *Management Control Systems*. Illinois: Irwin.

Anthony, R. and Young, D. (2000) *Management Control in Non-Profit Organisations*. Thousand Oaks: Sage.

Baker, H. and Jennings, K. (1999) 'Dysfunctional Organisational Control Mechanisms: An Example', *Journal of Applied Management Studies*, 8 (2), 231–9.

Barnard, L. and Von Solms, R. (2000) 'A Formalized Approach to the Effective Selection and Evaluation of Information Security Controls', *Computers and Security*, 19 (2), 185–95.

Bedeian, A. (1993) *Management*. Fort Worth: Dryden Press.

Bhimani, A. (1999), 'Mapping Methodological Frontiers in Cross-national Management Control Research', *Accounting Organizations and Society*, 24 (5/6), 413–40.

Brophy. S. (1985) *The Strategic Management of Irish Business*. Dublin: Smurfit Publications.

Bruns, W. and McFarlan, F. (1987) 'Information Technology Puts Power in Control Systems', *Harvard Business Review*, 65 (5) 89–94.

Burris, B. (1989) 'Technocracy and Transformation of Organizational Control', *Social Science Journal*, (26), 313–33.

Chapman, P. (1999) 'Managerial Control Strategies in Small Firms', *International Small Business Journal*, 17 (2), 75–82.

Daft, R. and Macintosh, N. (1984) 'The Nature and Use of Formal Control Systems for Management Control and Strategy Implementation', *Journal of Management*, 10 (1), 43–66.

Davies, A. and Kochhar, A. (2000) 'A Framework for the Selection of Best Practices', *International Journal of Operations and Production Management*, 20 (10), 1203–18.

Davis, R. (1951) *The Fundamental of Top Management*. New York: Harper Row.

Donnelly, J., Gibson, J. and Ivancevich, J. (1981) *Fundamentals of Management*. Texas: Business Publications.

Dunbar, R. (1981) 'Designs for Organisational Control', in Nystrom, P. and Starbuck, W. (eds) *Handbook of Organisational Design*. London: Oxford University.

Flamholtz, E. (1979) 'Behavioural Aspects of Accounting\Control Systems', in Kerr, S. (ed.) *Organisational Behaviour*. Ohio: Grid.

Fuld, M. (1986) 'Cultivating Home Grown Spies', *Wall Street Journal*, 17 March, 20.

Gavin, M., Green, S. and Fairhurst, G. (1995) 'Managerial Control Strategies for Poor Performance Over Time and the Impact of Subordinate Reactions', *Organizational Behavior and Human Decision Processes*, 63 (2), 207–21.

Giglioni, G. and Bedeian, A. (1974) 'A Conspectus of Management Control Theory', *Academy of Management Journal*, 17 (2), 292–305.

Gurnani, H. (1999) 'Pitfalls in Total Quality Management Implementation: The Case of a Hong Kong Company', *Total Quality Management*, 10 (2), 209–29.

Herzlinger, R. and Nitterhouse, D. (1999) *Financial Accounting and Managerial Control for Nonprofit Organisations*. Thousand Oaks: Sage.

Hiyassat, M. (2000) 'Applying the ISO Standards to a Construction Company: A Case Study', *International Journal of Project Management*, 18 (4), 275–81.

Hutchinson, R. (2000) 'Project Change Control', *Project Manager Today*, 12 (5), 18–21.

Jermier, J. (1998) 'Introduction: Critical Perspectives on Organizational Control', *Adminsinistrative Science Quarterly*, 43 (2), 235–56.

Kald, M., Nilsson, F. and Rapp, B. (2000) 'On Strategy and Management Control: The Importance of Classifying the Strategy of the Business', *British Journal of Management*, 11 (3), 197–212.

Keil, M. and Montealegre, R. (2000) 'Cutting Your Losses: Extricating Your Organisations When a Big Project Goes Awry', *Sloan Management Review*, 41 (3), 55–69.

Kirsch. L. (1996) 'The Management of Complex Tasks in Organizations: Controlling the Systems Development Process', *Organization Science*, 7 (1), 1–21.

Koontz, H. and Bradspies, R. (1980) 1980 in text 'Managing Though Feedforward Control', in C. O'Donnell and H. Weihrich (eds) *Management: A Book of Readings*. New York: McGraw-Hill.

Lawler, E. (1976) 'Control Systems in Orgnaisations', in Dunnette, M. (ed.) *Handbook of Industrial and Organizational Psychology*. Chicago: Rand McNally.

Lawler, E. and Rhode, J. (1991) 'Information and Control in Organisations', in Robey, D. (ed.) *Designing Organisations*. Illinois: Irwin.

Matyas, S. and Stapleton, J. (2000) 'A Biometric Standard for Information Management and Security', *Computers and Security*, 19 (5), 428–42.

Modell, S. (2000) 'Integrating Management Control and Human Resource Management in Public Health Care: Swedish Case Study Evidence', *Financial Accountability and Management*, 16 (1), 33–54.

Mulqueen, E. (2000) 'Roads Authority Pay £2.8 Million After Mistake' *Irish Times*, 20 July.

Naveh, E. and Halevy, A. (2000) 'A Hierarchical Framework for a Quality Information System', *Total Quality Management*, 11 (1), 87–112.

Nilsson, F. (2000) 'Parenting Styles and Value Creation: A Management Control Approach', *Management Accounting Research*, 11 (1), 89–113.

Otley, D. (1999) 'Performance Management: A Framework for Management Control Systems Research', *Management Accounting Research*, 10 (4), 363–82.

Phyrr, P. (1970) 'Zero Based Budgeting', *Harvard Business Review*, 60, (6).

Pomerantz, F. (1979) 'Pre-emptive Auditing: Future Shock or Present Opportunity?', *Journal of Accounting, Auditing and Finance*, Summer, 352–6.

Rothschild, J. and Ollilainen, M. (1999) 'Obscuring but not Reducing Managerial Control: Does TQM Measure up to Democracy Standards?', *Economic and Industrial Democracy*, 20 (4), 583–623.

Sridhar, S. and Balachandran, B. (1997) 'Incomplete Information, Task Assignment and Managerial Control Systems', *Management Science*, 43 (6), 764–78.

Stewart, T. (1990) 'Why Budgets are Bad for Business', *Fortune*, 4 June, 115–19.

Storey, D. (1994) *Understanding the Small Business Sector*. London: Routledge.

Sunday Tribune (1994) 'Aer Lingus: £12 Million in Overpayment to Suppliers', Business Section, C1, 12 June.

Tood, J. (1977) 'Management Control Systems: A Key Link between Strategy, Structure and Employee Performance', *Organisation Dynamics*, Spring, 65–78.

Van der Wiele, T., Dale, B. and Williams, R. (2000a) 'Business Improvement Through Quality Management Systems', *Management Decisions*, 38 (1), 19–25.

Van der Wiele, T., Williams, R. and Dale, B. (2000b) 'ISO 9000 Series Registration to Business Excellence: The Migratory Path', *Business Process Management Journal*, 10 (1), 417–28.

Wall, T., Corbett, J., Martin, R., Clegg, C. and Jackson, P. (1990) in text 'Advanced Manufacturing Technology, Work Design and Performance: A Change Study', *Journal of Applied Psychology*, 75, 691–7.

Webb, S. (2000) 'Crimes and Misdemeanours: How to Protect Corporate Information in the Internet Age', *Computers and Security*, 19 (2), 128–33.

Weihrich, H. and Koontz. W. (1993) *Management: A Global Perspective*. New York: McGraw-Hill.

Weiner, N. (1949) *Cybernetics or Control and Communication in Animal and Machine*. Mass: MIT Press.

Whitley, R. (1999) 'Firms, Institutions and Management Control: The Comparative Analysis of Coordination and Control Systems', *Accounting Organizations and Society*, 24 (5/6), 507–24.

Chapter 11

Operations Management

....

11.1 Introduction

This chapter explains and describes the key aspects of operations management. Along with finance and marketing, the management of operations plays a vital role: without the successful production and delivery of a product or service there are no products to sell and no profits to measure.

The last quarter of the twentieth century saw rapid advances in the development and complexity of operations management. The global scale of manufacturing caused changes in how products were sourced and produced. More centralised distribution networks reduced the time from order to delivery. Information technology and the Internet have brought about closer information networks between suppliers, producers, and customers, allowing new models of supply, manufacture and delivery to be advanced. Ireland, as a gateway location to the rest of the EU, hosts many multinational firms which are at the leading edge of operations management (Dell, Hewlett Packard, Microsoft) and are also influential to Irish supply firms. The core principles of operations management are currently being redefined, in favour of more direct supply lines from producer to customer, and many traditional distributors and wholesalers are re-evaluating their function.

In this chapter, the key elements of operations management: process planning and management, the supply chain, quality and inventory management are outlined. The management of innovation, now considered a key input to the development of national industrial strategy, is discussed, and the chapter concludes with a case study from an Irish firm, referencing some of the issues involved in the actual practice of operations management.

11.2 Management of operations

In exploring this area of functional management, two terms need clarification. The first is the term 'operations', which is instinctively understood to involve a PROCESS or a series of planned events. In the specific context of business, an OPERATION is a transformational process, by which inputs (materials, labour, and knowledge) are transformed into outputs (goods and services). Feedback from customers is used to make adjustments to the transformation process and to the combination of inputs used (see Figure 11.1).

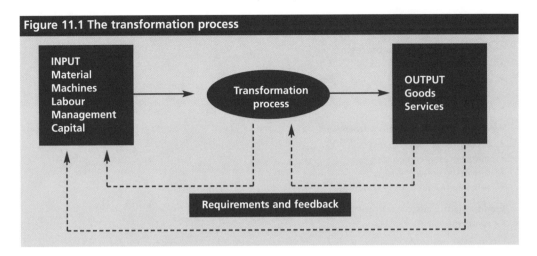

Figure 11.1 The transformation process

An operation therefore harnesses resources in order to produce a good or to supply a service. Banks, manufacturing organisations, fast-food chains and theatres are examples of the diverse operations produced and offered for sale for the benefit of a customer. Russell and Taylor (2000) suggest that operations can take many different forms and the process can be:

▶ physical, as in manufacturing
▶ locational, as in retailing
▶ physiological, as in health care
▶ psychological, as in entertainment,
▶ informational, as in communications.

It could be argued that the management of operations is in fact an integral part of every manager's job. The management of operations is agreed to be a core function within any organisation: without the smooth working of this core all other aspects of the organisation will malfunction. It is useful to make a distinction between transformed and transforming resources. *Transformed* resources have been treated or operated on in a certain way, for example, materials or information, prepared or cut to a certain specification. *Transforming* resources are the enabling factors that allow the transformation to take place, for example, trained staff, facilities. Usually, one of the transformed resources is dominant in an operation—manufacturing is primary involved with materials, banks are engaged with customers, hospitals process information about patients. Slack *et al.* (1998) distinguish three categories of organisations from this perspective (see Figure 11.2):

The function of operations management involves the design and operation of productive systems. Wild (1995) suggests that there are four different types of operations, each of which needs a different managerial approach:

▶ manufacturing—where the physical output differs from the input
▶ transport—where something is moved, without any change in physical resources
▶ supply—where the ownership of goods changes without a change in form
▶ services—where the customer or something belonging to the customer receives intangible treatment.

Figure 11.2 Operations classified by primarily transformed resources

Predominantly materials processors:
- all manufacturers
- retail operations
- warehouses
- postal service

Predominantly information processors:
- accountants
- market research companies
- university research units
- telecommunications companies

Predominantly customers processors:
- hairdressers
- hotels
- hospitals
- theatres

Source: Slack *et al.* (1998).

Operations managers are responsible for handling the transformation process, be it in product, service or mixed product/service situations. Operations managers make decisions in five main areas:

▶ quality—managing quality issues, controlling quality and improving it

▶ process—selecting and designing the transformation process, selecting and using the appropriate technology, layout of facilities

▶ capacity—forecasting demand, making decisions about facility location, planning at top and detailed levels, including project planning

▶ inventory—planning appropriate levels of inventory and methods of control, linking inventory and methods of control, linking inventory to production planning and scheduling

▶ people: managing the workforce, designing and improving jobs (Boaden 1998).

The rest of this chapter includes a discussion of the first four of these areas of responsibility, while the subject of people management is addressed separately in Chapter 7.

11.2.1 Operations and strategy

At the centre of strategy development is the recognition and enhancement of core competences: areas in which the firm has a strong or superior performance in comparison with competitors. From the strategist's point of view, Russell and Taylor (2000) make the distinction between order qualifiers and order winners. Order qualifiers are characteristics of a product or service that qualify it to be considered for purchase by a buyer,for example, within a certain price range, or specified features. An order winner is a characteristic of a product that wins orders in the marketplace—the final factor in the purchasing decision. For example, an order might be won on the basis of flexibility, short time to delivery, or the most features for a certain price. Order qualifiers and order winners can evolve and change over time, as can core competences. From the viewpoint of the operations manager, it is interesting that the most frequently quoted sources of competitive advantage—cost, quality, flexibility and speed—are all related to how operations are managed.

Most organisations strive to compete on cost, no matter what price segment they compete in. Almost every market has competitors at the low cost or discount end of the market. Cost reductions may be brought about by reconfiguring operations, introducing new technology or more flexible working practices, or by asking customers to do some of the work involved in production or delivery. For example, RyanAir has developed many cost-saving elements in its operations which have given it enduring cost advantages. It selected airports which did not have intensive passenger traffic, where it could negotiate lower charges and turn around its aircraft more quickly. RyanAir staff are flexible and working agreements are negotiated directly without dealing with unions. The company website allows customers to book directly and also saves on the commission payable to travel agents. These cost advantages have allowed RyanAir to build a significant market with tourists and business people alike (O'Higgins 1999).

A firm competing on QUALITY offers customers certainty or written guarantees about the product or service on offer. While quality is often talked about in a defensive way, in the sense of zero defects and minimising errors, the concept of quality allows the firm some imagination in the particular offer being made. There is often scope to offer a product which is low quality and low cost (for example, cheap clothing which is fashionable) or of reasonable cost and higher than average quality (Marks and Spencer). Issues to be considered in evaluating the quality of operations include looking at customer perceptions and expectations, the relevance of quality standards and awards, competitor performance on quality, and the resources to innovate. For example, Waterford Crystal realised that younger people wanted lighter crystalware in more modern designs. The response was to offer a new range of stemware, branded Marquis, which was imported rather than hand blown, of a different level of quality and significantly more affordable than the traditional ranges of crystal.

FLEXIBILITY means the freedom to respond to changes or customer demands. Traditional manufacturing through the mode of mass production resisted flexibility—remember Henry Ford's old adage that the customer could have any colour s/he wanted—as long as it was black. Modern operations are responsive to market needs and can use technology to facilitate closer contacts with customers and suppliers. For example, Dell Computer builds machines according to customer specifications. The Dell website and call centres allow customer 24-hour-a-day contact. Suppliers are linked into this build-to-order system and must be able to perform within tight deadlines. This flexibility gives Dell an insight into customer requirements and an advantage in anticipating future market demands.

The final core competence—speed—means building faster movements or new adaptations into an operation. Speed may refer to waiting times, production times, the time it takes to get information, or the time it takes to ship and deliver orders. Placing speed and faster turnaround times at the core of the operation can enable a complete reconfiguration of systems to take place. The new providers of financial services, such as Northern Rock, do their business by phone or on the Internet, eliminating the need for a costly branch network. This system facilitates the development of a customer DATABASE, allowing more information and better service to customers. Cost savings can be passed on by way of more competitive interest rates, further enhancing the advantage.

In most cases, the operations manager will have to trade-off one source of core competence against another, as it is not possible to achieve everything at once. The typical trade-off is between price and quality, where constant adjustments are made to achieve a compromise that is acceptable to the customer. Modern practice is to achieve an improvement in one area without any diminution in performance elsewhere. The concept of WORLD-CLASS MANUFACTURING (WCM) refers to the aim of achieving excellence on all fronts. As can be seen from the case at the end of this chapter, the aim of being 'world class' involves a team effort undertaken in stages over a period of time.

11.3 Quality management

The evolution of the principles of quality and the concept of total quality management (TQM) have already been addressed in Chapter 1 and Chapter 10. The purpose of this section is to outline the principles and practice of quality management from the point of view of the operations manager.

In simple terms, quality can be defined as 'fitness for the intended purpose' (Juran 1988). But this definition suggests a conformist approach, and also makes the point that quality is an elusive concept: dependent on the market and customer group concerned. For example, quality clothes designed for young children might be well stitched, in bright colours and have easy fastenings. The older children's market, on the other hand, might be more concerned with high fashion and the most modern fabrics.

Crosby (1992) talked about quality as 'getting everyone to do what they have agreed to do and to do it right the first time'. Crosby's definition refers to two ideas: the integrative nature of quality being felt throughout the whole organisation; and the concept of 'zero defects' now widely practised in both manufacturing and service companies. The current idea of quality, as suggested by Ho (1999) is that of 'providing extraordinary customer satisfaction'. This calls for imagination in seeing things from the eyes of the customer and then deciding on the particular product offer which will give value, pleasure and customer loyalty, often referred to as 'zero defections'.

Exhibit 11.1 TQM at Analog Devices

Analog Devices is a multinational company manufacturing computer peripherals in Ireland. The principles of TQM have been integrated into its company ethos for several years. The TQM programme at Analog is centred around four main principles:

- **Focus on customers**. Analog focuses on what will satisfy the customer in order to concentrate and align its continuous improvement. Customer satisfaction is the only lasting means of achieving business success.

- **Continuous improvement**. The company insists on continually analysing what it is doing and modifying it to address changing customer needs and the competitive environment. It focuses on the key activities that make a big difference in the company's quality and performance.

- **Total company improvement**. Everyone is involved in the processes of continuous improvement and customer focus. Great importance is placed on people's active participation.

- **Networking**. TQM begins and ends with education. Mutual learning happens both inside and outside the organisation and accelerates the rate of learning.

Source: Ingle (1999).

Garvin (1987) suggests that there are eight dimensions of quality:

▶ performance
▶ features
▶ conformance
▶ reliability
▶ durability
▶ serviceability
▶ aesthetics
▶ perceived quality.

The first four features are regarded as intrinsic and measurable, while the second four features are extrinsic and less easily measured. The ranking of these dimensions involves constantly shifting standards of quality, and sometimes the end user is left unsure what to expect from complex products and services which are not always designed with user friendliness in mind.

Exhibit 11.2 Meeting customer expectations: cars versus computers

At a computer conference, the president of Microsoft reportedly compared the computer industry with the car industry and stated: 'If General Motors had kept up with technology like the computer industry has, we would all be driving twenty-five dollar cars that got a thousand miles to the gallon.'

In response, the following was circulated on the Internet, much to the enjoyment of all. If cars had developed like PC software ...

1. For no reason whatsoever your car would crash twice a day.
2. Every time they repainted the lines on the road you would have to buy a new car.
3. Occasionally, your car would die on the road for no reason, and you would just accept this, restart, and drive on.
4. Occasionally, executing a manoeuvre, such as a left turn, would cause your car to shut down and refuse to restart, in which case you would have to reinstall the engine.
5. You would have to buy more seats.
6. Apple would produce a car that was reliable, five times as fast, easy to drive, but would only run on 5 per cent of the roads.

Source: Peters (1999).

For services, the dimensions of quality are distinctly different and more related to the time factor and the relationship between employee and customer. Evans and Lindsay (1996) identify the dimensions of service quality as:

▶ timeliness
▶ completeness
▶ courtesy

- ▶ consistency
- ▶ accessibility
- ▶ accuracy
- ▶ responsiveness.

The intangible nature of services means there is only one opportunity to get it 'right first time' and unsatisfactory service encounters remain in the customer's mind and can result in word-of-mouth criticism. For manufactured goods, by contrast, there is the opportunity to improve on defective items as they come off the production line and the chance to repair or replace defective items.

The costs of achieving good quality are in two categories: prevention costs and appraisal costs:

PREVENTION COSTS are the costs of trying to ensure that poor quality goods do not reach the customer. Prevention costs include the costs of planning a quality programme; product design; process planning; training; and a quality management information system.

APPRAISAL COSTS are the costs of measuring quality. Such costs would include the costs of inspection and testing; the costs of the equipment for this process; and the labour cost of the time spent on quality inspection and information. These costs have to be balanced against the costs of poor quality, which can be grouped into internal and external failure costs. INTERNAL FAILURE COSTS include the costs of scrap and rework, the costs of process failure, and downtime costs. EXTERNAL FAILURE COSTS occur after the product has been delivered and include customer complaint costs, the cost of product returns, claims on guarantees, product liability costs and the cost of lost sales (Russell and Taylor 2000).

Figure 10.18 in the previous chapter shows the four distinct phases in the development of quality management systems up to the present. The initial step was quality through inspection, but inspection always took place at the end of a process and was soon observed to be inadequate. The next step was the development of quality control techniques which involved more detailed monitoring of the manufacturing process and the application of statistical process control (SPC) techniques, which involved sampling from the production line to ensure that specifications are being met. By the 1970s, the quality assurance approach was aiming for 'zero defects' and using groups and quality circles to make quality an objective throughout the whole organisation. The most recent concept of Total Quality Management (TQM) views quality as affecting and involving groups outside the organisation—typically suppliers and customers—as well as the internal groups already mentioned. The TQM philosophy sees quality as a vision of 'continuous improvement', which requires the instigation of change throughout the organisation, an openness to new ideas and ways of operating, and a commitment to employee quality and empowerment. The demands of the TQM philosophy are such that it demands strategic vision and committed leadership if it is to be implemented. The payoff is in profitability: research proves that high quality, in the long run, results in higher profits. In the short term, the costs of implementing TQM initiatives may hurt profits, so there is a leap of faith needed by management, employees and shareholders alike to await the payoff from their vision (see Figure 10.18).

11.3.1 Quality standards in Ireland

Externally audited quality standards are available through three accredited organisations in Ireland. The standards cover manufactured goods, services and the management of the human resources function. The achievement of a recognised quality standard brings benefits to both the company and the customer. For the company, there should be increased productivity, less waste, a better image and a distinct marketing benefit. Many large organisations, for example, only want to do business with suppliers that have achieved recognised quality standards. For the customer, a recognised quality system brings about more confidence and trust, increases fitness for use and reduces the time needed to search through a list of suppliers.

Excellence Ireland, an associate company of the European Foundation for Quality Management (EFQM), operates two quality mark (Q-Mark) programmes. The Quality Systems Q-Mark is focused on setting up and maintaining standards for the way a business operates. Companies are required to document procedures on the key activities in the organisation and produce a quality manual that describes how the quality system operates. The Q-Mark based on Business Excellence looks at all aspects of the business and represents a move away from quality assurance models to continuous improvement and world-class standards. It focuses on the results achieved by the organisation and the internal resources that are available to generate these results. Companies applying for recognition under this scheme complete a submission document for submission to Excellence Ireland. This is reviewed and assessed, then is there is a site visit and the submission is assessed. More companies are currently choosing the Business Excellence scheme because of its focus on business improvement.

The National Standards Authority of Ireland (NSAI) is the state certification body for the International Standards Organisation, Geneva, (ISO) 9000 and ISO 14001 standards. The ISO 9000 family of standards comprises 17 different standards, of which only ISO 9001, ISO 9002 and ISO 9003 are quotable, or audited, standards. The remaining 14 standards are guidelines. The vast majority of firms are registered under ISO 9001 or ISO 9002. The three quotable standards are:

▶ ISO 9001—Quality Systems model for quality assurance in design, development, production, installation and servicing

▶ ISO 9002—Quality Systems model for quality assurance in production, installation and servicing

▶ ISO 9003—Quality Systems model for quality assurance in final inspection and test.

As ISO 9000 is a harmonised European and International standard, certification to the standard opens up international markets to companies and is part of the EU drive to harmonise technical standards throughout Europe. Applications for registration for any of the three ISO standards are required to have a documented quality system in the form of a Quality Manual, supported by relevant procedures manuals and work instructions. The formal application for certification and the Quality Manual are assessed by NSAI. Significant variations or omissions are notified to the applicant and then a formal assessment, taking two to six days is carried out at the applicant's premises. Any areas of non-conformance are reported to the applicant and when remedial action has been verified, an application for registration can be made to NSAI. On approval, the company is awarded 'Registered Firm' status and is listed as an ISO registered supplier. There is an ongoing surveillance inspection programme by NSAI to ensure standards are being maintained.

A second set of standards accredited by NSAI concerns Environmental Management Systems (EMS). As can be seen in Chapter 12, firms are increasingly responsible for environmental protection and the two standards available allow this to be verified by an independent body. The two standards are:

▶ ISO 14001—Environmental Management Systems
▶ EMAS—Eco-Management and Audit Scheme.

Firms may apply for one or both standards and the validation process is similar to that described for the ISO 9000 series.

The third set of standards recognises best practice in the field of training and development and is administered through FAS. The Excellence Through People quality training award encourages organisations to develop the full potential of their employees. In the UK, a similar scheme, Investors in People, operates with the same objectives. By the end of 1999, 79 Irish firms had been awarded the standard by FAS.

11.4 Process design and planning

A process is the means by which chosen inputs are transformed into outputs. The process chosen reflects the strategy for how the product is to be offered and delivered in the marketplace. For example, there is a wide selection of restaurants offering meals away from home. Their points of difference centre around how the meal is prepared and delivered: compare this process in a fast-food outlet and in an expensive restaurant. The process by which the meal is prepared and delivered reflects the restaurant's competitive strategy and is reflected in the price the customer is willing to pay. A firm's process strategy defines its:

▶ capital intensity—the mix of capital and labour used in the production process
▶ process flexibility—the ease with which resources can be changed in response to changes in supply or market conditions
▶ customer involvement—the role of the customer in the production process (Russell and Taylor, 2000).

Figure 11.3 illustrates the range of processes and production environments. The first situation is the PROJECT process, which represents a one-off production, usually of high value and over a defined period of time. Examples are the construction of a building or a large consultancy assignment. Most of the work is usually done at the customer's site, and there is considerable variation between one project assignment and the next. There is limited potential for automation, and a core of experienced staff and expert knowledge management are critical factors. Managing this type of process calls for the ability to plan, co-ordinate and control diverse and complex operations. Major projects are often seen to fall behind schedule or go over budget, indicating that this is a far from perfect science. A parallel type of process is seen in craft production, in which customised skills are used to produce an individual product or service. Craft industries thrive on the fact that consumers often seek items that are unique, and the Irish craft industry now has about 3,000 employees involved in small-scale production.

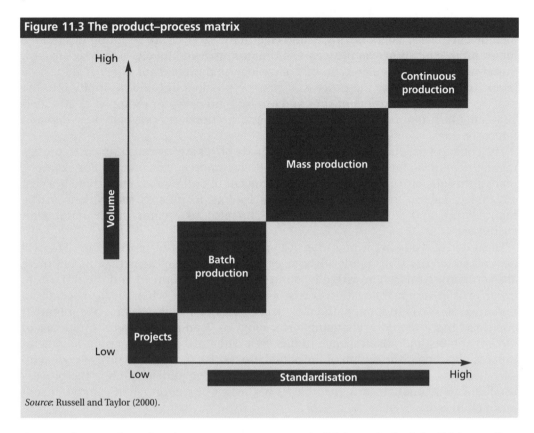

Figure 11.3 The product–process matrix

Source: Russell and Taylor (2000).

A second type of production, BATCH PRODUCTION, is fairly typical of the Irish small to medium-sized enterprise (SME). Products are produced in batches at regular intervals, with most of the work being in machining or preparation, rather than in final assembly. Examples include bakeries and education. The advantages are in being able to produce some variety of products using the same equipment; the problems are in the time delay between batches and the effect of machinery breakdowns. In some cases, the batch may be finished elsewhere in order to cut costs or add value. For example, Cuisine de France uses par-baking techniques to deliver partly prepared bread, which is then freshly baked on the retailer's premises. The customer sees a fresh warm crusty loaf and is willing to pay more for this distinctive product.

LINE or MASS PRODUCTION refers to a situation where a linear sequence of operations is dedicated to production of a particular good or service. Examples include fast food, cars and computers. The product is one that sells at high volumes and at a stable demand. Mass production usually uses standardised labour and is increasingly tending towards automation, computer-integrated manufacturing (CIM) and the use of cells or workstations with flexible work teams. The advantages are in scale and cost; the problems lie in the lack of flexibility and the ownership of a particular level of technology which may go out of date. The increasing trend for 'mass customisation' places strains on this process; many manufacturers have cut back on the options or extras they offer, or have adopted 'build to order' systems to solve this problem.

CONTINUOUS PRODUCTION is used for standardised products where the demand is high or there is a need for continuous supply. The process may involve the synthesis of several inputs to produce the final product and is usually capital-intensive. Examples include chemicals, alcoholic drinks and electricity. Services are adopting this model; for example, education over the web. Continuous processes involve a high set-up cost, investment in a particular type of technology and significant costs if there is a breakdown or failure in the process. It may be possible to build flexibility into the process by having a number of sites and levels of intensity; for example, electricity is generated at a number of power stations and production is regulated by demand forecasts.

The choice of production process will be made on taking into account costs, profits, market demands and the technological and economic environments. For example, many firms outsource the production of inputs or of entire products if there is a cost advantage. Labour and skill shortages are leading to process innovations in the manufacture and servicing of products and also to greater involvement with customers.

The initial decision in the planning of a process is whether to 'make or buy'. This will depend on the cost and supply advantages associated with either situation, but there are now some firms where virtually all production is outsourced and the firm's core expertise is in design, innovation or customer relationships. When the firm decides to undertake its own production, the next decision is the actual selection of equipment and machinery. Rapidly changing technology is leading to major problems of incompatibility and obsolescence in this area. The third area of decision making in process planning is the design of the actual process itself, which involves drawing up specifications, preparing a bill of materials and routing and scheduling the process itself. For new products and greenfield sites, it can be a bumpy path until efficient production is achieved.

Exhibit 11.3 Dell Computer: built to order

Dell Computer is a billion-dollar computer manufacturer, founded by Michael Dell in Austin, Texas, in 1986. The firm produces for the European market from its manufacturing plant in Limerick and uses the 'made-to-order' model to sell to their customers: large and small companies, government, education and home users.

Once an order for a laptop or desktop model is received, manufacturing breaks it down into a list of the parts required. When the specification sheet is generated, it is barcoded so that if a customer calls enquiring about his or her order, s/he can be informed about its status and shipment date. After the sale, the barcode is used for service enquiries to tell the technician the exact configuration of the system.

Manufacturing starts with the assembly of the motherboard with the microprocessor and RAM as ordered. Then the other optional parts (disk drives, DVD, etc.) are assembled into a bin of parts pulled from stock. The bin and the motherboard is forwarded to a manufacturing cell for assembly, wiring and testing. Software is then loaded and tested before the system is boxed with peripherals such as a keyboard, mouse and instruction manuals.

Dell is always striving to improve product quality and reduce the failure rate of its machines. For example, the firm decreased the number of human interactions with the hard drive during assembly from 30 to 15 'touches' and found that the rate of rejected hard drives fell by 40 per cent and overall PC failure dropped by 20 per cent.

The Dell process has become a model for efficiency in the industry. The entire process from order to product shipment can be 36 hours. Parts are ordered on a just-in-time basis and Dell operates on 13 days of inventory, compared to 75 days of some competitors. It deals with a small number of suppliers who warehouse their components as near as possible to the factory. Shipment of finished goods is contracted out. After the sale, the first line of support is over the telephone or the web. This solves 90 per cent of problems, and Dell has third-party maintenance agreements to provide on-site service to customers. These process innovations away from the traditional manufacturer–retailer model have given Dell significant cost savings as well as the differential advantage of a more direct relationship with its customers.

Source: Rangan and Bell (1998).

11.4.1 Current techniques in process planning

Many of the current developments in process planning originated in the objective of a firm or a department wanting to become more competitive—in terms of speed, cost, service or whatever. The more successful ideas have been taken up and adopted globally and the learning process has led to further refinement and adaptation. This section looks at developments that are most relevant to Irish operations.

At a general level, the concept of FACTORY AUTOMATION (FA) has become appealing. The core of FA consists of robots and computerised machine tools, supplemented by automated warehouses and automated guided vehicles (Ho 1999). This system reduces labour costs, allows 24-hour operations and facilitates the operation of flexible manufacturing systems (FMS) which can be rapidly adjusted to patterns of market demand. FA systems are also applied in services, where technology can be used to reduce the human input to the service process, for example, Internet banking. FA systems are more relevant to large-scale operations and are increasingly seen at new plants where systems can be installed without disturbing established methods.

JUST-IN-TIME (JIT) SYSTEMS were originally introduced by an engineer in Toyota to improve efficiency. JIT uses a 'pull' system for materials and parts to cut down wastage and stockholding. The ideal of the JIT system is of zero stocks, where parts and materials are introduced to the production line exactly as needed. This reduces the amount of inventory held, speeds the turnaround time on orders and offers huge potential cost savings. A JIT system involves the nomination of preferred suppliers who work closely with the manufacturer to co-ordinate deliveries and undertake some of the responsibility for holding stock. The Internet has further streamlined the idea: many 'virtual' retailers electronically forward customer orders to their suppliers, who handle the rest of the process themselves.

Another simple and useful concept originating in Japan is that of ERROR-PROOFING (*Poka-Yoka* in Japanese). Following on Crosby's message that quality means getting things 'right first time', fool-proofing means putting systems in place that will minimise the potential for errors. With many workplaces relying more on contract and casual labour, the need for error-proofing has become more urgent, and the incidence of product recalls which are costly and embarrassing for manufacturers is another good reason for error-proofing. If a firm can succeed in fool-proofing its product or service it has the potential to win customer confidence. For example, the Audi A2 car was launched in Spring 2000 with a completely sealed engine, except for an access point for oil and water. The manufacturers say the engine will need minimal maintenance and this will reduce running costs.

In the 1970s, MANUFACTURING-REQUIREMENTS PLANNING (MRP) SYSTEMS were introduced as a way of solving ever more complex manufacturing orders. For example, a factory producing batteries sells many different sizes and packs, under different brand names, to a wide spectrum of customers. MRP systems use information technology to calculate parts requirements, schedule work and purchase orders, and calculate the time and materials costs of a product. MRP system are the focal point of any large-scale producer's information system and play a key role in computer-integrated manufacturing systems (CIM). Global producers are now using a broader vision of MRP—enterprise resource planning (ERP)—to plan and co-ordinate between their various operations and locations.

BUSINESS PROCESS RE-ENGINEERING (BPR) is a process approach that was developed in the early 1990s (Hammer and Champy 1993). It involves the radical redesign of business as a whole, or of individual work processes, in order to improve business effectiveness. Hammer and his colleagues judged that continuous improvement efforts (*Kaizen* in Japanese) often did not bring significant changes, or the efforts hit a wall. BPR philosophy was a response to the need for radical change and redirection in markets that are characterised by speed and innovation (see Table 11.1).

Table 11.1 *Kaizen* versus BPR: similarities and differences		
	Continuous improvement (Kaizen)	**BPR**
Common point	Focus on the customer	
Starting point	Not under competitive pressure to take immediate action	The company has the resources to handle the transformation
D Strategy	Continuous small steps	Infrequent big leaps
I F Approach	Start with what you have	Start with 'clean sheet'
F E Methodology	Change what you have and learn	Forget and start again
R E Process	Simultaneous processes	Selective, one at a time
N C Value added	Eliminate non-value-added processes	Minimise inputs, add value to outputs
E Human resource	People involved in the operations	BPR project team
S Technology	Less technology required	More technology required

Source: Ho (1999).

The BPR process begins with analysing the nature of the business process and understanding how value is added. The technique of value engineering is used to look at the various functions undertaken, the costs involved and whether these processes are worthwhile, should be outsourced, or could be done away with altogether. Customer research is applied to understand demand and market trends. Another BPR technique—benchmarking—involves looking at best practice either in the industry or the process, for example, the top quality providers of excellent service. The information gathered from benchmarking is used to measure how far the organisation or process is from best practice and to judge what can be done to improve the situation. The first wave of BPR work in the early 1990s resulted in massive downsizing by organisations in the search to cut costs. The current focus of BPR efforts is more focused on the whole supply chain, where virtual connections can be used to streamline activities (Caulkin 1999).

The final technique currently being applied in process planning is WORLD-CLASS MANUFACTURING. WCM is seen as a holistic effort, integrating the techniques of TQM, BPR, JIT and employee involvement, in an effort to achieve standards that are of world class. Keegan and Lynch (1995) define this concept as 'the pursuit of superior performance in quality, lead time, cost and customer service through continuous improvement in Just-in-Time Manufacturing, Total Quality Management and employee involvement'. The term itself was coined by an American researcher, Schonberger (1986, 1990), to describe what he had observed being practised in the best of the Japanese companies he studied. The application of the WCM philosophy involves a re-examination of processes, culture and the operational links throughout the whole supply chain. The concept of WCM has now evolved into the 'world-class business' and the 'world-class cluster' concepts. The efforts of a medium-sized Irish firm to adopt WCM are discussed in the case study at the end of this chapter.

Exhibit 11.4 WCM and Microsoft Ireland

Microsoft Ireland supplies the European market with Microsoft licensed software from its location in Dublin. Since 1989, the company has been addressing WCM issues and has used the advantage of continuous new product development to build the WCM approach into new operations.

The first area to be addressed was the links with suppliers: the vendor base was reduced from 40 to 10. Sole-sourcing arrangements were entered into through the development of strategic partnerships with vendors. Next, the software distribution process was examined to establish more direct relationships with channel partners. This resulted in warehousing space being reduced by 75 per cent. Analysis of the business process led to a decision that Microsoft channel partners would concentrate on selling and Microsoft national subsidiaries would focus on marketing and no longer have a direct sales function.

The outcome of WCM efforts to date has been a shorter supply chain capable of delivering a diverse range of products with fewer transactions. The advantages quantified include:

- lead time cut from 8 weeks to 1 day
- raw material turns increased from 6 to 80
- work-in-progress reduced from 4 weeks to 4 hours
- finished-goods stock reduced from 10 weeks to 4
- introduction of ISO 9002.

Source: Keegan and Lynch (1995) Hill (2000).

11.5 Logistics and supply chain management

LOGISTICS MANAGEMENT is the means whereby the needs of customers are satisfied through the co-ordination of the materials and information flows that extend from the marketplace, through the firm and its operations, and beyond that to suppliers. Figure 11.4 shows the internal and external channels involved.

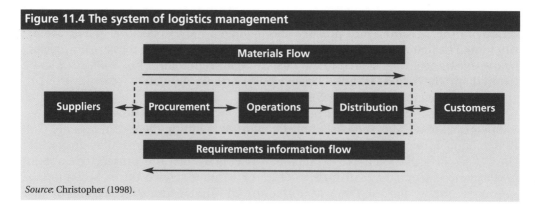

Figure 11.4 The system of logistics management

Source: Christopher (1998).

The management of the logistics function offers three opportunities:

▶ to save costs
▶ to add value
▶ to build competitive advantage.

Logistics management is primarily concerned with optimising flows within the organisation. A more recent development is SUPPLY CHAIN MANAGEMENT, which recognises the need to develop partnerships and co-operative agreements with external channel members—typically suppliers and distributors. This differs from vertical integration, where the firm maintains ownership of each channel member. Supply chain management is representative of the trend towards global outsourcing being practised by large firms, leaving them free to concentrate on core competences. Supply chain management can thus be seen as the management of upstream and downstream relationships with suppliers and customers to deliver superior customer value at less cost to the supply chain as a whole (Christopher 1998). Successful management involves a network of relationships which are becoming ever more complex.

Exhibit 11.5 A cola can's long and weary journey to Tesco

Next time you sip from a can of cola, consider the number of value streams you hold in your hand. The product you are consuming is composed of three separate elements: cola liquid, the can, and the cardboard packaging around the pack of cans. Of the three, the can itself has the longest value stream.

It starts at a mine in Australia where bauxite is scooped as ore and then every few weeks a shipment goes off to a reduction mill. After another few weeks at the mill, when two tons of alumina have been processed—enough to fill a vast ore carrier—it sets sail for Norway or Sweden. The journey takes four weeks and then the alumina might sit around for two months before being smelted. In two hours, the load is reduced to one ton of aluminium and stored in ingots for a few weeks before shipping to a hot rolling mill in Germany or Sweden. Two weeks later, the ingots are placed between rollers and reduced into coils in a process which takes about one minute. After storage for about four weeks, the coils are sent to another mill where they are rolled to a thickness of 0.3 millimetres and cut into sheets. After another month in storage, the sheets are loaded on to trucks and make the sea crossing to the can maker in England.

After being stored for two weeks, the aluminium sheets are converted into finished painted cans in a process that takes about ten seconds. The cans are palletised and spend four weeks in a warehouse before going to the bottler. After four days there, the cans are filled at a rate of 1,500 a minute. The filled cans are palletised and spend four weeks in a warehouse before trucking to a Tesco regional distribution centre.

Exhibit 11.5 A cola can's long and weary journey to Tesco *contd.*

From here, the pace quickens. After three days, the pallets are broken into cartons for overnight delivery to one of the stores. Once there, they are shelved and usually sold inside two days. The entire procedure has taken 319 days, with an actual processing time of three hours. The product is stationary for 99 per cent of the time, picked up and put down 30 times and moved through 14 stages of storage. In addition, 24 per cent of the aluminium is used up in the production process and only 16 per cent of the cans used are ever recycled, although it takes 20 times more energy to produce a new can.

By the way, when you are finished your drink, what were you thinking of doing with that can?

Source: Womack and Jones (1996).

Organisations implementing a globalised supply chain have developed several techniques to enhance the process. The FOCUSED FACTORY, which limits production to one line or product type allows for economies in manufacturing and in distribution. Companies can switch production between plants depending on costs, demand and exchange rates. The risks are in focusing production on just one line and the possible high costs of distribution which can cancel out some earlier cost savings. A second technique is the *centralisation of inventories*, which offers cost savings and a better level of customer service. Information systems allow the centralisation to be done electronically: the stocks need not be in the same physical location. Alongside these trends for centralisation came the need for postponement and localisation:

▶ POSTPONEMENT refers to the idea of building a product on a common platform and then delivering the part-completed product for finishing as determined by market needs or customer specifications. For example, a washing machine manufacturer might build a core washing machine platform, which is finished as a top-loading machine for the French market and a front loader for the Irish market.

▶ LOCALISATION refers to the extent to which the product must be modified to suit local market needs. Software packages need to be modified by language and by customer group, for example.

From the retailer's perspective, the philosophy of EFFICIENT CONSUMER RESPONSE (ECR) has been developed to place the focus on customer demand as the driver of production and supply. Companies using ECR track the sales of product lines through the retail shelves, monitor the outcomes of SALES PROMOTIONS, and assess how well their stocking of the shelves matches with consumer demand. The practice of ECR seeks to avoid the situation where too much stock is in situ relative to sales, or where a much sought product is out of stock, leaving customers disappointed. Finally, information technology and the Internet are facilitating the development of the 'virtual' supply chain. This allows for more sharing of real-time information between manufacturers and their suppliers. As the boundaries between channel members are becoming blurred, changes being implemented include co-operative product development, modular manufacturing, co-ownership of facilities and the sharing of customer and market data. The desired outcomes include quicker response times, a deeper understanding of customer and supplier concerns, and a lower failure rate at product development.

11.6 Inventory management

For the operations manager, the objective of inventory management is to have adequate stocks to meet production and customer demands, while at the same time keeping costs down. It is estimated that on average 30 per cent of the cost of manufactured goods is tied up with inventory costs—the most significant single element of production costs—so it is evident that there is a major interest in reducing this area of expense. The tradition of keeping large amounts of inventory in storage in warehouses has been affected by product obsolescence, more volatile patterns of demand and the trend towards JIT manufacturing. The types of inventory held illustrate the challenge that is involved in managing the situation:

▶ raw materials
▶ purchased parts and supplies
▶ labour
▶ work-in-progress
▶ component parts
▶ working capital
▶ tools and equipment.

This list relates to manufactured goods. In the service sector, the problem is that most services cannot carry a stock, but instead must try to match capacity as closely as possible to customer demand. For example, a hotel must anticipate seasonal peaks and troughs and develop its pricing policy accordingly.

Companies developing an inventory strategy will look at the benefits of the JIT approach and balance these against the requirements to hold buffer stocks. Firms implementing JIT experience problems if suppliers themselves have difficulties in fulfilling the terms of the contract. JIT also puts pressure on suppliers to take responsibility for stock holding and has been blamed for increasing costs at this part of the supply chain.

The costs of carrying inventory are broken down into three areas. *Carrying* costs are the costs of holding items in inventory. This involves the cost of the stock, warehousing and transportation. Other costs include DEPRECIATION, obsolescence, spoilage and theft. In all, carrying costs can account for 10-40 per cent of manufacturing costs. A second area at issue is the expense associated with *ordering* inventory. These costs are incremental rather than directly variable with every unit of production. For example, a larger order may qualify for a quantity discount and for faster delivery. Ordering costs include the administration of the purchasing function, receiving, inspection and handling costs, and usually bear an inverse relationship to carrying costs. The third area is the cost of *stockouts*. If there is insufficient stock to meet demand, there are the OPPORTUNITY COSTS of lost profits, the costs of delayed production if the stockout involves materials or parts, and the loss of customer good will and loyalty. The development of computerised MRP systems (see 11.4.1) was undertaken to reduce these three areas of cost and to increase flexibility in adjusting to changes in demand of supply conditions.

The basic economic order quantity model, shown in Figure 11.5, was developed to minimise the sum of carrying costs and ordering costs. The model has also been adapted to other applications, for example, CATEGORY MANAGEMENT in the retail trade, which focuses on the management of a particular category of goods on the shelf in order to maximise profits for both the retailer and the supplier.

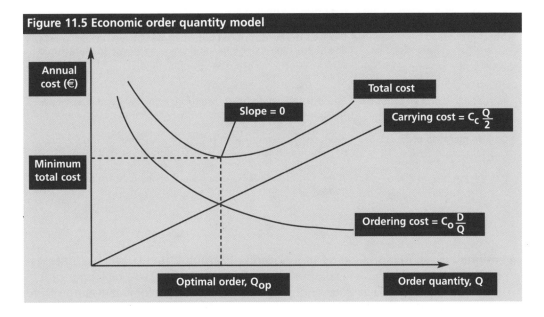

Figure 11.5 Economic order quantity model

Annual cost (€)

Total cost

Slope = 0

Carrying cost = $C_c \frac{Q}{2}$

Minimum total cost

Ordering cost = $C_o \frac{D}{Q}$

Optimal order, Q_{op}

Order quantity, Q

11.7 Managing innovation

The development of new products, processes and services is the life blood of the firm, particularly in the current world of changing technologies and shorter PRODUCT LIFE CYCLES. The operations manager is involved in two different elements of the innovation process:

▶ the development and testing of new ideas
▶ the production of the new product or service when the idea is finalised.

A third role for the operations manager is that of process improvement. An example of this work was developed by the Bank of Ireland and branded '100y2k', or '100 steps to better banking'. The scheme involved making one hundred improvements to banking services by the end of the year 2000, resulting in significant savings and better service to customers.

From a strategic point of view, innovation is the way to achieve the 'first mover advantage'. New product development can also be the catalyst for process improvement or change (see Table 11.2).

Table 11.2 A Typology of product innovation	
New products	Introduced to the market for the first time, this category would include radical product developments or those based on new patents or technologies.
Transfer products	Products newly introduced but which had previously been made elsewhere. This might include products being manufactured under licence or whose introduction depended on the purchase of new machinery.
Technically improved products	Products that were being produced previously and which have since been modified to improve their technical performance
Design-improved products	Products that were being produced previously and have since been modified to improve their fashion or aesthetic appeal
Unchanged products	Those products that have remained unchanged from an earlier period.

Source: Roper and Hewett-Dundas (1998).

In national terms, Ireland's record of innovation is around the EU average. Business expenditure on research and development was €679 million in 1997, or 1.1 per cent of GDP, on a par with the EU average. Indigenous firms accounted for just over one-third of this expenditure (36 per cent) with foreign-owned firms making up the rest (64 per cent). The main message from this data is that Ireland needs to improve its investment in innovation if it is to sustain its position as a high-tech economy. In response, the government announced the establishment of the Technology Foresight Foundation in Spring 2000 to increase R & D spend, with funds being targeted at the software, electronics, biotechnology and food sectors (Ahlstrom, 2000).

International data on patent applications collected by the OECD (Organisation for Economic Co-operation and Development) (1998) places Ireland 13th in a table of 24 countries rating patent applications per 10,000 of population. The highest-ranking country was Switzerland, and Ireland was marginally ahead of France. An analysis of patent applications by place of residence gives more revealing information, with 2 per cent of Irish patent applications being made by Irish residents, compared to 86 per cent in Japan and 19 per cent on average throughout the EU. The remaining 98 per cent of Irish patent applications were from non-residents or international corporations. As Roper and Hewitt-Dundas suggest (1998), this reflects the extent to which technological progress in Ireland is dependent on progress elsewhere and the importance of technology transfer (see Chapter 13).

From an operational point of view, a major issue in the development of innovative products is whether the work should be conducted internally or involve external partners. About a quarter to a third of Irish manufacturing businesses involve other companies or agencies at some point. These collaborative or sub-contract relationships may involve customers, suppliers, other players in the industry, consultants, research bodies, universities or government agencies. Irish companies tend to prefer the sub-contract type of relationship and, somewhat surprisingly, large firms are more likely to involve external links than small firms. All categories of firm favour multifunctional teams in the innovation process, but they tend to be involved more at the earlier stages of development, with up to five functions being represented on a team. In summary, Irish innovators fall into three main groups:

▶ **Top-down innovators**. About 40 per cent of firms adhere to the model of innovation as a top-down process. This means that only one functional group at a time is involved and the development process is sequential. The preferred model of innovation in most sectors is the concurrent one: where several projects are in hand at various stages of development at any one time.

▶ **Technical team players**. About half of Irish firms use a multifunctional team for the technical element of product development, but the marketing strategy seems to be the preserve of the marketing function.

▶ **Total team players**. Around 10 per cent of Irish firms involve teams at every stage of the development process (Roper and Hewitt-Dundas 1998).

11.8 Health and safety

The provision of a safe place of work which meets the requirements of health standards and legislation is most often the responsibility of the operations manager. Health and safety issues are particularly topical in the current economic climate. The rapid expansion of business activities leads to shortcuts being taken in health and safety and employees may turn a blind eye or be uninformed until an accident or fatality occurs. The day-to-day issue of sick leave is also an important concern for Irish employers; those that are more proactive have occupational health programmes to improve the health and safety of employees and also to reduce the amount of time and productivity lost through sick leave (see Table 11.3).

Table 11.3 Health and safety statistics, Ireland 1999

Total number of injuries reported	8,005
Total number of workplace fatalities	69
Total number of dangerous occurrences	1,373
Total number of accidents involving more than three days absence	14,900
Number of employees suffering from occupation-related illness	54,400
Number of employee's liability insurance claims allowed (1998)	9,270

Source: Health and Safety Authority (1999).

The regulation of workplace health and safety in Ireland draws on two sources: *common law* and *statute law*. Under common law, employers must exercise reasonable care towards employees and protect them against injury. Injuries involved range from the physical to the psychological, including stress and bullying. The Irish courts have determined that employers must:

▶ provide a safe system of work
▶ ensure that fellow workers are competent
▶ provide supervision
▶ provice a safe place of work.

These rights are more firmly laid out in statute laws passed in 1989 and 1993. The Safety, Health and Welfare at Work Act 1989 applies to employers, employees, suppliers, persons designing or constructing the workplace and persons affected by work activities. The Act states that it is the duty of the employer to ensure the safety, health and welfare at work of all employees. Work systems must be planned, as far as is practicable, without risk to health and safety. The employer must provide relevant information, instruction, training and supervision. Protective clothing and equipment must be provided where appropriate. The employer must prepare a safety statement identifying the risks and hazards to health and safety at that workplace, the arrangements provided to safeguard against these risks and the names of those in charge of safety matters. Employees may elect their own safety representative, who can, subject to prior notice, carry out inspections of possible hazards in the workplace. The Act also established the National Authority for Occupational Safety and Health, known as the Health and Safety Authority, empowered to inspect and enforce workplace practice of the legislation. In 1999, the Authority found that the level of compliance with legislation was low, particularly in the agriculture and construction sectors. The Authority is implementing a preventive approach and building up the level of consultation and partnership as a way of improving compliance levels.

The 1993 Safety, Health and Welfare at Work Regulations support the duties set out in the 1989 Act. Employers are required to take into account the evaluation of unavoidable risks, the combating of risks at source, the replacement of dangerous articles or substances, the drawing up of a prevention policy, the adoption of work to suit the individual employee and the provision of adequate training and instruction. Detailed requirements are specified in relation to a safe place of work, health surveillance, visual display units, electricity and the notification of accidents. This Act has been updated through regulations applying to particular sectors, for example, fishing vessels, as each industry tends to have unique and specific features in its workplace environment. During 1999, the Health and Safety Authority carried out 8,729 inspections and brought about 1,529 enforcement actions. The outcome of these actions ranged from improvement directions and notices to the prosecution of employers. A major review of the current legislation is under way with the aim of achieving better compliance and more effective monitoring of the situation.

11.9 Summary of key propositions

▶ An operation, in the context of manufacturing or service processes, involves a transformation process.

▶ The management of operations is a key element of business strategy. A core competence in operations can give advantages in supply chain management, in the production process, or in the order-to-delivery time for customers.

▶ The principles and practice of quality management are a core responsibility of the operations manager. The dimensions of quality differ between services and manufactured goods. The costs of achieving quality have to be measured against the costs of poor-quality products.

▶ There are two types of audited quality standard in Ireland: the Q-Mark and the ISO 9000 series. The choice of standard will depend on the rigour of audit required and the value the organisation places on the standard awarded.

▶ There are four different production methods: project, batch, mass and continuous production. The choice of production process will be made on consideration of costs, profits, market demands, technology and the economic environment.

▶ Current techniques applied to process planning include factory automation, flexible manufacturing systems, just-in-time systems, error-proofing, manufacturing-requirements planning systems, business process re-engineering, and world-class manufacturing.

▶ Logistics management is primarily concerned with optimising flows within the organisation. Supply chain management involves co-operation and partnerships with external members of the supply and distribution channel.

▶ Inventory costs account for 30 per cent on average of the cost of finished goods: therefore, a well-planned inventory management strategy can offer significant advantages.

▶ The management of innovation draws strongly on the resources of the operations department. On a national scale, Ireland's innovation capability is around the EU average and needs to improve.

▶ Safety, health and welfare issues at work are protected by legislation. The operations manager is responsible for its practice and enforcement.

Discussion questions

❶ Operations management is in fact a key element of every manager's job. Discuss.

❷ How do services operations differ from manufacturing operations? Analyse how these differences affect the job of the operations manager in each situation.

❸ Have you ever bought a product that turned out to be defective? How did the supplier respond to your complaint? How would you rate the quality management approach practised by the manufacturer of the product?

❹ A small furniture manufacturer in your locality is looking for advice on how to improve quality standards. Write a short report to the owner outlining the main principles of quality management and the relevant quality standards to consider.

❺ Dublin Airport is experiencing problems with increasing passenger numbers and an unsatisfactory infrastructure. (Note: It may be more appropriate to select an airport near your own location.)
   a. Research the process used for handling airplane and passenger traffic at the airport.
   b. Map the processes that need to be improved.
   c. Suggest how these processes need to be improved.
   d. What investment would this require and how could it be funded?

❻ Assess the impact of new production techniques such as business process re-engineering or JIT on:
   a. the production process
   b. the employees
   c. the product or service
   d. the organisational strategy.

❼ Analyse the supply chain for any product you have purchased recently.
   a. What changes or improvements would you propose to add value to the product?
   b. Write a letter or e-mail to the operations manager of the company concerned, outlining your suggested improvements. Discuss the response you receive.

❽ Visit any large-scale producer or service provider in your area.
   a. Describe and map the production process being employed.
   b. Assess the type of technology being applied.
   c. Analyse likely changes in the production process in the light of industry developments.

❾ You have been asked to speak at the next meeting of your local small-business forum on the subject of 'Patenting: applications, process and future for Ireland'. Prepare a 20-minute presentation on the subject, bearing in mind the needs of the small-business sector.

❿ Analyse the climate for innovation in Ireland.

⓫ Prepare a short essay discussing the operational aspects of the development of a new product.

⓬ Analyse the strengths and weaknesses of the current health and safety legislation in Ireland and compare these with the situation in any other EU state.

Concluding case: Introducing world-class manufacturing at Dubarry Shoes

Dubarry Shoes is situated in Ballinasloe, a medium-sized town in the west of Ireland. The Scott family ran the business until 1983 when there was a MANAGEMENT BUYOUT by the company's cost accountant and design manager. The company at that time was essentially a traditional, production-led firm.

In 1986, the National Development Corporation, then the state agency for developing Irish industry through investment, took a 39 per cent equity stake in Dubarry. The company was now producing ranges of traditional styles of men's and women's shoes, school shoes, and a range of deck shoes which was very price competitive and a strong seller.

In 1988, the company relocated to a new building just outside the town. This move was linked to a determined effort to expand the business. The company then employed 147 people. It purchased a new state-of-the-art CAD (computer-aided design) system, and decided to look at how to improve production operations.

In 1992, the company became more aware of the need to develop and improve its internal operations. In the middle of that year it had a technology audit done by the relevant state agency. This highlighted the need for a documented quality system. A quality co-ordinator was appointed and the company began to work towards a quality system. Two years later, it achieved ISO 9001.

At that time, there was a lot of interest in using teams to improve production. As a result, Dubarry decided to look at one of the best-known examples—K Shoes—and, in 1995, a small group visited K Shoes in England to look at its modular manufacturing system. K had started using production teams in 1991. The company had suffered a dramatic drop in its workforce and was losing money. In addition, it felt that it could not compete with cheap imports, and, in order to improve quality and to strengthen the business, it began introducing teams.

K found that using teams improved job satisfaction and reduced absenteeism. However, it was not plain sailing. The first module made a substantial loss in its initial year, but the situation improved each year until they were at or near break-even when Dubarry arrived in 1995. Despite K's difficulties, Dubarry was sufficiently impressed to begin introducing teams on the factory floor.

Early in 1996, Dubarry took another step towards improving its internal operations by deciding to implement WCM. It met with Forbairt (now Enterprise Ireland) to seek support for its introduction. In January 1997, Dubarry was informed that it would receive state support to introduce WCM over a period of 18 months to two years.

Production operations

Dubarry produces two ranges of shoes per year, spring/summer and autumn/winter. The marketing area observes market trends and provides a range brief. This identifies what is selling well and what the market is saying about the various designs on offer. It then makes suggestions for the coming season. Following this, the design area makes a number of prototypes. These are either new styles or modifications of current ones. Then a number of meetings are held with marketing and engineering and amendments are made until agreement is reached. The samples are then produced and distributed to the shops. Following the market's reaction and a minimum order, the company produces the new range.

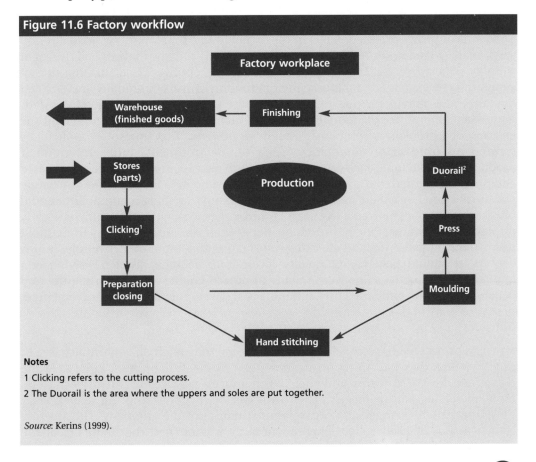

Figure 11.6 Factory workflow

Factory workplace

Warehouse (finished goods) ← Finishing ←

Stores (parts)   Production   Duorail[2]

Clicking[1]   Press

Preparation closing   Moulding

Hand stitching

Notes

1 Clicking refers to the cutting process.

2 The Duorail is the area where the uppers and soles are put together.

Source: Kerins (1999).

Introducing WCM at Dubarry

The initial steps to progress production efficiency were the technology audit in 1992 and then the ISO standard in 1994. Since the achievement of ISO 9001, Dubarry had become familiar with outsiders investigating its work process and testing its progress. The ISO experience heightened quality awareness and made the work operations more visible. However, many felt that they had not reaped the full benefits of this process. Although gaining accreditation to the standard had encouraged them to inspect work processes, it did not facilitate the necessary improvements. The company became involved in the WCM process partly to resolve this weakness. It felt that WCM would provide the skills necessary to improve the work system, which the ISO process had only recently begun to reveal.

With financial support from Forbairt, Dubarry decided to introduce WCM techniques to the factory floor. The WCM process was introduced in two phases. The first phase ran from February to December 1997, and the second phase from January to December 1998. First there were the early training workshops, consisting of a one-day management workshop, and a two-day supervisors' workshop. Over the following three months a management–union agreement was formulated. This was to underpin the change process necessary for the successful introduction of WCM. Under the terms of the agreement, no layoffs would result from the introduction of WCM, and a joint forum was set up to monitor developments.

To study Dubarry, three external consultants visited the company. Their report advised that modular manufacturing should be introduced in all areas of production. This would improve production by rapidly reducing lead times, improving quality and stock management, and reducing rejects and rework. Finally, they argued, it would simplify paperwork and reporting procedures. The report advised that the role of supervisors be expanded to increase their autonomy and accountability. It suggested that this role should include responsibility for efficiency, output, quality, safety, housekeeping and worker morale. Regarding quality, the report recommended the creation of a problem-solving environment so powerful that unresolved difficulties created an immediate emergency. Such an environment, built on modular production, would force each error and its underlying cause to be rectified at once. In addition, it suggested that specific quality targets be defined for each area and actual results measured on a daily basis. As part of the change, quality accountability should be specifically assigned and the targets and corrective actions should be visibly displayed in each area. Finally, the quality department should move away from its old reactive role of gathering and checking information to a more proactive role. In this context, it should help to set quality levels and facilitate problem-solving and improvement initiatives to ensure quality improved continually. Regarding the skill deficiencies, it recommended that a training and development plan be implemented.

Outcome

Six WCM project teams were set up and met the steering team on a monthly basis. At each meeting, they had to report on how they matched their team targets. At the outset, all the WCM teams and their 28 members were trained in project work, problem solving and teamwork. Their own weekly meetings and the related work slowly but surely changed the organisational nature of the company. The steering team was not in itself a new phenomenon, as it contained the members of the company executive. In contrast, the six WCM teams were new. They created completely new organisational linkages and strengthened collaborative structures that had previously been weak or non-existent. The composition and focus of the teams was important. The new style, material, and production groups reflected the efforts to deal with the work process from beginning to end. These three teams reflected a fundamentally different approach to a departmental approach. The quality and housekeeping teams focused on the underpinning support of the process. The hand-stitching team, on the other hand, dealt with an operation that was significantly outside the company's control but had an important bearing on its efficiency.

The company was now changing. Before the WCM project, each of the 28 team members had, for the most part, had a role within a particular department. Now they held additional responsibilities that went beyond their department and impacted on other areas of the company. As the groups grew in confidence and ability, they created political habitats that provided their own perspective and rationale and acted as a counter-pull to departmental influence.

At the core of the department was the specialised worker. Prior to this, the formal company thread ran from managing director to executive director to departments and then to individuals. The few modules that existed were as much a curiosity as anything else. Six relatively powerful planning teams now added to the team experience within Dubarry. Where before, many of their members rarely met senior management, they worked with them now on a monthly basis. The teams provided an additional fulcrum for expertise and perspective. Now as their knowledge and experience grows, they strengthen cross-departmental links and perspectives. This becomes possible because of a new and more broadly based conceptualisation that provides a necessary skill base to the effective implementation of modules.

Conclusion

Dubarry has begun a process of continuous improvement that will keep it busy for several years. It had already gone through significant change over the previous decade, and managed to survive and thrive, whereas most other shoe companies in Ireland have closed. Dubarry has also survived in a world where many other sectors, especially the high-tech ones, attract attention more easily. It does not produce an exciting product. Shoes are old hat. However, Dubarry has proven that even the oldest of hats can become exciting. Today it continues to produce high-quality and attractive products for its many satisfied customers.

Case adapted from Kerins (1999), by kind permission of the publishers.

Case questions

❶ Evaluate the WCM process as it has evolved to date at Dubarry. What steps do you think the firm should take to continue this initiative?

❷ Compare and contrast the production strengths and weaknesses of Dubarry with any other shoe company you are familiar with. Based on this analysis, what are the most urgent issues for the production manager at Dubarry to consider?

❸ The process of benchmarking involves looking at best practice either within the industry, or in a completely different field, in order to learn what improvements a firm can undertake.

    a. Suggest what types of firms and industry sectors the production team at Dubarry might benchmark.

    b. Select one of the firms or industry sectors you have nominated, and prepare a brief report on the areas of difference and improvement that Dubarry might consider.

❹ Evaluate the future of the shoe manufacturing sector in Ireland.

Keep up to date

www.dubarry.ie.
Conferring authority for the Qmark standard: www.excellence-ireland.ie.
National Standards Authority of Ireland: www.nsai.ie.
Health and Safety Authority: www.hsa.ie.
National Accreditation Board: www.forfas.ie/nab.
European Foundation for Quality Management: www.efqm.org.

Bibliography

Ahlstrom, D. (2000) 'Foresight Foundation Given Task of Making us Trailblazers', *Irish Times*, 9 March.

Boaden, R. (1998) 'Operations Management', in Hannigan, T. (1998) *Management: Concepts and Practices*, 2nd edition. London: Financial Times/Pitman Publishing.

Caulkin, S. (1999) 'Hammer breaks down the walls', *Observer*, 21 November.

Christopher, M. (1998) *Logistics and Supply Chain Management*, 2nd edition. London: Financial Times/Prentice Hall.

Crosby, P. B. (1992) *Completeness*. New York: Penguin Books.

Dale, B. and Plunkett, J. (1990) *Managing Quality*. Herts: Phillip Allan.

Evans, J. R. and Lindsay, W. M. (1996) *The Management and Control of Quality*. St Paul: West Publishing.

Garvin, D. A. (1987) 'Competing on the Eight Dimensions of Quality', *Harvard Business Review*, November–December.

Hammer, M. and Champy, J. (1993) *Reengineering the Corporation*. London: Nicholas Brealey.

Hayes, R. and Wheelwright, S, (1984) *Restoring the Competitive Edge: Competing through Manufacturing*. New York: John Wiley.

Hill, T. (2000) *Operations Management*. London: Macmillan.

Ho, S. K. (1999) *Operations and Quality Management*. London: International Thomson Business Press.

Ingle, R. (1999) 'TQM is Making its Impact on Irish Business', *Irish Times*, 25 January.

Juran, J. (1998) *Juran on Planning for Quality*. New York: Free Press.

Keegan, R. and Lynch, J. (1995), *World Class Manufacturing in an Irish Context*. Dublin: Oak Tree Press.

Kerins, A. (1999) *Sole Survivors: How Exceptional Companies Survive and Thrive at the Edge*. Dublin: Oak Tree Press.

National Authority for Occupational Safety and Health (Health and Safety Authority), Annual Report 1999.

OECD (Organisation for Economic Co-operation and Development) (1998) 'Main Science and Technology Indicators', 1997, 2, Paris: OECD.

O'Higgins, E. (1999) 'RyanAir: The Low Fares Airline', Cranfield: European Case Clearing House, Case 399–122–1.

Peters, G. (1999) *Waltzing with the Raptors: A Practical Roadmap to Protecting Your Company's Reputation.* New York: John Wiley.

Rangan, V. and Bell, M. (1998) 'Case Study: Dell Online', *Journal of Interactive Marketing*, 12 (4).

Roper, S. and Hewitt-Dundas, N. (1998) *Business Innovation in Ireland: Lessons for Managers.* Dublin: Oak Tree Press.

Russell, R. and Taylor, B. (2000) *Operations Management*, 3rd edition. New Jersey: Prentice Hall.

Schonberger, R. (1986) *World Class Manufacturing.* New York: Free Press.

Schonberger, R. (1990) *Building a Chain of Customers.* New York: Free Press.

Slack, N., Chambers, S., Harland, C., Harrison, A. and Johnston, R. (1998) *Operations Management*, 2nd edition. London: Financial Times/Pitman Publishing.

Wild, R. (1995) *Production and Operations Management: text and cases.* London: Cassell.

Womack, S. and Jones, D. (1996) *Lean Thinking: Banish Waste and Create Wealth in Your Corporation.* New York: Simon and Schuster.

Chapter 12 Business Ethics and Social Responsibility

12.1 Introduction

This chapter attempts to outline a range of views and issues around the themes of BUSINESS ETHICS and SOCIAL RESPONSIBILITY. The reader will be given an understanding of the terms 'business ethics' and 'social responsibility' and an outline of the key differences between these terms. The stakeholder view of business is examined, and the perspectives of stakeholder groups are analysed in an Irish context. The policies and procedures of CORPORATE GOVERNANCE are explained, with a view to understanding how governance and ethics practices can influence business strategy and decision making. Current issues for ethical businesses—the environment, WHISTLEBLOWING and crisis management are discussed. The case study at the end of the chapter gives insights into an Irish dimension on these questions.

12.2 The philosophy of business

Earlier in this book, the issues of corporate objectives and mission statements were discussed in some detail (Chapter 4). But before agreeing on a purpose and a set of objectives, every business organisation must clarify its fundamental purpose or reason for being in business. The twenty-first century has already witnessed a significant change in business attitudes, based on a widening of the business agenda (see Exhibit 12.1).

Exhibit 12.1 Typical business attitudes, twentieth and twenty-first century

Typical twentieth-century views:

Success is its own justification (the end justifies the means)
Leadership (right or wrong) is all powerful
We inform others on a 'need to know' basis
Business is serious and demands total commitment
Younger employees are better, cheaper and more docile
Our tribe is better than your tribe
There are winners and losers (and some survivors)
Non-profit-activities are second rate
My importance is proportional to what I take

Twenty-first-century views may be:

Long-term sustainable success depends on an ethical approach
Leadership reaches further by empowering others

Exhibit 12.1 Typical business attitudes, twentieth and twenty-first century *contd.*

Openness is the best long-term policy
Business with a shared purpose should be fun
The old and the young benefit from working together
Pool tribal strengths for the benefit of all
Win–win solutions are better in the long run
Worth is as important as wealth
Giving can be a sign of strength

Source: Davies (1999).

The broader business agenda which is now prevalent is influenced by the context within which business transactions take place. The Victorian view of business as a means of generating profits and providing employment has evolved into a wider, more inclusive philosophy of business, which moves from the concept of 'doing things right', to a more fundamental examination of whether business is, in fact, 'doing the right things'. The scale and pace of business growth is now such that global companies such as Microsoft generate more wealth than many national economies and have global power to match.

Davies (1997) presents five different ethical perspectives of modern-day business:

❶ **The Western Christians theological perspective**. This view suggests that Christian views will influence the operations of business. The principles of justice, respect and reconciliation will influence business decisions.

❷ **The industrial democracy perspective**. The separation of ownership and liability under company law has meant that shareholders have no formal responsibility for employees or for the community. However, the emergence of a philosophy of corporate governance towards the end of the twentieth century, suggests that business organisations should operate within a democratic framework. This view proposes that stakeholders in a business, such as employees and customers, should have a say in how the business is run and regulated.

❸ **The ecosystems perspective**. Advances in business have had serious effects on our personal and physical environments. Technological advances have positive and negative effects on the ecosystem and these effects should be measured and evaluated before proceeding with a new technology such as the use of pesticides. Business, by its nature, tends to take a short-term view of the physical environment, whereas the ecosystem demands a long-term global perspective. The ecosystem's perspective demands that ecological issues be raised to the top of the business agenda and that businesses would be evaluated according to how well they perform in relation to these issues.

❹ **The 'Friedmanite' perspective**. In 1970, the economist Milton Friedman published a landmark article 'The Social Responsibility of Business is to Increase its Profits'. In this article he defined the responsibilities of business and compared them with the responsibilities of government, charities and trade associations. The wrong-doings of business need to be reviewed by other parties, argued Friedman, but business is operating correctly if it reaches the profit objective. This perspective highlights the need for a careful and well-thought-through position on business ethics, in order that the criteria aspired to can be carefully applied and evaluated. Friedman's philosophy also suggests that organisations with too much of a focus on ethical issues may lose sight of the core objective of profits.

❺ The virtues perspective. The concept of this approach is to focus on the virtues of the individuals involved in the organisation. Solomon (1993) views the business as a community and as 'a culture with shared values and larger concerns'. Business, he suggests, exists to enrich society as well as to line people's pockets. This enrichment process depends on the character of individuals and in particular on the virtues of honesty, fairness and trust. As character is formed in youth, the argument is that business ethics should focus on character development and on how the organisation we are involved with will make us better people over the duration of our working lives. The virtues philosophy proposes that ethical issues be considered as part of the process of developing individuals.

Willmott and Flatters (1999) suggest that a new political economy is emerging: an economy which 'is an attempt to marry the principles of social cohesion and basic welfare with the economic necessity of enterprise and capitalism'. The development of this new economy is being driven by two factors: globalisation and the emergence of social capitalism.

The **globalisation** of business has affected every aspect of operations. Global sourcing has allowed companies to choose more competitive suppliers, regardless of location. Deregulation of trade, supported by the World Trade Organisation (WTO) and the EU, encourages business to open up to free competition and lower prices. Information technology has opened up global superhighways for the exchange of goods and ideas. Klein (2000) suggests that the move towards globalised corporate power and corporate branding has unwittingly militarised opposition. Highlighting the consequences of global brands for employees, human rights and the environment, her book has become a core text for anti-globalisation activists.

Globalisation can also be argued to be of most benefit to the richer economies where the resources already exist to take advantage of the new opportunities. This increasing polarisation between the 'have's and the 'have not's has driven the search for a more caring and inclusive version of capitalism. These efforts, typified by the Blair and Clinton governments, try to balance the laws of the market with the need to be inclusive and socially just. The modern organisation is reflecting this approach by adapting to the need for partnerships with a range of interest groups, for fair and equal treatment and for companies to be socially responsible.

Exhibit 12.2 Your own shopping experiences

Having just finished your college class in business ethics, you decide to call in to your local supermarket and do some shopping on the way home. While making your choices from the shelf displays, you are surprised at how many ethics-related questions occur to you:

- Are the vegetables guaranteed pesticide free?
- Did the coffee producer pay a fair price for the coffee beans purchased from a third-world supplier?
- Why do people buy cigarettes when one-third of smokers (including the Marlboro man himself) die from cancer?
- Is this piece of steak free from hormones and BSE?

Exhibit 12.2 Your own shopping experiences *contd.*

- Have those Spanish strawberries received irradiation treatment to keep them fresh for days after picking?
- Are these cornflakes made from genetically modified maize?
- Are the shop workers being paid fairly and above the minimum wage?
- Are the plastic bags recyclable?
- Does the retailer return any of the profits made into the community?

Do you know the answers to any of these questions? Should you be concerned? Can you suggest what issues in business ethics concern you personally?

12.3 Social responsibility

Dalton and Cosier (1982) describe four types of activities carried out by organisations:

▶ legal and responsible acts

▶ legal but irresponsible acts

▶ illegal but responsible acts

▶ illegal and irresponsible acts.

This typology illustrates the widening dimensions of business decision making. It is no longer enough to merely keep within the boundaries of the law: organisations must also consider the responsibilities involved in decision making, and how business decisions will be viewed by audiences outside the boundaries of the organisation. Companies such as The Body Shop and Marks and Spencer, influenced by the personalities of their founders, have expressed a vision of corporate responsibility which extends beyond mere profits.

Drucker (1989) pointed out that social responsibility is the remit of the individual manager. 'It requires of the manager that he assumes responsibility for the public good, that he subordinate his actions to an ethical standard of conduct, and that he restrain his self-interest and his authority wherever their exercise would infringe upon the common good and upon the freedom of the individual.'

Figure 12.1 The continuum towards citizenship

Minimalist	Discretionary	Strategic
Compliance with legislation integrated into business	Philanthropy/charitable giving	Citizenship

Source: McIntosh *et al.*, (1998).

Based on the continuum shown in Figure 12.1, McIntosh *et al.* (1998) present four models of social responsibility, which are not mutually exclusive, but represent different modes of corporate behaviour:

❶ *Business is amoral* based on profit making, and has no responsibility other than its economic and legal obligations.

❷ *Business is a moral activity* based on profit making and has an obligation to act for social betterment, meaning the betterment of the whole of society.

❸ *A business is a community* based on a corporate identity, which may be just for profit, not just for profit, or not at all for profit, and which recognises that a business has a social and economic role.

❹ *A business is a network*—it does not have a corporate identity and is neither moral nor amoral in its purpose; it is fluid and may be transitory and based on project management.

Elkington (1997) describes the 'triple bottom line' that businesses today must address, which covers the economic, environmental and social performance of the organisation. He argues that economic performance is dependent on successful social and environmental performance, rather than the other way around. This wider assessment of business relationships and responsibilities has led to a consideration of a wider agenda for business performance. Sharplin (1985) proposes that the relationships between business and society should be defined in a new form of social contract. Figure 12.2 shows the complex web of relationships brought about by the social contract view; and also the extent of involvement by parties external to the organisation itself, such as the government and other distinct interest groups.

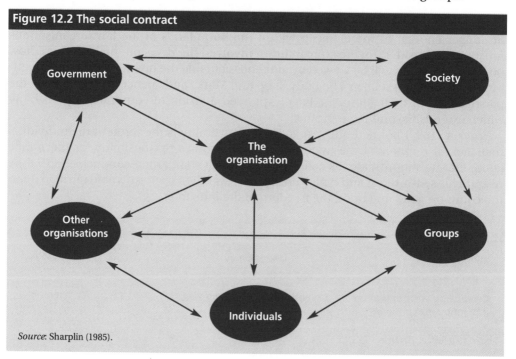

Figure 12.2 The social contract

Source: Sharplin (1985).

In the Irish context, the general public do not express a high level of trust in big business. Recent scandals in corporate Ireland have made the Irish public more suspicious of boardroom activities. Irish people are also quite community-minded rather than individualist, and express a willingness to fund better public services through the raising of taxing rates.

Exhibit 12.3 Responsible business: Irish perspectives

A survey of 500 Irish adults conducted in Ireland in 1999 looked at Irish attitudes to the conduct of businesses.

It found that 75 per cent of Irish consumers believe that companies are more interested in looking after their shareholders than their staff. Only 14 per cent of the Irish consumers trust Irish banks a great deal, compared with 30 per cent in a similar survey of UK citizens.

In general, 40 per cent of those questioned trust banks to some degree, and 26 per cent trust insurance companies. Irish-owned companies are nearly twice as likely to be trusted a great deal (50 per cent) as multinational companies (26 per cent). And 75 per cent of people trust An Post to be responsible and fair, while 64 per cent trust Eircom. Two-thirds of those questioned do not believe that industry and commerce pay enough attention to their social responsibilities.

Source: Amarach Consulting (2000).

12.4 The stakeholder view

In 1985, Freeman propounded the STAKEHOLDER approach to strategic management. He suggested that a range of interest groups outside of the organisation itself have an interest or a stake in how the business does business and goes about making its decisions. The groups he identified includes owners, employees, customers, suppliers and the community. Each group is in itself a wide audience, and each member of that audience differs in the extent of their involvement, interest and willingness to engage with the organisation.

The focus of stakeholder theory is that organisations should move from a *share*holder perspective to a *stake*holder perspective, where a stakeholder is defined as 'any group or individual that can affect or is affected by the achievement of the firm's objectives' (Freeman 1985). This idea is inherently attractive and acknowledges the ripple effect of business decisions on a wider audience. Companies adopting the principles of stakeholder management favour an inclusive approach, where a wide range of stakeholders is involved in the decision-making process. The Volkswagen motor company, for example, views its employees as 'workholders' and they receive part of their wages in 'time' shares. These shares can be cashed in to gain extra holidays, towards early retirement, or as a cushion against redundancy. The employees using this scheme become more involved with the company's performance. The company views the scheme as a way of negotiating more flexibility with employees, while improving performance and hence the security of employment (McIntosh *et al.* 1998).

The practice of the stakeholder approach raises several issues. First, the dialogue with stakeholders may turn out to be a lengthy and convoluted process. Peters (1999) suggests prioritising stakeholder groups according to their degree of concern with an issue at stake and the extent to which the groups are directly affected by the issue. The only problem with this approach is that, recently, organisations have experienced outside pressure from interest groups highly concerned with an issue, even if they are not directly affected by it. For example, the eco-warriors who camped in the Glen of the Downs in Wicklow, as a protest against the destruction of an ancient forest to make way for a wider road, were a group of people from outside the immediate area who shared a deep concern about environmental destruction. Their protest during 1997–2000 involved living in the forest, taking several court actions and serving prison sentences.

Table 12.1 Degrees of stakeholder concern

Little concern shown

Clarity of issue	Not represented by clear stakeholder view
Organisational status	Company perceived as having a limited impact on issue, no calls for action
Ethical status	Potential contravention of widely accepted local, legal or social norms

Moderately concerned

Stakeholder profile	Of concern to local, national, and international stakeholders
Clarity of issue	Clear majority stakeholder view, unfocused/indirect public campaign implicating company
Organisational status	Perceived as having significant influence on an issue, calls for long-term action by company
Ethical status	Potential contravention of widely accepted local, national and international legal or social norms.

Highly concerned

Stakeholder profile	Of concern to local, national and international stakeholders
Clarity of issue	Clear majority stakeholder view, well-organised/concerted public campaign directed at company
Organisational status	Seen as major influence on issue, consistent calls for action
Ethical status	Likely contravention of widely accepted local, national and international legal or social norms

Source: Peters (1999).

A second issue relates to where the interests of the business owners or shareholders fit in with the varying concerns of stakeholders. If the company spends too much time answering to the demands of stakeholder groups, the value of the company can languish and shareholder confidence is lost. A third issue is how much information to share with stakeholders (Table 12.2). This is a particular issue in Ireland, where companies are reluctant to conform to even the minimum reporting requirements set down in law. As a response to this issue, companies themselves may say that information is of no value to the uninformed audience, or that the information sought would be valuable to competitors.

However, societal demands are such that many organisations are now acknowledging the issue of stakeholder management and view it as an opportunity to pre-empt concerns which could otherwise have a whirlwind effect. Positive inclusion of stakeholder views may also be an effective means of avoiding the need for further legislation or regulation. Practitioners are now grappling with the question of how to measure and evaluate stakeholder involvement and response. The area of social and ethical audits is addressed in Section 12.9, but first, in the sections that follow, we look at the views of the most significant stakeholder groups in an Irish context.

Stakeholder	Information regularly obtained	Comment
Table 12.2 Typical information available to different stakeholders in a company		
Shareholders	Annual report and accounts	Limited to what the organisation wants its shareholders to know
Investment analysts, e.g. in stockbroking companies; also journalists	Regular updates of progress, sometimes face-to-face meetings	Better informed but still possible for the organisation to mislead
Main company board	Relatively full information but possible to mislead; legal obligation to be properly informed and to inform	Full disclosure of all issues is assisted by the character and independence of any non-executive directors
Senior managers	Detailed information in some areas but rely on managers to bring issues to their notice—remember Nick Leeson of Barings Bank?	Likely to be without the full picture available to the main board; can be the 'whistle-blower' of unethical, illegal or improper conduct
Managers	Some information but often incomplete	Can sometimes be the 'whistleblower' but under considerable pressure to conform to company rules
Employees	Usually only limited information unless the workers have representatives on a supervising board	New EU directives make senior representation more likely and offer some protection here

Source: Lynch (2000).

12.4.1 Owners and senior management

The owners and the board of management make decisions that will impinge on all the other stakeholders involved with an organisation. For this reason, they cannot afford to adopt a purely internal perspective on the decisions at hand. On the other hand, board-level decisions are made with major conflicts of interest at play. Owners and boards are under pressure from shareholders and potential investors to maximise profits. They can also be expected to behave with enlightened self-interest, in other words, to take decisions which will assure their own future and that of the organisation, or exonerate themselves from blame. Decisions made by a group of managers or a board can suffer from GROUP THINK where the views of the majority or the more powerful become the accepted decisions.

The decisions of the owner or the board will determine the future direction of the firm, the culture within the organisation and its attitude to other stakeholder groups. The large number of international firms with a presence in Ireland make an interesting case study in this regard. Many international firms came to Ireland in the 1960s and 1970s, to towns that had little experience of industrialisation. Throughout the 1980s, there was a national policy emphasis on the development of closer supply linkages between the multinationals and the local economy. In the 1990s, the Irish economy switched its focus to high-technology and service industries. By the end of the twentieth century, multinationals had successfully integrated into the Irish economy and were competing for a shrinking pool of skilled labour. Over the four decades, the orientation of the owners and managers had shifted from being the providers of jobs and wages in return for a generous level of grant support, to being participants in a local and European economy where research and knowledge are at a premium.

The current question facing owners and managers is how much information to disclose to stakeholder groups about current and future activities of the organisation. Terms used by boards and senior managers such as 'rightsizing', 'reengineering' and 'downshifting' are interpreted differently by the range of stakeholder groups. The use of public relations activities to communicate the corporate viewpoint has been unmasked through the efforts of pressure groups and monitoring authorities. For example, the cases of Shell and Brent Spar or British Nuclear Fuels at Sellafield, were both highlighted by the non-governmental organisation Greenpeace.

Exhibit 12.4 *Roger and Me*

Roger and Me is a documentary film produced and narrated by Michael Moore. The subject is Moore's home town of Flint in Michigan, the home of General Motors. From the mid-1970s to the early 1980s, Flint was affected by GM plant closures which reduced the workforce employed in the car plants there from 79,000 at peak to 49,000 in 1989.

In the film, Moore talks to people affected by the closure—employees, corporate management, publicists and townspeople. The company representatives talk about events in distant terms, mentioning plant closures and the loss of product lines. For those most directly involved in the situation, the employees, the language used is different, with people talking about job losses and the loss of their livelihood. There was little prospect of finding work at another car plant, because during this time most US motor companies relocated some production to Mexico, where wages were much lower and there was far less regulation of business and employment conditions.

The 'Roger' of the title was Roger Smith, the CEO of General Motors. Throughout the film, Moore attempts to meet Roger Smith to ask him directly about the closures. Along the way he meets a number of publicists and corporate spokespersons. In his quest for truth, he finds that the truth itself depends on whose shoes you are in—those of the corporate spokesman, the redundant employee, or some of the affluent members of Flint society who are totally unaffected by the closures. Michael Moore never gets to speak to Roger Smith face to face.

The film met with a range of reactions from the viewing public. Some applauded it as putting forward the views of the working person, most affected by corporate decisions, in an interesting way. Others saw it as a personal vendetta by Moore, and suggested that Flint had an unhealthy dependence on the motor industry for employment. Moore himself has since been making a successful career as a corporate commentator, comedian and larger than life personality.

Source: Moore (1989).

On a positive note, one term that has great currency in the boardroom of the early twenty-first century is the concept of GAINSHARING. The idea is that by sharing the gains made by the organisation and management with the workforce, employees become more directly involved as stakeholders in the fortunes of the company. The sharing of gains is usually negotiated in return for agreements about more flexible working conditions and productivity. Gainsharing is seen as a win–win situation in that there is mutual advantage for the employees and the management of the organisation.

A final issue for consideration in the boardroom concerns an organisation's ethical position as an employer. The rights expected by employees include the entitlement to a fair day's work and a fair day's pay, to a safe workplace, to equality of opportunity and to reward by merit and to the right to representation by a trade union. In Ireland, these rights are reflected in legislation on working time, minimum wages, anti-discrimination and pay, health and safety, equality, and in the Irish Constitution itself. Visionary employers, such as the ESB, have taken their own initiatives to inform employees of their rights.

Exhibit 12.5 The Electricity Supply Board: promoting equality

The ESB has an established Equality Office, as part of its human resources function. The Equality Office is responsible for informing employees of their personal rights and legislative entitlements and for promoting the equality agenda throughout the organisation. The work of the office includes:
- providing a flexible working environment by offering working conditions which allow for flexitime, work sharing, job sharing, crèche facilities and support for education
- clear guidelines on issues such as bullying and sexual harassment
- encouragement of more female apprentices
- training for local management and staff.

The ESB views affirmative action as a positive way of encouraging staff loyalty and enhancing the company's profile as an employer in an increasingly competitive and soon to be deregulated marketplace.

Source: ESB (1992, 1999).

12.4.2 Employees

Most people spend a significant part of their lifetimes at work, and most people work for some form of business organisation. Employee expectations for a working life are changing. Staff now expect to have a higher quality of working life, to be treated fairly, to be offered some options in managing the balance between work and personal responsibilities, to be offered training and educational facilities, and to have social and leisure opportunities through the workplace. In a tighter labour market, employers are also recognising the need to offer differential facilities and incentives to attract and retain key staff.

The UN Declaration of Human Rights, signed in 1948, sets down basic human rights, including rights relevant to the workplace. These include the right to fair and equal treatment, freedom from slavery, equality before the law, privacy, the right to be judged innocent until proven guilty, freedom of movement, freedom of beliefs, the right to assembly, the right to work and to join a trade union, the right to leisure and holidays, and the right to a decent standard of living. More recently, these rights have been specifically addressed in a European context through the EU Social Charter. The charter which has been signed by most EU states sets out worker entitlements in areas such as working time, holidays, a minimum wage, special leave entitlements, such as maternity and paternity leave, and health and safety in the workplace. In Ireland, the requirements of the Social Charter have been implemented through legislation and the establishment of monitoring bodies such as the Health and Safety Authority and the Equality Authority. The Equality Authority, established by the Employment

Equality Act 1998 is empowered to prevent discrimination in employment on nine grounds:

- ▶ marital status
- ▶ age
- ▶ religion
- ▶ membership of the traveller community
- ▶ disability
- ▶ race
- ▶ sexual orientation
- ▶ gender
- ▶ family status.

The 1998 Employment Equality Act also defines sexual harassment for the first time in Irish law, as 'Unwanted physical intimacy, requests for sexual favours, spoken words and gestures and the display or circulation of written words, pictures or other materials. Unwelcome requests or conduct that could reasonably be regarded as sexually or otherwise on the gender ground offensive, humiliating or intimidating, shall constitute sexual harassment.'

The Equality Authority is currently consulting with a wide range of employers and other relevant parties to develop a pro-active equality conscious approach to workplace issues and to enact more specific equal status legislation in the future.

Exhibit 12.6 Misogyny in government departments

A new report on gender equality in government departments found evidence of 'misogyny' and a 'macho culture' in some departments. The report, commissioned by an equality committee as part of the civil service's strategic management initiative, found that the lower grades in the service were overwhelmingly female, while the higher grades were dominated by men.

It found that, while female staff accounted for 54 per cent of higher executive officers, their proportion tapered off higher up the scale. The report states that in general: 'women progress less rapidly than men from every shared recruitment grade. Progress towards achieving gender balance remains painfully slow and cannot be achieved at assistant principal level or higher under prevailing conditions'.

One of the factors cited as responsible for women being promoted less was that they were more likely to job-share than men. Only 1 per cent of male civil servants were job-sharing at the time of the survey, while 14 percent of women were. Job-sharing had a negative image within the service among both women and men and was thought to imply a reduced commitment to the job and to have an adverse effect on promotion prospects. The report comments: 'Management at the core in most government departments is an almost exclusively male domain. This segregated pattern both reflects and helps to perpetuate the exclusion.'

Source: Coulter (2000).

BULLYING behaviour in the workplace is currently being highlighted as causing problems with work performance and having serious and stressful effects on the person being bullied. The Health and Safety Authority (1998) defines bullying as 'repeated aggression, verbal, psychological or physical, conducted by an individual or group against another person or person. Bullying is where aggression or cruelty, viciousness intimidation or a need to humiliate, dominate the relationships. Isolated incidents of aggressive behaviour, while to be condemned, should not be described as bullying.'

Exhibit 12.7 Bullying barometer

You are being bullied when:

- Your presence or opinions are ignored.
- You are denied information about your performance.
- You are given an unmanageable workload.
- You are given unreasonable deadlines.
- You are humiliated or ridiculed.
- Your work is excessively monitored.
- Gossip and rumour are spread about you.
- Faults are continually found with your work.

Source: Pollard (2000).

The effects of bullying are emotional, cognitive, behavioural and physiological. The most serious effects are anxiety, fear and depression, which can lead to suicide. The effects on the organisation as a whole can include:

▶ increased absenteeism

▶ low motivation

▶ reduced productivity

▶ reduced efficiency

▶ hasty decision-making

▶ poor industrial relations.

Those most vulnerable to bullying are individuals who are in some way different due to age, gender, education, shyness, disability, membership of a trade union, challenging behaviour (which can lead to victimisation), being new to the workforce or returning to work after a long absence, religion, noticeable physical characteristics, or a past personal history which the individual does not want disclosed, for example, having a prison record. The bullying can be by supervisors, an individual, or a group of work mates. Some Irish companies, both large and small, have an anti-bullying policy in place, which sets out informal and formal procedures to be followed where there is an indication of bullying behaviour. Under the 1989 Health and Safety at Work Act, employers are responsible for ensuring a safe place at work, in psychological and physical terms. Bullying policies may be addressed in the safety statement which employers are required to make under the Act. Work-related stress may be covered by the provisions of the Health and Safety Act, or it may be related to the issues of discrimination covered in the 1998 Employment Equality Act.

The current environment of partnership and co-determination in Irish industrial relations raises the question of the relevance of trade unions in modern industrial society. The right to be represented by a trade union and the right of the individual to choose whether he wants to be a member of a union, are both rights which are enshrined in Irish law. While unions are acknowledged to play a significant role in negotiating for better conditions and providing an employee 'voice', there is concern that the relevance of union membership is being eroded through the partnership approach and through the practice of human resource management, which, by taking a proactive approach to the management of resources, may sideline the impact and relevance of the trade unions collectivist approach. Flood and Stiles (1997) suggest that trade unions have an important regulatory impact on the ethical behaviour of managers. Non-union employees record greater pay dispersion, have fewer grievance and disciplinary procedures and higher labour turnover. Employee representation on boards of management is a logical way for unions to formalise their relationships with businesses, and this experience has been received differently throughout the EU. The experience of worker directors in Germany is supported by company law, whereas in Ireland and the UK the admission of worker directors to the board has been limited to the semi-state sector and to some private companies such as Waterford Glass.

The modern workplace demands a high level of competence and loyalty from the employee. This raises issues of confidentiality, security and privacy which are part of the legal and psychological contract between employer and employee. In the workplace, the employee is asked to provide personal information, handle confidential information and sign agreements relating to intellectual property rights on any innovative developments. The employer in turn, makes decisions with regard to salary and rewards, medical data and testing, surveillance of employees and access to personal information held on computer systems. While some of these concerns have been addressed through legislation on data protection and freedom of information, there is a continuing conflict between the employer's requirements for confidential information about the individual and the employee's willingness to surrender privacy and information which she may feel is of no relevance to work performance.

12.4.3 The financial institutions

Financial institutions have multiple roles and responsibilities in modern society. They invest money on behalf of other groups (institutional investors) or on behalf of individuals. Such investments require a long-term relationship between the parties concerned and a level of trust that monies invested will reap a fair return. Financial institutions also have an influential role in society in the way that they conduct their own business. In Ireland, the business of the financial institutions is monitored by the Minister for Finance, the Central Bank, the Ombudsman for the Credit Institutions and a range of voluntary codes of practice.

Financial institutions, in many instances, are dealing with clients who are looking for expertise, professionalism and impartiality. In recent years, a series of revelations about the behaviour of the financial institutions in Ireland, have shown that in some cases profit is more important than respect for the customer.

A significant development in the investment environment has been the rise of ethical investment funds. While socially responsible investment was initially seen as a protest movement against large corporations that were involved in defence contracts, tobacco and chemicals, it also revealed the influence of corporations on global issues, such as the environment, and the harmful consequences of their involvement. As the scope for ethics-conscious investors is widening, corporations are recognising the situation as an opportunity to examine their own activities, pre-empt attacks from pressure groups and widen their appeal to a broader range of investors.

Exhibit 12.8 Churning

Churning is the creation of excessive financial transactions for the purpose of generating commission, rather than in the best interests of the client. In June 1998, *Magill* magazine exposed a wholesale churning culture within the Irish Life insurance company. Irish Life is one of the country's largest companies (now known as Irish Life and Permanent). The practice was to convince customers that existing policies were no longer in their best interests and that new policies should be taken out. This did not benefit the customer at all, but generated commission for the insurance company employee.

The true extent of the churning and the amounts—believed to have been millions of pounds—of which customers were defrauded, have never been established independently. Some claims were brushed off. If, for instance, and insurance broker churned your Irish Life policy, you had no comeback. You were told the broker was your agent, not the insurance company's. Irish Life announced that over the previous five years it had sacked twenty-one employees for 'gross misconduct'. It condemned the *Magill* allegations as 'simply not true'. The company carried out a limited review-and-compensation exercise and the Oireachtas Committee on Enterprise and Small Business made an ineffective intervention, but everyone soon entered a 'forward-looking' mode.

Source: Summarised from Kerrigan and Brennan (1999).

The criteria used by ethical investment funds to determine their PORTFOLIO can be negative, positive and/or an active dialogue with companies. (McIntosh *et al.* 1998). Negative criteria involves drawing up a list of corporate activities which are deemed unacceptable, such as alcohol or animal testing, and excluding the companies with interests in these areas. Investors may be asked to specify their own individual criteria. The positive criteria approach means rewarding companies which have demonstrated commitment to issues such as community involvement, positive employment policies, or waste management. The active dialogue approach involves the investing body building closer relationships with the business community to encourage more positive improvements and indicate areas about which investors have expressed particular concern. This is particularly useful for firms which are keen to attract ethical investors, but do not yet measure up to all the requirements.

Exhibit 12.9 Ethical investing goes mainstream

Socially responsible investing (SRI) is becoming a buzzword in Britain, and interest is growing in Europe, particularly in countries with strong environmental records. Regulations introduced in Britain in 2000 make it obligatory for pension fund trustees to state the extent to which they take social, environmental or ethical considerations into account in choosing their investments. The publishers of the FTSE index are working on a new index series to be launched in summer 2001. Called FTSE4good, the indices will track ethical investments.

In Ireland, Friends First, a company with Quaker roots, is so far the only institution to offer an ethical fund. The fund excludes all companies involved in producing alcohol, those involved in animal testing, factory farming or military goods. Positive criteria include conservation, use of natural resources and avoidance of pollution. The fund has 30 per cent of its portfolio invested in Irish equities.

Source: O'Sullivan (2001).

The massive growth in the scale of global financial transactions in the 1980s led to revelations in the USA and the UK about the activities of insider traders. Employees within a financial organisation, either because of their rank or the nature of their duties, are privy to the most up-to-date information about financial markets and practices. This information can be exploited either for the gain of the individual or the financial institution, in a way that is unethical. International names such as Barings Bank and Drexel Burham Lambert are well known, but there are interesting examples of such activities closer to home.

Exhibit 12.10 Non-resident bank accounts

In Ireland, bank accounts opened by non-residents in the 1980s and 1990s were not liable for Deposit Interest Retention Tax (DIRT). This regulation offered an attractive loophole for tax evaders willing to open non-resident accounts and make a false declaration about their place of residence. By the late 1980s the Revenue Commissioners were aware of the problem with bogus non-residential accounts and asked the country's largest bank, AIB, to investigate its own situation. In 1991, AIB investigated 87,000 non-resident accounts and found that 53,000 of them, holding some €762 million on deposit, were bogus.

The extent of non-residential fraud was revealed in 1998 in the *Sunday Independent* and *Magill* magazine and had widespread reverberations. The Revenue Commissioners requested that all the banks involved check the bona fides of such accounts and began the process of collecting the DIRT tax due on such accounts. This process was reinforced by the extensive investigations of the Dáil Public Accounts Committee, which demanded that the banks account properly for the situation. Legislation was passed to establish more stringent criteria for non-residents, particularly since it emerged that the loopholes available had been used for money laundering. Some account holders who were proven to be fraudulent are suing the bank concerned, on the basis that they could not take advantage of a tax amnesty in 1993 and ended up paying more to the Revenue Commissioners when they were found out later. No individual bankers or account holders were prosecuted.

Source: Summarised from Kerrigan and Brennan (1999).

12.4.4 Suppliers

According to Knight (1974), the principles of fair competition in markets mean that:

▶ Prices are equivalent to those needed to provide an economic return to efficient companies.
▶ There is a choice of goods and services for consumers, recognising that there are different sections of market demand.
▶ Innovation is encouraged to allow the development of new processes, products, services and forms of business.
▶ There is fair trade between purchasers and sellers and fair competition between sellers.

The cut and thrust of modern business practices has enormous implications for supply-sector businesses. Concepts such as RE-ENGINEERING and JUST-IN-TIME manufacturing (see Chapter 11) have caused suppliers to be more cost-conscious and reduce delivery times. Larger suppliers have used their competitive strength to build monopolistic or cartel arrangements. Large companies are also in a strong position to dictate terms and conditions to smaller firms supplying them.

Exhibit 12.11 'Hello money'

For years, supermarkets extracted payments from suppliers in return for accepting their goods, or for placing the goods in prominent positions. This was known as 'hello money'. Suppliers could also be left waiting for six months to get paid, involuntarily providing the stores with credit. The 1987 Groceries Order Act banned 'hello money' and some other practices.

In 1998, a firm called Retail Logistics was set up by a former director of the Superquinn supermarket chain. While Retail Logistics was an independent company, an RTE investigation in 1999 revealed its links with the Superquinn chain of supermarkets. Suppliers who wanted to 'support' Superquinn could make payments to Retail Logistics. Superquinn provided management services to Retail Logistics, which paid fees for the services carried out.

Superquinn came under investigation by the Director of Consumer Affairs and announced that it would discontinue the practice. Suppliers were nervous about discussing the pressures on them to support supermarkets and claims that Superquinn was not the only chain requesting support were brushed aside.

Source: Summarised from Kerrigan and Brennan (1999).

EU regulations regarding the enforcement of free and fair competition rules led to the passing of the Competition Act in Ireland in 1991. The Act covers mergers, sale of a business, agreements between suppliers and resellers, refusal to supply and cartels. While the Act places obligations not to act in a way that might be anti-competitive, it is also of benefit to businesses as it provides protection against aggressive behaviour by larger businesses.

The Fair Trade movement began as an effort by non-government agencies working in third world countries to gain a more equal partnership for the goods produced, such as handicrafts and coffee. Oxfam first initiated the idea of selling Fair Trade goods through its chain of shops and clearly indicating the fair prices and simpler distribution chains involved. Fair Trade goods are growing sales at an average of 5 per cent in Europe. Items sold through Fair Trade principles include bananas, coffee, cocoa, tea and chocolate; in Ireland, Fair Trade now accounts for almost 1 per cent of the catering coffee market (Consumer Choice 1999).

12.4.5 Consumers

The concept of a fair deal for the consumer is most developed in northern European countries, where there are a number of Ombudsmen and a range of powerful consumer groups. Ireland lags behind in the area of a strong voice for the consumer, but perhaps this will change now that the sole Irish Commissioner at EU level has responsibility for consumer affairs.

When buying goods and services, consumers have intrinsic rights. These include the right to buy goods or services which are fairly priced, safe, perform to a reasonable standard, are fairly promoted and sold and give the buyer enough information to enable an informed choice to be made. These rights are supported by legislation in Ireland. The Sale of Goods Act 1980, the Consumer Information Act 1978 and the Consumer Credit Act 1995 are the most relevant pieces of legislation offering the consumer rights and redress. The modern principle of product liability places the onus on the manufacturer or service provider for defects or damages incurred through product usage or consumption.

A third area of interest in consumer ethics is the subject of advertising. The EU has stated that advertising must not mislead and that the consumer should have sufficient information to make a free choice. The Irish advertising industry's self-regulating body, the Advertising Standards Authority, states that all advertising should be 'legal, decent, honest and truthful and should be prepared with a sense of responsibility to the consumer and to society' (Office of the Director of Consumer Affairs 1999). However, the absence of strict regulation on product labelling and product claims of a scientific or medical nature leaves the Irish consumer reliant on the activities of the Director of Consumer Affairs or voluntary consumer groups such as the Consumers' Association.

The ethics involved in the actual act of consumption itself imply the consent of the consumer. There is also the relationship of trust with the supplier of goods and services which are implied to be safe and reasonable to use. The tobacco industry in Ireland offers an interesting example of the various interest groups and stakeholders involved in the production and consumption of a good which is proven to be harmful, yet is for sale in every shop and supermarket in Ireland and is actually enjoying a revival in sales due to the growth in the younger age groups' smoking habits.

Table 12.3 Smoking statistics, Ireland 2000

Percentage of cancers linked to smoking	30%
Number of people dying of smoking related illness every year	6,000-7,000
Percentages of adults who smoke	31% (was 28% in 1994)
Percentages of adult smokers who begin before age 18	80%
Percentage of 15-17 year olds who smoke	34%
Value of tobacco taxes to the Irish Exchequer in 1997	€915 million
Number of people employed by the tobacco industry in Ireland	1,000
Estimated value of the Irish cigarette market in 1999	€1.27 billion

Source: Sheridan (2000).

The ethics of consumption have been further blurred by the Internet and electronic shopping. In this marketplace, the consumer is buying goods which are only seen or described on screen, from a supplier who may be unknown, though possibly at a significant price discount. While consumers theoretically have the same rights when shopping electronically, the fact that much of the trade is across national borders makes it difficult or uneconomic to pursue rogue traders. There is also widespread concern about the distribution of offensive and illegal materials over the Internet, without any mechanisms to control purchasers and viewers of such materials. It remains to be seen whether the European Commission or individual governments will be able to organise a regulatory framework for this medium of distribution.

12.4.6 Government

The government of a nation acts both as a mirror to the society being governed and as a leader and instigator of change within the society. Almost every decision taken at government level has an ethical dimension, for example, social welfare, trade, wage agreements, taxation, health and education. Another consideration for a government in preparing solutions to a problem is whether to act through legislation or a self-regulatory framework. In recent years, government support of free-market economics in Ireland has led to PRIVATISATION of some state-run businesses; and self-regulation being preferred to complex legislation. The passing of the Freedom of Information Act, which allows any individual access to information held in any government department or body has been an important part of the progress towards providing information about how government decisions are made and more transparency about the decision-making process itself. The establishment of several Tribunals of Inquiry in the late 1990s (see Section 12.5) has proven an important system for investigating events outside of the traditional adversarial legal system, and the tribunals themselves have provided information about the close relationships between business and politics in Ireland.

Government bodies established to carry out an investigative role, for example, the Ombudsman, or the Health and Safety Authority, have complained of a lack of resources which restrains the proper fulfilment of their duties. Investigations can also be limited by a shortage of expertise and by weak legislation; for example, the fines for breaches of Health and Safety legislation are often very low. At a national level, there is also a lack of political will to pursue serious cases of fraud brought against businesses due to the conflict of interests between governments, politicians and business people. Few individuals have ever been jailed in the Republic of Ireland on foot of a serious fraud charge.

Exhibit 12.12 Patrick Gallagher

Patrick Gallagher inherited a building empire, the Gallagher Group, at the age of 22, after his father died in 1974. It was a time of office-block building and speculation, and Patrick Gallagher joined in the buying and selling activity. The company also established its own bank—Merchant Banking Limited, which channelled its own funds as well as taking deposits from the public. The Gallagher Group failed due to the collapse of a land deal based on a site in St. Stephen's Green, Dublin. The company liquidators found that most of the financial assets of Merchant Banking Limited had been syphoned off to fund the Gallagher Group. Merchant Banking Limited had a subsidiary in Belfast, Merbro Finance. In April 1988, Patrick Gallagher was arrested and charged with theft of money belonging to Merbro and with giving false information. He was sent to jail in Northern Ireland in 1990.

In the Republic of Ireland, the Gallagher Group liquidator found several possible offences in the company's practices. In 1991, the Director of Public Prosecutions, who had received the liquidator's report in 1984, decided not to proceed with a prosecution.

Patrick Gallagher completed his sentence and now lives outside Ireland.

Source: Summarised from Kerrigan and Brennan (1999).

12.4.7 Non-governmental organisations

NON-GOVERNMENTAL ORGANISATIONS (NGOs) represent a broad spectrum of organisations, voluntary or professional, whose purpose is to represent or campaign on an issue or an agenda. This loose description can cover everything from a residents' association to a highly organised body with many employees such as Greenpeace. As

NGOs have become more experienced and achieve success, the issues and agendas that they campaign about have moved from being peripheral to being mainstream on the business agenda. The current challenge to managers is to decide whether to consider relevant NGOs as adversaries or as partners to business. To date, NGOs have proven that they can be a powerful influence on the business agenda; and business managers have learnt that bringing on board the NGOs early on in the decision-making process may pre-empt difficulties later on, as well as being a positive influence on the overall process.

The growth of NGOs can be attributed to a loss of credibility of governments (Schwartz and Gibb 1999). The hierarchical structures of government are slow to recognise issues and emerging agendas and there is usually a significant time lag before the legislative framework processes those concerns. Citizens with particular interests or deeply felt concerns increasingly look to NGOs to speak and act for them. NGOs in turn have increasing legitimacy gained through public support, professional experience or a demonstrated commitment to an area of interest.

Exhibit 12.13 Activists: sizing up the problem

Company checklist

1. Are the arguments against the issue plausible?
2. Does the issue arouse emotion in the public's eye by being understandable, visual and touching?
3. Is the issue media-friendly?
4. Are there connections to other issues of the company or other companies?
5. How strong is the key activist group?
6. How isolated is the company?
7. How far have the dynamics of the crisis already evolved?
8. How easy is the solution?

Activist checklist

1. The campaign should have a clear aim or goal.
2. The issue is easily understood by the general public.
3. The issue has a high symbolic value.
4. The issue has the potential to damage the image of the company.
5. The opponent is strong enough, that is, No 'underdog' effect.
6. The issue can be 'packaged' in a campaign in which the public can get involved.
7. There are solutions that are confrontational.
8. There can be a dramatic element to the campaign to engage the media.

Source: Winter and Steger (1998).

One particular activity of NGOs—the organisation of boycotts—has a particular Irish interest. The word itself came into use after local people refused to co-operate with a West of Ireland landlord in the late 1800s, Captain Boycott. Global firms affected by NGO boycotts in recent decades include Nestlé, for its marketing of baby-milk powder in less-developed countries; Shell, for its support of the Nigerian military regime; and Disney, for business practices which were considered unChristian. Closer to home, Dunnes Stores was boycotted by many customers after some staff refused to handle goods from South Africa at the height of the apartheid regime. While the boycott is an extreme example of protest, companies can be seriously damaged if they misjudge or mishandle pressure-group campaigns. One way to anticipate points of contention is to analyse the issue from the viewpoints of the company and of the activist groups.

Activists tend to target companies that are well known and have some previous commitment to social and environmental causes (McIntosh *et al.* 1998). For example, McDonald's, being one of the higher profile fast-food chains, is vulnerable to the attentions of activist groups. So far, it has been criticised by environmentalists for its wasteful use of packaging, by parent and family groups for encouraging a fast-food culture and by local communities for the intrusive and bland design of its outlets. McDonald's outlets have been bombed and the company has been the subject of the longest libel trial in UK legal history. The company is the subject of several anti-McDonald's websites, the best known of which is McSpotlight (www.McSpotlight.org), the introductory page of which states:

McDonald's were chosen for this dubious honour because a) everyone's heard of them, b) they're bullies who threaten legal action on almost anyone who dares criticise them, c) there's stacks of information available about them, d) the nature of their business means loads of contemporary issues are relevant, e) they pioneered various unwelcome practices which other companies have followed and f) they take themselves far too seriously.

The Internet has altered the environment for pressure and activist groups in several interesting ways. First of all, it has lowered the cost of starting and communicating a campaign agenda. A pressure group can host its own site, be part of an umbrella site and provide links to other activist sites and the companies being targeted. The site can provide current information, leaflets and posters to print and likely targets for further action. E-mail facilities allow website visitors to send prepared messages and to circulate them to other likely campaign supporters. Internet archives can inform the general public long after a campaign has been dropped from the public domain. An example of the power of Internet campaigning was the conference of the World Trade Organisation in Seattle in 1999. A wide range of interest groups used the Internet to network and plan their activities for the week of the conference. WTO officials became aware of this but were powerless to stop it. Demonstrations and protests that were well organised and noticed by conference participants marked the week of the conference. The outcome of the conference was inconclusive and the activist groups viewed this as a success.

The disruption of the Grand National horse race at Aintree by animal rights campaigners is another sign of the sophistication of protest campaigns. The Grand National race attracts a betting audience of 15 million people and in addition to the disruption on the course, posters were used to target betting shops, veterinary offices and community centres. Another anti-vivisection organisation has targeted individual shareholders of a UK firm that uses live animals in its life sciences research. Investors received a letter asking them to sell their shares or risk protests outside their homes (Taylor 2000).

12.4.8 The community

'Community' suggests a grouping of interests between individuals, residents, companies, local social groups and other external groups with a particular interest or involvement. Communities themselves are evolving and developing organisms. It was seen in Exhibit 12.3 that Irish people feel that firms are not living up to their social responsibilities and communities also expect higher standards and more interaction from the businesses with which they are involved. Communities are increasingly willingly to marshal resources in support of issues which are of concern, for example, the siting of a toxic waste dump or the closure of a firm.

Some companies pride themselves on a high level of involvement with the local community and consider this approach an important input to business strategy. For example, the retail grocery group SuperValu sponsors the national Tidy Towns festival, while individual store owners contribute to local events and charities. For SuperValu, the returns are increased recognition of the brand name, closer links with the community and more loyalty from consumers. McIntosh *et al.* (1998) outline three levels of business involvement with the community:

▶ **charitable giving**—includes donations, social sponsorship, secondments and consultancy in-kind giving, matched giving, volunteering, collecting for charities from customers and staff

▶ **social investment**—through grants and donations, in-kind contributions, in-house training, supplier development, selection of specific community projects

▶ **commercial initiatives**—sponsorship, cause-related marketing, cash or in-kind contributions, staff development.

In some cases, these efforts may be supported by tax incentives, though in Ireland this is currently only available for some categories of charitable donations.

A community—employees, suppliers, customers and the physical environment—can feel the impact of a business long after a firm has closed its doors. For example, Mogul Ireland operated a zinc mine and dump near Silvermines, Co. Tipperary for 25 years, closing in 1982. As well as the loss of employment, the firm left behind an artificial lake of 150 acres of ore waste, including lead. The results of a report published in 2000 after a year-long investigation concluded that Silvermines was a safe area to live but recommended the resurfacing of the local school playground and that local fruit and vegetables should be washed and peeled. It also established that Mogul was legally responsible for the clean-up process, under the terms of the mining lease granted (O'Sullivan 2000).

Exhibit 12.14 Citizen Traveller

The Citizen Traveller Campaign is an attempt to build bridges and address misconceptions about the largest ethnic minority in Ireland—the 22,000 Travellers living in the state. The campaign will run from 2000 to 2003 and is allocated €1.1 million in funding from the Department of Justice, Equality and Law Reform. Its target audiences are individuals in the community and key opinion leaders such as politicians, the judiciary, the Gardai and the media. The campaign is using radio and outdoor advertising and also aims to encourage Travellers to take pride in their own cultural identity. It is the first campaign of its kind in Europe and a similar campaign in Australia focused on the Aboriginal population.

Source: Holland (2000)

Many firms are now practising a higher level of community involvement through more positive and inclusive employment policies. The Irish public sector, for example, has operated a 3 per cent quota for disabled employees, which has also forced the redesign of workspaces to be more inclusive. While operating a quota has been the subject of criticism, it is an initiative that has not yet been widely adopted by the private sector, and disability representative organisations still cite an unemployment figure of 80 per cent. The equality legislation now in force is causing a re-evaluation of these issues, helped by awareness initiatives from the Department of Justice, Equality and Law Reform and from the Equality Authority.

12.5 Business ethics

All business decisions, whether taken by an individual or a group, have an ethical dimension. There is, however, a distinction between a personal value system and the code of business behaviour as practised in the workplace. Hannigan (1998) talks about business ethics in the context of the 'actual value system'—the moral climate experienced by staff in their daily business lives which will determine the behaviour of the organisation as a whole—and a 'necessary value system', which is the minimum level of ethics (often equated with legal requirements) that has to exist for the organisation to survive.

Mullins (1999) offers three contrasting views on ethical business behaviour. Where people believe that ethical behaviour requires ethically based actions regardless of the consequences, their views are said to be *de-ontological*. For other people, it is the moral value of outcomes that is important, rather than the process by which outcomes are achieved: the ends justify the means. Values of this sort are said to be *teleological*. Other colleagues may have perceived that moral values show variations across cultures and social groupings and that moral views are therefore for the private judgement of each individual. This view is referred to as *ethical* or *moral relativism*.

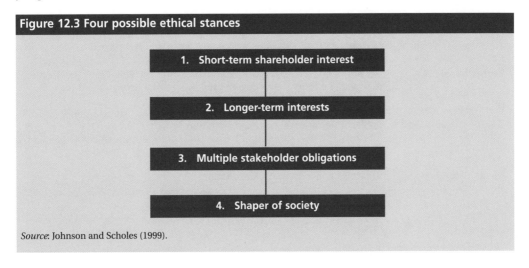

Figure 12.3 Four possible ethical stances

1. Short-term shareholder interest

2. Longer-term interests

3. Multiple stakeholder obligations

4. Shaper of society

Source: Johnson and Scholes (1999).

At the level of the organisation, Johnson and Scholes (1999) cite four possible ethical stances (see Figure 12.3). At one extreme are organisations that have taken the view that the only responsibility of business is the short-term interests of shareholders. The organisation will meet the rules laid down by government, but go no further. A second category of organisations recognises that well-managed stakeholder relationships can be of long-term benefit to shareholders. Ethical issues are therefore managed with an eye to long-term self-interest. A third group takes the view that the interests of multiple stakeholder groups should be explicitly incorporated in the organisation's purpose and strategy. These organisations will offer measures of performance that are wider than the 'bottom line'. The final group of organisations are at the ideological end of the spectrum. They are concerned with shaping society and are not overly concerned with the financial consequences of their decisions. This approach is more widely practised in the public sector or in private, family-owned firms that are not accountable to external shareholders.

Research by Alderson and Kakabadse (1994) compared the ethical attitudes of managers in Ireland, the UK and the USA. They found that Irish managers placed more emphasis than the other nationalities on the influence that increasing public concern about ethical standards has on business behaviour. This may be a result of increasing media coverage of business scandals in Ireland. Investigation of these issues through the media and tribunals has revealed close links between politicians, government and business.

Table 12.4 Recent political *cause célèbres* in Ireland

Instance	Issue	Outcome	Comment
Irish Sugar Company (1991)	Public duties/private interests	Resignation of Chief Executive	Increased awareness of public sector behaviour
Telecom Éireann (1991)	Public duties/private interests	Resignation of Chair of the Board	Increased reluctance of business élite to serve
Celtic Helicopters (1991)	Insider information	Weakened government reputation	Reinforced public disquiet
Beef Tribunal (1994)	Government mishandles export procedures	Criminal charges, destabilised government	Follows UK media story
C & D Petfoods (1994)	Public duties/private interests	No resignation	Taoiseach's judgement questioned
Hogan (February 1995)	Breach of convention	Resignation	Reinforced convention
Coveney (May 1995)	Public duties/private interests	Resignation and enquiry	Followed media investigation
Haughey (December 1996)	Unethical receipt of money	Enquiry	Followed media investigation
Burke (September 1997)	Unethical receipt of money	Resignation and enquiry	Followed media investigation

Source: Extracted from Collins (1999).

The study also revealed that more Irish managers believed business standards had fallen (37 per cent) than risen (12 per cent) over the past 10 years. The other 52 per cent felt that standards had stayed the same. More recent research by Murphy (1995) highlighted the inability or unwillingness of Irish managers to recognise and discuss specific ethical issues. This was in contrast to similar interviews with European managers where most did mention a specific ethical incident. This documented culture of secrecy in Ireland conflicts with public demands and political calls for more openness and transparency in all aspects of public life and business dealings.

12.6 Corporate governance

In the words of Monks and Minow (1991):

Corporations determine far more than any other institution the air we breathe, the quality of the water we drink, even where we live. Yet they are not accountable to anyone.

Their book looks at two issues at the forefront of the corporate governance agenda:

▶ accountability
▶ performance.

These issues were highlighted throughout the 1990s by business scandals involving abuse of chief executive power (Robert Maxwell), fraud (BCCI), insider trading (Guinness) and lack of management controls (Barings Bank). These and many other cases of fraud and mismanagement have emphasised the need for stricter controls on corporate behaviour, though the process is a continuing see-saw between the interests of owners, shareholders, board members and the other stakeholder groups.

Exhibit 12.15 The Cadbury Report: main recommendations

- The board must meet regularly, retain full control over the company, and monitor executive management.
- There should be clearly accepted division of responsibilities at the head of a company to ensure a balance of power and authority. When the chairman is also chief executive, it is essential that there should be a strong independent element on the board, with an appointed leader.
- Non-executive directors should be of high calibre and respected in their field. They should bring independent judgement in strategy, performance, executive pay, resources and standards of conduct.
- The majority of non-executive directors should be free of business connections with the company; terms should be specific and not more than three years. Reappointment should be only by shareholder approval.
- Non-executive directors should decide executive directors' pay.

Source: Cadbury Committee (1992).

The first influential report on corporate governance came from the Harvard Business School in 1991. The 'New Compact for Owners and Directors' set out five recommendations for owners and directors, the main ones of which were that directors should evaluate the performance of the chief executive regularly and that board members should be required to have set qualifications and be screened by outside directors. In the UK, the professional accounting bodies and the Stock Exchange commissioned the Cadbury Report, published in 1992. Its findings, presented in Exhibit 12.15, while regarded as a step in the right direction, were criticised for not being broad-ranging or strong enough.

The Greenbury report was published in the UK in 1995 following widespread protest at the remuneration of boards of the newly privatised utilities. Reporting on the remuneration of board directors, Greenbury prepared a code of practice that recommended more transparent disclosure of directors' salaries, benefits in kind, share options and bonuses. Looking at the Irish situation, the disclosure of the salaries paid to members of the board became a legal requirement in 2001. Table 12.5 shows the emerging trends.

Table 12.5 Irish chief executive salaries 2000 (€)

Name	Title	Company	Salary Euro 000
Michael J. Smurfit	Chairman/C.E.O.	Smurfit Group	6,758
Frank Bramble	Executive director (US)	AIB	1,700
Donal Geaney	Chairman/C.E.O.	Elan	1,600
Dermot Smurfit	Executive director (US)	Smurfit Group	1,300
Stephen Vernon	C.E.O.	Green Property	1,200
Tom Mulcahy	C.E.O.	AIB	1,200
Alan Smurfit	Executive director	Smurift Group	1,200
Tom Lynch	Finance director	Elan	1,099
Gary McGann	C.E.O.	Smurfit Group	1,000
Chris McGillivary	Executive director (US)	Waterford Wedgewood	1,000
Brendan Hopkins	Executive director	Independent News	974
Denis Brosnan	C.E.O	Kerry Group	846

Source: Carey (2001).

Note: Only refers to companies that have published their results in the first half of 2001.

As well as a regular salary, executive directors are paid a bonus, which may be related to performance targets, and may have share options and pension fund contributions. These rewards are agreed by a remuneration committee, which is made up of a small group of non-executive directors.

The Hampel Committee (1998) was set up in the UK to examine how the recommendations of the previous two reports could be implemented. It advised that implementation should be through the practice of fair principles and the use of self-regulation. It recommended that companies produce a narrative report explaining how the principles of honesty, integrity, objectivity, etc., are being applied. While Hampel has been criticised for not recognising the opportunity to deal with the strategic aspects of corporate governance, there is general agreement in the financial community that positive self-regulation is preferable to the prospect of government legislation.

Davies (1999) suggests two relevant approaches to improving standards of corporate governance. The first is the 'best practice' approach, whereby companies seek to attain the current level of 'best practice'. An example of this approach is the largest public pension fund in the USA, Calpers, which targets underperforming corporations in its portfolio, demanding changes in corporate governance as a driver of improved profitability. A second approach is that of strategic leadership, gained through the establishment of a creative and dynamic board of directors.

12.7 Whistleblowing

WHISTLEBLOWING occurs when an employee informs the public of inappropriate activities going on in the organisation. The whistleblower may be motivated by moral reasons, or may have been passed over for promotion or suffered some other injustice in the workplace. The consequences of whistleblowing are often extreme: loss of job and/or home, ostracism by peers, loss of family relationships, personal isolation and effects on physical health. Employers look on whistleblowers as disloyal and unworthy of trust, while their peers may regard them as weak or unbalanced. In Ireland and the UK, legislation has been passed to protect the whistleblower, as, without the courage of these individuals, many cases of malpractice and abuse of trust would never be exposed.

Beauchamp and Bowie (1993) contend that whistleblowing is only justified if the following traits are present:

❶ It is done based on an appropriate moral motive.

❷ The individual has exhausted all internal channels for dissent.

❸ The individual's belief regarding the inappropriate conduct is based on evidence that would persuade a reasonable person.

❹ The individual has carefully analysed the situation to determine the serious nature of the violation, the immediacy of the violation and specificity of the violation.

❺ The individual's action is commensurate with responsibility for avoiding and/or exposing moral violations.

In some cases, the whistleblower may be torn between his/her responsibilities as a professional and the need to preserve the confidentiality of clients or patients. As the need to blow the whistle arises from a lack of governance and managerial strength, organisations should attempt to improve performance in these areas. O'Higgins (2000) suggests three measures for avoiding the need for whistleblowing:

▶ Build procedures for reporting bad news into the everyday way of doing business. This has strategic as well as ethical merit.

▶ Staff will understand the benefits of reporting bad news if it is used constructively for learning purposes. Those who report bad news should not be punished or held responsible for other's wrong-doing.

▶ Build communications channels for reporting bad news. Use outside audits to examine the evidence objectively.

Exhibit 12.16 James Gogarty

James Gogarty was a senior executive with JMSE, a Dublin building firm. In June 1989 he received a letter from an executive of another building firm, Bovale Developments, inquiring about plans for around 700 acres of land in north Dublin owned by JMSE. Bovale were anxious to have the land re-zoned for housing developments and had contacts with the reigning political party, Fianna Fail. Later that same month, James Gogarty and an executive from Bovale, Michael Bailey, visited the home of Ray Burke, a government minister and county councillor and delivered a large amount of cash. These events were revealed at the Flood Tribunal in 1999.

The Tribunal was set up to investigate corruption in the planning process in Ireland. After years of rumours about bribes and numerous controversial planning decisions, some concerned conservationists, Michael Smith and Colm Mac Eochaidh, decided to offer a reward of €12,700 'for information leading to the conviction or indictment of persons for re-zoning corruption'. They placed an advertisement in the national newspapers, asking for replies to a firm of solicitors in Newry.

Within a few months 55 informants emerged. Among them was James Gogarty, now an elderly man with a grudge against JMSE, as he felt that the company had not given him a fair pension. The planning scandals exposed through the advertising were covered by the media and led to the establishment of a Tribunal of investigation. James Gogarty spent about three weeks giving evidence at the Tribunal. By June 2000, its findings had led to the resignation of Ray Burke from the Dail, and a criminal investigation into the affairs of former Dublin assistant city and county manager, George Redmond.

Source: Kerrigan and Brennan (1999); Battersby (2000).

12.8 Sustainable development

Since 1950, world population has more than doubled while the global economy has grown nearly sixfold. Water and timber use have tripled and paper use has increased sixfold. This overconsumption is happening in the more affluent nations: 20 per cent of the world's population consumes 80 per cent of the world's natural resources. These trends are being felt in Ireland, where our 'ecological footprint' is at least one and a quarter times its ideal size and growing (Enfo Ireland 1999).

The concept of sustainable development was developed as it became evident that the earth has finite resources and that the pace of human development is having a serious effect on those resources. The Brundtland Report (1987) described sustainable development as 'development that meets the needs of the present without compromising the ability of future generations to meet their needs'. The effects of business operations have commonly led to damage to the environment, either planned or by accident. This damage affects entire communities and unborn generations. McIntosh *et al.* (1998) suggest there are three fundamental shifts in perception necessary to adopt the principles of sustainability:

❶ Value the environment for the contribution it makes to life on earth, whether in terms of physical resources, recycling, beauty, and amenity or religious significance.

❷ All people have a right to environmental resources, including materials and beauty.

❸ Decision making about the use of environmental resources must be based on an awareness of all those who may be affected by the decision, including people in other parts of the world and unborn generations.

The practice of sustainable development can bring about significant business benefits—lower resource costs, cheaper and more effective waste disposal, better market acceptance and decreased liabilities.

In Europe, sustainability principles have been endorsed and validated by a range of organisations. The International Chamber of Commerce launched a Business Charter for sustainable Development in 1991. The European Eco-Management and Audit Scheme (EMAS) and the ISO 1400 Standard provide audit systems for compliance with environmental standards. The EU has established a number of Environmental Action programmes, planned to bring each member state to an agreed activity level in areas, such as recycling and CO_2 emissions. These programmes are based on principles such as 'prevention is better than cure' and 'the polluter pays.' All these developments have been a powerful influence on managers, who are now adopting the principles of product stewardship. This has involved looking at more environmentally friendly supply resources, the energy and resources used to manufacture a product and how a product can be disposed of or recycled at the end of its life. The Germans have been at the forefront of this movement, introducing the 'Green Point' eco-labelling system in 1978 and encouraging the recycling of cars and other large consumer goods.

Exhibit 12.17 Eco-efficiency in Ireland

The Kyoto Protocol, agreed by the United Nations in 1997, sets legally binding targets for greenhouse gases, under which, by 2008, Ireland has to limit the emission of greenhouse gases to 13 per cent above 1990 levels. EU Directives being implemented in Ireland also affect water usage and water quality. Among the issues of concern to the Department of the Environment with regard to sustainability are:

- Energy—there is discussion of an energy tax and a move away from fossil fuels.
- Water—the imposition of water charges and meters and an improvement in the quality of drinking water.
- Packaging and waste management—one third of the waste in landfill sites is discarded packaging. The infrastructure for waste management and recycling needs radical improvement. Efforts to introduce incineration as an alternative to landfill have met with vehement opposition from local communities.
- Transport—vehicles should meet emissions standards and be subject to a National Car Test.
- Public transport—over €2.5 billion is being allocated to improving the bus and rail network, particularly in the Dublin Region. Proposals for road pricing are being examined.

Source: Consumer Choice (2000); Enfo Ireland (1999).

12.9 Environmental and ethical audits

The audit process involves the examination of processes or procedures for the purpose of third-party verification. Though the idea of an audit of a company's ethical behaviour and practices is very new, the idea of environmental auditing is better established because it is partially required by legislation. In Ireland, some types of large scale industrial development require an Environmental Impact Statement (EIS) to be submitted as part of the planning process. Once the development is under way, however, there is no formal requirement for an environmental audit, but monitoring of emissions or waste discharge may be undertaken by the Environmental Protection Agency.

Many larger companies now publish an environmental statement as part of their annual report to shareholders, though it rarely has the weight of independent verification. However, it is an indication of shareholders' concerns that the firms they invest in should have positive and progressive environmental policies.

Firms that can be considered socially concerned, for example, The Body Shop or Ben & Jerry's, have so far engaged in the practice of the ETHICAL AUDIT. The questions that might be addressed in an ethical audit include:

▶ What are the values of the organisation?
▶ How were they derived?
▶ Are they consistent with the way the organisation works and what it does?
▶ Do they conform with the values of employees? (McIntosh *et al.* 1998)

An ethical audit can be extremely useful in assessing the organisation's current position on ethical issues and perhaps more important, the emerging or possible issues that will be revealed. An indication of the interest in the area is that the major accounting and business consultancies now offer an ethical audit service to their clients.

12.10 Ethics and strategy

So far, this chapter has outlined the many aspects of ethical philosophy and behaviour that are relevant to business decisions. A consideration of the ethical dimension broadens the horizons of decision makers involved in the process of strategic planning and evaluation (see Chapter 4).

Firstly, the process of engaging with stakeholders heightens the appreciation of the ramifications of a business decision, which otherwise may not be evident until after the decision is implemented. It may be decided to involve stakeholders actively in at least some aspects of the decision being made. This process will also broaden the environmental analysis that is undertaken as an input to the planning process. A third consideration is that more ethically founded decision making may actually improve profits and shareholder confidence. For example, when the Iceland frozen-food chain promised to make its products free of genetically modified ingredients, it did so in the hope that its core customers would now buy more from this guaranteed source. It also served as an important point of difference from its competitors, in an era when more affluent customers are seeking to 'do the right thing'. Finally, the concept of more ethically based decisions fits well with the concept of the learning organisation, as proposed by Senge (1990). The process of organisational learning and development has at its core engagement with the new stakeholder groups and the continuous reformulation of the corporate agenda for change (see Chapter 14).

12.11 Summary of key propositions

▶ The area of business ethics is of increasing relevance and interest to Irish business.
▶ The business agenda is broadening to include other motives outside of profits. This trend is being driven by the globalisation of business and increasing social consciousness.

▶ Organisations are aware of the need to behave in a manner that is socially responsible, but they differ in how they enact this responsibility, from being compliant with the legal minimum to a broader vision of corporate citizenship.

▶ The stakeholder approach suggests that firms have a variety of interest groups with an interest or stake in how the business decisions are made. These include owners and senior management, employees, financial institutions, suppliers, consumers, communities and government.

▶ All business decisions, whether taken by an individual or a group, have an ethical dimension. There are three contrasting views of ethical behaviour: de-ontological, teleological, and ethical relativism.

▶ Corporate governance is concerned with the control and conduct of the board of management. The Cadbury and Greenbury reports from the UK have made specific recommendations on corporate governance, and these have been influential in Ireland.

▶ Whistleblowing occurs when an employee informs the public of inappropriate activities going on in the organisation. It usually occurs as a result of a lack of governance and managerial strength.

▶ Sustainable development refers to 'development that meets the needs of the present without compromising the ability of future generations to meet their needs'. The practice of sustainable development can bring about lower resource costs, more effective disposal of waste, better market acceptance and decreased liabilities.

▶ More progressive firms, in response to shareholder and stakeholder concerns, are now undertaking environmental and ethical audits.

▶ A consideration of the ethical dimension broadens the horizons of decision makers involved in the process of strategic planning and evaluation.

Discussion questions

❶ Personal ethics should be kept separate from business ethics. Discuss.

❷ 'The business of business is to make a profit,' (Friedman). Outline any other objectives which might be pursued by a business and analyse their implications for bottom line profits.

❸ What are the advantages of having a worker representative on the board of directors? Select an Irish company that has worker representation at board level and analyse the input and effects of this structure.

❹ A well-known fast-food chain is proposing to open a new branch near your local school. As chairperson of the parents' committee, you are anxious to mount a campaign of opposition to this development and you have called a meeting of parents to discuss the issue.
   a. Prepare a report presenting your views to the meeting.
   b. What other stakeholder groups would you involve in the campaign?
   c. Briefly outline a campaign plan for the three months prior to the planning application for the fast-food outlet being considered by the local district council.

❺ Trade is better than aid. Discuss.

❻ You are the owner of a small convenience store. Having placed a sign in your window advertising for staff, you meet with a young woman who presents her CV and asks to be considered for the job. Closer perusal of her details reveals she is from a nearby housing scheme for settled Travellers.
   a. Would you employ this person?
   b. Analyse the consequences of your decision for all the parties involved.

❼ Select any one of the companies referred to in Table 12.4.
   a. What remuneration is awarded to members of the board of directors, other than the chief executive?
   b. Evaluate the company's performance in the light of this information.

❽ Mullins offers three perspectives on ethical behaviour, as outlined in section 12.4.
   a. Take any recent business decision that has been covered by the media and analyse which of these views influenced the decision.
   b. What was the outcome of the decision?

❾ Refer to Table 12.4. Select any one of the cases referred to and examine the relationship between business and politics.

❿ Select a company listed on the Irish Stock Exchange and carry out an environmental and ethical audit based on annual reports and other available information.
   a. How do you think this company compares with others in the same industry?
   b. How do you think it compares with best practice overall?
   c. As an advisor to the company, prepare a list of items for the agenda of the next board meeting, based on the findings of your audit of the company.

Concluding case: Banking and rural communities in Ireland

The threat of rural post office closures in the early 1990s caused a ground swell of opposition from communities who claimed the closures would devastate their towns and villages. Now small communities are up in arms again, this time over the withdrawal of banking facilities, which is happening quietly and continuously.

Those affected complain that the withdrawal of banking services will sound the death knell for their communities. As Mayo county councillor, Mr Jimmy Moloney, put it, nobody wants to set up business in a town that doesn't have a bank. He is very angry at the decision by the Bank of Ireland to close its sub-office in his home town of Foxford, in spite of vociferous protests.

Ms Marian Harkin, chairwoman of the Council for the West, said the fabric of rural Ireland and the opportunities available to people were slowly disintegrating. 'The White Paper on Rural Development promised people a choice to live, move to and work in rural areas. Unless these promises are underpinned by maintenance of a basic level of services and employment opportunities then these promises are hollow,' she said.

A rural sociologist, Father Harry Bohan, feels banks have a social obligation to the people in small communities who have made them what they are. 'At a time when urban growth is almost uncontrollable and when more and more people want to live in small communities, this is the very time that big organisations like the banks should be supporting that move and they should do so by retaining the services that people need rather than taking them away,' he said.

The situation in Foxford has been replicated in several other areas in the past 12 months.

In 1999, Allied Irish Banks closed 10 branches in the Republic, and a further sub-office closed at Sneem, Co. Kerry. The Bank of Ireland has also closed at least two sub-offices, one in Foxford, and the other in Louisburgh, Co. Mayo. National Irish Bank announced plans in February to close three of its agencies in Blacklion, Co. Cavan; Castlefin, Co. Donegal; and Drumkeerin, Co. Leitrim. They were scheduled to close in March 2000 but following an armed hold-up of staff at the Castlefin agency, the bank decided to close them immediately 'for security reasons'. In a further blow to the north-west it said the raid had also forced it within days to close two further sub-offices in Co. Donegal at Clonmany and Carrigart.

Dr Patrick Malone, secretary of the Sneem Development Co-operative Society, said the loss of the town's AIB sub-office on 17 February was a very serious blow to the town. Sneem is a prime tourist area, located on the Ring of Kerry with a thriving business community, including six restaurants, at least 20 guesthouses and 12 shops, which require access to banking facilities. 'Money changed outside Sneem is money lost to the town,' Dr Malone said. He also fears the move will result in elderly people hoarding money in their homes, making them even more vulnerable. 'The consequences really don't bear thinking about,' he said. 'Over the years, much lip service has been paid to regional development and inclusivity. The reality on the ground is that the noose is being progressively tightened around the necks of small communities, regardless of their contribution to the Celtic Tiger. 'Even AIB is not guiltless in this respect for, as sponsor of the Better Ireland Awards, it should be acutely aware of the needs of small communities and at the very least it should do nothing to compromise the expansion on business opportunities in those communities,' he added.

All the banks say that the closure of branches or sub-offices is an emotive issue and insist their decisions to withdraw services are not taken lightly. A spokesman for AIB said the bank opened and closed branches every year. Mr Turlough Crowe confirmed the bank withdrew services from Mountrath, Co. Laois; Enniscrone, Co. Sligo; Balla, Co. Mayo; Carlingford, Co. Louth; Mountbellew, Co. Galway; Blacklion, Co. Cavan; Bindon Street, Ennis; O'Connell Street, Limerick (there are two other branches on the street); and from Lansdowne Road and Ballyfermot in Dublin over the past twelve months. These were primarily 'commercial' decisions, he said, pointing out that new branches had opened in growth areas.

Bank of Ireland said a negligible amount of business was carried on in its Foxford outlet and it could not justify keeping it open. 'These are very carefully taken decisions. There is no wide-scale plan to reduce the number of branches we have, but we would look at the ones which have a low level of business like Foxford,' a spokesman said. Even before the raid on a sub-office of National Irish Bank in Castlefin, last week the bank had signalled its intention to close three of its sub-offices at the end of this month. 'Increasingly we are introducing new technology into our banks and we want people to start using it. Customers can phone us for a loan or a mortgage and using our laser cards they can pay for items at most shops and receive cash back in the process,' Ms Pamela Yeh, the bank's spokeswoman said.

People affected by the withdrawal of services are, however, not convinced that new technology is an acceptable substitute for good old-fashioned banking.

Case adapted from Donnellan (2000); www.aib.ie; www.ireland.com.

Case questions

❶ Analyse the effect of branch bank closures on the various stakeholder groups involved.

❷ Do you agree with the reasons given by the banks for the closures?

❸ What future do you forecast for the year 2020 in Ireland for:
   a. rural communities
   b. the nature of the Irish banking system
   c. the availability and delivery of public services, e.g. post offices, libraries, and hospitals.

Keep up to date

www.greenpeace.org.
www.earthwatch.org.
Shell's own site on the Brent Spar: www.shellexpro.brentspar.com.
McDonald's in the firing line: www.mcspotlight.org.
Green Net—facilitates over 200 protest groups: www.gn.apc.org.hostsite.
Online journal about ethical investment: www.greenmoney.com.
Shareholder activist group: www.lens-inc.com.
Enfo Ireland—environmental information service: www.enfo.ie.
Environmental Protection Agency: www.epa.ie.
Website subverting well-known global advertising campaings: www.subvertise.org.

Bibliography

Alderson, S. and Kakabadse, A. (1994) 'Business Ethics and Irish Management: A Cross Cultural Study', *European Management Journal*, 12, (4).

Amarach Consulting (2000) 'Responsible Business'. Report published by Amarach Consulting, Dublin and also at www.amarach.com.

Battersby, E. (2000) 'The Heritage Hero', *Irish Times*, 11 May.

Beauchamp, T. L. and Bowie, N. (1993) *Ethical Theory and Business*. Englewood Cliffs, New Jersey: Prentice Hall.

Brundtland, H. G. (1987) *Our Common Future*. Oxford: Oxford University Press.

The Cadbury Committee (1992) 'The Financial Aspects of Corporate Governance', London: Stock Exchange Council.

Carey, B. (2001) 'Open Season for executive pay'. *Sunday Tribune*, 20 May.

Collins, N. (1999) *Political Issues in Ireland Today*, Manchester: Manchester University Press.

Consumer Choice (1999) 'Fairtrade', December.

Consumer Choice (2000) 'Eco-Efficiency Drive', May.

Coulter, C. (2000) 'Misogyny Found in Government Departments', *Irish Times*, 23 March.

Dalton, D. R. and Cosier, R. A. (1982) 'The Four Faces of Social Responsibility', *Business Horizons*, 25 (3).

Davies, A. (1999) *A Strategic Approach to Corporate Governance*. Aldershot: Gower.

Davies, P. W. F. (1997) *Current Issues in Business Ethics*. London: Routledge.

Davis, A. (1999) *A Strategic Approach to Corporate Governance*. Aldershot: Gower.

Department of Justice, Equality and Law Reform (1999) *A Guide to the Employment Equality Act*. Dublin. Also available at www.equality.ie.

Donnellan, E. (2000) 'Rural Communities Angry at Bank Closures', *Irish Times*, 28 March.

Drucker, P. F.(1989) *The Practice of Management*. London: Heinemann.

Elkington, J. (1997) *Cannibals with Forks: The Triple Bottom Line of 21st Century Business*. Oxford: Clapstone.

Enfo Ireland (1999) *A Shopping and Investment Guide for Sustainable Living*. Dublin: Enfo.

ESB Equality Office (1992) 'Equal Opportunity'. Internal company publication.

ESB Equality Office (1999) 'Striking the Balance'. Internal company publication.

Flood, P. and Stiles, P. (1997) 'Trade Unions and Ethics', in Davies (1997).

Freeman, R. E. (1985) *Strategic Management: A Stakeholder Approach*. Boston: Ballinger.

Friedman, M. (1970) 'The Social Responsibility of Business is to Increase its Profits', *New York Sunday Times Magazine*, 13 September.

Greenbury, Sir Richard (1995) (Chair) Study Group on Directors' Remuneration. *Report of a Study Group*. London: Gee Publishing.

Hampel, Sir R., (1997) (Chair) Committee on Corporate Governance. Preliminary Report.

Hannigan, T. (1998) *Management: Concepts and Practices*, 2nd edition. London: Financial Times/Pitman.

Harvard Business Review Working Group on Corporate Governance (1991) 'A New Compact for Owners and Directors', *Harvard Business Review*, July–August.

Health and Safety Authority (1998) 'Bullying at Work', www.hsa.ie.

Holland, K. (2000) 'Bridging the Gap with Traveller Community', *Irish Times*, 28 February.

Johnson, G. and Scholes, K. (1999) *Exploring Corporate Strategy*, 5th edition. London: Prentice Hall.

Kerrigan, G. and Brennan, P (1999) *This Great Little Nation: The A–Z of Irish Scandals and Controversies*. Dublin: Gill & Macmillan.

Klein, (2000) *No Logo; Taking Aim at the Brand Bullies*. London: Flamingo.

Knight, A. (1974) *Private Enterprise and Public Intervention: The Courtaulds Experience*. London: George Allen & Unwin.

Lynch, R. (2000) *Corporate Strategy*, 2nd edition. Harlow: Financial Times/Prentice Hall.

McIntosh, M., Leipziger, D., Jones, K. and Coleman, G. (1998) *Corporate Citizenship: Successful Strategies for Responsible Companies*. London: Financial Times/Pitman.

Monks, R. A. G. and Minow, N. (1991) *Power and Accountability*. New York: Harper Business Books.

Moore, Michael (1989) *Roger and Me*. Documentary film, Warner Brothers.

Mullins, L. (1999) *Management and Organisational Behaviour*, 5th edition. London: Financial Times/Pitman.

Murphy, P. E. (1995) 'Irish Managers Views on Corporate Ethics', in Leavy, B. and Walsh, J.S. *Strategy and General Management*. Dublin: Oak Tree Press.

Office of the Director of Consumer Affairs (1999) 'Misleading Advertising', Dublin: Consumer Booklet.

O'Higgins, E. (2000) 'Switching on the Firm or Acting in the Public Interest?', *Irish Times*, 29 May.

O'Sullivan, J. (2001) 'Ethical investing goes mainstream as concerns about environment grow'. The *Irish Times*, 20 April.

O'Sullivan, K. (2000) 'Having to Live with the Threat of Toxic Waste', *Irish Times*, 28 June.

Peters, G. (1999) *Waltzing with the Raptors: A Practical Roadmap to Protecting Your Company's Reputation.* New York: Wiley.

Pollard, J. (2000) 'Please Sir, You're a Bully', *Observer*, 2 April.

Schwartz, P. and Gibb, B. (1999) *When Good Companies Do Bad Things.* New York: Wiley.

Senge, P (1990) *The Fifth Discipline.* New York: Doubleday.

Sharplin, A. (1985) *Strategic Management.* New York: McGraw-Hill.

Sheridan, K. (2000) 'Old Habits Die Hard', *Irish Times*, 24 June.

Solomon, R. C. (1993) *Ethics and Excellence: Co-operation and Integrity in Business.* New York: Oxford University Press.

Taylor, S. (2000) 'Shareholders in UK Targeted by Animal Rights Activists', *Irish Times*, 7 April.

Willmott, M. and Flatters, P. (1999) 'Corporate Citizenship: The New Challenge for Business?' *Consumer Policy Review*, 9 (6), November/December.

Winter, M. and Steger, U. (1998) *Managing Outside Pressure.* Chichester: Wiley.

Chapter 13 Entrepreneurship, Small Business and Innovation

13.1 Introduction

ENTREPRENEURSHIP is associated with the creation of new enterprises and new products, with the development of small business and with job creation. High profile entrepreneurs such as Denis O'Brien or Gillian Bowler have become well-known media personalities. The European Union has taken a particular interest in encouraging a higher rate of small business start-ups. All enterprises have their origins in a small or micro business, and a current focus of Irish policy making is the encouragement of high-potential growth enterprises which can be offered an accelerated programme of supports to encourage growth and improve the prospects of success.

The past decade has seen the arrival of a new generation of Irish entrepreneurs, particularly in the technological and service sectors. Irish businesses now compete on a world stage, and national competitiveness has taken significant strides forward. The economic, administrative and regulatory environments for entrepreneurs have improved significantly. Facing the twenty-first century, the new national agenda for enterprise is focused on making the most of opportunities—growing business, developing competitiveness and finding new ways of working. A positive vision at a national level is a further encouragement to individual enterprises to move forward and step up investment in research and business development (see Chapter 2).

In this chapter, the entrepreneurship process is analysed by looking at the traits and motivations of the entrepreneur. The business culture and climate for INNOVATION in Ireland are described. Guidelines for putting together a FEASIBILITY STUDY and BUSINESS PLAN are given. There are suggestions about the various modes of entry to business, and the influence of E-COMMERCE on the small business is highlighted. Strategies for building up and establishing the business are described and a list of relevant agencies and organisations offering support to enterprise is to be found in Appendix 1.

13.2 Enterprise: Economic and strategic perspectives

Economists have traditionally viewed enterprise as one of the factors of production, along with land, labour and capital. However, there is much debate in the literature as to whether enterprise is a causal factor in economic growth, or an effect, governed by the extent to which the other factors of production are in a favourable state. Supporters of the causal argument point to the emergence of newly industrialised countries (NICs), such as Korea, as evidence that an entrepreneurial framework can be the engine for economic growth. Economists who consider enterprise as an effect refer to nations like Japan, which in the post-war environment was poorly resourced with natural resources or capital, but willing to compensate through established frameworks and systems (Keritsu) which offered a higher input of enterprise. In more recent times, Porter (1990) has suggested how individual nations can act to improve competitive advantage through the analysis of four elements: factor conditions, demand conditions, competitive rivalry, and the presence of related supplier or support industries.

The term ENTREPRENEUR has its origins in the French verb *entreprendre*, meaning 'to undertake something'. Entrepreneurs were viewed as people undertaking risk. Cantillon (1931), an Irish businessman living in France in the eighteenth century, was the first economic commentator to identify an entrepreneur as a person who takes on uncertainty in the hope of making a profit. He observed that some traders 'buy at a certain price and sell at an uncertain price', and those who cope with this risk are the true entrepreneurs.

Another French writer, Say (1997), who ran a spinning factory, made the distinction between the interest payable on capital and the profit from enterprise. His view of the entrepreneur was of someone who was able to organise the factors of production to best advantage, and in return receive a wage for his input of enterprise—a scarce factor of production. This vision saw enterprise as a balancing element to achieve equilibrium within the factors of production. There was no mention of DYNAMISM, uncertainty, or innovation.

In Britain, Smith (1805), in his *Inquiry into the Nature and Causes of the Wealth of Nations*, made no distinction between profit gained through risk and interest gained on capital invested. His concept was that the capitalist employer accumulated capital as a return for his/her efforts and also made it available to be used by his/her workers. By failing to distinguish between enterprise and pure capital accumulation, Smith ignored the risk-bearing element of the business.

John Stuart Mill (1996) described the entrepreneur as a bearer of risk and supervisor of a business enterprise. He introduced the word 'entrepreneur' to the English language, using it to refer to an individual who founded a business.

Austrian economist Menger (1994) proposed that economic change does not result merely from circumstances, but from the individual's understanding and interpretation of those circumstances. For instance, a stock market crash occurs not just because the price of some stocks starts to fall, but because individuals interpret some event as a cause for concern and in turn decide to sell their stocks. The entrepreneur had particular calculating abilities and decision-making skills, which enabled him/her to deal with uncertainty more successfully.

Marshall (1920) introduced the dimension of leadership as being vital to the achievement of the entrepreneurial task. It was Schumpeter (1943) who described entrepreneurship as a force of 'creative destruction', whereby the existing ways of doing things are shattered by the creation of new processes or ways of getting things done: 'To act with confidence beyond the range of familiar beacons and to overcome that resistance require aptitudes that are present in only a small fraction of the population and define the entrepreneurial type as well as the entrepreneurial function'. Hayek (1949) viewed the process of innovation as something continuous and incremental, in contrast to Schumpeter's view of periods of continuity punctuated by entrepreneurial shocks. Keynes (1965) saw the entrepreneur playing the role of decision maker, selecting and planning investment decisions against a backdrop of uncertainty.

Arrow (1962) offered insights into why innovation is more likely to be introduced by a new entrant to a market than by the existing participants. By innovating, the new entrant can replace the current monopolist, a phenomenon that Arrow called the replacement effect. The theory of X-efficiency proposed by Leibenstein (1980) suggests that inefficient use of resources is the norm within firms. In this imperfect situation, enterprise is seen as having two roles. First of all, it is a 'gap filler', compensating for the inadequacies of factor utilisation. Its second role is more creative and expansive, helping the firm to connect with different markets and to grow.

More recent theoretical insights have focused on using the economists' frameworks to develop concepts that will help managers making strategic decisions. D'Aveni (1994) argues that in virtually all industries, the sources of competitive advantage are being created and eroded at an increasing rate. In such hypercompetitive environments, firms should aim to disrupt existing sources of advantage in the industry (including its own) and be prepared to create new ones. Hamel and Prahalad (1994) promoted two related ideas. They pointed out that certain global firms succeeded because of their obsession with becoming global leaders in their field—an obsession that they labelled 'strategic intent'. The focus of these firms was not always related to their existing resources and capabilities, and Hamel and Prahalad coined the term 'strategic stretch' in reference to the expansive and adaptive efforts made by organisations to meet the challenges of a new strategy. Barney (1991) developed the resource-based theory of the firm, suggesting that in order to develop a sustainable competitive advantage, a firm must build and enhance its stock of resources, (firm-specific factors) and capabilities (activities that it performs better than most of its competitors). These resources and capabilities are scarce and imperfectly mobile, so firms will not have a homogenous approach to the creation of value in a market.

Both the economists and the strategists view enterprise as a scarce and heterogeneous resource, and as an input to be combined with other elements in the quest to create something of value. To obtain some insights into the behavioural aspects of enterprise, other elements such as personality traits and innovation need analysis.

13.3 Traits of the enterprise

Many studies have attempted to analyse the psychological make-up and personality of the entrepreneur. It is certainly true that many high-profile entrepreneurs appear to share a common personality type. However, entrepreneurship is also a function of an individual's background and personal situation, and there are many potential entrepreneurs who lack the formal education or financial backing to bring their ideas to fruition. The individual's attitude to enterprise can develop and change over the lifetime of a career. For example, unemployment or redundancy are situational factors, which can often spur would-be entrepreneurs into action.

The most widely known psychological insight into the personal traits of the entrepreneur is that offered by McClelland (1961). He suggested that entrepreneurial behaviour is the result of a need for achievement—nAch for short. In this context, money has two functions:

▶ as a means of achieving the objective
▶ as a method of assessing performance.

An entrepreneur will see high profits as a positive indicator of performance, but may well want to reinvest those profits in the furtherance of the business. McClelland also suggested that if a society could lift the overall strength of the need for achievement, the level of entrepreneurial activity would increase, improving the rate of firm formation and economic growth. More recently, Timmons (1994) identified the key traits of the entrepreneur, based on an analysis of over 50 research studies. These traits include:

▶ total commitment, determination and perseverance
▶ a drive to achieve and grow
▶ opportunism and growth-orientation
▶ willingness to take initiative and personal responsibility
▶ persistence when problem solving
▶ low need for status and power
▶ calculatedly risk taking and risk seeking.

O'Farrell (1986) identified the following types of new firm founders, based on an Irish sample:

❶ **The graduate entrepreneur**. Typically a graduate of engineering or business, s/he is usually involved in high-value-added technology-based goods with export or import substitution potential.

❷ **The opportunist entrepreneur**. Usually of a lower middle-class background and educated to Leaving Certificate level, this person has typically held a variety of jobs and may have a family background in small business. S/he tends to have nursed an ambition to found his/her own business for a long time.

❸ **The craftsman entrepreneur**. Generally of a semi-skilled or skilled working-class background with a technical education or apprenticeship. S/he often starts a business on a part-time basis with little capital. S/he may have little business or management experience and is more likely to be limited to one or two products or services.

Exhibit 13.1 'Out on their own'

If I don't achieve my goal instantly, that doesn't mean that I will give up. I will always have it in the back of my mind and work patiently towards it. I am extremely persistent, single-minded, determined. If I don't get what I want in year one, I won't have forgotten it in year five. I never stop trying.

Gillian Bowler, Budget Travel

When I looked at all those grey faces crammed into the railway compartments, I decided I was never going to live like that, that I was never going to work for anybody else. If I ever made a conscious decision about my life, that was probably it. While I will never work for anybody else, funnily enough, I don't find working in partnerships any way difficult.

Mark Kavanagh, Hardwicke Property Ltd

Risk is the greatest of all aphrodisiacs. I like the feeling that you can be wrong but I like the odds to be in my favour even if ever so slightly. Once the risk goes out of a project, I lose interest. Risk is not a philosophy, it's an addiction.

John Teeling, Cooley Distillery

Source: Kenny (1991).

A 1999 survey sponsored by the Irish Business and Employers Confederation (IBEC) revealed four main reasons cited by owner–managers for setting up in business:

▶ dissatisfaction with previous employment
▶ long-standing objective
▶ spotted a business opportunity
▶ seeking independence.

The main concern expressed by survey participants was the fear of failure. However, nearly as many people stated that they had no fears when starting out. The key behaviour that the subjects linked to past business success was the ability to build effective working relationships, highlighting the importance of effective interpersonal skills.

Entrepreneurs come from the whole range of social classes, but many come from a background of self-employment, or from a family situation which emphasised self-reliance. Most have a strong work ethic, and have little time for leisure interests. All share a strong desire to learn, but due to pressures on their time, they seek flexible or applied learning opportunities, often not offered through the mainstream educational system. A darker side of the entrepreneur's background is that s/he may be a difficult employee, hating being told what to do (du Toit 1980). Another issue raised by Burns and Dewhurst (1996) is that members of ethnic minorities are more willing to take the opportunity for enterprise and accept the hardship necessary to achieve it. This has certainly been the experience of many Irish emigrants, and the recent arrival of a significant immigrant population in Ireland highlights a parallel opportunity.

These descriptions of psychological traits are not meant to imply that the possession of such traits is a formula for success. Other key factors are:

▶ the right product
▶ good timing
▶ the economic environment
▶ the availability of finance.

What does appear to be true is that successful entrepreneurs share at least some of the traits discussed. The literature on this subject now discusses the clustering of traits, and the need for learning or buying in expertise to fill in gaps (Carson *et al.* 1995). If notable traits are absent, a potential entrepreneur might compensate by the addition of partners or shareholders to the business, which is why JOINT VENTURES and PARTNERSHIPS are such a popular structure. Mentoring and networking schemes are now an important element in the process of nurturing small business growth (see Section 13.14)

13.4 The entrepreneurial process

Defining ENTREPRENEURSHIP has proved problematic because of the somewhat insubstantial nature of entrepreneurs and the changing nature of the entrepreneurial process in the modern, knowledge-based economy. A starting point is to view entrepreneurship as the process of wealth creation. Hisrich (1986) puts it like this:

Entrepreneurship is the dynamic process of creating increased wealth. This wealth is created by individuals who assume the major risks in terms of equity, time and/or career commitment, of providing value for some product or service. The product or service itself may or may not be new or unique but the entrepreneur must somehow infuse value by securing and allocating the necessary skills and resources.

Drucker (1985) offers a very succinct definition of the entrepreneur as someone 'who starts his own new and small business'. Carland *et al.* (1985) make the distinction between the small business venture and the entrepreneurial venture. A small business is independently owned but not necessarily dominant or superior in any way. An entrepreneurial venture is one that is characterised by innovative strategic practices. Carson *et al.* (1995) point out that the manager of the entrepreneurial process will be called on to perform a wide range of roles—innovator, change agent, risk taker, team builder, leader, negotiator and networker. Handy (1999) likens the entrepreneurial process to that of alchemy. He suggests that entrepreneurs are 'people who dream dreams and make them happen'. Such people are encouraged if there is a buzz around, or a creative cluster of people with the same interests. He sees new technology as a tremendous opportunity for small firms to become the leaders at innovation. Many large firms are now outsourcing so much of their operations that they rely on their contractors to tell them what is new.

Exhibit 13.2 John Rocha: profile of an entrepreneur

John Rocha believes in destiny. You win some, you lose some—he has done both. Life has a strange, quirky fatedness, he reckons. How else could a Christian Brothers boy from Hong Kong end up running an international business from Dublin? John Rocha went bust twice, staged three comebacks, and has diversified away from his roots in the fashion business. His interests include fashion design, corporate image and modern corporate concepts. His achievements include the designer label 'Chinatown', the launch of modern lines of crystal for Waterford Glass, the creation of a new design of corporate clothing for Virgin Airlines, and an ultra modern corporate interior design for the Morrisson Hotel in Dublin. He was British Designer of the Year in 1997.

Rocha is an archetypal outsider, a multicultural composite who holds a British passport. 'If you ask me where do I belong, it would be somewhere in the Irish Sea—born in Hong Kong, Chinese mother, Portuguese father, lived in Europe most of my life. If I were to say tomorrow that I am Irish, people would laugh at me. I always feel that to give up my British citizenship would almost betray my upbringing.' There's Rocha the man, and Rocha the brand; one trades on the other. His label, as established by his fashion designs, earns him the quality cachet, which he can use for other products. He designs everything himself.

He wouldn't have done it alone. 'One thing I learned from all my years in business is you really have to work with the experts. I didn't realise that when I started. I thought if I could design, everything would follow, but the designer is only part of the machinery.'

His experiences of failure have taught him not to rely on any one collaboration. As a point of principle, he has repaid all the debts incurred in his previous businesses—the Chinatown label and his design work for A-Wear and Brown Thomas.

'Success came late in my life, so I was quite lucky that it happened then, because now I can handle most things and I look on it as the icing on the cake.'

Sources: Ruane (1998) and author's own research.

13.5 Intrapreneurship

The term INTRAPRENEURSHIP refers to intra-company enterprise: the ability of any organisation to foster a climate that supports innovative behaviour. The innovation may involve a new product, process, service or system. Kanter (1989) views innovation as the process of bringing any new problem-solving idea into use. The challenge of intrapreneurship is to upset the old order in existing organisations. Yet, most large organisations, being motivated by short-term profits, present significant barriers to the entrepreneurial style of behaviour (Carter and Jones-Evans 2000). Entrepreneurial activity, by its nature, is long term and shows a high rate of failure before the ultimate goal is achieved. Any mistakes made will not reflect well on the career of the typical corporate manager. As an entrepreneurial project grows in scale, the original proposer may be replaced by a middle manager, lacking in the vision and imagination of his predecessor.

The emergence of a distinct style of corporation which expresses entrepreneurial flair—as reflected by the likes of Hewlett Packard, Virgin, and Apple—is the result of an awareness of key changes in corporate attitudes to risk. By the late 1960s, large firms, influenced by the likes of General Electric in the USA, were decomposing their operations into STRATEGIC BUSINESS UNITS (SBUs). The initial focus of SBU activity was on profits: large organisations were keen to identify which segments of their business were making a profit, and to make profit comparisons across business units. These smaller business unit structures consequently encouraged a climate for innovation and the ownership of innovative ideas by individuals or small project teams. The entrepreneurial style of management in the larger organisation has been practised and preached by the likes of Steve Jobs (Apple), Sir John Harvey Jones (ICI) and Fergal Quinn (Superquinn).

Exhibit 13.3 Branson and Virgin: fostering intrapreneurship

For Virgin, Richard Branson is the style, the package, the logo, the message. He seems the virtual businessman. Hardly anybody knows exactly what he does, what he manufactures, instead he appears, presides, enables.

If he can be everywhere, so can Virgin. Every so often, pundits say sternly that Branson is spreading the brand too thinly and he is going to come a cropper, but that's precisely the point. The brand can be spread everywhere, like margarine. Virgin airlines, Virgin cola, Virgin vodka, Virgin trains, Virgin cosmetics, Virgin financial services, Virgin weddings, Virgin supermodel agencies, Virgin radio, Virgin jeans, Virgin cinemas, Virgin insurance, Virgin condoms, Virgin clubs, Virgin lavatory paper. And of course, Virgin balloons.

'I do like challenge,' he says. It seems an understatement. 'What I like most of all is to learn. When I feel that I've learnt what there is to know about telecommunications or airlines or cosmetics—well, you name it—then I move on to something else. In the past two years, we've launched eight or nine different companies in eight or nine different sectors' ... He's the cheerleader, making us all join in, and we don't even realise he has left us behind and moved on to somewhere else, somewhere quite new, virgin fields, and he is beckoning us across to share it with him.

Source: Gerrard (1998).

Intrapreneurs and independent entrepreneurs have many characteristics in common. In the large organisation, enterprise can only flourish if the right climate is created.

Innovative activity needs the sponsorship of managers at all levels of the organisation, to overcome financial objections and ensure that vital ideas are not lost. The original proposer of a creative idea or concept must be continuously involved, otherwise, the passion for innovation will soon diminish. To build success, intrapreneurial teams must be established, which typically means crossing functional divides (Jones-Evans 2000). Modern organisations view joint ventures, TECHNOLOGY TRANSFER, academic–industrial consortia and PUBLIC–PRIVATE PARTNERSHIPS as models that overcome internal weaknesses within one single organisation. The intrapreneurial organisation has a high tolerance of failure, and seeks to find reward structures that acknowledge the effort of the individual.

Exhibit 13.4 Rules of the garage

Believe you can change the world.
Work quickly, keep the tools unlocked, work whenever.
Know when to work alone and when to work together.
Share—tools, ideas.
Trust your colleagues.
No politics. No bureaucracy. (These are ridiculous in a garage.)
The customer defines a job well done.
Radical ideas are not bad ideas.
Invent different ways of working.
Make a contribution every day.
If it doesn't contribute, it doesn't leave the garage.
Believe that together we can do anything.
Invent.

Source: Hewlett Packard Corporation (2000).

Learning from the flamboyant success of companies that are openly visionary, organisations now strive to encourage a particular style of intrapreneurial manager. To take up this function, the individual most be able to adopt a multidisciplinary role, be visionary and action-orientated, be able to build a coalition of supporters, and show persistence in overcoming failure (Pinchot 1986).

13.6 The climate for enterprise

According to the Task Force on Small Business (1994), the number of start-ups and the number of businesses in existence in Ireland is comparable to the European average. However, Ireland is above average in the number of business failures, for example, 56 per cent of grant-aided businesses set up in 1983 were not in existence 10 years later. The country is also lagging behind in the number of fast-growth firms it generates. In the USA, for example, the success of fast-growth firms has had a very positive impact on job creation.

Economic growth and buoyancy have created a much more encouraging environment for new venture creation. Irish industry has been performing very well in this climate. Between 1994 and 1997, Ireland's gross domestic product (GDP) growth averaged 7.7 per cent compared to the European average of 1.9 per cent. In 1998, there was a further surge in GDP growth to an estimated 11.4 per cent, almost three times the EU average (Enterprise Ireland 1998).

Membership of the EU has accelerated an awareness of globalisation within the Irish business community. Start-up firms are now aware of the need to tackle international markets at their initial phase of business development. Enterprise Ireland, the state agency responsible for industrial development, is supporting the market development plans of Irish businesses through sectoral support plans. An example of one such initiative is the Enterprise Ireland Trade and Technology Centre, located at the heart of Silicon Valley, California. The Centre was established to support the needs of firms needing a physical presence to build business and improve relationships through having a direct presence in the market. Globalisation also has a downside. The trends towards global sourcing and integration of the supply chain can put smaller firms at a disadvantage. Shorter product life cycles are placing new demands on manufacturing companies, and skill obsolescence is a major concern.

Research and development is a key issue for Irish firms. Spending on R & D is currently less than 2 per cent of industry sales, but this spending is planned to treble by 2001 (Enterprise Ireland 1998). Irish SMEs (small and medium-sized enterprises) have a significantly lower return on assets than in the rest of Europe, and WORLD-CLASS MANUFACTURING (WCM) and benchmarking initiatives are under way to redress this deficiency (see Chapter 11). Capitalising on technological opportunities in industries such as biotechnology, software and electronics, means drawing on resources outside of the level of the individual firm. NETWORKS are being drawn together at an industrial, regional and international level. From a broader perspective, the presence of an Irish community in every country of the world offers unique networking opportunities. The US/Ireland Business Partnership Programme, operated by the US Small Business Administration and Enterprise Ireland, has brought together Irish and US firms to discuss strategic partnership arrangements.

High potential start-ups tend to operate in high technology, knowledge-intensive areas of industry. A targeted support system is offered through Enterprise Ireland, and it also reaches recent start-ups that have set their sights on further expansion. For example, the biotechnology sector holds out great promise, but needs technical support and technology transfer processes to bridge the gap between the research laboratory and the commercially viable enterprise.

Easier access to VENTURE CAPITAL (see Section 13.13) and a stable interest rate climate have improved the investment environment for business start-ups. At state level, Enterprise Ireland now seeks equity participation in firms receiving targeted support, through the issue of ordinary or preference shares. This stakeholder approach is reaping positive financial returns, which facilitates investment in further business development.

13.7 State industrial policy

The development of Irish industrial policy is examined in Chapter 2. This section discusses industrial policy in the context of small business and enterprise.

The report of the Task Force on Small Business (1994) highlighted the gap in specific policy making which was directed at the encouragement and support of small business activity. It bemoaned the lack of any government body specifically responsible for small business issues. It highlighted the poor availability of start-up and seed capital, in marked contrast to the generous grant and tax supports available to multinationals choosing to locate in Ireland. It also pointed out that while the public sector was a customer to many small businesses, it was slow to settle accounts and had an adverse effect on the cash flow of small enterprises.

In response to both of these reports, the main changes made were:

▶ the establishment of the Department of Enterprise and Employment, giving acknowledgement to the pivotal role of enterprise in the national economy

▶ the establishment of the County Enterprise Boards, to embed enterprise at a local level

▶ the establishment of An Bord Bia, responsible for the food industry, the single largest area of Irish exports

▶ the establishment, in 1995, of the Small Business and Services Forum, to advise the Minister for Enterprise on issues impacting on the sector; representatives of the Forum are practitioners and members of small business associations

▶ a re-evaluation of industrial training and apprenticeship schemes co-ordinated by FAS, the national training agency

▶ greater emphasis on the links between enterprise and education, and on closer relationships between business and education

▶ the enactment of the Prompt Payment of Accounts Act 1997, which required that all public bodies settle their accounts payable by the due date, so as not to disadvantage businesses

▶ the reorganisation of the state agencies responsible for entrepreneurial activity. Ultimately, this resulted in the establishment of Enterprise Ireland in 1998. The new state agency combines the resources of three former bodies—Forbairt, Irish Trade Board, and the in-company training division of FAS. Enterprise Ireland sees its role as providing solutions to small business issues, and offers a tailored, one-stop approach.

A 1996 report by Forfas, the body responsible for the development of indigenous industry, gave pointers for the future development of Irish industry. It suggested that policy development should be aligned along three strands, which are separate but also interdependent areas. The first strand is the further development of a climate favourable to industry, through tax breaks, the availability of capital and a more distinct acknowledgement of the role of the entrepreneur in Irish society. A second strand is the development of a strong INFRASTRUCTURE—better telecommunications, logistics and energy supplies. A third strand considers the aspects of research and development, training and education. The report signalled the need to boost R & D spending within the indigenous sector, and highlighted the emerging skill gaps in key areas. Policy makers responded by allocating infrastructure and education as priority areas for EU Structural Funds during the period 1994–99. Changes in the taxation regime were also implemented, resulting in reductions in the rates of Corporation Tax, Capital Gains Tax, and Capital Acquisitions Tax.

By 1999, Enterprise Ireland was highlighting five elements in its strategy for building competitiveness and growth:

▶ establishing new businesses with high growth potential

▶ increasing the number of first-time exporters

▶ raising the number of companies with a significant overseas market presence

▶ increasing investment in R & D

▶ increasing investment in human resources development.

By early 2000, the 'Enterprise 2010' report (Forfas 2000) signalled the refinement and redirection of industrial policy towards more specific goals. The new agenda reflects both the success of earlier policy initiatives, and the need to focus on more targeted initiative to build on the economic gains of recent years. To ensure that the enterprise sector remains as the main engine of economic growth, the following changes are needed:

▶ acceleration of the shift towards high-growth, high-tech, high productivity activities and a shift from production-type activities to services-type activities

▶ a gradual shift in employment to higher-value-added sectors

▶ an increase in labour productivity in existing companies

▶ a deepening of the base of companies performing research and development

▶ reversing the trend of economic activity concentrating around a restricted number of major urban centres, in favour of a more balanced spatial and regional development

▶ a shift in development agency assistance from 'capacity' support (for example, support for building and equipment) to 'capability' support in areas such as human resource development, R & D, marketing and market development.

Indicating the priority of industrial issues at national level, the government has already made a partial response to this agenda. In March 2000, it announced the establishment of the Technology Foresight Foundation to oversee the investment of €711 million in technological research and development funds. The two key areas to be supported are information technology and biotechnology. The intention is to create more high-value jobs in enterprises, which will work at the leading edge of their technologies. The new Foundation is forecast to have as profound an effect on the future, as did the decisions in the early 1960s that first put Ireland on the path towards industrialisation (Ahlstrom 2000).

13.8 Support agencies for enterprise

A significant number of agencies, both publicly and privately funded, offer advice, grants, workspace and ongoing support. For the would-be entrepreneur, it can often be difficult to judge which of these agencies is the most appropriate to his/her needs. As the business is established and developed, the type of support needed changes, from day-to-day hand-holding, to a requirement for planning strategy, raising capital and developing exports. Geographical location is also a factor in the level of support available. The border counties and Gaeltacht areas benefit from a number of special schemes and certain areas of high unemployment throughout the state have been singled out for community enterprise schemes and local area partnerships.

The Department of Enterprise, Trade and Employment is responsible for overseeing the activities of the various government-funded agencies responsible for enterprise.

The Minister and the Department, in consultation with the government and special advisory groups, carry out the functions of policy development, implementation, and review. Forfas, the state policy and advisory board for industrial development and science and technology provides reports and expert committees to assist in these processes. Decisions made at EU level are also followed through by the Department through the implementation of Directives, the co-ordination of EU policy and raising awareness about such issues as e-commerce and the Euro currency.

13.8.1 Government-supported agencies

Enterprise Ireland, established in 1998, is the state body responsible for the encouragement and support of indigenous enterprise. The decision to centralise services available to start-up businesses was taken after several reports commented on the spread of agencies involved in the process.

An initial point of contact for the would-be entrepreneur is the telephone service, Enterprise Link (1850-353-333) provided by Enterprise Ireland. This service provides initial advice and directions as to the supports and services available for any sector of business activity.

Enterprise Ireland provides its services to indigenous firms in the manufacturing and international services sectors. Retailing and personal services are excluded from its remit, as are professional services that do not have the potential for internationalisation (for example, medical services, professional tax advice). The organisation is focused on industry sectors: science and innovation, investment services, food and consumer products, industrial products, software and international services, and technology services. Business proposals submitted to Enterprise Ireland must have the potential to employ 10 or more people and achieve a turnover of €952,000 within two years.

If a new business proposal or venture is within the brief of the organisation as described above, the company or venture team will be assigned an advisor to deliver a customised, integrated service. The main initiatives currently being undertaken by Enterprise Ireland are:

▶ in-company *Research, Technology and Innovation (RTI) Schemes*, which bring together all the financial supports available for company-led research. In 1998 there were 206 projects approved for grant payments of €24.5 million.

▶ the *Techstart Programme* places young technical graduates in small firms. In 1999 200 graduates were placed, with a continuing emphasis on the food sector, forest products and construction services, to help these companies develop more value-added products.

▶ initiatives in *R & D management* designed to improve the management of research, development and innovation in firms. Actions under the scheme include training courses, consultancy, overseas study visits and post-graduate qualifications.

▶ the *Services Sector Strategy*. The list of designated service sectors supported by Enterprise Ireland is being updated to include new emerging services such as electronic commerce, multimedia and logistics management services. This strategy is designed to help Irish businesses become 'early movers' in these electronic services sectors. A second initiative currently under development is designed to stimulate greater business activity in services and, in particular, internationally traded services.

FAS—the Training and Employment Authority—is responsible for industrial training. Its network of regional offices provide training and employment services relevant to the needs of small businesses. The Training Support Scheme assists SMEs in improving the level of skills in areas such as production, planning, marketing, languages, quality, technology, etc. Apprenticeship grants are available in some sectors to assist with the cost of training craftspeople. The Job Training Scheme enables and encourages employers to provide training to people who were previously unemployed. The Small Business Management Development Programme provides training on a one-to-one basis to the owner or manager of a business. FAS also operates a wide range of industry-related training courses, including an Enterprise course. One successful graduate of this course was Geoff Read, founder of Ballygowan Spring Water.

FAS has also undertaken a number of initiatives specifically targeted at the small business sector. The Community Enterprise programme provides training and employment grants towards the cost of employing enterprise workers and/or project managers. The 'Cluster' programme helps developing companies to strengthen their managerial capabilities through a training programme that is grant-supported and delivered in-house. The Co-Operative Development Unit promotes and assists individuals and groups who wish to organise themselves into worker CO-OPERATIVES. This option is useful for family businesses where there is no successor, and in rural areas. It offers an incentive to workers to stay in an area that might otherwise become depopulated (FAS 1998).

City and County Enterprise Boards (CEBs) are locally controlled enterprise development companies established in each County Council and urban local authority area in Ireland. The functions of the 35 CEBs are to develop indigenous enterprise appropriate to the local conditions and to stimulate economic activity at local level. The CEBs were established in 1993 in response to a perceived gap in the supports available to micro-enterprises (less than 10 people). During 1993–95, CEBs approved grants of €46.9 in respect of 4,339 projects, including 1,126 feasibility studies. The largest number of projects approved was in the services sector, and project proposers were individuals, existing micro-enterprises or community groups (Report of the City and County Enterprise Board Activities 1997)

Exhibit 13.5 County Enterprise Board support helps lever finance

Turning a kitchen sensation into a commercial success proved a little less difficult than the promoters of Ballymaloe Relish first expected. Initially promoter Yasmin Hyde was stunned by the success of the product. South Cork CEB approved grant aid of €33,000 for this enterprise towards the cost of plant and machinery. This helped develop the operation from a back kitchen initiative to a state-of-the-art food producing facility. The facility meets the highest international food hygiene standards. To quote the promoter: 'We must have had the very first grant aid application lodged with SCEB. Once they backed us, it started a spiral with the banks all coming on stream.'

Source: Report of the City and County Enterprise Board Activities (1997).

The **Business Innovation Centres** (BICs) are an initiative co-funded by the government and the EU. The six centres located in the main cities provide information and support services for potential and existing small businesses. The services include business counselling, assistance with trade and technical research, and project management advice. The EU linkage has fostered the development of NETWORKS for Irish business in such areas as technology transfer and MARKET RESEARCH. The BICs also have strong working relationships with other enterprise agencies.

Shannon Development offers similar services to Enterprise Ireland, in counties Limerick, Clare, North Tipperary, south-west Offaly and north Kerry. The Shannon Free Zone is a designated area with preferential tax incentives geared to attract multinational companies. In the Shannon area there is a focus on two differing types of enterprise: tourism and high technology start-ups. Shannon Development also operates a discretionary grants scheme for projects that do not qualify for assistance under any other state programme.

Údarás na Gaeltachta provides enterprise support services in the Gaeltacht areas of Donegal, Mayo, Galway, Kerry, Cork, Waterford and Meath. The schemes and supports available are similar to Enterprise Ireland. Údarás na Gaeltachta has made significant investments in enterprise and craft centres, to encourage the development of enterprise in what are mostly rural areas. The level of financial support offered is higher than elsewhere in the country, and the sectors experiencing success are tourism, crafts, seafood, light engineering and software businesses.

Other agencies relevant to the entrepreneur include:

▶ the **National Food Centre**—operates a range of services for the food industry, including product and process research, development and testing.
▶ the **National Microelectronics Centre** (NMRC)—provides design and evaluation services for the electronics industry.
▶ **Campus Innovation and Enterprise Centres**—attached to most universities and Institutes of Technology, and support ventures initiated by academics or graduates. These initiatives have received significant EU funding in support of the perception that the gap between academia and industry needs to be narrowed, and the pace of ground-breaking innovation needs to increase.
▶ **Bord Failte**—responsible for the tourism sector, it operates a range of financial and advisory supports, and the current focus of activities is on the provision of a better tourism infrastructure and a higher quality of facilities.
▶ **Bord Iascaigh Mhara** (BIM)—responsible for the development of fisheries and aquaculture, it offers capital grants and runs an industry-specific co-operative and small-business development scheme. The EU has targeted aquaculture as an area for specific supports, to compensate for problems being experienced in other aspects of fisheries activities.
▶ the offices of the **European Union** (centrally in Dublin, and nationally through the Business Innovation Centres)—offer information about EU programmes and sources of funding. Programmes of particular relevance include LEADER (rural enterprise), INTERREG (SMEs and co-ops) and STRIDE (links between research centres and industry). The EU is also a significant purchaser of goods and services from the Irish business community.
▶ the **International Fund for Ireland** (IFI)—provides seed capital and financial support for enterprise centres in the border counties of Cavan, Donegal, Leitrim,

Lough, Monaghan, Sligo and Northern Ireland. The Fund is co-ordinated through the Department of Foreign Affairs.

▶ the **Project Development Centre** (Dublin Institute of Technology)—offers a number of support programmes at pre-start-up, start-up and growth stages. The programmes provide a mixture of MANAGEMENT DEVELOPMENT, incubation space and facilities, business counselling, access to funding and access to the PDC's network of over three hundred entrepreneurs and associate professionals. Although located in Dublin's docklands, entrepreneurs nation-wide can access its support.

▶ **Area Development Partnerships**—to initiate a co-ordinated effort to target high unemployment areas, 12 Area Development Companies have been established in selected areas. The initiative is co-financed by the government and the EU, and each company has an enterprise officer who channels funds towards the establishment of micro-enterprises and co-operatives. In Dublin, for example, the Northside Partnership established the Greencaps, a co-operative company providing support services for passengers and ground services at Dublin Airport. This achieved the dual objectives of establishing a new enterprise while at the same time generating employment for the workers recruited to the scheme.

13.8.2 Privately funded agencies

Private enterprise has acted to support several initiatives through the provision of workspace and finance.

First Step raises funds through the private sector to assist entrepreneurs who would otherwise have difficulty raising capital. It works through existing community service groups and also provides a mentoring service. The **Liffey Trust** is a voluntary, privately funded body that operates its own enterprise centre. It provides manufacturing space, consultancy and support services at no charge, while the business is getting off the ground. The **Society of St Vincent de Paul** operates an Enterprise Support Scheme that offers seed capital and support. Other privately funded agencies of relevance to the entrepreneur include:

▶ the Chambers of Commerce
▶ the Small Firms Association
▶ the Irish Small and Medium Enterprise Association (ISME)
▶ the Small Business Units of the commercial banks
▶ business and financial consultants.

13.9 The small-business sector

The popularity of the small business and enterprise culture fosters many myths about the contribution that SMEs make to the nation's economic well-being. These ideas and assumptions have been greatly boosted by the Internet, where the high valuation placed on start-up e-businesses appeared for a while to offer a whole new economic paradigm. As the glow has dimmed, so has the distinction between the impact and behaviour of small and large firms.

According to Bhide (1999), a small minority of small businesses—about 10 per cent—generate profits or develop new technologies. The typical micro-enterprise just about breaks even, provides one or two jobs and is based in a mature industry. Most of these businesses survive on tiny amounts of capital and there is no clear path from small to larger enterprise. Only the exceptional companies will thrive, and 98 per cent of these attribute their success to 'exceptional execution of ordinary ideas'.

Exhibit 13.6 Start-ups versus established companies

Typical start-up companies:

- have little capital, few intellectual or other assets, novel ideas or experience
- pursue opportunities in niche markets requiring little investment, but where the likely pay-off is small and uncertainty high
- depend on the energy and opportunism of individuals; improvisation; tolerance of ambiguity; sketchy planning and little research
- focus on short-term cash flow.

Established companies:

- have ample capital, many tangible and intangible assets (patents, know-how, brands), extensive co-ordinating mechanisms
- pursue opportunities in mass markets requiring high investment but where the pay-off is high and uncertainty low
- depend on planning, wide-ranging co-ordination, long-term programmes to develop assets and markets
- focus on long-term profits.

Source: Bhide (1999).

These ideas are further reinforced by the statistics about small business in the Republic of Ireland. The Task Force on Small Business (1994) defined a small business as one employing 50 people or less or where annual turnover is less than €3.8 million. Of the small firms analysed by the Task Force, a little under half were run solely by their owner, and a little over half employed at least one person. Most businesses in Ireland were found to be small businesses, and most small businesses were very small. About 98 per cent of non-farm businesses were classified as very small, while 90 per cent of companies employed less than 10 people. 80 per cent of small businesses were in services. Since there is no particular agency registering small businesses, estimates have to be gathered from a number of sources.

Table 13.1 Profile of the Irish small-business sector

	1996	1997	1998
Number of new companies incorporated	16,112	19,023	N/A
Number of companies dissolved	10,280	3,132	N/A
New jobs created by small business	43,000	51,000	57,000 (est)
New business names registered	6,550	7,449	N/A

Sources: Companies Registration Office, Small Firms Association.

It can be seen that the small-business sector thrived through the late 1990s. There is little data on the long-term survival rate for small businesses. However, the Task Force report (1994) showed that 36 per cent of grant-aided firms in the manufacturing and international services sectors had gone out of business by the time they were nine years old. Indeed, as these figures only include grant-aided enterprises, they almost certainly understate the real closure rate.

Dun and Bradstreet, a private company which tracks firms that have defaulted on their debts, reported a dramatic climb in the number of company failures in Ireland during 1999. Of all company failures, 95 per cent fell under the official classifications of small businesses. Manufacturing companies experienced the highest failure rate (25 per cent of failures) followed by wholesaling (21 per cent) and construction (17 per cent). The factors causing the high rate of failure in 1999 included over optimistic forecasts, sectoral rationalisation and poor financial management.

Table 13.2 1990–2000 Irish company failures

Liquidations	1st Q	2nd Q	3rd Q	4th Q	Total
1990	134	152	124	115	525
1991	141	136	229	124	630
1992	149	174	149	147	619
1993	177	174	168	151	670
1994	219	161	136	118	634
1995	165	145	162	156	628
1996	194	141	158	162	655
1997	126	155	115	123	519
1998	176	157	150	155	638
1999	178	109	176	286	749
2000	225	180	191	175	771

Source: Dun and Bradstreet.

13.10 Screening new venture proposals

Investors and venture capital executives are continually analysing business proposals and evaluating risks and returns. Before a business proposal is put on the table, the proposer or venture team needs to be able to present a proposition that is high in credibility and low to moderate as a risk.

The initial step in developing the proposal is to test the concept or unique selling proposition (USP) and see if prospective buyers and users understand it. For example, Eircom nominated Ennis, Co. Clare as the 'technology town' of Ireland, to enable trials of new, information-age products and services.

If the initial concept looks feasible, then technical trials and tests will be underway to determine the specific nature and pricing of the product. In many cases there are also regulatory issues to consider, for example, food safety and packaging claims. Technical trials may be undertaken as part of a shared venture or co-operative agreement. For smaller firms, options such as TECHNOLOGY TRANSFER or LICENSING eliminate the need for technical tests altogether.

The design and aesthetics of products and of service environments has become a key point of difference. The Apple iMac is an example of a conventional product being designed in an exciting new format; this was particularly appreciated by graphic designers, key customers for Apple. All of a sudden, competitors rushed to modernise their grey and black personal computers.

A final issue worth considering is the possibility of building partnerships with prospective suppliers or buyers at this early stage. As well as being mutually advantageous, this strategy can help to raise issues that are more easily resolved at the development stage than immediately prior to the launch of the venture.

Some companies use a checklist or a rating scale to evaluate the business potential of an idea. For any idea, there are 10 key questions to be answered:

❶ What is the potential return on investment?

❷ What are the estimated monthly sales for at least the first three years?

❸ How long is the estimated growth period of the product's life cycle?

❹ What is the estimated start-up time before high-volume sales?

❺ How long will it take to pay back the capital investment?

❻ What is the probability of achieving a unique market position for the product?

❼ What effect will the business cycle have on the product or service?

❽ What is the potential for selling the product at a premium price?

❾ How easy is it to enter the market?

❿ How long will it take to test-market the product or service?

The business knowledge contained in this text gives guidelines to answering the above questions. Unless at least six of the responses are promising, the project will most likely be a failure.

13.11 Ways of entering business

One of the most interesting aspects of enterprise is the variety of ways of getting started. Choice of entry method depends on the degree of control sought by the entrepreneur, the expected life of the business and the anticipated entry costs.

SOLE TRADER. This is an attractive route for the person who is concerned with retaining ownership and control of his/her own business. It means that the profits of the business accrue entirely to the owner. A sole trader is not required to register his/her accounts, apart from the usual requirements for income tax, PRSI and VAT purposes. If the business name is different from the proprietor's name, it must be registered with the Registrar of Business Names. This form of business is most suited to an individual who wants to start small and stay small. It is most favoured by the proprietors of small retail outlets, pubs and small service businesses.

Along with the attractions, there are several disadvantages that cannot be ignored. A sole trader is personally liable for the debts of his/her business, and so risks losing his/her home and other assets should s/he encounter difficulties. The second major problem is raising finance. When an investor is considering backing a sole trader, s/he is supporting the individual as much as the business. There may be doubts as to whether the individual has all the necessary qualities for success. Many sole traders stay small, not by choice, but because of problems with working capital and cash flow. Problems with succession often mean that the business dies with the retirement or death of the owner.

PARTNERSHIP tries to deal with the limitations of the one-person business by involving two or more partners. There are two to twenty people to share the debts and the profits. Some of these may be 'sleeping partners' who have shares but take no part in the running of the firm. This business format seems most suited to financial and professional services.

Partnership offers the same advantages as sole trading except it also tries to spread the risk and responsibility. It is cheap and easy to set up, but care has to be taken in selecting partners who are reliable from a business point of view and who have compatible personalities. Difficulties may arise if there is a dispute among partners, or where one partner wants to withdraw his/her investment.

Most partnerships start off by drawing up a formal agreement setting out individual responsibilities, profit shares, voting rights and the action to be taken when difficulties arise, for example, the dissolution of a partnership, trading difficulties, withdrawal, retirement or death of existing partners, or the incorporation of new partners. In the standard partnership agreement, each partner is liable for the entire debts of the business. Voting rights and profits are usually allocated on the basis of equal shares, seniority, or capital invested.

LIMITED PARTNERSHIPS are where one or more partners limit his/her liability to the amount s/he has invested in the partnership. However, limited partners cannot take part in the management of the business. There must be one partner willing to accept limited liability.

LIMITED COMPANIES are separate legal entities, set up by reference to the rules of company law. The main advantage is that liability is limited to the company, so that the shareholders can only lose whatever amount of share capital they subscribe. A company can be set up from scratch, or an off-the-shelf company can be bought from a registration agent. A company must have a minimum of two directors, and a company secretary. Alternatively, this role can be performed by one of the directors or an outside agent such as a solicitor or an accountant. It must register a name that is acceptable to the Registrar of Companies. It files two documents that are essential for the formation of the company: the Memorandum of Association and the Articles of Association.

The Memorandum needs to be signed by the directors and states the company name, registered office, share capital and company objectives. The Articles of Association deal with the rules governing the internal workings of the firm and are signed by the directors. A Certificate of Incorporation must be received before the business can commence trading.

The limitation of liability means that a director's home and personal assets are safe. Sometimes the value of this clause is reduced in the case of a new company trying to borrow funds. The lender may ask for a personal guarantee as s/he may feel that the new business is a risky proposition. A limited company also operates around a more structured framework, as there are certain legal requirements with which it must comply. The main one is that it must file annual accounts with the Registrar of Companies. On the positive side, the preparation of annual accounts is a good method of control. There are also attractive tax advantages to a limited company. Income tax is paid only on salaries and benefits drawn, and retained profits are taxed at a low rate. There is a 10 per cent rate of Corporation Tax for companies engaged in manufacturing. A limited company can raise finance through the issue of shares or may qualify for the Business Expansion Scheme. Finally, it also has the advantage of spreading ownership, thereby diluting the risk.

The biggest drawback is cost—the cost of setting up and then complying with the requirements of the Companies Act. These factors deter many small firms from incorporation as limited companies. A tax disadvantage is that accumulated profits withdrawn from the company as DIVIDENDS, salaries, benefit in kind or loans are subject to additional taxation. Service companies complain that the tax advantages favour manufacturing activities. For all these reasons, the limited company structure is most favoured by those entering business with a number of shareholders, or in a situation where there are diverse interests that need legal regulation.

Table 13.3 Make-up of the Irish Register of Companies 1997

Type of company	Number of companies on the Register
Private limited	149,522
Public limited	749
Unlimited	5,535
Limited partnerships	302

Source: Companies Office Report (1997).

FRANCHISING can be defined as a contractual relationship between a franchisee (usually taking the form of a small business) and a franchisor (usually a larger business) in which the former agrees to produce or market a product or service in accordance with an overall 'blueprint' devised by the franchisor (Carter and Jones-Evans 2000). The relationship commences with the signing of a formal legal agreement. The franchisor usually provides advice, research and support with advertising, marketing and site selection. The franchisee usually pays an initial signing-up fee and also an ongoing royalty or service fee, based on turnover and/or a mark-up on the supplies bought from the franchisor. The franchisee provides some or all of the set-up capital, and is a legally separate entity to the franchisor. Most franchise names are from the USA, for example, McDonald's, Holiday Inn, Burger King and Pizza Hut. The best known Irish franchises are O'Brien's Sandwich Bars, Abrakebabra, Supermacs and Eddie Rocketts.

Franchise agreements are of three different types. Manufacturers use franchises as a way of distributing their product, for example, car dealers. A second situation is where the franchisor acts as wholesaler to the franchisee, for example, health foods or slimming products. The third and most common situation is where the franchisor offers a system, which may include a brand name, a known image and a unique system, for example, The Body Shop.

Franchising systems represent a pooling of resources between the parties involved, and therefore reduce the capital cost and risk involved in business expansion. Firms wishing to expand into other countries find franchising an attractive and quick way of entering the market, if there are potential franchisees with good skills and market knowledge available. Once procedural manuals and legal agreements have been drafted, the cost of expansion is usually limited to franchisee recruitment, training and overheads. Although the revenue from franchised units is lower than from company-owned outlets, so too is the capital investment from the franchisor.

Franchisees can be expected to be well motivated to perform in a business that usually represents their own personal investment.

For the franchisee, a business format franchise offers the opportunity to own a business, with a reduction in risk because of the relationship to a larger firm. The holder of a master franchise has rights to a particular region or country, with high potential rewards. She/he has support with management and marketing, usually a burden to the typical SME. The franchise agreement covers a defined territory, limiting competition. Operating costs may be lower due to a group-buying system and pooled marketing resources. The use of an already known brand name or system should make it easier to recruit customers.

The drawbacks to the franchising system are fairly obvious, and the reader may have observed some of these issues in practice. The franchisor may have difficulty exercising control over how the system is being operated, and over the level of profit being declared. If the franchisee is under performing, there may be little that can be done during the period of the agreement, unless the actual conditions are being breached. Change management can be a cumbersome process if the franchisees are well practised in the current system (see Chapter 14). The franchisee may be slow to feed back information, particularly if it will lead to the establishment of more outlets or the drawing up of a new type of agreement. The franchisor may also experience difficulty in recruiting the right franchisees, particularly at the start-up phase.

For the franchisee, tight external control mitigates against putting his/her own personal stamp on the business. A franchisee never fully owns the business and may be prohibited from selling it or passing it on to another family member. It may be that an independent business could be established for the same sort of capital, without the involvement of a franchise. Finally, competing outlets from other franchise operations can pose a threat, for example, in the fast-food business.

A recent report examined the potential of franchising as a system for Irish companies to expand their markets overseas (McGarry Consulting 1998). The report suggested that there is strong potential for the export of Irish business concepts to the European market. It proposed that the state sector could provide a rounded support package for franchisors. A further business opportunity suggested by the report is the potential for Irish companies or entrepreneurs to bid for master franchise rights for the UK and Ireland.

Licensing, technology transfers and joint ventures can be considered together because there is substantial similarity in the arrangements in each case.

LICENSING offers some of the same advantages as franchising, but it is a more straight-forward arrangement. Manufacturers are often actively searching for licensees, or open to offers to manufacture or distribute under a licensing agreement. Such contracts can be initiated directly, or as a result of a meeting through a business agency (for example, a Chamber of Commerce) or a trade show. The licencee usually pays an initial fee, plus royalties. In general, Irish firms are underutilising this business opportunity; as well as expanding business it can be a useful learning opportunity leading to a further network of contacts.

TECHNOLOGY TRANSFER agreements usually involve a larger firm sharing or extending some aspect of its technology, under a formal agreement, with a smaller firm. The larger firm gains market coverage and the smaller firm gains the technology and a higher knowledge base. More recently, technology transfer ideas have been applied in the university sector to speed up the transition from academic innovation to commercial production. Technology transfer agreements may qualify for special-status EU funding.

JOINT VENTURE agreements may cover two or more firms, and involve some sharing of resources in regard to products, services or markets. The venture may be initiated by the firms themselves, or by an external body. For example, Enterprise Ireland supported a BRANDING campaign for the Irish clothing industry. Called 'The Look is Ireland', the campaign co-ordinated the resources of the industry, without conflicting with the branding efforts of each firm.

CO-OPERATIVES are businesses owned and run jointly by its members, with the profits shared among them. The advantages are in the raising of capital and the feeling of democracy in the way the business is run. A co-op can be formed by seven or more people and must register with the Registrar of Friendly Societies. It may affiliate to an existing co-operative body (for example, the Irish Co-operative Society, ICOS, in the agricultural area) and adopt its model rules.

The Co-operative Development Unit attached to FAS, assists start-up co-operatives, and also suggests co-op structures as an option for family firms where there is no obvious successor, or for medium and large firms seeking to develop their staff and create new employment opportunities. In 1998, 17 new co-operatives were established, employing 76 people. Co-operative structures have particular appeal for craft businesses in rural areas, and women have found the structure of particular interest (FAS 1998).

Buying an existing business: An attractive option for the would-be entrepreneur is to buy a business that is currently trading. The size of such a commitment can vary enormously. The buyer can purchase existing plant and equipment, agree to hire the existing workforce, or just buy the company's name and good will.

The attractions of the buy-out or buy-in are obvious. The business is already up and running, so many of the pitfalls of a start-up are avoided. It has most likely passed the break-even stage. Its expertise, track record, earnings and reputation are known and act as a measure of its value. It may be possible to buy an existing business for less than it would cost to start from scratch. The purchaser hopes to turn the firm around from loss to profits, or improve on existing profits, though the failure rate is higher among those who aspire to turn around a business than among those who buy businesses that are already in profit.

On the other hand, the first question to be asked by the buyer is: Why is this firm for sale? The most common reasons are:

▶ It is a recent or consistent loss maker.
▶ The market has changed. The firm's plant may be outdated, and the employees in need of retraining.
▶ The owner wants to divest to pursue other interests, or to retire.
▶ A company wants to sell an unprofitable or an unacceptable profitable subsidiary or division. Retirement or DIVESTMENT are more attractive selling reasons than a history of consistent losses.

The buyout (or buy-in) itself can take a few forms:

▶ The purchaser is an individual who may fund the investment from savings, inheritance or a severance payment, or borrow part from a lending agency.

▶ The buyer is an existing group of employees or managers who raise joint funds and get the support of a bank or venture capital company. Management/employee buyouts are increasingly common, as it is easier to raise funds between a number of employees. If the business is already profitable, it is not too difficult to get lenders interested. An example of a successful MANAGEMENT BUYOUT in 1999 was the drinks company Cantrell & Cochrane.

▶ The purchaser is a company—many firms now feel it is less costly to buy-in than build a business from the ground up, and the number of acquisitions has increased steeply. It makes sense to limit ACQUISITIONS to businesses in a similar line, or those that afford a degree of forward or backward integration. The Smurfit Group and Kerry Group have made acquisitions in this way (see Table 13.4).

▶ The buyer is a company specialising in buy-ins. Its business is to buy firms, improve their profits and then maintain or resell them. One business personality well known in Ireland for this type of activity is John Teeling of CountyGlen and Cooley Distillery.

Exhibit 13.10 Top five Irish acquiring companies 1999

Bidder	Target	Deal value (€m)
Elan Corporation	Dura Pharmaceuticals (US)	2,100
Baltimore Technologies	Content Technologies (UK)	690
Elan Corporation	Liposome Company (US)	596
Greencore	Hazelwood Foods (UK)	588
Green Property	P&O Property portfolio (UK)	508
Total value of acquisition activity in Ireland in 2000		10 billion euros

Source: McGrath (2001).

The ideal business to buy is one that is well established in the marketplace, with proven products and a strong earnings record. The other cornerstone is cashflow: the buyer must be sure that the daily payment demands can be met, and that loans can be paid as they fall due. Only when this can be done with some margin of safety should the purchase contract be signed.

13.12 Feasibility studies and business planning

Having decided on the most suitable type of business organisation, the entrepreneur is now in a position to formulate a more concrete business proposal. If the proposal is a manufacturing or service idea requiring significant investment, the initial step will be to carry out a feasibility study. If the results of the feasibility study appear promising and if the problems raised can be resolved, a business plan is then formulated. If the proposal involves a tried and tested area, or if it is already within the field of the entrepreneur's experience, s/he may feel confident enough to proceed directly to the business planning stage.

13.12.1 The feasibility study

A feasibility study is an examination of all the factors relevant to the establishment of the business. The purposes of such a study are to prepare a plan of the requirements necessary to develop the manufacturing plan or service operation, to arrive at an estimate of the finance required to set up the business, and to examine the underlying key assumptions and timetable of events. It can be seen from the foregoing that a feasibility study demands extensive research and consideration. Professional consultants are often required to provide a research input, or to assist with the preparation of the feasibility study document. Outside assistance is also helpful in viewing the business from a different perspective and questioning the key assumptions and financial projections. Enterprise Ireland and the County Enterprise Boards provide financial support towards the cost of preparing a feasibility study involving manufacturing or international services, provided the proposal is not in an area in which overcapacity already exists.

The typical headings for a feasibility study would be as follows:

❶ Profile of the project promoter(s)
❷ Description of the business proposal
❸ Details of the product/service
❹ The market and customer base
❺ Capital requirements
❻ Employment
❼ Critical issues for the project, for example, market research, product trials
❽ Key assumptions and schedule of events.

Preparation of the feasibility study forces the entrepreneur into an examination of the crucial aspects of the business proposal. It also provides answers to the questions that will be posed by lenders and investors. If the outlook is positive, the information gathered for the feasibility study can be expanded upon in more detail in the business plan.

13.12.2 The business plan

The objective of the BUSINESS PLAN is to set out in detail the proposal for the establishment and management of the business. The plan sets targets that can act as yardsticks for measuring progress once the business is up and running. The preparation of a business plan is also an exercise in communication: the clarity of expression is a reflection of the extent to which the proposal has been planned and considered.

Exhibit 13.7 Differences between the feasibility study and the business plan

Feasibility study:
- a comprehensive analysis of information regarding the proposed venture
- written for the benefit of the entrepreneur
- regarded as a search for any factor which could prevent the project from succeeding
- details of the feasibility of the project for a certain level of investment
- details alternative promotional/marketing strategies that the business can use

Business plan:
- a programme of action outlining how the business will be conducted
- often written for potential investors as well as the entrepreneur
- a positive statement outlining the direction of the business
- states the necessary financial requirements of the business
- describes the marketing strategies that the business will use

Source: Bohan (1994).

A business plan may be prepared with a variety of audiences in mind:

▶ the entrepreneur, or entrepreneurial team
▶ the lending agency
▶ the investor
▶ the venture capitalist
▶ the grant giving authority, at local, national or European level
▶ key suppliers and customers.

The actual writing of the business plan is the responsibility of the entrepreneur or members of the venture team, though it may be necessary to call on expert advice as to the research and presentation of various aspects of the proposal. A balance sheet, cash flow and profit and loss statements covering five years of activity will be included in the financial plan. The financial forecasts will also give an analysis of the break-even point, return on investment, and best- and worst-case scenarios.

The following headings show the contents of a typical business plan:

❶ Executive summary
❷ Promoters and summary company details
❸ Outline of proposed venture
   a. Overview of proposed business
   b. History of the business
   c. Objectives and strategy
   d. Industry analysis
   e. Proposed product/service
   f. Break-even calculation
   g. Return on investment and financial ratios
❹ Market research and analysis
   a. Target market and customer profile
   b. Secondary research

   c. Primary research—method and findings

   d. Market positioning

   e. Market size and share

   f. The competition

❺ The marketing plan

   a. Sales plan

   b. Distribution strategy

   c. Pricing strategy

   d. Promotion plan

❻ Production/operations plan

   a. Premises

   b. Production/operations process

   c. Labour force

   d. Machinery and equipment

   e. Materials

   f. Suppliers

   g. Manufacturing/process costs

❼ The venture team

   a. Outline of proposed owners/shareholders

   b. The management team

   c. Responsibilities and organisation

   d. List of advisors used to date—solicitors, accountants, stage agencies, etc.

❽ Financial plan

   a. Sources of finance

   b. Profit and loss projections

   c. Cash flow projections

   d. Sales forecasts by project/service

   e. Sensitivity analysis

❾ Statement of strengths, weaknesses, opportunities and threats (SWOT) of business proposals

❿ Schedule of events proposed

⓫ Appendices.

The most common reasons why a start-up venture might fail to attract finance are listed below. These are useful pointers to remember when preparing and presenting a proposal:

❶ weakness in management (lack of motivation, no financial expertise, no feel for the market, no track record)

❷ inadequate personal finance

❸ poorly presented proposals

❹ inadequate security offered

❺ too many risks inherent in the venture

❻ overambitiousness

❼ lack of detail as to how the finance will be repaid

❽ product or service weakness

❾ insufficient market research.

❿ no clear source of competitive advantage.

⓫ intellectual property rights unavailable.

A useful example of the impact of these issues comes from the software industry.

Exhibit 13.8 Fledgling software companies: the pitfalls

- Not knowing or researching the market well enough
- Forgetting to protect the core business
- Not identifying what you do well and what you need help with
- Being reluctant to change
- Getting distracted by peripheral problems stemming from rapid growth
- Not identifying core competencies which help identify further product or business opportunities
- Failing to retain key staff
- Not employing validation procedures to assess future growth
- Floating on the stock market too soon.

Source: Prospectus (1998).

13.13 Sources of finance

The sources and availability of finance have expanded considerably throughout the last decade. A common factor highlighted in all public reports has been the scarcity of small-business and start-up capital, and this gap is being narrowed through more targeted schemes and more flexible solutions, such as the channelling of more government support through equity rather than straight grant support. The recent wave of successful new Irish enterprises has increased business confidence in investing in new projects. However, there is still a shortage of capital and a need for more structured schemes to target the start-up of the micro-business.

The reasons for this shortage of capital become more apparent when the issue of finance is examined from the lender's point of view. The lender is trying to evaluate the risk of the project proposal, counterbalanced by the possible rewards and the time frame involved. O'Kane (1995) suggests that banks measure lending proposals using three criteria—character, collateral and cash flow. If the proposer is already known to the bank, or has a track record and the experience to draw up a credible business plan, the chances of achieving the loan package sought are higher.

Venture capitalists and BUSINESS ANGELS are willing to live with a higher degree of risk but also screen a higher volume of proposals before settling on the few that are perceived to have a higher chance of success. Business angels are business individuals or companies with high net worth interested in fostering new enterprises, particularly in the e-commerce arena. Entrepreneurs in Ireland hoping to initiate e-commerce ventures are networking with potential business angels and venture capitalists at a monthly gathering called the 'First Tuesday' club. This informal gathering, held on the first Tuesday of every month in Dublin facilitates the initiation of relevant funding and support contacts. Virtual companies may also make their first funding contacts online, through incubators such as HotOrigin.com or BusinessIncubator.com.

Table 13.5 Sources of new venture finance in Ireland

Source	Examples
Equity	Owners' equity Seed capital Development capital
Bank loans	Enterprise loan schemes through clearing banks and ICC
Seed capital	Business Innovation Centres' seed capital fund
The Stock Exchange	Developing Companies Market
Tax incentives	Business Expansion Scheme
State agencies	Equity participation, development grants
Venture capital	ICC Software Fund
Short-term finance	Leasing, hire purchase, factoring

Table 13.6 Irish venture capital funds: summary of investments 1998 (€'000)

ACT Enterprise Fund	2,857
AWG Investment Fund	635
Bank of Ireland Entrepreneurs Fund	2,349
Campus Companies Venture Capital Fund	116
Dublin Seed Capital Fund	349
Enterprise 2000 Fund	127
First Step	546
Guinness Ulster Bank Equity	1,600
ICC Software Fund	3,809
Smurfit Venture Investments	1,378
Trinity Venture Fund	1,359
TOTAL	15,124

Source: Burke (2000).

A final issue to consider is the capital structure desired by the owner–manager or project proposer. If the business is family-owned, there may be a strong desire to retain ownership within the family, and a reluctance to cede a share to any outside interests. If the project proposed is capital-intensive or requires a heavy outlay on research and development, the only option may be to bring in additional investors. Having made that decision, considerable time and energy will be committed to consideration of the most suitable equity structure, and the time frame over which the financial commitment will be extended. The financial structure of the micro-business will be reshaped as the firm develops and grows. Start-up firms tend to rely on debt finance, and rely more on internal than external sources of finance. As the firm matures the reliance on debt declines (Carter and Jones-Evans 2000). Economic conditions are a huge influence: the buoyant Irish economy and low interest rate regime since the late 1990s caused a loosening of lending criteria and an uplift in the expectations of success.

13.14 Developing and nurturing new enterprises

As a business becomes established and experiences success, new challenges arise. These strategic issues will place demands on the founders of the enterprise which can be acknowledged and addressed, or ignored in the hope that they will disappear off the business agenda.

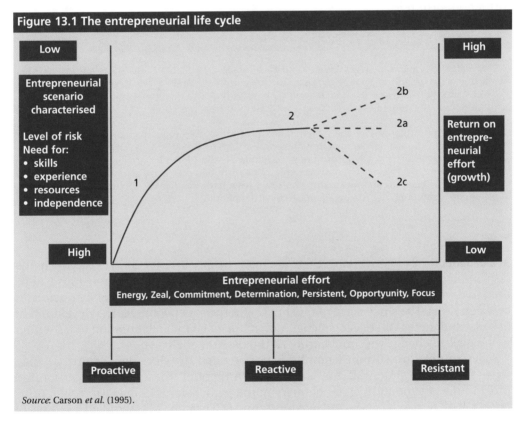

Figure 13.1 The entrepreneurial life cycle

Source: Carson et al. (1995).

As Figure 13.1 shows at the outset, the new enterprise is chaotic, creative and informal in style. There is ambiguity about roles, management skills may be limited or lack definition, and the enterprise is under the personal guidance of the founder. As business grows, there may be a sense that the venture is getting too big and that things are getting out of hand. There is a need for more formality; clearer structures emerge to impose control and accountability. The emergence of stability and greater special-isation may serve to dampen the spirit of entrepeneurialism. The original founders of the business may be supplemented or substituted by professional managers with a greater emphasis on the 'bottom line'. At this critical stage, the founder must give leadership and develop entrepreneurial teams to revitalise and renew the organisation. In many cases the founder or original visionary does not have the skills or experience to drive the business further, and success will depend on his/her willingness to build a team with complementary abilities.

One way for the new venture founder to improve his/her competencies and vision is through the use of NETWORKS. These can be of two types: personal, informal networks, or more formal arrangements between organisations. The personal contact network (PCN) is inherent to the venturer's way of doing business, in that the idea and gestation of the business will have arisen through the development of informal and unstructured personal contacts (Carson *et al.* 1995). As shown in Exhibit 13.16, government agencies and European policy makers have recognised the potential of PCNs, and are harnessing these networks for the purposes of creating and developing further opportunities.

Exhibit 13.9 The Plato Programme

The Plato Programme involves large companies assisting SMEs with advice on all aspects of managing the growth of their enterprises. The idea originated in Belgium 10 years ago, and has been successfully adopted in an increasing number of regions in Ireland. Plato Programmes are funded through County Enterprise Boards with funding from the EU.

Companies participating in the scheme are part of a two-year structured management development programme that puts them in contact with other SMEs and also with larger firms, which act as mentors and advisors to the participants. A recent Plato Programme in north Dublin had 85 businesses participating, of which only 17 per cent had previously attended management programmes. They received advice and mentoring from large companies within the same region, including Superquinn, Aer Rianta, Campbell Bewley and Irish Ferries.

Source: Adapted from Kerr (1999).

At a broader level of networking, there are many avenues for the SME to explore in the development of inter-organisational relationships (IORs). These relationships can be used to develop new products, build new markets, share risks and establish synergies between firms. The small scale of most new enterprises encourages the development of IORs, and there is increasing recognition of the need for collaboration as a solution to the pace of change without bearing all the risks on one's own.

Policy makers are currently emphasising the need to select new ventures which have significant potential for expansion, and offer these firms a structured programme of support to channel them on the path towards being fast-growth firms (FGFs). Irish research conducted by Murray and O'Gorman (1994) studied a sample of SMEs with the aim of discovering what characterised and differentiated the high-growth firms. Their research found that the most important management decision influencing growth was the choice of market. The choice of a high-growth-rate market resulted in a high growth rate for the company. High-growth companies focused on particular segments of the market, where they competed by differentiating their product and their company.

Exhibit 13.10 The Business Partnership Programme

Established by Enterprise Ireland, the Business Partnership Programme (BPP) aims to set up Irish firms with potential partnerships overseas for product or service licensing, technology transfer, joint ventures, contract manufacturing or collaborative R&D. The Irish firms involved are SMEs with a certain amount of financial and managerial resources. Overseas partners are quite similar, and so far have tended to come from the USA or EU. The typical partnership deal tends to be long term in nature, and so far 70 such agreements have been signed. About half the firms involved have been in the high tech and food sectors, and the BPP's own staff believe there is significant untapped potential out there.

Source: Latimore (1999).

A second conclusion from the Murray and O'Gorman study was that high-growth companies are more likely to export or make overseas investments. As many new venture start-ups are now in markets which are global, the venture team acknowledges the need to 'go international' from the outset. While SME scale might initially seem to discourage participation in international markets, the structure of this type of firm offers several clear advantages. SMEs can be more flexible and can communicate directly with customers, facilitating a faster reaction to market needs and the ability to customise where required. SMEs can be risk takers, attacking new or emerging market sectors that have been ignored or sidelined by larger enterprises. The SME can compensate for a lack of scale by entering joint ventures or co-operative networks (Hollensen 1998).

Internationalisation may occur simply because the SME's customers are a global group, or because the SME follows customers abroad. A third option is to encourage international customers to visit SME suppliers on their home territory, which can result in increased exports, as illustrated in Exhibit 13.11.

Exhibit 13.11 The Crafts Council of Ireland: helping Irish craft companies to export

'Showcase Ireland' is an annual international crafts, gift and fashion trade fair. It is held in mid-January in Dublin over four days. It brings together craftworkers from all over Ireland and world-wide buyers, and is now Ireland's largest manufacturers' fair. In the last five years buyer attendance at the fair has trebled, and sales in 1998 amounted to €61 million.

Business at the fair generates substantial further orders throughout the year. The demand for stands is constantly increasing and outstrips the space available.

'Showcase Ireland' is organised by the Crafts Council of Ireland, with the financial support of Enterprise Ireland and the European Union. Enterprise Ireland organises the inward buyers who visit the fair, representing craft, gift and department stores all over the world. 'Showcase Ireland' competes with other international craft fairs like Frankfurt, for example, to secure and increase international sales of Irish crafts.

The fair is divided into different sections. The 'Craft Village' highlights the best of contemporary Irish design. The 'New Faces' area is where the work of up-and-coming craftspeople is displayed. Other sections of the fair include the gift, knitwear and fashion exhibitions. Many craftspeople rely on the fair for more than 50 per cent of their orders. It is a unique opportunity for them to meet foreign buyers and increase export sales.

Source: Foley and Curley (1998).

The electronic business environment streamlines the potential for globalisation in a way that is particularly attractive to the new enterprise. A firm may choose to develop its own website, have a presence at a portal or retail site, or use e-commerce to streamline its dealings with suppliers and customers. The adoption of the electronic business model may eliminate the need for a tangible physical presence in the marketplace. As Exhibit 13.12 demonstrates, this 'virtual marketplace' is particularly attractive to the micro-business.

Exhibit 13.12 Selling speeches in cyberspace

Niamh Crowe sells speeches over the Internet. Her one-woman company 'Speech-writers.com' operates from her Dublin home. Her website attracts 60,000 hits per month from customers looking for prepared speeches for business or social occasions. More than 90 per cent of sales come from the USA, Australia and South America. But why would someone want to download a speech written by a complete stranger? 'The hassle factor is a major selling point,' says Crowe. 'Many people don't have the time. Or maybe they just lack confidence.'

Speechwriters went online in 1994, but business really boomed following the introduction of a fully automated service in 1999. The success of the business now poses a dilemma. 'I have to ask myself, do I need to grow bigger?' comments Crowe. 'And in doing so, could I sacrifice the very qualities that make the service so attractive?'

Source: Adapted from Power (1999).

A final cautionary note in the context of new-venture growth concerns the dangers of complacency and STRATEGIC DRIFT. Much success turns out to be transient, and the factors that have driven success may also be factors that cause market shakeout and business failure. Miller (1990) suggests that the excesses of success can cause a company to lose sight of its original vision and motivation. He calls this the Icarus Paradox. Icarus was a tragic figure of Greek mythology who died because he flew too close to the sun. His greatest asset, his wings, became his downfall as he was seduced into considering himself omnipotent. The same phenomenon is experienced in many organisations; the taste of success leads to specialisation and overconfidence. A drift away from the core needs of the market being served represents a path towards decline. A firm often finds that it has to move away from its original mission and the vision of its founders, but the message is that this move needs to be thought through and planned, rather than just being a series of events that develop and evolve.

13.15 Summary of key propositions

▶ Economists, psychologists and social commentators have viewed the subject of entrepreneurship in different terms.

▶ 'Intrapeneurship' refers to intra-company enterprise and the effort to foster a working climate that encourages creativity.

▶ Defining entrepreneurship has proved problematic, but must take in a broad range of perspectives.

▶ There is an important distinction between entrepreneurship and innovation.

▶ The climate for enterprise is very positive in Ireland, and the enterprise culture is blooming.

▶ The publication of recent government reports has resulted in the reorganisation of the government bodies responsible for industrial development in Ireland. Enterprise Ireland is the central agency now responsible for enterprise development.

▶ There is a wide range of agencies, both publicly and privately funded, involved in support schemes for new business. Support offered includes finance, training, business planning and mentoring schemes. Start-up enterprises are encouraged to take a strategic approach, and funding is more likely to be through equity than by direct grant aid.

▶ There are approximately 160,000 small firms in Ireland. Most businesses are small (98 per cent), and most small firms are very small (90 per cent of all companies employ less than 10 people).

▶ New product/service ideas must be put through a screening process in order to test their viability.

▶ There is a variety of ways of entering business—sole trader, partnership, limited company, etc. Choice of entry method depends on the degree of control sought by the entrepreneur, the expected life of the business and the anticipated costs.

▶ The initial step in exploring the viability of a business proposal is the preparation of a feasibility study. If the results of this study are promising, a business plan is then formulated.

▶ The new enterprise has a wide choice of financing options. The financial structure chosen will depend on the type of enterprise structure and the level of growth anticipated.

▶ Once the enterprise is established and stable, it must focus on building up its business. The management of a new firm must be aware of and anticipate the most common reasons for business failure.

Discussion questions

❶ Review the definitions of entrepreneurship proposed by various authors. In your opinion, which of these definitions is most accurate?

❷ Complete a personal profile of an individual entrepreneur, known either locally or nationally. How do his/her background and personal traits compare with those mentioned in this chapter?

❸ What type of business structure (for example, sole trader, partnership, etc.) is most commonly used by small firms? Why?

❹ Prepare a short case study of a recently established enterprise for presentation in class. The following headings should be addressed:

   ▶ details of the proprietors of the business
   ▶ product/service offered
   ▶ level of innovation
   ▶ sources of finance

- ▶ track record to date
- ▶ operational/managerial problems
- ▶ future prospects.

❺ Select an enterprise known to you which has encountered failure/liquidation in the last five years.
- ▶ Why did the business fail?
- ▶ Did the enterprise recommence business in either the same or a new format?
- ▶ Have any of the employees, to your knowledge, become entrepreneurs themselves?

❻ Can you think of any examples of successful business people who encountered failure? What effect did it have?

❼ Family-owned businesses often encounter problems with succession, leading to the sale or closure of the business. In your opinion, how can this problem be resolved?

❽ Compare and contrast the level of state financial support available for manufacturing and for service projects.

❾ Which state agencies could offer assistance to an entrepreneur in the following situations:
a. an individual buying a newsagent's shop
b. an experienced shop manager currently in employment planning to start a business in the food industry
c. the managing director of a timber firm examining the prospects for a new enterprise making pine furniture.

❿ Visit your nearest campus innovation centre or Enterprise Incubation Centre.
a. Compile a list of the firms in operation.
b. How long has each enterprise been in business?
c. How is each business financed?
d. Prepare a short profile of the owner or manager of one enterprise.

⓫ Research the rates of interest and the terms being offered to start-up enterprises by lending institutions.

⓬ As a would-be graduate, do you consider your career prospects lie in employment or in starting your own business? Why?

⓭ Discuss the impact of e-business on the SME, in the context of new venture creation and development.

Concluding case: Iona Technologies

Introducton

Iona Technologies is an Irish based software company established in 1991. It has evolved to become an established player in the global marketplace for very specialised software solutions. It was the first Irish software firm to float on the NASDAQ stock market, in February 1997.

The start-up

Dr Chris Horn, a lecturer in computer science, established Iona Technologies as a campus company at the University of Dublin in 1991. He also led a team of researchers who worked on new methods of programming using a combination of object technology and networking. At the university, Dr Horn had attracted significant research funding for his studies.

The other members of the management team on board at the start-up were Dr Sean Baker, also an academic, Annrai O'Toole, who had been a research student at the college, and Colin Newman, who is credited with formalising the early business and marketing practices within the company.

'The classic problem is having a really good idea, but no good management ability,' says Dr Horn. 'When we started we were conscious we didn't have good marketing experience, so early on we brought in additional management on the marketing, sales and financial side at both board and senior management level.'

Iona's products are in the middleware section of the software business, providing solutions that allow different types of computer systems to talk to each other. Middleware systems ideally enable software components from different systems to be snapped together. Those systems must be reliable as the typical applicants involve mission critical systems with a low tolerance of failure. Iona's core technology; an implementation of Common Object Request Broker Architecture (CORBA) competes directly with products offered by IBM, Inprise, BEA, and Oracle. The company first generated substantial profits in 1997, and now employs over 600 people from its head office in Ballsbridge, Dublin, and also at locations in the USA, Hong Kong and Australia.

Launching new software products

The launch of a new software product on the market is the culmination of a complex process, involving not just the development of the software product itself, but also a thorough analysis of the legal and marketing issues to be considered. For a company like Iona, active in international markets, the process is even longer and more involved.

Any new piece of software that is regarded as significantly different needs patent protection, which can take up to 18 months to be issued. One of the drawbacks to this system is that the idea has to be kept confidential until the patent is issued, so production cannot take place beforehand. It is also advisable to register a trademark in each market where the product is to be sold. There are several examples of European software products entering the US market, only to find other products there carrying the same name. Iona has used the brand name 'Orbix' for its software products, and its advertising slogan 'Orbix everywhere' communicates the interconnections that are enabled by its products.

Introducing new customers to a new piece of software is a challenging task. In the words of Noel Toolan, a past marketing director of the company: 'You never get fired for buying technology from the big guy. So our job is to break through the barrier and establish Iona as a force in the market.' To encourage the trial of the new software, Iona issues it to prospective users for 60 days at about 5 per cent of the purchase price. At the end of that period, the product automatically ceases to operate, and the customer can opt to buy the full package, or return the trial system. The company also exhibits at major trade shows, and quickly follows up on all leads gained. By 1999, with Iona's market capitalisation exceeding $1 billion, it was in a position to launch a new advertising campaign featuring an army of worker bees singing 'Let's get together'. The company has also acquired a number of software distribution firms and signed a licensing deal with Sun Microsystems.

The firm is also building its sales and marketing support operations. 'When we went public in 1997, we did very well selling sub-$250K contracts,' says Dr Horn, 'but now we also have to sell directly to the chief executive and chief technical officers.' This is a more difficult sell, as both the technology and the company itself are still relatively new.

As Iona strives to become a mainstream software supplier, it is encountering competition from the likes of IBM and Oracle. These firms have the advantage of being US based and having large armies of sales people on the ground. Iona's answer to these competitors is upfront and aggressive. 'We have a very unique attitude to the software business,' says Annrai O'Toole, chief technical officer. 'We believe in making a profit, a foreign concept to many companies in Silicon Valley.'

Financing company development

Iona's start-up as a campus company could be said to be a reasonably sheltered one. The confines of the university setting encouraged the research and development phase, while the campus company designation required that 15 per cent of the equity share be allocated to the college.

As Iona grew to the stage of being confident about its products and markets, the management team focused on preparing a strong business plan to attract substantial investment. Initially, the company undertook training and consultancy work while pitching for European funds to support product development.

Iona Technologies was the first Irish software firm to float on the US NASDAQ stock market in February 1997. The IPO (Initial Public Offering) was carefully planned to happen at a time when Iona was hitting the profit phase. In the words of Dr Horn: 'The very worst thing you can possibly do is go public, and then miss your first quarter.' The listing on NASDAQ followed 18 months of time-consuming work. The company had to issue a prospectus and detail its profit projections. The managing director made presentations to investment houses world-wide, explaining how a little-known Irish software house represented a rising star. The board had to be in place and have a management structure that was prepared for growth.

The firm's shares floated at $18, and initially were a runaway success, peaking at $50 a share during the period 1997–99. Since then, fortunes have been mixed, as is typical of the software industry.

Current outlook

Iona's current challenge is to manage growth. Their products face stiff international competition. There is limited legal protection of intellectual property in the software business, and other firms may develop superior technologies. The management team is grappling with a skill shortage, which is affecting information technology industries world-wide. The firm needs to nurture existing staff if it is to harvest the knowledge base represented by the global potential of its products. Iona is currently examining the potential of further mergers and acquisitions, a sign that, as a company it, too, is coming of age.

Case questions

❶ Look up Iona's current share price on the NASDAQ. Would you regard the shares as a good investment?

❷ The transition from a medium-sized to a large company does not happen in every enterprise. Evaluate the factors that have caused Iona to achieve such growth, and discuss the extent to which further expansion is feasible and advisable.

❸ Consider the management team at Iona.
   a. Is the team, at present, sufficient to carry forward the momentum for future growth?
   b. What additions or changes to the management team would you consider necessary, in this knowledge-based industry?
   c. Prepare a list of strategic issues to be considered at the next board meeting of Iona Technologies.

Case adapted from Healy (2000); Iona Technologies Annual Report (1998); *Sunday Business Post* (1999); Lyons (1998); McGee (1999); McKay (1999).

Keep up to date

www.iona.com
www.enterprise-ireland.ie
www.pdc.ie: Project Development Centre
www.hotorigin.com: Irish portal for start-up e-businesses
www.businessincubator.com
www.firsttuesday.ie: Meeting place for e-business entrepreneurs and financiers
www.cro.ie: Companies Registration Office
www.forfas.ie
www.irlgov.ie/entemp: Department of Enterprise and Employment

Bibliography

Ahlstrom, D. (2000) 'Foresight Foundation Given Task of Making us Trailblazers' *Irish Times*, 9 March.

Arrow, K. (1962) 'Economics, Welfare and the Allocation of Resources for Inventions', in R. Nelson (ed.) *The Rate and Director of Inventive Activity*. Princeton NJ: Princeton University Press.

Barney, J. (1991) 'Firm Resources and Sustained Competitive Advantage', *Journal of Management*, 17, 99–120.

Bhide, A. (1999) *The Origin and Evolution of New Business*. London: Oxford University Press.

Bohan, P. (1994) *Notes on Enterprise Development*. Dublin: The Marketing Institute.

Burns, P. and Dewhurst, J. (1996) *Small Business and Entrepreneurship*. Basingstoke: Macmillan.

Cantillon, R. (1931) *'Essai sur la nature du commerce en général'*, edited with an English translation by Henry Higgs. London: Macmillan.

Carland, J. W., Hoy, F., Boutlon, W. R. and Carland, J. A. C. (1984) 'Differentiating Entrepreneurs from Small Business Owners: A Conceptualisation', *Academy of Management Review*, 9 (2), 354–9.

Carson, D., Cromie, S., McGowan, P. and Hill, J. (1995) *Marketing and Entrepreneurship in SMEs: An Innovative Approach*. Hemel Hempstead: Prentice-Hall. Chapters 2 and 4.

Carter S. and Jones-Evans, D. (2000) *Enterprise and Small Business: Principles, Practice and Policy*. Harlow: Prentice Hall.

Companies Registration Office: www.cro.ie.

Department of Enterprise and Employment (1998) *Companies Office Report 1997*. Dublin: Government Publications.

D'Aveni, R. (1994) *Hypercompetition: Managing the Dynamics of Strategic Manoeuvring*. New York: Free Press.

Drucker, P. F. (1985) *Innovation and Entrepreneurship*. London: Heinemann.

du Toit, D. E. (1980) 'Confessions of a Successful Entrepreneur', *Harvard Business Review*, November–December.

Dun and Bradstreet, www.dbireland.com.

Enterprise Ireland Annual Report 1998: Dublin.

FAS Annual Report (1998) Dublin: Government Publications.

Foley, E. and Curley, C. (1998) 'The Crafts Council of Ireland: Helping Irish Craft Companies to Export', in S. Hollensen *Global Marketing*.

Forfas (1996) Shaping Our Future: A Strategy for Enterprise in Ireland in the 21st Century. Dublin: Government Publications.

Forfas (2000), Enterprise 2010, www.forfas.ie.

Gerrard, N. (1998) 'Why do we Love Richard Branson?', *Observer*, 8 February.

Hamel, G. and Prahalad, C. K. (1994) *Competing for the Future*. Cambridge, MA: Harvard Business School Press.

Handy, C. (1999) *The New Alchemists*. London: Hutchinson.

Hayek , F.A. (1949) *Individualism and economic order*. London: Routledge and Kegan Paul.

Healy, Y (2000) 'Boffins have to do the business', *Irish Times*, 15 February.

Hewlett Packard Corporation: www.hp.com.

Hisrich, R. D. and Peters, M. P. (1989*) Entrepreneurship*. New York: Irwin.

Hollensen, S. (1998) *Global Marketing: A Market-Responsive Approach*. Hemel Hempstead: Prentice Hall.

Iona Technologies Annual Report (1998) Dublin.

Irish Business and Employers Confederation: www.IBEC.ie.

Kanter, R.M. (1989) *When Giants Learn to Dance*. Simon and Schuster: London.

Kenny, I. (1991) *Out on Their Own: Conversations with Irish Entrepreneurs*. Dublin: Gill & Macmillan.

Kerr, C. (1999) 'Small Businesses Warm to the Plato Philosophy', *Irish Independent*, 24 June.

Keynes, J.M. (1965) *A Treatise on Money*. London: Macmillan.

Latimore, J. (1999) 'SMEs: Take Your Partners for Growth', *Irish Times*, 26 January.

Liebenstein, H. (1980) *Inflation, income distribution and x-efficiency theory*. London: Croom Helm.

Lyons, M. (1998) 'Launching software is patently difficult', *Irish Times*, 23 January.

Marshall, A. (1920) *Principles of Economics: An Introductory volume*. 8th ed. London: Macmillan.

McClelland, H. (1960) *The Achieving Society*. New York: Van Nostrand.

McGarry Consulting (1998), *The Franchise Option*. Dublin: Report to Enterprise Ireland.

McGee, J. (1999) 'Into Orbix', *Business and Finance*, 28 January.

McGrath, B. (2001) 'Business makes a big deal of 2000', *Irish Times*, 6 January.

McKay, N.(1999) 'Iona aims to make it in first division', *Irish Times*, 5 February.

Menger, C. (1994) *Carl Menger's lectures*, ed. and trans. by E.W. and M. Streissler, Aldershot: Edward Elgar.

Mill, J.S. (1996) *Essays on economics and society*. London: Routledge.

Miller, D. (1990) *The Icarus Paradox: How Exceptional Companies Bring About Their Own Downfall*. New York: Harper Collins.

Murray, J. A. and O'Gorman, C. (1994) 'Growth Strategies for the Smaller Business', *Journal of Strategic Change*, 1, (3).

O'Farrell, P. N. (1986) *Entrepreneurs and Industrial Change*. Dublin: Irish Management Institute.

O'Kane, B. (1995) *Starting a Business in Ireland*, 2nd edition. Dublin: Oak Tree Press.

Pinchot, G. (1986) *Intrapreneuring*. New York: Harper Row.

Porter, M. E. (1990) *The Competitive Advantage of Nations*. New York: Free Press.

Power, E. (1999) 'Unaccustomed As She Was', *Irish Times*, 11 November.

Prospectus Management Consultants (1998) *The Irish Software Industry*. Report commissioned by the Irish Software Industry Association, Dublin.

Report of the City and County Enterprise Board Activities 1993–1995 (1997) Dublin: Government Publications.

Ruane, M. (1998) 'If At First You Don't Succeed', *Irish Times*, 23 April, 15.

Say, J.B. (1997) *An Economist in Troubled Times*; J.B. Say, Writings selected and translated by R.R. Palmer, Princeton, N.J.: Princeton University Press

Schumpeter, J. (1942) *Capitalism, Socialism and Democracy*. London: Allen and Unwin.

Small Business and Services Forum (1999) *Annual Report on Small Business in Ireland*. Dublin: Government Publications Office.

Smith, A. (1805) *An Inquiry into the Nature and Causes of the Wealth of Nations*. London: T. Cadell and W. Davies Publishers.

Sunday Business Post (1999) 'IT Road Warriors', 21 November 1999.

Task Force on Small Business (1994) Dublin: Government Publications.

Timmons, J. A. (1994) *New Venture Creation: Entrepreneurship for the 21st Century*. Boston, MA: Irwin.

Chapter 14

The Management of Change

14.1 Introduction

This chapter examines the management of change within organisations. Due to the changing nature of the business environment (discussed in Chapter 3), the management of change has become a top priority for all managers, irrespective of the organisation within which they work. Change is occurring at a far greater pace than before and the changes themselves are fundamental. Organisations face unique sets of factors forcing change and four broad trends that are driving change—globalisation, developments in information and communication technology, the changing nature of the labour force, and the changing nature of work—are identified and discussed, along with potential sources of resistance to such change. A model of strategic change is outlined and applied to an Irish example. Finally, factors which contribute to the successful management of change are considered.

14.2 The nature and importance of change

The whole area of change and change management has become one of the most important issues in the field of management. Change can be viewed as perceived or felt differences in circumstances and behaviour, to such an extent that a situation becomes or is made different (Mills and Murgatroyd 1991). Therefore, change is concerned with different circumstances and behaviour.

The 1990s were a decade of highly significant change for organisations and indeed the entire world. In 1990 the Internet was largely limited to use in scientific exchange and some government communications. In 2000 almost 1 billion people world-wide are communicating and transacting business deals via the Internet. This marks one of the most phenomenal changes to the conduct of business affairs since the industrial revolution. In addition, industry boundaries have been eroded, major technological advances have occurred, previously closed markets have been opened and global competition has significantly increased (Hitt 2000). In the midst of all of this upheaval the manner in which business is conducted is changing rapidly and strategic discontinuity rather than continuity is the norm.

Change has become an important issue for managers due to the nature of the business environment. Instead of a stable and certain environment, organisations are now faced with complexity, uncertainty and DYNAMISM, all of which demand change. Such change, however, is very different in both nature and duration to other periods of change faced by organisations. First, the current period of change contains fundamental changes rather than minor changes. These changes are so important that they require changes in the way we think and view the world, sometimes referred to as *paradigm shifts*.

Second, the period of change appears to be one long process of continuous change. Previous changes facing organisations had clearly identifiable beginnings and ends. For example, an organisation was able to recognise a given change and alter its behaviour in some way to accommodate the change and then carry on its operations. Today, however, organisations are caught up in one long continuous process of change. As soon as an organisation responds to one set of changing circumstances it is faced with another. Organisations, therefore, have to constantly adapt in order to meet changes or to anticipate future developments in the business environment. Change, therefore, has assumed paramount importance for organisations due to its nature and duration.

Organisations which fail to respond to and anticipate change find themselves either out of business or with severe competitive difficulties. The Internet revolution has taken its toll on many established organisations. In the retail book industry in the USA Barnes & Noble was severely effected by the emergence of Amazon.com which provides books over the Internet. If Barnes & Noble could have anticipated such changes they could have established their own online book service before Amazon and thus developed a strong market share.

Not only is change occurring in all parts of the world, it is also affecting each of the major functions within organisations. Its not uncommon for employees to be involved in more than one change intervention at a time, further complicating matters (Cutcher-Gershenfeld *et al.* 1997). The changing nature of the business environment is forcing organisations to introduce strategic change and to develop new managerial skills to deal with new issues. Figure 14.1 provides a summary of the nature of the business environment and the managerial skill requirements to compete in such a marketplace, as identified by Hitt (2000).

Figure 14.1 The business current environment: key managerial requirements

Business environment	Managerial requirements
Intense competition	Flexibility and agility
Continuous and rapid change	Building human capital
Strategic discontinuity	Creating, diffusing and applying knowledge
Fundamental and paradigm change	Developing a global market
	Building core competencies

Source: Hitt (2000).

According to Hitt (2000) the changing nature of the business environment demands a new mindset which is global in orientation and permits strategic flexibility. Managers must be able to strike a balance between constant and fluid situations. Organisations also must have a highly developed source of human capital to draw on. This involves training employees to ensure they have a wide portfolio of skills, which generate flexibility. To manage in a business environment characterised by constant change, employees need to think laterally or 'outside of the box'. This involves opening the mind to new possibilities and eventualities which would previously have been incomprehensible.

As ARTIFICIAL INTELLIGENCE becomes more developed and widespread, human capital will be required to effectively harness and apply artificial intelligence with other technologies. Organisations must develop a culture of career flexibility within their workforce. Another key managerial skill is that of creating, diffusing and applying knowledge. Such organisations require a process of continuous learning and should always be open to learning new concepts. Continuous learning organisations develop a culture of innovation.

To facilitate the development of a global market the organisation will have to develop a multinational culture. This can be facilitated by the development of multicultural work teams and management teams which help to promote the development of a more global approach. In addition, multicultural work teams produce greater diversity of thought and can generate more innovation. The final managerial challenge associated with the changing nature of the environment is the need to build up dynamic core competencies in the context of organisational vision. It is critically important that core competencies do not become core rigidities as was the case with IBM in the mid-1990s (Hitt 2000).

Having outlined the nature of the business environment and the critically important managerial requirements for global success, it is necessary to consider the specific factors which are forcing organisations to change.

14.3 Factors forcing change

Organisations operating in both developed and developing countries are facing enormous pressure to change. Such pressures for change can come from two sources, namely, those internal to the organisation and those external to the organisation. While internal pressures for change (such as the long tenure of a CEO or management team; see Boeker 1997) are important, they are heavily influenced by developments in the external environment. For this reason, our analysis here will focus mainly on factors in the external business environment which are driving change. Internal pressures will be considered later during the discussion on the change process.

Each organisation faces a unique set of factors which shape change depending on the nature of the industry and the characteristics of the organisation. However, it is possible to identify broad factors which are forcing organisations world-wide to change their strategies and operations, as illustrated in Figure 14.2.

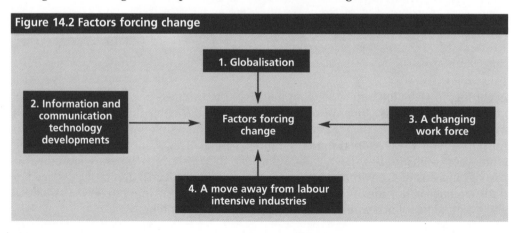

Figure 14.2 Factors forcing change

14.3.1 Globalisation

Organisations currently face competition on a global scale. Markets which were previously served by domestic operators have typically been opened up to foreign competition from aggressive new entrants, and are becoming borderless. Organisations, therefore, confront competition, not only from national competitors, but also international competitors. The trend towards globalisation has resulted from the emergence and development of a number of important industrial economies which have provided intense competition in established markets, especially that of high technology:

▶ the emergence of industrialised countries including the 'four dragons' of South Korea, Taiwan, Hong Kong and Singapore

▶ the emergence of the Single European Market

▶ the move from planned economies to more open-market-based economies in eastern Europe and the former Soviet Union.

▶ developments in the Asia/Pacific region

▶ developments in the Americas.

All of these factors have heightened the trend towards global markets and consequently global competition and GLOBAL STRATEGIES. Globalisation is now a powerful force facing organisations, and one that cannot be ignored. An example of an industry that largely ignored the trend towards global competition during the early 1980s is the US automobile industry. Throughout the 1960s and 1970s the US market had been dominated by US manufacturers: General Motors, Ford and Chrysler. However, the early 1980s saw the emergence of Japanese competitors into this previously domestic US market. Within a few years, companies like Honda, Nissan and Toyota had overtaken the US manufacturers in their home market. The US manufacturers closed 13 plants during this period. In contrast, the Japanese opened 11 plants (Hitt *et al.* 1992). The Japanese success was primarily due to its high quality/modest price strategy and the fact that the US manufacturers failed to respond to the global competition that confronted them.

The global nature of the auto market has continued into the new millennium with significant MERGER and ACQUISITION activity. For example, Daimler-Benz and Chrysler have merged, while Peugeot has acquired Nissan. There have also been strategic alliances between Japanese and US manufacturers. Many of the key players in the industry today sell their products on a global basis. As a result, there have been moves to standardise operations. For example, the Ford Motor Company plans to automate and standardise brand images across global websites and sales materials. The rationale behind the move is to a have globally uniform image on all Ford websites and print advertising.

As a result of the trend towards globalisation, the number and strength of international and MULTINATIONAL CORPORATIONS (MNCs) has increased significantly. Such corporations are now the major players in the world economy. Trends towards privatisation and deregulation have also contributed to global expansion. Where markets have opened through deregulation, large multinationals have frequently entered the scene. The privatisation of large state-owned organisations has resulted in leaner, more efficient and therefore more competitive organisations.

The emergence and expansion of corporations of this nature, such as McDonald's, Ford, Intel and IBM, create pressure for domestic organisations. In order to compete with emerging global players, smaller domestic organisations have had to introduce strategic change in relation to their structures, culture and operations. Recent moves towards deregulation in a number of markets in Ireland, including telecommunications and public utilities, has meant that many Irish organisations are facing global competition. Organisations such as Eircom have responded by attempting to place the company in a sound competitive position. Therefore, globalisation is an important development driving change for many organisations.

14.3.2 Information and communication technology developments

The pace of technological change in both manufacturing and information is occurring at a quicker rate than ever before. Technological developments have led to the introduction of computer-aided design (CAD) and computer-aided manufacturing (CAM) techniques and, recently, organisations have started to experiment with COMPUTER-INTEGRATED MANUFACTURING (CIM). The CIM system involves the use of networks of computers to link the order, production, sale and distribution of a product. For example, a customer could place an order for a product by computer. This would then be relayed to a factory computer which sends instructions to factory machines outlining what needs to be produced, the mode of distribution and materials needed from outside suppliers. In this way the organisation can operate a JUST-IN-TIME (JIT) manufacturing system which reduces the costs of holding inventory.

Technological innovations and changing customer demands have resulted in a shorter product life cycle and reduced lead times for producing new products. Organisations can therefore no longer rely on technological leadership and innovation to provide a long-term source of competitive advantage. Product life cycles and lead times used to be as long as 10 years but now they are reduced to a few months. For example, when General Electric first produced X-ray machines, it enjoyed a competitive advantage for many years based on that technological innovation. Today General Electric has to innovate at a far quicker pace to enjoy any form of competitive advantage from its technology (Potts and Behr 1987). Intel creates sophisticated products so quickly that in some cases in less than a year a new product has cannibalised an old one. This also gives the company little time to recoup their enormous R & D investment. The current pace of technological innovation demands that organisations be adaptive and flexible in order to compete effectively.

However, the most dramatic and influential changes are occurring in the area of information and communications technology, where developments have far-reaching affects on the management and operation of work. Systems such as management information systems (MIS) and financial information systems (FIS) have facilitated the dissemination of timely and accurate information throughout the organisation. These information systems have resulted in the elimination of layers of middle managers whose prime function was to relay information up and down the hierarchy. This has led to huge reductions in costs. These systems also make the control of operations much easier as the remaining managers can now spend more of the day facilitating the completion of work, rather than controlling the work of employees.

Technological developments such as teleconferencing, video-conferencing, faxes and e-mail have greatly facilitated information exchange between people, regardless of physical distance. A key result of such developments is that people no longer need to be in close physical proximity to work collectively with others. Increasingly it has become possible for people to work from their homes and to communicate by phone, fax and computer. So while the Industrial Revolution resulted in people moving to central bases such as factories, revolutions in information technology mean that the reverse can now happen with people working in isolation from their homes (see Section 14.3.4 for a fuller discussion).

The emergence of e-business and the use of the Internet for business purposes has probably been the most significant change to the conduct of business in the last decade. It is having a profound effect on the operation, relationships and structures within modern organisations (McKenney 1995). Organisations now have electronic links to suppliers and customers, connecting manufacturing and inventory functions to aid reordering. It is also effecting and re-engineering all organisational processes from logistics, distribution and manufacturing.

In Ireland, the B2C (business-to-customer) e-business market is valued at €48.25 million (McCall 2000). It is predicted to grow to €934.5 million by 2002. Following the international pattern, B2B (business-to-business) is by far the largest market in Ireland with a current value of €120 million, predicted to grow €3.35 billion by 2002.

The development of both B2C and B2B types of business transactions are producing enormous change for organisations world-wide. B2B transactions allow organisations to purchase supplies of raw materials over the Internet, and also to sell their products to other businesses over the Internet. Organisations that fail to develop an e-presence in the market will find that their market share is eroded over time as more businesses develop online facilities.

Not only is e-business revolutionising how organisations conduct business with one another, it is also having a profound effect on B2C transactions. Many organisations are dealing with customers directly through online facilities. Customers wishing to purchase goods on line simply have to log on to the organisation's website and can purchase goods with a credit card. Organisations that fail to use this important sales medium will end up losing market share, as was the case of Barnes & Noble with the arrival of Amazon.com. Many new companies have been established to provide shopping facilities on line. Older more established retail outlets have also been forced to provide online facilities in order to compete with the aggressive new entrants.

B2C business techniques are becoming ever more sophisticated and appealing to customers. For example, General Motors have developed a new website where customers can custom order the car of their choice which is then delivered within 10 days. This allows the customer much greater choice and control of the product that they purchase.

The Internet revolution has therefore had a huge impact on business and organisations, forcing fundamental change upon them. The conduct of business in many sectors has been significantly changed, for example, air travel, retail and banking. For some sectors, most notably banking, the development of online banking facilities could eventually lead to a situation where traditional bank branches are no longer necessary. This could result in a fundamental restructuring of the banking industry. In Ireland both Allied Irish Bank and Bank of Ireland have 5 per cent of their customers online, of which about 80 per cent is B2B banking. The level of business done in this manner is predicted to treble by 2003 (O'Halloran 2000).

There is some disagreement among commentators about the long-term impact of

Internet banking on traditional branch banking. Some argue that conventional banking will always have a role in society due to the fact that people like face-to-face contact, particularly in relation to financial affairs. Customers unfamiliar with the Internet are unlikely to embrace or trust a comparatively new insecure medium. It has also been argued that the introduction of automated teller machines (ATMs) did not result in the predicted job losses and that Internet banking will be no different.

While it is impossible to predict with any certainty the extent of erosion faced by traditional banking there is no doubt that online banking is set to grow over the next decade. It provides a much cheaper distribution channel for customers. In the USA a branch transaction costs $1.07, a telephone transaction $0.52, ATM $0.27 and online transactions $0.01. This data alone suggests that online banking will be an integral part of the future and will have implications for banks.

The outcome of all of the combined technological developments is that the modern organisation is in a state of transformation. The introduction of the information and communication technology can lead to significant cost savings and increased efficiency. As more organisations adopt such techniques, competitors are compelled to do the same in order to remain competitive. Therefore, information and communications technology, while producing enormous benefits in terms of savings, also force organisations to keep up to date with new technology.

14.3.3 The changing nature of the labour force

The nature of the world labour force is changing significantly in terms of composition and also values and expectations held. A number of important trends are emerging in the composition of the world labour force. The average age of the labour force is projected to increase significantly. The trend towards an older labour force is most pronounced in the developed regions of the world. Older workers generally cost an organisation more as their wages are higher and health-care and pension costs increase in line with age. As a result, organisations located within the developed world are faced with the challenge of maintaining competitiveness in the face of increased costs. Unless such increased costs can be matched with higher productivity, organisations within these regions will be faced with a loss of competitive advantage. In contrast to the trends in most of the developed countries, Ireland still has a relatively young population, as shown in Figure 14.3.

Figure 14.3 Irish population by age 1990–97

Age	0–14	15–24	25–44	45–64	65+	Total
1990	954.6	594.1	949.1	608.1	400	3,505.8
1991	940.6	601.6	959	621.7	402.9	3,525.7
1992	930.8	610.2	970.7	637	405.8	3,554.5
1993	917	615.9	979	654.3	407.9	3,574.1
1994	898.6	621	986.5	671.1	408.7	3,585.9
1995	877.9	625.6	999.6	686.8	411.4	3,601.3
1996	859.4	625.6	1,016	703.8	413.9	3,626.1
1997	845.5	642.5	1,033	722.4	416.5	3,660.6

Source: Labour Force Survey (1997).

It is likely that in years to come the Irish labour force will also age. Irish companies can perhaps learn some lessons from other countries faced with this situation currently. The number of women in the labour force has also significantly increased. The developing regions show the most potential for future growth as relatively few women have entered the labour force to date. Similar trends can also be found in Ireland where the number of women working outside of the home has increased significantly. Figure 14.4 illustrates this trend.

Figure 14.4 Women in the Irish labour force (000s) 1992–97

	1992	1993	1994	1995	1996	1997
Total number of women at work	401	412	431	459	494	513
Total female labour force	454.8	471.7	487.1	507.6	546.3	561.1
Total female population	1,786	1,796	1,802	1,812	1,825	1,843
Total labour force (%)	33	34.1	34.6	35.2	36.7	35.7

Source: Labour Force Survey (1997).

As the number of women in the labour force increases, working conditions and patterns of consumer demand will change. It is likely that demand for fast foods, crèche facilities, day care and home cleaners will increase in line with female participation in the labour force. Organisations will continue to implement equal opportunities in the hiring and promotion of personnel. Women are likely to seek time away from work for family commitments. It is likely that the trend towards increased part-time and temporary work will continue to meet this demand. Figure 14.5 shows how part-time, temporary and short-term-contract employment has increased in Ireland in recent years.

Figure 14.5 Trends in part-time, temporary and short-term-contract employment 1990–99 IDA Ireland, Enterprise Ireland and Údarás na Gaeltachta (excludes Shannon Development)

	1990	1991	1992	1993	1994	1995	1996	1997	1998	1999
Overall total	14,345	13,337	14,654	17,807	22,881	26,518	25,139	29,820	31,894	33,244
Irish-owned	8,575	8,235	8,627	10,589	12,009	13,233	13,608	14,270	14,967	16,173
Foreign-owned	5,770	5,102	6,027	7,218	10,872	13,285	11,531	15,550	16,927	17,071

Source: Forfas Employment Survey 1999.

Part-time temporary and short-term-contract employment rose by 131.7 per cent over the 10-year period 1990–99 and by 4.2 per cent in 1999. This follows an increase of 7.0 per cent in 1998. A decline occurred in 1996 by 1,379 (-5.2 per cent) and in the following year (1997) grew by 18.6 per cent. The decline in 1996 was mainly attributable to employees in this category moving into permanent employment in a number of companies in the foreign-owned electronics sector. The growth in part-time, temporary and short-term-contract employment since 1996 was significant at 32.2 per cent, and appears to indicate that the decline in 1996 was a one-off occurrence.

Employment in this category in Irish-owned companies grew by 7,598 (88.6 per cent) over the 1990–99 period to 16,173 jobs in 1999. An increase of 1,206 jobs (8.1 per cent) was recorded in 1999. 1991 was the only year where a decline occurred decreasing in that year by 4.0 per cent to a level of 8,235 jobs.

Employment in this category in foreign-owned companies grew by 195.9 per cent (11,301) jobs over the 10-year period 1990–99. An increase of 144 jobs in this category was recorded in 1999, a rise of 0.9 per cent. In line with the overall decrease in this category in 1991, foreign-owned companies also recorded a decline of 11.6 per cent. The overall decline, which occurred in 1996, was due to a decrease of 13.2 per cent in this category of employment in foreign-owned companies.

The world labour force is predicted to increase significantly in the developing regions of the world. However, most of the well paid jobs continue to be generated in the developed world. The result is a mismatch between available jobs and workers. Consequently, it is predicted that the labour force will be increasingly mobile. Employees are also expected to become less loyal to one particular organisation and to change occupations several times during their career (Handy 1989). Due to increased mobility on the part of labour, it is predicted that the world's labour force will become more global in nature, with an increased standardisation of practices throughout the world. Already a degree of standardisation has developed in relation to holiday periods (five weeks) and the length of the working week (40 hours) in the EU, USA and Japan. These trends are likely to develop further, which means that organisations will have to keep up to date with new developments.

The values and expectations of the labour force are also changing considerably. In general, employees are now better educated, less-unionised and possess different values and attitudes when compared to previous generations. Younger workers are demanding more opportunities and more enjoyment from their work. They are less willing to accept traditional authority and are increasingly demanding more autonomy and a say in decisions that affect both themselves and the business. Improving the quality of working life has become an important goal for many employees. Organisations, therefore, have to respond to such changes and provide opportunities for employees in order to compete effectively in the labour market.

All of the foregoing changes in the world labour force herald changes for organisations which in future will be faced with an older labour force, higher rates of female participation and increased mobility of labour and standardisation of work practices.

14.3.4 The changing nature of work

In recent years there has been a marked shift in employment away from traditional labour-intensive industries (for example, iron and steel, and coal mining) to knowledge-based industries and services. According to Handy (1989), 30 years ago nearly half of all employees were involved in the manufacturing sector. In the USA alone the figure had dropped to 18 per cent by the early 1990s. Handy (1989) predicts that this figure could be as low as 10 per cent in another 30 years' time.

Traditional labour-intensive industries employed large numbers of people at cheap rates who were heavily supervised by a hierarchical management structure. Employees were mainly hired on a full-time basis, to be used for the benefit of the organisation. The demise of the mass-manufacturing organisation has seen the end of mass-employment organisations.

While labour-intensive industries have been declining, knowledge-based industries have increased in number (Drucker 1992). Examples of knowledge-based industries include journalism, publishing, education and finance. In contrast to the traditional labour-intensive industries, organisations involved in knowledge-based industries create added value from the information and creativity put in, rather than from muscle power. These organisations generally employ fewer people who think creatively, aided by information technology. Even industries which were traditionally labour-intensive, such as agriculture and construction, have recently invested in knowledge and machines to replace muscle power.

The move towards knowledge-based industries and organisations means that different people and indeed different forms of organisation are required. These organisations recognise that they cannot do everything themselves. Instead, they sub-contract or outsource work to specialist agencies, while retaining a core group of talented and energetic people. These organisations are also flatter and more adaptive.

There have also been moves towards the service sector on a world-wide basis. Figure 14.6 illustrates the trend towards employment in the service sector in Ireland from 1975 to 1997.

Figure 14.6 Employment changes by sector in Ireland 1975–97

	Agriculture		Industry		Services		Total
	000s	%	000s	%	000s	%	
1975	238	22.1	337	31.4	498	46.4	1,073
1980	209	18	371	32	576	49.8	1,156
1985	171	15.8	306	28.3	602	55.7	1,079
1989	163	14.9	306	28.3	621	56.9	1,090
1992	154	13.4	319	27.8	672	58.6	1,145
1993	144	12.5	313	27.1	695	60.3	1,152
1994	142	11.9	333	28	713	60	1,188
1995	143	11.4	349	27.9	756	60.5	1,248
1996	138	10.6	355	27.3	804	61.9	1,297
1997	134	10	386	28.8	818	61.1	1,338

Source: Labour Force Survey (1997).

Social changes and increases in the female labour participation rate have led to a greater reliance on services provided by others. Society itself becomes more like the knowledge-based organisation in that it contracts out services that it is either not good at or does not have the time to complete as cost effectively. The result has been a significant increase in the services sector. While some services are knowledge-based, most of them are not; for example, cleaning, transport and catering. It is in these areas that those who were previously employed in labour-intensive industry will find employment (Handy 1989).

As with knowledge-based industries, the service-based organisation requires a different type of organisation. Service-based organisations have to be flexible to meet changing consumer demands. Such flexibility is ensured by the use of part-time and temporary workers in conjunction with a small core of full-time staff as discussed earlier. Therefore, the shift towards knowledge-based and service-based industries has had an enormous influence not only on the type of people employed but also on the type of organisation required. All of this has led to considerable change for traditional organisations.

Not only is the type of work changing, the physical location of work is also undergoing significant change. The advent of computer-based technology has resulted in a number of alternative work forms beyond the conventional work setting. Teleworking, as this new trend is called, includes:

▶ home-based telecommuting
▶ satellite offices
▶ neighbourhood work centres
▶ and mobile working, as explained in Figure 14.7.

Figure 14.7 Types of teleworking

1. Home-based telecommuting. Employees work at home on a regular basis.
2. Satellite offices. Employees work outside the home yet away from the conventional office in a location convenient to customers and employees.
3. Neighbourhood work centres. Employees work in a satellite office which houses more than one organisation's employees.
4. Mobile working. Employees work outside the conventional office on a mobile basis and communicate with the office by using electronic means.

Source: Curled and Bailey (1999).

It is estimated that about 3–8 per cent of the workforce in the USA is involved in teleworking. The main differences between teleworking and conventional forms is the lack of the key components of conventional work:

▶ personal supervision
▶ face-to-face communications
▶ working side by side with co-workers.

It is expected that the number of employees involved in teleworking will increase significantly over the next decade. The main advantages associated with teleworking include:

▶ less commuting time
▶ cost savings
▶ less stress
▶ increased job satisfaction.

The main challenges include professional and social isolation and decreased office presence and influence (Curled and Bailey 1999).

The combined impact of the four main factors forcing change outlined above means that organisations are facing an unprecedented amount of change in their external environments. Organisations can no longer ignore developments in the external environment as they now affect almost every aspect of the organisation from operations and production to employees and consumer demand patterns. Hitt (2000:9) has suggested that a useful analogy of the current business environment can be found in a soccer match:

Typically in a soccer match, two teams play each other for a defined period of time at a previously agreed date and time. They play on a field of known proportions that is level with a prescribed set of rules that are enforced by referees. Winners and losers are easily identified at the end of the match ... In contrast the manager of a business often must prepare to compete against 20, 30 or more other businesses simultaneously. The firm must compete in multiple markets and often in multiple countries each of which has its own rules and referees (government officials). Therefore if a firm operates in a market across 20 different countries, there may be 20 separate sets of rules to which it must conform. Furthermore, while financial records provide data on firm performance there are multiple measures by which to measure a firm's success. Also the field on which business takes place it not level.

14.4 Resistance to change

Organisations facing change will inevitably encounter a degree of resistance even with sufficient planning. Organisations by their very nature are designed to ensure stability over time, so some resistance to change is natural in any organisation. Such resistance can be overt and take the form of strikes, reductions in productivity and even sabotage. More covert examples of resistance to change include increased absenteeism, loss of employee motivation and a higher rate of accidents or errors in the workplace. The most damaging form of resistance occurs when employees refuse to participate in or commit to the process of change when given the opportunity to do so (Neumann 1989).

Resistance to change originates from two main sources, namely, the individual and the organisation, as illustrated in Figure 14.8. In an environment characterised by constant change, it is vitally important that both managers and employees are aware of the reasons and sources of resistance to change if the process is to be successful (Spector 1989).

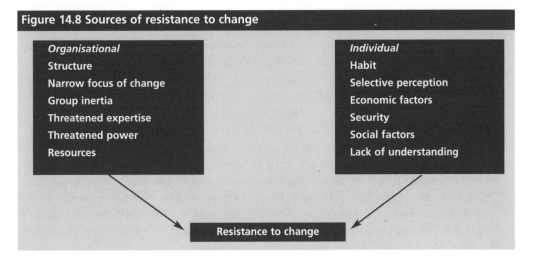

Figure 14.8 Sources of resistance to change

Organisational	Individual
Structure	Habit
Narrow focus of change	Selective perception
Group inertia	Economic factors
Threatened expertise	Security
Threatened power	Social factors
Resources	Lack of understanding

Resistance to change

14.4.1 Organisational sources of resistance

Katz and Kahn (1978) have identified six main organisational sources of resistance to change:

❶ **Organisational structure** can be an important source of resistance to change, primarily due to the fact that it is designed to maintain stability over time. All organisations need a structure to ensure stability and continuity in order to function effectively. Consequently, employees are assigned established roles, and procedures are designed to achieve tasks. However, these structures (for example, bureaucratic structures) become very rigid as they develop, which mitigates against change. Over time, tall hierarchies, narrowly defined jobs, and hierarchical authority block change. Because they were designed to ensure stability, they emphasise a narrow and limited outlook and prevent the circulation of new ideas. Hannan and Freeman (1984) refer to this as structural inertia.

❷ **Narrow focus of change**. Frequently, change programmes take a limited or narrow focus by attempting to introduce piecemeal changes in particular areas. In taking such an approach, the important interdependencies between elements in the organisation, such as people, structures and systems, are largely ignored. For example, an organisation could change the structure of tasks by introducing teams, yet still reward employees for individual achievements and retain a culture that emphasises competition between individuals. In this case the organisation has changed the structure but not the culture or the systems. Therefore, employees will resist change because the culture and systems do not back up the change. Organisations should consider carefully the interdependencies between areas to avoid resistance to change.

❸ **Group inertia**. Inertia is the innate desire to retain the status quo even when the present situation is inferior compared to something new (Stanislao and Stanislao 1983). Group inertia occurs when the group, either formal or informal, refuses to change its behaviour patterns and consequently group norms act as a barrier to change, especially if individual attempts at change are dependent on corresponding change by the group.

❹ **Threatened expertise**. Organisational change programmes can have an important impact on the level of expertise held by key individuals or groups. If the specialised expertise of an individual or group is threatened, their natural reaction is to resist such change. For example, many organisations are introducing multiskilling, whereby employees are trained to complete a wide range of tasks rather than one or two very specific skills. Craft unions resist such changes because they perceive that this dilutes the expertise of craft workers who have served an apprenticeship and have years of experience in a particular trade, such as mechanics or painting.

❺ **Threatened power and influence**. Organisational change programmes frequently involve a redistribution of power and influence much like a political cabinet reshuffle, in that there are nearly always winners and losers. When an individual, a group or department controls a resource, such as people, money or information, they have power. Once a position of power has been established such individuals or groups resist any change which is viewed as reducing their power and influence. For example, attempts to decentralise decision making from middle-management levels to the shop floor have frequently met with resistance from middle managers. The reason for such resistance is the perception that such decentralisation will reduce the decision-making power and influence of middle managers.

❻ **Resources**. Organisational change programmes that attempt to alter the allocation of scarce resources will meet with resistance from individuals or groups that currently enjoy a favourable allocation and who are likely to lose out. Resources include people, money and information. For example, if an organisation decides to reduce employment in marketing from 30 to 15 and concurrently decides to increase employment in finance from 20 to 30, it is quite likely that marketing will resist this move because it marks a reduction in the prestige and resources associated with the area.

The six organisational sources of resistance to change are primarily associated with people and social relationships. Many of the sources discussed are connected with the loss of power, influence, resources or the status quo.

14.4.2 Individual sources of resistance to change

Researchers such as Nadler (1983) and Stanislao and Stanislao (1983) have identified a number of individual sources of resistance to change. By drawing together elements of this research, it is possible to identify six main sources of resistance to change which are associated with the individual. Individual resistance to change arises from basic human characteristics, such as attitudes and needs.

❶ **Habit**. As individuals complete the various tasks assigned to them, habits develop. It becomes easier to do the job in the same manner each day whereby the steps are repeated over and over again. An established habit allows an individual to adjust to and cope with the work environment and, therefore, provides a degree of comfort. Changing this habit may result in a resistance to change due to the fact that breaking a habit, by learning something new, is more difficult than leaving things as they are.

  The extent to which a habit develops into a major source of resistance depends on whether individuals see any advantage from the change. If the rewards associated with the change are seen as great, and more than offset the loss of breaking the habit, then resistance should not be a problem. If, on the other hand, no rewards or compensation are associated with the change, then individuals will more than likely resist the change.

❷ **Selective perception**. Individuals tend to selectively perceive or view things that match their current understanding of the work environment or the world around them. When individuals have developed an understanding of reality through their values and attitudes, they are hesitant to alter this understanding. In resisting change, individuals frequently only listen to things that they agree with, they 'forget' other viewpoints and misunderstand communications which, if viewed correctly, would not match their understanding of reality. For example, if an individual is told to make certain changes, s/he may be selective about those areas which s/he will change and ignore those which are perceived to be at odds with the individual's beliefs and attitudes.

❸ **Economic factors**. While individuals are not motivated solely by money, economic factors still remain important. Employees spend time learning how to perform their job successfully and getting good performance appraisals and possibly a bonus. Therefore, any change in established work practices or social relations threaten an individual employee's economic security in two main ways:

▶ The individual's income may be reduced through change.

▶ Individuals may feel that change requires new learning to achieve the same level of performance as before, which means that income will be lower during the learning period.

❹ **Security**. Individuals like to feel comfortable and secure in completing things the same way. In doing so they gain a degree of security in their jobs and in their lives. When the status quo is threatened by change, employees feel their security is at risk, and consequently they resist such change. Confronting any form of the unknown makes the individual anxious and insecure. Insecurity arises not only from the change itself but also from the prospective outcomes of such change; for example, employees may turn down an overseas promotion due to insecurity and fear of the unknown.

❺ **Social factors**. Individuals may resist change due to social factors, particularly the fear of what others will think. The work group may exert peer pressure on the individual to resist change. The groups norms serve as a guide to what behaviour is acceptable and unacceptable to the group. If an individual's behaviour is contrary to the group s/he may be ostracised in some way. If acceptance of the group is important to the individual then s/he will go along with the group view, even if that means resisting change which s/he would otherwise have supported. However, the opposite also holds true in that employees who may individually resist the change are carried along by the group which favours the change.

❻ **Lack of understanding**. Resistance to change frequently results from a lack of understanding by the individual. If s/he does not understand the rationale for the change, the change itself and any consequences, then s/he will resist the change. Employees will not take on board changes which they do not fully understand. In many cases individuals will resist the change rather than clarify the position. It is therefore up to the organisation to fully explain to its employees the details of any change programme.

In combining both organisational and individual sources of resistance to change, there are potentially 12 different sources. An example of resistance to change in an Irish context can be seen in Team Aer Lingus and Irish Steel. In both cases, the craft unions resisted change and were initially unwilling to accept required changes in work practices, even when the survival of both organisations was in question. The main source of their resistance centred around the loss of expertise by the craft workers which would be a result of the changes, together with a fear of the unknown, and insecurity. Eventually, when it became obvious that both Irish Steel and Team Aer Lingus would close, agreement was reached, but not without intense resistance to change (Flynn 1994).

The organisation has to understand each source of resistance before it can attempt to manage or overcome it. Resistance to change should not necessarily be viewed as a bad thing in fact it can have important contributions to make to the change programme. Where legitimate concerns about issues are raised, the organisation can benefit from a re-evaluation or checking of certain elements. It could be the case that important issues have been overlooked. Resistance to change ensures that decisions are fully researched and considered before implementation. Re-evaluating a change programme in response to employee resistance can also have symbolic significance in that it shows management cares about its employees' views (Pfeffer 1981).

14.5 Planned organisational change

The strategic change literature can be broadly classified as either content or process driven. The *content* school concentrates on antecedents and consequences of change, normally studying large numbers of organisations quantitatively (see Gibbs 1993; Ginsberg and Bucholtz 1990). In contrast, the *process* school concentrates on the role played by managers in the strategic change process, by examining a small number of organisations qualitatively (see Whipp *et al.* 1989; Webb and Dawson 1991).

It is important to distinguish between change that inevitably happens to all organisations and that which is essentially planned by organisational members (Cummings and Huse 1989). According to Goodman and Kurke (1982), planned organisational change is a set of activities and processes designed to change individuals, groups, structures and processes. Organisations typically introduce changes in response to external pressures. However, they also make changes in anticipation of future problems. Effective organisations anticipate future changes *and* react to current changes by planning and developing strategies to meet such changes.

Planned organisational change, either reactive or anticipatory, is the deliberate effort by organisational members to improve organisational performance. Planned organisational change programmes tend to have two main goals. First, such programmes are designed to improve organisational flexibility and adaptability in response to changes in the business environment. Second, they aim to change individual behaviour within the organisation, which, according to Beer *et al.* (1990), should be the primary focus of all planned organisational change programmes.

As planned organisational change requires a systematic process of moving from one condition or state to another, this chapter focuses on the process models of strategic change. Two approaches to change based on this process are examined below—Lewin's model of change and a model of strategic change.

14.6 Lewin's model of change

Lewin (1951) argued that efforts to bring about change should be viewed as a multi-stage process, rather than merely one step which would achieve the aim of the change programme. Lewin's model of organisational change consists of three steps—unfreezing, change and refreezing as shown in Figure 14.9.

The first stage, UNFREEZING, is the process by which organisational members become aware of the need for change. Employees who are most affected by the intended change must be made aware of the need for change and the rationale behind its introduction. This stage of the change process attempts to make employees dissatisfied with the current state of affairs, so that they will be motivated to change. For example, if employees are made aware of the fact that a crisis is facing the organisation, they are more likely to feel the need for change and will be more open to it.

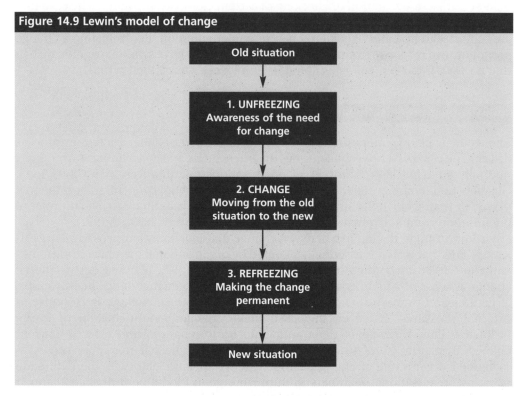

Figure 14.9 Lewin's model of change

The second stage is *change*, which is the movement from the old situation to the new one. The change itself could involve the introduction of new technology or a change in the structure, systems or culture of the organisation.

The final stage of the process is called REFREEZING which makes the new behaviour or change a permanent feature of the organisation. Refreezing can be achieved through training and development sessions and rewarding new behaviour. This stage is critically important in the process because unless the new behaviour is made permanent, the organisation and its members will revert back to the old situation. Frequently during management training sessions, new skills and techniques are learned. Yet when the manager returns to the work environment, the new skills are forgotten and the manager reverts back to his/her old behaviour. The reason for this reversion is that the new skills were not refrozen or made permanent in any way either through rewards or follow-up training sessions.

Lewin's model of organisational change is perhaps the most simple and straightforward available. For this reason it has been incorporated into many other models of planned organisational change. However, it has been criticised for viewing organisations as closed systems, and for the notion of equilibrium which lies at the heart of the approach. Organisational life is rarely based on equilibrium but on a constant battle for power. The model also ignores the role of factors forcing change, how change is actually introduced and what organisations can do to ensure successful change. The next model of organisational change to be examined seeks to overcome many of these inadequacies.

14.7 A model of strategic change

Strategic change is any change in the strategies pursued by the organisation. It can occur in relation to employees, technology, structure and culture. The nature of the changes in the current business environment have forced many organisations to make significant changes in the strategies employed.

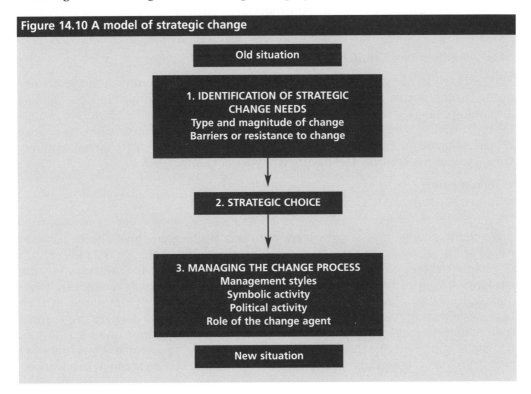

Figure 14.10 A model of strategic change

Old situation

1. IDENTIFICATION OF STRATEGIC CHANGE NEEDS
Type and magnitude of change
Barriers or resistance to change

2. STRATEGIC CHOICE

3. MANAGING THE CHANGE PROCESS
Management styles
Symbolic activity
Political activity
Role of the change agent

New situation

Strategic change can take a number of different forms. REORIENTATION, or corporate-level strategic change, occurs when an organisation moves into new markets or industries and discards or reduces involvement in others. REVITALISATION occurs when an organisation's performance is mediocre or poor, but survival is still possible. For example, the organisation may have certain problems, such as a reduction in market share, which means that it has to revitalise its current market position. The most serious form of strategic change is a TURNAROUND strategy which occurs when the survival of the organisation is at stake due to serious losses and poor performance. A turnaround strategy is, therefore, designed to turn around the organisation's fortunes.

Effective management of strategic change has become vitally important for managers in the current business environment. One of the biggest mistakes which organisations frequently make is to embark on a change programme without a carefully planned strategy for managing the overall process (Kotter and Schlesinger 1979). According to Nadler (1981) organisational change is successful when:

▶ The organisation is moved from its current state to some planned future state that will exist after the change.

▶ The functioning of the organisation in the future state meets expectations.

▶ The transition is accomplished without excessive costs to the organisation and the individual.

These factors are important to consider when planning and implementing change. In order to introduce strategic change effectively a model of strategic change is outlined in Figure 14.10 which shows each of the main steps an organisation should go through when implementing change.

14.7.1 Identification of strategic change needs

The first step in the strategic change process is to clearly identify strategic change needs. In other words, the organisation needs to identify and understand what factors are forcing change, why the organisation needs to change and what barriers to change the organisation is likely to encounter. An examination of the factors forcing change should indicate to the organisation the nature and extent of change required. Organisations are typically faced with two types of change:

▶ incremental

▶ transformational.

Incremental change is a step-by-step, non-radical change, where the beliefs and values of the organisation are maintained. Transformational change is a radical form of change whereby the established beliefs and values of the organisation are challenged. Poor performance over a long period of time generally requires transformational change. Having established the nature of the change required, it then becomes necessary to identify the likely sources of resistance to change. The 12 main sources of resistance to change were discussed above (see Sections 14.4.1 and 14.4.2). It is vitally important that the organisation identifies potential sources of resistance to change so that attempts to manage and overcome them can be planned in advance.

14.7.2 Strategic choice

Strategic choice involves choosing the most effective strategy to meet the strategic change needs. In choosing the strategy, the issue is subjected to the normal decision-making and problem-solving processes. Alternatives are generated, evaluated and one particular strategy chosen. Organisations try to choose strategies that they think will meet the needs of environmental changes while minimising the sources of resistance to change. Top management play a very important role in choosing the strategy to be pursued and therefore, the process is influenced by their perceptions, attitudes and values.

14.7.3 Managing the change process

Having made a choice about which strategy to introduce, the organisation then moves on to implement the relevant changes. To manage the change process successfully, the organisation and those involved in implementing the change should concentrate on management styles, symbolic and political activity and the role of the change agent.

Management styles are the techniques used by managers or CHANGE AGENTS in introducing change. The change agent is the person responsible for managing the change effort. The various management styles are designed to overcome resistance to change, and the style used will depend on the extent and nature of resistance to change in any given situation. According to Kotter and Schlesinger (1979) there are six main styles of management associated with introducing change:

- *Education and communication* are appropriate where problems and resistance are caused by insufficient information or misinformation. Such a style requires an atmosphere of trust between the sides involved. Education and communication are generally more effective if they take place before the change is implemented. However, this style is costly and time-consuming as it involves mass briefings. Organisations dealing with large numbers of employees can use small group briefings to ensure effective communication.

- *Participation* is appropriate where the commitment and participation of employees is vital to the success of the change programme. It is an effective way of overcoming resistance based on lack of awareness or a narrow focus of change. Employees who are involved in the change process are also more likely to accept changes. Participation usually involves project teams or task forces who generate ideas and give advice on implementing change. Once again, this style is time-consuming and costly.

- *Support and facilitation* are appropriate management styles when employees are experiencing difficulty in coming to terms with the new changes. Support and facilitation help to overcome resistance arising from a fear of the unknown and the need for security. Schneider *et al.* (1996) have argued that creating the correct climate and culture for change determines whether change will be successful. This style of management involves providing support mechanisms for employees to help them cope with change. Most frequently organisations provide additional training or extra emotional support while employees get used to the changes. A problem associated with this style is that while it may help people through the change process, it does not necessarily win their commitment and support. It is also time-consuming and can fail.

- *Negotiation and agreement* is a useful management style when groups or key individuals are negatively affected by the change, yet have sufficient power to resist and interrupt the introduction of change. A good example is a TRADE UNION whose primary concern is to protect the welfare of its members. Trade unions resist any change that negatively affects their members. By engaging in negotiation before implementation, the organisation may find the change process runs more smoothly. If any other problems arise during the course of implementation, then both sides can refer to the written agreement to sort out problems. This method is most appropriate for overcoming resistance to change arising from threatened expertise, power, resources and group factors. The possibility of rewards, such as increased wages or perks, can also be examined to reinforce the direction of change (Nadler 1981).

- *Manipulation* of the situation by the agent can make it easier to introduce change. For example, it has been established that crisis situations are more likely to motivate people to change. So organisations can attempt to exaggerate the extent of the situation facing the organisation, to make it appear as if the organisation is in a crisis. This style is often used when resistance is caused by habit, resource allocation, economic and group factors.

▶ *Coercion* involves the explicit use of power by issuing directives to employees about the changes being implemented. Managers or the change agent resort to coercion if all other methods have failed to reduce resistance to change. It is generally recognised as the least successful method of introducing change. Even when coercion is applied, and employees accept change, it can have long-term negative effects on employee attitudes and behaviour.

Each of the management styles described above is appropriate for particular situations. Education and communication are most effective for incremental change or where transformational change is being introduced over a long period of time. Manipulation and coercion are effective if there is a crisis or a need for rapid transformational change. Participation and negotiation are intermediate styles whereby transformational change can be achieved with less risk, but they are also effective for incremental change (Nutt 1989).

Symbolic activity. While the style of management used can help overcome resistance to change and can aid the implementation of change, symbolic activity plays an equally important role. In Chapter 1, organisational culture was referred to as the beliefs, values and attitudes of the organisation. In implementing change managers must ensure that such change is apparent in the day-to-day experiences of employees and can be grasped by them. It is through symbolic means and organisational culture that the organisation can achieve this. For example, the organisation could introduce decentralised decision making throughout the organisation yet senior managers could still take all decisions themselves without delegating to middle managers. In this situation middle managers do not see apparent changes in their experience of work. As a result, they will be reluctant to delegate any of their decision-making power. All elements of the organisation's culture must reinforce the direction of the change if it is to be successful.

The most powerful symbol of all in any organisational change process is the behaviour of the change agent(s), whether they be the CEO, senior management or an external consultant. Whether consciously or unconsciously, the language and behaviour of the change agent(s) must reinforce the changes. It is essential that their behaviour corresponds with the strategic change, to build commitment to the change process and ensure that the process is not undermined.

Political activity. When change takes place in the organisation, especially transformational change, there is nearly always an alteration of power structures. In order to achieve a reconfiguration of the power base, the change agent must understand the political processes and systems, and how strategic change can be implemented within the political context. Any manager who is faced with change needs to consider how it can be implemented from a political perspective. According to Johnson and Scholes (1993) there are four main political mechanisms which can be used to build a power base, encourage support, overcome resistance and achieve commitment:

▶ The control and manipulation of resources. Identification by the change agent with important resource areas and the ability to withdraw or reallocate resources can be important in overcoming resistance to change and persuading others to accept.

▶ Relationships with powerful groups. Association by the change agent with internal/ external stakeholders and trade unions can become an important power base, especially for an external change agent who does not have a personal power base.

▶ Sub-systems. Acceptance of and communication about the change process is important throughout the organisation. Therefore, how well the various sub-systems are handled is important. An effective change agent will build up powerful alliances and networks of people within the sub-systems. This can be very effective for overcoming resistance from powerful groups. It is important, however, not to alienate existing elites within the organisation.

▶ Symbolic mechanisms. These can be used to break with existing paradigms and to reward those who accept the changes. Creating stories and rituals around those who have facilitated the changes will help to spread the change.

These four mechanisms are important for introducing change through the political processes of the organisation. Problems arise when the change agent aligns him/herself too closely with particular groups and alienates others. In addition, changing the power structure of the organisation can lead to instability.

The role of the change agent. A change agent is a person or group responsible for managing the change effort. The change agent can either be an external consultant or an internal person or group. An internal change agent is likely to know the organisation, employees, tasks, politics and culture, which may help in interpreting data and understanding systems. However, an insider might be too close to be objective. An external person has the advantage of being objective and having a fresher outlook. However, s/he will lack knowledge of the organisation and will have to build a power base from which to work. Many organisations still opt for an external change agent.

Unless the change agent is a top manager or CEO then his/her power base will not come from a hierarchical position and legitimate authority within the organisation. While support of the top-management team helps the change agent, s/he has to develop other sources of power to move the process of change forward. Beer (1980:78) identifies five sources of power which the change agent can develop:

▶ High status afforded to the change agent by organisational members who believe that s/he shares similar attitudes and behaviour is an important source of power.

▶ Another source of power is trust, which can be built up by consistent handling of people and information.

▶ Expertise in the area of change management and previous experience can be an important source of power.

▶ Established credibility from the management of other change programmes also establishes power.

▶ Dissatisfied internal groups may see the change agent as an opportunity to introduce changes favourable to them, and will consequently give the change agent a certain amount of power.

Successful change agents typically possess a number of important characteristics:

▶ They have a clarity of vision which can be communicated to others. Many successful change agents carefully use METAPHORS to describe the need for and process of change. The use of metaphors in introducing change is particularly noticeable at the diagnosis and intervention stages (Akin and Palmer 2000).

▶ They recognise the importance of the context in which the change is occurring and are sensitive to the type of change needed and the resistance to change.

▶ They use appropriate styles of management.

▶ They use symbolic actions where necessary.

▶ They use political processes to build a power base.

▶ They have good INTERPERSONAL SKILLS and an ability to spread enthusiasm to others.

14.8 Successful change programmes

Following a clearly defined model of strategic change is not sufficient to ensure success. Organisations that follow models of this nature still end up with programmes which have been a failure. Researchers at the Harvard Business School investigating the effects on performance of change interventions in Fortune 100 organisations found that only 30 per cent of these initiatives produced an improvement in bottom line results and only 50 per cent lead to an increase in share price (Hitt 2000). Yet other organisations can introduce change with very positive results. So what is it about some organisational change programmes that make them successful? Pascale *et al.* (1997) have argued that one of the biggest problems with organisational change is that the burden of change typically rests with a few people. They suggest that organisations should involve employees, instil mental disciplines and establish focus and urgency to maintain involvement.

Pettigrew and Whipp (1991) conducted research in the UK in a number of industries from publishing to automobiles. They identified organisations which had introduced strategic change programmes and pinpointed aspects of their successful programmes. Based on their research, they argue that successful strategic change depends on the presence of five interrelated elements, as shown in Figure 14.11.

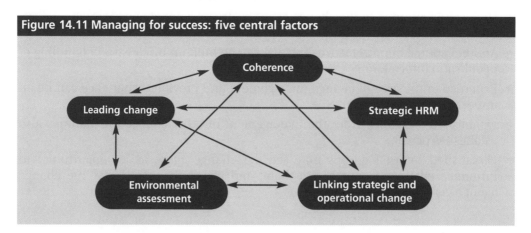

Figure 14.11 Managing for success: five central factors

❶ **Environmental assessment**. Organisations which introduce successful change programmes assessed their external environment very carefully, went beyond acquiring and processing data and became open learning systems. External developments within the business environment were effectively communicated to employees and championed by a change agent.

❷ **Leading change**. Pettigrew and Whipp (1991) found that success depended on the ability of the change agent to establish and develop a context for change both in cultural terms and the capabilities of the organisation. Styles of management were used which were tailored to the context, and the change agent altered the approach where necessary.

❸ **Strategic human resource management**. Successful organisations integrated their HRM policies with their strategic changes. Training and development, employee relations and rewards were all designed to facilitate the introduction of the desired changes.

❹ **Linking strategic and operational change**. Organisations which have successfully managed strategic change have effectively linked strategic change with operational change. In other words, there has been a clear connection and consistency between strategic, tactical and operations plans.

❺ **Coherence**. The most complex factor arises from the demands of the previous four. Pettigrew and Whipp (1991) found that success depended on coherence across all aspects of the organisation as follows:

▶ consistency between intended strategy, strategic objectives, operational plans and the behaviour of the change agent

▶ consistency between the direction of strategic change and the environmental changes

▶ a feasible strategy in terms of resources required, organisational structure and the changes required to the organisational culture

▶ a strategic direction that is clearly related to achieving competitive advantage.

The next section applies the model of strategic change to an Irish organisation that introduced change and evaluates its success using the Pettigrew and Whipp (1991) framework.

14.9 Managing strategic change in Irish Ferries

In 1965 the government purchased the British and Irish Steampacket Co. Ltd (shortened to B & I). B & I, therefore, became a semi-state body involved in the transport of both passengers and cargo from Ireland to the UK and Europe. By 1985, however, B & I was in severe financial difficulties. At the end of that year, the company's consolidated balance sheet showed an accumulated loss of €114.2 million of which €72.3 million had been incurred in 1984 and 1985 alone.

In order to improve the competitive position of B & I, a private consultant was appointed as chairman of the company, to revitalise B & I and to return it to profitability. Despite attempts to improve performance, B & I still incurred significant losses, turnover fell from €126.9 million in 1985 to €79 million in 1989 and passenger numbers fell by 20 per cent and cargo by 17 per cent over the same period (Nolan 1994). Therefore, commercial viability had not been achieved for the long term and by the early 1990s B & I was once more in severe trouble.

14.9.1 Identifying strategic change needs

Three main factors were forcing B & I to change by the beginning of 1990. One of the major factors forcing change was the poor financial performance of B & I. Between 1987 and 1991 B & I lost over €35.6 million, as shown in Figure 14.12.

Figure 14.12 B & I: financial losses 1987–91	
	Millions (€)
1987	25,335
1988	1,949
1989	1,856
1990	4,343
1991	2,168

B & I was also burdened by high debts incurred through loans (see Figure 14.13).

Figure 14.13 B & I: loans 1987–91	
	Millions (€)
1987	43,324
1988	39,507
1989	36,580
1990	35,590
1991	38,194

Turnover had also been declining since the early 1980s. While the turnover had increased since 1988, it was still much lower than it had been in 1987, as illustrated in Figure 14.14.

Figure 14.14 B & I: turnover 1987–91	
	Millions (€)
1987	103,840
1988	74,900
1989	79,000
1990	84,140
1991	92,091

B & I was therefore making significant financial losses, burdened by debt and below average turnover. If B & I continued to perform badly it could no longer exist as a viable entity without considerable state aid.

The second factor forcing change within B & I was its purchase by the Irish Continental Group (ICG) for €10.79 million in January 1992. ICG operated a ferry service from Rosslare to France and had been established in 1988, receiving BES funding. ICG recognised the crisis situation facing B & I and was determined to force through significant changes which would safeguard its investment. The image of B & I as an outdated and inefficient operator would have to be changed to make ICG's investment viable. The most important change produced by the ICG purchase was the move from a semi-state body to a private commercial entity. In order to survive without state aid, B & I would have to improve its financial performance, compete against low-cost operators and develop more harmonious employee relations.

The final factor forcing change was increased competition in the transport market between Ireland and the UK and Europe. Liberalisation of the air travel market between the UK and Ireland and the consequential fare wars between RyanAir and Aer Lingus from 1986 onwards led to a significant reduction in the number of people travelling by sea as it became cheaper to fly. As a result, demand for sea travel declined significantly.

Consequently, competition between established sea operators became more intense with each one fighting to maintain passenger numbers. Sealink, B & I's most competitive rival, operated with much lower costs which made it difficult for B & I to compete effectively. Therefore, B & I was faced with competition on two fronts—from alternative forms of transport and also from operators like Sealink.

The combined forces amounted to a crisis situation which demanded strategic change to turn around the fortunes of the company. However, like any long-established organisation, B & I displayed an inherent resistance and suspicion to the proposed changes. The strongest resistance came from the trade unions as the changes threatened their power, expertise and their membership base which would be reduced through voluntary redundancy.

14.9.2 Strategic choice

Having considered both the factors forcing change and the resistance to change, B & I generated a number of strategic options. A choice was made in favour of a strategy to reduce the price of the product and to increase quality in order to achieve competitive advantage. The strategic plan required a restructuring and rationalisation of each business area within B & I and contained the following important changes.

Organisational structure. B & I was restructured into three businesses:

▶ Ferry Services, which provides the transportation of passengers, vehicles and freight on two routes between Ireland and the UK

▶ European Container Service, which operates container services between Ireland and the UK using a fleet of 1,200 containers

▶ Dublin Ferryport Terminals which provides cargo handling for roll-on-roll-off vessels by B & I and third-party operators.

Management structure:

▶ After the acquisition, ICG personnel were placed on the board of B & I. Old board members, who had been politically appointed non-executive directors, were removed. The new management structure therefore, was a mixture of B & I and ICG.

Reductions in staff:

▶ In order to reduce the number of staff, cut costs and reduce the age profile of the company, which was heavily biased towards people in pensionable categories, 235 voluntary redundancies were planned. The expected cost of the redundancies was in the region of €10.1 million.

Culture change:

▶ The culture of B & I would have to change from having a semi-state-owned culture to a private industrial enterprise. Therefore, the culture would have to be far more cost-conscious and commercial in nature. The old image of B & I which had been built up in the public's mind would also have to be changed.

Control systems:

▶ The final change was the introduction of more formal control systems to provide budgeting and estimates of future income and expenditure.

14.9.3 Managing strategic change

▶ **Management style**. To overcome the main sources of resistance to change, B & I embarked on a style emphasising education, communication, participation and negotiation. Before the takeover by ICG there were a series of written communications from ICG to all B & I employees explaining the changes. Once the official takeover had occurred, management continued using participation and negotiation to introduce change. Although the process was a long, drawn-out one, B & I persevered.

▶ **Culture and symbolic activity**. It is important that change agents exemplify behaviour consistent with the planned change in order to generate commitment from employees. In seeking to make B & I more competitive, the company was willing to make a substantial financial investment in improving quality and image, showing the process of change was not all in one direction. The first symbolic move of this nature made by the company to demonstrate its faith in the programme and its employees, was the introduction of the new *Isle of Inishfree* in 1992 and a £2.54 million refurbishment of the *Isle of Inishmore* in 1993.

▶ **Political activity**. The main change agents who were the top managers in B & I used political processes to change the power base and to achieve commitment from employees. The change agents used symbolic political mechanisms to break away from the established beliefs and values associated with the conduct of industrial relations. Essentially, management tried to reduce the power base of the unions by adopting a much tougher stance than before. The balance of power was shifted from the unions back towards management. Previously, disputes went to the Labour Court who issued a recommendation which was used as a basis for further negotiations by the unions. The new management team made it clear that Labour Court recommendations were the final outcome and harshly implemented those decisions. At the same time, the company increased communications with employees and developed important alliances within the sub-systems.

▶ **The role of the change agent**. The most important change agent was the new managing director who spearheaded change within B & I by attacking taken-for-granted ways of doing things. He dealt with resistance to change and earned the support and commitment of staff, and possessed a vision to acquire bigger ships to achieve economies of scale in order to reduce costs, which he implemented with great success. Finally, he recognised the importance of communications in implementing change and built up an important power base.

14.9.4 A successful change programme?

Since the introduction of the change programme, B & I has improved its financial performance significantly; it has increased turnover and expanded into new commercial ventures. The successful management of strategic change was achieved by the application of five key factors which Pettigrew and Whipp (1991) outlined. The changing nature of the business environment was carefully considered, including the trend towards larger ships to reduce costs and increase capacity (See Curran 1993). By identifying this trend, B & I was able to react successfully. The role of the change agent was effectively handled by the managing director who had the necessary vision and communications skills to implement the changes.

Strategic and operational change were effectively linked through proper communications between different levels. A human resources director was introduced onto the board of B & I which was a significant move towards having HR polices integrated with strategic change. Finally, the B & I change programme was coherent, with consistency between the need for change, the strategy chosen, operational plans and the end result of achieving competitive advantage.

14.10 Summary of key propositions

▶ The management of change has become one of the most important issues for managers due to the nature of the business environment. The changes represent fundamental shifts and are occurring at a continuous pace.

▶ While each organisation faces a unique set of factors that shape the need for change, it is possible to identify four important developments affecting most organisations: globalisation; information and communication technology developments; a changing labour force; and the changing nature of work.

▶ Organisations inevitably face resistance to change as the organisation itself is designed to maintain stability over time. Organisational sources of resistance to change include: organisational structure; narrow focus of change; group inertia; threatened expertise and power; and resource allocation. Individual sources of resistance to change include: habit; selective perception; economic factors; security; social factors; and lack of understanding.

▶ Change inevitably happens to all organisations. However, an organisation can plan to introduce change. Planned change is a set of activities designed to change individuals, groups, structures and systems. Planned change is normally introduced to increase organisational flexibility and adaptability and to change a particular element of individual behaviour.

▶ Lewin argued that the process of change occurred in three stages: unfreezing; change; and refreezing. This approach, while having been widely adopted, has been criticised for its simplicity.

▶ Strategic change is a change in the strategy pursued by an organisation and occurs in three main stages: an identification of strategic change needs; strategic choice; and management of the change process.

▶ When managing the introduction of change managers should pay special attention to styles of managing; symbolic activity; political activity; and the role of the change agent.

▶ The change agent is charged with a very important role within the management of the change process. S/he should have a clear vision, recognise the context of change, use suitable styles of management, symbolic and political activity and have good interpersonal skills and an ability to spread enthusiasm to others.

▶ Pettigrew and Whipp found that organisations who successfully implemented strategic change had five things in common: a careful assessment of the environment; appropriate leadership; strategic HRM; a link between strategic and operational change; and, most importantly of all, coherence between all of the elements.

Discussion questions

❶ Why has the management of change become so important in recent years?

❷ Explain the four main forces driving organisational change. Which one has most impact on Irish industry?

❸ Explain the major sources of organisational resistance to change. Find an example of the one you think is most important.

❹ Explain the major sources of individual resistance to change. Which one have you experienced?

❺ What can an organisation do to manage resistance to change?

❻ Explain Lewin's three-step model of change. Why has it been criticised?

❼ What is planned organisational change? What does it generally seek to achieve?

❽ What is strategic change? Why has it become so important? Find some examples of organisations that have introduced strategic changes.

❾ Explain the different management styles that can be used when introducing change. Under which circumstances are they appropriate?

❿ What steps can be taken by the change agent to ensure that strategic change is implemented successfully?

⓫ Apply the model of strategic change to an organisation with which you are familiar.

⑫ Critically evaluate the five-factor change framework developed by Pettigrew and Whipp. Can you think of anything else which should have been included?

Concluding case: Marks and Spencer—a time for change

Marks and Spencer is a British-owned company involved in the high-quality retail clothing and food business. In addition to a dominant presence in the UK market, Marks and Spencer also has outlets in the Republic of Ireland, including Dublin (Mary's Street, Grafton Street and Liffey Valley Centre) and Cork. The company has traditionally been synonymous with good quality and value, and its reputation was unrivalled in the high street.

Marks and Spencer (M & S) was the result of a successful business partnership between Michael Marks and Thomas Spencer who formed a private limited company in 1903. By 1926 the company became public and business blossomed for M & S. Early growth of the company was achieved by increasing the number of retail outlets, and the company gained an early lead in market-share battles by concentrating on the production of its own brand products under the St Michael trademark. In the post-war period sales continued to grow, mainly due to an increase in size of the retail outlets. In the 1970s M & S introduced the concept of high-quality, pre-cooked, ready-prepared foods, which was a highly innovative and successful move for the company. Like many other companies during the 1970s and 1980s, M & S began to diversify operations. Early moves on the international front included the purchase of D'Allairds in Canada and Brooks Brothers and King Supermarkets in the USA. Expansion in the European market soon followed with the opening of retail outlets in France, Spain and Germany, among others. However, despite attempts to geographically diversify M & S remained heavily reliant on the UK market in terms of sales and profits.

Throughout the 1990s M & S retained its reputation as a high-quality producer and its position as the premier high street retailer in the UK market. Despite the recession of the early 1990s M & S continued to post profits. Its success was often attributed to its high-quality, good-value approach, good employment relations, excellent customer service, downward pressure on suppliers to reduce costs and successful diversification into the high-quality food market.

However, in 1998 the company encountered the first signs of trouble. Early indications of the problems which would have to be faced by M & S came in the form of poor sales figures in both clothing and food sectors. In May 1999 M & S announced that its profits had fallen from €1.4 billion to €831.6 million. Sales were particularly disappointing within the UK market, on which the company was heavily reliant. While the fortunes of M & S began to dip, the fate of their competitors could not have been more different. Companies such as NEXT still produced healthy profits and an increasing share of the market. There are numerous reasons why M & S failed to stay competitive.

M & S failed to keep up with advances made by their main competitors in both the clothing and food sectors. Their main competitors in clothing are companies like NEXT and Arcadia, while in the food sector M & S has to compete with the supermarket giants such as Tesco and Asda-Walmart. Recently the major supermarkets have introduced clothing lines for customers. For example, Asda-Walmart has introduced its George range of clothing and is even planning to open stand-alone clothes stores to sell its new range, especially in areas where planning permission for food stores is difficult.

In relation to the food market M & S is being slowly squeezed by the big supermarkets who can offer equal product quality at a lower price. One of the main reasons that the big supermarkets can offer lower prices is that they source cheaper overseas suppliers for much of their produce. An added bonus for these supermarkets is the strength of Sterling which once again makes for cheaper goods. The big supermarkets also invest heavily in advertising and the discounting of prices. For example, Asda-Walmart announced in March 2000 that it was reducing prices on 4000 items by an average of 15 per cent. The cuts were also reinforced by a nation-wide advertising campaign. The supermarket giants have also developed new distribution channels for the sale of their products, such as mail order and the Internet.

In contrast, M & S appears to have stagnated and not responded to changing customer demand and developments within the marketplace. While the big supermarkets enjoyed lower costs in their supply chain by sourcing overseas suppliers, M & S found no such cost advantages with its heavily reliance on UK suppliers. While its competitors invested in advertising, M & S pursued its policy of no advertising despite the pressure for market share. M & S were very slow to introduce Internet sales and did so in response to their rivals. However, this gave competitors of M & S a strong lead in Internet sales. Another reason why M & S lost sales was that it refused to accept credit cards other than its own. While M & S still leads the UK clothing market with a 13 per cent market share this lead is being significantly reduced. The trend in the food sector is also alarming, with M & S having 3 per cent of the market compared to Tesco's 19 per cent.

M & S have also faced difficulties with its overseas investments. The Brooks Brothers clothing chain which M & S acquired in 1988 has not performed particularly well. However, its Kings Supermarkets have performed reasonably well in the New Jersey niche market. Sales in Europe have also been poor particularly in Spain, Germany and France. M & S have recently announced their intention of divesting all such investment.

As well as facing pressure from external sources, the company also has many internal problems. Like many organisations, as they grow and mature their structures become bureaucratic and centralised over time, which in turn makes them difficult to change. M & S has become so bureaucratic and centralised in its structure that the important links between decision makers and customers have been eroded. The organisational culture of M & S also needs to change to take into account the changing nature of the business and the need for change. The supply chain no longer reflects what customers want. While many other organisations have attempted to decentralise control to the store level M & S has failed to move beyond centralised control which prevents close customer contact. The head office has also become overstaffed.

Case adapted from Marks and Spencer website; *Business and Finance* (2000). Davies (1999); Merriden (2000).

Case questions

❶ Identify the strategic change needs of M & S.

❷ What strategies should the organisation now pursue?

❸ How should M & S manage the strategic change process?

Keep up to date

www.Marks-and-Spencer.com.

Bibliography

Akin, G. and Palmer, I. (2000) 'Putting Metaphors to Work for Change in Organisations', *Organisation Dynamics*, 28 (3), 67–77.

Beer, M. (1980) *Organisational Change and Development: A Systems View*. California: Goodyear.

Beer, M., Eisenstat, R. and Spector, B. (1990) 'Why Change Programmes Do Not Produce Change', *Harvard Business Review*, 68 (6), 158–66.

Boeker, W. (1997) 'Strategic Change; the Influence of Managerial Characteristics and Organisational Growth', *Academy of Management Journal*, 40 (1), 152–71.

Business and Finance (2000) 'St Michael Needs Rescuing', Global View, 9 March.

Carnall, C. (1990) *Managing Change in Organisations*. New York: Prentice Hall.

Cronin. C. (1993) 'ICG Battens Down', *Business and Finance*, 14 January, 44–5.

Cummings, T. and Huse, E. (1989) *Organisational Development and Change*. St Paul: West.

Curled, N. and Bailey, D. (1999) 'Telework: The Advantages and Challenges of Working Here, There, Anywhere, Anytime', *Organisational Dynamics*, 28 (2), 55.

Curran, R. (1993) 'Stena Speed to Challenge B & I Route', *Sunday Business Post*, 11 July.

Cutcher-Gershenfeld, J., Kossek, E. and Sandling, H. (1997) 'Managing Concurrent Change Initiatives; Integrating Quality and Work/Family Strategies', *Organisation Dynamics*, 25 (3), 21–38.

Davies, G. (1999) 'The Evolution of Marks and Spencer', *The Service Industries Journal*, 19 (3), 60–73.

Dineen, D. (1992) 'Atypical Work Patterns in Ireland: Short Term Adjustments of Fundamental Changes', *Administration*, 40 (3), 248–74.

Drucker,P. (1992) 'The New Society of Organisations', *Harvard Business Review*, 70 (5).

Flynn, G. (1994) 'Craftsmen: The Last of the Dinosaurs', *Business and Finance*, 13 October, 18–23.

Gibbs, P. (1993) 'Determinants of Corporate Restructuring: The Relative Importance of Corporate Governance, Take-over Threat and Free Cash Flow', *Strategic Management Journal*, 14, 51–68.

Ginsberg, A. and Bucholtz, A. (1990) 'Converting to for Profit Status: Corporate Responsiveness to Radical Change', *Academy of Management Journal*, 33, 445–77.

Goodman, P. and Kurke, L. (1982) 'Studies of Change in Organisations: A Status Report', in Goodman, P. *et al.* (eds) *Change in Organisations*. San Francisco: Jossey Bass.

Handy, C. (1989) *The Age of Unreason*. London: Business Books.

Hannan, M. and Freeman, J. (1984) 'Structural Inertia and Organisational Change', *American Sociological Review*, 49, 149–64.

Hitt, M. (2000) 'The New Frontier: Transformation of Management for the New Millennium', *Organisation Dynamics*, 28 (3), 7–18.

Hitt, M., Hoskisson, R. and Harrison, J. (1992) 'Strategic Competitiveness in the 1990s: Challenges and Opportunities for US Executives', *Academy of Management Review*, 15 (2), 7–22.

Johnson, G. (1991) 'The Global Work Force 2000: A New World Labour Market', *Harvard Business Review*. 69 (2), 115–27.

Johnson. G. and Scholes, K. (1993) *Exploring Corporate Strategy: Text and Cases.* Cambridge: Prentice Hall.

Kanter, R. (1989) *When Giants Learn to Dance.* New York: Simon & Schuster.

Kanter, R. (1991) 'Transcending Business Boundaries: 12,000 World Managers View Change', *Harvard Business Review,* 69 (3), 151–64.

Katz, D. and Kahn, R. (1978) *The Social Psychology of Organisations.* New York: Wiley.

Kotter, P. and Schlesinger, L. (1979) 'Choosing Strategies for Change', *Harvard Business Review,* 57 (2), 106–14.

Labour Force Survey (1997). Central Statistics Office, Dublin.

Lewin, K. (1951) *Field Theory in Social Science.* New York: Harper Row.

McCall, B. (2000) 'The Future is E', E Business Supplement, *Irish Times,* 28 June.

McKenney, J. (1995) *Waves of Change: Business Evolution through Information Technology.* Boston: HBS Press.

Merriden, T. (2000) 'A Turnaround in Progress', *Management Review,* January, 24–8.

Mills, A. and Murgatroyd, S. (1991) *Organisational Rules.* London: Prentice Hall.

Nadler, D. (1981) 'Managing Organisational Change: An Integrative Approach', *Journal of Applied Behavioural Science,* 17, 191–211.

Nadler, D. (1983) 'Concepts for the Management of Organisational Change', in Hackman, J., Lawler, E. and Porter, L. (eds) *Perspectives on Behaviour in Organisations.* New York: McGraw-Hill.

Neumann, J. (1989) 'Why People Do Not Participate in Organisational Change', in Woodman, R. and Pasmore, W. (eds) *Research in Organisational Change and Development.* Connecticut: JAI Press.

Nolan, J. (1994) 'The Management of Strategic Change in B & I Line'. Unpublished Final Year BBS Project: University of Limerick.

Nutt, P. (1989) 'Identifying and Appraising How Managers Install Strategy', *Strategic Management Journal,* 8 (1), 1–14.

O'Halloran, B. (2000) 'Will Clicks Replace Clerks?', *Business and Finance,* 9 March, 10–11.

Pascale, R., Millemann, M. and Gioja, L. (1997) 'Changing the Way we Change', *Harvard Business Review,* 75 (6), 126–39.

Peters, T. (1990) 'Prometheus Barely Unbound', *Academy of Management Executive,* 4 (4), 70–84.

Pettigrew, A. and Whipp, R. (1991) *Managing Change for Competitive Success.* London: Basil Blackwell.

Pfeffer, J. (1981) 'Management as Symbolic Action: The Creation of Organisational Paradigms', in Cummings, L. and Staw, B. (eds) *Research in Organisational Behaviour.* Connecticut: JAI Press.

Potts, M. and Behr, P. (1987) *The Leading Edge.* New York: McGraw-Hill.

Rajagopalan, N. and Spreitzer, G. (1997) 'Towards a Theory of Strategic Change: A Multi Lens Perspective and Integrative Framework', *Academy of Management Review,* 22 (1), 48–80.

Schneider, B., Brief, A. and Guzzo, R. (1996) 'Creating a Climate and Culture for Sustainable Organisational Change', *Organisation Dynamics,* 24 (4), 7–19.

Spector, B. (1989) 'From Bogged Down to Fired Up: Inspiring Organisational Change', *Sloan Management Review,* 30 (4), 29–34.

Stanislao, J. and Stanislao, B. (1983) 'Dealing with Resistance to Change', *Business Horizons,* 26 (4), 74–8.

Webb, J. and Dawson, P. (1991) 'Measure for Measure: Strategic Change in an Electronics Instruments Corporation', *Journal of Management Studies*, 28, 191–206.

Whipp, R., Rosenfeld, R. and Pettigrew, A. (1989) 'Culture and Competitiveness: Evidence from two Mature UK Industries', *Journal of Management Studies*, 26, 561–85.

Appendix

Republic of Ireland

ACT Venture Capital Ltd
Jefferson House
Eglinton Road
Dublin 4
Tel: 01 260 0966
Fax: 01 260 0538

Allied Irish Bank
Enterprise Development Bureau
Bankcentre
Ballsbridge
Dublin 4
Tel: 01 660 0311
Fax: 01 608 999136

An Bord Bia
Clanwilliam Court
Lower Mount Street
Dublin 2
Tel: 01 668 5155
Fax: 01 668 7521

Area Development Management Ltd
Holbrook House
Holles Street
Dublin 2
Tel: 01661 3611
Fax: 01 661 0411

Area Partnership, Ballyfermot
343 Ballyfermot Road
Dublin 10
Tel: 01626 9222
Fax: 01 626 3416

Area Partnership, Ballymun
North Mall
Ballymun Town Centre
Dublin 11
Tel: 01 842 3612
Fax: 01 842 7004

Area Partnership, Blanchardstown
Deanstown House
Main Street
Blanchardstown
Dublin 15
Tel: 01 820 9550
Fax: 01 820 9551

Area Partnership, Bray
5 Carlton Terrace
Novara Avenue
Bray
Co Wicklow
Tel: 01 286 8266
Fax: 01 286 8700

Area Partnership, Canal Communities
197 Tyrconnell Road
Inchicore
Dublin 10
Tel: 01 473 2196
Fax: 01 453 4857

Area Partnership, Clondalkin
Camac House
Unit 4, Oakfield Industrial Estate
Clondalkin
Dublin 22
Tel: 01 457 6433
Fax: 01 457 7145

Area Partnership, Chonamara agus Aran
(Connemara and Aran)
Ionad Fiontar
Rosmuc
Contae na Gaillmhe
Tel: 091 574 353
Fax: 091 574 047

Area Partnership, Cork City
Sunbeam Industrial Park
Millfield
Mallow Road
Cork
Tel: 021 302310
Fax: 021 302081

Area Partnership, County Cavan
Lynton House
Farnham Street
Cavan
Tel: 049 31029
Fax: 049 31117

Area Partnership, County Leitrim
Church Street
Drumshambo
Co Leitrim
Tel: 078 41740
Fax: 078 41741

Area Partnership, County Sligo
Co Sligo Development Centre
Cleveragh Road
Sligo
Tel: 071 41138
Fax: 071 41162

Area Partnership, County Wexford
Millpark Road
Enniscorthy
County Wexford
Tel: 054 37206
Fax: 054 37026

Area Partnership, Drogheda,
12A North Quay
Drogheda
County Louth
Tel: 041 42088
Fax: 041 43358

Area Partnership, Dublin Inner City
Equity House
Upper Ormond Quay
Dublin 7
Tel: 01 872 1321

Area Partnership, Dublin Northside
Bunratty Drive
Coolock
Dublin 17
Tel: 01 848 5630
Fax: 01 848 5661

Area Partnership, Dublin Southside
45 Upper Georges Street
Dun Laoghaire
County Dublin
Tel: 01 230 1011
Fax: 01 230 1713

Area Partnership, Dundalk
Partnership Court
Park House
Dundalk
County Louth
Tel: 042 30288
Fax: 042 305552

Area Partnership, Finglas/Cabra
Rosehill House
Finglas Road
Dublin 11
Tel: 01 836 1666
Fax: 01 864 0211

Area Partnership, Galway City
Kiltartan House
Foster Street
Galway
Tel: 091 566617
Fax: 091 566618

Area Partnership, Inishowen
2 Victoria Villas
St Mary's Road
Buncrana
County Donegal
Tel: 077 62218/63480
Fax: 077 62990

Area Partnership, Kimmage/
Walkinstown/Crumlin/Drimnagh
Unit 5
105 Longmile Road
Dublin 12
Tel: 01 456 7501
Fax: 01 456 7502

Area Partnership, Limerick
25 The Tait Centre
Dominic Street
Limerick
Tel: 061 4199388
Fax: 061 418098

Area Partnership, Longford
6 Church Street
Longford
Tel: 043 45555
Fax: 043 48105

Area Partnership, Mayo
Lower Main Street
Foxford
County Mayo
Tel: 094 567745
Fax: 094 56749

Area Partnership, Monaghan
Dublin Road
Castleblayney
County Monaghan
Tel: 042 49500
Fax: 042 49504

Area Partnership, North West
Kildare/North Offaly
Edenderry Business Park
Edenderry
County Offaly
Tel: 0405 32688
Fax: 0405 32690

Area Partnership, Roscommon
c/o ACC Offices
Main Street
Roscommon
Tel: 0903 27424
Fax: 0903 27478

Area Partnership, Tallaght
Unit 19 The Village Green
Tallaght
Dublin 24
Tel: 01 459 7990
Fax: 01 459 7991

Area Partnership, Thir Chonaill
(Tyrconnell)
MFG Teo
Aonad Eargail 1
An tEastat Tionscail
Na Doiri Beaga
Tir Chonaill
Contae Dun na nGall
Tel: 075 32017
Fax: 075 32428

Area Partnership, Tralee
37 Ashe Street
Tralee
County Kerry
Tel: 066 29544
Fax: 066 29544

Area Partnership, Waterford
Unit 4
Westgate Business Centre
Tramore Road
Waterford
Tel: 051 841740
Fax: 051 843153

Area Partnership, Wexford
Cornmarket
Mallin Street
Wexford
Tel: 053 23994
Fax: 053 21024

Bank of Ireland
Enterprise Support Unit
Head Office
Lower Baggot Street
Dublin 2
Tel: 01 661 5933
Fax: 01 676 3493

Bolton Trust
Powerhouse
Pigeon House Harbour
Ringsend
Dublin 4
Tel: 01 668 7155
Fax: 01 668 7945
(run with the support of the Dublin
Institute of Technology)

Bord Failte (Irish Tourist Board)
Baggot Street Bridge
Dublin 2
Tel: 01 602 4000
Fax: 01 602 4100
Website: www.failte.ie

Bord Iascaigh Mhara (Irish Fisheries
Board)
Crofton Road
Dun Laoghaire
Co Dublin
Tel: 01 284 1544
Fax: 01 284 1123

Business Information Centre
Central Library
ILAC Centre
Henry Street
Dublin 1
Tel: 01 873 4333
Fax: 01 872 1451

Business Innovation Centre, Cork
IDA Enterprise Centre
North Mall
Cork
Tel: 021 397711
Fax: 012 395393
E-mail: postmaster@corkbic.com

Business Innovation Centre, Dublin
The Tower
IDA Enterprise Centre
Pearse Street
Dublin 2
Tel: 01 671 3111
Fax: 01 671 3330
E-mail: dbic@indigo.ie

Business Innovation Centre, Limerick
The Innovation Centre
National Technological Park
Plassey
Limerick
Tel: 061 338177
Fax: 061 338065
E-mail: postmaster@shannon-dev.ie

Business Innovation Centre, West
Hardiman House
5 Eyre Square
Galway
Tel: 091 567974
Fax: 091 567980
E-mail: bicgwy@iol.ie

Central Statistics Office
Ardee Road
Dublin 6
Tel: 01 497 7144
Fax: 01 497 2360
Website: www.cso.ie

Central Statistics Office
Skehard Road
Mahon
Cork
Tel: 021 359000
Fax: 021 359090

Chambers of Commerce of Ireland
22 Merrion Square
Dublin 2
Tel: 01 661 2888
Fax: 01 661 2811

Companies Registration Office
Parnell House
14 Parnell Square
Dublin 1
Tel: 01 804 5200
Fax: 01 804 5222
Website: www.cro.ie

Co-operation Ireland
37 Upper Fitzwilliam Street
Dublin 2
Tel: 01 661 0588

County Enterprise Board, Carlow
98 Tullow Street
Carlow
Tel: 0503 30880
Fax: 0503 30717
E-mail: cceb@indigo.ie

County Enterprise Board, Cavan
17 Farnham Street
Cavan
Tel: 049 433 2427
Fax: 049 433 1384
E-mail: cceb@tinet.ie

County Enterprise Board, Clare
Enterprise House
Mill Road
Ennis
County Clare
Tel: 065 684 1922
Fax: 065 684 1887
E-mail: cceb@iol.ie

County Enterprise Board, Cork City
1-2 Bruach na Laoi
Union Quay
Cork
Tel: 021 96 1828/1839
Fax: 021 96 1869
E-mail: corkceb@iol.ie

County Enterprise Board, North Cork
26 Bank Place
Mallow
County Cork
Tel: 022 43235
Fax: 022 43247
E-mail: corknenet@iol.ie

County Enterprise Board, South Cork
Unit 2
Frankfield Business Paek
Ballycurreen
Cork
Tel: 021 975281
Fax: 021 975287
E-mail: info@sceb.ie

County Enterprise Board, West Cork
8 Kent Street
Clonakilty
County Cork
Tel: 023 34700
Fax: 023 34702
E-mail: enterprise@wceb.ie

County Enterprise Board, Donegal
County House
The Diamond
Lifford
County Donegal
Tel: 074 72351
Fax: 074 42042
E-mail: donegalceb@tinet.ie

County Enterprise Board, Dublin City
17 Eustace Street
Dublin 2
Tel: 01 677 6068/6078
Fax: 01 677 6093
E-mail: dceb@indigo.ie

County Enterprise Board, Fingal
Upper Floor Office Suite
Mainscourt
23 Upper Main Street
Swords
County Dublin
Tel: 01 890 0800
Fax: 01 813 9991
E-mail: ceb@fingal.ie

County Enterprise Board, South Dublin
No 3 Village Square
Old Bawn Road
Tallaght
Dublin 24
Tel: 01 405 7073/74, 452 5416
Fax: 01 451 7477
E-mail: sdubceb@itw.ie

County Enterprise Board,
Dun Laoghaire/Rathdown
Dundrum Office Park
Main Street, Dundrum
Dublin 16

Tel: 01 205 1100
Fax: 01 298 6827
E-mail: venturl@venturepoint.ie

County Enterprise Board, Galway
City/County
Wood Quay Court
Wood Quay
Galway
Tel: 091 565269
Fax: 091 565384
E-mail: lynche@iol.ie

County Enterprise Board, Kerry
County Buildings
Ratasc
Tralee
County Kerry
Tel: 066 712 1111
Fax: 066 712 6712
E-mail: kerryceb@kerrycoco.ie

County Enterprise Board, Kildare
The Woods
Clane
County Kildare
Tel: 045 861707
Fax: 045 861712
E-mail: info@kildareceb.ie

County Enterprise Board, Kilkenny
42 Parliament Street
Kilkenny
Tel: 056 522662
Fax: 056 51649
E-mail: kceb@kceb.ie

County Enterprise Board, Laois
IBS House
Dublin Road
Portlaoise
County Laois
Tel: 0502 61800
Fax: 0502 61797
E-mail: laoisceb@tinet.ie
Website: www.dpsnet.com/lceb

County Enterprise Board, Leitrim
Carrick-on-Shannon Business Park
Dublin Road
Carrick-on-Shannon
County Leitrim
Tel: 078 20450
Fax: 078 21491
E-mail: leitceb@iol.ie

County Enterprise Board, Limerick City
The Granary
Michael Street
Limerick
Tel: 061 312611
Fax: 061 311889
E-mail: info@limceb.ie

County Enterprise Board, Limerick
County Buildings
79/84 O'Connell Street
Limerick
Tel: 061 319319
Fax: 061 319318/318478
E-mail: lcoeb@lcoeb.iol.ie

County Enterprise Board, Longford
Great Water Street
Longford
Tel: 043 46231
Fax: 043 41233
E-mail: enterprise@tinet.ie

County Enterprise Board, Louth
Partnership Court
The Ramparts
Dundalk
County Louth
Tel: 042 932 7099
Fax: 042 932 7101
E-mail: info@lceb.org

County Enterprise Board, Mayo
Spencer Street
Castlebar
County Mayo
Tel: 094 24444
Fax: 094 24416
E-mail: info@mayoceb.iol.ie

County Enterprise Board, Meath
Navan Enterprise Centre
Trim Road
Navan
County Meath
Tel: 046 27444
Fax: 046 27356
E-mail: mhceb@meath.com
Website: www.meath.com

County Enterprise Board, Monaghan
Courthouse
Monaghan
Tel: 047 71818
Fax: 047 84786
E-mail: info@mceb.ie

County Enterprise Board, Offaly
Cormac Street
Tullamore
County Offaly
Tel: 0506 52971
Fax: 0506 52973
E-mail: offalyceb@tinet.ie

County Enterprise Board, Roscommon
Abbey Street
Roscommon
Tel: 0903 26263/26765
Fax: 0903 25474
E-mail: rosceb@iol.ie

County Enterprise Board, Sligo
Sligo Development Centre
Cleveragh Road
Sligo
Tel: 071 46792
Fax: 071 44779
E-mail: sceb@iol.ie

County Enterprise Board, Tipperary
North Riding
Summerhill
Nenagh
County Tipperary
Tel: 067 33086
Fax: 067 33605
E-mail: info@ntippceb.iol.ie

County Enterprise Board, Tipperary
South Riding
1 Gladstone Street
Clonmel
County Tipperary
Tel: 052 29466
Fax: 052 26512
E-mail: toss@sera.ie

County Enterprise Board, Waterford City
Enterprise House
New Street Court
Waterford
Tel: 051 852 883
Fax: 051 877 494
E-mail: wceb@tinet.ie

County Enterprise Board, Waterford
County
The Courthouse
Dungarvan
County Waterford
Tel: 058 44811
Fax: 058 44817
E-mail: waterfordceb@tinet.ie

County Enterprise Board, Westmeath
Enterprise Centre
Bishopsgate Street
Mullingar
County Westmeath
Tel: 044 49222
Fax: 044 49009
E-mail: wceb@iol.ie

County Enterprise Board, Wexford
16/17 Mallin Street
Cornmarket
Wexford
Tel: 053 22965/24407/24850
Fax: 053 24944
E-mail: info@wexfordceb.ie

County Enterprise Board, Wicklow
1 Main Street
Wicklow
Tel: 0404 67100
Fax: 0404 67601

E-mail: wicklowceb@tinet.ie
Website: www.wicklow.ie

Department of Enterprise, Trade and
Employment
Kildare Street
Dublin 2
Tel: 01 631 2121
Website: www.irlgov.ie\entemp

Dublin Inner City Partnership
Equity House
Upper Ormond Quay
Dublin 7
Tel: 01 872 1321
Fax: 01 872 1330

Enterprise Ireland
Glasnevin
Dublin 9
Tel: 01 857 0000
Fax: 01 808 2020
Website: www.enterprise-ireland.ie

Enterprise Ireland
Merrion Hall
Strand Road
Sandymount
Dublin 4
Tel: 01 857 0000
Fax: 01 206 6400

Enterprise Ireland
Wilton Park House
Wilton Place
Dublin 2
Tel: 01 857 0000
Fax: 01 808 2802
(Enterprise Ireland has regional offices
in Clare, Cork, Donegal, Dublin, Galway,
Kerry, Limerick, Louth, Sligo, Waterford
and Westmeath—see local telephone
directories for details)

Enterprise Link
Tel: 1850 35 33 33

European Commission
Jean Monnet Centre
39 Molesworth Street
Dublin 2
Tel: 01 662 5113
Website: www.europa.org

FAS The Training and Employment
Authority
27-33 Upper Baggot Street
Dublin 4
Tel: 01 607 5000
Fax: 01 607 0600
Website: www.fas.ie

FAS Regional Offices—see local
telephone directories

First Step
Jefferson House
Eglinton Road
Dublin 4
Tel: 01 260 0988
Fax: 01 260 0989

Forfas
Wilton Park House
Wilton Place
Dublin 2
Tel: 01 607 3000
Fax: 01 607 3030
E-mail: forfas@forfas.ie
Website: www.forfas.ie

ICC Bank
72-74 Harcourt Street
Dublin 2
Tel: 01 415 5555
Fax: 01 671 7797
Website: www.icc.ie

ICC Bank
ICC House
46 Grand Parade
Cork
Tel: 021 277166
Fax: 021 270267

ICC Bank
Odeon House
Eyre Square
Galway
Tel: 091 566 445
Fax: 091 566 811

ICC Bank
ICC House
Charlotte Quay
Limerick
Tel: 061 317 577
Fax: 061 311 462

Industrial Development Authority
Wilton Park House
Wilton Place
Dublin 2
Tel: 01 603 4000
Fax: 01 603 4040

International Fund for Ireland
PO Box 2000
Dublin 2
Tel: 01 478 0655
Fax: 01 475 1351

International Fund for Ireland
PO Box 2000
Belfast
BT4 2QY
Tel: 08 01232 768832
Fax: 08 01232 763313
(operating in Northern Ireland and
Counties Donegal, Leitrim, Louth,
Monaghan and Sligo)

Inner City Enterprise
56 Gardiner Street
Dublin 1
Tel: 01 836 4076
Fax: 01 836 3742
Website: www.ice.ie

Irish Business and Employers
Confederation (IBEC)
84 Lower Baggot Street
Dublin 2

Tel: 01 660 1011
Fax: 01 660 1717
Website: www.ibec.ie

Irish Small and Medium Enterprises
Association (ISME)
17 Kildare Street
Dublin 2
Tel: 01 662 2755
Fax: 01 661 2157

Liffey Trust
117 Upper Sheriff Street
Dublin 1
Tel: 01 836 4645
Fax: 01 874 0298

National Food Centre
Dunsinea
Castleknock
Dublin 15
Tel: 01 805 9500

National Irish Bank
7/8 Wilton Place
Dublin 2
Tel: 01 678 5066
Fax: 01 678 5949

National Microelectronics Applications
Centre
National Technological Park
Plassey
Limerick
Tel: 061 334699
Fax: 061 330316

National Microelectronics Research
Centre
Lee Maltings
Prospect Row
Cork
Tel: 021 903000
Fax: 021 2702271

Patents Office
45 Merrion Square
Dublin 2

Tel: 01 661 4144
Fax: 01 676 0416

Project Development Centre
Docklands Innovation Park
128-130 East Wall Road
Dublin 3
Tel: 01 240 1300
Fax: 01 240 1310
E-mail: info@docklands-innovation.com
Website: www.docklands-innovation.com
www.pdc.ie

Revenue Commissioners
Dublin Castle
Dublin 2
Tel: 01 679 2777
Fax: 01 838 7355
Website: www.revenue.ie

Saint Paul's Area Development
Enterprise Limited (SPADE)
St Paul's
North King Street
Dublin 7
Tel: 01 677 1026
Fax: 01 677 1558

Saint Vincent De Paul
8 Cabra Road
Dublin 7
Tel: 01 838 4164
Fax: 01 838 7355

Shannon Development
Town Centre
Shannon
County Clare
Tel: 061 361555
Fax: 061 361903
Website: www.shannon-dev.ie

Shannon Development
Brendan Street
Birr
County Offaly
Tel: 0509 20440
Fax: 0509 20660

Shannon Development
Clare Business Centre
Francis Street
Ennis
County Clare
Tel: 065 20165/6
Fax: 061 21234

Shannon Development
The Granary
Michael Street
Limerick
Tel: 061 410777
Fax: 061 315315634

Shannon Development
Silverline Building
Connolly Street
Nenagh
County Tipperary
Tel: 067 32100
Fax: 067 33418

Shannon Development
Bay 5 Workspace
Newcastlewest Industrial Estate
Newcastlewest
County Limerick
Tel: 069 62977
Fax: 069 62898

Shannon Development
Memorial Hall
Denny Street
Tralee
County Kerry
Tel: 066 24988
Fax: 066 24267

Small Firms Association
84 Lower Baggot Street
Dublin 2
Tel: 01 660 1011
Fax: 01 661 2861

Smurfit Job Creation Enterprise Fund
c/o Smurfit Venture Investments
Limited
2 Clanwilliam Court
Lower Mount Street
Dublin 2
Tel: 01 478 4091
Fax: 01 475 2362
Webiste: www.smurfit-venture.ie

Údarás na Gaeltachta
Na Forbacha
Gaillimh
Tel: 091 503100
Fax: 091 503101
Website: www.udaras.ie

Údarás na Gaeltachta
35 Bothar Siolbhroin
Baile Atha Cliath 4
Tel: 01 605 2100
Fax: 01 605 2101

Údarás na Gaeltachta
An Phriomh Sraid
Beal an Mhuirthead
Contae Maigh Eo
Tel: 097 81418
Fax: 097 82179

Údarás na Gaeltachta
Sraid an Doirin
An Daingean
Contae Chiarrai
Tel: 066 50100
Fax: 066 50101

Údarás na Gaeltachta
Na Doiri Beaga
Co Dun na nGall
Tel: 075 60100
Fax: 075 60101

Údarás na Gaeltachta
Baile Mhic Ire
Maigh Chromtha
Contae Chorcaigh
Tel: 026 45366
Fax: 026 45423

Ulster Bank
Small Business Section
33 College Green
Dublin 2
Tel: 01 677 7623
Fax: 01 702 5230

Northern Ireland

Business Library
The Belfast Education and Library Board
Belfast Public Libraries
Central Library
Royal Avenue
Belfast BT1 1EA

Confederation of British Industry
Fanum House
108 Great Victoria Street
Belfast BT2 7PD
Tel: 02890 326658

Co-operation Ireland
7 Botanic Avenue
Belfast BT7 1JG
Tel: 02890 321462

Department of Employment, Trade and
Industry
Netherleigh
Massey Avenue
Belfast BT4 2JP
Tel: 02890 529900

European Commission
Windsor House
9-15 Bedford Street
Belfast BT2 7EG
Tel: 02890 240708

Federation of Small Business
3 Farrier Court
Glengormley
Newtownabbey
County Antrim
Tel: 02890 844079

Industrial Development Board
64 Chichester Street
Belfast BT1 4JX
Tel: 02890 233233

Institute of Directors
Manley House
Dargan Crescent
Belfast BT3 9JP
Tel: 02890 370107

Law Society
90 Victoria Street
Belfast BT1 3JZ
Tel: 02890 231614

L.E.D.U.
Upper Galwally
Belfast BT8 4TB

L.E.D.U.
13 Shipquay Street
Derry BT48 6DJ
Tel: 02871 267257

LEDU
6-7 The Mall
Newry BT34 1BX
Tel: 02830 262955

Newry and Mourne Enterprise Agency
WIN Industrial Estate
Canal Quay
Newry
Tel: 02830 267011

Northern Ireland Business Club
Portview Trade Centre
310 Newtownards Road
Belfast BT4 1HT
Tel: 02890 453260

Northern Ireland Chamber of
Commerce
22 Great Victoria Street
Belfast BT2 7BJ
Tel: 02890 244113

Northern Ireland Chamber of Trade
Bank of Ireland Buildings
92–100 Royal Avenue
Belfast BT1 1DL
Tel: 02890 230444

Northern Ireland Training Council
Association
14–16 Westbank Road
Newtownabbey
Tel: 02890 775573

Noribic Innovation Centre
9 Shipquay Street
Derry
Tel: 02871 264242

Omagh Business Club
Omagh Enterprise Complex
Gortrush Industrial Estate
Omagh
County Tyrone
Tel: 02882 249494

The Training and Employment Agency
Clarendon House
9–21 Adelaide Street
Belfast BT2 8DJ
Tel: 02890 244300

Glossary

Acquisitions The purchase of a controlling interest in one company by another. Acquisitions can be friendly or hostile.

Appraisal costs The costs of measuring quality. Such costs include the costs of inspection and testing, the costs of the equipment for this process, and the labour cost of the time spent on quality inspection and information.

Artificial intelligence The ability of appropriately programmed computers to display levels of intelligence normally associated with human beings.

Activity ratios Ratios used to determine how efficiently an organisation uses its resources.

Asset turnover ratio The ratio between an organisation's sales and total assets. It indicates how efficiently an organisation is using its assets.

Authority Power that has been legitimised in a specific social context. In an organisation authority is the power to perform or command.

Autonomy The extent to which employees are free to take action based on their own initiative.

Bad debts Bad debts arise when debtors can not pay the organisation what they owe. Such debts are essentially unrecoverable.

Balance of payments The difference between payments into and out of the country, in a given period of time.

Balance of trade The excess of imports over exports, or exports over imports traded by a country.

Batch production The production of a product in predetermined batches at regular intervals.

Branding Giving a name, sign or symbol to items or services, so that they can be identified in a manner which would differentiate them from competitors' goods. Branding a good/service aids customers in differentiating between items/services offered by different companies.

Break-even analysis A method of assessing the relationship between costs, revenues and the volume produced.

Break-even point The point at which total revenue equals total expenditure and consequently no loss is made.

Budget A statement of plans and expected outcomes expressed in numerical terms for different organisational activities.

Bullying 'Repeated aggression, verbal, psychological or physical, conducted by an individual or group against another person or persons' (Health and Safety Authority).

Bureaucracy An approach to management/structure which emphasises detailed rules and procedures, a clearly outlined organisational hierarchy and mainly impersonal relationships between organisational members.

Business Angel An individual or company of high net worth interested in investing in new, high risk enterprises.

Business ethics The examination of the ethical or moral aspects of business policies or decisions.

Business-level strategies Organisational strategies which relate to the operation of a single business.

Business plan A plan setting out the objectives, strategies and activities of a business over a specified time period.

Business process re-engineering The radical redesign of the business process as a whole, or of individual work processes in order to improve business effectiveness.

Business to business (B2B) The interchange of goods or services from one business to another through electronic means.

Business to custom (B2C) The interchange of goods or services from a business to a customer through electronic means.

Business unit A distinct business area within an organisation usually producing a particular product/service.

Category management The management of a particular category of conumer products in order to maximise profits for both the retailer and supplier.

Chain of command A systematic ordering of positions and duties that defines a managerial authority.

Change agent A person or group responsible for managing the change effort in the organisation. The change agent can be an internal or external person(s).

Churning The creation of excessive financial transactions for the purpose of generating commission.

Classical management An approach to management that emphasises universal approaches to internal efficiency in order to increase organisational success.

Closed system A system that does not depend on, is not influenced by nor interacts with its external environment.

Coalition An alliance of individuals or group who come together to achieve a specific goal.

Cognitive dissonance Conflicting attitudes experienced by individuals.

Common agricultural policy An EU policy to control the price and distribution of agricultural goods within the community. CAP imposes a minimum price and if a farmer is unable to sell goods they are then bought through intervention. Supply often exceeds demand and butter mountains and wine lakes have resulted.

Competitive niche Specialisation by an organisation in a narrow segment of a given market.

Computer-aided design (CAD) The use of computer technology to design products and services.

Computer-aided manufacturing (CAM) The use of computer technology to manufacture products and services.

Computer-integrated manufacturing The use of CAD and CAM to sequence and optimise a number of production processes.

Conceptual skills The ability to see an organisation as a whole.

Concurrent controls Controls that monitor the transformation of inputs into outputs to make sure that they meet standards.

Contingency A situation or the characteristics of a situation which affect the practice of management.

Contingency management An approach to management that emphasises that managerial practice depends on a given set of contingencies or factors, i.e. the situation at hand. It therefore emphasises that there is no one best way to manage in all situations. It is sometimes called situational management.

Contingency planning A sophisticated planning process that identifies alternative courses of action to be implemented if the key characteristics of a situation change.

Contingency theory This is dedicated to examining the fit between a leader's behaviour and the specific environment in which s/he manages (see also **Leadership**).

Continuous production A continual process involving the synthesis of

several inputs to produces the final product.

Control The management function which measures actual performance and compares it to established standards and then takes corrective action.

Co-operative A business owned and run jointly by the members, with the profits shared among them.

Co-ordination The process of integrating various individuals, work groups and business units to achieve organisational goals.

Corporate governance The regulation of the performance of the board of directors through a recognised code of practice.

Corporate-level strategies Organisational strategies which may extend across several industry sectors.

Cost leadership A competitive strategy involving an aggressive pursuit of operating efficiency by an organisation so that it can be a low cost producer.

Critical path The most direct path or sequence of activities in a PERT chart.

Current assets Assets acquired by the organisation for disposal in the course of trade and which can be renewed again.

Current ratio The ratio between an organisation's current assets and current liabilities used to assess liquidity.

Database A collection of information stored in an orderly way in a computer.

Debt equity ratio The ratio between an organisation's total liabilities and total equities used to assess an organisation's debt financing.

Delegation The process by which new or additional responsibilities are assigned to a subordinate by a superior.

Demarcation lines The strict lines separating one area of work from another.

Depreciation The loss in value of capital goods over a period of time.

Differentiation A competitive strategy involving attempts by an organisation to develop goods or service that are viewed industry wide as unique in some important way.

Direct marketing Interactive system of marketing that uses one or more media to effect a measurable response and/or transaction in order to communicate directly and personally with the would-be buyer.

Diversification A growth strategy whereby an organisation expands into new business areas outside of its original core capability.

Divestment When a company sells off or offloads businesses or divisions that are no longer relevant to the business strategy.

Dividend Payment from an organisation's post-tax profits to its shareholders.

Dynamic environment The degree to which environmental elements change.

Dynamism In relation to the economy—a phenomena of growth and change.

E-business The interchange of goods and services from business to business, or business to consumer, by electronic means.

EC/EU Commission The Commission consists of two commissioners from the larger countries and one from the smaller members. They act to ensure that rules and principles are respected.

E-commerce The conduct of commercial transactions and relationships through electronic media.

Economies of scale Savings which arise due to the fact that the average unit cost of producing an item decreases as the volume of production increases.

Effective managers Active leaders who create a work environment that provide both the opportunity and the incentive to achieve high performance.

Effectiveness The degree to which the outputs of the organisation correspond to the outputs that organisations and individuals in the external environment want.

Efficiency The achievement of objectives or targets at the least cost, resources or other undesirable outcomes.

Efficient consumer response The use of information technology to track consumer demand patterns and develop an efficient and responsive supply system.

Employee relations This includes all employer–employee interactions, incorporating both union and non-union approaches to workforce management.

Employment Appeal Tribunal (EAT) A quasi-judicial tribunal that administers a number of legislative acts in the area of employment and hears appeals from the rights commissioner service.

Enterprise Either a business organisation, as in a state enterprise; or an economic system in which people are free to do business more or less as they wish, as in 'free enterprise'; or in the context of this book, the quality exemplified by the risk-taking businessperson.

Entrepreneur A person viewed as undertaking a risk.

Entrepreneurship The activity of creating a new enterprise or business entity, and the undertaking of risk.

Environment All factors affecting the organisation yet which lie outside of the organisation's boundary.

Environmental complexity The number of environmental elements that affect organisational decision making.

Environmental management Proactive strategies designed to change the environmental context within which the organisation operates.

Environmental uncertainty A situation in which managers have little information about environmental events or their effect on the organisation.

Equality officer This role was set up under the equality legislation to investigate claims of inequitable practices by organisations based on nine possible grounds from discrimination.

Error-proofing Putting systems in place that will minimise the potential for errors.

Ethical audit Audit of the ethical behaviour of a company, for the purpose of third-party verification.

European Exchange Rate Mechanism The mechanism for controlling the exchange rates of the EU members currencies relative to one another.

European Monetary System A system whereby the currencies members of the EU are tied to one another through a grid of currency parities.

European Union A political and economic alliance of countries within Europe, where barriers to trade and business activity have been removed to encourage economic growth within the region.

Existence-relatedness-growth (ERG) Advanced by Alderfer, it provides a means of understanding employee motivation. It argues that employee motivation can be understood with reference to these three key needs.

Expectancy The belief held by the individual that a specific level of effort will be followed by a specific level of performance (see also **Expectancy theory**).

Expectancy theory Advanced by Vroom, this is a model of motivation. It argues that work motivation is a product of two distinct individual beliefs: the relationship between effort and performance; and the importance of particular work outcomes (see also **Expectancy; Instrumentality; Valence**).

Expert power Power that arises from the possession of knowledge or specialised skills.

External failure costs The externally accrued costs of a failure in quality systems, which can include customer complaint costs, the cost of product returns, claims or guarantees, product liability costs and the cost of lost sales.

Factory automation The use of robots and computerised technology to automate a production process.

Feasibility study A document detailing all the factors relevant to the establishment of a new business.

Feedback controls Controls used to monitor outputs to make sure they meet standards.

Feedforward controls Controls used to monitor inputs to make sure they meet standards.

Finished goods All items a manufacturer has made for sale to customers.

Fixed costs Costs that do not vary with the level of output.

Flexibility The freedom to change operational practices in response to changes in demand.

Focus A competitive strategy pursued by an organisation by concentrating on a specific geographical market or customer grouping.

Focused factory Manufacturing plant which limits production to one line, with the aim of achieving economies of scale and a unique competitive advantage.

Foreign direct investment Investment by a foreign company in another country usually by establishing a business facility.

Franchise An arrangement whereby a company sells limited rights to use its brand name to a franchisee in return for a lump sum payment and a share of the franchisee's profits.

Franchising A contract between a franchisor and a franchisee, to distribute a product or service, in accordance with an overall blueprint devised by the franchisor.

Free trade Trade between nations which is free of all restrictions such as tariffs, quotas and protection of domestic industries by subsidisation.

Front-line managers Managers responsible for directly managing operational employees and resources.

Functional departmentalisation A method of co-ordinating activities based on each of the major functions undertaken by the organisation.

Gainsharing The sharing of financial gains with the workforce. Gains may be negotiated on the basis of increased productivity and/or more flexible working conditions. Gains might include higher salaries, bonuses, additional annual leave, flexitime, share options or profit shares.

Gantt chart A non-financial method of control that illustrates across time the sequence of activities comprising a project.

Geographical departmentalisation A method of co-ordinating activities based on the various regions served by the organisation.

Global strategies A strategy of global competition based on the assumption that no differences exist among countries with respect to consumer tastes, competitive conditions, operations and political, legal, economic and social environments.

Goal displacement A condition that occurs when people lose sight of the original goal and a new, possibly less important, goal arises.

Gross domestic product The total value of output produced in a country.

Gross national product (GNP) The total value of output produced in a given country plus net property income from abroad.

Group think The mode of thinking that people engage in when seeking agreement becomes so pervasive in a group that it overrides a realistic consideration of alternative solutions.

Human resource management (HRM) This refers to the management of employees through the development of a strategic corporate approach. The key principle is the incorporation of people issues into strategic decision making (see also **Personnel management**).

Human resource planning This refers to the specification and determination of future human resource needs in line with the organisation's strategic development plans.

Hygiene factors Derived from Herzberg's 'Two-factor theory' of work motivation, these are associated with the job context rather than its actual content.

Incentives A motivational force that stimulates people to greater activity or increased efficiency. Encourages an employee to work harder and be more productive.

Indigenous company A company originated in the native/home country, that is, it is not a foreign-owned company.

Industrial relations This refers to the rules, practices and conventions governing interrelations between management and the workforce; normally involves collective employee representation and bargaining.

Information processing The organising, manipulation, calculation and sorting of data.

Infrastructure The basic structure of a nation's economy, including transportation, communications and other public services on which economic activity relies.

Innovation A critical part of the business process. It is a new concept or approach in the product cycle. It is the addition of new elements to products or services, or to the methods of producing/providing them. Innovation is not the creation of an entirely new product, this is invention. Innovation allows one to gain a competitive edge over competitors.

Instrumentality The probability assumed by the individual that a particular level of achieved task performance will lead to specific work outcomes (see also **Expectancy theory**).

Interest The price paid to borrow money which is paid to the lender by the borrower.

Interest rates The price charged for the hire of money by the hirer and received by the lender of the money. Interest is the reward paid to those who lend money.

Internal failure costs The internal costs related to a failure in quality systems. Includes the costs of scrap and rework, the costs of process failure, and downtime costs.

Interpersonal skills The ability to work effectively with other people.

Intrapreneurship Enterprise within the organisation; the ability to foster an internal climate and systems that support innovative behaviour.

Inventory turnover ratio The ratio between an organisation's cost of goods sold and the inventory used to identify the number of times the inventory has been sold in a given period.

Irish Congress of Trade Unions (ICTU) The central co-ordinating body for the Irish trade union movement.

Job characteristics model Advanced by Hackman and Oldham, it seeks to identify job characteristics which satisfy higher order needs and which provide opportunities for achieving this satisfaction. It assumes that tasks are determined in terms of five core dimensions which are related to three critical psychological states and certain personal and work outcomes (see also **Motivation theory**).

Job description An account of the responsibilities and tasks associated with a particular job.

Job design Also referred to as job redesign or work structuring, it relates to the establishment of groups of tasks/activities to form a particular job.

Job diagnostic survey A measurement tool in the form of a questionnaire devised by Hackman and Oldham to test the job characteristics model.

Job enlargement An individualistic approach to job design which focuses on the horizontal extension of the job as a means of broadening job scope and creating a more satisfying job (see also **Job design**).

Job enrichment An individualistic approach to job design which focuses on the vertical extension of the job as a means of broadening job scope and establishing a more challenging, satisfying job (see also **Job design**).

Job production This relates to the production of one-off or small quantities of a wide variety of specialised goods/items (see also **Production management**).

Job shop An organisation with a large variety of products each produced in single quantities.

Job specialisation Activities which are narrowed down to simple routine tasks.

Joint venture A business venture entered into jointly by two or more partners. Their aim is to share the risk of new ventures, to benefit from synergy through the combining of each partner's resources, or to enter new markets.

Just-in-time (JIT) systems A system of zero stockholding, where parts and materials are delivered directly from suppliers to the production line as needed.

Key result areas Areas vital to the organisation's continued existence.

Labour Court Established originally under the Industrial Relations Act of 1946 as the principal institution for facilitating the settlement of industrial disputes. This role was modified by the

Industrial Relations Act of 1990.

Labour Relations Commission A tripartite body with statutory authority charged with the general responsibility of promoting good industrial relations.

Leadership The process of influencing an individual or group through deciphering his/her/its objectives and directing and motivating behaviour in pursuit of these objectives.

Legitimate power Power based on an individual's position in the organisational hierarchy.

Lending agencies A finance company, bank, loan organisation or the like that lends money and makes money by advancing money to others.

Levelling effect When an individual's thinking is brought into line with the average quality of a group's thinking.

Licensing An agreement to produce or supply a product or service under terms and conditions defined in a legal agreement.

Limited company A form of company that can be established by law with limited legal liability. Liability is usually limited by the value of shares owned, and this enables the directors personal assets to be protected in the event of the failure of the firm.

Limited partnership Where one or more partners limits his/her liability to the amount s/he has invested in the partnership, but s/he cannot take part in the management of the business.

Line authority The authority that follows an organisation's direct chain of command.

Line (mass) production A linear sequence of operations dedicated to production of a particular product.

Liquidity A measure of an organisation's ability to cover short-term debts.

Localisation The extent to which a product has to be modified to suit local market conditions.

Logistics management The co-ordination of the materials and information flows through the firm and its suppliers into the marketplace and the end customer.

Management Activities that make up the management process. The major management functions are planning, organising, staffing, leading and controlling.

Management buyout The buyout of the ownership of a firm by some or all of the management team.

Management by exception A control tool that permits only significant deviations between planned and actual performance to be brought to the manager's attention.

Management development Leadership training for middle- or top-level personnel to upgrade their skills.

Management process The process involving the five management functions of planning, organising, staffing, leading and controlling.

Managerial grid Advanced by Blake and Mouton, it provides a framework for understanding and applying effective leadership. Five key managerial styles result from combining two fundamental ingredients of managerial behaviour—a concern for production and a concern for people (see also **Leadership**).

Manufacturing-requirements planning (MRP) systems Computerised systems used to plan supply requirements, schedule production, manage a purchasing system and calculate manufacturing costs.

Market research The process of methodically examining the market for an existing product or a new product. That part of marketing research that deals with the pattern of a market, measuring the extent and nature of a market and identifying a market.

Mass production A production system in which large batches of standard products are manufactured in assembly line fashion by combining parts in a specified manner.

Matrix structure A method of co-ordinating activities that crosses product departmentalisation with functional departmentalisation.

Merger The combining of two or more entities through the direct acquisition by one of the net assets of the other.

Metaphor The application of a name or descriptive phrase to an object or action to which it is imaginatively, rather than literally, related.

Middle managers Managers in charge of plants and departments who have responsibility for the performance of their particular unit and how it relates to the rest of the organisation.

Motivation The forces that act on, or that are within an individual which cause him/her to behave in a particular, goal-directed fashion.

Motivators Derived from Herzberg's 'Two-factor theory' of work motivation, they are related to job content or to what the individual does in his/her work.

Multinational corporation (MNC) An organisation that operates and competes in several different countries.

Networks A system of linking organisations together in any formal or informal relationship.

Non-programmed decision A new unstructured decision which the organisation has not encountered before. As a result decision rules can not be applied.

Non-governmental organisations (NGOs) The broad spectrum of organisations, voluntary and professional, whose purpose is to represent or campaign on a single issue or agenda, or represent a particular group of interests.

Objective probability The likelihood of an event occurring based on hard quantitative data.

Open system A system that depends on, is influenced by and constantly interacts with its external environment.

Operation A transformational process by which inputs (materials, labour, and knowledge) are converted into outputs (goods and services).

Opportunity costs The cost of not doing something. The opportunity cost is the reward that would have come from the best course of action that the business did not follow.

Organisational chart A diagram of all the positions in the organisational hierarchy.

Organisational culture The common set of beliefs and expectations shared by members of the organisation.

Partnership A business format where two or more people are involved in the ownership and management of the company.

Performance appraisal The process of evaluating an employee's job and organisational-related performance and his/her future potential.

Personnel management This refers to either the specialist professional function performed by personnel managers or to all those people in an organisation with responsibilities for people management issues.

Person specification This sets out the knowledge, skills, abilities and other characteristics required by an individual to perform a given job.

PERT analysis A network analysis system whereby events in a project are identified along with the time taken to complete them. A network is developed showing relationships between the sequence of each event. A critical path can then be established.

Portfolio A collection of securities owned by an individual or an organisation.

Postponement The concept of building a product on a common platform and then finishing it according to market needs or customer specifications.

Prevention costs The costs of trying to ensure that poor quality goods do not reach the customer.

Price competition Competition based on offering the lowest price.

Privatisation The transfer of ownership of an organisation from the public to the private sector. Public sector organisations are sometimes called nationalised organisations or industries.

Process The means by which the chosen inputs are transformed into outputs.

Product A bundle of features both tangible and intangible which are presented to the prospective customer.

Product departmentalisation A method of co-ordinating activities based on the products produced by the organisation.

Production management This refers to the management of the transformation of the material resource inputs into outputs of goods and services.

Production planning and control system A means of ensuring that the correct quantity of a product is produced at the right time, at the right quality and at the most acceptable cost.

Product life cycle The stages of market acceptance of any goods. The stages are: introduction, growth, maturity and decline.

Product mix A composite of items offered for sale by a company.

Productivity The relationship between the total amount of goods or services being produced (output) and the organisational resources needed (inputs) to produce the goods or services.

Programmed decision A routine decision which is well structured, repetitive, occurs at lower levels in the organisation with short-term results.

Project A one-off production, usually of high value, with a defined budget and time horizon, and requiring a combination of inputs and skills.

Protectionism policies Used to protect a country's domestic industry. These include embargoes which prohibit the importation of certain goods, quotas which limit the amount of certain goods which may be imported and tariffs which impose a duty on the importation of certain goods.

Public–private partnership Agreement between public bodies and private companies, usually for the purpose of sharing the costs of a major infrastructural project.

Quality Fitness for intended purpose. Can be measured on eight dimensions performance, features, conformance, reliability, durability, serviceability, aesthetics and perceived quality.

Quality circle A group of employees who meet regularly to identify and solve quality problems or to make suggestions as to how quality can be improved.

Quick asset ratio Ratio between an organisation's total liabilities and total assets less inventory. It is used to measure an organisation's ability to meet financial obligations.

Rate of return (on investment) The amount earned in direct proportion to the capital invested.

Ratio analysis A control tool based on the process of generating information that summarises the financial position of an organisation by calculating ratios based on various financial measures appearing on balance sheets and income statements.

Recruitment The process of identifying and attracting potential job candidates.

Reengineering The re-shaping of business processes or practices.

Refreezing The process of making new behaviour permanent after a change programme has been introduced.

Reorientation A process that occurs when an organisation moves its resources into more attractive markets and industries.

Revitalisation A process an organisation goes through when its performance is unsatisfactory, designed to give the organisation new life.

Reward system This refers to the organisation's approach to compensating employees for job performance.

Rights Commissioners People charged with the responsibility for investigating individual disputes relating to pay and conditions. The recommendations made by them are generally not binding.

Sales promotions Short-term incentives to encourage product trial, shift brand loyalty, or increase product usage.

Satisficing Accepting the first minimally acceptable solution to a problem.

Scalar principle A structure in which each person is part of one chain of command that extends from the top to the bottom of the organisation.

Science Organised knowledge of relevance to an area of practice.

Scientific analysis The use of scientific methods to analyse a problem.

Scientific management An approach to management that emphasises the one best way to perform a task by applying scientific methods of inquiry.

Scientific method A problem-solving approach that involves 1) observing a system; 2) constructing a framework that is consistent with the observation and from which the consequences of altering the system can be predicted; 3) predicting how various changes would influence the system, i.e. cause and effect relationships; 4) testing to see if these changes influence the system as intended.

Segmentation The categorising of consumers into a number of different segments, each of which has a distinctive feature. Its purpose is to identify more precisely the target market for a particular product or service.

Selection This refers to the process of evaluating and choosing the most suitable candidate from a pool of candidates established through recruitment.

Self-managed teams A group of employees who have the day-to-day responsibility for managing themselves and the work they do.

Small open economy An economy which is small relative to its trading partners and is open in that it imports and exports a significant amount of goods and services.

Social responsibility Examination of the societal responsibilities and consequences of any business decision.

Sole trader A business owned and operated by one person.

Specialisation The number of distinct occupational titles or activities accomplished within the organisation. High specialisation means that there are many different functions or activities within the organisation.

Staff authority The authority to provide advice and expertise to help line units in achieving their goals.

Staff unit A unit that contributes indirectly to accomplishing an organisation's objectives.

Stakeholder Any individual or group with a direct or potential interest or stake in the organisation.

State intervention The extent of government involvement in industry.

Strategic business unit (SBU) A business operation or product group with designated responsibility for profits.

Strategic drift A loss of focus on core objectives and strategy, often caused by an excess of success.

Strategy A general and broad plan developed to achieve long-term organisational objectives.

'Strong man' theory Associated with leadership style, this is based on the principle of autonomy.

Structural funds EU assistance in the form of grants in order to help regions whose development is lagging. The aim is to reduce differences between regions and create a better economic and social balance between EU member states.

Structural imperatives Factors that determine how the organisation should be structured for effectiveness.

Subjective probability The likelihood of an event occurring based on personal judgement.

Subjectivity This relates to or arises from a person's emotions or prejudices.

Substitute products Items that can easily replace one another in either production or in consumption.

Sub-system A system created as part of the process of the overall management system.

SuperLeadership An approach to leadership that emphasises the central role of the followers. The central role of the leader is to help the followers to become self-leaders.

Supply chain management The development of partnerships or agreements with members of the distribution channel.

Sustainable development Development that meets the needs of the present without compromising the ability of future generations to meet their needs.

SWOT analysis An analysis of the internal strengths and weaknesses of the organisation, and also studying the external factors of opportunities and threats, all of which effect the organisation.

Synergy The creation of a whole that is greater than the sum of its parts.

System A set of interdependent parts or elements which function as a whole in achieving certain goals or objectives.

Tariff A list of customs duties to be paid on imports or exports; they are imposed for protection or revenue purposes.

Technology transfer An agreement involving the transfer or use of technology between firms.

Theory The systematic grouping of interdependent principles that provide a framework for drawing together significant knowledge.

Theory X This focuses on managerial assumptions about employees. It argues that managers perceive employees to have an inherent dislike of work and will avoid it where possible (see also **Theory Y**).

Theory Y This focuses on managerial assumptions about employees. It argues that managers perceive employees to enjoy work and derive satisfaction from the performance of their duties (see also **Theory X**).

Time and motion study The study of the time and number of motions necessary to perform a task.

Top managers Managers who determine the form of an organisation and define its overall character, mission and direction.

Total costs The total of fixed and variable costs.

Total quality management (TQM) A systematic approach to improving the production of goods and services.

Trade union An organisation dedicated to uniting workers with common interests, and defining, articulating and collectively advancing those interests.

Trait theory This argues that leaders are born and not made, and are endowed with key characteristics which other individuals do not possess (see also **Leadership**).

Turnaround A situation in which a business has sustained serious losses and needs radical changes if it is to survive.

Two-factor theory Advanced by Herzberg, it provides a means of analysing employee motivation. It suggests that factors leading to job satisfaction are distinct from those leading to job dissatisfaction (see also **Hygiene factors; Motivators**).

Unfreezing The process by which people become aware of the need for change.

Unit production A production system in which either one or a small number of finished products are manufactured according to customer specifications.

Unity of command The idea that no subordinate should report to more than one supervisor. It is designed to ensure that conflicts in instructions are reduced and that personal responsibility is increased.

Universal principles of management Management principles that are universal or applicable to all types of organisations and all organisational levels.

Valence The value the individual attaches to specific work outcomes (see also **Expectancy theory**).

Variable budget Budgets that distinguish between fixed and variable costs and which show how budget expenses vary as the volume of output increases.

VAT Value Added Tax is an indirect tax levied by the government on particular goods and services. VAT is added on at the point of purchase by the selling organisation. It is therefore a commercial tax.

Venture capital Capital offered for the start-up of new enterprises, in a situation that is perceived to be higher risk than lending to existing businesses.

Whistleblowing The release of internal company information concerning inappropriate business activity, by an employee. Usually arises from a lack of governance and/or professional conduct by management.

World-class manufacturing A holistic effort, integrating the techniques of total quality management, business process re-engineering, just-in-time manufacturing and employee involvement, in an effort to achieve standards that are world class.

Zero-based budget A budgeting process whereby each budget starts from zero and carries nothing forward from the last one. It is designed to eliminate inefficiencies which are carried forward from one budget to the next.

Index